Why Do You Need this New Edition?

If you're wondering why you should buy this new edition of *Reading Across the Disciplines: College Reading and Beyond* here are 7 good reasons!

1. **A new introduction** to the text, "Ten Success Strategies for Learning and Studying Academic Disciplines," provides numerous practical tips for reading in the disciplines to help you develop new skills, acquire the right tools, and learn the specialized vocabulary of different disciplines

2. **A new introduction to Part Two**, "Reading Across the Disciplines," explains how the chapters in this book are designed to give you the reading practice you need across various course areas and how the exercises and activities that accompany them will prepare you to be a successful student in future academic courses.

3. **Two new readings in Chapter 1** provide ample opportunities for you to apply and practice active reading skills.

4. **Expanded coverage in Chapter 9** of how to evaluate electronic sources shows you how to determine the accuracy, authority, objectivity, and usability of online sources.

5. **A new psychology textbook selection** at the end of the text gives you multiple opportunities to apply the strategies you have learned.

6. **New readings** on learning principles and video games, relationships and technology, culture and non-verbal communication, product placement, and stem cell research are informative and interesting and provide plenty of practice with important reading skills.

7. **MyReadingLab icons** included in the text send you to MyReadingLab for all of the additional practice you need for key reading skills.

PEARSON
Longman

Reading Across the Disciplines

Reading Across the Disciplines

College Reading and Beyond

Fourth Edition

Kathleen T. McWhorter
Niagara County Community College

Longman

New York   San Francisco   Boston
London   Toronto   Sydney   Tokyo   Singapore   Madrid
Mexico City   Munich   Paris   Cape Town   Hong Kong   Montreal

Acquisitions Editor: Kate Edwards
Development Editor: Gillian Cook
Marketing Manager: Tom DeMarco
Production Manager: Stacey Kulig
Project Coordination, Text Design, and Electronic Page Makeup: Pre-Press PMG
Cover Designer/Manager: Wendy Ann Fredericks
Cover Photos: Clockwise from top left: Erich Lessing/Art Resource, NY; Francesca Tesoriere/Age Fotostock; Louise Gubb/Corbis News; and Ed Young/AG Stock USA
Photo Researcher: Clare Maxwell
Senior Manufacturing Buyer: Dennis J. Para
Printer and Binder: Courier Corporation
Cover Printer: Coral Graphics Services

For permission to use copyrighted material, grateful acknowledgment is made to the copyright holders on pp. 671–678, which are hereby made part of this copyright page.

Library of Congress Cataloging-in-Publication Data

McWhorter, Kathleen T.
   Reading across the disciplines : college reading and beyond / Kathleen T. McWhorter. — 4th ed.
      p. cm.
   Includes bibliographical references and index.
   ISBN-13: 978-0-205-66273-9 (alk. paper)
   ISBN-10: 0-205-66273-0 (alk. paper)
   1. College readers.   2. Reading (Higher education)   3. Interdisciplinary approach in education.   I. Title.
   PE1122.M37 2009
   428.6—dc22   2008045505

Copyright © 2009 by Pearson Education, Inc.

All rights reserved. No part of this publication may be reproduced, stored in a retrieval system, or transmitted, in any form or by any means, electronic, mechanical, photocopying, recording, or otherwise, without the prior written permission of the publisher. Printed in the United States.

3 4 5 6 7 8 9 10—CRK—12 11 10

Longman
is an imprint of

Student Edition ISBN 13: 978-0-205-66273-9
Student Edition ISBN 10:   0-205-66273-0
Annotated Instructor's Edition ISBN 13: 978-0-205-66278-4
Annotated Instructor's Edition ISBN 10:   0-205-66278-1

www.pearsonhighered.com

Brief Contents

Detailed Contents

Preface

Reading Across the Disciplines, Fourth Edition, is designed to improve college students' reading and thinking skills through brief skill instruction and extensive guided practice with academic discipline-based readings. The text is structured around 12 academic disciplines. The 36 readings—all of which aim to motivate students—are selected from college textbooks as well as from books, periodicals and popular magazines, newspapers, and Internet sources. The objective is to show the relevance of college studies to events and issues in everyday life through the use of engaging readings.

PURPOSE

The primary purposes of the text are to teach essential college reading skills and to guide their application in each of 12 academic disciplines. The text develops basic vocabulary and comprehension skills, as well as inferential and critical-reading and -thinking skills. In addition to developing overall reading skills, the text also introduces students to content-specific reading skills. Each chapter in Part Two, "Readings for Academic Disciplines," begins with a tip list for applying reading and thinking skills to text with the unique characteristics of the discipline. Questions and activities that precede and follow each reading demonstrate the application of vocabulary, comprehension, and critical-reading and -thinking skills to the particular discipline.

Another important goal of the text is to demonstrate to students the relevance and utility of college courses to their daily lives. The book attempts to answer the long-standing question frequently asked by students, "Why do I have to take a course in history, biology, etc.?" The book presents readings that show students how academic disciplines embrace and investigate topics of interest and concern to everyday human experience.

CONTENT OVERVIEW

The book is organized into three parts:

- **Part One, "A Handbook for Reading and Thinking in College,"** presents a brief skill introduction. Written in handbook format (1a, 1b, etc.), this part introduces students to essential vocabulary, comprehension, critical-reading, and reading-rate skills.

- **Part Two, "Readings for Academic Disciplines,"** has 12 chapters, each containing readings representative of a different academic discipline. Each chapter has three reading selections. The readings in each chapter are chosen from textbooks, books, periodicals, newspapers, and Internet sources that contain material relevant to the discipline. The readings in each chapter vary in length as well as difficulty. Within each chapter, readings are arranged from least to most difficult, providing students with the opportunity to strengthen their skills, experience success, and build positive attitudes toward reading. Each reading is accompanied by an extensive apparatus that guides student learning.

- **Part Three, "Textbook Chapter Reading,"** contains a complete psychology textbook chapter. This chapter enables students to practice skills on a larger piece of writing and to apply the skills they have developed in the preceding parts. Apparatus is provided for each major section of the chapter.

FEATURES

Reading Across the Disciplines guides students in learning reading and thinking skills essential for college success.

Students Approach Reading as Thinking

Reading is approached as a thinking process—a process of interacting with textual material and sorting, evaluating, and reacting to its organization and content. The apparatus preceding and following each reading focuses, guides, and shapes the students' thought processes.

Students Develop Active Reading Skills

Students learn to approach reading as a process that requires involvement and response. In doing so, they are able to master the skills that are essential to college reading. The reading apparatus provides a model for active reading.

Students Learn Essential Reading Skills

Vocabulary, comprehension, and critical-reading skills are presented concisely in Part One, "A Handbook for Reading and Thinking in College," and are accompanied by several exercises.

Students Learn Discipline-Specific Reading Skills

The high-interest readings in Part Two are grouped according to academic discipline. Each chapter begins with a brief list of tips for reading and learning within the particular discipline. Students are encouraged to apply these techniques as they read the selections within the chapter.

Students Learn as They Work

Unlike many books, which simply test students after they have read a selection, this text teaches students as they work. Some of the apparatus provides new material on vocabulary, methods of organizing information, transitions, and reading/study strategies.

Students Understand the Importance of Academic Disciplines to Their Daily Lives

Through the high-interest topics selected, students will come to understand the relevance of various academic disciplines to their daily lives, careers, and workplace.

Students Learn Visually

Increasingly, college students are becoming visual learners, and visual literacy is critical to success in today's world. To promote visual learning, this text is four-color and contains numerous photographs, graphics, graphic organizers (maps), charts, and diagrams.

Students Appreciate Consistent Format

Because students often need structure and organization, this text uses a consistent format for each reading selection. Students always know what to expect and what is expected of them.

Students Can Build Success by Progressing from Less to More Difficult Readings

The readings within each chapter are organized conceptually from less to more difficult. Instructors may choose a starting level that is appropriate for their classes. By starting with a relatively easy reading, students can build confidence and success before approaching more challenging readings.

Students Refer to Part One, "A Handbook for Reading and Thinking in College," to Get Help Answering Questions

The activities following each reading are parallel to the topics in Part One of the book, which presents a brief skill overview in a handbook format. For example, if students have difficulty answering inferential questions, they may refer to the section in Part One that explains how to make inferences. The handbook also includes a section on reading and evaluating electronic sources.

Format of the Apparatus

The apparatus for each reading selection follows a consistent format. The sections vary in the number of questions and the specific skills reviewed. Each reading selection has the following parts:

- **Headnote.** A headnote introduces the reading, identifies its source, provokes the students' interest, and most important, establishes a framework or purpose for reading.
- **Previewing the Reading.** Students are directed to preview the reading using the guidelines provided in Part One and to answer several questions based on their preview.

- **Making Connections.** This brief section encourages students to draw connections between the topic of the reading and their own knowledge and experience.
- **Reading Tip.** The reading tip is intended to help students approach and work through the reading. A different reading tip is offered for each reading. For example, a reading tip might suggest how to highlight to strengthen comprehension or how to write annotations to enhance critical thinking.
- **Reading Selection/Vocabulary Annotation.** Most reading selections contain difficult vocabulary words that are essential to the meaning of the selection. Often these are words that students are unlikely to know and cannot figure out from context. These words are highlighted, and their meanings are given as marginal annotations. Preferable to a list of words preceding the reading, this format allows students to check meanings on an as-needed basis, within the context of the selection. Annotations are also used occasionally to provide necessary background information that students may need to grasp concepts in a reading.
- **Understanding the Thesis and Other Main Ideas.** This section helps students figure out the thesis of the reading and identify the main idea of selected paragraphs.
- **Identifying Details.** This section focuses on recognizing the relationship between main ideas and details, as well as distinguishing primary from secondary details. The format of questions within this section varies to expose students to a variety of thinking strategies.
- **Recognizing Methods of Organization and Transitions.** This part of the apparatus guides students in identifying the overall organizational pattern of the selection and in identifying transitional words and phrases within the reading. Prompts are provided that serve as teaching tips or review strategies.
- **Reviewing and Organizing Ideas.** Since many students are proficient at literal recall of information but have difficulty seeing relationships and organizing information into usable formats for study and review, this section emphasizes important review and organizational skills such as paraphrasing, mapping, outlining, and summarizing.
- **Figuring Out Inferred Meanings.** The ability to think inferentially is expected of college students. This section guides students in making inferences based on information presented in the reading selection.
- **Thinking Critically.** This section covers essential critical-thinking skills including distinguishing fact from opinion, identifying the author's purpose, recognizing bias, evaluating the source, identifying tone, making judgments, and evaluating supporting evidence.
- **Building Vocabulary.** The first part of this section focuses on vocabulary in context, while the second is concerned with word parts. Using words from the reading selection, exercises are structured to encourage students to expand their vocabulary and strengthen their

word-analysis skills. A brief review of the meanings of prefixes, roots, and suffixes used in the exercise is provided for ease of reference and to create a meaningful learning situation. The third vocabulary section focuses on a wide range of interesting features of language, drawing upon unusual or striking usage within the reading. Topics such as figurative language, idioms, and connotative meanings are included.

- **Selecting a Learning/Study Strategy.** College students are responsible for learning and studying what they read; many use the same study method for all disciplines and all types of material. This section helps students to choose appropriate study methods and to adapt their study methods to suit particular academic disciplines.

- **Exploring Ideas Through Discussion and Writing.** Questions provided in this section are intended to stimulate thought, provoke discussion, and serve as a springboard to writing about the reading.

- **Beyond the Classroom to the Web.** These activities draw on the skills students have learned by directing them to the Internet, where they are asked to read particular articles. These activities also demonstrate the relevance of the academic discipline beyond the classroom and provide guidance in using Web sources.

FEATURES OF THE FOURTH EDITION

The goal of this revision was to give greater emphasis to the skills beginning college students need to succeed in a variety of academic disciplines. The revision also recognizes and addresses new technology that has entered the learning environment, including e-books, online study groups, and course management systems. Readings have also been replaced with new selections on current and relevant topics.

NEW Ten Success Strategies for Learning and Studying Academic Disciplines

This new introduction to the book provides students with basic skills they need to succeed in the numerous academic disciplines they will study and addresses the new technology available to enhance communication and learning. Students learn to

- Develop new skills appropriate for each discipline.
- Acquire the right tools to enhance learning.
- Learn the technical and specialized language of each discipline.
- Communicate with classmates (e-mail, online study groups, IM, etc.).
- Communicate with professors.
- Develop new means of acquiring information.
- Use new information sources (databases, discipline-specific learning aids, and so on).
- Record and organize information using a computer.

- Approach online courses.
- Develop academic integrity (avoid plagiarism, cyberplagiarism, etc.).

NEW Introduction to Part Two, "Readings for Academic Disciplines"

This section acquaints students with the structure of the apparatus following each reading and demonstrates its utility as they work within a new academic discipline.

NEW Complete Textbook Chapter

A new psychology textbook chapter has been chosen for Part Three. The chapter, titled "Memory," is representative of the organization and structure of typical textbook chapters. Its content is particularly relevant to students as they develop learning strategies for academic disciplines. The chapter covers encoding, storage, and retrieval of information and contains a variety of practical applications.

NEW Reading Selections

Eight new reading selections have been added. Seven are on the topics of video games, online dating, cultural differences in nonverbal communication, issue-oriented and street art, product placement in the media, DNA fingerprinting, and stem cell research. A new poem by Gladys Cardiff explores traditions passed through generations.

NEW Readings in Part One

Two new readings, one on commercial jingles, another on snitching, have been added to Part One to provide skill application and practice.

EXPANDED Coverage of Evaluating Online Sources

Chapter 9 has been revised to drop information that has become common knowledge and to add information and exercises on evaluating Web sites, including new material on objectivity, authority, and usability.

MyReadingLab **NEW Linkage to MyReadingLab**

Icons throughout Part One link content to coverage on the MyReadingLab site, the extensive online reading skills resource, where students can obtain further practice in the skills indicated.

BOOK-SPECIFIC ANCILLARIES

- **Annotated Instructor's Edition.** The Annotated Instructor's Edition is identical to the student text, but it includes answers printed directly on the pages where questions and exercises appear. ISBN 0-205-66278-1

- **Test Bank.** This supplement contains numerous tests for each chapter, formatted for easy distribution and scoring. It includes content review quizzes and skill-based mastery tests for Part One and a discipline-based test and two discipline-based mastery tests for Part Two. ISBN 0-205-66276-5
- **Instructor's Manual.** The manual includes teaching suggestions for each section of Part One. For each reading in Part Two, the manual provides numerous suggestions for introducing the reading and offers a variety of follow-up activities designed to review and reinforce skills. ISBN 0-205-66277-3
- **Expanding Your Vocabulary.** Instructors may choose to shrink-wrap *Reading Across the Disciplines* with a copy of *Expanding Your Vocabulary*. This book, written by Kathleen McWhorter, works well as a supplemental text providing additional instruction and practice in vocabulary. Students can work through the book independently, or units may be incorporated into weekly lesson plans. Topics covered include methods of vocabulary learning, contextual aids, word parts, connotative meanings, idioms, euphemisms, and many more interesting and fun topics. The book concludes with vocabulary lists and exercises representative of ten academic disciplines. To preview this book, contact your Longman sales consultant for an examination copy.

ACKNOWLEDGMENTS

I wish to express my gratitude to my reviewers for their excellent ideas, suggestions, and advice on the preparation and revision of this text:

Maria Spelleri, Manatee Community College; Sylvia D. Ybarra, San Antonio College; Valerie Hicks, Community College Beaver County; Lynette D. Shaw-Smith, Springfield College Illinois/Benedictine University; Kathleen S. Britton, Florence-Darlington Technical College; Kimberly S. Hall, Harrisburg Area Community College; Debra Herrera, Cisco Junior College; Michael Vensel, Miami Dade College; and Anne Hepfer, Seattle University.

I also wish to thank Gill Cook, my development editor, for her creative vision of the project, her helpful suggestions, and her assistance in preparing and organizing the manuscript. I am particularly indebted to Kate Edwards, acquisitions editor, for her enthusiastic support, valuable advice, and expert guidance of the revision.

KATHLEEN T. MCWHORTER

STRATEGIES

Ten Success Strategies for Learning and Studying Academic Disciplines

Ten SUCCESS STRATEGIES FOR LEARNING AND STUDYING ACADEMIC DISCIPLINES

Each academic discipline has a specialized approach for studying the world. To illustrate, let's choose human beings and consider how various disciplines might approach their study.

- An ARTIST might consider a human being as an object of beauty and record a person's fluid, flexible muscular structure and meaningful facial expressions on canvas.

- A PSYCHOLOGIST might study what human needs (love, safety, etc.) are fulfilled by various behaviors.

- A HISTORIAN might research the historical importance of human actions and decisions—their decisions to enter wars or form alliances with other countries.

- An ANTHROPOLOGIST might trace the evolution of the human race.

- An ECONOMIST might focus on the supply of and demand for essential human goods (food, clothing, transportation) and the amount of business they generate.

- A BIOLOGIST would categorize the human as *Homo sapiens*.

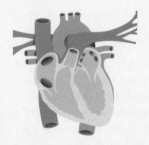

- A PHYSIOLOGIST would be concerned with human bodily functions (breathing, heart rate, temperature).

- A MATHEMATICIAN might calculate human life expectancies based on lifestyle, gender, race, and so forth.

Each academic discipline, then, approaches a given object or event with a different focus or perspective. Each has its own special purposes and interests that define the scope of the discipline. You will find that each discipline also has its own methodology for studying the topics with which it is concerned. Because each discipline is unique, each requires somewhat different study and learning strategies. The purpose of this introduction is to show you how to modify and adapt your learning, thinking, and study strategies to best apply them to a variety of specific academic areas.

STRATEGY 1

Develop New Skills for Each Academic Discipline

In college, you are likely to encounter disciplines with which you have had no prior experience. Anthropology, political science, or organic chemistry, for example, may be new to you. In the beginning, these new fields of study may seem unfamiliar or foreign. One student described this feeling as "being on the outside looking in," watching other students participate in the class but being unable to do so himself. At first, you may feel lost, confused, or frustrated in such courses, due to your unfamiliarity with the specialized language, the types of learning and thinking expected of you, and the conventions, approaches, and methodology of the discipline.

Strategies for Reading in New Disciplines

When approaching a new field of study, try the following:

- **Spend more time than usual reading and studying.** You are doing more than reading and studying: you are learning how to learn as well. That is, you are trying to discover what is important and what is the best way to learn it. For example, in chemistry, formulas are important, and you need to work out a way to organize, learn, and remember them. In business marketing and advertising, case studies are common, so you need to develop a system for identifying and summarizing what they demonstrate.

- **Overlearn until you discover more about what is expected.** Until you do discover what is important and do figure out the best way to learn it, learn more information than you may need. That is, err in the direction of learning too much, rather than too little. For example, in a criminal justice class, until you know whether the instructor's focus is on trends, patterns, and theories or on facts, research findings, and specific laws, it is safer to learn both.

- **Since you do not know what information you will be expected to know for exams and quizzes and the form in which you will be asked to deliver it (essays, multiple choice, short answer, and so forth), use several different methods to learn the same information.** For example, in an anthropology course, you might learn events and discoveries chronologically (according to occurrence in time) as well as comparatively (according to similarities and differences among various discoveries). In an accounting course, you might organize information by procedures as well as by controlling principles. In a sociology course, you might highlight textbook information (to promote factual recall) as well as write outlines and summaries (to interpret and consolidate ideas). You might also draw diagrams that map the relationships between concepts and ideas.

- **Look for similarities between the new subject matter and other academic fields that are familiar to you.** If similarities exist, you may be able to modify or adapt learning approaches and strategies you are already familiar with to fit your new field of study. For instance, if you are familiar with mathematics, some of the learning strategies you use in that discipline may apply to physics and chemistry.

- **Establish an overview of the field.** Spend time studying the table of contents of your textbook; it provides an outline of the course. Look for patterns, progression of ideas, and recurring themes, approaches, or problems.

- **Obtain additional reference materials, if necessary.** Some college texts delve into a subject immediately, providing only a brief introduction to or overview of the discipline in the first chapter. If needed, spend an hour or so in the library or online getting a more comprehensive overview of the field. Many libraries provide research guides both in print and on the Web. Check to see what your library offers. These guides usually list the most important reference books (some available electronically) in the field. The reference materials, which may include specialized encyclopedias and dictionaries, will provide you with the key concepts, names, dates, statistics, and events for specific disciplines. With this information, you will be able to delve further into the topics as you search for books, articles, and other documents in the library's online resources (catalogs and databases). Find out whether your library has a librarian assigned to the discipline; if so, this person will be a key contact for you. The librarian is already an expert at finding resources and can save you a great deal of time looking for relevant material. Use the following sources, as well:

STUDY AIDS FOR ACADEMIC DISCIPLINES

ACADEMIC DISCIPLINE	STUDY AID WEBSITES
Social Sciences	http://owl.english.purdue.edu/owl/resource/559/01/
Communication/Speech	http://www.muskingum.edu/~cal/database/content/speech.html
Anthropology	http://chss2.montclair.edu/anthropology/bettergrades.htm
Arts/Humanities/Literature	http://muskingum.edu/~cal/database/content/literature3.html http://www.muskingum.edu/~cal/database/content/art.html
Political Science/Government/History	http://www.unc.edu/depts/wcweb/handouts/polisci.html
Business/Advertising/Economics	http://www.scsv.nevada.edu/~roncron/studytips.html
Technology/Computers	http://web.grinnell.edu/careerdevelopment/makingchoices/math.html
Health-Related Fields	www.sarc.sdes.ucf.edu/ss87.pdf http://mtsu32.mtsu.edu:11024/Lecture_Materials/advice_&_study_tips.htm http://medi-smart.com/study-tips.htm
Life Sciences	http://www.newsdesk.umd.edu/culture/2006/scinotes/ http://wc.pima.edu/~carem/BIOSTUDY.html

STRATEGY 2

Acquire the Right Tools

To be successful in any discipline you need the right tools. These include the following: a collegiate dictionary, subject area dictionaries, access to useful Web sites, and documentation guides.

A Collegiate Dictionary

Regardless of the field you are studying, you need a collegiate dictionary. Many are available in paperback editions. Online dictionaries are available and offer the added advantage of offering an audio function that allows you to hear how a word is pronounced. Here are several useful sites.

- **Dictionary.com** (http://www.dictionary.com). This site gives you meanings from several different sources and allows you to compare them. Following are examples for the word *metabolism*.

Dictionary.com Unabridged (b 1.1)

> **me·tab·o·lism** Audio Help [m*uh*-**tab**-*uh*-liz-*uh* m] Pronunciation Key – Show IPA Pronunciation
> —*noun*
>
> 1. *Biology, Physiology.* the sum of the physical and chemical processes in an organism by which its material substance is produced, maintained, and destroyed, and by which energy is made available. Compare ANABOLISM, CATABOLISM.
> 2. any basic process of organic functioning or operating: *changes in the country's economic metabolism.*
>
> [Orgin: 1875–80; < Gk *metabol* ē *change (meta–* META– + *bol* ē a throw) + –ISM]

American Heritage Dictionary

me · tab · o · lism   Audio Help (mĭ–tăb′ə-lĭz′əm) Pronunciation Key n.

1. The chemical processes occurring within a living cell or organism that are necessary for the maintenance of life. In metabolism some substances are broken down to yield energy for vital processes while other substances, necessary for life, are synthesized.

2. The processing of a specific substance within the living body: *water metabolism; Iodine metabolism.*

[From Greek metabolē, *change,* from metaballein, *to change*: meta-, *meta-* + ballein, *to throw*; see gʷela- in Indo-European roots.]

- **Merriam-Webster Online** (http://www.m-w.com). This site allows you to enter a word or phrase and check the site's dictionary, thesaurus, Spanish-English dictionary, and/or medical dictionary for its meaning.

- **American Heritage Online** (http://www.bartleby.com). This site allows you to select from among a variety of reference books, including *American Heritage Collegiate Dictionary, Roget's Thesaurus, Bartlett's Quotations, Gray's Anatomy,* and so forth.

Subject Area Dictionaries

Many academic fields have specialized dictionaries that list most of the important words used in that discipline. These dictionaries list specialized meanings for words and suggest how and when to use them. The field of nursing, for instance, has *Taber's Cyclopedic Medical Dictionary.* Other subject area dictionaries include *A Dictionary of Anthropology, The New Grove Dictionary of Music and Musicians,* and *A Dictionary of Economics.*

Find out whether there are subject area dictionaries for the disciplines you are studying. Most libraries have copies of specialized dictionaries in the reference section, and you can also access numerous subject area dictionaries online.

Useful Web Sites

The Internet has a wealth of information on learning and studying each academic discipline. For example, the site http://apphysicsb.homestead.com/study.html contains useful information on how to study physics. Do a Google search to find useful information on each academic discipline you are studying. The table below lists useful online references for each of the academic disciplines covered in this book.

DISCIPLINE	USEFUL ONLINE REFERENCE
Social Sciences	Online Dictionary of the Social Sciences http://bitbucket.icaap.org/
Communication/Speech	Glossary of Communication http://www.jyu.fi/viesti/verkkotuotanto/ci/ glossary.shtml
Anthropology	What Is Anthropology http://www.aaanet.org/about/WhatisAnthropology.cfm
Arts/Humanities/Literature	Humanities Glossary http://www.foreignlanguages.eku.edu/humanities/ glossary.php
Public Policy/Contemporary Issues	Political Economy and Public Policy Glossary http://www.laits.utexas.edu/gov310/PEP/glossary.html
Political Science/Government/History	Political Science Terms http://www.nelson.com/nelson/polisci/glossary.html
Business/Advertising/Economics	New York Times Financial and Business Terms http://www.nytimes.com/library/financial/ glossary/bfglosa.htm
Technology/Computers	How to Study Computer Science http://www.aihorizon.com/essays/basiccs/general/ starting_out.htm
Health-Related Fields	Online Medical Encyclopedia http://www.nlm.nih.gov/medlineplus/encyclopedia.html
Life Sciences	Life Science Glossary http://www.biochem.northwestern.edu/holmgren/ Glossary/Definitions.html
Physical Sciences/Mathematics	Physical Sciences Resource Center http://www.psrc-online.org/search/ browse.cfm?browse=gsss ChemiCool http://www.chemicool.com/ Wolfram's MathWorld http://mathworld.wolfram.com/ Planet Math Encyclopedia http://planetmath.org/encyclopedia
Workplace/Career Fields	Career Competencies http://www.bgsu.edu/offices/sa/career/ page19374.html

Documentation Guides

Most academic fields of study have preferred methods of crediting sources used when writing papers. Be sure to find out what documentation style your instructor requires and obtain the appropriate style guide in print or locate a reliable Web site that summarizes the guidelines.

The most common documentation styles are

- **MLA** (Modern Language Association). Used in English, some humanities, and foreign languages.

- **APA** (American Psychological Association). Widely used in the social sciences.

- **CSE** (Council of Science Editors). Used in the life sciences, physical sciences, and mathematics.

- **Chicago Style.** Commonly used in history, art history, philosophy, and some humanities.

STRATEGY 3

Learn the Language of the Discipline

White blood cell

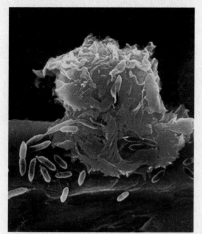

Each academic discipline has its own set of specialized words that allow precise communication through accurate and concise descriptions of events, principles, concepts, problems, and occurrences. One of the first tasks you face in a new course, then, is to learn the specialized language of that course. This task is especially important in introductory courses in which the subject is new and unfamiliar. In an introductory psychology course, you must learn many new terms—*assimilation, autonomic nervous system, conditioning, reinforcement, defense mechanism,* and *extinction* are a few examples. You will encounter this specialized terminology in class lectures and in textbooks and will be expected to use it in assignments and exams.

A white blood cell ingests bacteria using phagocytosis.

Class Lectures

Often, the first few lectures in a course are devoted to acquainting you with the nature and scope of the field and introducing you to its specialized language. Use the following tips below and shown in the sample notes to keep track of and learn new terms throughout each course.

- **Record accurately each new term for later review and study.**

- **Pay attention to clues about what is important.** Good lecturers give students clues to what terms and definitions are important to record. Some instructors make a habit of writing new words on the chalkboard, as a means of emphasis. Other instructors may emphasize new terms and definitions by slowing down, almost dictating, so that you can record definitions. Still other instructors may repeat a word and its definition several times or offer several variations of meaning.

- **Develop a consistent method for easily identifying new terms and definitions recorded in your notes.** You might circle or draw a box around each new term; or, as you review your notes, underline each new term in red; or write "def." in the margin each time a definition is included. The particular mark or symbol you use is a matter of preference; what is important is to find some way to mark definitions for further study.

```
                        Sample Lecture Notes
              A. Types of Aging
   def         ┌ 1. Primary ─┬ normal progressive aging
   def         └ 2. Secondary ─┬ aging due to extrinsic factors
                     ▪ ex. Disease, smoking, environmental pollution
```

Textbook Assignments

The first few chapters within a textbook are generally introductory. They are written to familiarize you with the subject of study and acquaint you with its specialized language. For example, in a widely used psychology textbook, 34 new terms are introduced in the first two chapters (40 pages), and in a popular chemistry book, 56 specialized words are introduced in the first two chapters (28 pages). Some of the words in each are words common in everyday usage that have specialized meanings when used in these disciplines. For example, the word *drive* is commonly used to mean "to control a vehicle," but in psychology it means a biologically based motivation. *Ground*, commonly used to refer to the solid surface we stand on, means background—the area around and between figures—in the field of visual arts. Other technical terms are used only in the subject area. For example, the terms *distal tubing, endodermis,* and *photosynthesis* are unique to biology-related fields.

Textbook authors use various means to emphasize and explain new terminology. These include the following:

- **Typeface variations**. Use of italics, boldface type, or colored print to identify important terms and/or definitions.

- **Marginal definitions**. New terms defined in the margin of a page next to where they appear in the body of the text.

- **"New Terminology" or "Vocabulary" lists**. These appear at the beginning or end of each chapter.

- **Glossaries**. These are comprehensive lists of terms introduced throughout a text and are usually found at the end. They include the meanings of terms and sometimes page references for where they are used in the text.

STRATEGY 4

Communicate with Classmates

Your classmates are valuable and important resources, and computers and the Internet offer new and convenient ways of communicating, sharing information, and studying with them. Talking with classmates in person or by phone was once the primary form of communication. Now there are many new options; use each of the following to learn more effectively.

New Options for Communication

- **Email.** It is helpful to get the e-mail addresses of several classmates. If you miss a class or are confused by an assignment, you can contact a classmate and get help immediately. Your e-mail address is the first information many people will get about you—keep it simple: yourfirstname. yourlastname is fine, h0tR@v3rGur1 is not.

- **Instant Messaging (IM).** Instant messaging allows you to talk back and forth with classmates through your computer, as long as you are both online at the same time. You can discuss assigned readings, quiz each other in preparation for a test, practice for a class discussion, or set up a study group. Choose an IM partner who is serious and respectful of your time constraints. It is too easy to waste valuable time chatting about nonessen-tials. Since there are many different chat programs, try one that operates on multiple networks, like Trillian, which supports AOL Instant Messenger, MSN Messenger, Yahoo! Messenger, and IRC. You'll still need separate accounts with each service, but you'll have fewer programs running.

- **Online Study Group.** If everyone in your group takes notes on a computer, sharing them is easy. IM, e-mail, and other programs, such as Skype, make it easy to stay in contact with classmates. Group chat rooms that offer text and audio are preferable to walking a mile in the rain to a study group. List your classes in Facebook, then click on them to see everyone taking that class.

■ **Professor Operated Message Boards.** For some courses, your professor may create a message board where class members can post and share information. Remember that anything you post here is public—available for anyone to read. Avoid posting complaints about assignments or the workload for the course. Instead, use it positively. Get other students' points of view on topics and issues. Find out about useful study tips, sources of information, or course deadlines that other students have posted.

■ **Social Networks.** Many students communicate through social networks such as MySpace or Facebook, usually for nonacademic purposes. They may post photographs, status updates, or party announcements. Whatever you post may be public information, although some networks do allow you to give access to your postings only to specified users. Use these networks with caution, and be sure not to give personal information that may jeopardize your safety or security. If you are using a public network, remember that what you post now may hurt you later. Many employers check these networks to learn about the background of potential employees. You would not want a potential employer to see a photo of you in embarrassing or inappropriate poses, for example.

■ **Cell Phones.** Turn your phone off during class, and leave it off; texting, or worse, talking, will anger your professor.

STRATEGY 5

Communicate with Your Professors

Your instructors are valuable resources; there are a variety of possible ways to communicate with them other than through traditional means such as in-person contact before and after class or during office hours

Options for Communicating with Professors

■ **Email.** Many professors give students an e-mail address at which to contact them. Some professors check their e-mail several times a day; others may check it as little as once a week. Until you are certain a professor checks his or her e-mail frequently, do not e-mail time-sensitive questions or information.

Although e-mail is more informal than other types of writing, use a more formal level of communication with professors than you would with friends. Use correct grammar, spelling, and punctuation; avoid slang. Do not be overly friendly or familiar, and don't send attachments or pictures unless requested. Some professors won't discuss grades or other personal information over e-mail.

■ **Phone.** Be especially cautious with professors' phone numbers, and always ask about appropriate calling times. It's all right to call an office number at 2 a.m., but not a home number.

■ **Instant Messaging.** Most professors do not communicate with students over IM. If you have one who does, treat his or her screenname like a home phone number; scrub your profile and other shared information.

STRATEGY 6

Develop New Means of Acquiring Information

While print textbooks, instructor handouts, and print library sources are still the most important sources of information, you also need to be familiar with new information delivery systems, including e-books, course management systems, online class notes, and online information sources.

Reading E-books

E-books are textbooks that you can purchase in electronic form. E-books have one major advantage—they are usually much cheaper than print textbooks. They are also convenient, portable via computer, and much lighter than hardbacks. Use the following suggestions for reading e-books:

■ If the e-book is in PDF format, use the search function to find useful information not only in the chapter you're currently studying, but elsewhere in the text.

■ Not everyone can study on a computer, especially if it requires reading pages of plain text. If you have this problem and have an e-book as a required text, print it out or look for a paper edition.

Using Course Management Web Sites

A course management Web site is sponsored and controlled by the professor. The site allows the professor to post the course syllabus, assignments, or tests and quizzes. Students may submit assignments to the professor through the site, and the professor may send feedback and/or graded assignments back to students. The site can also be used to organize discussion groups, send e-mail, and post announcements.

When using a course management Web site, be sure you do not submit materials too soon. Once you click "send," your work is submitted. Take enough time to be sure your work is top quality and does not need further revision. Some sites allow you to resubmit in case of errors, but don't count on it.

Make sure you're using the latest version of your Web browser and have the most recent plug-ins for QuickTime, Flash, and anything else the course management site requires. While most work with Firefox, some are still Internet Explorer only.

Reading/Using Online Notes

Some professors post online notes on their Web sites. They may be guides to upcoming lectures, summaries of previous lectures, or supplementary information. They are useful because they identify what the professor feels is important and necessary to learn. Here are a few tips.

- **Do not skip the lecture and rely on online notes.** Online notes are intended to help you in class. They are a teaching/learning tool.

- **Do not use online notes as a substitute for taking your own notes in class.** Lectures often cover different aspects of the material and go into greater detail. Missing a lecture also means missing the class discussion, one of the best ways to understand concepts.

- **Devise a system whereby you place your own notes beside the online notes.** Use a split page or double column page. If they are in PowerPoint, print the slides and write in the white space.

- **Reading online notes will not ensure that you have learned the material.** Unlike notes that you have taken yourself, you have little ownership of them. You have not thought about the material, condensed it, and expressed it in your own words. To learn the material, try to interact with it by summarizing, rewriting, reorganizing, or testing yourself on it.

STRATEGY 7 Use New Means of Acquiring Information

The Internet contains a vast amount of information that is not organized in any particular way. Search engines can help you locate the information you need. Don't be afraid to try new ones. Google is very useful, but it's not the only one. If you want to search a number of engines or organize your results by cluster, try Dogpile.com and mamma.com for multiengine search, and Clusty.com for a more organized approach. Once you find information on a Web site, be sure to evaluate its purpose, content, and accuracy using the suggestions in Chapter 9. In general, take everything online with a grain of salt and remember that you need at least a two-source confirmation.

Using Electronic Databases

Electronic databases are closed collections of articles; they do not include books. Electronic databases can be searched rapidly using very specific queries. School libraries usually purchase access to these databases for students, faculty, and staff to use on- and off-campus. Some articles are full-text; others are not. You might have to get the article in print from the library or request it through interlibrary loan. You will also need to know how many articles the professor requires and if they need to be peer-reviewed.

Many professors require a combination of sources, including books, articles, and Web sites. Databases provide *articles only,* which do not always provide the breadth and depth of information found in books. Here are a few tips for using databases:

- **Take time to get to know your database**. If you want to search for two different terms, you need to know whether & or *AND* or + will get you there. No two databases are the same.

- **Know that there are many different databases.** Each provides significantly different information. Go to the right database, and you'll find crafting the right query much easier. Ask your librarian for help.

- **Make sure you know what information you need to do electronic searches when you're not at the library**—the password for one campus computer system might not work for another.

- **Check the availability of the service.** Don't assume it is always available.

- **If you can e-mail yourself articles, do so instead of printing them.** You'll save on paper and it's easier to copy and paste quotes than to retype them. As always, attribute properly.

- **Understand that Lexis-Nexis is a huge, comprehensive database, but it can be difficult to use.** Don't try to learn Lexis when you have a paper due; take an afternoon and toss queries at it until you know what kinds of questions it'll respond to.

STRATEGY 8

Use New Means of Recording Information

Computers offer students new and more efficient ways of recording information. Some students bring laptop computers to class and use them to take notes.

Using Computers to Take Notes

Here are some helpful hints for using a computer for taking notes in class:

- Take all your notes for each class in the same document.
- Set your word processor to save automatically every few minutes in case of a power surge or outage.
- Bring your AC adapter even if you don't think you need it. When you do need it, you'll be glad.
- Turn down your screen brightness to stretch a dying battery.
- If you get to class a few minutes early, turn on your laptop right away so if it makes an annoyingly loud startup noise no one cares.

Information from Web sites can be printed, copied, or cut and pasted into a document on your computer. (If you copy something, be sure to fully note the source and give credit to that source if you use the information in a paper or class discussion.)

Using Computers to Organize Information

A computer provides easy and efficient ways of organizing information for study and review. Here are a few tips:

- Keep all your notes for each class in one file. This makes review easy: print your notes and read, repeating as desired.
- Set your word processor to auto-save often.
- Take advantage of different text colors to set off important information.

Computers can also be used to help you manage your time efficiently. Programs such as Google Calendar and FutureMe offer a customized daily agenda and reminder e-mails, helpful for both the short and long term.

STRATEGY 9

Become Familiar with Online Courses

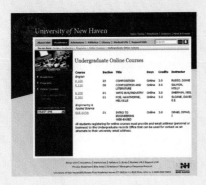

Many colleges now offer students the opportunity to enroll in courses online. Rather than attending class, students complete all or most of the course requirements electronically. Professors post reading assignments, sponsor and monitor discussions, and interact with individual students by e-mail. Some online classes are conducted in real time; both professor and students are online together at given times. Other classes permit students to work independently, choosing times when they want to participate, work, and study.

Tips for Taking Online Courses

While online courses may seem easy, they require a great deal of self-discipline and the ability to work alone. Use the following tips for taking online courses.

- **Avoid taking online courses during your first semester or first year.** It is better to learn what is expected in college classes by attending traditional classes. Once you are familiar with college expectations, you will be better prepared to take an online course.

- **Read, read, read.** Reading is your primary source of information. You read textbooks and communications from professors and other students. If you aren't a strong reader or feel as if you need personal contact with a professor and in-person support from other students, an online course may not be appropriate for you.

- **Keep up with the work.** Most students who fail online courses fail because they fall hopelessly behind with the required reading and written assignments and cannot catch up.

- **Devote specific hours each week to the online course.** Make a work/study schedule and follow it as you would for any other class.

- **Keep your focus.** Turn off music, instant messaging, and e-mail when you study.

STRATEGY 10 Demonstrate Academic Integrity

Academic integrity refers to honest and ethical conduct by both students and professors. It involves doing your own work, not representing the work of others as your own, and conducting yourself in class in a manner that's serious and respectful to others.

Avoiding Cheating

There are many forms of cheating, and you are likely to see some students engaging in it. Students who cheat on homework or exams are, in the long run, cheating themselves. They are cheating themselves out of the education they are in college to obtain. Obvious forms of cheating involve sharing homework assignments or exchanging information with other students on exams. Other, less obvious, but still very serious, forms of cheating include the following:

- Using unauthorized notes during an exam
- Changing exam answers after grading and requesting regrading
- Falsifying or making up results for a lab report
- Submitting the same paper twice for more than one course without instructor authorization
- Not following rules on take home exams
- Using someone else's work or ideas as if they are your own (plagiarism)

What Constitutes Plagiarism

Plagiarism means borrowing someone else's ideas or exact wording without giving that person credit. If you take information on Frank Lloyd Wright's architecture from a reference source, but do not indicate where you found it, you have plagiarized. If you take the six-word phrase "Martinez, the vengeful, despicable drug czar" from an online news article on the war on drugs, you have plagiarized. Plagiarism is intellectually dishonest because you are taking someone else's ideas or wording and passing them off as your own. There are academic penalties for plagiarism. You may receive a failing grade on your paper or you may fail the entire course. At some institutions you can even be academically dismissed.

Plagiarism can be intentional (planned) or unintentional (done by accident or oversight). Either way it carries the same academic penalty. If you buy a paper from an Internet site or deliberately copy and paste a section of an article from a Web site into your paper, your plagiarism is intentional. If you take notes from a source and copy exact wording, forget to enclose the wording in quotation marks, and later use that exact wording in your paper, your plagiarism is unintentional, but it is still serious and dishonest. Here are some guidelines that will help you understand exactly what is considered plagiarism.

WHAT IS PLAGIARISM?

- *Plagiarism* is the use of another person's words without giving credit to that person.
- *Plagiarism* is using another person's theory, opinion, or idea without listing where the information was taken from.
- *Plagiarism* results when the exact words of another person are not placed inside quotation marks. Both the quotation marks and a citation (reference) to the *original source* are needed.
- *Paraphrasing* (rewording) another person's words without giving credit to him or her is still *plagiarism*.
- Using facts, data, graphs, charts, and so on without stating where they were taken from is *plagiarism*.
- Using commonly known facts or information is **not** *plagiarism* and you need not give a source for such information. For example, the fact that Neil Armstrong set foot on the moon in 1969 is widely known and does not require documentation.

Avoiding Plagiarism

As you write papers for college classes, you will probably use sources to locate the information you need. As you read and take notes, and, later, as you write the paper, you need to know the rules for indicating that you have taken information or ideas from the work of other people. The purposes of identifying your sources are to help others who want to look further into the ideas of that author, find that source, and to give credit to the person who originally wrote the material or thought of the idea.

Here are some suggestions for avoiding plagiarism.

HOW TO AVOID PLAGIARISM

- When you take notes from a source, place anything you copy directly in quotation marks.
- As you read and take notes, separate your ideas from ideas taken from sources so you do not mistakenly present ideas from sources as your own. One way to do this is to use different colors of ink for each; another is to use different sections of a notebook page for information from sources and for your own ideas.
- Keep track of all sources you use, marking where each idea came from.
- When paraphrasing someone else's words, change as many words as possible and try not to follow the exact same organization. Give credit for where the information came from.
- Write paraphrases without looking at the original text so you rephrase information using your own words.
- When writing a paper, use quotation marks to designate exact quotations.
- Use citations to indicate the source of quotations and all ideas and information that are not your own. A citation is a parenthetical notation referring to a complete listing of sources used at the end of the paper.

Avoiding Cyberplagiarism

Cyberplagiarism is a special type of plagiarism; it involves borrowing information from the Internet without giving credit to the source posting the information. It is also called **cut and paste plagiarism**, referring to the ease with which a person can copy something from an Internet document and paste it into his or her own paper. Numerous Web sites offer student papers for sale on the Internet. The term *cyberplagiarism* also refers to using these papers and submitting them as one's own. Use the following suggestions to avoid unintentional cyberplagiarism:

- **If you copy exact words from an Internet source, put them in quotation marks in your notes, along with the name of the author, title of the article, title of the website, publisher, date of publication, and date of access.** Be sure to consult a style manual for details on how to indicate in your paper which material is borrowed and how to write a list of works you used in your paper.
- **List sources for all the information you include in your notes** regardless of whether it takes the form of direct quotes, paraphrases, or summaries of someone else's ideas.
- **Never copy and paste directly from a Web site into your paper** without enclosing the words in quotation marks and listing the source.
- **List the source for any information, facts, ideas, opinions, theories, or data you use from a Web site.**

Instructors have access to Web sites that can easily and quickly identify papers that have been shared or purchased, so most instructors can easily spot an intentionally plagiarized paper.

PART ONE

A Handbook for Reading and Thinking in College

1 Active Reading and Thinking Strategies

What does it take to do well in biology? In psychology? In history? In business? In answer to these questions, college students are likely to say:

- "Knowing how to study."
- "You have to like the course."
- "Hard work!"
- "Background in the subject area."
- "A good teacher!"

Students seldom mention reading as an essential skill. In a sense, reading is a hidden factor in college success. When you think of college, you think of attending classes and labs, completing assignments, studying for and taking exams, and writing papers. A closer look at these activities, however, reveals that reading is an important part of each.

Reading stays "behind the scenes" because instructors rarely evaluate it directly. Grades are based on production: how well you express your ideas in papers or how well you do on exams. Yet reading is the primary means by which you acquire your ideas and gather information.

Throughout this handbook you will learn numerous ways to use reading as a tool for college success.

1a   ACTIVE READING: THE KEY TO ACADEMIC SUCCESS

MyReadingLab

To practice active reading skills, go to

➤ Study Plan
➤ Reading Skills
➤ Active Reading Strategies

Reading involves much more than moving your eyes across lines of print, more than recognizing words, and more than reading sentences. Reading is thinking. It is an active process of identifying important ideas and comparing, evaluating, and applying them.

Have you ever gone to a ball game and watched the fans? Most do not sit and watch passively. Instead, they direct the plays, criticize the calls, encourage the players, and reprimand the coach. They care enough to get actively involved in the game. Just like interested fans, active readers get involved. They question, challenge, and criticize, as well as understand. Table 1.1 on page 28 contrasts the active strategies of successful readers with the passive ones of less successful

TABLE 1.1 ACTIVE VERSUS PASSIVE READING

ACTIVE READERS . . .	PASSIVE READERS . . .
Tailor their reading to suit each assignment.	Read all assignments the same way.
Analyze the purpose of an assignment.	Read an assignment because it was assigned.
Adjust their speed to suit their purpose.	Read everything at the same speed.
Question ideas in the assignment.	Accept whatever is in print as true.
Compare and connect textbook material with lecture content.	Study lecture notes and the textbook separately.
Skim headings to find out what an assignment is about before beginning to read.	Check the length of an assignment and then begin reading.
Make sure they understand what they are reading as they go along.	Read until the assignment is completed.
Read with pencil in hand, highlighting, jotting notes, and marking key vocabulary.	Read.
Develop personalized strategies that are particularly effective.	Follow routine, standard methods. Read all assignments the same way.

readers. Not all strategies will work for everyone. Experiment to discover those that work particularly well for you.

> ## NOW PRACTICE . . . ACTIVE READING

Consider each of the following reading assignments. Discuss ways to get actively involved in each assignment.

1. Reading two poems by Maya Angelou for an American literature class.

   _____

   _____

2. Reading the procedures for your next biology lab.

   _____

   _____

3. Reading an article in *Newsweek* magazine assigned by your political science instructor in preparation for a class discussion.

   _____

   _____

Previewing is a means of familiarizing yourself with the content and organization of an assignment *before* you read it. Think of previewing as getting a "sneak preview" of what a chapter or reading will be about. You can then read the material more easily and more rapidly.

How to Preview Reading Assignments

Use the following steps to become familiar with the content and organization of a chapter, essay, or article.

1. **Read the title.** The title indicates the topic of the article or chapter; the subtitle suggests the specific focus of, or approach to, the topic.
2. **Check the author and the source of an article and essay.** This information may provide clues about the article's content or focus.
3. **Read the introduction or the first paragraph.** The introduction or first paragraph serves as a lead-in, establishing the overall subject and suggesting how it will be developed.
4. **Read each boldface (dark print) heading.** Headings label the contents of each section and announce the major topic covered. If there are no headings, read the first sentence of each paragraph. The first sentence of the paragraph is often the topic sentence, which states the main idea of the paragraph. By reading first sentences, you will encounter most of the key ideas in the article.
5. **Read the first sentence under each major heading.** The first sentence often states the central thought of the section. If the first sentence seems introductory, read the last sentence; often this sentence states or restates the central thought.
6. **Note any typographical aids.** Colored print, boldface font, and italics are used to emphasize important terminology and definitions, distinguishing them from the rest of a passage. Material that is numbered 1, 2, 3; lettered a, b, c; or presented in list form is also of special importance.
7. **Note any graphic aids.** Graphs, charts, photographs, and tables often suggest what is important. Be sure to read the captions of photographs and the legends on graphs, charts, or tables.
8. **Read the last paragraph or summary.** This provides a condensed view of the article or chapter, often outlining the key points.
9. **Read quickly any end-of-article or end-of-chapter material.** This might include references, study questions, discussion questions, chapter outlines, or vocabulary lists. If there are study questions, read them through quickly because they tell you what is important to remember in the chapter. If a vocabulary list is included, rapidly skim through it to identify the terms you will be learning as you read.

A section of an interpersonal communication textbook chapter discussing the breakup of a relationship is reprinted here to illustrate how previewing is done. The portions to focus on when previewing are shaded. Read only those portions. After you have finished, test how well your previewing worked by answering the questions that follow, titled, "What Did You Learn from Previewing?"

Ending a Relationship

1   Some relationships, of course, do end. Sometimes there is simply not enough to hold the couple together. Sometimes there are problems that cannot be resolved. Sometimes the costs are too high and the rewards too few, or the relationship is recognized as destructive and escape is the only alternative. As a relationship ends, you're confronted with two general issues: (1) how to end the relationship, and (2) how to deal with the inevitable problems that relationship endings cause.

The Strategies of Disengagement

2   When you wish to exit a relationship you need some way of explaining this—to yourself as well as to your partner. You develop a strategy for getting out of a relationship that you no longer find satisfying or profitable. The table identifies five major disengagement strategies (Cody 1982). As you read down the table, note that the strategies depend on your goal. For example, you're more likely to remain friends if you use de-escalation than if you use justification or avoidance (Banks, Altendorf, Greene, and Cody 1987). You may find it interesting to identify the disengagement strategies you have heard of or used yourself and see how they fit in with these five types.

Dealing With a Breakup

3   Regardless of the specific reason, relationship breakups are difficult to deal with; invariably they cause stress. You're likely to experience high levels of distress over the breakup of a relationship in which you were satisfied, were close to your partner, had dated your partner for a long time, and felt it would not be easy to replace the relationship with another one (Simpson 1987, Frazier and Cook 1993).

4   Given both the inevitability that some relationships will break up and the importance of such breakups, here are some suggestions to ease the difficulty that is sure to be experienced. These suggestions apply to the termination of any type of relationship—between friends or lovers, through death, separation, or breakup.

Break the Loneliness-Depression Cycle

5   The two most common feelings following the end of a relationship are loneliness and depression. These feelings are significant; treat them seriously. Realize that depression often leads to serious illness. In most cases, fortunately, loneliness and depression are temporary. Depression, for example, usually does not last longer than three or four days. Similarly, the loneliness that follows a breakup is generally linked to this specific situation and will fade when the situation changes. When depression does last, is especially deep, or disturbs your normal functioning, it's time for professional help.

FIVE DISENGAGEMENT STRATEGIES

Think back to relationships that you have tried to dissolve or that your partner tried to dissolve. Did you or your partner use any of the strategies listed here? These strategies are taken from research by Michael Cody (1982).

STRATEGY	FUNCTION	EXAMPLES
Positive tone	To maintain a positive relationship; to express positive feelings for the other person	I really care for you a great deal but I'm not ready for such an intense relationship.
Negative identity management	To blame the other person for the breakup; to absolve oneself of the blame for the breakup	I can't stand your jealousy, your constant suspicions, your checking up on me. I need my freedom.
Justification	To give reasons for the breakup	I'm going away to college for four years; there's no point in not dating others.
Behavioral de-escalation	To reduce the intensity of the relationship	Avoidance; cut down on phone calls; reduce time spent together, especially time alone.
De-escalation	To reduce the exclusivity and hence the intensity of the relationship	I'm just not ready for so exclusive a relationship. I think we should see other people.

Take Time Out

6   Resist the temptation to jump into a new relationship while the old one is still warm or before a new one can be assessed with some objectivity. At the same time, resist swearing off all relationships. Neither extreme works well.

7   Take time out for yourself. Renew your relationship with yourself. If you were in a long-term relationship, you probably saw yourself as part of a team, as part of a couple. Now get to know yourself as a unique individual, standing alone at present but fully capable of entering a meaningful relationship in the near future.

Bolster Self-Esteem

8   When relationships fail, self-esteem often declines. This seems especially true for those who did not initiate the breakup (Collins and Clark 1989). You may feel guilty for having caused the breakup or inadequate for not holding on to the relationship. You may feel unwanted and unloved. Your task is to regain the positive self-image needed to function effectively.

9   Recognize, too, that having been in a relationship that failed—even if you view yourself as the main cause of the breakup—does not mean that you are a failure. Neither does it mean that you cannot succeed in a new and different relationship. It does mean that something went wrong with this one relationship. Ideally, it was a failure from which you have learned something important about yourself and about your relationship behavior.

Remove or Avoid Uncomfortable Symbols

10   After any breakup, there are a variety of reminders—photographs, gifts, and letters, for example. Resist the temptation to throw these out. Instead, remove them. Give them to a friend to hold or put them in a closet where you'll not see them. If possible, avoid places you frequented together. These symbols will bring back uncomfortable memories. After you have achieved some emotional distance, you can go back and enjoy these as reminders of a once pleasant relationship. Support for this suggestion comes from research showing that the more vivid your memory of a broken love affair—a memory greatly aided by these relationship symbols—the greater your depression is likely to be (Harvey, Flanary, and Morgan 1986).

Seek Support

11   Many people feel they should bear their burdens alone. Men, in particular, have been taught that this is the only "manly" way to handle things. But seeking the support of others is one of the best antidotes to the unhappiness caused when a relationship ends. Tell your friends and family of your situation—in only general terms, if you prefer—and make it clear that you want support. Seek out people who are positive and nurturing. Avoid negative individuals who will paint the world in even darker tones. Make the distinction between seeking support and seeking advice. If you feel you need advice, seek out a professional.

Avoid Repeating Negative Patterns

12   Many people repeat their mistakes. They enter second and third relationships with the same blinders, faulty preconceptions, and unrealistic expectations with which they entered earlier ones. Instead, use the knowledge gained from your failed relationship to prevent repeating the same patterns.

13   At the same time, don't become a prophet of doom. Don't see in every relationship vestiges of the old. Don't jump at the first conflict and say, "Here it goes all over again." Treat the new relationship as the unique relationship it is. Don't evaluate it through past experiences. Use past relationships and experiences as guides, not filters.

—From De Vito, Joseph A. *The Interpersonal Communication Book*, 9e. Published by Allyn and Bacon, Boston, MA. Copyright © 2001 by Pearson Education. Reprinted by permission of the publisher.

➤ WHAT DID YOU LEARN FROM PREVIEWING?

Without referring to the passage, answer each of the following true/false questions.

_____ 1. To end a relationship you need to find a way to explain the breakup to yourself and to your partner.

_____ 2. The breakup of a relationship almost always causes stress.

_____ 3. The two most common feelings following the end of a relationship are anger and fear of desertion.

_____ 4. After a breakup occurs, it is important to keep letters and photographs as reminders of the relationship at its best.

_____ 5. One mistake people often make after a breakup is to enter into a new relationship too soon.

You probably were able to answer all (or most) of the questions correctly. Previewing, then, does provide you with a great deal of information. If you were to return to the passage from the textbook and read the entire section, you would find it easier to do than if you hadn't previewed it.

Why Previewing Is Effective

Previewing is effective for several reasons:

- **Previewing helps you to make decisions about how you will approach the material.** On the basis of what you discover about the assignment's organization and content, you can select the reading and study strategies that will be most effective.
- **Previewing puts your mind in gear and helps you start thinking about the subject.**
- **Previewing also gives you a mental outline of the chapter's content.** It enables you to see how ideas are connected, and since you know where the author is headed, your reading will be easier than if you had not previewed. Previewing, however, is never a substitute for careful, thorough reading.

> **NOW PRACTICE . . . PREVIEWING**

Assume you are taking a psychology course. Your instructor has assigned the following article from Wiretap, *an online news and culture magazine. Preview the article using the procedure described in this section. When you have finished, answer the questions that follow.*

Deadly Silence: Stop Snitching's Fatal Legacy
By Ayah Young

1   In 2004, a DVD called *Stop Snitching* began to circulate in Baltimore, Maryland. The homemade film featured self-proclaimed drug dealers who issued violent threats against people who reported any information about their crimes to the police. An immediate underground success, this film brought snitching to the forefront of

hip-hop culture and soon after its release, t-shirts with an image of a stop sign bearing the phrase "Stop Snitching" began to appear on the streets. The message was assimilated into hip-hop lyrics, and in October of 2005, stop snitching was brought to a national audience by an article about the t-shirts in the *New York Times*.

Snitching's Many Meanings

2   So what exactly is snitching? Dr. Rick Frei, an applied psychology professor at the Community College of Philadelphia has been working with a team of student researchers to determine just that. In an effort known as the Snitching Project, Frei and his students developed a questionnaire that they administered to nearly 1500 community college students. The resulting data illustrated that a wide variety of definitions exist. While 82.6 percent of students polled identified that ratting someone else out to get out of a crime would be considered snitching, other activities—tattling on a brother or sister, reporting a classmate cheating on an exam, helping the police set someone up, picking a suspect out of a police lineup, or answering questions from police at the scene of the crime—could also be considered snitching.

3   Cooperating witnesses often fear retaliation from those they've informed upon, and frequently the fear of physical harm or death is so intense that it causes witnesses to remain silent. Without witnesses to speak out, more crimes go unsolved. So when the "Stop Snitching" campaign became national, its reception by police and the general public was less than favorable. People were quick to blame the t-shirts, and hip-hop, as the cause of the problem.

4   In a 60 *Minutes* special called "Stop Snitching" that aired on April 22, 2007, social activist and author Geoffrey Canada placed blame for unsolved crimes in urban communities directly on hip-hop, stating emphatically, "Rappers are preaching anarchy." He went on to articulate, "The message is, go out and do things that will destroy you, that will get you locked up in jail, that will ruin your relationships, that will estrange you from your kids, that's what this music is preaching." He believes that some hip-hop music is the driving force behind violence in the streets.

5   Geoffrey Canada's hostility toward this music stems from a personal experience. Israel Ramirez, a student whom he mentored and loved like a son, was shot and killed while providing security on the set of a Busta Rhymes music video. With a possible dozen witnesses to the crime, and no one willing to speak with the police, it's easy to see how Canada would readily place the blame of this unsolved crime on hip-hop itself.

6   In another famous instance from the same show, rapper Cam'ron controversially outlined his "code of ethics" to host Anderson Cooper. "If I knew a serial killer was living next door to me, I wouldn't call and tell anybody on him." This clip outraged average Americans and sensationalized the correlation between hip-hop and the credo of street silence.

7   The music industry has long been blamed for violent behavior. When the infamous shootings occurred at Columbine High School in 1999, the media was quick to implicate Marilyn Manson's music as a cause for Klebold and Harris' killing spree.

8   But does music shape society? Or is music merely a reflection of preexisting ideals within society? As a part of the Snitching Project's study, participants were asked about their music listening habits. The report stated, "While over one-third of all students said that they listened to music that explicitly said snitching was bad, only 5.5 percent of students said that the music that they listened to influenced their opinion of snitching." In a discussion with Dr. Frei he explained, "It may be that people are not really influenced by the music that they listen to. Or it might be that people seek out music that confirms their own personal worldview. While the 'Stop Snitching' campaign has probably influenced some people, I think most people didn't trust the police long before Cam'ron ever recorded a song."

Informant Woes

9   In an era where each is out to get their own, the problem of snitches working with the police is very different. The same message, lacking the community context, makes for an entirely different reality. Individuals, who may be trying to save themselves jail time, can make a deal with the police in exchange for information regarding another wanted party. When that person gets locked up, the snitch gains enemies, further perpetuating violence on the streets.

10   Police work with snitches and informants has a checkered history. Tafari explains how in his work, he has frequently encountered kids brought in on charges who don't know their rights. They are offered a deal and are willing to say just about anything to get off the hook. "The really bad part is that these deals they cut with people might not even be [based on] the truth."

11   This issue of false information has serious real-life implications. In a study conducted by the Northwestern University School of Law Center on wrongful convictions, they found that of 111 capital cases studied since 1973, 45 percent of wrongful convictions were a result of snitches. That's an overwhelming percentage of people who were given death sentences as a result of bad information.

Snitching Solutions?

12   So what is to be done? We can't just ban "Stop Snitching" messages from the culture and hope that the problem goes away. Ethan Brown, the author of *Snitch: Informants, Cooperators, and the Corruption of Justice,* suggests that we restore faith in the legal system by refocusing our federal sentencing policies, including placing limits on the number of times that an individual can provide assistance in an investigation in exchange for a reduced sentence, and requiring that information provided by cooperators be corroborated with evidence. These suggestions, if put into practice, could have an extremely positive effect on the quality of "justice" in America.

13   But while these measures may help to reduce crime and unjust sentencing, they are a band-aid solution for the issue's root cause. Beyond our current judicial system lies the reality that high levels of crime in this country often stem from a history of institutionalized racism and classism that denies some populations opportunities for fair work opportunities and safer environments. This lack of resources and development has had a disastrous effect on America's low-income urban communities. As Abel Habtegeorgies bluntly stated, "If our urban areas weren't so neglected and if greater investment in communities like parks and recreation programs, job training programs, and jobs existed, you wouldn't have people resorting to illegal opportunities."

14   With continual cuts to vital resources like education, it is not likely that we will see the government step in to enhance these kinds of services anytime soon. The task of revitalizing these communities has fallen on the shoulders of concerned citizens and grassroots organizations like the Ella Baker Center, Elementz, Youth Uprising, and H.O.M.E.Y, who are engaging youth and community members in constructive dialogue and offering them inspiration, training and empowerment. And there are people like Dr. Frei who are working to understand social attitudes about snitching and building classroom curriculum to address the issue.

15   While the work these people and organizations do is vital to the future of our cities, it is important to remember that to create radical change in our society requires everyone's participation, consciousness and diligence. So the next time you see a "Stop Snitching" shirt or read about uncooperative witnesses, ask yourself: "What is my community or city doing to empower itself, form stronger familial bonds and improve not just my safety, but everyone's?" If you don't have a good answer, it's time to get to work, and clean our collective dirty laundry.

—Reprinted from WiretapMag.org

1. What is the overall subject of this article?

_____

2. How did the topic of this reading become popular?

_____

_____

3. Why are some people afraid to snitch?

_____

4. Who or what is being blamed for unsolved crimes in urban areas?

_____

5. What solution does the author offer to the problem of "stop snitching"?

_____

6. On a scale of 1 to 5 (1 = easy, 5 = very difficult), how difficult do you expect the article to be? _____

1c   **ACTIVATING BACKGROUND KNOWLEDGE**

After previewing your assignment, you should take a moment to think about what you already know about the topic. Whatever the topic, you probably know *something* about it: This is your background knowledge. For example, a student was about to read an article titled "Growing Urban Problems" for a sociology class. His first thought was that he knew very little about urban problems because he lived in a rural area. But when he thought of a recent trip to a nearby city, he remembered seeing the homeless people and crowded conditions. This recollection helped him remember reading about drug problems, drive-by shootings, and muggings.

Activating your background knowledge aids your reading in three ways. First, it makes reading easier because you have already thought about the topic. Second, the material is easier to remember because you can connect the new information with what you already know. Third, topics become more interesting if you can link them to your own experiences. Here are some techniques to help you activate your background knowledge.

- **Ask questions, and try to answer them.** If a chapter in your biology textbook titled "Human Diseases" contains headings such as "Infectious diseases," "Sexually transmitted diseases," "Cancer," and "Vascular diseases," you might ask and try to answer such questions as the following: What kinds of infectious diseases have I seen? What caused them? What do I know about preventing cancer and other diseases?
- **Draw on your own experience.** If a chapter in your business textbook is titled "Advertising: Its Purpose and Design," you might think of several ads you have seen and analyze the purpose of each and how it was constructed.
- **Brainstorm.** Write down everything that comes to mind about the topic. Suppose you're about to read a chapter in your sociology textbook on domestic violence. You might list types of violence—child abuse, rape, and so on. You might write questions such as "What causes child abuse?" and "How can it be prevented?" Alternatively, you might list incidents of domestic violence you have heard or read about. Any of these approaches will help to make the topic interesting.

> **NOW PRACTICE . . . ACTIVATING BACKGROUND KNOWLEDGE**

Use one of the three strategies listed above to discover what you already know about snitching.

1d   CHECKING YOUR COMPREHENSION

What happens when you read material you can understand easily? Does it seem that everything "clicks"? Do ideas seem to fit together and make sense? Is that "click" noticeably absent at other times?

Table 1.2 lists and compares common signals to assist you in checking your comprehension. Not all the signals appear at the same time, and not all the signals work for everyone. But becoming aware of these positive and negative signals will help you gain more control over your reading.

TABLE 1.2 COMPREHENSION SIGNALS

POSITIVE SIGNALS	NEGATIVE SIGNALS
You feel comfortable and have some knowledge about the topic.	The topic is unfamiliar, yet the author assumes you understand it.
You recognize most words or can figure them out from context.	Many words are unfamiliar.
You can express the main ideas in your own words.	You must reread the main ideas and use the author's language to explain them.
You understand why the material was assigned.	You do not know why the material was assigned and cannot explain why it is important.
You read at a regular, comfortable pace.	You often slow down or reread.
You are able to make connections between ideas.	You are unable to detect relationships; the organization is not apparent.
You are able to see where the author is leading.	You feel as if you are struggling to stay with the author and are unable to predict what will follow.
You understand what is important.	Nothing (or everything) seems important.

▶ NOW PRACTICE . . . CHECKING YOUR COMPREHENSION

Read the article titled "Deadly Silence: Stop Snitching's Fatal Legacy" that appears on page 33. Be alert for positive and negative comprehension signals as you read. After reading the article, answer the following questions.

1. On a scale of 1 to 5 (1 = very poor, 5 = excellent), how would you rate your overall comprehension? _____

2. What positive signals did you sense? List them below.

_____

_____

_____

3. What negative signals did you experience, if any? List them below.

_____

_____

_____

4. In which sections was your comprehension strongest? List the paragraph
   numbers. _____

5. Did you feel at any time that you had lost, or were about to lose,
   comprehension? If so, go back to that part now. What made it difficult to
   read?

_____

_____

1e   STRENGTHENING YOUR COMPREHENSION

Here are some suggestions to follow when you realize you need to strengthen
your comprehension.

1. **Analyze the time and place in which you are reading.** If you've been
   reading or studying for several hours, mental fatigue may be the source of
   the problem. If you are reading in a place with distractions or interruptions,
   you might not be able to understand what you're reading.
2. **Rephrase each paragraph in your own words.** You might need to approach
   complicated material sentence by sentence, expressing each in your own words.
3. **Read aloud sentences or sections that are particularly difficult.** Reading out
   loud sometimes makes complicated material easier to understand.
4. **Reread difficult or complicated sections.** In fact, at times several readings are
   appropriate and necessary.
5. **Slow down your reading rate.** On occasion, simply reading more slowly and carefully will provide you with the needed boost in comprehension.
6. **Write questions next to headings.** Refer to your questions frequently and jot
   down or underline answers.
7. **Write a brief outline of major points.** This will help you see the overall organization and progression of ideas.
8. **Highlight key ideas.** After you've read a section, go back and think about and underline what is important. Underlining forces you to sort out what is important,
   and this sorting process builds comprehension and recall. (Refer to 7a for suggestions on how to highlight effectively.)
9. **Write notes in the margins.** Explain or rephrase difficult or complicated ideas or
   sections.

10. **Determine whether you lack background knowledge.** Comprehension is difficult, or at times impossible, if you lack essential information that the writer assumes you have. Suppose you are reading a section of a political science text in which the author describes implications of the balance of power in the Third World. If you do not understand the concept of balance of power, your comprehension will break down. When you lack background information, take immediate steps to correct the problem:

   - Consult other sections of your text, using the glossary and index.
   - Obtain a more basic text that reviews fundamental principles and concepts.
   - Consult reference materials (encyclopedias, subject or biographical dictionaries).
   - Ask your instructor to recommend additional sources, guidebooks, or review texts.

2 Vocabulary Building

Your vocabulary can be one of your strongest assets or one of your greatest liabilities. It defines and describes you by revealing a great deal about your level of education and your experience. Your vocabulary contributes to that all-important first impression people form when they meet you. A strong vocabulary provides both immediate academic benefits and long-term career effects. This chapter describes two methods of strengthening your vocabulary: using context clues and word parts.

2a USING CONTEXT CLUES

Read the following brief paragraph in which several words are missing. Try to figure out the missing words and write them in the blanks.

> Rate refers to the _____ at which you speak. If you speak too _____, your listeners will not have time to understand your message. If you speak too _____, your listeners' minds will wander.

Did you insert the word *speed* in the first blank, *fast* in the second blank, and *slowly* in the third blank? Most likely you correctly identified all three missing words. You could tell from the sentence which word to put in. The words around the missing words—the sentence context—gave you clues as to which word would fit and make sense. Such clues are called **context clues.**

While you probably won't find missing words on a printed page, you will often find words that you do not know. Context clues can help you to figure out the meanings of unfamiliar words.

MyReadingLab

To practice vocabulary skills go to

➤ Study Plan
➤ Reading Skills
➤ Vocabulary

Example:

> **Phobias,** such as fear of heights, water, or confined spaces, are difficult to eliminate.

From the sentence, you can tell that *phobia* means "fear of specific objects or situations."

Here's another example:

> The couple finally **secured** a table at the popular, crowded restaurant.

You can figure out that *secured* means "got or took ownership of" the table.

There are four types of context clues to look for: (1) definition, (2) example, (3) contrast, and (4) logic of the passage.

Definition Clues

Many times a writer defines a word immediately following its use. The writer may directly define a word by giving a brief definition or a synonym (a word that has the same meaning). Such words and phrases as *means, is, refers to,* and *can be defined as* are often used. Here are some examples:

> **Corona** refers to *the outermost part of the sun's atmosphere.*
>
> A **soliloquy** is *a speech made by a character in a play that reveals his or her thoughts to the audience.*

At other times, rather than formally define the word, a writer may provide you with clues. Punctuation is often used to signal that a definition clue to a word's meaning is to follow. Punctuation also separates the meaning clue from the rest of the sentence. Three types of punctuation—commas, parentheses, and dashes—are used in this way. In the examples below, notice that the meaning clue is separated from the rest of the sentence by punctuation.

1. Commas

> *Five-line rhyming poems,* or **limericks,** are among the simplest forms of poetry.
>
> **Equity,** *general principles of fairness and justice,* is used in law when existing laws do not apply or are inadequate.

2. Parentheses

> **Lithium** (*an alkali metal*) is so soft it can be cut with a knife.
>
> A leading cause of heart disease is a diet with too much **cholesterol** (*a fatty substance made of carbon, hydrogen, and oxygen*).

3. Dashes

> Our country's **gross national product**—*the total market value of its national output of goods and services*—is increasing steadily.
>
> Ancient Egyptians wrote in **hieroglyphics**—*pictures used to represent words.*

Facets—*small flat surfaces at different angles*—bring out the beauty of a diamond.

▶ NOW PRACTICE . . . USING DEFINITION CLUES 1

Read each sentence and write a definition or synonym for each boldfaced word or phrase. Use the definition context clue to help you determine word meaning.

1. The judge's **candor**—his sharp, open frankness—shocked the jury.

   _____

2. A **chemical bond** is a strong attractive force that holds two or more atoms together.

   _____

3. Hearing, technically known as **audition,** begins when a sound wave reaches the outer ear.

   _____

4. A **species** is a group of animals or plants that share similar characteristics and are able to interbreed.

   _____

   _____

5. Many diseases have **latent periods,** periods of time between the infection and the first appearance of a symptom.

   _____

▶ NOW PRACTICE . . . USING DEFINITION CLUES 2

Read the following paragraphs and use definition clues to help you determine the meaning of each boldfaced word or phrase.

During **adolescence** (the period of growth from childhood to maturity), friendship choices are directed overwhelmingly to other students in the same school. Adolescent students may be involved in an informal network of friendship subsystems that operate primarily within the boundaries of the school world.

Cliques are relatively small, tightly knit groups of friends who spend considerable and often exclusive time with each other. Although cliques are the most common and important friendship structure for adolescents, not everyone belongs to one; in fact, fewer than half of adolescents do. About 30 percent of students are **liaisons**—individuals who have friends from several different cliques but belong to none. The remaining students are **social isolates**—individuals with few friends. Schools also contain **crowds**, which are loose associations of cliques that usually get together on weekends.

—adapted from Rice and Dolgin,
The Adolescent: Development, Relationships, and Culture, pp. 250–251

1. adolescence _____

2. cliques _____

_____

3. liaisons _____

4. social isolates _____

5. crowds _____

Example Clues

Writers often include examples that help to explain or clarify a word. Suppose you do not know the meaning of the word *toxic*, and you find it used in the following sentence:

> **Toxic** materials, such as arsenic, asbestos, pesticides, and lead, can cause bodily damage.

This sentence gives four examples of toxic materials. From the examples given, which are all poisonous substances, you could conclude that *toxic* means "poisonous."

Examples

> Perceiving, learning, and thinking are examples of **cognitive** processes.

Cognitive processes, then, are mental processes.

> **Legumes**, such as peas and beans, produce pods.

Legumes, then, are vegetable plants that produce pods.

> Many **pharmaceuticals**, including morphine and penicillin, are not readily available in some countries.

From the examples of morphine and penicillin, you know that pharmaceuticals are drugs.

> **NOW PRACTICE . . . USING EXAMPLE CLUES 1**

Read each sentence and write a definition or synonym for each boldfaced word or phrase. Use the example context clue to help you determine word meaning.

1. The child was **reticent** in every respect; she would not speak, refused to answer questions, and avoided looking at anyone.

   _____

2. Instructors provide their students with **feedback** through test grades and comments on papers.

   _____

3. Clothing is available in a variety of **fabrics,** including cotton, wool, polyester, and linen.

   _____

4. **Involuntary reflexes,** like breathing and beating of the heart, are easily measured.

   _____

5. The student had a difficult time distinguishing between **homonyms**— words such as *see* and *sea*, *wore* and *war*, and *deer* and *dear*.

   _____

> **NOW PRACTICE . . . USING EXAMPLE CLUES 2**

Read the following paragraphs and use definition and example clues to help you determine the meaning of each boldfaced word or phrase.

Freshwater lakes have three life zones. The **littoral zone,** nearest to shore, is rich in light and nutrients and supports the most diverse community—from cattails and bulrushes close to shore, to water lilies and algae at the deepest reaches of the zone. Inhabitants include snails, frogs, minnows, snakes, and turtles, as well as two categories of the microscopic organisms called plankton: photosynthetic **phytoplankton,** including bacteria and algae, and nonphotosynthetic **zooplankton,** such as protists and tiny crustaceans.

The **limnetic zone** is the open-water region of a lake where enough light penetrates to support photosynthesis. Inhabitants of the limnetic zone include cyanobacteria, zooplankton, small crustaceans, and fish. Below the limnetic zone lies the **profundal zone,** which is too dark for photosynthesis. This zone is inhabited primarily by decomposers and detritus feeders, such as bacteria, snails, and insect larvae, and by fish that swim freely among the different zones.

—adapted from Audesirk, Audesirk, and Byers, *Life on Earth,* pp. 622–624, 632

1. littoral zone _____

_____

2. phytoplankton _____

_____

3. zooplankton _____

_____

4. limnetic zone _____

_____

_____

5. profundal zone _____

_____

Contrast Clues

It is sometimes possible to determine the meaning of an unknown word from a word or phrase in the context that has an opposite meaning. Notice, in the following sentence, how a word opposite in meaning from the boldfaced word provides a clue to its meaning:

> One of the dinner guests **succumbed** to the temptation to have a second piece of cake, but the others resisted.

Although you may not know the meaning of *succumbed*, you know that the one guest who succumbed was different from the others who resisted. The word *but* suggests this. Since the others resisted a second dessert, you can tell that one guest gave in and had a piece. Thus, *succumbed* means the opposite of *resist*; that is, "to give in to."

Examples

> Most of the graduates were **elated,** though a few felt sad and depressed.
> (The opposite of *sad and depressed* is joyful.)

> The old man acted **morosely,** whereas his grandson was very lively.
> (The opposite of *lively* is quietly and sullenly.)

> The gentleman was quite **portly,** but his wife was thin.
> (The opposite of *thin* is heavy or fat.)

> ### NOW PRACTICE ... USING CONTRAST CLUES 1

Read each sentence and write a definition or synonym for each boldfaced word. Use the contrast clue to help you determine word meaning.

1. Some city dwellers are **affluent;** others live in or near poverty.

   _____

2. I am certain that the hotel will hold our reservation; however, if you are **dubious,** call to make sure.

   _____

3. Although most experts **concurred** with the research findings, several strongly disagreed.

   _____

4. The speaker **denounced** certain legal changes while praising other reforms.

   _____

5. When the couple moved into their new home, they **revamped** the kitchen and bathroom but did not change the rest of the rooms.

   _____

> ### NOW PRACTICE ... USING CONTRAST CLUES 2

Read the following paragraph and use contrast clues to help you determine the meaning of each boldfaced word. Consult a dictionary, if necessary.

The Whigs chose General William Henry Harrison to run against President Martin Van Buren in 1840, using a **specious** but effective argument: General Harrison is a plain man of the people who lives in a log cabin. Contrast him with the suave Van Buren, **luxuriating** amid "the Regal Splendor of the President's Palace." Harrison drinks ordinary hard cider with his hog meat and grits, while Van Buren **eschews** plain food in favor of expensive foreign wines and fancy French cuisine. The general's furniture is **unpretentious** and sturdy; the president dines off gold plates and treads on carpets that cost the people $5 a yard. In a country where all are equal, the people will reject an **aristocrat** like Van Buren and put their trust in General Harrison, a simple, brave, honest, public-spirited common man. (In fact, Harrison came from a distinguished family, was well educated and financially comfortable, and certainly did not live in a log cabin.)

—adapted from Carnes and Garraty, *The American Nation,* p. 267

1. specious _____

2. luxuriating _____

3. eschews _____

4. unpretentious _____

5. aristocrat _____

Logic of the Passage Clues

Many times you can figure out the meaning of an unknown word by using logic and reasoning skills. For instance, look at the following sentence:

> Bob is quite **versatile;** he is a good student, a top athlete, an excellent car mechanic, and a gourmet cook.

You can see that Bob is successful at many different types of activities, and you could reason that *versatile* means "capable of doing many things competently."

Examples

> When the customer tried to pay with Mexican **pesos,** the clerk explained that the store accepted only U.S. dollars.

Logic tells you that customers pay with money; *pesos,* then, are a type of Mexican currency.

> We had to leave the car and walk up because the **incline** was too steep to drive.

Something that is too steep must be slanted or have a slope; *incline* means a slope.

> Since Reginald was nervous, he brought his rabbit's foot **talisman** with him to the exam.

A rabbit's foot is often thought to be a good luck charm; *talisman* means a good luck charm.

NOW PRACTICE . . . USING LOGIC OF THE PASSAGE CLUES 1

Read each sentence and write a definition or synonym for each boldfaced word. Use information provided in the context to help you determine word meaning.

1. The foreign students quickly **assimilated** many aspects of American culture.

_____

2. The legal aid clinic was **subsidized** by city and county funds.

_____

3. When the bank robber reached his **haven,** he breathed a sigh of relief and began to count his money.

_____

4. The teenager was **intimidated** by the presence of a police officer walking the beat and decided not to spray-paint the school wall.

_____

5. If the plan did not work, the colonel had a **contingency** plan ready.

_____

> ## NOW PRACTICE . . . USING LOGIC OF THE PASSAGE CLUES 2

Read the following paragraphs and use the logic of the passage clues to help you choose and circle the correct meaning of each boldfaced word or phrase.

The map of the geography of languages is not **static.** The use of some languages is expanding because the speakers of those languages are **diffusing** around the world, are gaining greater power and influence in world affairs, or are winning new **adherents** to their ideas.

For international **discourse,** English is the world's leading **lingua franca,** partly because of its widespread use in science and business. Many multinational corporations have designated English their corporate language, whatever the languages of their home countries might be.

—adapted from Bergman and Renwick, _Introduction to Geography_, p. 263

1. static
   a. difficult
   b. unchanging
   c. unfit
   d. unlikely

2. diffusing
   a. spreading
   b. revealing
   c. being eliminated
   d. causing confusion

3. adherents
   a. opponents
   b. meanings
   c. supporters
   d. power

4. discourse
   a. communication
   b. problems
   c. currency exchange
   d. society

5. lingua franca
   a. international currency
   b. form of negotiation
   c. language held in common by many countries
   d. corporate policy

SUMMING IT UP

CONTEXT CLUES

CONTEXT CLUE	HOW TO FIND MEANING	EXAMPLE
Definition	1. Look for words that announce that meanings are to follow (*is, refers to, means*).	Broad, flat noodles that are served with sauce or butter are called **fettucine.**
	2. Look for parentheses, dashes, or commas that set apart synonyms or brief definitions.	Psychologists often wonder whether **stereotypes**—the assumptions we make about what people are like—might be self-fulfilling.
Example	Figure out what the examples have in common. (Peas and beans both are vegetables and both grow in pods.)	Most **condiments,** such as pepper, mustard, and cat-sup, are used to improve the flavor of foods.
Contrast	Look for a word or phrase that is the opposite in meaning of a word you don't know.	Before their classes in manners, the children were disorderly; after "graduation" they acted with much **decorum.**
Logic of the Passage	Use the rest of the sentence to help you. Pretend the word is a blank line and fill in the blank with a word that makes sense.	On hot, humid afternoons, I often feel **languid.**

2b   LEARNING PREFIXES, ROOTS, AND SUFFIXES

Suppose that you came across the following sentence in a human anatomy textbook:

> Trichromatic plates are used frequently in the text to illustrate the position of body organs.

If you did not know the meaning of *trichromatic,* how could you determine it? There are no clues in the sentence context. One solution is to look up the word in a dictionary. An easier and faster way is to break the word into parts and analyze the meaning of each part. Many words in the English language are made up of word parts called **prefixes, roots,** and **suffixes.** These word parts have specific meanings that, when added together, can help you determine the meaning of the word as a whole.

The word *trichromatic* can be divided into three parts: its prefix, root, and suffix.

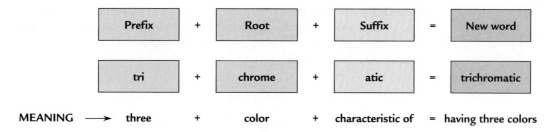

| Prefix | + | Root | + | Suffix | = | New word |
| tri | + | chrome | + | atic | = | trichromatic |

MEANING ⟶   three   +   color   +   characteristic of   =   having three colors

You can see from this analysis that *trichromatic* means "having three colors."

Here are two other examples of words that you can figure out by using prefixes, roots, and suffixes:

> The parents thought the child was **unteachable.**
>
> **un-** = not
> **teach** = help someone learn
> **-able** = able to do something
> **unteachable** = not able to be taught

> The student was a **nonconformist.**
>
> **non-** = not
> **conform** = go along with others
> **-ist** = one who does something
> **nonconformist** = someone who does not go along with others

The first step in using the prefix-root-suffix method is to become familiar with the most commonly used word parts. The prefixes and roots listed in Tables 2.1 and 2.2 (pages 53–56) will give you a good start in determining the meanings of thousands of words without looking them up in the dictionary. Before you begin to use word parts to figure out new words, there are a few things you need to know:

1. **In most cases, a word is built upon at least one root.**
2. **Words can have more than one prefix, root, or suffix.**
   a. Words can be made up of two or more roots (*geo/logy*).
   b. Some words have two prefixes (*in/sub/ordination*).
   c. Some words have two suffixes (*beauti/ful/ly*).
3. **Words do not always have a prefix and a suffix.**
   a. Some words have neither a prefix nor a suffix (*read*).
   b. Others have a suffix but no prefix (*read/ing*).
   c. Others have a prefix but no suffix (*pre/read*).
4. **The spelling of roots may change as they are combined with suffixes.** Some common variations are included in Table 2.2.

5. **Different prefixes, roots, or suffixes may have the same meaning.** For example, the prefixes *bi-*, *di-*, and *duo-* all mean "two."
6. **Sometimes you may identify a group of letters as a prefix or root but find that it does not carry the meaning of that prefix or root.** For example, the letters *mis* in the word *missile* are part of the root and are not the prefix *mis-*, which means "wrong; bad."

Prefixes

Prefixes appear at the beginnings of many English words. They alter the meaning of the root to which they are connected. For example, if you add the prefix *re-* to the word *read*, the word *reread* is formed, meaning "to read again." If *pre-* is added to the word *reading*, the word *prereading* is formed, meaning "before reading." If the prefix *post-* is added, the word *postreading* is formed, meaning "after reading." Table 2.1 lists 62 common prefixes grouped according to meaning.

> **NOW PRACTICE . . . USING PREFIXES 1**

Read each of the following sentences. Use your knowledge of prefixes to fill in the blank and complete the word.

1. A person who speaks two languages is _bi_ lingual.
2. A letter or number written beneath a line of print is called a _sub_ script.
3. The new sweater had a snag, and I returned it to the store because it was _im_ perfect.
4. The flood damage was permanent and _ir_ reversible.
5. I was not given the correct date and time; I was _mis_ informed.
6. People who speak several different languages are _poly_ lingual.
7. A musical _inter_ lude was played between the events in the ceremony.
8. I decided the magazine was uninteresting, so I _dis_ continued my subscription.
9. Merchandise that does not pass factory inspection is considered _____ standard and is sold at a discount.
10. The tuition refund policy approved this week will apply to last year's tuition as well; the policy will be _in_ active to January 1 of last year.

TABLE 2.1 COMMON PREFIXES

PREFIX	MEANING	SAMPLE WORD
Prefixes referring to amount or number		
mono-/uni-	one	monocle/unicycle
bi-/di-/du-	two	bimonthly/divorce/duet
tri-	three	triangle
quad-	four	quadrant
quint-/pent-	five	quintet/pentagon
dec-/deci-	ten	decimal
centi-	hundred	centigrade
homo-	same	homogenized
mega-	large	megaphone
milli-	thousand	milligram
micro-	small	microscope
multi-/poly-	many	multipurpose/polygon
nano-	extremely small	nanoplankton
semi-	half	semicircle
equi	equal	equidistant
Prefixes meaning "not" (negative)		
a-	not	asymmetrical
anti-	against	antiwar
contra-/counter-	against, opposite	contradict
dis-	apart, away, not	disagree
in-/il-/ir-/im-	not	incorrect/illogical/irreversible/impossible
mal-	poorly, wrongly	malnourished
mis-	wrongly	misunderstand
non-	not	nonfiction
un-	not	unpopular
pseudo-	false	pseudoscientific
Prefixes giving direction, location, or placement		
ab-	away	absent
ad-	toward	adhesive
ante-/pre-	before	antecedent/premarital
circum-/peri-	around	circumference/perimeter

(continued on next page)

(continued from preceding page)

PREFIX	MEANING	SAMPLE WORD
com-/col-/con-	with, together	compile/collide/convene
de-	away, from	depart
dia-	through	diameter
ex-/extra-	from, out of, former	ex-wife/extramarital
hyper-	over, excessive	hyperactive
hypo-	below, beneath	hypodermic
inter-	between	interpersonal
intro-/intra-/in-	within, into, in	introduction
post-	after	posttest
pre-	before	preview
re-	back, again	review
retro-	backward	retrospect
sub-	under, below	submarine
super-	above, extra	supercharge
tele-	far	telescope
trans-	cross, over	transcontinental

► NOW PRACTICE . . . USING PREFIXES 2

Read the following paragraph and choose the correct prefix from the box below to fill in the blank next to each boldfaced word part. One prefix will not be used.

multi	uni	pseudo
tri	bi	sub

Neurons, or nerve cells, can be classified structurally according to the number of axons and dendrites that project from the cell body. (1) __uni__ **polar** neurons have a single projection from the cell body and are rare in humans. (2) __bi__ **polar** neurons have two projections, an axon and a dendrite, extending from the cell body. Other sensory neurons are (3) __pseudo__ **unipolar** neurons, a (4) __sub__ **class** of bipolar neurons. Although only one projection seems to extend from the cell body of this type of neuron, there are actually two projections that extend in opposite directions. (5) __multi__ **polar** neurons, the most common neurons, have multiple projections from the cell body; one projection is an axon, all the others are dendrites.

—adapted from Germann and Stanfield, *Principles of Human Physiology*, p. 174

TABLE 2.2 COMMON ROOTS

COMMON ROOT	MEANING	SAMPLE WORD
anthropo	human being	anthropology
archaeo	ancient or past	archeology
aster/astro	star	astronaut
aud/audit	hear	audible
bene	good, well	benefit
bio	life	biology
cap	take, seize	captive
cardi	heart	cardiology
chron(o)	time	chronology
corp	body	corpse
cred	believe	incredible
dict/dic	tell, say	predict
duc/duct	lead	introduce
fact/fac	make, do	factory
geo	earth	geophysics
graph	write	telegraph
gyneco	woman	gynecology
log/logo/logy	study, thought	psychology
mit/miss	send	permit/dismiss
mort/mor	die, death	immortal
neuro	nerve	neurology
path	feeling	sympathy
phono	sound, voice	telephone
photo	light	photosensitive
port	carry	transport
pulmo	lungs	pulmonary
scop	seeing	microscope
scrib/script	write	inscription
sen/sent	feel	insensitive
spec/spic/spect	look, see	retrospect
tend/tent/tens	stretch or strain	tension
terr/terre	land, earth	territory
theo	god	theology

(continued on next page)

(continued from preceding page)

COMMON ROOT	MEANING	SAMPLE WORD
ven/vent	come	convention
vert/vers	turn	invert
vis/vid	see	invisible/video
voc	call	vocation

Roots

Roots carry the basic or core meaning of a word. Hundreds of root words are used to build words in the English language. Thirty-seven of the most common and most useful are listed in Table 2.2. Knowledge of the meanings of these roots will enable you to unlock the meanings of many words. For example, if you know that the root *dic/dict* means "tell or say," then you have a clue to the meanings of such words as *dictate* (to speak for someone to write down), *diction* (wording or manner of speaking), or *dictionary* (book that "tells" what words mean).

➤ NOW PRACTICE . . . USING ROOTS 1

Use the list of common roots in Table 2.2 to determine the meanings of the following words. Write a brief definition or synonym for each, checking a dictionary if necessary.

1. photocopy
   light copy, duplicate

2. visibility
   seeing

3. credentials
   believable evidence

4. speculate
   _____

5. terrain
   _____

6. audition

_____

7. astrophysics

_____

8. chronicle

_____

9. autograph

_____

> **NOW PRACTICE . . . USING ROOTS 2**

Read the following paragraph and choose the correct root from the box below to fill in the blank next to each boldfaced word part. One root will not be used.

graph	scope ✓	mit
astro ✓	photo ✓	logy

You might think that the easiest way to discover extrasolar planets, or planets around other stars, would be simply to (1) _photo_ **graph** them through a powerful (2) **tele** _scope_. Unfortunately, current observational (3) **techno** _logy_ cannot produce such images. The primary problem arises from the fact that any light that an orbiting planet might (4) **trans** _mit_ would be overwhelmed by light from the star it orbits. For example, a Sun-like star would be a *billion times* brighter than the reflected light from an Earth-like planet. Because even the best telescopes blur the light from stars at least a little, finding the small blip of planetary light amid the glare of scattered starlight would be very difficult. For now, (5) _astro_ **nomers** must rely on techniques that observe the star itself to find indirect evidence of planets.

—adapted from Bennett, Donahue, Schneider, and Voit,
The Cosmic Perspective, p. 218

Suffixes

Suffixes are word endings that often change the tense and/or part of speech of a word. For example, adding the suffix *-y* to the noun *cloud* forms the adjective *cloudy*.

Accompanying the change in part of speech is a shift in meaning (*cloudy* means "resembling clouds; overcast with clouds; dimmed or dulled as if by clouds").

Often, several different words can be formed from a single root word by adding different suffixes.

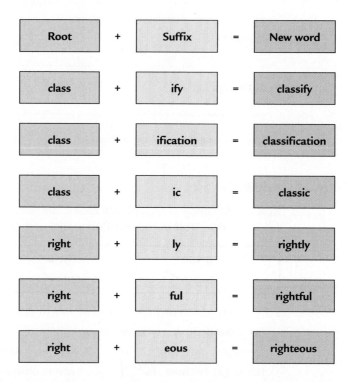

If you know the meaning of the root word and the ways in which different suffixes affect the meaning of the root word, you will be able to figure out a word's meaning when a suffix is added. A list of common suffixes and their meanings appears in Table 2.3.

You can expand your vocabulary by learning the variations in meaning that occur when suffixes are added to words you already know. When you find a word that you do not know, look for the root. Then, using the sentence the word is in, figure out what the word means with the suffix added. Occasionally you may find that the spelling of the root word has been changed. For instance, a final *e* may be dropped, a final consonant may be doubled, or a final *y* may be changed to *i*. Consider the possibility of such changes when trying to identify the root word.

TABLE 2.3 COMMON SUFFIXES

SUFFIX	SAMPLE WORD
Suffixes that refer to a state, condition, or quality	
-able	touchable
-ance	assistance
-ation	confrontation
-ence	reference
-ible	tangible
-ic	chronic
-ion	discussion
-ish	girlish
-ity	superiority
-ive	permissive
-less	hopeless
-ment	amazement
-ness	kindness
-ous	jealous
-ty	loyalty
-y	creamy
Suffixes that mean "one who"	
-an/-ian	Italian
-ant	participant
-ee	referee
-eer	engineer
-ent	resident
-er	teacher
-ist	activist
-or	advisor
Suffixes that mean "pertaining to or referring to"	
-ac	cardiac
-al	autumnal
-ary	secondary
-hood	brotherhood
-ship	friendship
-ward	homeward

Examples

The article was a **compilation** of facts.

 root + suffix

compil(e) + -ation = something that has been compiled, or put together into an orderly form

We were concerned with the **legality** of our decision to change addresses.

 root + suffix

legal + -ity = pertaining to legal matters

Our college is one of the most **prestigious** in the state.

 root + suffix

prestig(e) + -ous = having prestige or distinction

> ## NOW PRACTICE . . . USING SUFFIXES 1

For each of the words listed, add a suffix so that the new word will complete the sentence. Write the new word in the space provided. Check a dictionary if you are unsure of the spelling.

1. converse

   Our phone _____ lasted ten minutes.

2. assist

   The medical _____ labeled the patient's blood samples.

3. qualify

   The job applicant outlined his _____ to the interviewer.

4. intern

   The doctor completed her _____ at Memorial Medical Center.

5. eat

   We did not realize that the blossoms of the plant could be

   _____ .

6. audio

   She spoke so softly that her voice was not _____ .

7. season

   It is usually very dry in July, but this year it has rained constantly. The weather isn't very _____ .

8. permit

   The professor granted her _____ to miss class.

9. instruct

   The lecture on Freud was very _____.

10. remember

    The wealthy businessman donated the building in _____ of his deceased father.

➤ NOW PRACTICE . . . USING SUFFIXES 2

Read the following paragraph. For each pair of words in parentheses, underline the word that correctly completes the sentence.

How do new species form? Most evolutionary (1) (biologists / biological) believe that the most common source of new species, especially among animals, has been geographic isolation. When an (2) (impassable / impassor) barrier physically separates different parts of a population, a new species may result. Such physical separation could occur if, for example, some members of a population of land-dwelling organisms drifted, swam, or flew to a remote (3) (oceany / oceanic) island. Populations of water-dwelling organisms might be split when (4) (geological / geologist) processes such as volcanism or continental drift create new land barriers that divide previously (5) (continuous / continuation) seas or lakes. You can probably imagine many other scenarios that could lead to the geographic subdivision of a population.

—adapted from Audesirk, Audesirk, and Byers, *Life on Earth*, p. 237

SUMMING IT UP

WORD PARTS

WORD PARTS	LOCATION	HOW TO USE THEM
Prefixes	Beginnings of words	Notice how the prefix changes the meaning of the root or base word. (How does meaning change when *un-* is added to the word *reliable*?)
Roots	Beginning or middle of words	Use roots to figure out the basic meaning of the word.
Suffixes	Endings of words	Notice how the suffix changes the meaning of the root or base word. (How does meaning change when *-ship* is added to the word *friend*?)

3 Thesis, Main Ideas, Supporting Details, and Transitions

Most articles, essays, and textbook chapters contain numerous ideas. Some are more important than others. As you read, your job is to sort out the important ideas from those that are less important. For exams your instructors expect that you have discovered and learned what is important in assigned chapters. In class, your instructors expect you to be able to discuss the important ideas from an assignment. In this section, you will learn to identify the thesis of a reading assignment and to distinguish main ideas and supporting details. You will also learn about transitions that writers use to link ideas together.

3a IDENTIFYING THE THESIS

The **thesis** is what the entire reading selection is about. Think of it as the one most important idea that the entire article or assignment is written to explain. In articles and essays the thesis is quite specific and is often stated in one sentence, usually near the beginning of the article. In textbook chapters the thesis of the entire chapter is much more general. Individual sections of the chapter may have more specific theses. A psychology textbook chapter on stress, for example, may have as its thesis that stress can negatively affect us, but there are ways to control it. A section within the chapter may discuss the thesis that there are five main sources of stress. A magazine article on stress in the workplace, because it is much shorter, would have an even more specific thesis. It might, for instance, express the thesis that building strong relationships with coworkers can help to alleviate stress.

Now reread the article from *Wiretap* magazine on the topic of snitching that appears on p. 33. Do not continue with this section until you have read it.

The thesis of this reading is that the trend toward stopping snitching is dangerous and unhealthy. The remainder of the article presents evidence that supports this thesis.

➤ **NOW PRACTICE . . . IDENTIFYING THESIS STATEMENTS**

Underline the thesis statement in each group of sentences.

1. a. Monotheism is a belief in one supreme being.

    b. Polytheism is a belief in more than one supreme being.

    c. Theism is a belief in the existence of a god or gods.

    d. Monotheistic religions include Christianity, Judaism, and Islam.

2. a. Vincent Van Gogh is an internationally known and respected artist.

    b. Van Gogh's art displays an approach to color that was revolutionary.

    c. Van Gogh created seventy paintings in the last two months of his life.

    d. Van Gogh's art is respected for its attention to detail.

3. a. The Individuals with Disability Education Act offers guidelines for inclusive education.

    b. The inclusive theory of education says that children with special needs should be placed in regular classrooms and have services brought to them.

    c. The first movement toward inclusion was mainstreaming—a plan in which children with special needs were placed in regular classrooms for a portion of the day and sent to other classrooms for special services.

    d. Families play an important role in making inclusive education policies work.

4. a. Stress can have a negative effect on friendships and marital relationships.

    b. Stress can affect job performance.

    c. Stress is a pervasive problem in our culture.

    d. Some health problems appear to be stress related.

3b   FINDING MAIN IDEAS

MyReadingLab

To practice your skills on main ideas go to

➤ Study Plan
➤ Reading Skills
➤ Main Idea

A paragraph is a group of related sentences that express a single idea about a single topic. This idea is called the **main idea.** All the other sentences in the paragraph support this main idea. These sentences are called **supporting details.** Not all details in a paragraph are equally important.

In most paragraphs the main idea is expressed in a single sentence called the **topic sentence.** Occasionally, you will find a paragraph in which the main idea is not expressed in any single sentence. The main idea is **implied;** that is, it is suggested but not directly stated in the paragraph.

You can visualize a paragraph as shown in the accompanying diagram.

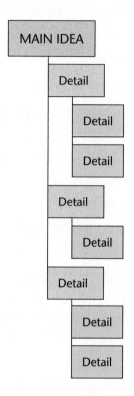

How to Find the Main Idea

We have defined a paragraph as a group of related ideas. The sentences are related to one another, and all are about the same person, place, thing, or idea. The common subject or idea is called the **topic**—what the entire paragraph is about. As you read the following paragraph, you will see that its topic is elections.

> Americans elect more people to office than almost any other society. Each even year, when most elections occur, more than 500,000 public officials are elected to school boards, city councils, county offices, state legislatures, state executive positions, the House of Representatives and the Senate, and of course, every fourth year, the presidency. By contrast with other countries, our elections are drawn-out affairs. Campaigns for even the most local office can be protracted over two or three months and cost a considerable amount of money. Presidential campaigns, including the primary season, last for at least ten months, with some candidates beginning to seek support many months and, as noted earlier, even years before the election.
>
> —Baradat, *Understanding American Democracy*, p. 163

Each sentence of this paragraph discusses or describes elections. To identify the topic of a paragraph, then, ask yourself: *"What or who is the paragraph about?"*

The **main idea** of a paragraph is what the author wants you to know about the topic. It is the broadest, most important idea that the writer develops throughout the paragraph. The entire paragraph explains, develops, and supports this main idea. A question that will guide you in finding the main idea is *"What key point is the author making about the topic?"* In the paragraph above, the writer's main idea is that elections in the United States are more numerous and more drawn out than in other countries.

The Topic Sentence

Often, but not always, one sentence expresses the main idea. This sentence is called the **topic sentence**.

To find the topic sentence, search for the one general sentence that explains what the writer wants you to know about the topic. A topic sentence is a broad, general statement; the remaining sentences of the paragraph provide details about or explain the topic sentence.

In the following paragraph, the topic is the effects of high temperatures. Read the paragraph to find out what the writer wants you to know about this topic. Look for one sentence that states this.

> Environmental psychologists have also been concerned with the effects that extremely high temperatures have on social interactions, particularly on aggression. There is a common perception that riots and other more common displays of violent behaviors are more frequent during the long, hot days of summer. This observation is largely supported by research evidence (Anderson, 1989; Anderson & Anderson, 1984; Rotton & Frey, 1985). C. A. Anderson (1987, 1989) reported on a series of studies showing that violent crimes are more prevalent in hotter quarters of the year and in hotter years, although nonviolent crimes were less affected. Anderson also concluded that differences in crime rates between cities are better predicted by temperature than by social, demographic (age, race, education), and economic variables. Baron and Ransberger (1978) point out that riots are most likely to occur when the outside temperature is only moderately high, between about 75° and 90°F. But when temperatures get much above 90°F, energy (even for aggression) becomes rapidly depleted, and rioting is less likely to occur.
>
> —Gerow, *Psychology: An Introduction*, p. 553

The paragraph opens with a statement and then proceeds to explain it by citing research evidence. The first sentence of the paragraph functions as a topic sentence, stating the paragraph's main point: High temperatures are associated with aggressive behavior. Here are some tips that will help you find the main idea.

1. **Identify the topic.** As you did earlier, figure out the general subject of the entire paragraph. In the preceding sample paragraph, "high temperatures and aggressive behavior" is the topic.

2. **Locate the most general sentence (the topic sentence).** This sentence must be broad enough to include all of the other ideas in the paragraph. The topic sentence in the sample paragraph ("Environmental psychologists have also been concerned with the effects that extremely high temperatures have on social interactions, particularly aggression.") covers all of the other details in the paragraph.

3. **Study the rest of the paragraph.** The main idea must make the rest of the paragraph meaningful. It is the one idea that ties all of the other details together. In the sample paragraph, sentence 2 explains and elaborates upon the topic sentence. Sentences 3, 4, 5, and 6 report results of research that suggest high temperature and aggressive behavior are related.

The topic sentence can be located anywhere in the paragraph. However, there are several positions where it is most likely to be found.

Locating the Topic Sentence

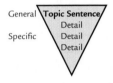

Topic Sentence First.   Most often the topic sentence is placed first in the paragraph. In this type of paragraph, the author first states his or her main point and then explains it.

> There is some evidence that colors affect you physiologically. For example, when subjects are exposed to red light respiratory movements increase; exposure to blue decreases respiratory movements. Similarly, eye blinks increase in frequency when eyes are exposed to red light and decrease when exposed to blue. This seems consistent with intuitive feelings about blue being more soothing and red being more arousing. After changing a school's walls from orange and white to blue, the blood pressure of the students decreased while their academic performance improved.
>
> —DeVito, *Interpersonal Communication*, p. 182

Here the writer first states that there is evidence of the physiological effects of color. The rest of the paragraph presents that evidence.

Topic Sentence Last.   The second most likely place for a topic sentence to appear is last in the paragraph. When using this arrangement, a writer leads up to the main point and then directly states it at the end.

> Is there a relationship between aspects of one's personality and one's state of physical health? Can psychological evaluations of an individual be used to predict physical as well as psychological disorders? Is there such a thing as a disease-prone personality? Our response is very tentative, and the data are not all supportive, but for the moment we can say yes, there does seem to be a positive correlation between some personality variables and physical health.
>
> —Gerow, *Psychology: An Introduction*, p. 700

In this paragraph, the author ponders the relationship between personality and health and concludes with the paragraph's main point: that they are related.

Topic Sentence in the Middle.   If it is placed neither first nor last, then the topic sentence appears somewhere in the middle of the paragraph. In this arrangement, the sentences before the topic sentence lead up to or introduce the main idea. Those that follow the main idea explain or describe it.

> There are 1,500 species of bacteria and approximately 8,500 species of birds. The carrot family alone has about 3,500 species, and there are 15,000 known species of wild orchids. Clearly, the task of separating various living things into their proper groups is not an easy task. Within the insect family, the problem becomes even more complex. For example, there are about 300,000 species of beetles. In fact, certain species are disappearing from the earth before we can even identify and classify them.
>
> —Wallace, *Biology: The World of Life,* p. 283

In this paragraph, the author first gives several examples of living things for which there are numerous species. Then he states his main point: Separating living things into species is not an easy task. The remainder of the paragraph offers an additional example and provides further information.

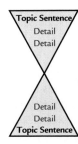

Topic Sentence First and Last.   Occasionally the main idea is stated at the beginning of a paragraph and again at the end, or elsewhere in the paragraph. Writers may use this organization to emphasize an important idea or to explain an idea that needs clarification. At other times, the first and last sentences together express the paragraph's main idea.

> Many elderly people have trouble getting the care and treatment they need for ailments. Most hospitals, designed to handle injuries and acute illness that are common to the young, do not have the facilities or personnel to treat the chronic degenerative diseases of the elderly. Many doctors are also ill-prepared to deal with such problems. As Fred Cottrell points out, "There is a widespread feeling among the aged that most doctors are not interested in them and are reluctant to treat people who are as little likely to contribute to the future as the aged are reputed to do." Even with the help of Medicare, the elderly in the United States often have a difficult time getting the health care that they need.
>
> —Coleman and Cressey, *Social Problems,* p. 277

The first and last sentences together explain that many elderly people in the United States have difficulty obtaining needed health care.

> ## NOW PRACTICE . . . FINDING MAIN IDEAS 1

Underline the topic sentence(s) of each of the following paragraphs.

Paragraph 1

Evidence suggests that groups given the right to vote do not immediately exercise that right. In recent elections, young people have not voted at a high rate—

always well below 50 percent. Since the passage of the Twenty-sixth Amendment in 1971, the addition of 18- to 20-year-olds to the electorate has contributed to a lower turnout. After the passage of the Nineteenth Amendment in 1920, many women were slow to use their new right. The difference in turnout between men and women has not been significant in recent decades, though. By the 1988 presidential election, it was fairly easy for most Americans to register and vote; yet only about 50 percent turned out to vote. What causes low turnout? How serious is it?

—Keefe et al., *American Democracy,* p. 178

Paragraph 2

The symbols that constitute language are commonly referred to as words—labels that we have assigned to concepts, or our mental representations. When we use the word *chair* as a symbol, we don't use it to label just one specific instance of a chair. We use the word as a symbol to represent our concept of chairs. As symbols, words need not stand for real things in the real world. We have words to describe objects or events that cannot be perceived, such as *ghost* or, for that matter, *mind*. With language we can communicate about owls and pussycats in teacups and a four-dimensional, time-warped hyperspace. Words stand for cognitions, or concepts, and we have a great number of them.

—Gerow, *Psychology: An Introduction,* p. 250

Paragraph 3

Body mass is made up of protoplasm, extracellular fluid, bone, and adipose tissue (body fat). One way to determine the amount of adipose tissue is to measure the whole-body density. After the on-land mass of the body is determined, the underwater body mass is obtained by submerging the person in water. Since water helps support the body by giving it buoyancy, the apparent body mass is less in water. A higher percentage of body fat will make a person more buoyant, causing the underwater mass to be even lower. This occurs because fat has a lower density than the rest of the body.

—Timberlake, *Chemistry,* p. 30

Paragraph 4

Early biologists who studied reflexes, kineses, taxes, and fixed action patterns assumed that these responses are inherited, unlearned, and common to all members of a species. They clearly depend on internal and external factors, but until recently, instinct and learning were considered distinct aspects of behavior. However, in some very clever experiments, Jack Hailman of the University of Wisconsin showed that certain stereotyped behavior patterns require subtle forms of experience for their development. In other words, at least some of the behavior normally called instinct is partly learned.

—Mix, *Biology, The Network of Life,* p. 532

Paragraph 5

On election day in 1972, at 5:30 p.m. Pacific Standard Time, NBC television news declared that Richard Nixon had been reelected president. This announcement came several hours before the polls were closed in the western part of the United States. In 1988, polls in a dozen western states were still open when CBS and ABC announced that George Bush had been elected president. These developments point to the continuing controversy over the impact of election night coverage on voter turnout.

—Keefe et al., *American Democracy,* p. 186

Paragraph 6

According to economic data, a tiny segment of the American population owns most of the nation's wealth. The wealthiest 1 percent (900,000 households with about $6 trillion net worth) own more than the least affluent 99 percent of Americans (84 million households with about $5 trillion net worth). Or, from another angle, the top 1 percent of the population owns about 38 percent of all wealth in the United States while the bottom 80 percent of the population accounts for about 17 percent of the national wealth (Mishel et al., 2001). To give you a more personalized view of the gap between rich and poor consider this: Bill Gates owns "more wealth than America's 100 million poorest people" (Greider et al., 1998:39).

—Thompson and Hickey, *Society in Focus,* p. 198

Paragraph 7

A gunnysack is a large bag, usually made of burlap. As a conflict strategy, gunnysacking refers to the practice of storing up grievances so we may unload them at another time. The immediate occasion for unloading may be relatively simple (or so it might seem at first), such as someone's coming home late without calling. Instead of arguing about this, the gunnysacker unloads all past grievances. As you probably know from experience, gunnysacking begets gunnysacking. When one person gunnysacks, the other person often reciprocates. Frequently the original problem never gets addressed. Instead, resentment and hostility escalate.

—DeVito, *Human Communication,* 9th edition, p. 217

Paragraph 8

As just about everyone today knows, e-mail has virtually become the standard method of communication in the business world. Most people enjoy its speed, ease and casual nature. But e-mail also has its share of problems and pitfalls, including privacy. Many people assume the contents of their e-mail are private, but there may in fact be any number of people authorized to see it. Some experts have even likened e-mail to postcards sent through U.S. mail: They pass through a lot of hands and before a lot of eyes, and, theoretically, many different people can read them.

—adapted from Ebert and Griffin, *Business Essentials,* p. 64

Paragraph 9

Patrescence, or becoming a father, usually is less socially noted than matrescence. The practice of **couvade** is an interesting exception to this generalization.

Couvade refers to "a variety of customs applying to the behavior of fathers during the pregnancies of their wives and during and shortly after the births of their children" (Broude 1988:902). The father may take to his bed before, during, or after the delivery. He may also experience pain and exhaustion during and after the delivery. More common is a pattern of couvade that involves a set of prohibitions and prescriptions for male behavior. Couvade occurs in societies where paternal roles in child care are prominent. One interpretation views couvade as one phase of men's participation in parenting: Their good behavior as expectant fathers helps ensure a good delivery for the baby. Another interpretation of couvade is that it offers support for the mother. In Estonia, a folk belief is that a woman's birth pains will be less if her husband helps by taking some of them on himself.

—adapted from Miller, *Cultural Anthropology,* pp. 144–145

Paragraph 10

Everything moves. Even things that appear at rest move. They move relative to the sun and stars. As you're reading this you're moving at about 107,000 kilometers per hour relative to the sun. And you're moving even faster relative to the center of our galaxy. When we discuss the motion of something, we describe motion relative to something else. If you walk down the aisle of a moving bus, your speed relative to the floor of the bus is likely quite different from your speed relative to the road. When we say a racing car reaches a speed of 300 kilometers per hour, we mean relative to the track. Unless stated otherwise, when we discuss the speeds of things in our environment we mean relative to the surface of the earth; motion is relative.

—adapted from Hewitt, *Conceptual Physics,* p. 39

> ### NOW PRACTICE . . . FINDING MAIN IDEAS 2

Underline the topic sentence of each of the following paragraphs.

Symbols and Superstitions On the surface, many marketing images have virtually no literal connection to actual products. What does a cowboy have to do with a bit of tobacco rolled into a paper tube? How can a celebrity such as basketball star Michael Jordan enhance the image of a cologne? The meanings we impart to these symbols are largely influenced by our culture, so marketers need to take special care that the symbol they use in a foreign market has the meaning they intended. Even the same product may be used quite differently and take on a different meaning to people. In parts of rural India, for example, the refrigerator is a status symbol, so people want a snazzy-looking one that they can keep in the living room to show off to visitors.

For assistance in understanding how consumers interpret the meanings of symbols, some marketers are turning to a field of study known as **semiotics,** which examines how people assign meanings to symbols. For example, although the American cowboy on packs of Marlboro cigarettes is a well-known symbol of the frontier spirit in many countries, people in Hong Kong see him as a low-status laborer.

Philip Morris has to make sure he's always pictured riding a white horse, which is a more positive symbol in that country. Even something as simple as a color takes on very different meanings around the globe. Pepsodent toothpaste found this out when it promised white teeth to people in Southeast Asia, where black or yellow teeth are status symbols.

Marketers also need to be concerned about taboos and superstitions. For example, the Japanese are superstitious about the number four. *Shi,* the word for "four," is also the word for "death," so Tiffany sells glassware and china in sets of five in Japan. In some Arab countries, alcohol and pork are forbidden to Islamic consumers (even stuffed pig toys are taboo), and advertisers may refrain from showing nudity or even the faces of women in photos, which some governments prohibit.

—Solomon and Stuart, *Marketing: Real People, Real Choices,* p. 108

> ## NOW PRACTICE . . . FINDING MAIN IDEAS 3

After reading the following passage, in the space provided write the letter of the choice that best completes each of the statements below.

Picking Partners

Just as males and females may find different ways to express emotions themselves, the process of partner selection also shows distinctly different patterns. For both males and females, more than just chemical and psychological processes influence the choice of partners. One of these factors is *proximity,* or being in the same place at the same time. The more you see a person in your hometown, at social gatherings, or at work, the more likely that an interaction will occur. Thus, if you live in New York, you'll probably end up with another New Yorker. If you live in northern Wisconsin, you'll probably end up with another Wisconsinite.

The old adage that "opposites attract" usually isn't true. You also pick a partner based on *similarities* (attitudes, values, intellect, interests). If your potential partner expresses interest or liking, you may react with mutual regard known as *reciprocity.* The more you express interest, the safer it is for someone else to return the regard, and the cycle spirals onward.

Another factor that apparently plays a significant role in selecting a partner is *physical attraction.* Whether such attraction is caused by a chemical reaction or a socially learned behavior, males and females appear to have different attraction criteria. Men tend to select their mates primarily on the basis of youth and physical attractiveness. Although physical attractiveness is an important criterion for women in mate selection, they tend to place higher emphasis on partners who are somewhat older, have good financial prospects, and are dependable and industrious.

—Donatelle, *Health: The Basics,* 5th ed., p. 105

_____ 1. The thesis of the entire selection is
     a. several factors influence choice of partners.
     b. physical attraction is more important to men than for women.
     c. proximity is the key to mate selection.
     d. opposites attract.

_____ 2. The topic sentence of the first paragraph begins with the words
     a. "For both."
     b. "One of these."
     c. "The more."
     d. "Just as."

_____ 3. The topic of the second paragraph is
     a. physical attraction.
     b. interaction.
     c. the old adage.
     d. similarities.

_____ 4. In the second paragraph, the topic sentence begins with the words
     a. "You also pick."
     b. "The more you express."
     c. "If your potential."
     d. "The old adage."

_____ 5. The topic sentence of the third paragraph is the
     a. first sentence.
     b. second sentence.
     c. third sentence.
     d. fourth sentence.

3c   FINDING THE IMPLIED MAIN IDEA

Although most paragraphs do have a topic sentence, some do not. This type of paragraph contains only details or specifics that, taken together, point to the main idea. The main idea, then, is implied but not directly stated. In such paragraphs you must infer, or reason out, the main idea. This is a process of adding up the details and deciding what they mean together or what main idea they all support or explain. Use the following steps to grasp implied main ideas.

■ Identify the topic by asking yourself, "What is the one thing the author is discussing throughout the paragraph?"

- Decide what the writer wants you to know about the topic. Look at each detail and decide what larger idea each explains.
- Express this idea in your own words.

Here is a sample paragraph; use the above questions to identify the main idea.

> Severe punishment may generate such anxiety in children that they do not learn the lesson the punishment was designed to teach. Moreover, as a reaction to punishment that they regard as unfair, children may avoid punitive parents, who therefore will have fewer opportunities to teach and guide the child. In addition, parents who use physical punishment provide aggressive models. A child who is regularly slapped, spanked, shaken, or shouted at may learn to use these forms of aggression in interactions with peers.
>
> —Newcombe, *Child Development*, p. 354

The topic of this paragraph is punishment. The author's main point is that punishment has negative effects. You can figure out this writer's main idea even though no single sentence states this directly. You can visualize this paragraph as follows:

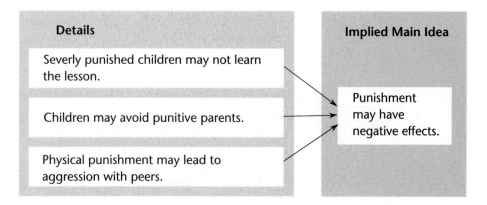

NOW PRACTICE . . . FINDING IMPLIED MAIN IDEAS 1

After reading each of the paragraphs, complete the diagram that follows by filling in the missing information.

Paragraph A

The average American consumer eats 21 pounds of snack foods in a year, but people in the West Central part of the country consume the most (24 pounds per person) whereas those in the Pacific and Southeast regions eat "only" 19 pounds per person. Pretzels are the most popular snack in the mid-Atlantic area, pork rinds are most likely to be eaten in the South, and multigrain chips turn up as a favorite in the West. Not surprisingly, the Hispanic influence in the Southwest has influenced snacking preferences—consumers in that part of the United States eat about 50 percent more tortilla chips than do people elsewhere.

—adapted from Solomon, *Consumer Behavior*, p. 184

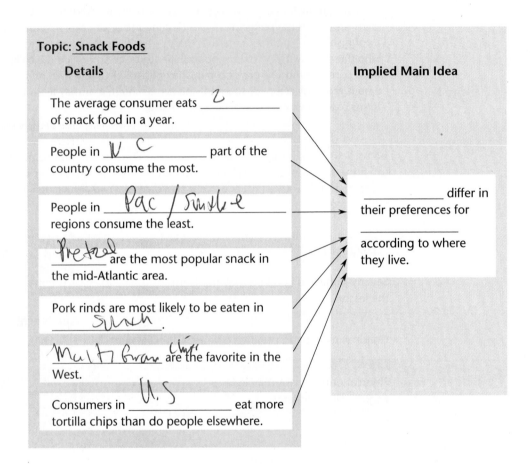

Topic: <u>Snack Foods</u>

Details

The average consumer eats __2__ of snack food in a year.

People in __N C__ part of the country consume the most.

People in __Pac / Swthe__ regions consume the least.

__Pretzel__ are the most popular snack in the mid-Atlantic area.

Pork rinds are most likely to be eaten in __Sunth__.

__Multi Gran Chips__ are the favorite in the West.

Consumers in __U.S__ eat more tortilla chips than do people elsewhere.

Implied Main Idea

_____ differ in their preferences for _____ according to where they live.

Paragraph B

The constellation [group of stars] that the Greeks named Orion, the hunter, was seen by the ancient Chinese as a supreme warrior called *Shen.* Hindus in ancient India also saw a warrior, called *Skanda,* who rode a peacock. The three stars of Orion's belt were seen as three fishermen in a canoe by Aborigines of northern Australia. As seen from southern California, these three stars climb almost straight up into the sky as they rise in the east, which may explain why the

Chemehuevi Indians of the California desert saw them as a line of three sure-footed mountain sheep.

—adapted from Bennett et al., *The Cosmic Perspective*, p. 28

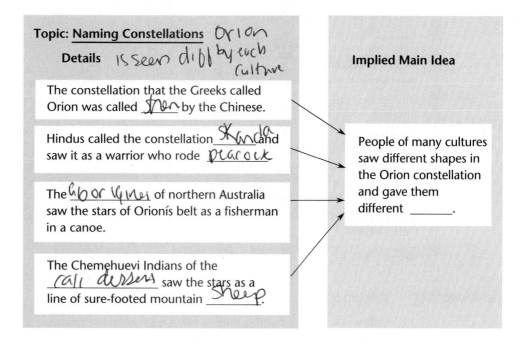

Topic: Naming Constellations Orion

Details is seen diff by each culture

The constellation that the Greeks called Orion was called _Shen_ by the Chinese.

Hindus called the constellation _Skanda_ and saw it as a warrior who rode _peacock_

The _Gboor Gime_ of northern Australia saw the stars of Orionís belt as a fisherman in a canoe.

The Chemehuevi Indians of the _Cali desserv_ saw the stars as a line of sure-footed mountain _sheep_.

Implied Main Idea

People of many cultures saw different shapes in the Orion constellation and gave them different _____.

Paragraph C

first of all

Initially, many computers entered homes as children's games. But the trend spread fast, from simple games to more sophisticated ones. Soon they became a favorite pastime both for children and young adults. This group of people showed an almost natural ability to adapt to computers; software developers saw the opportunity for the market and developed increasingly challenging games as well as educational programs. Many parents were then tempted to buy computers for home use and this, in turn, led to a situation where people of all ages and backgrounds saw the benefit of computers not only for young people but also for adults who used them for personal and business purposes.

—Bandyo-padhyay, *Computing for Non-specialists*, p. 4

Topic: Computers

Details	Implied Main Idea

Computers first entered homes as _____ .

As games became more _____, they became popular for both children and _____ .

_____ developed increasingly challenging games as well as _____ for this market.

People of all ages and backgrounds began to see the benefit of _____ for personal and _____ purposes.

The use of _____ at home has grown from children's entertainment to many _____ applications.

> **NOW PRACTICE . . . FINDING IMPLIED MAIN IDEAS 2**

Write a sentence that states the main idea for each of the following paragraphs.

Paragraph 1

During the 1960s, police went from walking "beats" [regular routes] to riding in squad cars. While squad cars provided a faster response to emergency calls, they also changed the nature of social interaction between police officers and the public. Much police work had been highly personal, as officers strolled the sidewalks talking to storekeepers and homeowners, but it became much more impersonal, with less contact between officers and citizens. Since the 1960s, technological advances have provided more elaborate means of communication and surveillance, better-equipped squad cars, and more sophisticated weaponry. Unfortunately criminals have benefited from increased technology as well. This increased technology and other developments have led many city leaders to question contemporary policing practices and some to accentuate the need to reemphasize police–community relations.

—Thompson and Hickey, *Society in Focus,* p. 162

Main idea: The advancement of technology so between and policing

The changing in police work

Paragraph 2

When a homemaker is killed in an auto accident, that person's family can often sue for the value of the services that were lost. Attorneys (who rely on economists) are often asked to make an attempt to estimate this value to present to the court. They add up the cost of purchasing babysitting, cooking, housecleaning, and tutoring services. The number turns out to be quite large, often in excess of $30,000 a year. Of course one of the problems in measuring the value of unremunerated housework in such a way is that we could often purchase the services of a full-time live-in housekeeper for less money than if we paid for the services of the various components of housekeeping. And what about quality? Some homemakers serve fabulous gourmet meals; others simply warm up canned and frozen foods. Should they be valued equally? Another problem lies in knowing when to stop counting. A person can hire a valet to help him or her get dressed in the morning. Should we therefore count the time spent in getting dressed as part of unpaid work? Both men and women perform services around the house virtually every day of the year. Should all of those unremunerated services be included in a "new" measure of GDP [Gross Domestic Product]? If they were, measured GDP would be increased dramatically.

—Miller, *Economics Today*, p. 185

Main idea: __hard to get accurate price__

Paragraph 3

In 1970 the federal government passed the Comprehensive Drug Abuse, Prevention and Control Act (also known as the Controlled Substance Act). That act did not contain a rigid penalty system but rather established only upper bounds for the fines and prison terms to be imposed for offenses. In 1984 the act was amended in order to impose fixed penalties, particularly for dealers. For anyone caught with more than 1 kilogram of heroin, 50 grams of cocaine base, or 1,000 kilograms of marijuana, the applicable penalty was raised to imprisonment from 10 years to life plus a fine of $4 million. A variety of other prison penalties and fines were outlined in that amendment. Another amendment passed in 1988 included the death penalty for "drug kingpins."

—Miller, *Economics Today*, p. 513

Main idea: __Drug amendments and__
__rules__
__Penalties have__

Paragraph 4

As recently as 20 years ago, textbooks on child psychology seldom devoted more than a few paragraphs to the behaviors of the neonate—the newborn through the first 2 weeks of life. It seemed as if the neonate did not do much worth writing about. Today, most child psychology texts devote substantially more space to discussing the abilities of newborns. It is unlikely that over the past 20 years neonates have gotten smarter or more able. Rather, psychologists have. They have devised new and clever ways of measuring the abilities and capacities of neonates.

—Gerow, *Psychology: An Introduction*, p. 319

Main idea: _The Uncover the unknown nenote_

➤ NOW PRACTICE . . . FINDING IMPLIED MAIN IDEAS 3

After reading each of the following paragraphs, select the letter of the choice that best answers the questions that follow.

Paragraph A

John Kennedy, the first "television president," held considerably more public appearances than did his predecessors. Kennedy's successors, with the notable exception of Richard Nixon, have been even more active in making public appearances. Indeed, they have averaged more than one appearance every weekday of the year. Bill Clinton invested enormous time and energy in attempting to sell his programs to the public. George W. Bush has followed the same pattern.

—Edwards et al., *Government in America*, p. 422

_____ 1. What is the topic?
   a. the presidency
   b. the effects of television
   c. President Kennedy
   d. public appearances of the president

_____ 2. What main idea is the writer implying?
   a. U.S. presidents all enjoy being in the public eye.
   b. The successors of President Kennedy have tried to imitate him.
   c. Presidents have placed increasing importance on making public appearances.
   d. Presidents spend too much time making public appearances.

Paragraph B

When speaking on the telephone be sure to speak clearly, enunciating carefully. It is also a good practice to speak just a bit slower than if you were talking with someone face-to-face. When responding to an answering machine or voice mail, be brief but to the point. Give your name, telephone number, and a brief explanation of why you called. State what time would be best to return your call.

It is also helpful to give your phone number a second time as a conclusion to your message.

—adapted from Cook, Yale, and Marqua, *Tourism: The Business of Travel*, p. 370

_____ 3. What is the topic?

    a. telephone manners

    b. public speaking

    c. telemarketing

    d. customer service

_____ 4. What is the writer saying about the topic?

    a. People today have terrible phone manners.

    b. Telephone manners are not as important as those used in face-to-face conversations.

    c. Speaking on the telephone requires clarity, brevity, and conciseness.

    d. Telephone messages should be kept to a minimum.

Paragraph C

All the nutrients in the world are useless to humans unless oxygen is also available. Because the chemical reactions that release energy from foods require oxygen, human cells can survive for only a few minutes without oxygen. Approximately 20% of the air we breathe is oxygen. It is made available to the blood and body cells by the cooperative efforts of the respiratory and cardiovascular systems.

—adapted from Marieb, *Anatomy and Physiology*, p. 9

_____ 5. What is the topic?

    a. humans

    b. nutrients

    c. oxygen

    d. the respiratory system

_____ 6. What main idea is the writer implying?

    a. All chemical reactions require oxygen.

    b. Oxygen is vital to human life.

    c. Less than a fourth of the air we breathe is oxygen.

    d. The respiratory system and the cardiovascular system work together.

_____ 7. Which one of the following details does *not* support the paragraph's implied main idea?

    a. All the nutrients in the world are useless to humans.

  b. The chemical reactions that release energy from foods use oxygen.

  c. Plants release oxygen into the air through the process of photosynthesis.

  d. The respiratory and cardiovascular systems supply oxygen to the blood and body cells.

Paragraph D

People's acceptance of a product may be largely determined by its packaging. In one study the very same coffee taken from a yellow can was described as weak, from a dark brown can as too strong, from a red can as rich, and from a blue can as mild. Even your acceptance of a person may depend on the colors worn. Consider, for example, the comments of one color expert: "If you have to pick the wardrobe for your defense lawyer heading into court and choose anything but blue, you deserve to lose the case. . . ." Black is so powerful it could work against the lawyer with the jury. Brown lacks sufficient authority. Green would probably elicit a negative response.

—adapted from DeVito, *Messages: Building Interpersonal Communication Skills*, p. 161

_____ 8. What is the topic?

  a. packaging

  b. marketing

  c. colors

  d. dressing for success

_____ 9. What is the writer saying about the topic?

  a. Colors influence how we think and act.

  b. A product's packaging determines whether or not we accept it.

  c. A lawyer's success depends on the color of his or her wardrobe.

  d. Color experts consider blue to be the most influential color.

_____ 10. Which one of the following details does *not* support the paragraph's implied main idea?

  a. The same coffee is judged differently depending on the color of the coffee can.

  b. The colors a person is wearing may influence your opinion of that person.

  c. Lawyers who wear blue in court deserve to be defeated.

  d. Green is not considered a good color to wear in the courtroom.

► **NOW PRACTICE . . . FINDING STATED AND IMPLIED MAIN IDEAS**

Turn to the article titled "Deadly Silence: Stop Snitching's Fatal Legacy" on p. 33. Using your own paper, number the lines from 1 to 15, to correspond to the 15 paragraphs in the article. For each paragraph number, if the main idea is stated, record the sentence number in which it appears (first, second, etc.). If the main idea is unstated and implied, write a sentence that expresses the main idea.

3d RECOGNIZING SUPPORTING DETAILS

MyReadingLab

To practice your skills on details, go to

► Study Plan
► Reading Skills
► Supporting Details

Supporting details are those facts and ideas that prove or explain the main idea of a paragraph. While all the details in a paragraph do support the main idea, not all details are equally important. As you read, try to identify and pay attention to the most important details. Pay less attention to details of lesser importance. The key details directly explain the main idea. Other details may provide additional information, offer an example, or further explain one of the key details.

Figure A shows how details relate to the main idea and how details range in degree of importance. In the diagram, more important details are placed toward the left; less important details are closer to the right.

Figure A

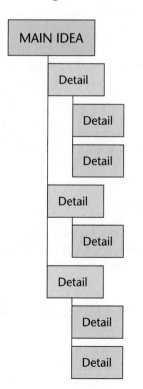

Figure B

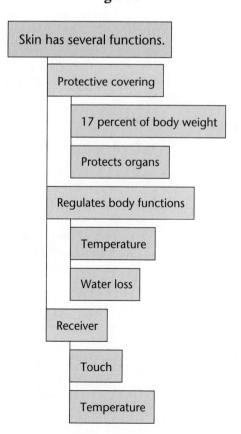

Read the following paragraph and study Figure B.

> The skin of the human body has several functions. First, it serves as a protective covering. In doing so, it accounts for 17 percent of the body weight. Skin also protects the organs within the body from damage or harm. The skin serves as a regulator of body functions. It controls body temperature and water loss. Finally, the skin serves as a receiver. It is sensitive to touch and temperature.

From this diagram you can see that the details that state the three functions of skin are the key details. Other details, such as "protects the organs," provide further information and are at a lower level of importance.

Read the following paragraph and try to pick out the more important details.

> Many cultures have different rules for men and women engaging in conflict. Asian cultures are more strongly prohibitive of women's conflict strategies. Asian women are expected to be exceptionally polite; this is even more important when women are in conflict with men and when the conflict is public. In the United States, there is a verbalized equality; men and women have equal rights when it comes to permissible conflict strategies. In reality, there are many who expect women to be more polite, to pursue conflict in a nonargumentative way, while men are expected to argue forcefully and logically.

This paragraph could be diagrammed as follows (key details only):

> **Many cultures have different rules for men and women engaging in conflict.**
>
> > Rules in Asian cultures
> >
> > Rules in the United States

NOW PRACTICE . . . RECOGNIZING SUPPORTING DETAILS 1

Each of the following topic sentences states the main idea of a paragraph. After each topic sentence are sentences containing details that may or may not support the topic sentence. Read each sentence and put an "S" beside those that contain details that support the topic sentence.

1. **Topic Sentence:** Malmo is one of Sweden's leading environmentally conscious cities known for its responsible use of natural resources.

_____ a. Most of the city's electricity comes from nuclear and hydropower.

_____ b. Many residents use green roofing (botanical roof gardens) that add insulation to buildings.

_____ c. Malmo is home to 280,000 people and is the third largest city in Sweden.

_____ d. Forty percent of the city's commuters travel by bicycle.

_____ e. Many of the neighborhoods, with their canals, harbors, and beaches, face the problem of beach erosion.

2. **Topic Sentence:** *Mens rea,* a term that refers to a person's criminal intent when committing a crime, or his or her state of mind, can be evaluated in several ways.

_____ a. Confessions by criminals are direct evidence of their criminal intent.

_____ b. Circumstantial evidence can be used to suggest mental intent.

_____ c. *Actus rea* is a person's actions that make up a crime.

_____ d. A person may unknowingly commit a crime.

_____ e. Expert witnesses may offer an opinion about a person's criminal intent.

3. **Topic Sentence:** Food irradiation is a process in which food is treated with radiation to kill bacteria.

_____ a. Gamma radiation is made up of radioactive cobalt, cesium, and X-rays.

_____ b. The radioactive rays pass through the food without damaging it or changing it.

_____ c. The newest form of irradiation uses electricity as the energy source for irradiation.

_____ d. Irradiation increases the shelf life of food because it kills all bacteria present in the food.

_____ e. *E. coli,* salmonella, and listeria cause many illnesses each year.

4. **Topic Sentence:** Overtraining is the most common type of fitness-related injury, and it can be easily avoided.

_____ a. A physical fitness program will improve your health and well-being.

_____ b. Our bodies usually provide warning signs of potential muscle damage.

_____ c. People often injure themselves by doing too much too soon when they exercise.

_____ d. To avoid injury, do not rely solely on repetitive motion activities like running or step aerobics.

_____ e. Varying an exercise program can allow muscles time to rest and recover from strain.

5. **Topic Sentence:** Frank Lloyd Wright was a radically innovative architect.

_5_ a. Wright believed that buildings fit their surroundings.

_5_ b. He popularized the use of steel cantilevers in homes at a time when they were only used commercially.

_____S_____ c. He built the Kaufmann Residence over a waterfall without disturbing it.

_____ d. Wright had plans to build a mile-high skyscraper but died before he could do so.

_____S_____ e. Wright designed the Guggenheim Museum.

> ## NOW PRACTICE . . . RECOGNIZING SUPPORTING DETAILS 2

Underline only the most important details in each of the following paragraphs.

Paragraph 1

Physical dependence is what was formerly called addiction. It is characterized by *tolerance* and *withdrawal*. *Tolerance* means that more and more of the drug must be taken to achieve the same effect, as use continues. *Withdrawal* means that if use is discontinued, the person experiences unpleasant symptoms. When I quit smoking cigarettes, for example, I went through about five days of irritability, depression, and restlessness. Withdrawal from heroin and other narcotics is much more painful, involving violent cramps, vomiting, diarrhea, and other symptoms that continue for at least two or three days. With some drugs, especially barbiturates, cold-turkey (sudden and total) quitting can result in death, so severe is the withdrawal.

—Geiwitz, *Psychology,* p. 512

Paragraph 2

The two most common drugs that are legal and do not require a prescription are caffeine and nicotine. *Caffeine* is the active ingredient in coffee, tea, and many cola drinks. It stimulates the central nervous system and heart and therefore is often used to stay awake. Heavy use—say, seven to ten cups of coffee per day—has toxic effects, that is, it acts like a mild poison. Prolonged heavy use appears to be addicting. *Nicotine* is the active ingredient in tobacco. One of the most addicting of all drugs and one of the most dangerous, at least when obtained by smoking, it has been implicated in lung cancer, emphysema, and heart disease.

—Geiwitz, *Psychology,* p. 513

Paragraph 3

Hypnosis today is used for a number of purposes, primarily in psychotherapy or to reduce pain, and it is an acceptable technique in both medicine and psychology. In psychotherapy, it is most often used to eliminate bad habits and annoying symptoms. Cigarette smoking can be treated, for example, by the suggestion that the person will feel nauseated whenever he or she thinks of smoking. Sufferers of migraine headaches treated with hypnotic suggestions to relax showed a much greater tendency to improve than sufferers treated with drugs; 44 percent were headache-free after 12 months of treatment, compared to 12 percent of their drug-treated counterparts.

—Geiwitz, *Psychology,* p. 229

Paragraph 4

There are four main types of sunglasses. The traditional *absorptive* glasses soak up all the harmful sun rays. *Polarizing* sunglasses account for half the market. They're the best buy for knocking out glare, and reflections from snow and water, but they may admit more light rays than other sunglasses. *Coated* sunglasses usually have a metallic covering that itself reflects light. They are often quite absorptive, but a cheap pair of coated glasses may have an uneven or nondurable coating that could rub off after a short period of time. New on the market are the somewhat more expensive *photochromatic* sunglasses. Their chemical composition causes them to change color according to the brightness of the light: in the sun, they darken; in the shade, they lighten. This type of sunglasses responds to ultraviolet light only, and will not screen out infrared rays, so they're not the best bet for continual exposure to bright sun.

—George, *The New Consumer Survival Kit,* p. 14

Paragraph 5

In simplest outline, how is a President chosen? First, a candidate campaigns within his party for nomination at a national convention. After the convention comes a period of competition with the nominee of the other major party and perhaps the nominees of minor parties. The showdown arrives on Election Day. The candidate must win more votes than any other nominee in enough states and the District of Columbia to give him a majority of the electoral votes. If he does all these things, he has won the right to the office of President of the United States.

— "ABC's of How a President Is Chosen," *U.S. News and World Report,* p. 45

> **NOW PRACTICE . . . RECOGNIZING SUPPORTING DETAILS 3**

Reread the article "Deadly Silence: Stop Snitching's Fatal Legacy" on p. 33 and underline the most important supporting details in each paragraph.

3e   RECOGNIZING TRANSITIONS

Transitions are linking words or phrases used to lead the reader from one idea to another. If you get in the habit of recognizing transitions, you will see that they often guide you through a paragraph, helping you to read it more easily.

In the following paragraph, notice how the underlined transitions lead you from one important detail to the next.

The principle of rhythm and line also contributes to the overall unity of the landscape design. This principle is responsible for the sense of continuity between different areas of the landscape. <u>One</u> way in which this continuity can be developed is by extending planting beds from one area to another. <u>For example</u>, shrub beds developed around the entrance to the house can be continued around the sides and into the backyard. Such an arrangement helps to tie the front and rear areas of the property together. <u>Another</u> means by which rhythm is given to a design is to repeat shapes, angles, or lines between various areas and elements of the design.

—Reiley and Shry, *Introductory Horticulture*, p. 114

Not all paragraphs contain such obvious transitions, and not all transitions serve as such clear markers of major details. Often, however, transitions are used to alert you to what will come next in the paragraph. If you see the phrase *for instance* at the beginning of a sentence, then you know that an example will follow. When you see the phrase *on the other hand*, you can predict that a different, opposing idea will follow. Table 3.1 lists some of the most common transitions used within a paragraph and indicates what they tell you.

TABLE 3.1   COMMON TRANSITIONS

TYPES OF TRANSITIONS	EXAMPLES	WHAT THEY TELL THE READER
Time or Sequence	first, later, next, finally	The author is arranging ideas in the order in which they happened.
Example	for example, for instance, to illustrate, such as	An example will follow.
Enumeration	first, second, third, last, another, next	The author is marking or identifying each major point (sometimes these may be used to suggest order of importance).
Continuation	also, in addition, and, further, another	The author is continuing with the same idea and is going to provide additional information.
Contrast	on the other hand, in contrast, however	The author is switching to a different, opposite, or contrasting idea than previously discussed.
Comparison	like, likewise, similarly	The writer will show how the previous idea is similar to what follows.
Cause and Effect	because, thus, therefore, since, consequently	The writer will show a connection between two or more things, how one thing caused another, or how something happened as a result of something else.

▶ NOW PRACTICE . . . RECOGNIZING TRANSITIONS 1

Select the transitional word or phrase from the box below that best completes each of the following sentences.

another	however	more important
for example	because	

1. The function of taste buds is to enable us to select healthy foods. _____ function is to warn us away from foods that are potentially dangerous, such as those that are sour or bitter.

2. Michelangelo considered himself to be primarily a sculptor; _____, the Sistine Chapel ceiling painting is one of his best known works of art.

3. Failure to floss and brush teeth and gums can cause bad breath. _____, this failure can also lead to periodontal disease.

4. Businesses use symbols to stand for a product's qualities; _____, the golden arches have come to represent the McDonald's chain.

5. In the 1800s, the "Wild West" was made up of territories that did not belong to states. _____ there was no local government, vigilantes and outlaws ruled the land, answering only to U.S. marshals.

▶ NOW PRACTICE . . . RECOGNIZING TRANSITIONS 2

Select the transitional word or phrase from the box below that best completes each of the following sentences. Two of the transitions in the box may be used more than once.

on the other hand	for example	because	in addition
similarly	after	next	however
also			

1. Typically, those suffering from post-traumatic stress disorder are soldiers after combat. Civilians who have experienced events such as the World Trade Center destruction can _____ experience this syndrome.

2. Columbus was determined to find an oceanic passage to China _____ finding a direct route would mean increased trading and huge profits.

3. In the event of a heart attack, it is first important to identify the symptoms. _____, call 911 or drive the victim to the nearest hospital.

4. In the 1920s, courtship between men and women changed dramatically. _____, instead of paying calls at the woman's home with her parents there, men now invited women out on dates.

5. Direct exposure to sunlight is dangerous because the ultraviolet rays can lead to skin cancer. _____, tanning booths also emit ultraviolet rays and are as dangerous as, if not more dangerous than, exposure to sunlight.

6. Lie detector tests are often used by law enforcement to help determine guilt or innocence. _____, because these tests often only have an accuracy rate of between 60% and 80%, the results are not admissible in court.

7. The temporal lobes of the brain process sound and comprehend language. _____, this area of the brain is responsible for storing visual memories.

8. The theory of multiple intelligences holds that there are many different kinds of intelligence, or abilities. _____, musical ability, control of bodily movements (athletics), spatial understanding, and observational abilities are all classified as different types of intelligence.

9. During World War II, Japanese Americans were held in relocation camps. _____ the war was over, the United States paid reparations and issued an apology to those who were wrongfully detained.

10. Support continues to grow for the legalization of marijuana. _____, legalization has not yet been passed in any state and it is unlikely this will happen anytime soon.

▶ NOW PRACTICE . . . RECOGNIZING TRANSITIONS 3

Many transitions have similar meanings and can sometimes be used interchangeably. Match each transition in column A with a similar transition in column B. Write the letter of your choice in the space provided.

Column A	Column B
_____ 1. because	a. therefore
_____ 2. in contrast	b. also
_____ 3. for instance	c. likewise
_____ 4. thus	d. after that
_____ 5. first	e. since
_____ 6. one way	f. finally
_____ 7. similarly	g. on the other hand
_____ 8. next	h. one approach
_____ 9. in addition	i. in the beginning
_____ 10. to sum up	j. for example

> ### NOW PRACTICE . . . RECOGNIZING TRANSITIONS 4

Each of the following beginnings of paragraphs uses a transitional word or phrase to tell the reader what will follow in the paragraph. Read each, paying particular attention to the underlined word or phrase. Then, in the space provided, describe as specifically as you can what you would expect to find next in the paragraph.

1. Price is not the only factor to consider in choosing a pharmacy. Many provide valuable services that should be considered. For instance . . .

   _____

2. There are a number of things you can do to prevent a home burglary. First, . . .

   _____

3. Most mail order businesses are reliable and honest. However, . . .

   _____

   _____

4. One advantage of a compact stereo system is that all the components are built into the unit. Another . . .

   _____

5. To select the presidential candidate you will vote for, you should examine his or her philosophy of government. Next . . .

   _____

4 Organizational Patterns

MyReadingLab

To practice using organizational patterns, go to

➤ Study Plan
➤ Reading Skills
➤ Patterns of Organization

Most college students take courses in several different disciplines each semester. They may study psychology, anatomy and physiology, mathematics, and English composition all in one semester. During one day they may read a poem, solve math problems, and study early developments in psychology.

What few students realize is that a biologist and a psychologist, for example, think about and approach their subject matter in similar ways. Both carefully define terms, examine causes and effects, study similarities and differences, describe sequences of events, classify information, solve problems, and enumerate characteristics. The subject matter and language they use differ, but their approaches to the material are basically the same. Researchers, textbook authors, and your professors use standard approaches, or **organizational patterns**, to express their ideas.

In academic writing, commonly used organizational patterns include definition, classification, order or sequence, cause and effect, comparison and contrast, and listing/enumeration. Other important patterns include statement and clarification, summary, generalization and example, and addition.

These patterns can work for you in several ways:

- **Patterns** help you anticipate the author's thought development and thus focus your reading.
- **Patterns** help you remember and recall what you read.
- **Patterns** are useful in your own writing; they help you organize and express your ideas in a more coherent, comprehensible form.

The following sections describe each pattern listed above. In subsequent chapters, you will see how these patterns are used in specific academic disciplines.

4a DEFINITION

Each academic discipline has its own specialized vocabulary. One of the primary purposes of introductory textbooks is to introduce students to this new language. Consequently, definition is a commonly used pattern throughout most introductory-level texts.

Suppose you were asked to define the word *comedian* for someone unfamiliar with the term. First, you would probably say that a comedian is a person who entertains. Then you might distinguish a comedian from other types of entertainers by saying that a comedian is an entertainer who tells jokes and makes others laugh. Finally, you might mention, by way of example, the names of several well-known comedians who have appeared on television. Although you may have presented it informally, your definition would have followed the standard, classic pattern. The first part of your definition tells what general class or group the term belongs to (entertainers). The second part tells what distinguishes the term from other items in the same class or category. The third part includes further explanation, characteristics, examples, or applications.

You can visualize the definition pattern as follows:

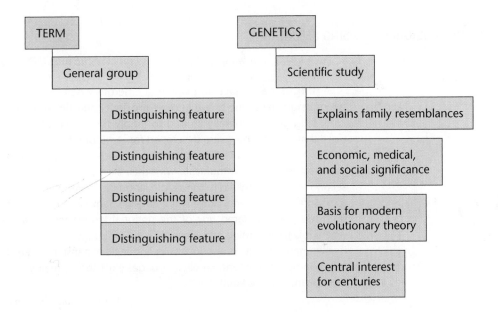

See how the term *genetics* is defined in the following paragraph, and notice how the term and the general class are presented in the first sentence. The remainder of the paragraph presents the distinguishing characteristics.

Genetics is the scientific study of heredity, the transmission of characteristics from parents to offspring. Genetics explains why offspring resemble their parents and also why they are not identical to them. Genetics is a subject that has considerable economic, medical, and social significance and is partly the basis for the modern theory of evolution. Because of its importance, genetics has been a topic of central interest in the study of life for centuries. Modern concepts in genetics are fundamentally different, however, from earlier ones.

—Mix, Farber, and King, *Biology, The Network of Life,* p. 262

Writers often provide clues called **transitions** that signal the organizational pattern being used. These signals may occur within single sentences or as connections between sentences. (Transitional words that occur in phrases are italicized in the box below to help you spot them.)

TRANSITIONS FOR THE DEFINITION PATTERN

genetics *is* . . .
bureaucracy *means* . . .
patronage *refers to* . . .
aggression *can be defined* as . . .
deficit is *another term* that . . .
balance of power *also means* . . .

> **NOW PRACTICE . . . USING DEFINITION**

Read each of the following paragraphs and answer the questions that follow.

A.   A **pidgin** is a contact language that emerges when different cultures with different languages come to live in close proximity and therefore need to communicate. Pidgins are generally limited to highly functional domains, such as trade, since that is what they were developed for. A pidgin therefore is no one's first language. Many pidgins of the Western hemisphere developed out of slavery, where owners needed to communicate with their slaves. A pidgin is always learned as a second language. Tok Pisin, the pidgin language of Papua New Guinea, consists of a mixture of many languages, some English, Samoan, Chinese, and Malayan. Tok Pisin has been declared one of the national languages of Papau New Guinea, where it is transforming into a **creole,** or a language descended from pidgin with its own native speakers and involving linguistic expansion and elaboration. About two hundred pidgin and creole languages exist today, mainly in West Africa, the Caribbean, and the South Pacific.

—Miller, *Cultural Anthropology,* pp. 308–309

1. What term is being defined?

   _____

2. Explain the meaning of the term in your own words.

   _____

   _____

3. Give an example of the term. _____

B.   The **integumentary** system is the external covering of the body, or the skin. It waterproofs the body and cushions and protects the deeper tissues from injury. It also excretes salts and urea in perspiration and helps regulate body temperature.

Temperature, pressure, and pain receptors located in the skin alert us to what is happening at the body surface.

—Marieb, *Essentials of Human Anatomy and Physiology,* p. 3

4. Define the integumentary system in your own words.

_____

5. List three things the integumentary system does.

_____

_____

4b CLASSIFICATION

If you were asked to describe types of computers, you might mention PC's, laptops, and BlackBerries. By dividing a broad topic into its major categories, you are using a pattern known as *classification.*

This pattern is widely used in many academic subjects. For example, a psychology text might explain human needs by classifying them into two categories: primary and secondary. In a chemistry textbook, various compounds may be grouped and discussed according to common characteristics, such as the presence of hydrogen or oxygen. The classification pattern divides a topic into parts, on the basis of common or shared characteristics.

Here are a few examples of topics and the classifications or categories into which each might be divided.

- **Movies:** comedy, horror, mystery
- **Motives:** achievement, power, affiliation, competency
- **Plants:** leaves, stem, roots

Note how the following paragraph classifies the various types of cancers.

The name of the cancer is derived from the type of tissue in which it develops. Carcinoma (carc = cancer; omo = tumor) refers to a malignant tumor consisting of epithelial cells. A tumor that develops from a gland is called an adenosarcoma (adeno = gland). Sarcoma is a general term for any cancer arising from connective tissue. Osteogenic sarcomas (osteo = bone; genic = origin), the most frequent type of childhood cancer, destroy normal bone tissue and eventually spread to other areas of the body. Myelomas (myelos = marrow) are malignant tumors, occurring in middle-aged and older people, that interfere with the blood-cell-producing function of bone marrow and cause anemia. Chondrosarcomas (chondro = cartilage) are cancerous growths of cartilage.

—Tortora, *Introduction to the Human Body,* p. 56

You can visualize the classification pattern as follows:

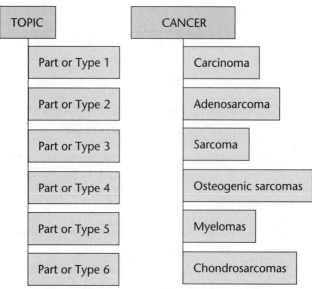

TOPIC	CANCER
Part or Type 1	Carcinoma
Part or Type 2	Adenosarcoma
Part or Type 3	Sarcoma
Part or Type 4	Osteogenic sarcomas
Part or Type 5	Myelomas
Part or Type 6	Chondrosarcomas

TRANSITIONS FOR THE CLASSIFICATION PATTERN

There are *several kinds* of chemical bonding . . .
There are *numerous types of* . . .
Reproduction can be *classified as* . . .
the human skeleton is *composed of* . . .
muscles *comprise* . . .
one type of communication . . .
another type of communication . . .
finally, there is . . .

> **NOW PRACTICE . . . USING CLASSIFICATION**

Read each of the following paragraphs and answer the questions that follow.

A.   The reptiles made one of the most spectacular adaptive radiations in all of Earth history. One group, the pterosaurs, took to the air. These "dragons of the sky" possessed huge membranous wings that allowed them rudimentary flight. Another group of reptiles, exemplified by the fossil *Archaeopteryx,* led to more successful flyers: the birds. Whereas some reptiles took to the skies, others returned to the sea, including fish-eating plesiosaurs and ichthyosaurs. These reptiles became proficient swimmers, but retained their reptilian teeth and breathed by means of lungs.

—Tarbuck and Lutgens, *Earth Science,* p. 309

1. List the classification of reptiles included in this paragraph.

   _____

2. Highlight the transitional words used in the paragraph.

   _____

B.   From the hundreds of billions of galaxies, several basic types have been identified: spiral, elliptical, and irregular. The Milky Way and the Great Galaxy in
Andromeda are examples of fairly large **spiral galaxies**. Typically, spiral galaxies
are disk-shaped with a somewhat greater concentration of stars near their centers, but there are numerous variations. Viewed broadside, arms are often seen
extending from the central nucleus and sweeping gracefully away. One type of
spiral galaxy, however, has the stars arranged in the shape of a bar, which rotates
as a rigid system. This requires that the outer stars move faster than the inner
ones, a fact not easy for astronomers to reconcile with the laws of motion.
Attached to each end of these bars are curved spiral arms. These have become
known as **barred spiral galaxies**. The most abundant group, making up 60
percent of the total is the **elliptical galaxies**. These are generally smaller than
spiral galaxies. Some are so much smaller, in fact, that the term dwarf has been
applied. Because these dwarf galaxies are not visible at great distances, a survey
of the sky reveals more of the conspicuous large spiral galaxies. As their name im-
plies, elliptical galaxies have an ellipsoidal shape that ranges to nearly spherical,
and they lack spiral arms. Only 10 percent of the known galaxies lack symmetry
and are classified as **irregular galaxies**. The best-known irregular galaxies, the
Large and Small Magellanic Clouds in the Southern Hemisphere, are easily visible
with the unaided eye.

—Tarbuck and Lutgens, *Earth Science*, pp. 620–621

3. What are the three primary classifications of galaxies?

   _____

4. What determines how a galaxy is classified?

   _____

5. Highlight the transitional words used in the paragraph.

   _____

4c   ORDER OR SEQUENCE

If you were asked to summarize what you did today, you probably would mention key events in the order in which they occurred. In describing how to write
a particular computer program, you would detail the process step-by-step. In

each case, you are presenting information in a particular sequence or order. Each of these examples illustrates a form of the organizational pattern known as *order* or *sequence*. Let's look at several types of order.

Chronology

Chronological order refers to the sequence in which events occur in time. This pattern is essential in the academic disciplines concerned with the interpretation of events in the past. History, government, and anthropology are prime examples. In various forms of literature, chronological order is evident; the narrative form, used in novels, short stories, and narrative essays, relies on chronological order.

You can visualize the chronological order pattern as follows:

The following paragraph uses chronology to describe how a conflict in Kosovo developed into an allied operation in Europe.

In 1999, a smoldering conflict in Kosovo, another of the provinces of the former Yugoslavia, led to war. In an effort to stop Slobodan Milosevic, the Serbian leader responsible for the devastation of Bosnia, from squelching a movement for autonomy in Kosovo, NATO, now 50 years old, launched an American-led bombing campaign. Milosevic responded with an even more violent "ethnic cleansing" campaign that drove hundreds of thousands of Kosovars from their homes. Even without the introduction of ground troops, this ultimately successful air assault was the largest allied operation in Europe since World War II.

—Nash et al., *The American People,* p. 1099

TRANSITIONS FOR CHRONOLOGICAL ORDER

in ancient times . . .
at the start of the battle . . .
on September 12 . . .
the *first* primate species . . .
later efforts . . .
Other chronological transitions are *then, before,
during, by the time, while, afterward, as, after, thereafter,
meanwhile,* and *at that point.*

➤ NOW PRACTICE . . . USING ORDER OR SEQUENCE

Read each of the following textbook excerpts and answer the questions that follow.

A. **Railroads: Pioneers of Big Business**

Completion of efficient and speedy national transportation and communications networks encouraged mass production and mass marketing. Beginning in 1862, federal and state governments vigorously promoted railroad construction with land grants from the public domain. Eventually, railroads received lands one and a half times the size of Texas. Local governments gave everything from land for stations to tax breaks.

With such incentives, the first transcontinental railroad was finished in 1869. Four additional transcontinental lines and miles of feeder and branch roads were laid down in the 1870s and 1880s. By 1890, trains rumbled across 165,000 miles of tracks. Telegraph lines arose alongside them.

—Nash et al., *The American People*, pp. 611–613

1. What events does the excerpt detail?

_____

2. What is the importance of these events?

_____

3. Highlight the transitional words used in the excerpt.

_____

B. **U.S. Intervention in Vietnam**

The pretext for full-scale intervention in Vietnam came in late July 1964. On July 30, South Vietnamese PT (patrol torpedo) boats attacked bases in the Gulf of Tonkin inside North Vietnamese waters. Simultaneously, the *Maddox*, an American destroyer, steamed into the area to disrupt North Vietnamese communication facilities. On August 2, possibly seeing the two separate missions as a combined maneuver against them, the North Vietnamese sent out several PT boats to attack the destroyer. The *Maddox* fired, sinking one of the attackers, then radioed the news to Washington. Johnson ordered another ship into the bay. On August 3 both destroyers reported another attack, although somewhat later, the commander of the *Maddox* radioed that he was not sure. Nonetheless, the president ordered American planes to retaliate by bombing inside North Vietnam.

—Wilson et al., *The Pursuit of Liberty*, p. 493

4. What events in history does this paragraph describe?

_____

_____

5. Highlight the transitional words used in the paragraph.

_____

_____

Process

In disciplines that focus on procedures, steps, or stages by which actions are accomplished, the process pattern is often employed. These subjects include mathematics, natural and life sciences, computer science, and engineering. The pattern is similar to chronology, in that the steps or stages follow each other in time. Transitional words and phrases often used in conjunction with this pattern are similar to those used for chronological order. You can visualize the process pattern as follows:

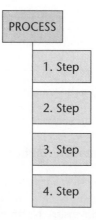

Note how this pattern is used in a paragraph explaining what occurs in the brain during sleep.

Let us track your brain waves through the night. As you prepare to go to bed, an EEG records that your brain waves are moving along at a rate of about 14 cycles per second (cps). Once you are comfortably in bed, you begin to relax and your brain waves slow down to a rate of about 8 to 12 cps. When you fall asleep, you enter your *sleep cycle,* each of whose stages shows a distinct EEG pattern. In Stage 1 sleep, the EEG shows brain waves of about 3 to 7 cps. During Stage 2, the EEG is characterized by *sleep spindles,* minute bursts of electrical activity of 12 to 16 cps. In the next two stages (3 and 4) of sleep, you enter into a very deep state of relaxed sleep. Your brain waves slow to about 1 to 2 cps, and your breathing and heart rate decrease. In a final stage, the electrical activity of your brain increases; your EEG looks very similar to those recorded during stages 1 and 2. It is during this stage that you will experience REM sleep, and you will begin to dream.

—Zimbardo and Gerrig, *Psychology and Life,* p. 115

> ## NOW PRACTICE . . . USING PROCESS

Read each of the following textbook excerpts and answer the questions that follow.

A.   Should you eat less fat? Scientists doing medical research think you probably should; they recommend no more than 30% fat in our diets, whereas the average American diet is estimated to contain 34% fat. Perhaps you're convinced that you should cut down on fatty foods, but you can't imagine watching the Super Bowl without a big bag of chips at your side. The chemists at Procter & Gamble have been trying to resolve your dilemma by developing an edible substance with the rich taste and smooth texture of fat molecules but without the calories. Olestra seems to meet these criteria.

Fat digestion is an enzyme-mediated process that breaks fat molecules into glycerol and fatty acids, which are then able to enter the bloodstream. Olestra is a hexa-, hepta-, or octa-ester of fatty acids (derived from vegetable oil, such as soybean oil or cottonseed oil) and sucrose. Because the body contains no digestive enzymes that convert Olestra's fat-like molecules into their smaller components of sucrose and fatty acids, and because Olestra is too large to enter the bloodstream undigested, the compound passes through systems unchanged.

—Bishop, *Introduction to Chemistry,* p. 749

1. What process does this passage explain?

_____

2. Why is Olestra not digested?

_____

_____

B.   BMI [body mass index] is an index of the relationship of height and weight. It is one of the most accurate indicators of a person's health risk due to excessive weight, rather than "fatness" per se. Although many people recoil in fright when they see they have to convert pounds to kilograms and inches to meters to calculate BMI, it really is not as difficult as it may seem. To get your kilogram weight, just divide your weight in pounds (without shoes or clothing) by 2.2. To convert your height to meters squared, divide your height in inches (without shoes) by 39.4, then square this result. Sounds pretty easy and it actually is. Once you have these basic values, calculating your BMI involves dividing your weight in kilograms by your height in meters squared.

$$BMI = \frac{\text{Weight (in lbs)} \times 2.2 \text{ (to determine weight in kg)}}{(\text{Height [in inches]} \div 39.4)^2 \text{ (to determine height in meters squared)}}$$

Healthy weights have been defined as those associated with BMIs of 19 to 25, the range of the lowest statistical health risk. A BMI greater than 25 indicates overweight and potentially significant health risks. The desirable range for females is between 21 and 23; for males, it is between 22 and 24. A body mass index of over 30 is considered obese. Many experts believe this number is too high, particularly for younger adults.

—Donatelle, *Access to Health*, p. 264

3. What process is being described in this paragraph?

_____

4. How do you convert height in inches to meters squared?

_____

5. What does BMI measure and why is it useful?

_____

_____

Order of Importance

Ideas can be organized in a pattern that expresses order of priority or preference. Ideas are arranged in one of two ways: from most to least important, or from least to most important. In the following paragraph, the causes of the downward trend in the standard of living are arranged in order of importance.

The United States' downward trend in standard of living has many different causes, of which only a few major ones can be identified here. Most important is probably deindustrialization, the massive loss of manufacturing jobs as many U.S. corporations move their production to poor, labor-cheap countries. But deindustrialization hurts mostly low-skilled manufacturing workers. Most of the well-educated, high-skilled employees in service industries are left unscathed. Deindustrialization alone is therefore not enough to explain the economic decline. Another major factor is the great increase in consumption and decrease in savings. Like their government, people spend more than they earn and become deeply in debt. Those who do practice thrift still have an average rate of savings significantly lower than in countries with fast-growing economies. The habits of high consumption and low saving may have resulted from the great affluence after the Second World War up until the early 1970s (Harrison, 1992).

—Thio, *Sociology,* p. 255

Order of importance is used in almost every field of study.

TRANSITIONS FOR ORDER OF IMPORTANCE
is *less* essential than . . .
more revealing is . . .
of *primary* interest is . . .
Other transitions that show the order of importance are *first, next, last, most important, primarily,* and *secondarily.*

➤ NOW PRACTICE . . . USING ORDER OF IMPORTANCE

Read the following paragraph and answer the questions that follow.

Media resources are being reassembled in a new pattern, with three main parts. The first is the traditional mass media that will continue to be for a long time the most important element in the pattern in terms of their reach and influence. The second consists of the advanced electronic mass media, operating primarily within the new information utility, and competing increasingly with older media services. Finally, there are newer forms of personal electronic media, formed by clusters of like-minded people to fulfill their own professional or individual information needs. Internet chat rooms and personalized Web pages are fast-expanding examples of this development. Each of these parts of the evolving mass-communications pattern deserves separate scrutiny.

—Dizard, *Old Media, New Media,* p. 179

1. What does this paragraph describe?

   _____

2. Write the transitional words used in the paragraph.

   _____

3. Why is traditional mass media the most important type of resource?

_____

4. Which type of media resource competes the most with the traditional mass media?

_____

5. What are some examples of personal electronic media?

_____

Spatial Order

Information organized according to its physical location, or position or order in space, exhibits a pattern that is known as **spatial order**. Spatial order is used in academic disciplines in which physical descriptions are important. These include numerous technical fields, engineering, and the biological sciences.

You can see how the following description of a particular type of blood circulation relies on spatial relationships.

> Pulmonary circulation conducts blood between the heart and the lungs. Oxygen-poor, CO_2-laden blood returns through two large veins (venae cavae) from tissues within the body, enters the right atrium, and is then moved into the right ventricle of the heart. From there, it is pumped into the pulmonary artery, which divides into two branches, each leading to one of the lungs. In the lung, the arteries undergo extensive branching, giving rise to vast networks of capillaries where gas exchange takes place, with blood becoming oxygenated while CO_2 is discharged. Oxygen-rich blood then returns to the heart via the pulmonary veins.
>
> —Mix, Farber, and King, *Biology: The Network of Life,* pp. 663–664

Diagramming is of the utmost importance in working with this pattern; often, a diagram accompanies text material. For example, a diagram makes the functions of the various parts of the human brain easier to understand. Lecturers often refer to a visual aid or chalkboard drawing when providing spatial descriptions.

TRANSITIONS FOR SPATIAL ORDER

the *left side* of the brain . . .
the *lower* portion . . .
the *outer* covering . . .
beneath the surface . . .
Other spatial transitions are *next to, beside,
to the left, in the center,* and *externally.*

> **NOW PRACTICE . . . USING SPATIAL ORDER**

Read the following passage and answer the questions that follow.

Skeletal muscle tissue is named for its location—attached to bones. Skeletal muscle tissue is also *voluntary* because it can be made to contract by conscious control. A single skeletal muscle fiber (cell) is cylindrical and appears *striated* (striped) under a microscope; when organized in a tissue, the fibers are parallel to each other. Each muscle fiber has a plasma membrane, the **sarcolemma**, surrounding the cytoplasm, or **sarcoplasm**. Skeletal muscle fibers are multinucleate (more than one nucleus), and the nuclei are near the sarcolemma.

—Tortora, *Introduction to the Human Body*, p. 77

1. Briefly describe skeletal muscle tissue.

    _____

    _____

2. Highlight the transitional words in the paragraph.

    _____

3. How are skeletal muscle fibers or cells arranged in a tissue?

    _____

4. Where can the sarcolemma (or plasma membrane) be found in muscle fibers?

    _____

5. Where are the nuclei in the skeletal muscle fibers located?

    _____

4d   CAUSE AND EFFECT

The **cause-and-effect** pattern expresses a relationship between two or more actions, events, or occurrences that are connected in time. The relationship differs, however, from chronological order in that one event leads to another by *causing* it. Information that is organized in terms of the cause-and-effect pattern may:

- explain causes, sources, reasons, motives, and action
- explain the effect, result, or consequence of a particular action
- explain both causes and effects

You can visualize the cause and effect pattern as follows:

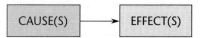

Cause and effect is clearly illustrated by the following passage, which gives the sources of fashions or the reasons why fashions occur.

> Why do fashions occur in the first place? One reason is that some cultures, like ours, *value change:* what is new is good, even better. Thus, in many modern societies clothing styles change yearly, while people in traditional societies may wear the same style for generations. A second reason is that many industries promote quick changes in fashion to increase sales. A third reason is that fashions usually trickle down from the top. A new style may occasionally originate from lower-status groups, as blue jeans did. But most fashions come from upper-class people who like to adopt some style or artifact as a badge of their status. But they cannot monopolize most status symbols for long. Their style is adopted by the middle class, maybe copied or modified for use by lower-status groups, offering many people the prestige of possessing a high-status symbol.
>
> —Thio, *Sociology,* p. 534

The cause-and-effect pattern is used extensively in many academic fields. All disciplines that ask the question "Why" employ the cause-and-effect thought pattern. It is widely used in the sciences, technologies, and social sciences.

Many statements expressing cause-and-effect relationships appear in direct order, with the cause stated first and the effect following: "When demand for a product increases, prices rise." However, reverse order is sometimes used, as in the following statement: "Prices rise when a product's demand increases."

The cause-and-effect pattern is not limited to an expression of a simple one-cause, one-effect relationship. There may be multiple causes, or multiple effects, or both multiple causes and multiple effects. For example, both slippery road conditions and your failure to buy snow tires (causes) may contribute to your car sliding into the ditch (effect).

In other instances, a chain of causes or effects may occur. For instance, failing to set your alarm clock may force you to miss your 8:00 a.m. class, which in turn may cause you not to submit your term paper on time, which may result in a penalty grade.

TRANSITIONS FOR THE CAUSE-AND-EFFECT PATTERN

stress *causes* . . .
aggression *creates* . . .
depression *leads to* . . .
forethought *yields* . . .
mental retardation *stems from* . . .
life changes *produce* . . .
hostility *breeds* . . .
avoidance *results in* . . .
Other cause-and-effect transitions are *therefore,*
consequently, hence, for this reason, and *since.*

> NOW PRACTICE . . . USING CAUSE AND EFFECT

Read each of the following paragraphs and answer the questions that follow.

A.   All objects continually radiate energy. Why, then, doesn't the temperature of all objects continually decrease? The answer is that all objects also continually absorb radiant energy. If an object is radiating more energy than it is absorbing, its temperature does decrease; but if an object is absorbing more energy than it is emitting, its temperature increases. An object that is warmer than its surroundings emits more energy than it receives, and therefore it cools; an object colder than its surroundings is a net gainer of energy, and its temperature therefore increases. An object whose temperature is constant, then, emits as much radiant energy as it receives. If it receives none, it will radiate away all its available energy, and its temperature will approach absolute zero.

—Hewitt, *Conceptual Physics,* p. 272

1. Explain why some objects that radiate energy increase in temperature.

   _____

   _____

2. What happens to an object that radiates energy but does not absorb any?

   _____

3. Highlight the transitional words used in the paragraph.

   _____

4. What causes an object's temperature to remain constant?

   _____

5. What is the effect of an object being warmer than its surroundings?

   _____

B.   It's the end of the term and you have dutifully typed the last of several papers. After hours of nonstop typing, you find that your hands are numb, and you feel an intense, burning pain that makes the thought of typing one more word almost unbearable. If you are like one of the thousands of students and workers who every year must quit a particular task due to pain, you may be suffering from a **repetitive stress injury (RSI)**. These are injuries to nerves, soft tissue or joints that result from the physical stress of repeated motions. One of the most common RSIs is **carpal tunnel syndrome**, a product of both the information age and the age of technology in general. Hours spent typing at the computer, flipping groceries through computerized scanners, or other jobs "made simpler" by technology can result in irritation to the median nerve in the wrist, causing numbness, tingling, and pain in the fingers and hands.

—Donatelle, *Access to Health,* p. 516

6. What is the cause of RSIs?

_____

7. What kind of damage causes carpal tunnel syndrome?

_____

8. What do students often do that can cause RSIs?

_____

9. What kinds of symptoms can result from RSI?

_____

10. Highlight the transitional words used in the passage.

_____

4e COMPARISON AND CONTRAST

The **comparison organizational pattern** is used to emphasize or discuss similarities between or among ideas, theories, concepts, or events, whereas the **contrast pattern** emphasizes differences. When a speaker or writer is concerned with both similarities and differences, a combination pattern is used. You can visualize these three variations of the pattern as follows:

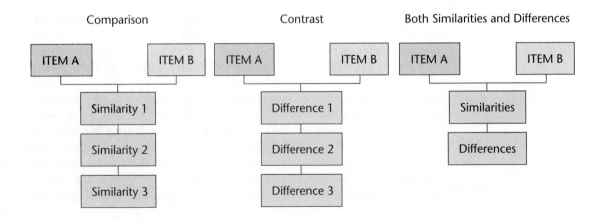

The comparison-and-contrast pattern is widely used in the social sciences, where different groups, societies, cultures, or behaviors are studied. Literature courses may require comparisons among poets, among several literary works, or among stylistic features. A business course may examine various management styles, compare organizational structures, or contrast retailing plans.

A contrast is shown in the following paragraph, which describes the purchasing processes of small and large businesses.

> Small businesses are likely to have less formal purchasing processes. A small retail grocer might, for example, purchase a computer system after visiting a few suppliers to compare prices and features, while a large grocery store chain might collect bids from a specified number of vendors and then evaluate those bids on pre-established criteria. Usually, fewer individuals are involved in the decision-making process for a small business. The owner of the small business, for example, may make all decisions, and a larger business may operate with a buying committee of several people.
>
> —Kinnear, Bernhardt, and Krentler, *Principles of Marketing,* p. 218

Depending on whether a speaker or writer is concerned with similarities, differences, or both similarities and differences, the pattern might be organized in different ways. Suppose a professor of American literature is comparing the work of two American poets, Walt Whitman and Robert Frost. Each of the following organizations is possible:

1. **Compare and then contrast the two.** That is, first discuss how Frost's poetry and Whitman's poetry are similar, and then discuss how they are different.
2. **Discuss by author.** Discuss the characteristics of Whitman's poetry, then discuss the characteristics of Frost's poetry, then summarize their similarities and differences.
3. **Discuss by characteristic.** For example, first discuss the two poets' use of metaphor, next discuss their use of rhyme, and then discuss their common themes.

TRANSITIONS THAT SHOW CONTRAST

unlike Whitman, Frost . . .
less wordy *than* Whitman . . .
contrasted with Whitman, Frost . . .
Frost *differs from* . . .
Other transitions of contrast are *in contrast, however, on the other hand, as opposed to,* and *whereas.*

> **TRANSITIONS THAT SHOW COMPARISON**
> *similarities between* Frost and Whitman . . .
> Frost is *as* powerful *as* . . .
> *like* Frost, Whitman . . .
> *both* Frost and Whitman . . .
> Frost *resembles* Whitman in that . . .
> Other transitions of comparison are *in a like manner,*
> *similarly, likewise, correspondingly,* and *in the same way.*

➤ NOW PRACTICE . . . USING COMPARISON AND CONTRAST

Read each of the following paragraphs and answer the questions that follow.

A.   When considering the relationship of Congress and the president, the basic differences of the two branches must be kept in mind. Members of Congress are elected from narrower constituencies than is the president. The people usually expect the president to address general concerns such as foreign policy and economic prosperity, while Congresspersons are asked to solve individual problems. There are structural differences as well. Congress is a body composed of hundreds of independent people, each with a different power base, and it is divided along partisan lines. Thus, it is difficult for Congress to act quickly or to project unity and clear policy statements.

—Baradat, *Understanding American Democracy,* p. 300

1. What two branches of the government are discussed?

   _____

2. Does this paragraph mainly use comparison, contrast, or both?

   _____

3. Explain how the two branches are similar and/or different.

   _____

   _____

4. Why is it difficult for Congress to act quickly?

   _____

   _____

5. Highlight the transitional words in the paragraph.

   _____

B.   What are the main characteristics of this new postindustrial society? Unlike the industrial society from which we are emerging, its hallmark is not raw materials and manufacturing. Rather, its basic component is *information.* Teachers pass on knowledge to students, while lawyers, physicians, bankers, pilots, and interior decorators sell their specialized knowledge of law, the body, money, aerodynamics, and color schemes to clients. Unlike the factory workers in an industrial society, these workers don't *produce* anything. Rather, they transmit or use information to provide services that others are willing to pay for.

—Henslin, *Social Problems,* p. 154

6. What two things are being compared or contrasted?

_____

7. What is the postindustrial society based upon?

_____

8. What did most workers in the industrial society do at their jobs?

_____

9. How is information connected to money in the postindustrial society?

_____

10. Highlight the transitional words used in the paragraph.

_____

4f   LISTING/ENUMERATION

If asked to evaluate a film you saw, you might describe the characters, plot, and technical effects. These details about the film could be arranged in any order; each detail provides further information about the film, but they have no single order in which they must be discussed. This arrangement of ideas is known as **listing** or **enumeration**—giving bits of information on a topic by stating them one after the other. Often there is no particular method of arrangement for those details.

You can visualize the listing/enumeration patterns as follows:

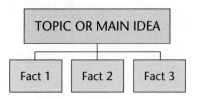

The following list of managers' difficulties in problem solving could have been presented in any order without altering the meaning of the paragraph.

Although accurate identification of a problem is essential before the problem can be solved, this stage of decision making creates many difficulties for managers. Sometimes managers' preconceptions of the problem prevent them from seeing the situation as it actually is. They produce an answer before the proper question has ever been asked. In other cases, managers overlook truly significant issues by focusing on unimportant matters. Also, managers may mistakenly analyze problems in terms of symptoms rather than underlying causes.

—Pride, Hughes, and Kapoor, *Business,* p. 189

This pattern is widely used in college textbooks in most academic disciplines. In its loosest form, the pattern may be simply a list of items: factors that influence light emission, characteristics of a particular poet, a description of an atom, a list of characteristics that define poverty.

Somewhat tighter is the use of listing to explain, support, or provide evidence. Support may be in the form of facts, statistics, or examples. For instance, the statement, "The incidence of white collar crime has dramatically increased over the past ten years" would be followed by facts and statistics documenting the increase.

TRANSITIONS FOR LISTING

one aspect of relativity . . .
a second feature of relativity . . .
also, relativity . . .
there are *several characteristics of* . . .
(1) . . . , *(2)* . . . , *and (3)* . . . ,
(a) . . . , *(b)* . . . , *and (c)* . . . ,
Other transitional words and phrases are *in addition, first, second, third, finally,* and *another.*

▶ NOW PRACTICE . . . USING LISTING

Read the following paragraphs and answer the questions that follow.

A.   Minorities come into existence, then, when, due to expanded political boundaries or migration, people with different customs, languages, values or physical characteristics come under control of the same state organization. There, some groups who share physical and cultural traits discriminate against those with different traits. The losers in this power struggle are forced into minority group status; the winners enjoy the higher status and greater privileges that their dominance brings. Wagley and Harris noted that all minorities share these five characteristics: (1) They are treated unequally by the dominant group. (2) Their physical or cultural traits are held in low esteem by the dominant group. (3) They tend to feel strong group solidarity because of their physical or cultural traits—and the disabilities these traits bring. (4) Their membership in a minority group is not voluntary but comes through birth. (5) They tend to marry within their group. Sharing cultural or physical traits, having similar experiences of discrimination, and marrying within their own group create a shared identity—sometimes even a sense of common destiny. These shared experiences, however, do not mean that all minority groups have the same goals.

—Henslin, *Social Problems,* p. 252

1. What does this paragraph list?

_____

2. How do minority groups come into existence?

_____

_____

_____

B.   Voters make two basic decisions at election time. The first is whether to vote. Americans' right to vote is well established, but in order to do so citizens must go through the registration process. America's unique registration system is one major reason why turnout in American elections is much lower than in most other democracies. The 1996 election was another in a long string of low-turnout elections. Second, those who choose to vote must decide for whom to cast their ballots. Over a generation of research on voting behavior has helped political scientists understand the dominant role played by three factors in voters' choices: party identification, candidate evaluations, and policy positions.

—Edwards, *Government in America,* p. 330

3. What does this paragraph list?

_____

_____

4. Highlight the transitional words used in the paragraph.

_____

5. What is the major reason why voter turnout is low in America?

_____

4g   MIXED PATTERNS

Organizational patterns are often combined. In describing a process, a writer may also give reasons why each step must be followed in the prescribed order. A lecturer may define a concept by comparing it with something similar or familiar. Suppose an essay in your political science textbook opens by stating, "The distinction between 'power' and 'power potential' is an important one in considering the balance of power." You might expect a definition pattern (where the two terms are defined), but you also might anticipate that the essay would discuss the difference between the two terms (contrast pattern).

> ▶ NOW PRACTICE . . . USING ORGANIZATIONAL PATTERNS 1

For each of the following topic sentences, anticipate what organizational pattern(s) the paragraph is likely to exhibit. Record your prediction in the space provided.

1. The Enlightenment celebrated the power of reason; however, an opposite reaction, Romanticism, soon followed.

   Pattern: _____

2. Psychogenic amnesia—a severe and often permanent memory loss—results in disorientation and the inability to draw on past experiences.

   Pattern: _____

3. Several statistical procedures are used to track the changes in the divorce rate.

   Pattern: _____

4. The GNP (gross national product) is an economic measure that considers the total value of goods and services that a country produces during a given year.

   Pattern: _____

5. Large numbers of European immigrants first began to arrive in the United States in the 1920s.

   Pattern: _____

6. There are sources of information about corporations that might help an investor evaluate them. One of the most useful is the Value Line Investment Survey.

   Pattern: _____

7. Diseases of the heart and blood vessels—cardiovascular diseases—are the leading cause of death in the United States today.

   Pattern: _____

8. The spinal cord is located within the spinal column; it looks like a section of rope or twine.

   Pattern: _____

9. Think of the hardware in a computer system as the kitchen in a short-order restaurant: It's equipped to produce whatever output a customer (user) requests, but sits idle until an order (command) is placed.

   Pattern: _____

10. The purpose of a résumé is to sell the qualities of the person writing it; it should include several important kinds of information.

    Pattern: _____

> **NOW PRACTICE . . . USING ORGANIZATIONAL PATTERNS 2**

Read each of the following paragraphs and identify the primary organizational pattern used in each.

Paragraph 1

Ours is an ethnically, religiously, and racially diverse society. The white European Protestants, black slaves, and Native Americans who made up the bulk of the U.S. population when the first census was taken in 1790 were joined by Catholic immigrants from Ireland and Germany in the 1840s and 1850s. In the 1870s, Chinese migrated to America, drawn by jobs in railroad construction. Around the turn of the twentieth century, most immigration was from eastern, central, and southern Europe, with its many ethnic, linguistic, and religious groups. Today, most immigration is from Asia and Latin America.

—Greenberg and Page, *The Struggle for Democracy*, p. 71

Pattern: _____

Paragraph 2

Anthropology is the study of human beings from their origins to the present time. It is concerned with humans as both natural and social beings, and, as such, overlaps with other academic disciplines such as sociology, psychology, biology, and history. Because the field of anthropology is so complex and diverse, it is commonly divided into four branches. Cultural anthropology focuses on the behavior of human beings in social groups. Archaeology is the study of people who lived in the past; it concentrates on material goods that humans left behind. Physical anthropology studies the biological development of human beings. Anthropological linguistics is the study of human language, both historical and modern and focuses on the development, change, and use of language.

—Tortora, *Introduction to the Human Body*, p. 77

Pattern: _____

Paragraph 3

The process of digestion begins at the upper end of the gastrointestinal tract. The *mouth* is where food enters and where the processes of mechanical breakdown and digestion begin. In the mouth, food is chewed (a process called **mastication**) and mechanically broken down into smaller particles by the cutting and grinding actions of the teeth. The food is also mixed with **saliva,** which lubricates it and contains an enzyme which begins the digestion of carbohydrates by breaking down starch and glycogen.

From the mouth, the food-saliva mixture is propelled by the tongue into the **pharynx** (commonly known as the *throat*), a common passageway for food and air. From the pharynx, the passageways for food and air diverge. Whereas air enters the larynx and trachea and proceeds toward the lungs, food enters the esophagus, which runs parallel to the trachea.

The **esophagus** is a muscular tube whose primary function is to conduct food from the pharynx to the stomach. It can easily stretch to accommodate food as it is swallowed; when food is not present, however, it is normally collapsed.

—adapted from German and Stanfield, *Principles of Human Physiology,* pp. 606–607

Pattern: _____

Paragraph 4

By far the most important committees in Congress are the standing committees. Currently 16 standing committees in the Senate and 22 in the House receive the bills that are introduced in Congress. The standing committees are assigned subject-matter jurisdiction by the rules of their respective house, and their titles reflect their general area of expertise. Hence, we have the Senate Finance Committee, the House Agriculture Committee, the Senate Budget Committee, the House Judiciary Committee, and so on. The authority of the standing committees includes the power to study legislation, to subpoena witnesses or information, to remand bills to subcommittees, to vote bills dead, to table bills (putting them aside, thus allowing them to die quietly at the end of the congressional term), to amend bills, to write bills (amending a bill or writing an entirely new version of a bill is called **marking-up**), or to report the bill to the floor.

—Baradat, *Understanding American Democracy,* p. 202

Pattern: _____

Paragraph 5

Not all tumors are **malignant** (cancerous); in fact, most are benign (noncancerous). Benign and malignant tumors differ in several key ways. Benign tumors are generally composed of ordinary-looking cells enclosed in a fibrous shell or capsule that prevents their spreading to other body areas. Malignant tumors, in contrast, are usually not enclosed in a protective capsule and can therefore spread to other organs. Unlike benign tumors, which merely expand to take over a given space, malignant cells invade surrounding tissue, emitting clawlike protrusions that disrupt chemical processes within healty cells.

—adapted from Donatelle, *Health: The Basics,* p. 324

Pattern: _____

4h   OTHER PATTERNS OF ORGANIZATION

Although the patterns presented in the previous sections are the most common, writers do not limit themselves to these six patterns. Especially in academic writing, you may also find statement and clarification, summary, generalization and example, and addition. Transitions associated with these different patterns are listed in the "Summing It Up" table on pages 120–121.

Statement and Clarification

Many writers make a statement of fact and then proceed to clarify or explain that statement. For instance, a writer may open a paragraph by stating that "The best education for you may not be the best education for someone else." The remainder of the paragraph would then discuss that statement and make its meaning clear by explaining how educational needs are individual and based on one's talents, skills, and goals. Here is a sample paragraph about sex ratios.

> Sex ratios in the poor countries do not show a consistent pattern. In some poor countries men outnumber women, but in others, in tropical Africa, for example, women outnumber men. In fact, variations in sex ratios can be explained only by a combination of national economic and cultural factors. In the countries of North America and Europe and in Japan, women may suffer many kinds of discrimination, but they are not generally discriminated against when it comes to access to medical care.
>
> —Bergman and Renwick, *Introduction to Geography,* p. 185

Notice that the writer begins with a statement about sex ratios in poor countries and then goes on to clarify this fact. The author uses the transitional phrase "in fact."

Summary

A summary is a condensed statement that provides the key points of a larger idea or piece of writing. Frequently, summaries at the end of each chapter provide a quick review of the chapter's contents. Often writers summarize what they have already said or what someone else has said. For example, in a psychology textbook you will find many summaries of research. Instead of asking you to read an entire research study, the textbook author will summarize the study's findings. Other times a writer may repeat in condensed form what he or she has already said as a means of emphasis or clarification.

In the following paragraph about the magazine industry, the author uses the summary method of organization.

> In summary, the magazine industry is adapting to the new world of electronic multimedia information and entertainment, with formats that will be quite different

from the familiar ones. Computer-generated publishing has become the norm in the magazine business, expanding beyond its uses in producing newsletters and other specialized publications. Most general circulation magazines already rely heavily on desktop computers, interacting with other electronic equipment to produce high-quality, graphics-filled products.

—Dizard, *Old Media, New Media,* p. 169

Notice that the author summarizes many facts about how the magazine industry uses electronic multimedia information and that the transitional phrase "in summary" is used.

Generalization and Example

Examples are one of the best ways to explain something that is unfamiliar or unknown. Examples are specific instances or situations that illustrate a concept or idea. Often writers make a general statement, or generalization, and then explain it by giving examples to make its meaning clear. In a social problems textbook, you may find the following generalization: Computer theft by employees is on the increase. The section may then go on to offer examples from specific companies in which employees insert fictitious information into the company's computer program and steal company funds.

In the following paragraph about dreams, the writer uses generalization and example.

Different cultures place varying emphases on dreams and support different beliefs concerning dreams. For example, many people in the United States view dreams as irrelevant fantasy with no connection to everyday life. By contrast, people in other cultures view dreams as key sources of information about the future, the spiritual world, and the dreamer. Such cultural views can influence the probability of dream recall. In many modern Western cultures, people rarely remember their dreams upon awakening. The Parintintin of South America, however, typically remember several dreams every night (Kraeke, 1993) and the Senoi of Malaysia discuss their dreams with family members in the morning (Hennager, 1993).

—Davis and Palladino, *Psychology,* p. 210

Notice that the author begins with the generalization that different cultures place different emphases on dreams and then goes on to give examples of the way specific cultures treat dreams. Note the use of the transitional phrase "for example."

Addition

Writers often introduce an idea or make a statement and then supply additional information about that idea or statement. For instance, an education textbook may introduce the concept of home schooling and then provide in-depth information about its benefits. This pattern is often used to expand, elaborate, or discuss an idea in greater detail.

In the following paragraph about pathogens, the writer uses addition.

> Some pathogens [disease-causing organisms] evolve and mutate naturally. Also, patients who fail to complete the full portion of their antibiotic prescriptions allow drug-resistant pathogens to multiply. The use of antibiotics in animal feed and to spray on fruits and vegetables during food processing increases opportunities for resistant organisms to evolve and thrive. Furthermore, there is evidence that the disruption of Earth's natural habitats can trigger the evolution of new pathogens.
>
> —Bergman and Renwick, *Introduction to Geography,* p. 182

Notice that the writer states that some pathogens mutate naturally and then goes on to add that they also mutate as a result of human activities. Note the use of the transitional words "also" and "furthermore."

> ## NOW PRACTICE . . . USING ORGANIZATIONAL PATTERNS 3

For each of the following statements, identify the pattern that is evident and write its name in the space provided. Choose from among the following patterns: process, statement and clarification, summary, generalization and example, addition, and spatial order.

1. If our criminal justice system works, the recidivism rate—the percentage of people released from prison who return—should decrease. In other words, in a successful system, there should be a decrease in the number of criminals who are released from prison and become repeat offenders.

   Pattern: _____

2. Students who are informed about drugs tend to use them in moderation. Furthermore, they tend to help educate others.

   Pattern: _____

3. A successful drug addiction treatment program would offer free or very cheap drugs to addicts. Heroin addicts, for example, could be prescribed heroin when under a physician's care.

   Pattern: _____

4. In conclusion, it is safe to say that crime by women is likely to increase as greater numbers of women assume roles traditionally held by men.

   Pattern: _____

5. The pollutants we have just discussed all involve chemicals; we can conclude that they threaten our environment and our well-being.

   Pattern: _____

6. Sociologists study how we are socialized into sex roles, the attitudes expected of males and females. Sex roles, in fact, identify some activities and behaviors as clearly male and others as clearly female.

Pattern: _____

7. Patients often consult a lay referral network to discuss their medical problems. Cancer patients, for instance, can access Internet discussion groups that provide both information and support.

Pattern: _____

> ## NOW PRACTICE . . . USING ORGANIZATIONAL PATTERNS 4

Read each of the following paragraphs and identify the predominant organizational pattern used. Write the name of the pattern in the space provided. Choose from among the following patterns: statement and clarification, summary, generalization and example, and addition.

1. **Managing Emotional Responses**

Have you gotten all worked up about something you thought was happening only to find that your perceptions were totally wrong or that a communication problem had caused a misrepresentation of events? If you're like most of us, you probably have. We often get upset not by realities but by our faulty perceptions. For example, suppose you found out that everyone except you is invited to a party. You might easily begin to wonder why you were excluded. Does someone dislike you? Have you offended someone? Such thoughts are typical. However, the reality of the situation may have absolutely nothing to do with your being liked or disliked. Perhaps you were sent an invitation and it didn't get to you.

—Donatelle, *Access to Health*, p. 81

Pattern: _____

2. A serious problem with some drugs is addiction, or drug dependence. That is, people come to depend on the regular consumption of a drug in order to make it through the day. When people think of drug addiction, they are likely to think of addicts huddled in slum doorways, the dregs of society who seldom venture into daylight—unless it is to rob someone. They don't associate addiction with "good," middle-class neighborhoods and "solid citizens." But let's look at drug addiction a little more closely. Although most people may think of heroin as the prime example of an addictive drug, I suggest that nicotine is the better case to consider. I remember a next-door neighbor who stood in his backyard, a lit cigarette in his hand, and told me about the operation in which one of his lungs was removed. I say "I remember," because soon after our conversation he died from his addiction.

—Henslin, *Social Problems*, p. 93

Pattern: _____

3.   In short, the view that a drug is good or bad depends not on objective conditions but on subjective concerns. It is a matter of how people define matters. People's definitions, in turn, influence how they use and abuse drugs, whether or not a drug will be legal or illegal, and what social policies they want to adopt. This is the central sociological aspect of drug use and abuse, one that we shall stress over and over in this chapter.

—Henslin, *Social Problems,* p. 91

Pattern: _____

4.   Human migration has by no means come to an end. Large-scale migrations still make daily news. The United Nations' Universal Declaration of Human Rights affirms anyone's right to leave his or her homeland to seek a better life elsewhere, but it cannot guarantee that there will be any place willing to take anyone. As in the past, the major push and pull factors behind contemporary migration are economic and political. Also, people are trying to move from the poor countries to the rich countries and from the politically repressed countries to more democratic countries. In addition, millions of people are fleeing civil and international warfare. Pressures for migration are growing, and in coming years they may constitute the world's greatest political and economic problem.

—Bergman and Renwick, *Introduction to Geography,* p. 197

Pattern: _____

5.   Be careful not to evaluate negatively the cultural differences you perceive. Be careful that you don't fall into the trap of ethnocentric thinking, evaluating your culture positively and other cultures negatively. For example, many Americans of Northern European descent evaluate negatively the tendency of many Hispanics and Southern Europeans to use the street for a gathering place, for playing Dominoes, and for just sitting on a cool evening. Whether you like or dislike using the street in this way, recognize that neither attitude is logically correct or incorrect. This street behavior is simply adequate or inadequate for *members of the culture.*

—DeVito, *Human Communication,* p. 103

Pattern: _____

SUMMING IT UP

PATTERNS AND TRANSITIONS

PATTERN	CHARACTERISTICS	TRANSITIONS
Definition	Explains the meaning of a word or phrase	Is, refers to, can be defined as, means, consists of, involves, is a term that, is called, is characterized by, occurs when, are those that, entails, corresponds to, is literally
Classification	Divides a topic into parts based on shared characteristics	Classified as, comprises, is composed of, several varieties of, different stages of, different groups that, includes, one, first, second, another, finally, last
Chronological Order	Describes events, processes, procedures	First, second, later, before, next, as soon as, after, then, finally, meanwhile, following, last, during, in, on, when, until
Process	Describes the order in which things are done or how things work	First, second, next, then, following, after that, last, finally
Order of Importance	Describes ideas in order of priority or preference	Less, more, primary, first, next, last, most important, primarily, secondarily
Spatial Order	Describes physical location or position in space	Above, below, beside, next to, in front of, behind, inside, outside, opposite, within, nearby
Cause and Effect	Describes how one or more things cause or are related to another	*Causes:* because, because of, for, since, stems from, one cause is, one reason is, leads to, causes, creates, yields, produces, due to, breeds, for this reason
		Effects: consequently, results in, one result is, therefore, thus, as a result, hence
Comparison and Contrast	Discusses similarities and/or differences among ideas, theories, concepts, objects, or persons	*Similarities:* both, also, similarly, like, likewise, too, as well as, resembles, correspondingly, in the same way, to compare, in comparison, share

(continued on next page)

(continued from preceding page)

PATTERN	CHARACTERISTICS	TRANSITIONS
		Differences: unlike, differs from, in contrast, on the other hand, instead, despite, nevertheless, however, in spite of, whereas, as opposed to
Listing/Enumeration	Organizes lists of information: characteristics, features, parts, or categories	The following, several, for example, for instance, one, another, also, too, in other words, first, second, numerals (1., 2.), letters (a., b.), most important, the largest, the least, finally
Statement and Clarification	Indicates that information explaining an idea or concept will follow	In fact, in other words, clearly, evidently, obviously
Summary	Indicates that a condensed review of an idea or piece of writing is to follow	In summary, in conclusion, in brief, to summarize, to sum up, in short, on the whole
Generalization and Example	Provides examples that clarify a broad, general statement	For example, for instance, that is, to illustrate, thus
Addition	Indicates that additional information will follow	Furthermore, additionally, also, besides, further, in addition, moreover, again

5 Making Inferences

MyReadingLab

To practice making inferences, go to

➤ Study Plan
➤ Reading Skills
➤ Inference

Look at the photograph below, which appeared in a psychology textbook. What do you think is happening here? What is the man's occupation? What are the feelings of the participants?

In order to answer these questions, you had to use any information you could get from the photo and make guesses based on it. The facial expression, body language, clothing, and other objects present in this photo provided clues. This reasoning process is called "making an inference."

5a MAKING INFERENCES FROM THE GIVEN FACTS

An **inference** is a reasoned guess about what you don't know made on the basis of what you do know. Inferences are common in our everyday lives. When you get on an expressway and see a long, slow-moving line of traffic, you might predict that there is an accident or roadwork ahead. When you see a puddle of water under the kitchen sink, you can infer that you have a plumbing problem.

The inferences you make may not always be correct, even though you based them on the available information. The water under the sink might have been the result of a spill. The traffic you encountered on the expressway might be normal for that time of day, but you didn't know it because you aren't normally on the road then. An inference is only the best guess you can make in a situation, given the information you have.

➤ NOW PRACTICE . . . MAKING INFERENCES 1

Study the photograph below. Use your skills in making inferences to write a statement explaining what is happening in this photograph.

_____

_____

_____

_____

_____

➤ NOW PRACTICE . . . MAKING INFERENCES 2

Read each of the following statements. Place a check mark in front of each sentence that follows that is a reasonable inference that can be made from the statement.

1. Twice as many couples seek marriage counseling as did 20 years ago.
   _____ a. There are more married people now than 20 years ago.
   _____ b. There has been an increased demand for licensed marriage counselors.
   _____ c. Marriage is more legalistic than it used to be.
   _____ d. Couples are more willing to discuss their differences than they were 20 years ago.

2. More than half of all Americans are overweight.
   _____ a. Many Americans are at high risk for heart disease.
   _____ b. Teaching children about nutrition and exercise should be a high priority in public schools.
   _____ c. Americans place great emphasis on appearance.
   _____ d. The weight-loss industry is an important sector of business.

3. Many courts now permit lawyers to file papers and handle some court work over the Internet.
   _____ a. Courtrooms will no longer be needed.
   _____ b. Attorneys will be able to check the status of their cases from their home computers.
   _____ c. Some cases may proceed more quickly now.
   _____ d. More lawyers will carry laptops.

5b   MAKING INFERENCES FROM WRITTEN MATERIAL

When you read the material associated with your college courses, you need to make inferences frequently. Writers do not always present their ideas directly. Instead, they often leave it to you to add up and think beyond the facts they present. You are expected to reason out or infer the meaning an author intended (but did not say) on the basis of what he or she did say. In a sense, the inferences you make act as bridges between what is said and what is not said, but is meant.

Each inference you make depends on the situation, the facts pr[ ]
your own knowledge and experience. Here are a few guidelines to help you see
beyond the factual level and make solid inferences.

Understand the Literal Meaning

Be sure you have a firm grasp of the literal meaning. You must understand the
stated ideas and facts before you can move to higher levels of thinking, which
include inference making. You should recognize the topic, main idea, key details, and organizational pattern of each paragraph you have read.

Notice Details

As you are reading, pay particular attention to details that are unusual or stand
out. Often such details will offer you clues to help you make inferences. Ask
yourself:

- What is unusual or striking about this piece of information?
- Why is it included here?

Read the following excerpt, which is taken from a business marketing textbook, and mark any details that seem unusual or striking.

Marketing in Action

Dressing Up the Basics in Idaho

In almost any grocery store across the United States, consumers can purchase
ten pounds of Idaho-grown potatoes for less than $5.00. Despite this fact, Rolland
Jones Potatoes, Incorporated, has been extremely successful selling a "baker's
dozen" of Idaho potatoes for $18.95. The potatoes are wrapped in a decorative
box that uses Easter grass.

The Baker's Dozen of Idaho potatoes is only one example of a growing phenomenon. Laura Hobbs, marketing specialist for the Idaho Department of
Agriculture, reports that more than 200 Idaho farms produce specialty or value-
added products. These goods typically consist of basic farm commodities that
have been "dressed-up" with packaging. Consumers can choose from these products: microwave popcorn that comes on the cob and pops right off the cob, a
bag of complete chili ingredients that makers claim won't cause embarrassing
side-effects, and chocolate-covered "Couch Potato Chips."

Idaho farmers are supported by two groups, the Idaho Specialty Foods
Association and Buy Idaho, whose goals are to help producers market and promote unique items. With the help of the groups, Idaho farmers are getting quite
savvy. The marketers have discovered, for example, that packaging certain items

together can increase their attractiveness. Hagerman's Rose Creek Winery found that sales of its wines soared when they were packaged in gift baskets with jars of Sun Valley brand mustard.

According to Hobbs, consumers attracted to the unique packaging provide a market for an endless variety of products, all of which are standard commodities transformed into new products through packaging. The value added through the unique packaging also provides opportunities to charge prices in ranges far above the prices of standard products—like $18.95 for 12 potatoes!

—Kinnear, Bernhardt, and Krenther, *Principles of Marketing,* p. 301

Did you mark details such as the price of $18.95 for potatoes, corn that pops right off the cob, and chocolate-covered potato chips?

Add Up the Facts

Consider all of the facts taken together. To help you do this, ask yourself such questions as the following:

- What is the writer trying to suggest from this set of facts?
- What do all these facts and ideas seem to point toward or add up to?
- Why did the author include these facts and details?

Making an inference is somewhat like assembling a complicated jigsaw puzzle; you try to make all the pieces fit together to form a recognizable picture. Answering these questions will require you to add together all the individual pieces of information, which will enable you to arrive at an inference.

When you add up the facts in the article "Dressing Up the Basics in Idaho," you realize that the writer is suggesting that people are willing to pay much more than a product is worth if it is specially packaged.

Be Alert to Clues

Writers often provide you with numerous hints that can point you toward accurate inferences. An awareness of word choices, details included (and omitted), ideas emphasized, and direct commentary can help you determine a textbook author's attitude toward the topic at hand. In the foregoing excerpt, the authors offer clues that reveal their attitude toward increased prices for special packaging. Terms such as *dressed-up* and the exclamation point at the end of the last sentence suggest that the authors believe that the products mentioned are not worth their price.

Consider the Author's Purpose

Also study the author's purpose for writing. If an author's purpose is to persuade you to purchase a particular product, as in an advertisement, as you begin reading you already have a clear idea of the types of inferences the writer hopes you will make. For instance, here is a magazine ad for a sound system:

If you're in the market for true surround sound, a prematched system is a good way to get it. The components in our system are built for each other by our audio engineers. You can be assured of high performance and sound quality.

Verify Your Inference

Once you have made an inference, check that it is accurate. Look back at the stated facts to be sure that you have sufficient evidence to support the inference. Also, be certain that you have not overlooked other equally plausible or more plausible inferences that could be drawn from the same set of facts.

> **NOW PRACTICE . . . MAKING INFERENCES 3**

Study the cartoon below and place a check mark after each statement that is a reasonable inference that can be made from the cartoon.

_____ 1. The cartoonist thinks workers are physically abused.

_____ 2. The cartoonist is critical of those in management.

_____ 3. Many conflicts exist between workers and supervisors.

_____ 4. The cartoonist believes that people change when they become managers.

_____ 5. The cartoonist is a labor relations specialist.

"We get it, Tom—you're management now."

> **NOW PRACTICE . . . MAKING INFERENCES 4**

Read each of the following statements. Place a check mark in front of each sentence that follows that is a reasonable inference that can be made from the statement.

1. Political candidates must now include the Internet in their campaign plans.

    _____ a. Political candidates may host online chats to assess voter opinion.

    _____ b. Informal debates between candidates may be conducted online.

    _____ c. Internet campaigning will drastically increase overall campaign expenditures.

    _____ d. Television campaigning is likely to remain the same.

2. Half of the public education classrooms in the United States are now hooked up to the Internet.

    _____ a. Children are more computer literate than their parents were when they were in school.

    _____ b. Students now have access to current world news and happenings.

    _____ c. Books are no longer considered the sole source of information on a subject.

    _____ d. Teachers have become better teachers now that they have Internet access.

3. The Internet can make doctors more efficient through the use of new software and databases that make patient diagnosis more accurate.

    _____ a. The cost of in-person medical care is likely to decrease.

    _____ b. Doctors may be able to identify patients with serious illness sooner.

    _____ c. Doctors are likely to pay less attention to their patients' descriptions of symptoms.

    _____ d. Information on the symptoms and treatment of rare illnesses is more readily available.

> **NOW PRACTICE . . . MAKING INFERENCES 5**

Read each of the following passages. Using inference, determine whether the statements following each passage are true or false. Place an X next to each untrue statement.

A.   The United Nations Population Division predicts that by 2025, world population will increase to about 9 billion people. More disturbing, whereas the United Nations earlier predicted that the world population would stabilize at around 10 billion, it has revised its estimate to close to 11 billion, or even as high as

14 billion. These projections have prompted concerns that overpopulation and food scarcity are the principal threats to the planet's future. The United Nations sponsored an International Conference on Population and Development held in Cairo in 1994. There, a World Programme of Action was developed to shift the focus of dismal demographic projections toward concern about a gender-sensitive, humanistic approach to population control.

—Thompson and Hickey, *Society in Focus*, p. 544

_____ 1. If the projections are inaccurate, the world community no longer needs to be concerned about overpopulation.

_____ 2. Previous approaches to population control have not been gender sensitive.

_____ 3. If population increases more rapidly than predicted, there will be even greater food shortages.

_____ 4. The United Nations has developed adequate responses to food scarcity.

_____ 5. By 2050, world population will have increased to 20 billion.

B.   Blowfish is one of the most prized delicacies in the restaurants of Japan. This fish is prized not only for its taste, but for the tingling sensation one gets around the lips when eating it. In blowfish TTX (a neurotoxin) is concentrated in certain organs, including the liver and gonads. Its preparation takes great skill and can only be done by licensed chefs who are skilled at removing the poison-containing organs without crushing them, which can lead to contamination of normally edible parts. The toxin cannot be destroyed by cooking. Lore has it that the most skilled chefs intentionally leave a bit of the poison in, so that diners can enjoy the tingling sensation caused by blockage of nerve signals from the sense receptors on the lips.

—adapted from Germann and Stanfield, *Principles of Human Physiology*, p. 185

_____ 6. Consuming TTX has potentially dangerous consequences.

_____ 7. The United States has strict rules about the preparation of blowfish.

_____ 8. Japanese diners enjoy blowfish partly because of the sense of danger involved.

_____ 9. TTX causes blockage of signals from nerves.

_____ 10. Blowfish is always unsafe to eat.

C.   Through your parents, teachers, and the media, your culture instills in you a variety of beliefs, values, and attitudes—about success (how you define it and how you should achieve it); the relevance of a person's religion, race, or nationality; the ethical principles you should follow in business and in your personal life. These teachings provide benchmarks against which you can measure yourself. Your ability to, for example, achieve what your culture defines as success, will contribute to a positive self-concept. Your failure to achieve what your culture teaches (for example, not being married by the time you're thirty) will contribute to a negative self-concept.

—DeVito, *Essentials of Human Communication,* pp. 36–37

_____ 11. People with positive self-concepts often have achieved their culture's notion of success.

_____ 12. Most cultures do not believe that race or religion are relevant.

_____ 13. People often ignore their culture's beliefs about ethical principles.

_____ 14. Self-concept is affected by both success and failure.

_____ 15. Your self-concept can never change.

➤ NOW PRACTICE . . . MAKING INFERENCES 6

Read each of the following paragraphs. A number of statements follow them; each statement is an inference. Label each inference as either:

PA—Probably accurate—there is substantial evidence in the paragraph to support the statement.

IE—Insufficient evidence—there is little or no evidence in the paragraph to support the statement.

A.   While working for a wholesale firm, traveling to country stores by horse and buggy, Aaron Montgomery Ward conceived the idea of selling directly to country people by mail. He opened his business in 1872 with a one-page list of items that cost one dollar each. People could later order goods through a distributed catalog and the store would ship the merchandise cash on delivery (COD). The idea was slow to catch on because people were suspicious of a strange name. However, in 1875 Ward announced the startling policy of "satisfaction guaranteed or your money back." Contrasting with the former retailing principle of caveat emptor (Latin for "buyer beware"), this policy set off a boom in Ward's business.

—Frings, *Fashion: From Concepts to Consumer,* p. 11

_____ 1. Aaron Ward had experience in sales before he began his own business.

_____ 2. Country people were targeted because they do not have access to stores in cities.

_____ 3. Ward's mistake was to give every item on the list the same price.

_____ 4. Other stores in operation at the time did not offer money back guarantees.

_____ 5. Other mail order businesses quickly followed Ward's success.

B.   Artist Georgia O'Keefe was born in Sun Prairie, Wisconsin, and spent her childhood on her family's farm. While in high school, she had a memorable experience that gave her a new perspective on the art-making process. As she passed the door to the art room, O'Keefe stopped to watch as a teacher held up a jack-in-the-pulpit plant so that the students could appreciate its unusual shapes and subtle colors. Although O'Keefe had enjoyed flowers in the marshes and meadows of Wisconsin, she had done all of her drawing and painting from plaster casts or had copied them from photographs or reproductions. This was the first time she realized that one could draw and paint from real life. Twenty-five years later she produced a powerful series of paintings based on flowers.

—adapted from Preble and Preble, *Artforms,* p. 34

_____ 6. O'Keefe's artistic style was influenced by her high-school art teacher.

_____ 7. O'Keefe's paintings from plaster casts were unsuccessful.

_____ 8. O'Keefe was deeply influenced by nature.

_____ 9. O'Keefe was not influenced by modern art.

_____ 10. O'Keefe never copied flowers from other paintings.

➤ NOW PRACTICE . . . MAKING INFERENCES 7

Read the following paragraphs and the statements following them. Place a check mark next to statements that are reasonable inferences.

August Vollmer was the chief of police of Berkeley, California, from 1905 to 1932. Vollmer's vision of policing was quite different from most of his contemporaries. He believed the police should be a "dedicated body of educated persons comprising a distinctive corporate entity with a prescribed code of behavior." He was critical of his contemporaries and they of him. San Francisco police administrator Charley Dullea, who later became president of the International Association of Chiefs of Police, refused to drive through Berkeley in protest against Vollmer. Fellow California police chiefs may have felt their opposition to Vollmer was justified, given his vocal and strong criticism of other California police departments. For example, Vollmer publicly referred to San Francisco cops as "morons," and in an interview with a newspaper reporter, he called Los Angeles cops "low grade mental defectives."

Because of his emphasis on education, professionalism, and administrative reform, Vollmer often is seen as the counterpart of London's Sir Robert Peel and is sometimes called the "father of modern American policing." Vollmer was decades ahead of his contemporaries, but he was not able to implement significant change in policing during his lifetime. It remained for Vollmer's students to implement change. For example, O.W. Wilson, who became chief of police of Chicago, promoted college education for police officers and wrote a book on police administration that reflected many of Vollmer's philosophies. It was adopted widely by police executives and used as a college textbook well into the 1960s.

Vollmer is credited with a number of innovations. He was an early adopter of the automobile for patrol and the use of radios in police cars. He recruited college-educated police officers. He developed and implemented a 3-year training curriculum for police officers, including classes in physics, chemistry, biology, physiology, anatomy, psychology, psychiatry, anthropology, and criminology. He developed a system of signal boxes for hailing police officers. He adopted the use of typewriters to fill out police reports and records, and officers received training in typing. He surveyed other police departments to gather information about their practices. Many of his initiatives have become common practice within contemporary police departments.

—Fagin, *Criminal Justice*, p. 195

_____ 1. Vollmer did not have a college degree.

_____ 2. Most police officers of Vollmer's time had limited educations.

_____ 3. Vollmer believed police should be held accountable for their actions.

_____ 4. Sir Robert Peel dramatically changed policing procedures in England.

_____ 5. Vollmer received support from most police officers on the street.

_____ 6. Vollmer would support technological advances in policing.

_____ 7. Police departments of Vollmer's time were run with a careful eye toward accuracy.

_____ 8. Vollmer outlawed billy clubs.

6 Critical Reading

MyReadingLab

To practice thinking critically, go to

➤ Study Plan
➤ Reading Skills
➤ Critical Thinking

In college you will be reading many new kinds of material: research articles, essays, critiques, reports, and analyses. Your instructors expect you to be able to do much more than understand and remember the basic content. They often demand that you read critically, interpreting, evaluating, and reacting to assigned readings. Specifically, an instructor may expect you to do all of the things listed above. To meet these expectations, you'll need to distinguish facts from opinions, identify the author's purpose, recognize the author's tone, detect bias, evaluate data and evidence, understand connotative language, and interpret figurative language.

6a   IS THE MATERIAL FACT OR OPINION?

When working with any source, try to determine whether the material is factual or an expression of opinion. **Facts** are statements that can be verified—that is, proven to be true or false. **Opinions** are statements that express feelings, attitudes, or beliefs and are neither true nor false. Below are examples of each:

Facts

1. More than one million teenagers become pregnant every year.
2. The costs of medical care increase every year.

Opinions

1. Government regulation of our private lives should be halted immediately.
2. By the year 2025, most Americans will not be able to afford routine health care.

Facts, once verified or taken from a reputable source, can be accepted and regarded as reliable information. Opinions, on the other hand, are not reliable sources of information and should be questioned and carefully evaluated. Look for evidence that supports the opinion and indicates that it is reasonable. For example, opinion 2 is written to sound like a fact, but look closely. What basis does the author have for making that statement?

Some authors are careful to signal the reader when they are presenting an opinion. Watch for words and phrases such as:

According to	It is believed that	Possibly
Apparently	It is likely that	Seemingly
In my opinion	One explanation is	This suggests
In my view	Presumably	

In the following excerpt from a social problems textbook, notice how the author carefully distinguishes factual statements from opinion using qualifying words and phrases (shown here underlined).

Economic Change, Ideology, and Private Life

It seems clear that there has been a major change in attitudes and feelings about family relationships since the eighteenth century. It is less clear how and why the change came about. One question debated by researchers is: In what social class did the new family pattern originate—in the aristocracy, as Trumbach (1978) believes, or in the upper gentry, as Stone (1977) argued, or in the working class, as Shorter (1975) contended? Or was the rise of the new domesticity a cultural phenomenon that affected people in all social categories at roughly the same time? Carole Shammas (1980) has found evidence of such a widespread cultural change by looking at the kinds of things people had in their homes at various times in the past, as recorded in probate inventories. She found that in the middle of the eighteenth century all social classes experienced a change in living habits; even working-class households now contained expensive tools of domesticity, such as crockery, teapots, eating utensils, and so on. Thus, according to Shammas, the home was becoming an important center for social interaction, and family meals had come to occupy an important place in people's lives.

—Skolnick, *The Intimate Environment: Exploring Marriage and the Family,* p. 96

Other authors do just the opposite; they try to make opinions sound like facts, as in opinion 2, or they mix fact and opinion without making clear distinctions. This is particularly true in the case of *expert opinion,* which is the opinion of an authority. Ralph Nader represents expert opinion on consumer rights, for example. Textbook authors, too, often offer expert opinion, as in the following statement from an American government text.

Ours is a complex system of justice. Sitting at the pinnacle of the judicial system is the Supreme Court, but its importance is often exaggerated.

—Lineberry, *Government in America,* p. 540

The author of this statement has reviewed the available evidence and is providing his expert opinion as to what the evidence indicates about the Supreme Court. The reader, then, is free to disagree and offer evidence to support an opposing view.

The article, "Deadly Silence: Stop Snitching's Fatal Legacy," reprinted in Chapter 1, contains numerous examples of expert opinion, as well. The opinions of Frei, Canada, and Tafari, experts in their fields, are given as evidence.

NOW PRACTICE . . . DISTINGUISHING FACT AND OPINION 1

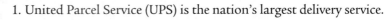

Read each of the following statements and identify whether it is fact (F), opinion (O), or expert opinion (EO).

___F___ 1. United Parcel Service (UPS) is the nation's largest delivery service.

___O___ 2. United Parcel Service will become even more successful because it uses sophisticated management techniques.

_____ 3. Americans spend $13.7 billion per year on alternative medicine.

___O___ 4. The best way to keep up with world news is to read the newspaper.

_____ 5. A community, as defined by sociologists, is a collection of people who share some purpose, activity, or characteristic.

___F___ 6. The Bill of Rights comprises the first ten amendments to the Constitution.

___F___ 7. Archaeologists believe that the stone monument known as Stonehenge was built to serve a religious purpose.

___EO___ 8. According to Dr. Richard Sobol, a communication specialist, conflict in interpersonal relationships is not only inevitable, it can also be beneficial.

___O___ 9. The finest examples of landscape photography can be found in the work of Ansel Adams.

___F___ 10. The symbol of Islam—a crescent and star—appears on the flags of nations that have a Muslim majority, such as Turkey and Pakistan.

NOW PRACTICE . . . DISTINGUISHING FACT AND OPINION 2

Each of the following paragraphs contains both facts and opinions. Read each paragraph and label each sentence as fact, opinion, or expert opinion.

A.   1. Almost half of all Americans drink coffee every day, making it the most widely consumed drug in the United States. 2. Some people believe its popularity can be explained by the "wake-up" effect of caffeine, a critical element of many people's morning ritual. 3. A five-ounce cup of coffee contains between

65 and 115 milligrams of caffeine, depending on the brand of coffee and the strength of the brew. 4. In addition to enhancing mental alertness and reducing fatigue, the stimulant effects of caffeine include increases in urinary output, insomnia, irregular heartbeat, and indigestion. 5. Apparently, these rather unpleasant side effects are not enough to deter millions of Americans from their daily caffeine "fix."

—adapted from Donatelle, *Health: The Basics,* p. 215

Sentences: 1. _____ 2. _____ 3. _____ 4. _____ 5. _____

B.   1. Harriet Tubman was born a slave in Maryland in 1820 and escaped to Philadelphia in 1849. 2. Her own escape presumably required tremendous courage, but that was just the beginning. 3. Through her work on the Underground Railroad, Harriet Tubman led more than 300 slaves to freedom. 4. During the Civil War, Tubman continued her efforts toward the abolition of slavery by working as a nurse and a spy for the Union forces. 5. Today, Americans of all races consider Harriet Tubman one of the most heroic figures in our country's history.

Sentences: 1. _____ 2. _____ 3. _____ 4. _____ 5. _____

C.   1. Smokeless tobacco is used by approximately 5 million U.S. adults, most of whom are young males. 2. One explanation for the popularity of smokeless tobacco among young men is that they are emulating professional athletes who chew tobacco or use snuff. 3. In any major league baseball game, more than a few players with chewing tobacco bulging in their cheeks apparently believe the myth that smokeless tobacco is less harmful than cigarettes. 4. In reality, smokeless tobacco contains 10 times the amount of cancer-producing substances found in cigarettes and 100 times more than the Food and Drug Administration allows in foods and other substances used by the public. 5. Smokeless tobacco has been banned from minor league baseball, a move that should be extended to all professional sports to help discourage the use of smokeless tobacco products.

—adapted from Donatelle, *Access to Health,* pp. 372–373

Sentences: 1. _____ 2. _____ 3. _____ 4. _____ 5. _____

D.   1. Managed care plans have agreements with certain physicians, hospitals, and health care providers to give a range of services to plan members at a reduced cost. 2. There are three basic types of managed care plans: health maintenance organizations (HMOs), point-of-service plans (POSs), and preferred provider organizations (PPOs). 3. The PPO, in my opinion, is the best type of managed care plan because it merges the best features of traditional health insurance and HMOs. 4. As in traditional plans, participants in a PPO pay premiums, deductibles, and co-payments, but the co-pay under a PPO is lower (10 percent or less compared to the 20 percent co-pay under a traditional plan). 5. The best part of a PPO, though, is its flexibility: participants may choose their physicians and services from a list of preferred providers, or they may go outside the plan for care if they wish.

—adapted from Pruitt and Stein, *HealthStyles,* pp. 572–573

Sentences: 1. _____ 2. _____ 3. _____ 4. _____ 5. _____

E.   1. Some sociologists believe that if any nation deserves the "pro-family" label, it is Sweden. 2. The typical Swedish family today consists of two working parents, with the majority of women working part-time and more than 90 percent of men working full-time. 3. To support women's and men's dual roles in the family and work, the state has devised a benefit package that *all* families receive, regardless of class or income. 4. Benefits include public-supported child care, parental leave insurance for both men and women, a basic child allowance per year of around $900, and a housing allowance that is based on income and number of children in the family. 5. Despite deficiencies (for example, women occupy only 5 percent of upper management positions), the way Sweden combines family and employment appears to be far superior to the situations in most other countries.

—adapted from Thompson and Hickey, *Society in Focus,* p. 364

Sentences: 1. _____ 2. _____ 3. _____

4. _____ 5. _____

6b   WHAT IS THE AUTHOR'S PURPOSE?

MyReadingLab

To practice identifying author's purpose, go to

➤ Study Plan
➤ Reading Skills
➤ Purpose and Tone

Writers have many different reasons or purposes for writing. Read the following statements and try to decide why each was written:

1. About 14,000 ocean-going ships pass through the Panama Canal each year. This averages to about three ships per day.
2. *New Unsalted Dry Roasted Almonds.* Finally, a snack with a natural flavor and without salt. We simply shell the nuts and dry-roast them until they're crispy and crunchy. Try a jar this week.
3. Man is the only animal that blushes. Or needs to. (Mark Twain)
4. If a choking person has fallen down, first turn him or her face up. Then knit together the fingers of both your hands and apply pressure with the heel of your bottom hand to the victim's abdomen.
5. If your boat capsizes, it is usually safer to cling to the boat than to try to swim ashore.

Statement 1 was written to give information, 2 to persuade you to buy almonds, 3 to amuse you and make a comment on human behavior, 4 to explain, and 5 to give advice.

In each of the examples, the writer's purpose is fairly clear, as it is in most textbooks (to present information), newspaper articles (to communicate daily events), and reference books (to compile facts). However, in many other types of writing, authors have varied, sometimes less obvious, purposes. In these cases, an author's purpose must be inferred.

Often a writer's purpose is to express an opinion indirectly. The writer may also want to encourage the reader to think about a particular issue or problem. Writers achieve their purposes by manipulating and controlling what they say and how they say it.

Writers may vary their styles to suit their intended audiences. A writer may write for a general-interest audience (anyone who is interested in the subject but is not considered an expert). Most newspapers and periodicals, such as *Time* and *Newsweek,* appeal to a general-interest audience. The article "Deadly Silence: Stop Snitching's Fatal Legacy," seems to be written for the general public. It does not assume that readers have a special knowledge of police procedures or of research done on snitching.

On the other hand, a writer may have a particular interest group in mind. A writer may write for medical doctors in the *Journal of American Medicine,* for skiing enthusiasts in *Skiing Today,* or for antique collectors in *The World of Antiques.* A writer may also target his or her writing to an audience with particular political, moral, or religious attitudes. Articles in the *New Republic* often appeal to those interested in a particular political viewpoint, whereas articles in the *Catholic Digest* appeal to a specific religious group.

Depending on the group of people for whom the author is writing, he or she will change the level of language, choice of words, and method of presentation. One step toward identifying an author's purpose, then, is to ask yourself the question: Who is the intended audience? Your response will be your first clue to determining why the author wrote the article.

> **NOW PRACTICE . . . IDENTIFYING THE AUTHOR'S PURPOSE 1**

Read each of the following statements, find the author's purpose for each statement in the box below, and write it in the space provided.

to persuade	to entertain	to inform
to advise	to criticize	

_____ 1. If you are looking for specialized information on the Internet, the best approach is to use a metasearch engine such as ProFusion.

_____ 2. Good judgment comes from experience, a comes from bad judgment. (Will Rogers)

_____ 3. The Constitution of the United States prescri tion of powers among the executive, legislative, an cial branches of government.

_____ 4. Members of the art gallery enjoy benefits such as free admission and discounts on special gallery exhibits.

_____ 5. The governor's ill-advised plan to attach a "sin tax" to sales of tobacco and alcohol can only have a negative effect on tourism in our state.

> ## NOW PRACTICE . . . IDENTIFYING THE AUTHOR'S PURPOSE 2

Read each of the following statements and identify the author's purpose. Write a sentence that describes the intended audience.

1. Chances are you're going to be putting money away over the next five years or so. You are hoping for the right things in life. Right now, a smart place to put your money is in mutual funds or bonds.

   _____

   _____

2. Think about all the places your drinking water has been before you drink another drop. Most likely it has been chemically treated to remove bacteria and chemical pollutants. Soon you may begin to feel the side effects of these treatments. Consider switching to filtered, distilled water today.

   _____

   _____

3. Introducing the new, high-powered Supertuner III, a sound system guaranteed to keep your mother out of your car.

   _____

   _____

4. Bright and White laundry detergent removes dirt and stains faster than any other brand.

   _____

   _____

5. As a driver, you're ahead if you can learn to spot car trouble before it's too late. If you can learn the difference between drips and squeaks that occur under normal conditions and those that mean that big trouble is just down the road, then you'll be ahead of expensive repair bills and won't find yourself stranded on a lonely road.

_____

_____

6c   WHAT IS THE TONE?

MyReadingLab

To practice recognizing tone, go to

➤ Study Plan
➤ Reading Skills
➤ Purpose and Tone

The tone of a speaker's voice helps you interpret what he or she is saying. If the following sentence were read aloud, the speaker's voice would tell you how to interpret it: "Would you mind closing the door?" In print you cannot tell whether the speaker is polite, insistent, or angry. In speech you could tell by whether the speaker emphasized the word *would, mind,* or *door.*

Just as a speaker's tone of voice tells how the speaker feels, a writer conveys a tone, or feeling, through his or her writing. **Tone** refers to the attitude or feeling a writer expresses about his or her subject. The tone of the article "Deadly Silence: Stop Snitching's Fatal Legacy" is informative. The author presents statistics and other evidence to support the thesis.

A writer may adopt a sentimental tone, an angry tone, a humorous tone, a sympathetic tone, an instructive tone, a persuasive tone, and so forth. Here are a few examples of different tones. How does each make you feel?

■ **Instructive**

> When purchasing a piece of clothing, one must be concerned with quality as well as with price. Be certain to check for the following: double-stitched seams, matched patterns, and ample linings.

■ **Sympathetic**

> The forlorn, frightened-looking child wandered through the streets alone, searching for someone who would show an interest in helping her find her parents.

■ **Persuasive**

> Child abuse is a tragic occurrence in our society. Strong legislation is needed to control the abuse of innocent victims and to punish those who are insensitive to the rights and feelings of others.

■ **Humorous**

> Those people who study animal behavior professionally must ᵈ
> times when their cover is blown at a dinner party. The unfortunaᵗ
> are sure to be seated next to someone with animal stories. The conveᵗ
> tion will invariably be about some pet that did this or that, and nonsense
> is the *polite* word for it. The worst stories are about cats. The proud owners
> like to talk about their ingenuity, what they are thinking, and how they
> "miss" them while they're at the party. Those cats would rub the leg of a
> burglar if he rattled the Friskies box. (Marge Thielman Hastreiter, "Not
> Every Mother Is Glad Kids Are Back in School." *Buffalo Evening News*)

■ **Nostalgic**

> Things change, times change, but when school starts, my little grand-
> daughter will run up the same wooden stairs that creaked for all of the
> previous generations and I will still hate it when the summer ends.
> (Hastreiter)

In the first example, the writer offers advice in a straightforward, informative style. In the second, the writer wants you to feel sorry for the child. This is
accomplished through description. In the third example, the writer tries to
convince the reader that action must be taken to prevent child abuse. The use
of such words as *tragic, innocent,* and *insensitive* establish this tone. In the fourth
example, the writer pokes fun at cat owners, and in the fifth example, the writer
fondly reminisces about the start of school in the fall.

To identify an author's tone, pay particular attention to descriptive language and shades of meaning. Ask yourself: "How does the author feel about
his or her subject and how are these feelings revealed?" It is sometimes difficult
to find the right word to describe the author's tone. Table 6.1 on page 144 lists
words that are often used to describe the tone of a piece of writing. Use this list
to provoke your thinking when identifying tone. If any of these words are unfamiliar, be sure to check their meanings in a dictionary.

> **NOW PRACTICE . . . RECOGNIZING TONE 1**

*Read each of the following statements, choose a word from the box that describes
the tone it illustrates, and write it in the space provided.*

optimistic	angry	admiring	cynical/bitter
excited	humorous	nostalgic	disapproving
formal	informative	sarcastic	

_____ 1. Taking a young child to a PG-13 movie is inappropriate and shows poor judgment on the part of the parents.

_____ 2. The brown recluse spider has a dark, violin-shaped marking on the upper section of its body.

_____ 3. The dedication and determination of the young men and women participating in the Special Olympics were an inspiration to everyone there.

_____ 4. The first tomato of the summer always makes me think fondly of my grandfather's garden.

_____ 5. Nobody is ever a complete failure; he or she can always serve as a bad example.

_____ 6. The councilman once again demonstrated his sensitivity toward the environment when he voted to allow commercial development in an area set aside as a nature preserve.

_____ 7. The success of the company's youth mentoring program will inspire other business groups to establish similar programs.

_____ 8. Professional athletes have no loyalty toward their teams or their fans anymore, just their own wallets.

_____ 9. We were thrilled to learn that next year's convention will be held in San Antonio—we've always wanted to see the Alamo!

_____ 10. To be considered for the president's student-of-the-year award, an individual must demonstrate academic excellence as well as outstanding community service, and the individual must furnish no fewer than four letters of reference from faculty members.

▶ NOW PRACTICE . . . RECOGNIZING TONE 2

Read each of the following statements, paying particular attention to the tone. Then write a sentence that describes the tone. Prove your point by listing some of the words that reveal the author's feelings.

1.   No one says that nuclear power is risk-free. There are risks involved in all methods of producing energy. However, the scientific evidence is clear and obvious. Nuclear power is at least as safe as any other means used to generate electricity.

_____

_____

2.   The condition of our city streets is outrageous. The sid[...]
     littered with paper and other garbage—you could trip whil[...]
     store. The streets themselves are in even worse condition. Deep [...]
     and crumbling curbs make it unsafe to drive. Where are our city tax[...]
     going if not to correct these problems?

     _____

     _____

     _____

3.   I am a tired American. I am tired of watching criminals walk free while they
     wait for their day in court. I'm tired of hearing about victims getting hassled
     as much or more than criminals. I'm tired of reading about courts of law that
     accept lawsuits in which criminals sue their intended victims.

     _____

     _____

     _____

4.   Cross-country skis have heel plates of different shapes and materials.
     They may be made of metal, plastic, or rubber. Be sure that they are tacked
     on the ski right where the heel of your boot will fall. They will keep snow
     from collecting under your foot and offer some stability.

     _____

     _____

     _____

5.   In July of 1986 my daughter, Lucy, was born with an underdeveloped
     brain. She was a beautiful little girl—at least to me and my husband—but
     her disabilities were severe. By the time she was two weeks old we knew that
     she would never walk, talk, feed herself, or even understand the concept of
     mother and father. It's impossible to describe the effect that her five-and-a-
     half-month life had on us; suffice it to say that she was the purest
     experience of love and pain that we will ever have, that she changed us for-
     ever, and that we will never cease to mourn her death, even though we know
     that for her it was a triumphant passing.

     —Armstrong, "The Choices We Made," p. 165

     _____

     _____

     _____

     _____

TABLE 6.1 WORDS FREQUENTLY USED TO DESCRIBE TONE

abstract	condemning	formal	joyful	reverent
absurd	condescending	frustrated	loving	righteous
amused	cynical	gentle	malicious	sarcastic
angry	depressing	grim	melancholic	satiric
apathetic	detached	hateful	mocking	sensational
arrogant	disapproving	humorous	nostalgic	serious
assertive	distressed	impassioned	objective	solemn
awestruck	docile	incredulous	obsequious	sympathetic
bitter	earnest	indignant	optimistic	tragic
caustic	excited	indirect	outraged	uncomfortable
celebratory	fanciful	informative	pathetic	vindictive
cheerful	farcical	intimate	persuasive	worried
comic	flippant	ironic	pessimistic	
compassionate	forgiving	irreverent	playful	

6d   IS THE AUTHOR BIASED?

Bias refers to an author's partiality, inclination toward a particular viewpoint, or prejudice. A writer is biased if he or she takes one side of a controversial issue and does not recognize opposing viewpoints. Perhaps the best example of bias is in advertising. A magazine advertisement for a new car model, for instance, describes only positive, marketable features—the ad does not recognize the car's limitations or faults. In some material the writer might be direct and forthright in expressing his or her bias; other times a writer's bias might be hidden and only discovered through careful analysis.

Read the following description of the environmental protection group Greenpeace. The author expresses a favorable attitude toward the organization and a negative one toward whale hunters. Notice, in particular, the underlined words and phrases.

Greenpeace is an organization <u>dedicated</u> to the preservation of the sea and its great mammals, notably whales, dolphins, and seals. Its ethic is <u>nonviolent</u> but its aggressiveness in <u>protecting</u> our oceans and the life in them is becoming <u>legendary.</u> In their roving ship, the *Rainbow Warrior,* Greenpeace volunteers have <u>relentlessly hounded</u> the <u>profiteering</u> ships of any nation harming the resources Greenpeace deems to be the property of the world community. Whales, they believe, belong to us all and have a right to exist no matter what the demand for shoe-horns, cosmetics, and machine oil.

—Wallace, *Biology: The World of Life,* p. 518

To identify bias, use the following suggestions:

1. **Analyze connotative meanings.** Do you encounter a large number of positive or negative terms used to describe the subject?
2. **Notice descriptive language.** What impression is created?
3. **Analyze the tone.** The author's tone often provides important clues.
4. **Look for opposing viewpoints.**

> **NOW PRACTICE . . . DETECTING BIAS 1**

Read each of the following statements and place a check mark in front of each one that reveals bias.

_____ 1. Testing the harmful effects of cosmetics on innocent animals is an outrage.

_____ 2. Judaism, Christianity, and Islam share a common belief in an all-powerful creator.

_____ 3. One of Shakespeare's wittiest and most delightful romantic comedies is *The Taming of the Shrew.*

_____ 4. Each fall, thousands of greater sandhill cranes leave their nesting grounds in Idaho and fly south to the Rio Grande.

_____ 5. A laissez-faire policy asserts that businesses should be able to charge whatever they want for their goods and services without interference from the government.

_____ 6. Campaign finance reform is essential to restoring both the integrity of the election process and the faith of Americans in our political system.

_____ 7. The longest siege of the Civil War took place in Petersburg, Virginia, when Union troops blocked Confederate supply lines from June 1864 to April 1865.

_____ 8. Students should not waste their time joining fraternities and sororities; they should concentrate on their academic coursework.

_____ 9. Bicycling is the only way to fully experience the beautiful scenery of southern France.

_____ 10. The hardware in a computer system includes the physical system itself, which may consist of a keyboard, a monitor, a central processing unit (CPU), and a printer.

> **NOW PRACTICE . . . DETECTING BIAS 2**

Read the following passage and underline words and phrases that reveal the author's bias.

Not unlike drugs or alcohol, the television experience allows the participant to blot out the real world and enter into a pleasurable and passive mental state. The worries and anxieties of reality are as effectively deferred by becoming absorbed in a television program as by going on a "trip" induced by drugs or alcohol. And just as alcoholics are only inchoately aware of their addiction, feeling that they control their drinking more than they really do ("I can cut it out any time I want— I just like to have three or four drinks before dinner"), people similarly overesti-mate their control over television watching. Even as they put off other activities to spend hour after hour watching television, they feel they could easily resume liv-ing in a different, less passive style. But somehow or other while the television set is present in their homes, the click doesn't sound. With television pleasures avail-able, those other experiences seem less attractive, more difficult somehow.

—Winn, *The Plug-In Drug*

6e   HOW STRONG ARE THE DATA AND EVIDENCE?

Many writers who express their opinions or state viewpoints provide the reader with data or evidence to support their ideas. Your task as a critical reader is to weigh and evaluate the quality of this evidence. You must examine the evidence and assess its adequacy. You should be concerned with two factors: the type of evidence being presented, and the relevance of that evidence. Various types of evidence include:

- personal experience or observation
- expert opinion
- research citation
- statistical data
- examples, descriptions of particular events, or illustrative situations
- analogies (comparisons with similar situations)
- historical documentation
- quotations

Each type of evidence must be weighed in relation to the statement it sup-ports. Acceptable evidence should directly, clearly, and indisputably support the case or issue in question.

> NOW PRACTICE . . . EVALUATING DATA AND EVIDENCE

Refer to the article "Deadly Silence: Stop Snitching's Fatal Legacy," on page 33. For each of the following paragraphs, identify the type(s) of evidence the author provides.

1. Paragraph 2 _____

2. Paragraph 5 _____

3. Paragraph 6 _____

4. Paragraph 10 _____

5. Paragraph 11 _____

6f   HOW IS CONNOTATIVE LANGUAGE USED?

Which of the following would you like to be a part of: a crowd, mob, gang, audience, congregation, or class? Each of these words has the same basic meaning: "an assembled group of people." But each has a different *shade* of meaning. *Crowd* suggests a large, disorganized group. *Audience,* on the other hand, suggests a quiet, controlled group. Try to decide what meaning each of the other words in the list suggests.

This example shows that words have two levels of meanings—a literal meaning and an additional shade of meaning. These two levels of meaning are called denotative and connotative. A word's **denotative meaning** is the meaning stated in the dictionary—its literal meaning. A word's **connotative meaning** is the additional implied meanings, or nuances, that a word may take on. Often the connotative meaning carries either a positive or negative, favorable or unfavorable impression. The words *mob* and *gang* have a negative connotation because they imply a disorderly, disorganized group. *Congregation, audience,* and *class* have a positive connotation because they suggest an orderly, organized group.

Here are a few more examples. Would you prefer to be described as "slim" or "skinny"? As "intelligent" or "brainy"? As "heavy" or "fat"? As "particular" or "picky"? Notice that each pair of words has a similar literal meaning, but that each word within the pair has a different connotation.

Depending on the words they choose, writers can suggest favorable or unfavorable impressions of the person, object, or event they are describing. For example, through the writer's choice of words, the two sentences below create two entirely different impressions. As you read them, notice the underlined words that have a positive or negative connotation.

> The <u>unruly</u> crowd <u>forced</u> its way through the restraint barriers and <u>ruthlessly attacked</u> the rock star.
>
> The <u>enthusiastic</u> group of fans <u>burst</u> through the fence and <u>rushed</u> toward the rock star.

When reading any type of informative or persuasive material, pay attention to the writer's choice of words. Often a writer may communicate subtle or hidden messages, or he or she may encourage the reader to have positive or negative feelings toward the subject.

➤ NOW PRACTICE . . . USING CONNOTATIVE LANGUAGE 1

For each of the following pairs of words, underline the word with the more positive connotation.

1. request   demand
2. overlook   neglect
3. ridicule   tease
4. display   expose
5. garment   gown
6. gaudy   showy
7. artificial   fake
8. costly   extravagant
9. choosy   picky
10. sieze   take

➤ NOW PRACTICE . . . USING CONNOTATIVE LANGUAGE 2

For each of the following sentences, underline the word in parentheses that has the more appropriate connotative meaning. Consult a dictionary, if necessary.

1. The new superintendent spoke (extensively / enormously) about the issues facing the school system.

2. The day after we hiked ten miles, my legs felt extremely (rigid /stiff).

3. Carlos thought that he could be more (productive / fruitful) if he had a home office.

4. The (stubborn / persistent) ringing of the telephone finally woke me up.

5. The investment seemed too (perilous / risky) so we decided against it.

6g   HOW IS FIGURATIVE LANGUAGE USED?

Figurative language is a way of describing something that makes sense on an imaginative level but not on a literal or factual level. Many common expressions are figurative:

> The exam was a piece of cake.
>
> Sam eats like a horse.
>
> He walks like a gazelle.

In each of these expressions, two unlike objects are compared on the basis of some quality they have in common. Take, for example, Hamlet's statement "I will speak daggers to her, but use none." Here the poet is comparing the features of daggers (sharp, pointed, dangerous, harmful) with something that can be used like daggers—words.

Figurative language is striking, often surprising, even shocking. This reaction is created by the unlikeness of the two objects being compared. To find the similarity and understand the figurative expression, focus on connotative meanings rather than literal meanings. For example, in reading the lines

> A sea
>
> Harsher than granite

from an Ezra Pound poem, you must think not only of rock or stone but also of the characteristics of granite: hardness, toughness, impermeability. Then you can see that the lines mean that the sea is rough and resistant. Figurative words, which are also called figures of speech, are used to communicate and emphasize relationships that cannot be communicated through literal meaning. For example, the statement by Jonathan Swift, "She wears her clothes as if they were thrown on by a pitchfork," creates a stronger image and conveys a more meaningful description than saying "She dressed sloppily."

The three most common types of figurative expressions are similes, metaphors, and symbols. Similes make the comparison explicit by using the word *like* or *as*. Metaphors, on the other hand, directly equate the two objects. Here are several examples of each.

■ Similes

> We lie back to back.
>
> Curtains lift and fall,
>
> like the chest of someone sleeping.
>
> —Kenyon
>
> Life, like a dome of many-colored glass,
>
> stains the white radiance of Eternity.
>
> —Shelley

■ **Metaphors**

> My Life has stood—a Loaded Gun—
> In Corners—till a Day
> The Owner passed—identified—
> And carried Me away—
>
> —Emily Dickinson

> . . . his hair lengthened into sunbeams . . .
>
> —Gustave Flaubert

➤ **NOW PRACTICE . . . USING FIGURATIVE LANGUAGE 1**

Each of the following sentences uses figurative language. For each figurative expression, write the letter of the choice that best explains its meaning.

_____ 1. Craig looked <u>like a deer caught by headlights</u> when I found him eating the last piece of pie.

a. startled into immobility

b. worried he would be injured

c. comfortable in the spotlight

d. ready to be admired

_____ 2. Rosa was <u>walking on air</u> after she learned that she had made the dean's list.

a. hurrying

b. happy and lighthearted

c. unable to get her footing

d. numb

_____ 3. Throughout my grandmother's life, her church has been her <u>rock</u>.

a. hard

b. unfeeling

c. source of strength

d. heavy weight

_____ 4. Our computer is a <u>dinosaur.</u>

a. very large

b. frightening

c. unique

d. outdated

_____ 5. The food at the sales meeting tasted <u>like cardboard.</u>
   a. artificial
   b. tasteless
   c. stiff
   d. sturdy

> **NOW PRACTICE . . . USING FIGURATIVE LANGUAGE 2**

Study the figurative expression in each of the following statements. Then, in the space provided, explain the meaning of each.

1. Hope is like a feather, ready to blow away.

   _____

   _____

   _____

2. Once Alma realized she had made an embarrassing error, the blush spread across her face like spilled paint.

   _____

   _____

   _____

3. A powerboat, or any other sports vehicle, is a hungry animal that devours money.

   _____

   _____

   _____

4. Sally's skin was like a smooth, highly polished apple.

   _____

   _____

   _____

5. Upon hearing the news, I took shears and shredded my dreams.

   _____

   _____

   _____

SUMMING IT UP

CRITICAL-READING QUESTIONS	BENEFITS
Is the material fact or opinion?	Facts are verifiable statements; you can determine whether they are true or false. Opinions express attitudes, feelings, or personal beliefs. By distinguishing statements of fact from opinions you will know what ideas to accept or verify and which to question.
What is the author's purpose?	Authors usually address specific audiences. Depending on their purpose, authors adjust content, language, and method of presentation to suit their audience. Recognizing the author's purpose will help you to grasp meaning more quickly and evaluate the author's work.
What is the tone?	Tone refers to the attitude or feeling an author expresses about his or her subject. Recognizing tone will help you evaluate what the writer is attempting to accomplish through his or her writing.
Is the author biased?	Bias refers to an author's partiality toward a particular viewpoint. Recognizing tone will help you evaluate whether the author is providing objective, complete information or selectively presenting information that furthers his or her purpose.
How strong are the data and evidence?	Data and evidence are used to support statements, opinions, and viewpoints. By evaluating the data and evidence, you will be able to decide whether to accept a writer's position.
How is connotative language used?	Connective language refers to a word's implied meanings or nuances. By analyzing connotative language you will uncover writers' efforts to create favorable or unfavorable impressions of their subjects.
How is figurative language used?	Figurative language is a way of describing something that makes sense on an imaginative level but not on a literal level. It compares two unlike things that have some quality in common. By understanding figurative language you will more fully appreciate the writer's use of language and gain a fuller understanding of how the writer views his or her subject.

7 Organizing Ideas

Have you ever wondered how you will learn all the facts and ideas from your textbooks and instructors? The key to handling the volume of information presented in each course is a two-step process. First, you must reduce the amount to be learned by deciding what is most important, less important, and unimportant to learn. Then you must organize the information to make it more meaningful and easier to learn. This section describes three strategies for reducing the information—textbook highlighting, annotating, and paraphrasing—and three means of organizing the information—outlining, mapping, and summarizing.

7a   HIGHLIGHTING

MyReadingLab

To practice highlighting, go to

➤ Study Plan
➤ Reading Skills
➤ Notetaking and Highlighting

Highlighting is an excellent way to improve your comprehension and recall of textbook assignments. Highlighting forces you to decide what is important and sort the key information from less important material. Sorting ideas this way improves both comprehension and recall. To decide what to highlight, you must think about and evaluate the relative importance of each idea. To highlight most effectively, use these guidelines.

1. **Analyze the assignment.** Preview the assignment and define what type of learning is required. This will help you determine how much and what type of information you need to highlight.
2. **Assess your familiarity with the subject.** Depending on your background knowledge, you may need to highlight only a little or a great deal. Do not waste time highlighting what you already know.
3. **Read first, then highlight.** Finish a paragraph or self-contained section before you highlight. As you read, look for signals to organizational patterns (see Chapter 4). Each idea may seem important as you first encounter it, but you must see how it fits in with the others before you can judge its relative importance.

4. **Use the boldface headings.** Headings are labels that indicate the overall topic of a section. These headings serve as indicators of what is important to highlight.

5. **Highlight main ideas and only key supporting details.** Avoid highlighting examples and secondary details.

6. **Avoid highlighting complete sentences.** Highlight only enough so that your highlighting makes sense when you reread it. In the following selection, note that only key words and phrases are highlighted. Now read only the highlighted words. Can you grasp the key idea of the passage?

Biomes

By using imagination, we can divide the earth's land into several kinds of regions called biomes, areas of the earth that support specific assemblages of plants. As would be expected, certain kinds of animals occupy each type of biome, since different species of animals are dependent on different sorts of plant communities for food, shelter, building materials, and hiding places. . . .

Tropical rain forests are found mainly in the Amazon and Congo Basins and in Southeast Asia. The temperature in this biome doesn't vary much throughout the year. Instead, the seasons are marked by variation in the amount of rainfall throughout the year. In some areas, there may be pronounced rainy seasons. These forests support many species of plants. Trees grow throughout the year and reach tremendous heights, with their branches forming a massive canopy overhead. The forest floor, which can be quite open and easy to travel over, may be dark and steamy. Forests literally swarm with insects and birds. Animals may breed throughout the year as a result of the continual availability of food. Competition is generally considered to be very keen in such areas because of the abundance of species.

—Wallace, *Biology: The World of Life*, pp. 708, 710

7. **Move quickly through the document as you highlight.** If you have understood a paragraph or section, then your highlighting should be fast and efficient.

8. **Develop a consistent system of highlighting.** Decide, for example, how you will mark main ideas, how you will distinguish main ideas from details, and how you will highlight new terminology. Some students use a system of single and double highlighting, brackets, asterisks, and circles to distinguish various types of information; others use different colors of ink or combinations of pens and pencils.

9. **Use the 15–25 percent rule of thumb.** Although the amount you will highlight will vary from course to course, try to highlight no more than 15 to 25 percent of any given page. If you exceed this figure, it often means that you are not sorting ideas as efficiently as possible. Other times, it may mean that you should choose a different strategy for reviewing the material. Remember, the more you highlight, the smaller your time-saving dividends will be as you review. The following excerpt provides an example of effective highlighting.

Temperate deciduous forests once covered most of the eastern United States and all of Central Europe. The dominant trees in these forests are hardwoods. The areas characterized by such plants are subject to harsh winters, times when the trees shed their leaves, and warm summers that mark periods of rapid growth and rejuvenation. Before the new leaves begin to shade the forest floor in the spring, a variety of herbaceous (nonwoody) flowering plants may appear. These wildflowers are usually perennials, plants that live and produce flowers year after year. In the early spring, they don't have time to manufacture the food needed to grow and bloom suddenly. Instead, they draw on food produced and stored in underground parts during the previous year. Rainfall may average 75 to 130 centimeters or more each year in these forests and is rather evenly distributed throughout the year.

—Wallace, *Biology: The World of Life,* pp. 712–713

> ## NOW PRACTICE . . . HIGHLIGHTING 1

Read the following pairs of paragraphs, which have been highlighted in two different ways. Look at each highlighted version, then write your answers to the questions that follow in the spaces provided.

Example A

Murders, especially mass murders and serial murders, fascinate the public and criminologists. Murder is the least committed crime but receives the most attention. Murder trials often capture the attention of the entire nation. The O. J. Simpson murder trial was one of the most watched television programs in the history of network Nielson ratings.

—Fagin, *Criminal Justice,* p. 89

Example B

Murders, especially mass murders and serial murders, fascinate the public and criminologists. Murder is the least committed crime but receives the most attention. Murder trials often capture the attention of the entire nation. The O. J. Simpson murder trial was one of the most watched television programs in the history of network Nielson ratings.

1. Is Example A or Example B the better example of highlighting? _____

2. Why isn't the highlighting in the other example effective?

_____

_____

Example C

Air pollution results when several factors combine to lower air quality. Carbon monoxide emitted by automobiles contributes to air pollution, as do smoke and other chemicals from manufacturing plants. Air quality is usually worst in certain geographic locations, such as the Denver area and the Los Angeles basin, where pollutants tend to get trapped in the atmosphere. For this very reason, the air around Mexico City is generally considered to be the most polluted in the entire world.

—Ebert and Griffin, *Business Essentials,* p. 71

Example D

Air pollution results when several factors combine to lower air quality. Carbon monoxide emitted by automobiles contributes to air pollution, as do smoke and other chemicals from manufacturing plants. Air quality is usually worst in certain geographic locations, such as the Denver area and the Los Angeles basin, where pollutants tend to get trapped in the atmosphere. For this very reason, the air around Mexico City is generally considered to be the most polluted in the entire world.

3. Is Example C or Example D the better example of effective highlighting?

_____

4. Why isn't the highlighting in the other example effective?

_____

_____

➤ NOW PRACTICE . . . HIGHLIGHTING 2

Highlight the following article, "How Commercial Jingles Work."

Fully Annotate

How Commercial Jingles Work
by Tim Faulkner

1   Does this sound familiar? It's the middle of the day, you're at work, you've long since eaten lunch, and nothing out of the ordinary is happening. Then, all of a sudden, you hear a voice in your head singing "bah-da-ba-ba-bah, I'm lovin' it" over and over, and it won't go away. And now you're craving French fries. That's what a good jingle does; it gets in your head and won't leave.

2   A Jingle is a radio or TV advertising slogan set to a (hopefully) memorable melody. Jingles are written explicitly about a product—they can be original works designed to describe a product or service, or to help consumers remember information about a product. As long as the slogan is instantly catchy—and hard to forget—there's almost no limit to what advertisers can say in a jingle. It can be a slogan, a phone number, a radio or TV station's call letters, a business's name or even the benefits of a certain product. In this article, we'll take a look at this unique advertising technique to find out how commercial jingles worm their way into our psyches.

"Bah-da-ba-ba-bah . . ."

Jingle History

3   Jingles have been around since the advent of commercial radio in the early 1920s, when advertisers used musical, flowery language in their ads. But it was on Christmas Eve, 1926 in Minneapolis, Minn., that the modern commercial jingle was born when an a cappella group called the Wheaties Quartet sang out in praise of a General Mills breakfast cereal. Executives at General Mills were actually about to discontinue Wheaties when they noticed a spike in its popularity in the regions where the jingle aired. So the company decided to air the jingle nationally, and sales went through the roof. Eighty years later, Wheaties is a staple in kitchens across the globe.

4   There is some debate about this historical tidbit, though. Some point to a 1905 song called "In My Merry Oldsmobile," by Gus Edwards and Vincent Bryan, as the world's first jingle. But the song itself predates commercial radio—Oldsmobile appropriated it for radio in the late 1920s. So, we could probably more accurately call it the world's first pop song licensed for advertising.

5   In the early 1930s radio was enjoying a golden age, but there were strict advertising rules. Direct advertising during prime-time hours was prohibited, so advertisers started using a clever loophole—the jingle. Jingles could mention a company or product's name without explicitly shilling that product. For example, the introduction to "The Adventures of the Jenkins Family" program began with a sing-songy "Oh, my! It's Eskimo Pie!"

6   A good jingle can do wonders for business—it can save a dying brand, introduce a new item to a broader audience and rejuvenate a lackluster product. The histories of the jingle and commercial radio are inextricably entwined. Prior to the popularization of radio, products were sold on a one-on-one basis (at the store, or by a traveling

---

Top 10 Commercial Jingles

1. "You Deserve a Break Today" (McDonald's, 1974)
2. "Be All That You Can Be" (U.S. Army, 1983)
3. "Pepsi Cola Hits the Spot" (1954)
4. "M'mmm M'mmm Good" (Campbell's Soup, mid-1930s)
5. "See the USA in Your Chevrolet" (1978)
6. "I Wish I Were an Oscar Mayer Weiner" (1963)
7. "Double Your Pleasure, Double Your Fun" (Wrigley's Doublemint Gum, 1986)
8. "Winston Tastes Good Like a Cigarette Should" (1954)
9. "It's the Real Thing" (Coca-Cola, 1975)
10. "A Little Dab'll Do Ya" (Brylcreem, mid-1950s)

[source: Ad Age]

---

salesman), and advertisements from those days reflect that. They are very direct, matter-of-factly describing the benefits of their product over their competitor's. But as the radio audience grew, advertisers had to convince the public of the superiority of a product they couldn't see—for this purpose, jingles were ideal. In the 1950s, jingles reached their commercial and artistic peak. Famous songwriters penned slogans, and the copyrights were granted to jingle composers rather than the manufacturing company.

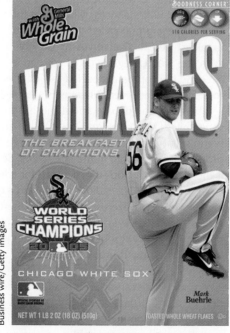

Business wire/Getty images

"Have you had your Wheaties today?"

Why are jingles so catchy?

7   Jingles are written to be as easy to remember as nursery rhymes. The shorter the better, the more repetition the better, the more rhymes the better. If you're being indecisive in the deodorant aisle and you suddenly hear a voice in your head singing "by . . . Mennen," you might drop a Speed Stick (manufactured by Mennen) into your basket without a second thought. Jingles are designed to infiltrate your memory and stay there for years, sometimes popping up from out of nowhere. You probably fondly remember all of the words to the Oscar Mayer B-O-L-O-G-N-A song, the "plop plop fizz fizz" chorus of the Alka-Seltzer jingle, and countless other melodies from your childhood.

8   Psyohologists and neurologists who study the effects of music on the brain have found that music with a strong emotional connection to the listener is difficult to forget. It was this discovery that led marketers to license pop songs for advertising instead of commissioning original jingles. It turns out that some pop songs contain **earworms**: pleasantly melodic, easy-to-remember "hooks" that have the attributes of a typical jingle. Earworms, also known by their German name, "ohrwurm," are those tiny, 15- to 30-second pieces of music that you can't get out of your head no matter how hard you try (the phenomenon is also called Song Stuck Syndrome, repetuneitis, the Jukebox Virus and melodymania). The word "earworm" was popularized by James Kellaris, a marketing professor at the University of Cincinnati, who has done a great deal (for better or worse) to bring this phenomenon to the forefront of the study of advertising techniques.

9   We don't know much about what causes earworms, but it could be the repeating of the neural circuits that represent the melody in our brains. It might also have to do with some of the findings of researchers Alan Baddely and Graham Hitch, and the model of **working memory**, the part of the brain that practices and repeats verbal information [source: Models of Working Memory]. In 1947 Baddely and Hitch discovered what they called the **phonological loop**, which is composed of the **phonological store** (your "inner ear," which remembers sounds in chronological order) and the **articulatory rehearsal system** (your "inner voice"

Justin Sullivan/Getty images

"The most refreshing taste around. . . . the one that never lets you down."

> ### Give Me a Break, Give Me a Break . . .
>
> Professor Kellaris has noted that experience is highly individual, but through several surveys he's been able to compile a list of the tunes (not necessarily jingles) most frequently cited as earworms. He calls it "The Playlist from Hell" [source: Earworms Research].
>
> - The "Baby Back Ribs" Chili's jingle
> - Baha Men: "Who Let the Dogs Out?"
> - Queen: "We Will Rock You"
> - The "Give Me a Break" Kit-Kat jingle
> - Lalo Schifrin: "Mission: Impossible Theme"
> - The Village people: "YMCA"
> - Tag Team: "Whoomp, There It Is"
> - The Tokens: "The Lion Sleeps Tonight"
> - Richard Sherman: "It's a Small World"

which repeats these sounds in order to remember them). This area of the brain, is vital in early childhood for developing vocabulary and in adulthood for learning new languages.

10   Researchers have noted that the shorter and simpler the melody, the more likely it is to get stuck in your head—that is why some of the most common earworms are jingles and the choruses of pop songs. Earworms tend to occur more often in musicians than nonmusicians and in women more than men. Those suffering from obsessive-compulsive disorder can be particularly irritated by earworms. Sometimes, actually hearing the offending refrain (or replacing it with something equally infectious) can clear an earworm from the mind, but, unfortunately, there is no surefire way to get rid of them.

11   But now that jingles have been largely supplanted in advertising by pop songs, do they still have a future? Before we can answer that, we'll look more closely at their decline in popularity.

The Future of Jingles

12   Jingles were an advertiser's dream for the same reason the public can grow to hate them: You can't get them out of your head. But, as with most other stimuli, the more you experience them, the less of an effect they have on you. The widespread use of jingles on radio and TV has caused the newest generation of consumers to see them as hokey.

13   As we've mentioned, the commercial licensing of pop songs caused the decline of the jingle. In 1987, the Beatles tune "Revolution" was licensed for a Nike shoe campaign, which would prove to be the start of a revolution in advertising. As markets became increasingly clogged with indistinguishable products, it was no longer possible (or relevant) to tout the absolute supremacy of a product. To gain a loyal

brand following, a good product was simply not enough—a company now had to represent a lifestyle or an identity. Piggybacking on emotional and cultural experience became the most effective way to sell products. It's widely known that most humans have a deep emotional connection to music—so instead of trying to form a new connection with consumers, why not let the *Rolling Stones, Mike and the Mechanics, Fall Out Boy,* or *Bob Seger* do it for you?

14   Music purists derided the commercialization of their favorite tunes, and musicians who wanted to be considered "serious artists" vowed never to allow their songs to be used in a marketing campaign. In the 1980s, Sting famously rebuffed an offer to use the *Police* song "Don't Stand So Close To Me" in a deodorant commercial (but he and his music later went on to star in a Jaguar campaign in 2000). But for all the cries of ruination, these ad campaigns have significantly helped revive the music of several critically acclaimed but widely unknown musicians—like Nick Drake, *Stereolab and Spiritualized.* In fact, marketers are quick to point out that much of the hype surrounding the licensing of pop songs for commercials comes from major record labels. Major labels are in crisis mode, desperately seeking new ways to promote their albums. Deals with advertisers—and prime-time shows like "Grey's Anatomy"—have helped record companies find new ways to promote their music and create additional revenue streams.

15   Product placement, the conspicuous inclusion of name-brand products in TV shows and movies, has also gained hold in recent years. With the invention of the digital video recorder (DVR), viewers can now fast-forward through commercials, forcing companies to find more clever ways to advertise their products.

16   Fashion is cyclical, though, and advertising is no exception to the rule. The ubiquity that led to the demise of jingles and the rise of licensed music is causing the pendulum to swing the other way. The cost of licensing music is getting higher as it becomes more popular, and jingles are being rediscovered for their promotional value in small and local markets. There may never be another "I'm stuck on Band-Aid, 'cause Band-Aid's stuck on me," but the jingle has proven itself as a tried-and-true technique for advertisers trying to worm their way into our brains.

7b   ANNOTATING

In many situations, highlighting alone is not a sufficient means of identifying what to learn. It does not give you any opportunity to comment on or react to the material. For this, you might want to use annotation. Annotating is an active reading process. It forces you to keep track of your comprehension as well as react to ideas. The chart on page 162 suggests various types of annotation used in marking a political science textbook chapter.

➤ NOW PRACTICE . . . ANNOTATING 1

Review the chart on p. 162 and then add annotations to the reading "How Commercial Jingles Work" on page 156.

MARGINAL ANNOTATION	TYPES OF ANNOTATION		EXAMPLE
	Circling unknown words		. . . redressing the apparent (asymmetry) of their relationship
	Marking definitions	def	To say that the balance of power favors one party over another is to introduce a disequilibrium.
	Marking examples	ex	. . . concessions may include negative sanctions, trade agreements . . .
	Numbering lists of ideas, causes, reasons, or events	①	components of power include self-image, population, ② natural resources, and geography ③ ④
	Placing asterisks next to important passages	*	Power comes from three primary sources . . .
	Putting question marks next to confusing passages	? ⟶	war prevention occurs through institutionalization of mediation . . .
	Making notes to yourself	Chech def in soc text	power is the ability of an actor on the international stage to . . .
	Marking possible test items	T	There are several key features in the relationship . . .
	Drawing arrows to show relationships		. . . natural resources . . . , . . . control of industrial manufacture capacity
	Writing comments, noting disagreements and similarities	Can terrorism be prevented through similar balance?	war prevention through balance of power is . . .
	Marking summary statements	sum	the greater the degree of conflict, the more intricate will be . . .

> NOW PRACTICE . . . ANNOTATING 2

Add annotations to the reading "Economic Change, Ideology, and Private Life" on page 134.

7c   PARAPHRASING

A **paraphrase** is a restatement of a passage's ideas in your own words. The author's meaning is retained, but your wording, *not* the author's, is used. We use paraphrasing frequently in everyday speech. For example, when you relay a message from one person to another you convey the meaning but do not use the person's exact wording. A paraphrase can be used to make a passage's meaning clearer and often more concise. Paraphrasing is also an effective learning and review strategy in several situations.

First, paraphrasing is useful for portions of a text for which exact, detailed comprehension is required. For example, you might paraphrase the steps in solving a math problem, the process by which a blood transfusion is administered, or the levels of jurisdiction of the Supreme Court. Below is a paraphrase of a paragraph from "How Commercial Jingles Work."

A SAMPLE PARAPHRASE

PARAGRAPH	PARAPHRASE
There is some debate about this historical tidbit, though. Some point to a 1905 song called "In My Merry Oldsmobile," by Gus Edwards and Vincent Bryan, as the world's first jingle. But the song itself predates commercial radio—Oldsmobile appropriated it for radio in the late 1920s. So, we could probably more accurately call it the world's first pop song licensed for advertising.	Some dispute that jingles began with the Wheaties commercial. Some people think the first jingle was a song titled "In My Merry Oldsmobile," written in 1905 by Gus Edwards and Vincent Bryan. However, the song was published before the fisrt radio commercial. Oldsmobile decided to use the song in their commercials in the late 1920s. Actually, then, the song was the first to be licensed and used in advertising.

Paraphrasing is also a useful way to be certain you understand difficult or complicated material. If you can express the author's ideas in your own words, you can be certain you understand it, and if you find yourself at a loss for words—except for those of the author—you will know your understanding is incomplete.

Paraphrasing is also a useful strategy when working with material that is stylistically complex, poorly written, or overly formal, awkward, or biased. Use the following suggestions to paraphrase effectively.

1. **Read slowly and carefully.**
2. **Read the material through entirely before writing anything.**
3. **As you read, pay attention to exact meanings and relationships among ideas.**
4. **Paraphrase sentence by sentence.**
5. **Read each sentence and express the key idea in your own words.** Reread the original sentence; then look away and write your own sentence. Then reread the original and add anything you missed.
6. **Don't try to paraphrase word by word. Instead, work with ideas.**
7. **For words or phrases you are unsure of** or that are not words you feel comfortable using, check a dictionary to locate a more familiar meaning.
8. **You may combine several original sentences into a more concise paraphrase.**

> **NOW PRACTICE . . . USING PARAPHRASING 1**

Read each paragraph and the paraphrases following them. Answer the questions about the paraphrases.

Paragraph A

The use of silence can be an effective form of communication, but its messages and implications differ cross culturally. In Siberian households, the lowest status person is the in-marrying daughter, and she tends to speak very little. However, silence does not always indicate powerlessness. In American courts, comparison of speaking frequency between the judge, jury, and lawyers shows that lawyers, who have the least power, speak most, while the silent jury holds the most power.

—Miller, *Cultural Anthropology,* p. 302

Paraphrase 1

Silence carries a message as well as serves as a form of communication. Young married Siberian women speak very little, lawyers (who are powerless) speak a great deal, and the jury (which is most powerful) is silent.

Paraphrase 2

Silence is a way to communicate, but its meaning varies from culture to culture. In Siberia, women have low status in their husband's family and speak very little. In American courts, however, the most powerful group, the jury, is silent, while the least powerful—attorneys—speak the most.

Paraphrase 3

Silence has many meanings. Siberian women speak very little, indicating their low status. Lawyers speak a great deal, while a jury is silent.

1. Which is the best paraphrase of the paragraph? _____

2. Why are the other paraphrases less good? Answers will vary.

_____

_____

_____

_____

_____

Paragraph B

Today, the dominant family form in the United States is the child-free family, where a couple resides together and there are no children present in the household. With the aging of the baby boomer cohort, this family type is expected to increase steadily over time. If current trends continue, nearly three out of four U.S. households will be childless in another decade or so.

—Thompson and Hickey, *Society in Focus,* p. 355

Paraphrase 1

A child-free family is one where two adults live together and have no children. It is the dominant family form.

Paraphrase 2

The child-free family is dominant in the U.S. Baby boomers are having fewer children. Three out of four homes do not have children in them.

Paraphrase 3

The child-free family is dominant in the U.S. As baby boomers get older, there will be even more of these families. Three-quarters of all U.S. homes will be childless ten years from now.

3. Which is the best paraphrase of the paragraph?_____

4. Why are the other paraphrases less good?

_____

_____

_____

_____

> **NOW PRACTICE . . . PARAPHRASING 2**

Write a paraphrase of paragraph 3 in the reading "How Commercial Jingles Work" on page 157.

7d   OUTLINING TO ORGANIZE IDEAS

MyReadingLab

To practice outlining, go to

> Study Plan
> Reading Skills
> Outlining and Summarizing

Outlining is a writing strategy that can assist you in organizing information and pulling ideas together. It is also an effective way to pull together information from two or more sources—your textbook and class lectures, for example. Finally, outlining is a way to assess your comprehension and strengthen your recall. Use the following tips to write an effective outline.

1. **Read an entire section and then jot down notes.** Do not try to outline while you are reading the material for the first time.
2. **As you read, be alert for organizational patterns** (see Chapter 4). These patterns will help you organize your notes.
3. **Record all the most important ideas in the briefest possible form.**

4. **Think of your outline as a list of the main ideas and supporting details of a selection.** Organize it to show how the ideas are related or to reflect the organization of the material.

5. **Write in your own words; do not copy sentences or parts of sentences from the selection.** Use words and short phrases to summarize ideas. Do not write in complete sentences.

6. **Use a system of indentation to separate main ideas and details.** As a general rule, the greater the importance of an idea, the closer it is placed to the left margin. Ideas of lesser importance are indented and appear closer to the center of the page. Your notes might follow a format such as this:

OUTLINE FORMAT

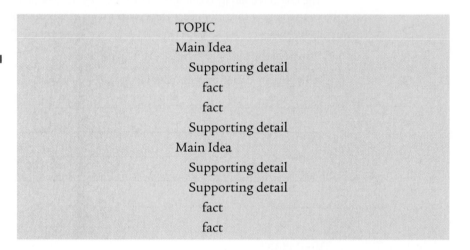

TOPIC

Main Idea

   Supporting detail

      fact

      fact

   Supporting detail

Main Idea

   Supporting detail

   Supporting detail

      fact

      fact

To further illustrate the techniques of outlining, study the notes shown in the sample outline below. They are based on a portion (paragraph 1 and the table included in the reading) of the textbook excerpt "Ending Relationships" on page 30.

A SAMPLE OUTLINE

I. Ending Relationships

  A. How to Break Up (Disengage)

    1. Five Strategies

      a) use a positive tone and express positive feelings

      b) blame the other person (negative identity management)

      c) give reasons for breakup (justification)

      d) reduce the strength of the relationship by avoiding the person or spending less time with him or her (behavioral de-escalation)

      e) reduce exclusivity (de-escalation)

    2. Strategy used depends on a person's goal

> **NOW PRACTICE . . . OUTLINING 1**

Read the following passage and complete the outline.

Gender Characteristics

Masculinity refers to attributes considered appropriate for males. In American society, these traditionally include being aggressive, athletic, physically active, logical, and dominant in social relationships with females. Conversely, femininity refers to attributes associated with appropriate behavior for females, which in America include passivity, docility, fragility, emotionality, and subordination to males. Research conducted by Carol Gilligan and her students at Harvard's Gender Studies Department indicate that children are acutely aware of and feel pressure to conform to these powerful gender traits by the age of 4. Some people insist that gender traits such as male aggressiveness are innate characteristics linked to sex and do not depend on cultural definitions. However, the preponderance of research indicates that females and males can be equally aggressive under different social and cultural conditions and that levels of aggression vary as widely within the sexes as between them.

—adapted from Thompson and Hickey, *Society in Focus,* p. 285

Gender Characteristics

A. Masculinity

    1. attributes society believes appropriate for males

    2. include ——————————————————————————

    ————————————————————————————————

B. Femininity

    1. ————————————————————————————————

    2. include ——————————————————————————

    and subordination to males

C. —————— are aware of and feel pressure to conform to gender

    expectations by ——————

D. Link to Sex

    1. some people believe linked to sex

    2. research shows both sexes can be equally aggressive and levels of

    ————————————————————————————————

> **NOW PRACTICE . . . OUTLINING 2**

Finish outlining the textbook excerpt "Ending a Relationship" on page 30.

7e   MAPPING TO SHOW RELATIONSHIPS

Mapping is a way of drawing a diagram to describe how a topic and its related ideas are connected. Mapping is a visual means of learning by writing; it organizes and consolidates information.

This section discusses four types of maps: conceptual maps, process diagrams, part and function diagrams, and time lines.

Conceptual Maps

A conceptual map is a diagram that presents ideas spatially rather than in list form. It is a "picture" of how ideas are related. Use the following steps in constructing a conceptual map.

1. **Identify the topic and write it in the center of the page.**
2. **Identify ideas, aspects, parts, and definitions that are related to the topic.** Draw each one on a line radiating from the topic.
3. **As you discover details that further explain an idea already recorded, draw new lines branching from the idea that the details explain.**

A conceptual map of Part One of this book is shown below. This map shows only the major topics included in Part One. Maps can be much more detailed and include more information than the one shown, depending on the purpose for drawing it.

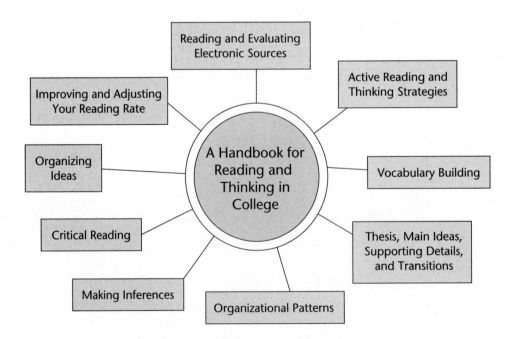

> ### NOW PRACTICE . . . DRAWING A CONCEPTUAL MAP 1

Read the following paragraph about social institutions. Complete the conceptual map that presents the ideas contained in this paragraph.

Society cannot survive without social institutions. A social institution is a set of widely shared beliefs, norms and procedures necessary for meeting the basic needs of society. The most important institutions are family, education, religion, economy, and politics. They have stood the test of time, serving society well. The family institution leads countless people to produce and raise children to ensure that they can eventually take over from the older generation the task of keeping society going. The educational institution teaches the young to become effective contributors to the welfare—such as the order, stability, or prosperity—of society. The religious institution fulfills spiritual needs, making earthly lives seem more meaningful and therefore more bearable or satisfying. The economic institution provides food, clothing, shelter, employment, banking, and other goods and services that we need to live. The political institution makes and enforces laws to prevent criminals and other similar forces from destabilizing society.

—Thio, *Sociology*, pp. 35–36

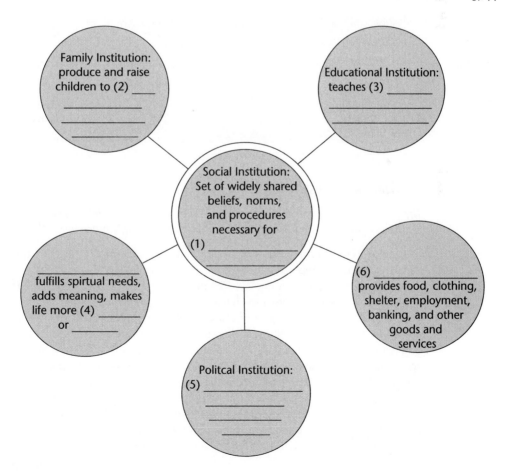

Family Institution: produce and raise children to (2) _____ _____ _____

Educational Institution: teaches (3) _____ _____ _____

Social Institution: Set of widely shared beliefs, norms, and procedures necessary for (1) _____ _____

_____ fulfills spirtual needs, adds meaning, makes life more (4) _____ or _____

(6) _____ provides food, clothing, shelter, employment, banking, and other goods and services

Politcal Institution: (5) _____ _____ _____ _____

> NOW PRACTICE . . . DRAWING A CONCEPTUAL MAP 2

Draw a conceptual map for the textbook excerpt "Ending a Relationship" on page 30.

Process Diagrams

In the technologies and the natural sciences, as well as in many other courses, *processes* are an important part of the course content. A diagram that visually describes the steps, variables, or parts of a process will make learning easier. For example, the diagram below visually describes the steps in the search process for using library sources.

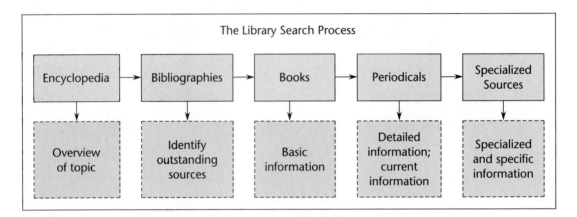

> NOW PRACTICE . . . DRAWING A PROCESS DIAGRAM 1

The following paragraph describes how a bill becomes a law. Read the paragraph and then complete the process diagram that illustrates this procedure.

Federal criminal laws must originate in the House of Representatives or the U.S. Senate. A senator or representative introduces a proposal (known as a bill) to create a new law or modify an existing law. The merits of the bill are debated in the House or Senate and a vote is taken. If the bill receives a majority vote, it is passed on to the other house of Congress where it is again debated and put to a vote. If any changes are made, the amended bill must be returned to the house of Congress where it originated and voted on again. This process continues until the House and Senate agree on a single version of the bill. The bill is then forwarded to the president, who can sign the bill into law, veto it or take no action, in which case the bill dies automatically when Congress adjourns. If the president vetoes a bill, Congress can pass the law over the president's veto by a two-thirds vote of both houses. Whether approved by the president and the Congress or by the Congress alone, a bill becomes a law when it is published in the *U.S. Criminal Codes.*

—Fagin, *Criminal Justice,* p. 107

Drawing a Process Diagram – 1

The Making of Federal Criminal Laws

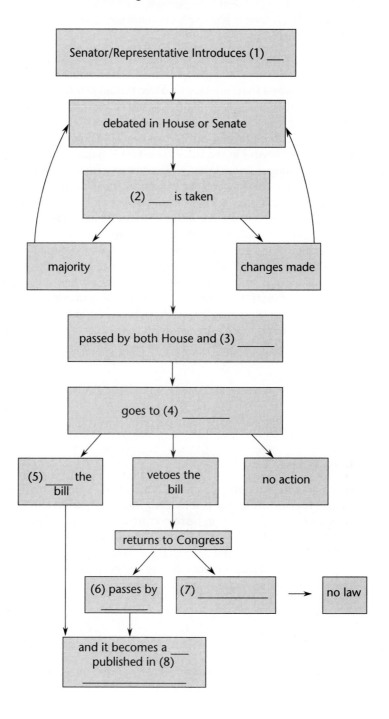

> **NOW PRACTICE . . . DRAWING A PROCESS DIAGRAM 2**

The following paragraph describes the sequential effects of taking the psychedelic drug LSD. Read the paragraph and then draw a process diagram that describes this response sequence. Compare your diagram with those of several other students.

Psychedelics are . . . a group of drugs that produce hallucinations and various other phenomena that very closely mimic certain mental disorders. These drugs include lysergic acid diethylamide (LSD), mescaline, peyote, psilocybin, and various commercial preparations such as Sernyl and Ditran.

Of these, LSD is probably the best known, although its use has apparently diminished since its heyday in the late 1960s. LSD is synthesized from lysergic acid produced by a fungus (ergot) that is parasitic on cereal grains such as rye. It usually produces responses in a particular sequence. The initial reactions may include weakness, dizziness and nausea. These symptoms are followed by a distortion of time and space. The senses may become intensified and strangely intertwined—that is, sounds can be "seen" and colors "heard." Finally, there may be changes in mood, a feeling of separation of the self from the framework of time and space, and changes in the perception of the self. The sensations experienced under the influence of psychedelics are unlike anything encountered within the normal range of experiences. The descriptions of users therefore can only be puzzling to nonusers. Some users experience bad trips or "bummers," which have been known to produce long-term effects. Bad trips can be terrifying experiences and can occur in experienced users for no apparent reason.

—Donatelle, *Health*, p. 179

Time Lines

When you are studying a topic in which the sequence or order of events is a central focus, a time line is a helpful way to organize the information. Time lines are especially useful in history courses. To map a sequence of events, draw a single line and mark it off in year intervals, just as a ruler is marked off in inches. Then write events next to the correct year. For example, the following time line displays major events during the presidency of Franklin D. Roosevelt. The time line shows the sequence of events and helps you to visualize them clearly.

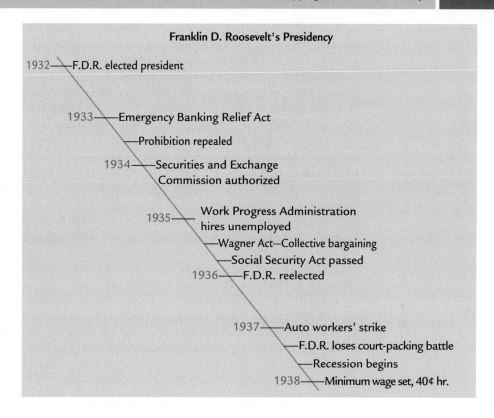

Franklin D. Roosevelt's Presidency

1932——F.D.R. elected president

1933——Emergency Banking Relief Act
——Prohibition repealed
1934——Securities and Exchange
Commission authorized

1935——Work Progress Administration
hires unemployed
——Wagner Act—Collective bargaining
——Social Security Act passed
1936——F.D.R. reelected

1937——Auto workers' strike
——F.D.R. loses court-packing battle
——Recession begins
1938——Minimum wage set, 40¢ hr.

> **NOW PRACTICE . . . DRAWING A TIME LINE**

The following passage reviews the chronology of events in public school desegregation. Read the selection and then draw a time line that will help you to visualize these historical events.

Desegregating the Schools

The nation's schools soon became the primary target of civil-rights advocates. The NAACP concentrated first on universities, successfully waging an intensive legal battle to win admission for qualified blacks to graduate and professional schools. Led by Thurgood Marshall, NAACP lawyers then took on the broader issue of segregation in the country's public schools. Challenging the 1896 Supreme Court decision (*Plessy v. Ferguson*) which upheld the constitutionality of separate but equal public facilities, Marshall argued that even substantially equal but separate schools did profound psychological damage to black children and thus violated the Fourteenth Amendment.

A unanimous Supreme Court agreed in its 1954 decision in the case of *Brown v. Board of Education of Topeka.* Chief Justice Earl Warren, recently appointed by President Eisenhower, wrote the landmark opinion which flatly declared that "separate educational facilities are inherently unequal." To divide grade-school children "solely because of their race," Warren argued, "generates a feeling of inferiority as to their status in the community that may affect their hearts and minds in a way unlikely ever to be undone." Despite this sweeping language, Warren realized that it would be difficult to change historic patterns of segregation quickly. Accordingly, in 1955 the Court ruled that implementation should proceed "with all deliberate speed" and left the details to the lower federal courts.

The process of desegregating the schools proved to be agonizingly slow. Officials in the border states quickly complied with the Court's ruling, but states deeper in the South responded with a policy of massive resistance. Local White Citizen's Councils organized to fight for retention of racial separation; 101 congressmen and senators signed a Southern Manifesto in 1956 which denounced the *Brown* decision as "a clear abuse of judicial power." School boards, encouraged by this show of defiance, found a variety of ways to evade the Court's ruling. The most successful was the passage of pupil-placement laws . . . .

Southern leaders mistook Ike's silence for tacit support of segregation. In 1957, Governor Orville Faubus of Arkansas called out the national guard to prevent the integration of Little Rock's Central High School on grounds of a threat to public order . . . .

Despite the snail's pace of school desegregation, the *Brown* decision led to other advances. In 1957, the Eisenhower administration proposed the first general civil-rights legislation since Reconstruction. Strong southern resistance and compromise by both the administration and Senate Democratic leader Lyndon B. Johnson of Texas weakened the bill considerably. The final act, however, did create a permanent Commission for Civil Rights, one of Truman's original goals. It also provided for federal efforts aimed at "securing and protecting the right to vote." A second civil-rights act in 1960 slightly strengthened the voting-rights section.

—Divine, *America Past and Present*, pp. 890–891

Part and Function Diagrams

In courses that deal with the use and description or classification of physical objects, labeled drawings are an important learning tool. In a human anatomy and physiology course, for example, the easiest way to learn the parts and functions of the brain is to draw it. To study it, you would sketch the brain and test your recall of each part and its function.

▶ NOW PRACTICE . . . DRAWING A PART AND FUNCTION DIAGRAM

The following paragraph describes the layers of the earth. Read the paragraph and then draw a diagram that will help you to visualize how the earth is structured.

Outer Layers of the Earth

The Earth's crust and the uppermost part of the mantle are known as the *lithosphere*. This is a fairly rigid zone that extends about 100 km below the Earth's surface. The crust extends some 60 km or so under continents, but only about 10 km below the ocean floor. The continental crust has a lower density than the oceanic crust. It is primarily a light granitic rock rich in the silicates of aluminum, iron, and magnesium. In a simplified view, the continental crust can be thought of as layered: On top of a layer of igneous rock (molten rock that has hardened, such as granite) lies a thin layer of sedimentary rocks (rocks formed by sediment and fragments that water deposited, such as limestone and sandstone); there is also a soil layer deposited during past ages in the parts of continents that have had no recent volcanic activity or mountain building.

Sandwiched between the lithosphere and the lower mantle is the partially molten material known as the *asthenosphere,* about 150 km thick. It consists primarily of iron and magnesium silicates that readily deform and flow under pressure.

—Berman and Evans, *Exploring the Cosmos,* p. 145

7f   SUMMARIZING TO CONDENSE IDEAS

MyReadingLab

To practice summarizing, go to

➤ Study Plan
➤ Reading Skills
➤ Outlining and Summarizing

Like outlining, summarizing is an excellent way to learn from your reading and to increase recall. A **summary** is a brief statement that reviews the key points of what you have read. It condenses an author's ideas or arguments into sentences written in your own words. A summary contains only the gist of the text, with limited explanation, background information, or supporting detail. Writing a summary is a step beyond recording the author's ideas; a summary must pull together the writer's ideas by condensing and grouping them. Before writing a summary, be sure you understand the material and have identified the writer's major points. Then use the following suggestions:

1. **As a first step, highlight or write brief notes on the material.**
2. **Write one sentence that states the writer's overall concern or most important idea.** To do this, ask yourself what one topic the material is about. Then ask what point the writer is trying to make about that topic. This sentence will be the topic sentence of your summary.
3. **Be sure to paraphrase, using your own words rather than those of the author.**
4. **Review the major supporting information that the author gives to explain the major idea.**
5. **The amount of detail you include, if any, depends on your purpose for writing the summary.** For example, if you are writing a summary of a television documentary for a research paper, it might be more detailed than if you were writing it to jog your memory for a class discussion.
6. **Normally, present ideas in the summary in the same order in which they appeared in the original material.**
7. **If the writer presents a clear opinion or expresses an attitude toward the subject matter, include it in your summary.**
8. **If the summary is for your own use only and is not to be submitted as an assignment, do not worry about sentence structure.** Some students prefer to write summaries using words and phrases rather than complete sentences.

A sample summary of the article "Ending a Relationship", which appears on page 30, is shown below.

A SAMPLE SUMMARY

> It is inevitable that some relationships do end. As a relationship ends, there are two concerns: how to end it and how to deal with the breakup. There are five ways to end a relationship, called disengagement strategies. They are: use a positive tone, blame the other person, give reasons for the breakup, reduce the intensity of the relationship, and reduce the exclusivity of the relationship. Breakups always cause stress. Six ways to deal with a breakup are to avoid loneliness and depression, avoid jumping into a new relationship, build self-esteem, get rid of hurtful reminders, seek help and support from family and friends, and avoid repeating the same mistakes.

➤ **NOW PRACTICE . . . SUMMARIZING 1**

Complete this summary of the passage about psychedelic drugs on page 172.

Psychedelic drugs cause _____ and can cause reactions mimicking _____. Examples of these drugs include _____. LSD is the best known and was most popular in _____. It is created from _____, which comes from a _____. Initially, it causes weakness, _____, and _____ and later a distortion of time and space. It causes senses to be _____. The drug affects _____, creates a feeling of distance, and creates changes in _____. The sensations resulting are outside _____. _____ can have _____ consequences and the reason for them is not understood.

—Donatelle, *Health: The Basics,* p. 179

➤ **NOW PRACTICE . . . SUMMARIZING 2**

Write a summary of the section titled "Why are jingles so catchy?" (paragraphs 7–11) of the article "How Commercial Jingles Work" on page 159.

8 Improving and Adjusting Your Reading Rate

The speed at which you read, called your reading rate, is measured in words per minute (WPM). What should your reading rate be? Is it better to be a fast or slow reader? You should be able to read at 100, 200, 300, and even 400 words per minute, depending on what you are reading and why you are reading it. You should be both a slow and a fast reader; when you are reading difficult, complicated material you should read slowly. When reading easy material or material that you do not have to remember for a test, you can afford to read faster. This section will offer some suggestions for improving your reading rate and explain how to adjust your reading rate.

8a IMPROVING YOUR READING RATE

Here are a few suggestions for improving your overall reading rate.

1. **Try to read a little faster.** Sometimes by just being conscious of your reading rate, you can improve it slightly.
2. **Be sure to preview** (see Chapter 1, Section 1b). Previewing familiarizes you with the material and allows you to understand what you are reading more easily, thereby enabling you to read slightly faster.
3. **Improve your concentration.** If your mind wanders while you are reading, it will cost you time. Eliminate distractions, read in a place conducive to study, use writing to keep you mentally and physically alert, and alternate between different types of reading assignments.
4. **Set time goals.** Before you begin an assignment, decide approximately how much time it should take. Without a time goal, it is easy to drift and wander through an assignment rather than working straight through it efficiently.

8b ADJUSTING YOUR RATE TO MEET COMPREHENSION DEMANDS

Do you read the newspaper in the same way and at the same speed at which you read a biology textbook? Do you read an essay for your English class in the same way and at the same speed at which you read a mystery novel? Surprisingly, many people do.

If you are an efficient reader, however, you read the newspaper more quickly and in a different way than you read a biology textbook. The newspaper is usually easier to read, and you have a different purpose for reading it. Efficient readers adapt their speed and comprehension levels to suit the material.

Rate and comprehension are the two main factors that you must keep in balance; as your reading rate increases, your comprehension may decrease. Your goal is to achieve a balance that suits the nature of the material and your purpose for reading it. The following steps will help you learn to vary your reading rate.

1. **Assess how difficult the assignment is.** Factors such as the difficulty of the vocabulary, length, and organization all affect text difficulty. Usually, longer or poorly organized material is more difficult to read than shorter or well-organized material. Numerous typographical aids (italics, headings, etc.) can make material easier to read. As you preview an assignment, notice these features and estimate how difficult the material will be to read. There is no rule to use when adjusting your speed to compensate for differing degrees of difficulty. Instead, use your judgment to adjust your reading rate and style to the material.

2. **Assess your familiarity with and interest in the subject.** Your knowledge of and interest in a subject influence how fast you can read it. Material you are interested in or that you know something about will be easier for you to read, and you can increase your speed.

3. **Define your purpose.** The reason you are reading an assignment should influence how you read it. Different situations demand different levels of comprehension and recall. For example, you can read an article in *Time* magazine assigned as a supplementary reading in your sociology class faster than you can read your sociology text, because the magazine assignment does not require as high a level of recall and analysis.

4. **Decide what, if any, follow-up activity is required.** Will you have to pass a multiple-choice exam on the content? Will you be participating in a class discussion? Will you summarize the information in a short paper? The activities that follow your reading determine, in part, the level of comprehension that is required. Passing an exam requires a very high level of reading comprehension, whereas preparing for a class discussion requires a more moderate level of comprehension or retention.

Table 8.1 on page 179 shows the level of comprehension required for various types of material and gives approximate reading rates that are appropriate for each level.

TABLE 8.1 LEVELS OF COMPREHENSION

DESIRED LEVEL OF COMPREHENSION	TYPE OF MATERIAL	PURPOSE IN READING	RANGE OF READING RATES
Complete, 100%	Poetry, legal documents, argumentative writing	Analysis, criticism, evaluation	Less than 200 WPM
High, 80–100%	Textbooks, manuals, research documents	High comprehension, recall for exams, writing research reports, following directions	200–300 WPM
Moderate, 60–80%	Novels, paperbacks, newspapers, magazines	Entertainment, enjoyment, general information	300–500 WPM

> ## NOW PRACTICE . . . ADJUSTING YOUR READING RATE

For each of the following situations, define your purpose and indicate the level of comprehension that seems appropriate.

1. Reading a credit card agreement or an insurance policy before signing it.

   Purpose: _____

   _____

   Comprehension level: _____

2. Reading a critical essay that analyzes a Shakespearean sonnet you are studying in a literature class.

   Purpose: _____

   _____

   Comprehension level: _____

3. Reading an encyclopedia entry on poverty to narrow down a term paper assignment to a manageable topic.

   Purpose: _____

   _____

   Comprehension level: _____

4. Reading a newspaper article on a recent incident in the Middle East for your political science class.

Purpose: _____

_____

Comprehension level: _____

5. Reading an excerpt from a historical novel set in the Civil War period for your American history class.

Purpose: _____

_____

Comprehension level: _____

9 Reading and Evaluating Electronic Sources

Most of today's college students and teachers learned to read using print text. We have been reading print text much longer than electronic text; consequently our brains have developed numerous strategies or "work orders" for reading traditional printed material.

Electronic text has a wider variety of formats and presents us with more variables than traditional text. Because electronic text is a relatively new form of text, our brains need to develop new strategies in order to understand Web sites. And because Web sites vary widely in both purpose and reliability, it is important that your reading be critical.

9a DEVELOPING NEW WAYS OF THINKING AND READING

The first step in reading electronic text easily and effectively is to understand how it is different from print text. A print source is linear—it goes in a straight line from idea to idea. Electronic sources, in contrast, tend to be multidirectional. Using links, you can skip around easily. (See the accompanying figure.) Therefore, reading electronic sources demands a different type of thinking from reading print sources.

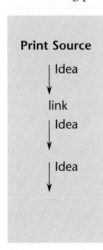

Print Source

Idea

link

Idea

Idea

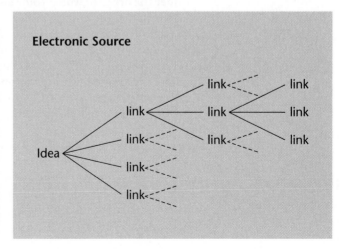

Electronic Source

Idea

link

link

link

link

link

link

link

link

link

link

Using electronic text also requires new reading strategies. You need to change and adapt how you read. To do this, focus on your purpose, pay attention to how information is organized, and use links to find the information you need.

Focus on Your Purpose

Focus clearly on your purpose for visiting the site. What information do you need? Because you must create your own path through the site, fix in your mind what you are looking for. If you don't, you may wander aimlessly, waste valuable time, or even become lost, following numerous links that lead you farther and farther away from the site at which you began.

Pay Attention to How Information Is Organized

Because you can navigate through a Web site in many different ways, it is important to have the right expectations and to make several decisions before you begin. Some Web sites are much better organized than others. Some have clear headings and labels that make it easy to discover how to proceed; others do not and will require more thought before you begin. For example, if you are reading an article with as many as 10 or 15 underlined words (links), there is no prescribed order to follow and these links are not categorized in any way. Below are some suggestions on how to stay organized when using a Web site.

1. **Use the site map, if provided, to discover what information is available and how it is organized.** A sample site map for the American Management Association Web site is shown on the facing page. Notice that the links are categorized according to the types of information (seminars, books, membership) a user may need.
2. **Consider the order in which you want to take in information.** Choose an order in which to explore links; avoid randomly clicking on link buttons. Doing so is somewhat like randomly choosing pages to read out of a reference book. Do you need definitions first? Do you want historical background first? Your decision will be partly influenced by your learning style.
3. **Consider writing brief notes to yourself as you explore a complicated Web site.** Alternatively, you could print the home page and jot notes on it. You can also save Web pages on to a disk or save them on your computer as a text file.
4. **Expect shorter, less detailed sentences and paragraphs.** Much online communication tends to be briefer and more concise than in traditional sources. As a result, you may have to mentally fill in transitions and make inferences about the relationships among ideas. For example, you may have to infer similarities and differences or recognize cause-and-effect connections on your own.

NEED HELP?
CALL 1.877.566.9441

Seminars | Corporate Solutions | Government Solutions | Events | Books & Self Study | Blended Learning | Membership | About AMA

Enter keywords, seminar number or your zip code   (Search)   Advanced Seminar Search

AMA Site Map

Seminars

› Browse by Subject
› Search by Location
› New Seminars
› Certificate Programs
› Best Selling Seminars
› Executive Conference Centers

Corporate Solutions

› Customized Programs
› On-site Training
› Top On-site Seminars
› Sexual Harassment Training
› Diversity Training
› Assessment Tools
› Success Stories

Government Solutions

› Federal Government Seminars
› GSA Approved Seminars
› Customized Programs
› Contract Vehicles

Special Events

› Upcoming Events
› On-Demand Webcasts
› AMA Podcasts
› Summaries of Recent Events

Books & Self Study

› Browse the Book List
› Featured Books
› Books in the News
› Self-Study Courses

eLearning

› Blended Learning
› e-Learning Solutions

Membership

› Members Web Site
› Your Member Account
› Join AMA

About AMA

› Board of Trustees
› Management Team
› Councils
› Research
› Worldwide
› Career Opportunities
› Faculty
› Partnerships & Sponsorships
› OE/Young adult program
› Executive Conference Centers
› Press Releases
› Related Links

Use Links to Find the Information You Need

Links are unique to electronic text. The suggestions below will help you use links to find the information you need.

1. **Plan on exploring links to find complete and detailed information.** Both remote links (those that take you to another site) and related links (within a site) are intended to provide more detailed information on topics introduced on the home page.

2. **As you follow links, be sure to bookmark your original site and other useful sites you come across so you can find them again.** Bookmarking is a feature of your Internet browser that allows you to record Web site addresses and access them later by simply clicking on the site name. Different Web browsers use different terms for this function. Firefox and Safari use the term *Bookmarks;* Microsoft

Explorer calls it *Favorites*. In addition, the browsers have a *History* or "Back" feature that allows a user to retrace the steps of the current search.

3. **If you use a site or a link that provides many pages of continuous paragraphs, print the material and read it offline.**

4. **If you find you are lacking background on a topic, use links to help fill in the gaps, or search for a different, less technical Web site on the same topic.**

▶ NOW PRACTICE . . . NEW WAYS OF THINKING AND READING 1

Visit one of the following Web sites. Locate the information needed and take brief notes to record what you find.

URL	Information to Locate
1. **http://www.consumer.gov**	List three tips for buying a used car.

_____

_____

_____

_____

| 2. **http://www.bls.gov.oco/** | What is the job outlook for CAD operators? |

_____

| 3. **http://thomas.loc.gov/ home/lawsmade.toc.html** | Why are lights and ringing bells used in parts of the Capitol building and U.S. House and Senate office buildings? |

_____

_____

_____

_____

▶ NOW PRACTICE . . . NEW WAYS OF THINKING AND READING 2

For one of the Web sites you visited above or a new site of your choice, follow at least three links and then answer the following questions.

1. What type of information did each contain?

_____

2. Was each source reliable? How do you know?

_____

3. Which was the easiest to read and follow? Why?

_____

9b   DISCOVERING THE PURPOSE OF WEB SITES

There are millions of Web sites and they vary widely in purpose. Table 9.1 below summarizes five primary types of Web sites.

9c   EVALUATING WEB SITES

Once you have become familiar with the organization of a Web site and determined its purpose, you should evaluate it. To do this, consider its content, accuracy, authority, objectivity, timeliness, and usability.

Evaluate the Content of a Web Site

When evaluating the content of a Web site, evaluate its appropriateness, its level of technical detail, its completeness, and its links.

Evaluate Appropriateness. To be worthwhile a Web site should contain the information you need. It should answer one or more of your search questions. If the site only touches upon answers to your questions but does not address them in detail, check the links on the site to see if they will lead you to more detailed information. If they do not, search for a more useful site.

Evaluate the Level of Technical Detail. A Web site should contain a level of technical detail that is suited to your purpose. Some sites may provide

TABLE 9.1 TYPES OF WEB SITES

TYPE	PURPOSE	DESCRIPTION	URL EXTENSION
Informational	To present facts, information, and research data	May contain reports, statistical data, results of research studies, and reference materials	.edu or .gov
News	To provide current information on local, national, and international news	Often supplements print newspapers, periodicals, and television news programs	.com
Advocacy	To promote a particular cause or point of view	Usually concerned with a controversial issue; often sponsored by nonprofit groups	.org
Personal	To provide information about an individual and his or her interests and accomplishments	May list publications or include the individual's résumé	URL will vary; may contain .com or .org or may contain a tilde (~)
Commercial	To promote goods or services	May provide news and information related to their products	.com

information that is too sketchy for your search purposes; others assume a level of background knowledge or technical sophistication that you lack. For example, if you are writing a short, introductory-level paper on threats to the survival of marine animals, information on the Web site of the Scripps Institution of Oceanography (**http://www.sio.ucsd.edu**) may be too technical and contain more information than you need. Unless you already have some background knowledge in that field, you may want to search for a different Web site.

Evaluate Completeness.   Determine whether the site provides complete information on its topic. Does it address all aspects of the topic that you feel it should? For example, if a Web site on important twentieth-century American poets does not mention Robert Frost, then the site is incomplete. If you discover that a site is incomplete, search for sites that provide a more thorough treatment of the topic.

Evaluate the Links.   Many reputable sites supply links to other related sites. Make sure that the links work and are current. Also check to see if the sites to which you were sent are reliable sources of information. If the links do not work or the sources appear unreliable, you should question the reliability of the site itself. Also determine whether the links provided are comprehensive or only present a representative sample. Either is acceptable, but the site should make clear the nature of the links it is providing.

➤ NOW PRACTICE . . . EVALUATING CONTENT

Evaluate the content of two of the following sites. Explain why you would either trust or distrust the site for reliable content.

1. **http://www.geocities.com/RainForest/6243/index.html**

   _____

   _____

   _____

2. **http://www1.umn.edu/ohr/careerdev/resources/resume/index.html**

   _____

   _____

   _____

3. **http://www.idausa.org/facts/pg.html**

   _____

   _____

   _____

Evaluate the Accuracy of a Web Site

When using information on a Web site for an academic paper, it is important to be sure that you have found accurate information. The site itself will also provide clues about the accuracy of the information it contains, so ask the following questions:

1. **Is the information presented on the site verifiable?** Compare it with other online sources or with print sources (periodicals and books) on the same topic. If you find a discrepancy between the Web site and other sources, do not trust the site.
2. **Is the information complete or in summary form?** If it is a summary, use the site to locate the original source. Original information is less likely to contain errors and is usually preferred in academic papers.
3. **Could the site be a spoof?** Some sites that appear serious are actually spoofs, hoaxes, or satires designed to poke fun at topics and issues. An example is **http://www.theonion.com**. This site appears to offer legitimate information but actually provides political and social commentary through made-up stories.
4. **Does the site contain current links to other sources?** Accurate sites often provide links where additional information can be found on the Internet.
5. **Does the site provide a list of works cited?** As with any form of research, the sources of information used on the Web site must be documented. If sources are not credited, you should question the accuracy of the site.

> **NOW PRACTICE . . . EVALUATING ACCURACY**

Evaluate the accuracy of two of the following Web sites.

1. **http://gunscholar.com/**

   _____

   _____

   _____

2. **http://freeyourmindonline.net/victorytax.html**

   _____

   _____

   _____

   _____

   _____

3. **http://www.maharanisindia.com/tsunami.html**

Evaluate the Authority of a Web Site

Before using information on a Web site, use the following questions to evaluate the authority of the person or group presenting the information.

1. **Who is the site's sponsor?** Is the sponsor a private individual, an institution, a corporation, a government agency, or a nonprofit organization? Who a site is sponsored by often suggests its purpose. For example, a Web site sponsored by Nike is designed to promote its products, while a site sponsored by a university library is designed to help students learn to use its resources more effectively. Often, the ending of the URL can help you identify the sponsor. The copyright indicates the owner of the site. Another way to check the ownership of a site is to locate the site's home page. You can do this by using only the first part(s) of its URL. For example, suppose you found a paper about Berlin during World War II on the Internet and you wanted to track its source. Its URL is **http://hti.math.uh.edu/curriculum/units/2004/01/04.01.09.php**. If you shorten it to **http://hti.math.uh.edu/**, this URL takes you to the University of Houston Teacher's Institute, where this paper was submitted as a curriculum unit. In general, if the individual, business, or agency sponsor is not identified, the site lacks authority.

2. **Who authored the site?** Is the author's name given, or only the Webmaster's name? (The Webmaster handles the technical details of the site but is not responsible for, and does not create, content.) If the author's name is not given, the site lacks authority. If the author's name is given, is the author an expert in his or her field? If not, the information may not be trustworthy.

3. **Is contact information provided for the author?** Often an e-mail address or other contact information is provided. If it is not, again, this is evidence that the source may not be reliable.

▶ **NOW PRACTICE . . . EVALUATING AUTHORITY**

Evaluate the authority of two of the following Web sites.

1. **http://www.angelfire.com/apes/howard/shakespeare.html**

_____

_____

2. **http://www.youmeworks.com/funny.html**

_____

_____

_____

_____

_____

_____

3. **http://sitemaker.umich.edu/huankgk.356/home**

_____

_____

_____

Evaluate the Timeliness of a Web Site

Although the Web is well known for providing up-to-the-minute information, not all Web sites are current. Evaluate a site's timeliness by checking:

- the date on which the Web site was posted (put on the Web).
- the date when the document you are using was added.
- the date when the site was last revised or updated.
- the date when the links were last checked.

This information is usually provided at the end of the site's home page or at the end of the document you are using.

> **NOW PRACTICE . . . EVALUATING TIMELINESS**

Evaluate the timeliness of two of the following Web sites, using the directions given for each site.

1. **http://www.hwg.org/resources/?cid=30**
   See when these links were last checked. Find out what the consequences of this are by checking the links yourself.

_____

_____

2. **http://www.nhm.org/cats/biblio.htm**
Evaluate whether this site provides timely information for children who want to read more about cats.

_____

_____

_____

3. **http://www.benbest.com/computer/y2kdec.html**
What is your reaction to this article? Explore the site for a more recent up-date. How does this add to the earlier pages?

_____

_____

Evaluate the Objectivity of a Web Site

When using a Web site to obtain information, be sure that the site is objective—that is, it treats the subject in a fair, unbiased manner. (See Chapter 6, Section 6d, p. 144 for more about bias.) Here are a few questions to ask:

1. **What is the goal of the Web site?** Is it to present information or to persuade you to accept a particular point of view or to take a specific action? If it is not to present information, you should question the site's objectivity.
2. **Is the site a mask for advertising?** Be cautious of sites that present information to persuade you to purchase a product or service. If a site resembles an infomercial you might see on television, be just as suspicious of it as you would be of an infomercial.
3. **Does the site present detailed information or focus on generalities?** If the site tends to focus on generalities, then you might suspect that its primary purpose is not to present information and it will not be useful as an in-depth information source.
4. **Are opinions clearly identified?** An author is free to express opinions, but they should be clearly identified as such. Look for words and phrases that identify ideas as opinions. (See Chapter 6, Section 6a, p. 134 for a list of these words and phrases.) If a site presents opinions as facts or does not distinguish between facts and opinions, it is an indication that the site is unreliable.

▶ NOW PRACTICE . . . EVALUATING OBJECTIVITY

Evaluate the objectivity of two of the following Web sites.

1. **http://www.peacenow.org/**

_____

_____

_____

_____

2. **http://kidshealth.org/research/vegan_baby.html**

_____

_____

3. **http://mccainforpresident.org/**

_____

_____

Evaluate the Usability of a Web Site

The design and ease of use of a site often provide clues to the care with which it was constructed. Be suspicious of carelessly put together sites. You might consider the following factors:

- **Navigability.** Is it easy to move around the site?
- **Links.** Do the links work?
- **Format.** Are the pages clear and easy to read or are they cluttered and disorganized?
- **Design.** Do the graphics, art, and buttons support the site's purpose?
- **Correctness.** Are there errors in spelling, grammar, or punctuation?

> **NOW PRACTICE . . . EVALUATING USABILITY**

Evaluate the usability of two of the following Web sites.

1. **http://www.bird-stamps.org/**

_____

_____

_____

_____

2. **http://www.vintage.org/**

_____

_____

_____

_____

3. http://www.designnation.co.uk/

_____

_____

_____

_____

▶ NOW PRACTICE . . . EVALUATING WEB SITES

Assume you are taking a sociology class and you have been given the following assignment:

Write a 5-page research paper comparing and contrasting men's and women's styles of communication. Use both online and print sources.

You have identified the following online sources. Which ones would be appropriate to use in your paper? Which ones would you question, and why? Be sure to evaluate each site for content, accuracy, authority, objectivity, timeliness, and usability.

http://ohioline.osu.edu/flm02/fs04.html

http://www.purdue.edu/UNS/html4ever/2004/040217.MacGeorge.sexroles.html

http://knowledge.emory.edu/article.cfm?articleid=1103

http://www.cbmw.org/Resources/Articles/Communication-between-Men-and-Women

http://www.crosswalk.com/spirituallife/women/1381415/

http://www.onlinedatingmagazine.com/columns/connect/02-menwomencommunication.html

http://janesanders.com/articles/article_biology.html

http://raysweb.net/poems/articles/tannen.html

http://www.usachcs.army.mil/TACarchive/ACCOMO/robertso.htm

http://www.negotiations.com/articles/gender-bender/

http://www.npr.org/templates/story/story.php?storyId=12633456

PART TWO

Readings for Academic Disciplines

Introduction: Reading Across the Disciplines

Brian was a first-year student taking a full-time course load: Introductory Psychology, College Writing, Biology, and World History. He had received good grades in high school and was confident he would do well at a community college where he was majoring in pre-elementary education. After about the fourth week of the term, Brian realized he was not doing as well as he expected to do in his courses. He spent approximately 30 hours per week studying, but was not earning top grades. He got C's on three biology labs, a B minus on a response essay for his writing class, a 70 on his first history exam, and 65, 75, and 70 on the first three psychology quizzes. Brian knew he would probably pass all of his courses, but his goal was to earn grades that would ensure his transfer to a four-year college of his choice.

Brian visited the campus Academic Skills Center and requested tutors for three of his courses. After the first few tutoring sessions he realized that his tutors used a unique approach to each of the disciplines. Specifically, they seemed to read, study, and think differently in each. Brian learned to vary his approach to the material he was studying in different courses. Before, he had studied each course the same way; now he has realized that different disciplines require specialized thinking skills.

Brian's realization is confirmed by a national research study titled "Understanding University Success"; it identified the critical thinking skills essential to success in various disciplines. The table on p. 196 demonstrates that different disciplines require different types of thinking and includes many of the skills identified in the research study. Study the table to get an idea of the types of thinking skills involved in each disciplinary grouping.

READINGS FOR ACADEMIC DISCIPLINES

Each college course you take will be different; in each you will be asked to master a unique set of information, learn new terminology, and demonstrate what you have learned. This section of the text provides you with opportunities to practice reading material from a wide range of disciplines, learn new terminology, and demonstrate your mastery of content through a variety of test-taking methods.

ADAPTING YOUR THINKING TO ACADEMIC DISCIPLINES

DISCIPLINE	SPECIALIZED TYPES OF THINKING REQUIRED	EXAMPLES
Social Sciences (sociology, psychology, anthropology, economics)	Evaluate ideas, make generalizations, be aware of bias, follow and evaluate arguments	Studying patterns of child development, examining causes of age discrimination, comparing cultures
Mathematics	Think sequentially, reason logically, evaluate solutions	Solving word problems, understanding theorems
Natural and Life Sciences (biology, chemistry, physiology, physics, astronomy, earth science)	Grasp relationships, ask questions, understand processes, evaluate evidence	Studying the theory of evolution, examining the question of life in outer space
Arts (music, painting, sculpture)	Evaluate the work of others, express your own ideas, critique your own work	Evaluating a sculpture, revising a musical score
Applied Fields (career fields, technology, business)	Follow processes and procedures, make applications, make and evaluate decisions	Evaluating a patient (nursing), finding a bug in a computer program (computer technology)

Part Two contains 36 readings, three readings for each of the following disciplines: social sciences, communication/speech, anthropology, arts/humanities/literature, public policy/contemporary issues, political science/government/history, business/advertising/economics, technology/computers, health-related fields, life sciences, physical sciences/mathematics, and workplace/career fields.

When taking courses in these fields, you will read textbooks, but you will also read a variety of print and online sources, as well. To give you practice reading a wide range of sources, most chapters in Part Two contain one textbook reading, and two non-textbook readings. The readings are preceded by information, tips, and questions intended to guide your reading. They are followed by questions that will help you evaluate your reading and practice with different test-taking formats. The types of questions and activities are intended to prepare you for future work in the different disciplines. They are in different formats so as to familiarize you with the variety of testing and evaluation methods used in these disciplines. Included are multiple-choice, fill-in-the-blank, true-false, and matching tests, as well as open-ended questions and brief writing assignments. Here is a review of the types of questions and activities you will work with.

- **Understanding the Thesis and Other Main Ideas.** These questions help you identify the most important information in each reading.

- **Identifying Details.** These questions help you discover the relationship between main ideas and details and distinguish between more and less important details.
- **Recognizing Methods of Organization and Transitions.** This activity guides you in discovering organizational patterns and using transitions.
- **Reviewing and Organizing Ideas.** This activity shows you how to learn the material in a reading. You will learn and practice a number of different review and study strategies, including mapping, summarizing, outlining, and paraphrasing.
- **Figuring Out Inferred Meanings and Thinking Critically.** These two sections demonstrate the types of thinking and reasoning that are expected in college courses. The questions take you beyond the literal (factual) content of the selection and guide you in applying many of the critical thinking skills you learned in Part One.
- **Building Vocabulary.** This section gives you practice in learning the terminology that is an essential part of each new academic discipline. You will learn how to use both context and word parts to master new terminology.
- **Selecting a Learning/Study Strategy.** Choosing appropriate learning and study methods is important in every discipline. This activity guides you in identifying appropriate ways to learn and study the material in a selection.
- **Exploring Ideas Through Discussion and Writing.** Because class participation is an important part of many college courses, this activity provides topics that can be used for class discussion. As many college courses involve writing papers and research reports and taking written exams, this activity also provides an opportunity for you to begin to apply your writing skills to various disciplines.
- **Beyond the Classroom to the Web.** Many instructors expect their students to extend and apply their learning to situations outside the classroom. This activity extends your learning beyond the reading selection and provides ways you can use or apply new information.

10 Social Sciences

The **social sciences** are concerned with the study of people, their history and development, and how they interact and function together. These disciplines deal with the political, economic, social, cultural, and behavioral aspects of people. Social scientists study how we live, how we act, how we dress, how we get along with others, and how our culture is similar to and different from other cultures. By reading in the social sciences, you will learn a great deal about yourself and those around you. In "Applying Principles of Learning to Video Games" you will read about efforts to use video game design principles in academic learning. "The New Flirting Game" examines a much more personal form of human interaction—flirtation. "Coming Into My Own" considers a social problem—racial discrimination—and shows how a black neurosurgeon dealt with it. Use the following tips when reading in the social sciences.

TIPS FOR READING IN THE SOCIAL SCIENCES

- **Pay attention to terminology.** The social sciences use precise terminology to describe their subject matter. Learn terms that describe behavior, name stages and processes, and label principles, theories, and models. Also learn the names of important researchers and theorists. As you read, highlight new terms. You can transfer them later to index cards or a vocabulary log for that course.

- **Understand explanations and theories.** The social sciences are devoted, in part, to explaining how people behave as they do. In this chapter you will read an explanation of how people flirt and why people tell stories, for example. As you read theories and explanations, ask these questions: What behavior is being explained? What evidence is offered that it is correct? Of what use is the explanation?

- **Look for supporting evidence.** As you read, look for details, examples, anecdotes, or research evidence that demonstrates that the writer's explanations are reasonable or correct. When reading "The New Flirting Game" look for the author's examples of women's flirting behaviors, for instance.

Often, too, in the social sciences, the examples and applications are highly interesting and will help you remember the theories they illustrate.

- **Make comparisons and connections.** Try to see relationships and make comparisons. Draw connections between topics. Draw charts or maps that compare different explanations, for example.

- **Make practical applications.** As you read, consider how the information is useful to you in real-life situations. Make marginal notes of situations that illustrate what you are reading about. Write comments, for example, about what you have observed about flirting or about instances of racial discrimination.

SELECTION 1

Applying Principles of Learning to Video Games

Samuel E. Wood, Ellen Green Wood, and Denise Boyd

This reading selection from a textbook titled *Mastering the World of Psychology* discusses how video game design principles can be used to make academic learning and instruction more engaging.

> **PREVIEWING THE READING**

Using the steps listed on page 29, preview the reading selection. When you have finished, complete the following items.

1. What is the subject of this selection?

   _____

2. List the five principles of learning that are described in this selection.

   a. _____

   b. _____

   c. _____

   d. _____

   e. _____

 MAKING CONNECTIONS

Think about a board game or a video game that you enjoy playing. What makes it engaging to you?

> **READING TIP**

As you read, look for and highlight the ways that game-based instruction can enhance learning.

Applying Principles of Learning to Video Games

1   Imagine that you are a **cybernetic** human who has narrowly escaped from the final battle in an alien war against planet Earth, only to find yourself marooned on a mysterious space station known as *Mastering the World of Psychology,* [the title of the textbook from which this reading was taken] or *MWP3E*, as it is more often called. To get back to Earth, you must unlock the secrets of *MWP3E.* You soon learn that *MWP3E* is inhabited by a ruthless alien army made up of killing machines who will stop at nothing to protect their secrets, even if they must resort to destroying every living being in the galaxy, including themselves, by means of a merciless horde of parasites. Your task seems impossible, but you have many weapons at your disposal. Do you think you are up to the challenge?

2   If you are one of the millions of college students who enjoy playing the video game *Halo,* these words have a familiar ring. Of course, learning psychology isn't among the obstacles that the game's heroes have to overcome. Suppose, though, that your psychology course was structured like a role-playing video game. Do you think you would learn more than you might from a conventional course?

3   Many educators argue that video game design principles should be incorporated into computer-assisted and online courses. To critics who scoff at the idea of game-based instruction, proponents point out that educational board games, for example, are a staple of both elementary and secondary classrooms. Thus, advocates say, using video games in classrooms represents nothing more than an update of an instructional resource that has been employed by teachers throughout the ages.

4   One of the most vocal advocates of applying video game design principles to instruction, Professor Rod Riegle of Illinois State University, launched what he claims to be the first role-playing game (RPG) online course in 2000. Riegle's undergraduate

education course features an interactive learning environment that includes sights, sounds, and language that are similar to those found in fantasy-based electronic games. Students are cast as "Change Agents" who must do battle against "Status Quo," a fictional character who represent forces in education that oppose new technologies and methods of instruction. Assignments consist of four **hierarchical** quests that require mastery of progressively difficult concepts and technological skills. When each quest is completed to Riegle's satisfaction, he awards students a title. "Future Lords" are students who have completed Quest 1, and "Hidden Masters" are those who have finished Quest 2. Those who have completed Quest 3 are known as "Infonauts," and their classmates who have finished Quest 4 are called "CyberGuides."

hierarchical (paragraph 4) organized according to different levels

5   Professor Riegle's course is very popular among students at Ilinois State University. However, before other educators adopt Riegle's strategies, most of them want to know how game-based instruction affects students' learning. Experiments carried out by Richard Mayer, an educational psychologist at the University of California at Santa Barbara, suggest that a game-based learning environment such as Riegle's RPG course could be quite effective if the instructor takes care to ensure that the structure of the course itself does not distract students from the content that they are expected to learn. However, the strongest argument in favor of game-based instruction is its potential for enhancing student engagement. To understand how a course that is structured like a video game might increase student engagement, we must understand why video games are engaging. Here's how the principles of learning can be used to explain how video games attract and hold players' interest.

- *Learning through association of stimuli:* The cues associated with games—their names, images, and sounds—trigger the emotions players experience while playing them, a set of feelings that are implied when we use the word "fun."
- *Learning through rewards:* With every new game, players experience both success and failure, and the consequences of their actions are immediate. Rewards of this kind exert a powerful influence on future behavior.
- *Learning through discovery:* The "Aha!" experiences that happen when players suddenly realize how to predict the appearance of an obstacle, learn how to escape from a trap, or find a shortcut from one level to the next have an important role in the "fun" experience of playing a video game.
- *Learning through exploration:* Whether players win or lose, each time they play a game, they become more familiar with its features. This knowledge helps them develop and execute strategies.
- *Learning through observation:* Playing video games with friends is yet another source of learning that keeps players coming back for more. Internet sites and magazines devoted to game-playing strategies are also important sources of observational learning. A possible downside of this principle is that players may imitate risky behaviors exhibited by a game's characters (e.g., reckless driving).

6   Applying learning principles to explain why video games are engaging calls attention to the practical value of psychological research. However, be forewarned that you will read about many experiments that seem to be far removed from everyday learning experiences. Remember, though, that the goal of psychologists is to identify general principles that explain and predict behavior across a variety of situations. Thus, these principles can be used to explain diverse learned behaviors—from those exhibited by maze-running laboratory rats to those of the 48% of college students who admit that they sometimes play video games when they should be studying and the 30% or so who say that they even play games while in class (Jones, 2003).

A.   UNDERSTANDING THE THESIS AND OTHER MAIN IDEAS

Select the best answer.

_____ 1. The authors' primary purpose in this selection is to
  a. promote video games as part of online instruction.
  b. compare conventional teaching methods with online instruction.
  c. identify different types of games that are used successfully in classrooms.
  d. explore the connection between learning and game-based instruction.

_____ 2. The topic of paragraph 3 is
  a. psychology.
  b. online courses.
  c. game-based instruction.
  d. elementary education.

_____ 3. The main idea of paragraph 4 is expressed in the
  a. first sentence.
  b. second sentence.
  c. third sentence.
  d. sixth sentence.

_____ 4. The primary question that is answered in paragraph 5 is:
  a. Do students like Professor Riegle's online course?
  b. What courses are most appropriate for game-based learning?
  c. How does game-based instruction influence students' learning?
  d. How can video games be adapted for use in the classroom?

_____ 5. The purpose of the bulleted list in paragraph 5 is to explain

    a. why video games interfere with learning.

    b. principles of learning that apply to video games.

    c. methods of video game development.

    d. principles of psychological research.

B. IDENTIFYING DETAILS

Indicate whether each statement is true (T) or false (F).

_____ 1. Professor Riegle claims to have launched the first role-playing game (RPG) online course.

_____ 2. Professor Riegle is an educational psychologist at the University of California at Santa Barbara.

_____ 3. The game character representing forces that oppose new technologies is known as "Status Quo."

_____ 4. Professor Riegle's game is called *MWP3E.*

_____ 5. Professor Riegle's RPG course is for undergraduate students in education.

C. RECOGNIZING METHODS OF ORGANIZATION AND TRANSITIONS

Complete the following statements by filling in the blanks.

1. In paragraph 3, the authors use the generalization and example pattern to explain why some educators like the idea of game-based instruction. Two transitional phrases that indicate this pattern are _____ and _____.

2. In paragraph 5, the authors use the _____ pattern to introduce the principles of learning as applied to video games.

3. In paragraph 6, the authors signal a change in thought with the transitional word _____.

D. REVIEWING AND ORGANIZING IDEAS: MAPPING

Complete the following map by filling in the blanks.

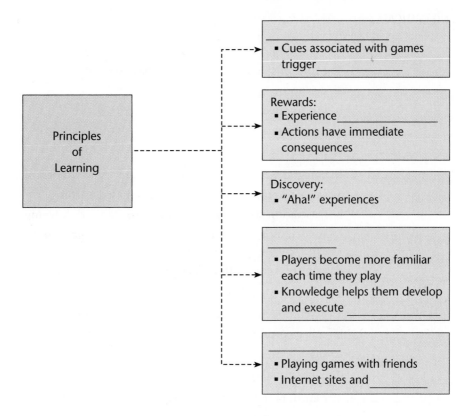

Principles of Learning

- Cues associated with games trigger _____

Rewards:
- Experience _____
- Actions have immediate consequences

Discovery:
- "Aha!" experiences

- Players become more familiar each time they play
- Knowledge helps them develop and execute _____

- Playing games with friends
- Internet sites and _____

➤ E. FIGURING OUT INFERRED MEANINGS

Indicate whether each statement is true (T) or false (F).

_____ 1. The video game described in the opening paragraphs is meant to resemble the game *Halo.*

_____ 2. Educational board games have been used successfully in classrooms for many years.

_____ 3. It can be inferred that critics of RPG courses object primarily to the violence in such games.

_____ 4. The structure and content of a course must be compatible for an RPG course to be effective.

_____ 5. RPG courses are designed mainly for students who already play video games in class.

> **F.   THINKING CRITICALLY**

Select the best answer.

_____ 1. The tone of this selection can best be described as
   a. disapproving.
   b. informative.
   c. incredulous.
   d. sensational.

_____ 2. In paragraph 5, the authors use the word "Aha!" to describe the
   a. sarcastic reaction of critics of game-based learning.
   b. frustration students sometimes associate with learning.
   c. sudden moment of understanding during a game or learning experience.
   d. irony of a connection between video games and learning.

_____ 3. The intended audience for this selection is most likely to be
   a. psychology students.
   b. college professors.
   c. video game designers.
   d. educational consultants.

_____ 4. The authors support their thesis with all of the following *except*
   a. examples and illustrations.
   b. statistical data.
   c. expert opinion.
   d. personal experience.

> **G.   BUILDING VOCABULARY**

> **Context**
Using context and a dictionary, if necessary, determine the meaning of each word as it is used in the selection.

_____ 1. ruthless (paragraph 1)
   a. careful
   b. merciless
   c. weak
   d. harmless

_____ 2. horde (paragraph 1)

    a. punishment

    b. field

    c. swarm

    d. portion

_____ 3. scoff (paragraph 3)

    a. ridicule

    b. imitate

    c. establish

    d. overlook

_____ 4. staple (paragraph 3)

    a. label

    b. lesson

    c. essential item

    d. fastener

_____ 5. exert (paragraph 5)

    a. depart

    b. put forth

    c. define

    d. breathe

➤ Word Parts

> ### A REVIEW OF PREFIXES, ROOTS, AND SUFFIXES
>
> AD- means *toward*
> PRO- means *supporting, favoring*
> VOC- means *call*
> -ENT means *one who*

Use your knowledge of word parts and the review above to fill in the blanks in the following sentences.

In this selection, the word *proponents* (paragraph 3) refers to people who
_____ something. Another word in this paragraph that
means the same thing is _____, which is used here to
describe those who speak in favor of using game-based instruction.

H. SELECTING A LEARNING/STUDY STRATEGY

Assume you will be tested on this reading on an upcoming exam. Evaluate the usefulness of the map you completed on page 205 as a study tool. How would you use it to study?

I. EXPLORING IDEAS THROUGH DISCUSSION AND WRITING

1. Evaluate the introduction to this selection. How successful was it in capturing your attention?

2. Think of a game that you enjoy playing, either a more traditional board game such as Monopoly or an online game. Apply the five learning principles to the game you have chosen and assess how well it reflects each principle.

3. Do you think game-based instruction would enhance your interest in learning? Identify specific courses that you think could benefit from game-based instruction. Which of your courses would *not* be enhanced by unconventional methods of instruction? Explain your answers.

J. BEYOND THE CLASSROOM TO THE WEB

Explore the site for a Economics 101 game **http://econ100.uncg.edu/dcl/econ100/.** *Be sure to go through each menu item to learn as much as possible about the game. How does this game reflect the principles outlined in the reading? Do you think you would enjoy learning about economics through this game?*

✔ Tracking Your Progress

Selection 1

Section	Number Correct	Score
A. Thesis and Main Ideas (5 items)	_____ x 5	_____
B. Details (5 items)	_____ x 4	_____
C. Organization and Transitions (4 items)	_____ x 3	_____
E. Inferred Meanings (5 items)	_____ x 4	_____
F. Thinking Critically (4 items)	_____ x 3	_____
G. Vocabulary		
1. Context (5 items)	_____ x 3	_____
2. Word Parts (2 items)	_____ x 1	_____
	TOTAL SCORE	_____ %

SELECTION
2

The New Flirting Game

Deborah A. Lott

This article first appeared in *Psychology Today*. Read it to discover how psychologists study the age-old custom of flirtation.

> ## PREVIEWING THE READING

Using the steps listed on page 29, preview the reading selection. When you have finished, complete the following items.

1. The subject of this reading is _____.

2. List at least three questions you expect to be able to answer after reading the article:

   a. _____

   b. _____

   c. _____

MAKING CONNECTIONS

Are these people flirting with each other? How can you tell?

> ## READING TIP

As you read, look for and highlight the qualities and characteristics of flirting. Highlighting will make it easier to review the reading and find information you need.

The New Flirting Game

1   We flirt with the intent of assessing potential lifetime partners, we flirt to have easy, no-strings-attached sex, and we flirt when we are not looking for either. We flirt because, most simply, flirtation can be a liberating form of play, a game with suspense and ambiguities that brings joys of its own. As Philadelphia-based **social psychologist** Tim Perper says, "Some flirters appear to want to prolong the interaction because it's pleasurable and erotic in its own right, regardless of where it might lead."

2   Here are some of the ways the game is currently being played.

social psychologist a person who studies how groups behave and how individuals are affected by the group

Taking the Lead

3   When it comes to flirting today, women aren't waiting around for men to make the advances. They're taking the lead. Psychologist Monica Moore, Ph.D., of Webster University in St. Louis, Missouri, has spent more than 2000 hours observing women's flirting maneuvers in restaurants, singles bars and at parties. According to her findings, women give nonverbal cues that get a flirtation rolling fully two-thirds of the time. A man may think he's making the first move because he is the one to literally move from wherever he is to the woman's side, but usually he has been summoned.

4   By the standards set out by **evolutionary psychologists**, the women who attract the most men would most likely be those with the most symmetrical features or the best hip-to-waist ratios. Not so, says Moore. In her studies, the women who draw the most response are the ones who send the most signals. "Those who performed more than 35 displays per hour elicited greater than four approaches per hour," she notes, "and the more variety the woman used in her techniques, the more likely she was to be successful."

evolutionary psychologists people who track how human behavior and psychological traits have developed and changed over the course of history

Sexual Semaphores

5   Moore tallied a total of 52 different nonverbal courtship behaviors used by women, including glancing, gazing (short and sustained), primping, preening, smiling, lip licking, pouting, giggling, laughing and nodding, as if to nonverbally indicate, "Yes! yes!" A woman would often begin with a room-encompassing glance, in actuality a casing-the-joint scan to seek out prospects. When she'd zeroed in on a target she'd exhibit the short darting glance—looking at a man, quickly looking away, looking back and then away again. There was something shy and indirect in this initial eye contact.

semaphores visual, nonverbal systems for sending information or signals

6   But women countered their shy moves with other, more aggressive and overt tactics. Those who liked to live dangerously took a round robin approach, alternately flirting with several different men at once until one responded in an unequivocal fashion. A few women hiked their skirts up to bring more leg into a particular man's field of vision. When they inadvertently drew the attention of other admirers, they quickly pulled their

skirts down. If a man failed to get the message, a woman might parade, walking across the room towards him, hips swaying, breasts pushed out, head held high.

Who's Submissive?

7   Moore observed some of the same nonverbal behaviors that Eibl Eibesfeldt and other **ethologists** had deemed universal among women: the eyebrow flash (an exaggerated raising of the eyebrows of both eyes, followed by a rapid lowering), the coy smile (a tilting of the head downward, with partial averting of the eyes and, at the end, covering of the mouth), and the exposed neck (turning the head so that the side of the neck is bared.

ethologists
people who study
behavior patterns

8   But while many ethologists interpret these signs as conveying female submissiveness, Moore has an altogether different take. "If these behaviors serve to orchestrate courtship, which they do, then how can they be anything but powerful?" she observes. "Who determined that to cover your mouth is a submissive gesture? Baring the neck may have a lot more to do with the neck being an erogenous zone than its being a submissive posture." Though women in Moore's sample used the coy smile, they also maintained direct eye contact for long periods and smiled fully and unabashedly.

9   Like Moore, Perper believes that ethologists have overemphasized certain behaviors and misinterpreted them as signifying either dominance or submission. For instance, says Perper, among flirting American heterosexual men and women as well as homosexual men, the coy smile is less frequent than direct eye contact and sustained smiling. He suggests that some cultures may use the coy smile more than others, and that it is not always a sign of deference.

10   In watching a flirtatious couple, Perper finds that a male will perform gestures and movements that an ethologist might consider dominant, such as sticking out his chest and strutting around, but he'll also give signs that could be read as submissive, such as bowing his head lower than the woman's. The woman may also do both. "She may drop her head, turn slightly, bare her neck, but then she'll lift her eyes and lean forward with her breasts held out, and that doesn't look submissive at all," Perper notes.

11   Men involved in these encounters, says Perper, don't describe themselves as "feeling powerful." In fact, he and Moore agree, neither party wholly dominates in a flirtation. Instead, there is a subtle, rhythmical and playful back and forth that culminates in a kind of physical **synchronization** between two people. She turns, he turns; she picks up her drink, he picks up his drink.

synchronization
happening at the
same time

12   Still, by escalating and de-escalating the flirtation's progression, the woman controls the pace. To slow down a flirtation, a woman might orient her body away slightly or cross her arms across her chest, or avoid meeting the man's eyes. To stop the dance in its tracks, she can yawn, frown, sneer, shake her head from side to side as if to say "No," pocket her hands, hold her trunk rigidly, avoid the man's gaze, stare over his head, or resume flirting with other men. If a man is really dense, she might hold a strand of hair up to her eyes as if to examine her split ends or even pick her teeth.

Learning the Steps

13   If flirting today is often a conscious activity, it is also a learned one. Women pick up the moves early. In observations of 100 girls between the ages of 13 and 16 at

shopping malls, ice skating rinks and other places adolescents congregate, Moore found the teens exhibiting 31 of the 52 courtship signals deployed by adult women. (The only signals missing were those at the more overt end of the spectrum, such as actual caressing.) Overall, the teens' gestures looked less natural than ones made by mature females: they laughed more boisterously and preened more obviously, and their moves were broader and rougher.

14   The girls clearly modeled their behavior on the leader of the pack. When the **alpha female** stroked her hair or swayed her hips, her companions copied quickly. "You never see this in adult women," says Moore, "Indeed, women go to great lengths to stand out from their female companions."

alpha female
the "first" female in a group, the leader whose behavior is copied by the others in the group

15   Compared with adults, the teens signaled less frequently—7.6 signs per hour per girl, as opposed to 44.6 per woman—but their maneuvers, though clumsy, were equally effective at attracting the objects of their desire, in this case, teen boys.

16   Some of the exhilaration of flirting, of course, lies in what is hidden, the tension between what is felt and what is revealed. Flirting pairs volley back and forth, putting out ambiguous signals, neither willing to disclose more than the other, neither wanting to appear more desirous to the other.

17   To observers like Moore and Perper, flirtation often seems to most resemble the antics of children on the playground or even perhaps the ritual peek-a-boo that babies play with their caregivers. Flirters jostle, tease and tickle, even sometimes stick out a tongue at their partner or reach around from behind to cover up their eyes. As Daniel Stern, researcher, psychiatrist, and author of *The Interpersonal World of the Infant* (Karnac, 1998), has pointed out, the two groups in our culture that engage in the most sustained eye contact are mothers and infants, and lovers.

18   And thus in a way, the cycle of flirting takes us full circle. If flirting sets us off on the road to producing babies, it also whisks us back to the pleasures of infancy.

A.   UNDERSTANDING THE THESIS AND OTHER MAIN IDEAS

Select the best answer.

_____   1. The author's primary purpose in "The New Flirting Game" is to
   a. expose the shallowness and superficiality of flirting behavior.
   b. teach women and men the modern methods of flirting.
   c. compare flirting behaviors of today with those of previous generations.
   d. describe how and why women and men flirt.

_____   2. The main idea of paragraph 1 is that women and men flirt
   a. to find lifetime partners.
   b. to have uncomplicated sex.
   c. as a game.
   d. for many different reasons.

_____ 3. The main idea of paragraph 3 is expressed in the
  a. first sentence.
  b. third sentence.
  c. fourth sentence.
  d. last sentence.

_____ 4. The topic of paragraph 6 is
  a. risky behavior.
  b. male responses.
  c. flirting tactics.
  d. flirting mistakes.

_____ 5. The main idea of paragraph 8 is that
  a. nonverbal flirting behaviors convey female submissiveness.
  b. women use both a smile and eye contact when flirting.
  c. the neck is an erogenous zone.
  d. nonverbal flirting behaviors are often powerful rather than submissive.

_____ 6. The statement that best expresses the main idea of paragraph 13 is
  a. "If flirting today is often a conscious activity, it is also a learned one."
  b. "Women pick up the moves early."
  c. "The only signals missing were those at the more overt end of the spectrum."
  d. "Overall, the teens' gestures looked less natural than ones made by mature females."

_____ 7. The main idea of paragraph 17 is that
  a. flirters are immature.
  b. flirtation resembles play.
  c. eye contact is important to mothers and infants.
  d. the eye contact between lovers is like that between mothers and infants.

B. IDENTIFYING DETAILS

Select the best answer.

_____ 1. According to Dr. Moore's research, the women who attract the most men are those
  a. with the most symmetrical features.
  b. with the best hip-to-waist ratios.
  c. who send the most signals.
  d. who are least interested in attracting men.

_____ 2. All of the following courtship behaviors are considered "sexual semaphores" *except*

    a. glancing and gazing.

    b. using suggestive language.

    c. primping and preening.

    d. smiling and laughing.

_____ 3. As described in the reading, one way that a woman can slow the
pace of a flirtation is by

    a. staring directly into the man's eyes.

    b. nodding as if in agreement.

    c. orienting her body toward him.

    d. crossing her arms across her chest.

_____ 4. Nonverbal flirting behaviors that are considered universal among
women include all of the following *except* the

    a. eyebrow flash.

    b. coy smile.

    c. wink.

    d. exposed neck.

_____ 5. As compared to the flirting behavior of adult women, the adolescent
girls observed by Dr. Moore did all of the following *except*

    a. exhibit many of the same courtship signals.

    b. look less natural in their gestures.

    c. go to greater lengths to stand out from their female companions.

    d. signal less frequently.

_____ 6. According to Dr. Moore's findings, women give nonverbal cues that
begin a flirtation

    a. one-third of the time.

    b. one-half of the time.

    c. two-thirds of the time.

    d. three-fourths of the time.

▶ C. RECOGNIZING METHODS OF ORGANIZATION AND TRANSITIONS

Complete the following statements by filling in the blanks.

1. Locate a phrase in paragraph 9 that indicates an example is to follow.

_____

2. In paragraphs 13–15, Dr. Moore's observations of adult women and adolescent girls are discussed using an organizational pattern called _____. A transitional phrase that helps identify the organizational pattern in this section is _____.

D. REVIEWING AND ORGANIZING IDEAS: PARAPHRASING

Complete the following paraphrase of paragraph 8 by filling in the blanks with the correct words or phrases.

Although many _____ believe these _____ convey female _____, Dr. Moore disagrees. She says that since these _____ seem to promote _____, they must be _____. She also disagrees that _____ is a _____ gesture and states that _____ may have more to do with it being an _____ than to it being a _____ posture. Women in Moore's _____ used the _____ but they also maintained _____ for extended periods and _____ fully and openly.

E. FIGURING OUT INFERRED MEANINGS

Indicate whether each statement is true (T) or false (F).

_____ 1. Some people enjoy flirting simply for the fun of it.
_____ 2. The people in the studies mentioned in the reading knew they were being observed.
_____ 3. Evolutionary psychology and social psychology are the same thing.
_____ 4. Flirting behaviors are the same in all cultures.
_____ 5. Teenage girls learn most of their flirting behaviors from watching adult women.

F. THINKING CRITICALLY

Select the best answer.

_____ 1. The author supports the thesis of "The New Flirting Game" primarily with
   a. cause and effect relationships.
   b. research evidence.
   c. personal experience.
   d. statistics.

_____   2. The author's tone throughout the article can best be described as
      a. serious and concerned.
      b. judgmental and opinionated.
      c. pessimistic and depressing.
      d. light and factual.

_____   3. Another appropriate title for this reading would be
      a. "The Modern Moral Decline."
      b. "Commitment in the Twenty-First Century."
      c. "The Art and Science of Flirting."
      d. "Nonverbal Communication Between Women and Men."

_____   4. In paragraph 3, the phrase "but usually he has been summoned" means that the man
      a. is usually the one who makes the first move.
      b. is expected to move from his location to the woman's.
      c. has been waved at from across the room.
      d. doesn't realize that he is responding to the woman's nonverbal invitation.

_____   5. The author ends the reading with
      a. a pleasing comparison.
      b. a warning.
      c. an appeal to action.
      d. a sympathetic note.

G.   BUILDING VOCABULARY

Context

Using context and a dictionary, if necessary, determine the meaning of each word as it is used in the selection.

_____   1. elicited (paragraph 4)
      a. expected from
      b. brought forth
      c. directed at
      d. returned to

_____   2. encompassing (paragraph 5)
      a. avoiding
      b. emptying

c. filling

d. including

_____   3. overt (paragraph 6)

a. obvious

b. secret

c. friendly

d. private

_____   4. dominance (paragraph 9)

a. control

b. stubbornness

c. friendliness

d. extroversion

_____   5. culminates (paragraph 11)

a. fears

b. concludes

c. recovers

d. begins

_____   6. congregate (paragraph 13)

a. depart

b. arrange

c. plan

d. gather

➤ Word Parts

A REVIEW OF PREFIXES MEANING "NOT"

Each of the following prefixes means *not*.

DE-

IN-

MIS-

NON-

UN-

Match each word in Column A with its meaning in Column B. Write your answers in the spaces provided.

Column A **Prefix + Root**	**Column B** **Meaning**
_____ 1. nonverbal	a. not on purpose
_____ 2. indirect	b. not understood correctly
_____ 3. unequivocal	c. without embarrassment
_____ 4. inadvertently	d. not spoken
_____ 5. unabashedly	e. without doubt
_____ 6. misinterpreted	f. without doubt or misunderstanding

> **Unusual Words/Understanding Idioms**

Indicate whether each statement is true (T) or false (F).

_____ 1. In paragraph 1, the phrase **no-strings-attached** sex means sex that is uncomplicated by expectations of commitment.

_____ 2. In paragraph 12, the phrase **to stop the dance in its tracks** means to bring an end to the flirtation.

> **H.   SELECTING A LEARNING/STUDY STRATEGY**

Discuss how visualization might help you learn the characteristics of flirting presented in this article.

> **I.   EXPLORING IDEAS THROUGH DISCUSSION AND WRITING**

1. The author uses terms that imply games or sports, such as the phrases "a round robin approach" (paragraph 6) and "volley back and forth" (paragraph 16). How do these phrases support her central thesis?

2. What images do the words *maneuvers* (paragraph 3) and *deployed* (paragraph 13) bring to mind?

3. Why is the reading called "The *New* Flirting Game"? What do you think the old flirting game consisted of?

➤ **J. BEYOND THE CLASSROOM TO THE WEB**

Visit *"Developing Flirt-Ability"* at **http://www.askheartbeat.com**.

Skim several articles. Compare the reliability of the articles on this Web site with Lott's article. Which is more likely to provide helpful information on dating and relationships? Why?

✔ Tracking Your Progress

Selection 2

Section	Number Correct		Score
A. Thesis and Main Ideas (7 items)	_____	x 4	_____
B. Details (6 items)	_____	x 3	_____
C. Organization and Transitions (3 items)	_____	x 2	_____
E. Inferred Meanings (5 items)	_____	x 3	_____
F. Thinking Critically (5 items)	_____	x 3	_____
G. Vocabulary			
1. Context (6 items)	_____	x 2	_____
2. Word Parts (6 items)	_____	x 1	_____
	TOTAL SCORE		_____%

SELECTION 3

Coming Into My Own

Ben Carson

This reading was taken from an autobiography titled *Gifted Hands: The Ben Carson Story*. In his book, Carson, a well-known neurosurgeon, describes his journey from his childhood in inner-city Detroit to a position as director of pediatric neurosurgery at Johns Hopkins Hospital.

▶ PREVIEWING THE READING

Using the steps listed on page 29, preview the reading selection. When you have finished, answer the following questions.

1. What is the setting of the first half of the reading?

   _____

2. What is the subject's profession in this reading?

   _____

 MAKING CONNECTIONS

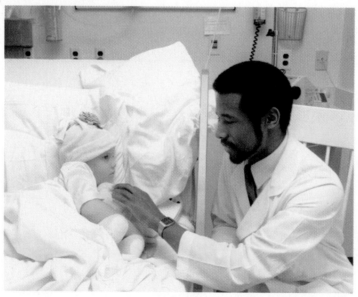

Dr. Benjamin Carson at Johns Hopkins Hospital. What do you suppose Dr. Carson is doing in this photo?

> **READING TIP**
>
> *As you read, notice situations that reveal racial discrimination or prejudice and how the author responded to them.*

Coming Into My Own

orderly
an attendant who does routine, nonmedical work in a hospital

intern
a recent medical school graduate undergoing supervised practical training

Intensive Care Unit
a specialized section of a hospital containing the equipment, medical and nursing staff, and monitoring devices necessary to provide care to extremely ill patients

1   The nurse looked at me with disinterest as I walked toward her station. "Yes?" she asked, pausing with a pencil in her hand. "Who did you come to pick up?" From the tone of her voice I immediately knew that she thought I was an **orderly**. I was wearing my green scrubs, nothing to indicate I was a doctor.

2   "I didn't come to pick up anyone." I looked at her and smiled, realizing that the only Black people she had seen on the floor had been orderlies. Why should she think anything else? "I'm the new **intern**."

3   "New intern? But you can't—I mean—I didn't mean to" the nurse stuttered, trying to apologize without sounding prejudiced.

4   "That's OK," I said, letting her off the hook. It was a natural mistake. "I'm new, so why should you know who I am?"

5   The first time I went into the **Intensive Care Unit**, I was wearing my whites (our monkey suits, as we interns called them), and a nurse signaled me. "You're here for Mr. Jordan?"

6   "No, ma'am, I'm not."

7   "You sure?" she asked as a frown covered her forehead. "He's the only one who's scheduled for respiratory therapy today."

8   By then I had come closer and she could read my name badge and the word *intern* under my name.

9   "Oh, I'm so very sorry," she said, and I could tell she was.

10   Although I didn't say it, I would like to have told her, "It's all right because I realize most people do things based on their past experiences. You've never encountered a Black intern before, so you assumed I was the only kind of Black male you'd seen wearing whites, a respiratory therapist." I smiled again and went on.

11   It was inevitable that a few White patients didn't want a Black doctor, and they protested to Dr. Long. One woman said, "I'm sorry, but I do not want a Black physician in on my case."

12   Dr. Long had a standard answer, given in a calm but firm voice. "There's the door. You're welcome to walk through it. But if you stay here, Dr. Carson will handle your case."

13   At the time people were making these objections, I didn't know about them. Only much later did Dr. Long tell me as he laughed about the prejudices of some patients. But there was no humor in his voice when he defined his position. He was adamant about his stance, allowing no prejudice because of color or ethnic background.

14   Of course, I knew how some individuals felt. I would have had to be pretty insensitive not to know. The way they behaved, their coldness, even without saying anything, made their feelings clear. Each time, however, I was able to remind myself they were individuals speaking for themselves and not representative of all Whites.

No matter how strongly a patient felt, as soon as he voiced his objection he learned that Dr. Long would dismiss him on the spot if he said anything more. So far as I know, none of the patients ever left!

15   I honestly felt no great pressures. When I did encounter prejudice, I could hear Mother's voice in the back of my head saying things like, "Some people are ignorant and you have to educate them."

16   The only pressure I felt during my internship, and in the years since, has been a self-imposed obligation to act as a role model for Black youngsters. These young folks need to know that the way to escape their often dismal situations is contained within themselves. They can't expect other people to do it for them. Perhaps I can't do much, but I can provide one living example of someone who made it and who came from what we now call a disadvantaged background. Basically I'm no different than many of them.

17   As I think of Black youth, I also want to say I believe that many of our pressing racial problems will be taken care of when we who are among the minorities will stand on our own feet and refuse to look to anybody else to save us from our situations. The culture in which we live stresses looking out for number one. Without adopting such a self-centered value system, we can demand the best of ourselves while we are extending our hands to help others.

18   I see glimmers of hope. For example, I noticed that when the Vietnamese came to the United States they often faced prejudice from everyone—White, Black, and Hispanics. But they didn't beg for handouts and often took the lowest jobs offered. Even well-educated individuals didn't mind sweeping floors if it was a paying job.

entrepreneurs
businesspeople

19   Today many of these same Vietnamese are property owners and **entrepreneurs**. That's the message I try to get across to the young people. The same opportunities are there, but we can't start out as vice president of the company. Even if we landed such a position, it wouldn't do us any good anyway because we wouldn't know how to do our work. It's better to start where we can fit in and then work our way up.

A.   UNDERSTANDING THE THESIS AND OTHER MAIN IDEAS

Select the best answer.

_____   1. The writer of "Coming Into My Own" can best be described as
a. a black respiratory therapist.
b. a white female nurse.
c. a black male doctor.
d. the white patient of a black doctor.

_____   2. The statement from the reading that best supports the writer's primary thesis is
a. "From the tone of her voice I immediately knew that she thought I was an orderly." (paragraph 1)
b. "It was inevitable that a few White patients didn't want a Black doctor." (paragraph 11)

      c. "I can provide one living example of someone who made it and who came from what we now call a disadvantaged background." (paragraph 16)

      d. "I see glimmers of hope." (paragraph 18)

_____ 3. According to the writer, the only pressure he felt during and after his internship has been from

      a. himself as he strives to be a role model for black youngsters.

      b. white nurses and doctors who treat him as less than equal.

      c. his parents and other family members because of their high expectations for him.

      d. members of other ethnic groups who resent his success.

_____ 4. The statement that best expresses the main idea of paragraph 17 is

      a. People should look to themselves rather than others to improve their situations.

      b. Adopting a self-centered value system is the only way to succeed in our culture.

      c. The racial problems in our society are primarily caused by misunderstanding.

      d. Extending help to others is not as important as getting ahead.

_____ 5. The topic of paragraph 18 is

      a. low-paying jobs.

      b. Vietnamese immigrants.

      c. prejudice among ethnic groups.

      d. education levels of immigrants.

_____ 6. The main point of paragraph 19 is expressed in the

      a. first sentence.

      b. second sentence.

      c. fourth sentence.

      d. last sentence.

B. IDENTIFYING DETAILS

Indicate whether each statement is true (T) or false (F).

_____ 1. The writer/intern was mistaken for both an orderly and a respiratory therapist.

_____ 2. The white patients who were prejudiced were careful to hide their feelings.

_____ 3. Many patients left the hospital immediately rather than be treated by a black doctor.

_____ 4. The writer came from a privileged background.

_____ 5. Many Vietnamese immigrants who started in low-paying jobs now own property.

C.   RECOGNIZING METHODS OF ORGANIZATION AND TRANSITIONS

Select the best answer.

_____ 1. In paragraphs 1–10, the writer describes the prejudice he has faced. The organizational pattern used in these paragraphs is

a. cause and effect.   c. enumeration.

b. time sequence.   d. comparison and contrast.

_____ 2. A phrase in paragraph 18 that indicates that the writer will illustrate his ideas is

a. But   c. For example

b. Even   d. If

D.   REVIEWING AND ORGANIZING IDEAS: SUMMARIZING

Complete the following summaries of paragraphs 5-10 and 11-13 by filling in the missing words and phrases.

Paragraphs 5–10: The nurse assumed that the writer was a _____ _____, not a _____. The writer understood that the nurse's assumption was based on her _____.

Paragraphs 11–13: Some _____ patients did not want to be treated by a _____ doctor. When they _____ to Dr. Long, his response was that _____ _____. Dr. Long later _____ about the patients' _____, but he also made it clear that he would not tolerate _____.

E.   FIGURING OUT INFERRED MEANINGS

Indicate whether each statement is true (T) or false (F).

_____ 1. From the situation described in paragraphs 1–4, it can be inferred that all orderlies are black males.

_____ 2. From the description of the writer's mother, it can be inferred that she believed that her son could change people's attitudes toward blacks.

_____ 3. From paragraphs 18–19, it can be inferred that the writer believes that immigrants are taking jobs away from blacks.

F. THINKING CRITICALLY

Select the best answer.

_____ 1. The writer's primary purpose in writing this article is to
   a. expose prejudice in the medical profession.
   b. persuade others, especially black youth, that it is possible to succeed in spite of prejudice and a disadvantaged background.
   c. discourage black males from becoming doctors.
   d. argue against affirmative action programs that offer "handouts" to minorities.

_____ 2. The writer supports his ideas primarily by
   a. describing his personal experience.
   b. reporting statistics.
   c. defining terms.
   d. citing facts.

_____ 3. By stating in paragraph 2 that he looked at the nurse "and smiled," the writer indicates that he
   a. was being sarcastic.
   b. understood the nurse's error and forgave her.
   c. was incredulous at being treated that way.
   d. thought the nurse was joking.

_____ 4. The writer's tone throughout the article can best be described as
   a. bitter.   c. encouraging.
   b. angry.   d. grateful.

G. BUILDING VOCABULARY

Context
Using context and a dictionary, if necessary, determine the meaning of each word as it is used in the selection.

_____ 1. prejudiced (paragraph 3)
   a. confused   c. inconsiderate
   b. biased   d. distracted

_____ 2. inevitable (paragraph 11)

    a. unfortunate   c. unavoidable

    b. disappointing   d. unexpected

_____ 3. adamant (paragraph 13)

    a. uncompromising   c. easygoing

    b. angry   d. humorous

_____ 4. pressing (paragraph 17)

    a. pushy   c. unnecessary

    b. urgent   d. minor

▶ Word Parts

```
┌─────────────────────────────────┐
│  A REVIEW OF PREFIXES           │
│  DIS- means not                 │
│  IN- means not                  │
└─────────────────────────────────┘
```

*Use your knowledge of word parts and the review above to choose the answer that best defines the **boldface** word in each sentence.*

_____ 1. "The nurse looked at me with **disinterest** as I walked toward her station." (paragraph 1)

    a. fascination   c. fear

    b. approval   d. indifference

_____ 2. "I would have had to be pretty **insensitive** not to know." (paragraph 14)

    a. concerned   c. unhappy

    b. not aware   d. emotional

_____ 3. ". . . I can provide one living example of someone who made it and who came from what we now call a **disadvantaged** background." (paragraph 16)

    a. wealthy   c. poor

    b. privileged   d. unlimited

▶ Unusual Words/Understanding Idioms

*Use the meanings given below to write a sentence using the **boldface** phrase.*

1. The expression **letting someone off the hook** (paragraph 4) means to release someone from an embarrassing situation or to forgive someone for an embarrassing mistake.

    Your sentence: _____

    _____

2. The phrase **looking out for number one** (paragraph 17) means to be concerned only with yourself or your own wants and needs.

Your sentence: _____

_____

H. SELECTING A LEARNING/STUDY STRATEGY

Assume you will be tested on this reading on an upcoming exam. Evaluate the usefulness of the summaries you completed above. Which other paragraphs would be useful to summarize?

I. EXPLORING IDEAS THROUGH DISCUSSION AND WRITING

1. Do you think the writer's response to prejudice was typical? How do you think you would react in a similar situation?
2. Have you observed or experienced situations in which someone revealed prejudice? How did you or the person handle the situation?

J. BEYOND THE CLASSROOM TO THE WEB

Vist the Academy of Achievement Gallery's site for Ben Carson at http://www.achievement.org/autodoc/page/carlpro-1. Read his profile and his biography. Read or watch the interview and explore the photo gallery. After reviewing all this additional information, how does your view of Ben Carson change, if at all?

✔ **Tracking Your Progress**

Selection 3

Section	Number Correct	Score
A. Thesis and Main Ideas (6 items)	_____ x 5	_____
B. Details (5 items)	_____ x 4	_____
C. Organization and Transitions (2 items)	_____ x 2	_____
E. Inferred Meanings (3 items)	_____ x 4	_____
F. Thinking Critically (4 items)	_____ x 4	_____
G. Vocabulary		
1. Context (4 items)	_____ x 3	_____
2. Word Parts (3 items)	_____ x 2	_____
	TOTAL SCORE	_____%

11 Communication/Speech

The field of **communication** is concerned with the exchange of information between individuals and groups through speaking, writing, or nonverbal communication (body language, such as gestures). Communication may be interpersonal, such as communication between two persons; may occur within a small group, such as a group of friends or a class discussion; and may also be public, in which a speaker addresses an audience. Communication skills are important for success in college, for finding and keeping a rewarding job, and for building and maintaining healthy, strong relationships with family, friends, and coworkers.

By studying communication, you will come to understand those around you and exchange ideas with them more effectively. "Reality TV: Race to the Bottom" reports the results of a research study analysing reality TV. "War: The Mother of All Words" explains how new words enter our language. In "Relationships and Technology" you will read about online dating and discover its advantages and disadvantages. Use the following tips when reading in the communication field.

TIPS FOR READINGS IN COMMUNICATION/SPEECH

- **Pay attention to processes.** In "War: The Mother of All Words," pay attention to the process by which new words enter our language.
- **Pay attention to principles—rules that govern how communication works.** When reading "Reality TV: Race to the Bottom," look for the principles on which reality TV is based.
- **Notice theories (explanations that attempt to describe how or why something happens).** In "Relationships and Technology" the author explains **how** online dating Web sites affect relationships.
- **Be alert for cultural differences.** Not all cultures and ethnic groups follow the same conventions and theories. Do you think online matchmaking described in "Relationships and Technology" would be considered appropriate in all cultures?
- **Pay attention to language and terminology.** In "War: The Mother of All Words" the author explores use of language associated with war.
- **Think critically.** As you read theories, ask challenging questions, such as "Does this information fit with what I already know and have experienced?" For example, when reading "Reality TV: Race to the Bottom," think of reality TV programs you have seen. Did they contain a great deal of the material the author considers offensive?

SELECTION
4

Reality TV: Race to the Bottom
Aubree Rankin

This selection appears on the Web site of the Parents Television Council. It reports on a study of reality TV carried out by this organization.

> ### PREVIEWING THE READING

Using the steps listed on page 29, preview the reading selection. When you have finished, complete the following items.

1. What is the subject of this selection?

   _____

2. List some of the shows mentioned.

   _____

3. List one reason the authors do not approve of reality TV shows.

   _____

 ### MAKING CONNECTIONS

These students are watching a reality TV show. What characteristics of reality TV make it appealing? Why do some people object to it?

> **READING TIP**
>
> *As you read, identify the purpose of the study, how it was conducted, its results, and the recommendations the authors make.*

Reality TV: Race to the Bottom

1   Reality shows have proliferated over the past five years. Today, reality shows constitute 13% of broadcast programming, up from 4% in 1999, according to a recent analysis by media negotiator Magna Global. Reality series are challenging the supremacy of top-rated scripted series; in the February 2004 sweeps, Donald Trump's reality series *The Apprentice* topped *C.S.I.* in the ratings.

2   Reality programs thrive on one-upmanship. ABC's *The Bachelor* lets a man pick a bride out of a group of single, attractive women hand-picked by the producers. Fox's *Married by America* lets the audience pick the bride. Producers of *Big Brother* hope for a "hook-up" they can televise nationally. Fox forces couples to "hook up" or get kicked off the island on *Paradise Hotel.* Every time a reality show ups the ante with outrageous behavior or shocking footage, it's encouraging subsequent shows to add more skin, more twists, and more shocking behavior, resulting in a perpetual race to the bottom.

3   There are also legitimate concerns about the messages inherent in many of these competitions. Television serves as a model for social behavior and interaction, especially for young viewers, many of whom pick up social cues from how they see their favorite TV personalities behave. Consider the lessons those children are learning from reality programs. "What you learn from a program like [*Survivor*] is to be a skunk, to be conniving and self-seeking. These are things most parents and society generally tried to teach us we're not supposed to be. But the reward doesn't go to the best person, it goes to the biggest rat," according to Robert Peters, president of Morality in Media.[1]

4   Beyond content concerns, there is also widespread concern about the voyeuristic aspects of today's reality shows. Cultural criminologist Mike Presdee of the University of Sunderland says of the trend, "We're becoming a nation of voyeurs. Is it cheap titillation, cheap entertainment? In *Big Brother*, people want to know if they're having

---

[1]McMullen, Cary. "Final Four: How Ethical is Reality TV?" *Lakeland Ledger.* D1. August 23, 2000.

sex or want to watch them going to the toilet. We know that those who brutalize others are brutalized in the process, even if it means they might well be willing to personally humiliate somebody, because they have seen it being done and think it is good fun. It is good fun, but it is also a form of mental cruelty. Domestic violence is not just physical, it includes mental violence, so what is the difference? Being cruel to somebody isn't just beating them up."[2]

5   There is also growing consensus within the medical community that reality TV is bad for the contestants as well. Newcastle University (UK) psychologist Joan Harvey told the Newcastle Journal that she believes reality-show participants don't realize just what they're getting themselves into when they sign on to do these shows. "The contestants go into it with a certain amount of ambition but an awful lot of naivete. They are probably not as extrovert [sic] as they perceive themselves to be. They are more vulnerable than they think. When your self-esteem does take a knock it can be quite catastrophic."[3] Indeed it can. One contestant voted off the original Swedish version of Survivor committed suicide a short time after he returned home, prompting the producers of many reality programs to keep psychologists on staff.[4]

6   Reality TV is a trend that's influencing all other areas of popular entertainment, and because such programs purport to show real people in real situations, the content can be far more explicit. Even the most envelope-pushing TV dramas wouldn't dare to use the sort of language that is constantly employed by contestants on some reality TV shows. Likewise, TV viewers watching sexual situations on scripted series know they're just watching two actors pantomiming physical intimacy. That's clearly not the case when sexual situations are presented on a reality series, making viewers voyeurs in a very real sense. For these reasons, the **PTC** chose to make television reality programs the subject of a second comprehensive content analysis.

PTC
Parents Television
Council, an
organization that
seeks decency and
responsibility in the
entertainment field.

7   How offensive has reality TV become? To answer that question, PTC analysts studied the first four episodes of twenty-nine different reality series airing on the seven broadcast networks (ABC, CBS, Fox, NBC, ITV, UPN, and the WB) between June 1, 2002, and August 31, 2003, for a total of 114.5 hours of reality programming, and found not only that reality series have grown raunchier over time, but also that they are qualitatively and quantitatively coarser than their scripted counterparts.

Major Findings

8   During our study period, there were an alarming 1,135 instances of foul language, 492 instances of sex, and 30 instances of violence logged on 114.5 hours of broadcast reality shows, for a total of 1,657 instances of offensive content, an average of 14.5 instances of offensive content per hour. This represents a 52.6% increase from the per-hour rate of offensive content on broadcast reality shows documented in the PTC's last study of the genre, *Harsh Reality,* released in October 2002.

[2]Morrison, Nick. "Can Reality TV Really Damage Your Health?" *The Northern Echo.* p. 10. June 9, 2003.
[3]Mapplebeck, Will. "How Reality TV Can Damage Your Health." Newcastle.co.uk. October 24, 2003.
[4]Goode, Erica. "Survivor's Nobler Roots: Psychologists Have Long Been Studying How Situations Influence Our Behaviour." *The Gazette.* A6. August 27, 2000.

9   To put this data in context, the PTC quantified the amount of sex and foul language on scripted broadcast series during the first two weeks of the November 2002 sweeps. Sex and foul language combined occurred on scripted series at a rate of 10.7 instances per hour, meaning there are on average 3.5 more instances per hour of sex and foul language on reality series than on scripted series.

10   Other findings include:

- The amount of bleeped profanities per hour has increased by 273% since the 2002 study. Verbal sexual references were also more frequent in recent reality series, increasing from 0.9 instances per hour to 3.31 instances per hour, an increase of 373% since 2002.
- Words and phrases that as yet the PTC has not recorded on scripted broadcast series were used on reality shows included in this study. In both instances the words were bleeped, but viewers were clearly able to decipher what was said.
- The two worst broadcast reality shows overall were CBS's *Big Brother 4,* with 41.8 instances of objectionable content per hour, and the WB's *The Surreal Life,* with 37.5.
- While innuendo far surpassed all other forms of sexual content in this study, nudity was the second-most-frequent type of sexual content on reality TV shows, followed by anatomical references and verbal or visual (images of pornographic magazines, for example) references to pornography.
- The PTC also counted sixteen instances of sexual activity on reality programs included in this study; two spoken references to masturbation; eighteen spoken references to kinky sexual practices; and two implied instances of oral sex.
- Reality series airing on the WB and UPN had the highest levels of offensive content, with 25.4 and 24.2 instances of offensive content per hour, respectively.
- The WB had the most foul-mouthed reality shows, with a per-hour rate of 20.1 instances of foul language.
- Reality series appearing on UPN contained the most sexual content, with 10.1 instances per hour.
- The WB's reality series contained the most violent content, with 1.7 instances of violence per hour of programming.
- Although CBS aired the most offensive reality series (*Big Brother 4*), it also aired some of the cleanest reality programs on broadcast TV.

Recommendations

11   If children are influenced by behaviors they see modeled by actors and actresses on scripted programs—and there's ample research to show that they are—common sense dictates that they will be equally influenced by behaviors they see modeled by real people on unscripted programs. Networks need to be held accountable for the dangerous and irresponsible messages they are communicating to young fans of the reality genre.

12   Sponsors also need to be held accountable for the messages they are helping to underwrite, particularly those companies that pay to have their products strategically placed on reality shows or underwrite prize competitions.

FCC   13   Networks are clearly pushing the envelope with reality series, so the **FCC** needs
Federal   to be vigilant in enforcing broadcast decency standards. Producers make choices
Communications   when editing the hundreds of hours of raw footage into each half-hour or hour-long
Commission, the   episode. When those producers choose to leave in explicit language or graphic con-
federal agency that   tent, they need to be held accountable every bit as much as the producers of
regulates television,   scripted series.
radio, satellite,
wire, and cable
broadcasting.

> **A.   UNDERSTANDING THE THESIS AND OTHER MAIN IDEAS**

Select the best answer.

_____ 1. The central thesis of this selection is that
   a. children should not watch reality TV.
   b. scripted programs are less offensive than reality shows.
   c. reality shows should be removed from broadcast television.
   d. people should be concerned about the content of reality TV shows.

_____ 2. The authors' primary purpose is to
   a. convince readers that reality TV contains questionable content.
   b. urge readers to contact sponsors, networks, and the FCC about the content of reality TV.
   c. present both sides of an argument about reality TV.
   d. compare and contrast the content of scripted and reality programs.

_____ 3. The main idea of paragraph 3 is that
   a. parents need to teach their children what is right.
   b. reality TV teaches children the wrong lessons.
   c. negative behavior is rewarded on reality shows.
   d. children should not watch *Survivor.*

_____ 4. The purpose of paragraph 7 is to
   a. list the networks that show offensive programs.
   b. ask how offensive reality TV has become.
   c. describe how the PTC study was conducted.
   d. give data on the offensive aspects of reality TV.

_____ 5. In the "Recommendations" section, the authors

    a. remind parents to talk to their children about TV choices.

    b. suggest that sponsors be held accountable for the content of the programs that they endorse.

    c. argue that the networks do not have control over what footage ends up on the screen.

    d. conclude that the FCC has been negligent in controlling offensive programming.

B. IDENTIFYING DETAILS

Indicate whether each statement is true (T) or false (F).

_____ 1. There are fewer reality shows on TV now than in 1999.

_____ 2. Many reality programs have psychologists on staff.

_____ 3. On scripted shows, sexual intimacy is pantomimed.

_____ 4. *Big Brother 4* was found to be the most offensive reality show.

_____ 5. WB had the least amount of profanity on its reality shows.

C. RECOGNIZING METHODS OF ORGANIZATION AND TRANSITIONS

Complete the following statements by filling in the blanks.

1. List two words or phrases used in paragraphs 3–5 that signal a transition.

    _____ .

2. In paragraph 6 the authors use the _____ organizational pattern to discuss reality TV and scripted shows.

D. REVIEWING AND ORGANIZING IDEAS: SUMMARIZING

Complete the following summary of paragraphs 11–13 by filling in the missing words or phrases.

Because _____ television programs affect the _____ of children, _____ TV will influence it as well. Many of the messages from reality TV are _____ and _____. _____ should be held accountable for the _____ content that they transmit. _____ and _____ are also responsible for what goes on the air. Finally, the _____ should be stricter in the enforcement of broadcast _____ standards.

➤ E. FIGURING OUT INFERRED MEANINGS

Indicate whether each statement is true (T) or false (F).

_____ 1. It is likely that reality shows will continue to grow in number on broadcast television.

_____ 2. Most children object to the offensive nature of reality TV shows.

_____ 3. It can be inferred that the PTC will study reality television again.

_____ 4. Objectionable content can be defined.

_____ 5. It can be inferred that the broadcast networks will continue using profanity if their ratings continue to rise.

➤ F. THINKING CRITICALLY

Select the best answer.

_____ 1. The PTC conducted the study because it
   a. wanted to see if objectionable content had increased since the original survey was performed.
   b. felt reality TV has not been properly researched.
   c. thought reality TV needed to be compared with scripted TV.
   d. was concerned about the future of reality TV.

_____ 2. The PTC studied how offensive reality TV has become by
   a. sending out surveys to television audiences.
   b. reading articles about reality TV.
   c. talking to scientists about objectionable television programming.
   d. watching many hours of television and recording instances of inappropriate content.

_____ 3. The report includes quotes from various individuals in order to
   a. impress readers.
   b. provide expert evidence to support the thesis.
   c. offer conflicting viewpoints.
   d. compare opinions.

_____ 4. The findings of the study
   a. demonstrate that reality TV contains what PTC considers objectionable material.
   b. offer data that do not support the PTC's thesis.
   c. are not relevant to the main idea of the report.
   d. cannot be challenged.

_____ 5. The overall tone of the report is

    a. disapproving.

    b. angry.

    c. malicious.

    d. frustrated.

G. BUILDING VOCABULARY

Context

Using context and a dictionary, if necessary, determine the meaning of each word as it is used in the selection.

_____ 1. proliferated (paragraph 1)

    a. increased in number   c. changed appearance

    b. improved   d. expanded

_____ 2. voyeuristic (paragraph 4)

    a. spying on for pleasure   c. glaring, staring

    b. watching from a distance   d. stalking

_____ 3. titillation (paragraph 4)

    a. pleasure   c. excitement

    b. amusement   d. fun

_____ 4. innuendo (paragraph 10)

    a. indirect remark   c. idea

    b. distraction   d. false impression

Word Parts

> **A REVIEW OF PREFIXES**
> **PER-** means *through*
> **CATA-** means *apart, down*
> **INTER-** means *between*

Use your knowledge of word parts and the review above to fill in the blanks in the following sentences.

1. A *perpetual* (paragraph 2) worry is one that carries _____ all aspects of your life, without interruption.

2. *Interaction* (paragraph 3) takes place when communication and sharing occurs _____ two or more people or between groups of people.

3. When a *catastrophic* event (paragraph 5) strikes, everything is torn completely _____ because of some sort of disaster.

➤ Unusual Words/Understanding Idioms

Use the meanings given below to write a sentence using the **boldface** *word or phrase.*

1. When someone acts like a **skunk** (paragraph 3), he or she is being obnoxious and hateful.

   Your sentence: _____

   _____

2. If a speaker **purports** (paragraph 6) to be an expert on a topic, she claims to know a great deal about the subject.

   Your sentence: _____

   _____

3. A company that **underwrites** (paragraph 12) an event gives it financial support and agrees with its purpose.

   Your sentence: _____

   _____

➤ H. SELECTING A LEARNING/STUDY STRATEGY

Select the best answer.

_____ Which of the following strategies would be most useful in preparing to answer the following essay question: "Explain why some people might find reality TV offensive."

   a. reread the report

   b. visualize a reality TV show

   c. use index cards to recall the facts about reality TV

   d. write a paragraph summarizing the main reasons

➤ I. EXPLORING IDEAS THROUGH DISCUSSION AND WRITING

1. Discuss reality TV. Which shows do you watch, if any, and why?

2. Take a poll among your friends, family members, and fellow students asking if they watch reality TV and, if so, which show is their favorite. Also ask if they find the material objectionable and if they think children should watch

reality TV. Write an essay that summarizes your experience and results. Compare your data with that of others in your class and that of the PTC study and other studies.

3. Discuss the different definitions for "objectionable content." Why is it so difficult to come to a consensus on this topic?

J. BEYOND THE CLASSROOM TO THE WEB

Visit the Web site for the Parents Television Council at **http://www.parentstv.org/.** *Explore the council's campaigns, publications, and other activities. How does your new knowledge of the organization affect your opinion of the reality TV report?*

✔ Tracking Your Progress

Selection 4

Section	Number Correct	Score
A. Thesis and Main Ideas (5 items)	_____ x 5	_____
B. Details (5 items)	_____ x 4	_____
C. Organization and Transitions (2 items)	_____ x 2	_____
E. Inferred Meanings (5 items)	_____ x 4	_____
F. Thinking Critically (5 items)	_____ x 4	_____
G. Vocabulary		
1. Context (4 items)	_____ x 2	_____
2. Word Parts (3 items)	_____ x 1	_____
	TOTAL SCORE	_____ %

SELECTION 5   War: The Mother of All Words

Brian Faler

This reading from the *National Journal* describes how new words enter our language, often through the experience of war. Read it to find out the origins of some common words and phrases, as well as some new words that you may not know.

> ## PREVIEWING THE READING

Using the steps listed on page 29, preview the reading selection. When you have finished, complete the following items.

1. What is the topic of this selection?

   _____

2. List four war-related words or phrases that the author mentions in this selection.

   a. _____

   b. _____

   c. _____

   d. _____

MAKING CONNECTIONS

The war in Iraq has had many effects on the lives of Americans as well as the citizens of Iraq. How do you think the war has changed our vocabulary?

lexicographers/ lexicon
people who write or compile dictionaries; the vocabulary of a language; a dictionary

kamikazes
Japanese pilots assigned to make suicidal crashes on targets

grunts
infantrymen, or foot soldiers, in the U.S. military

madrassa
a school or learning center that provides a general education and teaches the religious fundamentals of Islam

burqa
a veil or head covering worn by Muslim women

hawala
an informal and unregulated banking system used primarily in the Middle East, Africa, and Asia

Wahhabism
a Sunni fundamentalist Islamic movement and the dominant form of Islam in Saudi Arabia and Qatar

euphemistic
using a mild or pleasant expression to describe something unpleasant or offensive

> **READING TIP**

This reading introduces us to vocabulary that has its origins in a war setting. As you read, write down on a piece of paper each war-related word or term along with its definition, if it is given.

War: The Mother of All Words

1   When Christi Parsons needed an adjective to help describe a recent Elvis Presley impersonation contest, she turned to a rather curious phrase: "Elvis's moves seem to possess a weapons-grade charisma that can be passed on full-strength to imitators," the Chicago Tribune reporter wrote. Two days later, her colleague Steve Rosenbloom wrote of hockey legend Bobby Hull's "weapons-grade slap shot."

2   Do we have a new synonym for "potent"? Two newspaper articles may not make for a trend, but lexicographers and linguists say it would not be surprising if some of the language of the war on terrorism becomes a part of our permanent lexicon. Wars, they note, have always given us new words—from the "kamikazes" of World War II to the "grunts" of the Vietnam War to the Gulf War superlative "the mother of all . . . ," coined by Iraqi leader Saddam Hussein, when he promised "the mother of all battles." Now experts are poring over the language of the war on terrorism, looking for lasting contributions to the English tongue.

3   There would seem to be any number of candidates. For the past five months, the nation has been awash in war-related lingo. Our newfound interest in Islamic cultures—along with the omnipresent question "Why do they hate us?"—has introduced us to the madrassa and the burqa, hawala and Wahhabism. The threat of another attack has pushed the rarified language of national security—with its "dirty bombs" and "sleeper cells"—into everyday conversations. And the ongoing efforts to protect airline passengers have given us nouns such as "bag-matching" and the verb "wanding," which refers to the use of handheld metal detectors.

4   The American Dialect Society, an organization of lexicographers, recently announced the results of its widely reported Words of the Year contest. Among the picks: "Daisy cutter," the grim nickname for the 15,000-pound bomb that explodes just above ground level, was named most euphemistic. "Shuicide bomber" was dubbed the most creative. Least likely to succeed: "Osamaniac," a virtually unpronounceable word that supposedly describes someone who is sexually attracted to Osama bin Laden. "Let's roll," the phrase coined by Todd Beamer, a passenger on United Airlines Flight 93 who helped launch the attack against the hijackers over Pennsylvania, was named most inspirational. The society's word of the year: "9/11."

5   But as the group readily admits, its contest is only for fun and "to get our names in the newspapers," says its one-time president, R. W. Bailey. And the society's choices do not always stand the test of time. In 1990, for example, it named "Bushlips" the word of the year. That largely forgotten term was defined as "insincere political rhetoric" and referred to the former president's broken promise not to raise taxes.

6   The task of deciding which words actually make it into dictionaries, their editors say, is much more painstaking. "A lot of new words are just flashes in the pan," says Joseph Pickett, executive editor of the American Heritage Dictionary. "They last a few months and are never heard from again. And you don't want to fill up the dictionary with those because [it] will look ridiculous in five years."

7   And for collections with limited space—usually college dictionaries—adding new words, Pickett says, often means dropping others. Back in 1999, he thought he had a perfect candidate to drop from the 2000 edition—a seemingly inconsequential word not in general use. "Of all the things in the world, this has to be among the most trivial," Pickett says with a laugh, recounting his arguments to dump the word that, months later, during the Florida recount, became ubiquitous. The word was "chad."

chad
a tiny bit of paper
that is punched
from a ballot using
a punch-type
mechanical voting
machine

8   With all of that in mind—and with eight to 10 years separating individual editions of dictionaries—editors say that the only way to be sure of their choices is to simply wait and see which words take hold in the public's imagination. Pickett and others are willing to make a few predictions, though. They say that of all the ways of referring to the terrorist attacks—September 11, Terrible Tuesday, Black Tuesday, and, in Spanish, Negro Once—"9/11" seems to have become the most popular and is most likely to be included in their collections. They also say the war has given the phrase "Ground Zero" a new definition—the site of a disaster—that will also probably be included. Previously, the phrase referred only to the area immediately beneath a nuclear explosion.

9   More broadly, editors say, compared with previous conflicts, the war on terrorism has added relatively little to the language—and, they add, that's a good thing. Previous campaigns gave us so many words because, in part, the conflicts were so long—there was simply more time and many more experiences from which to develop new words and phrases, says Geoffrey Nunberg, usage editor of the American Heritage Dictionary.

10   And many of those words started out as slang among soldiers on the ground. "Basket case," for example, was originally used by British soldiers during World War I to refer to quadruple amputees; "SNAFU," an acronym for the phrase, "situation normal: all fouled up," was coined by American GIs during World War II. But this war, as Nunberg notes, has not gone on long and has involved relatively few troops. "Let's hope it doesn't have an effect on the language, because that will mean it's having a much bigger effect on American culture than it has," he says.

➤ A.   UNDERSTANDING THE THESIS AND OTHER MAIN IDEAS

Select the best answer.

_____ 1. The central thesis of the selection is that

   a. dictionary editors face a difficult task in choosing which words to include.

   b. many words and phrases in the English language have their origins in war.

   c. war-related words and phrases typically do not become a permanent part of the lexicon.

   d. the current war on terrorism has not resulted in any lasting additions to the language.

_____ 2. The author's primary purpose is to describe
   a. how words enter and become part of the language.
   b. what qualifies a word to be included in a dictionary.
   c. who decides what is included in a dictionary.
   d. which war-related words are most popular.

_____ 3. The topic of paragraph 2 is
   a. World War II.
   b. the Vietnam War.
   c. Saddam Hussein.
   d. war-related words.

_____ 4. The main idea of paragraph 3 is that
   a. the U.S. has a newfound interest in Islamic cultures.
   b. words from the war on terrorism may become part of our language.
   c. national security has become a topic of conversation.
   d. certain cultures seem to hate Americans.

_____ 5. The main idea of paragraph 4 is expressed in the
   a. first sentence.
   b. second sentence.
   c. third sentence.
   d. last sentence.

_____ 6. The American Dialect Society's word of the year was
   a. "daisy cutter."
   b. "shuicide bomber."
   c. "Osamaniac."
   d. "9/11."

_____ 7. The main idea of paragraph 7 is expressed in the
   a. first sentence.
   b. second sentence.
   c. third sentence.
   d. last sentence.

_____ 8. The statement that best expresses the main idea of paragraph 9 is
   a. "Compared with previous conflicts, the war on terrorism has added relatively little to the language."
   b. "That's a good thing."

c. "Previous campaigns gave us more words because the conflicts were so long."

d. "There were many more experiences from which to develop new words and phrases."

➤ B. IDENTIFYING DETAILS

Match each of the terms in Column A with its meaning in Column B.

Column A	Column B
_____ 1. weapons-grade (paragraph 1)	a. a bomb that explodes just above ground level
_____ 2. wanding (paragraph 3)	b. potent or powerful
_____ 3. daisy cutter (paragraph 4)	c. a chaotic situation (situation normal: all fouled up)
_____ 4. Ground Zero (paragraph 8)	d. the use of handheld metal detectors in airport security
_____ 5. snafu (paragraph 10)	e. the site of a disaster, or the area immediately beneath a nuclear explosion

➤ C. RECOGNIZING METHODS OF ORGANIZATION AND TRANSITIONS

Select the best answer.

_____ 1. The organizational pattern the author uses in paragraph 2 to tell about new words resulting from wars is

a. listing.

b. cause and effect.

c. definition.

d. comparison and contrast.

_____ 2. In paragraph 4, the organizational pattern the author uses to report the results of the word of the year contest is

a. cause and effect.

b. listing.

c. chronological order.

d. process.

_____ 3. The transitional word or phrase in paragraph 5 that indicates the author is going to illustrate his ideas is

a. but.

b. referred to.

        c. for example.

        d. defined as.

_____ 4. The transitional word in paragraph 8 that indicates that additional information will follow is

        a. though.

        b. also.

        c. previously.

        d. only.

_____ 5. In paragraphs 9–10, the author uses the comparison and contrast organizational pattern to discuss the difference between

        a. conflicts and wars.

        b. formal language and slang.

        c. World War I and World War II.

        d. previous conflicts and the war on terrorism.

_____ 6. In paragraph 10, the author uses the transitional phrase "for example" to

        a. contrast British and American soldiers.

        b. indicate the passage of time between the two world wars.

        c. illustrate slang among soldiers on the ground.

        d. show the cause and effect of war-related language.

▶ D. REVIEWING AND ORGANIZING IDEAS: PARAPHRASING

Use the following list of words to complete the paraphrase of paragraph 6.

dictionary	years	Joseph Pickett	include
American Heritage	difficult	disappear	absurd
editors	popular		

Dictionary _____ say that choosing which words to _____ is a difficult process. According to _____, the executive editor of the _____ Dictionary, many new words are temporarily popular but then _____. If the _____ contained words like that, it would seem _____ in five _____.

➤ **E. FIGURING OUT INFERRED MEANINGS**

Indicate whether each statement is true (T) or false (F).

_____ 1. It can be inferred that some popular words never appear in dictionaries.

_____ 2. Language experts look only at war-related language when they are searching for new words.

_____ 3. Many Americans began to be interested in Islamic cultures because of the war on terrorism.

_____ 4. The term "Osamaniac" will appear as a new word in the next edition of most dictionaries.

_____ 5. The American Dialect Society is very serious about its Words of the Year contest.

➤ **F. THINKING CRITICALLY**

Select the best answer.

_____ 1. The central thesis of the selection is supported primarily by
a. statistics.
b. personal experience.
c. expert opinions.
d. analogies.

_____ 2. The tone of the selection can best be described as
a. arrogant.
b. informative.
c. excited.
d. solemn.

_____ 3. Of the following words in paragraph 3, the one with a negative connotation is
a. candidate.
b. newfound.
c. threat.
d. language.

_____ 4. The term "daisy cutter" is euphemistic because it
a. uses a pleasant-sounding name to describe a bomb.
b. reveals exactly what the bomb is intended to do.
c. tells the opposite of what the bomb does.
d. makes fun of cutting daisies.

_____ 5. Of the following statements based on the selection, which one is an opinion?

   a. The American Dialect Society recently announced the results of its Words of the Year contest. (paragraph 4)

   b. Eight to ten years separate individual editions of dictionaries. (paragraph 8)

   c. They say that of all the ways of referring to the terrorist attacks, "9/11" seems to have become the most popular. (paragraph 8)

   d. Many of those words started out as slang among soldiers on the ground. (paragraph 10)

_____ 6. When the former president of the American Dialect Society says the contest is "to get our names in the newspapers" (paragraph 5), he is being

   a. earnest.

   b. humorous.

   c. indignant.

   d. serious.

_____ 7. The author includes the story about the word "chad" in paragraph 7 in order to illustrate that

   a. the process of adding and dropping words in dictionaries can be tricky.

   b. no words should be dropped from a dictionary when others are added.

   c. some words do not belong in the dictionary.

   d. politics should not affect which words are included in a dictionary.

G.   BUILDING VOCABULARY

Context

Using context and a dictionary, if necessary, determine the meaning of each word as it is used in the selection.

_____ 1. charisma (paragraph 1)

   a. appearance   c. personal magnetism

   b. ability   d. imitation

_____ 2. rarified (paragraph 3)

   a. unusual   c. simple

   b. cheerful   d. mistaken

_____ 3. rhetoric (paragraph 5)

    a. question   c. style

    b. language   d. payment

_____ 4. painstaking (paragraph 6)

    a. important   c. lengthy

    b. uncomfortable   d. careful

_____ 5. inconsequential (paragraph 7)

    a. uncertain   c. unimportant

    b. out of order   d. made up

_____ 6. ubiquitous (paragraph 7)

    a. not allowed   c. rewarding

    b. found everywhere d. invisible

➤ Word Parts

> **A REVIEW OF PREFIXES AND SUFFIXES**
> **SUPER-** means *above*
> **OMNI-** means *all*
> **QUAD-** means *four*
> **IN-** means *not*
> **-IST** means *one who*

Use your knowledge of word parts and the review above to fill in the blanks in the following sentences.

1. A *linguist* (paragraph 2) is _____ specializes in languages or linguistics.

2. The phrase "mother of all battles" is a *superlative* (paragraph 2) because it is describing a battle that is _____ all others in its intensity.

3. A person who is *insincere* (paragraph 5) is someone who is _____ serious or honest about his or her feelings.

4. A question that is *omnipresent* (paragraph 3) seems to be everywhere or in _____ places.

5. A person who is a *quadruple* (paragraph 10) amputee has had _____ limbs amputated or cut off.

➤ **Unusual Words/Understanding Idioms**

Use the meanings given below to write a sentence using the **boldface** *word or phrase.*

1. A person who has **coined** (paragraph 2) a word or phrase has created or invented it.

   Your sentence: _____

   _____

2. When someone refers to the English **tongue** (paragraph 2), he or she is talking about language.

   Your sentence: _____

   _____

3. When something does not **stand the test of time** (paragraph 5), it does not endure long enough to be considered serious or worthy.

   Your sentence: _____

   _____

4. People or things that are described as **flashes in the pan** (paragraph 6) seem to promise great success but fail or disappear.

   Your sentence: _____

   _____

➤ **H.   SELECTING A LEARNING/STUDY STRATEGY**

Assume you will be tested on this reading on an upcoming exam. Evaluate the usefulness of the word list you created while reading as well as the paraphrase you completed. What other study aids would help you prepare for a test on this reading?

➤ **I.   EXPLORING IDEAS THROUGH DISCUSSION AND WRITING**

1. This article first appeared during the early days of the war on terrorism, in 2002. Discuss new words or phrases—war-related or not—that have appeared since then. For each term, decide whether you think it will become part of our permanent lexicon or be considered a "flash in the pan."

2. Make a prediction about language. In the next ten years, where do you think some of the words and phrases joining our lexicon will come from? Consider various aspects of culture, including popular music, movies, politics, war, technology, and so on.

➤ J. BEYOND THE CLASSROOM TO THE WEB

Visit the Web site **http://www.dtic.mil/doctrine/jel/doddict/** *and explore the Department of Defense Dictionary. Choose five words that you use regularly, but have different meanings in the military. Find five words that are surprising, disturbing, or particularly interesting to you. Explain your choices.*

✔ Tracking Your Progress

Selection 5

Section	Number Correct		Score
A. Thesis and Main Ideas (8 items)	_____	x 4	_____
B. Details (5 items)	_____	x 3	_____
C. Organization and Transitions (6 items)	_____	x 1	_____
E. Inferred Meanings (5 items)	_____	x 3	_____
F. Thinking Critically (7 items)	_____	x 3	_____
G. Vocabulary			
1. Context (6 items)	_____	x 1	_____
2. Word Parts (5 items)	_____	x 1	_____
	TOTAL SCORE		_____%

SELECTION 6

Relationships and Technology

Joseph A. DeVito

Taken from a textbook titled *Interpersonal Messages: Communication and Relationship Skills,* this reading selection discusses the influence of technology on interpersonal relationships.

Preview
ABDG
 # 11
Fully annotated

PREVIEWING THE READING

Using the steps listed on page 29, preview the reading selection. When you have finished, complete the following items.

1. The subject of this selection is ——————————————————————

2. List two questions you expect to be able to answer after reading this selection:

   a. ————————————————————————————————

   b. ————————————————————————————————

MAKING CONNECTIONS

How do you typically use the Internet? Estimate what percentage of the total amount of time you spend on the Internet is spent in each of the following categories: social, work, school, entertainment, or news.

READING TIP

As you read, be sure to highlight the advantages and disadvantages of online relationships.

Relationships and Technology

1   Perhaps even more obvious than culture is the influence of technology on interpersonal relationships. Clearly, online interpersonal relationships are on the increase. The number of Internet users is rapidly increasing, and commercial websites devoted to

helping people meet other people are proliferating, making it especially easy to develop online relationships. Such websites as American Singles (**www.americansingles.com**) Friend Finder (**www.friendfinder.com**), Date (**www.date.com**), Match (**www.match.com**), Yahoo! Personals (**www.personals.yahoo**), Lavalife (**www.lavalife.com**), and Where Singles Meet (**www.wheresinglesmeet.com**) number their members in the millions, making it especially likely that you'll find someone you'd enjoy dating.

2   And not surprisingly, there are websites (for example, **www.comparedatingwebsites.com** and **www.homeandfamilyreview.com/dating.htm**) that offer comparisons of the various dating websites, distinguishing between those that are best for serious daters who are looking for lifetime commitment from those that are for people who want to find someone for casual dating. Lavalife, for example, has a pull down menu where you can indicate whether you want a casual date, a relationship, or an intimate encounter. And of course there are dating websites for different affectional orientations and different religious preferences.

3   Some dating websites—**eharmony.com** and **perfectmatch.com** are perhaps the most notable—have members complete extensive scientific questionnaires about their preferences and personalities which helps further in successfully matching people.

4   Some of these websites, for example, Yahoo! Personals and Friend Finder, give free trials so you can test the systems before registering or subscribing. And, to make these websites even more inviting, many of them offer chat rooms, dating and relationship advice, newsletters, and self-tests about love, relationships and dating.

5   Clearly, many people are turning to the Internet to find a friend or romantic partner. And, as you probably know, college students are making the most of sites such as Facebook.com and MySpace.com to meet other students on their own campus. In one study of MOOs (online role-playing games), 93.6 percent of the users formed ongoing friendships and romantic relationships. Some people use the Internet as their only means of interaction; others use it as a way of begining a relationship and intend to supplement computer talk later with photographs, phone calls, and face-to-face meetings. Interestingly, a *New York Times* survey found that by 2003 online dating was losing its earlier stigma as a last resort for losers.

6   Note that the importance of physical attractiveness enters the face-to-face relationship through nonverbal cues—you see the person's eyes, face, body—and you perceive such attractiveness immediately. In online relationships, just a few years ago, physical attractiveness could have only been signaled through words and descriptions. And in this situation the face-to-face encounter favored those who were physically attractive, whereas the online encounter favored those who were verbally adept at self-presentation. Today, with the numerous social networks such as MySpace, you can post your photo and reveal your attractiveness. Many of the online dating services (such as Friend Finder and Yahoo! Personals) now provide you with opportunities to not only post your photograph but also a voice introduction. Of course you still reveal more of yourself in face-to-face encounters, but the differences are clearly diminishing. Table A (p. 252) provides one example of the stages of Internet relationships.

7   Other research on Internet use finds that a large majority of users form new acquaintances, friendships, and romantic partnerships through the Internet. One study, published in 1996 found that almost two-thirds of newsgroup users had

affectional orientation an alternative term for sexual or romantic orientation

TABLE A ONLINE RELATIONSHIP STAGES

This table represents one attempt to identify the stages that people go through in Internet relationships. As you read down the table, consider how accurately this represents what you know of online relationships. How would you describe the way Internet relationships develop?

STAGE	BEHAVIOR
1. Curiosity	You explore and search for individuals through chat rooms and other online sources.
2. Investigation	You find out information about the individual.
3. Testing	You introduce various topics, looking for common ground.
4. Increasing frequency of contact	You increase the breadth and depth of your relationship.
5. Anticipation	You anticipate face-to-face interaction and wonder what that will bring.
6. Fantasy integration	You create a fantasy of what the person looks like and how the person behaves.
7. Face-to-face meeting	You meet face-to-face, and reality and fantasy meet.
8. Reconfiguration	You adjust the fantasy to the reality and may decide to end the relationship or to pursue it more vigorously.
9. Already separated	If you decide to maintain the relationship, you explore ways you can accomplish this.
10. Long-term relationship	You negotiate the new relationship, whether it will be maintained in its online form or in a new face-to-face form.

Source: This table is adapted from Leonard J. Shedletsky and Joan E. Aitken, *Human Communication on the Internet.* Published by Allyn and Bacon, Boston, MA. Copyright © by Pearson Education. By permission of the publisher. Adapted by permission of the publisher.

formed new relationships with someone they met online. Almost one-third said that they communicated with their partner at least three or four times a week; more than half communicated on a weekly basis. And, a study published in 2006 (Madden & Lenhart), found that 74 percent of Internet users who identify themselves as single and looking for romantic partners, used the Internet for this purpose.

8   Women, it seems are more likely to form relationships on the Internet than men. An early study showed that about 72 percent of women and 55 percent of men had formed personal relationships online. And women are more likely to use the Internet to deepen their interpersonal relationships.

9   As relationships develop on the Internet, **network convergence** occurs; that is, as a relationship between two people develops, they begin to share their network of other communicators with each other. This, of course, is similar to relationships formed through face-to-face contact. Online work groups also are on the increase and have been found to be more task oriented and more efficient than face-to-face groups. Online groups also provide a sense of belonging that may once have been thought possible only through face-to-face interactions.

Advantages of Online Relationships

10   There are many advantages to establishing relationships online. For example, online relationships are safe in terms of avoiding the potential for physical violence or sexually transmitted diseases. Unlike relationships established in face-to-face encounters, in which physical appearance tends to outweigh personality, relationships formed through Internet communication focus on your inner qualities first. Rapport and mutual self-disclosure become more important than physical attractiveness in promoting intimacy. And, contrary to some popular opinions, online relationships rely just as heavily on the ideals of trust, honesty, and commitment as do face-to-face relationships. Friendship and romantic interaction on the Internet are a natural boon to shut-ins and extremely shy people, for whom traditional ways of meeting someone are often difficult. Computer talk is empowering for those with "physical disabilities or disfigurements," for whom face-to-face interactions often are superficial and often end with withdrawal. By eliminating the physical cues, computer talk equalizes the interaction and doesn't put the disfigured person, for example, at an immediate disadvantage in a society in which physical attractiveness is so highly valued. On the Internet you're free to reveal as much or as little about your physical self as you wish, when you wish.

11   Another obvious advantage is that the number of people you can reach is so vast that it's relatively easy to find someone who matches what you're looking for. The situation is like finding a book that covers just what you need from a library of millions of volumes rather than from a collection holding only several thousand.

Disadvantages of Online Relationships

12   Of course, online relationships also have their disadvantages. For one thing, in many situations you can't see the other person. Unless you use a service that enables you to include photos or exchange photos or meet face-to-face, you won't know

"People are more frightened of being lonely than of being hungry, or being deprived of sleep, or having their sexual needs unfulfilled."—Fried Fromm Reichman

what the person looks like. Even if photos are posted or exchanged, how certain can you be that the photos are of the person or that they were taken recently? In addition, in most situations you can't hear the person's voice and this too hinders you as you seek to develop a total picture of the other person. Of course, you can always add an occasional phone call to give you this added information.

13   Online, people can present a false self with little chance of detection. For example, minors may present themselves as adults, and adults may present themselves as children in order to conduct illicit and illegal sexual communications and, perhaps, arrange meetings. Similarly, people can present themselves as poor when they're rich, as mature when they're immature, as serious and committed when they're just enjoying the online experience. Although people can also misrepresent themselves in face-to-face relationships, the fact that it's easier to do online probably accounts for greater frequency of misrepresentation in computer relationships.

14   Another potential disadvantage—though some might argue it is actually an advantage—is that computer interactions may become all-consuming and may substitute for face-to-face interpersonal relationships in a person's life.

15   Perhaps the clearest finding that emerges from all the research on face-to-face and online relationships is that people will seek out and find the relationship that works best for them at a given stage in their lives. For some that relationship will be online, for others face-to-face, for still others a combination. And just as people change, their relationship needs and wants also change, what works now may not work two years from now, and what doesn't work now may be exactly right in a few years.

Source: From DeVito, Joseph A. *Interpersonal Messages: Communication and Relationship Skills*, 1e. Published by Allyn and Bacon, Boston, MA. Copyright © 2008 by Pearson Education. Reprinted by permission of the publisher.

A.   UNDERSTANDING THE THESIS AND OTHER MAIN IDEAS

Select the best answer.

_____ 1. The author's primary purpose in this selection is to
  a. caution people to stay away from online relationships.
  b. promote specific Web sites for online relationships.
  c. describe how technology affects interpersonal relationships.
  d. identify cultural factors that influence interpersonal relationships.

_____ 2. The main idea of paragraph 1 is that
  a. culture has a major impact on interpersonal relationships.
  b. the number of Internet users is rapidly increasing.
  c. some Web sites are especially good at helping people meet.
  d. online interpersonal relationships are on the increase.

_____ 3. The main idea of paragraph 5 is expressed in the
  a. first sentence.
  b. second sentence.

     c. third sentence.

     d. last sentence.

_____ 4. The topic of paragraph 10 is

     a. online relationships.

     b. physical appearance.

     c. face-to-face interactions.

     d. self-disclosure.

_____ 5. The main idea of paragraph 12 is that online it is easy for people to

     a. establish meaningful relationships.

     b. detect misinformation about others.

     c. find someone who matches their needs.

     d. misrepresent themselves.

_____ 6. According to the selection, "network convergence" takes place when two people in an online relationship begin to

     a. look for common ground on a variety of topics.

     b. make plans to meet in person.

     c. share their network of other communicators.

     d. decide whether to continue the relationship.

B. IDENTIFYING DETAILS

Select the best answer.

_____ 1. According to the selection, the term MOOs refers to online

     a. newsgroups.

     b. dating services.

     c. role-playing games.

     d. chat rooms.

_____ 2. All of the following statements about online relationships are true *except*

     a. Men are more likely than women to form online relationships.

     b. Women are more likely than men to use the Internet to deepen their interpersonal relationships.

     c. Online work groups are more task oriented and more efficient than face-to-face groups.

     d. Online groups provide a sense of belonging for their members.

Based on the examples given in the selection, match each Web site in Column A with the description that corresponds to it in Column B.

Column A	Column B
_____ 3. friendfinder.com	a. provides comparisons of the various dating Web sites
_____ 4. lavalife.com	b. has a pull-down menu so users can indicate the type of relationship they seek
_____ 5. eharmony.com	c. allows users to post photographs and voice introductions
_____ 6. homeandfamilyreview.com	d. has members complete scientific questionnaires about their preferences and personalities

C.   RECOGNIZING METHODS OF ORGANIZATION AND TRANSITIONS

Complete the following statements by filling in the blanks.

In paragraph 6, the author uses the _____ organizational pattern to discuss the importance of physical appearance in face-to-face encounters versus online relationships. A transitional word that signals this pattern is _____.

D.   REVIEWING AND ORGANIZING IDEAS: MAPPING

Complete the following map of paragraphs 10–14 by filling in the blanks.

Online Relationships

Advantages	Disadvantages
1. The potential for _____ or sexually transmitted diseases is avoided.	1. Many times you will not be able to see what the person looks like.
2. The focus is on _____ rather than physical appearance.	2. It is hard to form a total picture of someone without seeing or hearing him or her.
3. Computer talk empowers those for whom traditional ways of meeting are difficult (for example, _____ _____).	3. People may _____ _____ (for example, minors posing as adults or adults posing as children).
4. Because such a huge number of people can be reached, it is relatively easy to find a match.	4. Computer interactions may become _____ and replace _____.

E.   FIGURING OUT INFERRED MEANINGS

Indicate whether each statement is true (T) or false (F).

_____ 1. Dating Web sites are designed for people who want a casual relationship only.

_____ 2. Many single Internet users look online for romantic partners.

_____ 3. For many people, online relationships are preferable to face-to-face interactions.

_____ 4. It can be inferred that most people looking for an online relationship are unconcerned about physical appearance.

F.   THINKING CRITICALLY

Select the best answer.

_____ 1. The author's tone can best be described as
   a. judgmental.
   b. lighthearted.
   c. concerned.
   d. objective.

_____ 2. The primary purpose of Table A is to
   a. compare the progression of online relationships with relationships based on traditional ways of meeting.
   b. recommend a series of steps for people who are thinking about entering an online relationship.
   c. identify the stages that people often go through in online relationships.
   d. describe acceptable and unacceptable behaviors for online dating.

_____ 3. Which one of the following words has a negative connotation?
   a. self-disclosure
   b. task oriented
   c. interactions
   d. disfigurements

_____ 4. The author supports his thesis by doing all of the following *except*
   a. giving examples and illustrations.
   b. describing his personal experience.
   c. citing research evidence.
   d. providing statistical support.

_____ 5. When the author states that "computer talk equalizes the interaction" (paragraph 10), he means that

    a. even people with limited technological skill can meet others online.

    b. people are more likely to be honest with each other online.

    c. people with physical issues are not at a disadvantage online.

    d. geographic distances do not matter in online relationships.

G. BUILDING VOCABULARY

▶ Context

Using context and a dictionary, if necessary, determine the meaning of each word as it is used in the selection.

_____ 1. proliferating (paragraph 1)

    a. ending

    b. growing

    c. altering

    d. continuing

_____ 2. stigma (paragraph 5)

    a. shame

    b. acceptance

    c. positive sign

    d. substitute

_____ 3. adept (paragraph 6)

    a. useless

    b. obvious

    c. skillful

    d. selfish

_____ 4. rapport (paragraph 10)

    a. information

    b. compatibility

    c. privacy

    d. safety

_____ 5. boon (paragraph 10)

    a. sound

    b. mistake

    c. emotion

    d. benefit

_____ 6. hinders (paragraph 11)

    a. invites in

    b. gets in the way

    c. pushes out

    d. delivers to

➤ Word Parts

A REVIEW OF PREFIXES
NON- means *not*
IL- means *not*
SUPER- means *above*
MIS- means *wrongly*

Match each word in Column A with its meaning in Column B. Write your answers in the spaces provided.

Column A

_____ 1. nonverbal

_____ 2. superficial

_____ 3. illicit

_____ 4. misrepresent

Column B

a. on the surface

b. give wrong or misleading information

c. not spoken

d. not permitted

➤ H. SELECTING A LEARNING/STUDY STRATEGY

Evaluate the effectiveness of the map you completed showing the advantages and disadvantages of online relationships. How else might you organize the material in this selection to study for an exam?

➤ I. EXPLORING IDEAS THROUGH DISCUSSION AND WRITING

1. What do you think of online relationships? If you have met people online, either for friendship or a romantic relationship, has your experience generally been positive or negative? Explain your answer.

2. Make a prediction about the future of online dating. Do you think the current trend will continue? Why or why not?

3. Reread Table A. Discuss whether the table accurately represents what you know about online relationships, and answer the question posed by the author in the table's caption: How would you describe the way Internet relationships develop?

4. Discuss the perception of online dating as "a last resort for losers" (paragraph 5). Do you agree with the 2003 *New York Times* survey that the stigma is disappearing?

J. BEYOND THE CLASSROOM TO THE WEB

Read these online dating tips from a university counseling center: **http:www.uwec .edu/counsel/pubs/datingonline.htm**. *Prepare a speech for new students at your school about online dating using this page, the reading and other information from your own experience.*

✔ **Tracking Your Progress**

Selection 6

Section	Number Correct		Score
A. Thesis and Main Ideas (6 items)	_____	x 4	_____
B. Details (6 items)	_____	x 3	_____
C. Organization and Transitions (2 items)	_____	x 3	_____
E. Inferred Meanings (4 items)	_____	x 3	_____
F. Thinking Critically (5 items)	_____	x 4	_____
G. Vocabulary			
1. Context (6 items)	_____	x 2	_____
2. Word Parts (4 items)	_____	x 2	_____
	TOTAL SCORE	_____%	

12 Anthropology

Anthropology is the study of humankind. It has five branches: cultural or social, linguistic, physical (or biological), archaeological, and applied. Anthropology attempts to understand all aspects that influence human thought and behavior. Anthropology stresses the importance of understanding the world from the perspective of different cultures, races, and ethnic groups. Studying anthropology will help you understand the world you live in and how people interact. You will study human relationships and their variations in different cultures. You will see that many modern-day traditions, problems, and issues are studied by anthropologists. In "To Love and to Cherish" you will examine the tradition of marriage ceremonies in a variety of religious groups. The textbook excerpt "Culture and Nonverbal Communication" describes cultural variations in gestures, facial expressions, eye communication, touch, and silence. The textbook excerpt "Play, Leisure, and Culture" explores the meaning of play and leisure and considers the role of games and sports. Use the following tips for reading in the field of anthropology.

TIPS FOR READINGS IN ANTHROPOLOGY	

- **Pay attention to terminology.** Like other social sciences, anthropology uses precise terminology to describe its subject matter. Also learn the names of important researchers and theorists. As you read, highlight new terms. You can transfer them later to index cards or a vocabulary log for the course.
- **Focus on patterns of behavior.** People in separate cultures often differ not only in how they behave, but also in how they think. They may differ in food gathering methods, social activities, or what they value as art, for example. Try to identify patterns of behavior.
- **Make comparisons between and among groups and cultures.** Try to see relationships and make comparisons. Draw charts or maps that compare different practices, beliefs, or family structures. In "To Love and to Cherish" you could construct a chart comparing various marriage rituals.
- **Make practical applications.** As you read, consider how the information is useful to you in real-life situations. Make marginal notes of situations that illustrate what you are reading about. For example, as you read think of situations in which you could use this information when traveling in foreign countries.

SELECTION 7

To Love and to Cherish
Michelle Kearns

From a four-part series published in *The Buffalo News* on religious ceremonies, this reading explores wedding ceremonies. Read it to discover the traditions that various cultures include in marriage ceremonies.

PREVIEWING THE READING

Using the steps listed on page 29, preview the reading selection. When you have finished, complete the following items.

1. What is the topic of this selection? _____

2. List at least four religious groups whose wedding customs are described:

   a. _____

   b. _____

   c. _____

   d. _____

MAKING CONNECTIONS

Think back to weddings that you have participated in or attended. How were they similar? How did they differ? What underlying theme(s) do they share?

> **READING TIP**

As you read, record the religious organizations mentioned, along with the traditions associated with each.

To Love and to Cherish

1   By government standards Beatrice Pardeep Singh-Arnone was married on a Tuesday by a judge in the town hall. "It still wasn't real for me," she said. Days later in the rose garden at Delaware Park [in Buffalo, NY], it was. She wore a red dress, the color of happiness. For her **Sikh** ceremony, parents exchanged carnation garlands to symbolize the new bond between the bride and groom's families. And Singh-Arnone and her husband made four trips around the holy book that is the foundation of the religion, which began in India. Each time, the couple walked to a different prayer reading about the physical, mental, soul-uniting and Godly aspects of their marriage. When they were done, friends and family showered them with flower petals, a kind of blessing.

Sikh
a follower of Sikhism—a branch of Hinduism marked by monotheism (having one god) founded in India in the 16th century

2   Wedding rituals vary from religion to religion—from circling a holy book, as Sikhs do, to marrying under a canopy or chupah to show the beginning of a home together, as Jews do. Still, there is usually something universal among them: Religious rituals try to fortify couples in their lives together by showing support from God and the family, said Trevor Watt, a Protestant theologian at the **Second Vatican Council** convened by Pope John XXIII in the 1960s. "The most meaningful wedding ceremonies are the ones that name and articulate the values held by the couple getting married and hopefully by the family and their social community," said Watt. And, he said, the best rituals express an inner conviction. In some ceremonies love and its various forms—such as, romantic, friendship, physical and emotional—are described because they give the marriage strength "to get beyond the hurts and the anger that are inevitable," he said. "The reason that we seek a wedding ceremony is it's an acknowledgement of something that's ultimate," continued Watt, who is a religion professor at Canisius College and an ordained United Church of Christ minister at the Westminster Presbyterian Church in Buffalo. "In the Christian tradition it's called God's love," he said, "like light it can be refracted into many different forms."

Second Vatican Council
a meeting held by the Pope to address questions and issues in the Catholic Church; many new policies and practices resulted from "Vatican II"

Christianity

3   For Catholics, the ceremony for the marriage **sacrament** gets part of its meaning from the bride and groom's work as ministers of their wedding service, said Father Matthew Zirnheld, a priest at Our Lady of Victory in Lackawanna. To prepare for their day, the couple has already planned for marriage by taking church classes about having children and keeping religion in their lives. The modern service has changed some to reflect that a bride is no longer considered a possession of the family, as she once was, Zirnheld said. She can decide to have her father escort her to the altar to begin the service, or not. Instead, he said, Catholics now emphasize the importance of couples entering a marriage freely—so there is nothing to hold them back from keeping the union together. "It's not a contract. A contract can be broken. It's a

sacrament
a formal Christian rite believed to be established by Jesus as a way to be with God

covenant," he said. The couple demonstrates this by leading the wedding, which is their public commitment to each other. They choose the prayers, readings, music, said Zirnheld, who leads the exchange of vows. As modern evidence of the couple's leading role, it has become popular, within the last decade or so, to illustrate the new union with a "unity candle," that is lit with separate candles held by the bride and groom, Zirnheld said.

4   These candles are also popular at the African Methodist Episcopal Church in Buffalo, where couples include African traditions along with more traditional protestant steps, said Reverend Richard Stenhouse. After going to the altar for blessings and to exchange rings and vows, they may jump over a broom. This practice comes from times of slavery. Slaves were not allowed to marry, so couples used this tradition to "cross over from being separate to joined," said Stenhouse. A bride and groom may use another African ritual of pouring some water, the essence of life, on the ground. "It gives honor and recognition to those who've gone before," he said.

5   At the Hellenic Orthodox Church of the Annunciation in Buffalo—part of the Eastern Orthodox church led by **patriarchs** rather than the pope—the traditional Greek service is designed as preparation for heaven. Father James Doukas, the priest, places crowns of beaded circles on the bride and groom's heads to indicate that they're queen and king of their household and ready to begin a heaven-worthy life. Then the couple walks around the altar table three times in tribute to Jesus, the martyrs and the saints. The couple sips from a cup of wine to indicate they will drink the happiness of life together, as well as the sorrow.

patriarchs
church leaders or bishops in the Orthodox faith

Judaism

6   Jewish weddings can vary between temples and movements, such as reform, which is more liberal, and orthodox, which is more conservative. Yet there are rituals common among them. One is the signing of the ktuba, a marriage contract describing the obligations to behave in an ethical and moral way. During the wedding ceremony, as the couple stands beneath a chupah, a rabbi reads the ktuba and offers seven blessings to encourage the couple to live in unity and love. When the service is over, the couple breaks a wine glass as reminder of the destruction of the temple in Jerusalem.

7   This is a signal for some that there is lots of work ahead, explained Rabbi Benjamin Arnold, of Temple Sinai in Amherst. "The wedding is a symbol of redemption and fulfillment," he said. "This wedding can be our inspiration." The couple sometimes retreats to a room with food, such as chocolate covered strawberries, so they can sit alone and break a pre-marriage fast. "It's a form of prayer, of asking God that he should be with this couple," said Rabbi Yirmiya Milevsky, of the Young Israel orthodox synagogue in Amherst.

Islam

8   Islam considers marriage a sacred duty, said Dawoud Adeyola, a leader of the Islamic Cultural Association of Western New York. "It's actually considered an act of worship," he said. Yet the ceremony itself is simple. First the couple must meet

certain pre-conditions—they can't be closely related, the husband has to be able to support his wife—and have two Muslim witnesses. Adeyola will read a verse from the Koran about all of humankind being created from a single soul. The groom promises or gives a dowry chosen by the bride—a house, a car or a piece of jewelry. And the bride or the groom proposes marriage, the other accepts and the ceremony is complete after a prayer, said Adeyola.

Koran
the holy book of Islam, containing what followers believe to be revelations of Allah as told to Muhammad

9   He has conducted spare ceremonies in a room and more elaborate ones in the rose garden at Delaware Park. It is important to dress up so that the couple stands out in recognition of the importance of the occasion. African Americans sometimes incorporate African traditions, such as African-style robes or food, said Adeyola remembering the yams served at his own Muslim wedding in 1969.

Lasting power

10   In the nearly five years since Singh-Arnone was married, she has had two children and life struggles. Her 2-year-old son, who is now fine, was born prematurely, which provoked a worrying few weeks. In such times she thinks back to her wedding and the memories of it nurture her still. "That was one of the most moving days of my life besides the birth of my children," she said. "I did feel surrounded by the presence of God." It was, she said, beyond happiness. It was bliss.

> **A.   UNDERSTANDING THE THESIS AND OTHER MAIN IDEAS**

Select the best answer.

_____ 1. The author's primary purpose in "To Love and to Cherish" is to
a. present research findings on the strength of religion-based marriages.
b. criticize couples who do not have a religious wedding ceremony.
c. encourage couples to put religion into their weddings.
d. describe various religious marriage traditions.

_____ 2. In paragraph 2, the author
a. introduces all the religions she will discuss further.
b. provides general information on the Sikh religion.
c. comments on the meaning and importance of rituals.
d. quotes people who have recently been married.

_____ 3. The topic of paragraph 3 is
a. the unity candle.
b. the Catholic ceremony.
c. Father Matthew Zirnheld.
d. marriage as a covenant.

_____ 4. All of the following are mentioned as reasons behind the rituals *except*

    a. to honor one's ancestors.

    b. to worship.

    c. to prepare for a large family.

    d. to seek redemption and fulfillment.

_____ 5. The main idea of paragraph 4 is

    a. candles are an important part of many ceremonies.

    b. couples may mix traditions from several cultures.

    c. an African tradition involves brooms.

    d. most rituals include recognition of people who have died.

B. IDENTIFYING DETAILS

Match the wedding ritual with the religious tradition as mentioned in the reading. The religions may be used more than once.

A.	Sikhism	D.	Hellenic Orthodox
B.	Catholicism	E.	Judaism
C.	African Methodist Episcopal	F.	Islam

_____ 1. The bride and groom lead the wedding.

_B_ 2. A priest places crowns on the heads of the couple.

_e_ 3. A wine glass is smashed.

_F_ 4. The couple walks around a holy book four times.

_C_ 5. Water is poured onto the ground.

_d_ 6. The bride and groom walk around the altar three times.

_f_ 7. A verse from the Koran is read.

_b_ 8. The couple takes pre-wedding classes.

_e_ 9. A marriage contract is signed.

_b_ 10. A unity candle is lit.

_d_ 11. The marriage ceremony is preparation for heaven.

_F_ 12. The bride chooses a dowry from the groom.

_A_ 13. The couple is blessed with flower petals.

_A_ 14. The parents exchange carnation garlands.

_f_ 15. The bride and groom jump over a broom.

➤ C. RECOGNIZING METHODS OF ORGANIZATION AND TRANSITIONS

Complete the following statements by filling in the blanks.

1. The author lists religious traditions and wedding ceremony characteristics using the organizational pattern called _____.

2. The _____ pattern is also used as the author examines similarities and differences among traditions.

➤ D. REVIEWING AND ORGANIZING IDEAS: OUTLINING

Complete the following outline of Beatrice Pardeep Singh-Arnone's experiences as described in the reading.

I. Civil ceremony
   A. Conducted by a _____
   B. Held in _____

II. Sikh ceremony
   A. Wore red dress—color of happiness
   B. Carnation garland exchange
      1. By parents
      2. Symbolizes _____
   C. Holy book
      1. Bride and groom walk _____
      2. Foundation of _____
      3. Reading about aspects of the marriage
         a. _____
         b. _____
         c. soul-uniting
         d. Godly
   D. Showered with flower petals as a blessing

➤ E. FIGURING OUT INFERRED MEANINGS

Indicate whether each statement is true (T) or false (F).

_____ 1. The Catholic couples are instructed on raising their children Catholic.
_____ 2. Ministers won't allow African customs at religious wedding ceremonies.

_____ 3. Some Jewish couples do not eat before their wedding.

_____ 4. The Islamic couples view marriage in a civic way only.

_____ 5. All Jewish wedding ceremonies contain the same rituals.

F.   THINKING CRITICALLY

Indicate whether each quote from the selection is fact (F) or opinion (O).

_____ 1. "It still wasn't real for me." (paragraph 1)

_____ 2. Wedding rituals vary from religion to religion. (paragraph 2)

_____ 3. "The most meaningful wedding ceremonies are the ones that name and articulate the values held by the couple getting married." (paragraph 2)

_____ 4. "A contract can be broken." (paragraph 3)

_____ 5. An African ritual uses water to give "honor and recognition to those who've gone before." (paragraph 4)

_____ 6. "This wedding can be our inspiration." (paragraph 7)

G.   BUILDING VOCABULARY

Context
Using context and a dictionary, if necessary, determine the meaning of each word as it is used in the selection.

_____ 1. fortify (paragraph 2)
   a. strengthen
   b. refresh
   c. control
   d. explain

_____ 2. articulate (paragraph 2)
   a. speak eloquently
   b. put into words
   c. make significant
   d. identify

_____ 3. inevitable (paragraph 2)
   a. certain to happen, unavoidable
   b. unthinkable, horrible
   c. painful, upsetting
   d. insurmountable, very difficult

_____ 4. covenant (paragraph 3)

      a. a bargain

      b. a settlement

      c. a binding agreement

      d. a fair offer

_____ 5. bliss (paragraph 10)

      a. complete happiness

      b. excitement

      c. sweet, nice

      d. pleasant

➤ Word Parts

> **A REVIEW OF PREFIXES**
> **RE-** means _back_
> **PRE-** means _before_

Use your knowledge of word parts and the review above to fill in the blanks in the following sentences.

1. When light is _refracted_ (paragraph 2) off a surface, it is bent _____ off its original path.

2. A baby that is born _prematurely_ (paragraph 10) is born _____ it is fully mature.

➤ Unusual Words/Understanding Idioms

Use the meanings given below to write a sentence using the **boldface** _word or phrase._

1. The **ultimate** (paragraph 2) sacrifice is one that is final and the utmost and best you could do for someone.

    Your sentence: _____

    _____

2. Someone who is **spare** (paragraph 9) with money is frugal and refrains from spending unnecessarily.

    Your sentence: _____

    _____

➤ H. SELECTING A LEARNING/STUDY STRATEGY

Suppose you had to study for an essay exam that asked you to summarize the wedding traditions of three religions. How would you prepare?

➤ I. EXPLORING IDEAS THROUGH DISCUSSION AND WRITING

1. Write about a time that you witnessed or participated in a religious ceremony. What rituals were involved? Did the wedding guests seem to recognize their significance?

2. A wedding is just the official beginning of a marriage. Discuss what couples really need to know about being husband and wife.

3. Discuss the wedding industry in America. Has it gotten out of control in terms of cost and importance in the lives of the bride and groom?

➤ J. BEYOND THE CLASSROOM TO THE WEB

Look at some sample nonreligious wedding ceremonies on the Web site at http://www.nonreligiousweddings.com/samples.html.

How do these compare with what you know about religious weddings from this reading and your life?

✔ Tracking Your Progress

Selection 7

Section	Number Correct	Score
A. Thesis and Main Ideas (4 items)	_____ x 5	_____
B. Details (10 items)	_____ x 2	_____
C. Organization and Transitions (2 items)	_____ x 2	_____
E. Inferred Meanings (7 items)	_____ x 4	_____
F. Thinking Critically (4 items)	_____ x 4	_____
G. Vocabulary		
1. Context (4 items)	_____ x 2	_____
2. Word Parts (2 items)	_____ x 2	_____
	TOTAL SCORE	_____%

SELECTION 8

Culture and Nonverbal Communication

Joseph A. DeVito

Taken from a textbook titled *Human Communication: The Basic Course*, this reading selection explores the effects of culture on different types of nonverbal communication.

> ### PREVIEWING THE READING

Using the steps listed on page 29, preview the reading selection. When you have finished, complete the following items.

1. What question do you expect the reading to answer?

   _____

2. List the five aspects of nonverbal communication that are explored in this selection.

   _____

   _____

MAKING CONNECTIONS

Think about the nonverbal gestures you sometimes use to communicate. Did you know that these gestures may not have the same meaning in other countries?

> ### READING TIP

As you read, underline examples of the different meanings of various types of nonverbal communication.

Culture and Nonverbal Communication

1   The importance of culture in certain areas of nonverbal communication has become the focus of sustained research. Here we consider just a sampling of research on gesture, facial expression, eye communication, touch, and silence.

Culture and Gesture

2   There is much variation in gestures and their meanings among different cultures. Consider a few common gestures that you might use even without thinking, but that could easily get you into trouble if you used them in another culture (also, take a look at Figure A):

- Folding your arms over your chest would be considered defiant and disrespectful in Fiji.
- Waving your hand would be insulting in Nigeria and Greece.
- Gesturing with the thumb up would be rude in Australia.
- Tapping your two index fingers together would be considered an invitation to sleep together in Egypt.
- Pointing with your index finger would be impolite in many Middle Eastern countries.
- Bowing to a lesser degree than your host would be considered a statement of your superiority in Japan.
- Inserting your thumb between your index and middle finger in a clenched fist would be viewed as a wish that evil fall on the person in some African countries.
- Resting your feet on a table or chair would be insulting and disrespectful in some Middle Eastern cultures.

Culture and Facial Expression

3   The wide variations in facial communication that we observe in different cultures seem to reflect different attitudes about what reactions are permissible in public rather

FIGURE A   SOME CULTURAL MEANINGS OF GESTURES

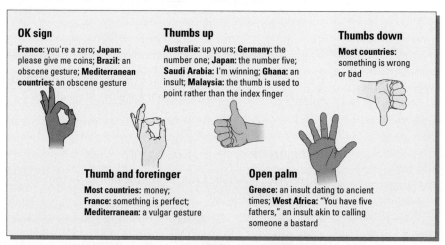

OK sign
France: you're a zero; **Japan:** please give me coins; **Brazil:** an obscene gesture; **Mediterranean countries:** an obscene gesture

Thumbs up
Australia: up yours; **Germany:** the number one; **Japan:** the number five; **Saudi Arabia:** I'm winning; **Ghana:** an insult; **Malaysia:** the thumb is used to point rather than the index finger

Thumbs down
Most countries: something is wrong or bad

Thumb and foretinger
Most countries: money; **France:** something is perfect; **Mediterranean:** a vulgar gesture

Open palm
Greece: an insult dating to ancient times; **West Africa:** "You have five fathers," an insult akin to calling someone a bastard

Cultural differences in the meanings of nonverbal gestures are often significant. The over-the-head clasped hands that signify victory to an American may signify friendship to a Russian. To an American, holding up two fingers to make a V signifies victory or peace. To certain South Americans, however, it is an obscene gesture that corresponds to the American's extended middle finger. This figure highlights some additional nonverbal differences. Can you identify others?

than differences in the way humans show emotions. For example, Japanese and American students watched a film of a surgical operation. The students were video-taped both in an interview situation about the film and alone while watching the film. When alone the students showed very similar reactions; in the interview, however, the American students displayed facial expressions indicating displeasure, whereas the Japanese students did not show any great emotion. Similarly, it's considered "forward" or inappropriate for Japanese women to reveal broad smiles, and so many Japanese women will hide their smile, sometimes with their hands. Women in the United States, on the other hand, have no such restrictions and so are more likely to smile openly. Thus, the difference may not be in the way people in different cultures express emotions but rather in the cultural rules for displaying emotions in public.

4   Similarly, people in different cultures may decode the meanings of facial expression differently. For example, American and Japanese students judged the meaning of a smiling and a neutral facial expression. The Americans rated the smiling face as more attractive, more intelligent, and more sociable than the neutral face. In contrast, the Japanese rated the smiling face as more sociable but not as more attractive—and they rated the neutral face as more intelligent.

Culture and Eye Communication

5   Not surprisingly, eye messages vary with both culture and gender. Americans, for example, consider direct eye contact an expression of honesty and forthrightness, but the Japanese often view this as a lack of respect. A Japanese person will glance at the other person's face rarely, and then only for very short periods. Interpreting another's eye contact messages with your own cultural rules is a risky undertaking; eye movements that you may interpret as insulting may have been intended to show respect.

Culture and Touch

6   In some cultures, some task-related touching is viewed negatively and is to be avoided. Among Koreans, it is considered disrespectful for a store owner to touch a customer in, say, handing back change; it is considered too intimate a gesture. Members of other cultures that are used to such touching may consider the Korean's behavior cold and aloof. Muslim children are socialized not to touch members of the opposite sex, a practice which can easily be interpreted as unfriendly by American children who are used to touching each other.

7   Some cultures—including many in southern Europe and the Middle East—are contact cultures; others are noncontact cultures, such as those of northern Europe and Japan. Members of contact cultures maintain close distances, touch one another in conversation, face one another more directly, and maintain longer and more focused eye contact. Members of noncontact cultures maintain greater distance in their interactions, touch one another rarely (if at all), avoid facing one another directly, and maintain much less direct eye contact. As a result, southern Europeans may perceive northern Europeans and Japanese as cold, distant, and uninvolved. Southern Europeans may in turn be perceived as pushy, aggressive, and inappropriately intimate.

Culture and Silence

8   All cultures do not view silence as functioning in the same way. In the United States, for example, silence is often interpreted negatively. At a business meeting or even in an informal social group, the silent member may be seen as not listening, having nothing interesting to add, not understanding the issues, being insensitive, or being too self-absorbed to focus on the messages of others. Others cultures, however, view silence more positively. In many situations in Japan, for example, silence is a response that is considered more appropriate than speech.

9   The traditional Apache, to take another example, regard silence very differently than do European Americans. Among the Apache, mutual friends do not feel the need to introduce strangers who may be working in the same area or on the same project. The strangers may remain silent for several days. This period enables them to observe and to form judgments about each other. Once this assessment is made, the individuals talk. When courting, especially during the initial stages, the Apache remain silent for hours; if they do talk, they generally talk very little. Only after a couple has been dating for several months will they have lengthy conversations. These periods of silence are generally attributed to shyness or self-consciousness; but the use of silence is explicitly taught to Apache women, who are especially discouraged from engaging in long discussions with their dates. Silence during courtship is a sign of modesty to many Apache.

10   Nonverbal messages serve important communications functions and vary from culture to culture. They help us form and manage impressions, form and define relationships, structure conversation and social interaction, influence others, and express emotions.

—From De Vito, Joseph A. *Human Communication: The Basic Course*, 11e. Published by Allyn and Bacon, Boston, MA. Copyright © 2009 by Pearson Education. Reprinted by permission of the publisher.

A.   UNDERSTANDING THE THESIS AND OTHER MAIN IDEAS

Select the best answer.

_____ 1. The author's primary purpose in this selection is to describe

    a. what elements are most important for effective communication.

    b. how nonverbal messages vary from culture to culture.

    c. why men and women communicate differently.

    d. how our senses help us send and receive messages.

_____ 2. The topic of paragraph 2 is

    a. cultures.

    b. communication.

    c. nonverbal gestures.

    d. the Middle East.

_____ 3. The main idea of paragraph 3 is expressed in the

    a. first sentence only.

    b. first and last sentences.

      c. second sentence.

      d. fourth sentence.

_____ 4. The main idea of paragraph 5 is that

      a. Japanese people do not value eye contact.

      b. Americans often misinterpret eye contact as insulting.

      c. eye contact messages vary from one culture to another.

      d. gender has no effect on eye contact behavior.

_____ 5. The topic of paragraph 6 is

      a. North American studies.

      b. touching.

      c. Korean culture.

      d. Muslim children.

➤ B.   IDENTIFYING DETAILS

Indicate whether each statement is true (T) or false (F).

_____ 1. Pointing with your index finger is a rude gesture in some Middle Eastern countries.

_____ 2. Folding your arms over your chest is considered a friendly gesture in Fiji.

_____ 3. The "thumbs down" gesture means the same thing in most countries.

_____ 4. In some Middle Eastern countries, it is offensive to rest your feet on a table or chair.

_____ 5. Waving your hand is insulting in Australia.

_____ 6. In Japan, bowing to a lesser degree than your host is considered a sign of respect.

➤ C.   RECOGNIZING METHODS OF ORGANIZATION AND TRANSITIONS

A primary organizational pattern used throughout the selection to describe cultural differences is comparison and contrast. For each of the paragraphs listed below, find two transitional words or phrases that identify this pattern.

1. Paragraph 3:   a. _____

                   b. _____

2. Paragraph 4:   a. _____

                   b. _____

D.   REVIEWING AND ORGANIZING IDEAS: MAPPING

Complete the following comparison-contrast chart of paragraphs 3-5 by filling in the blanks.

Nonverbal Communication	American	Japanese
Private facial expressions (response to film)	Similar	_____
Public facial expressions (response to film)	Indicated _____	Did not show emotion
Smiling in public	Women smile openly	Women _____
Decoding _____	Smiling face is more attractive, intelligent, and sociable than neutral face	Smiling face is more sociable and _____ is more intelligent
Eye contact	Direct eye contact expresses _____ _____	Direct eye contact shows _____

E.   FIGURING OUT INFERRED MEANINGS

Indicate whether each statement is true (T) or false (F).

_____ 1. Countries that share the same language use the same nonverbal gestures.

_____ 2. People traveling in other countries should always apply their own culture's rules to interpret nonverbal communication.

_____ 3. Americans are typically more open about expressing their emotions than other cultures.

_____ 4. It may be difficult for members of contact cultures and noncontact cultures to communicate with each other.

_____ 5. Silence may be interpreted positively or negatively, depending on the culture in which it is used.

_____ 6. Modesty is considered an attractive trait in a traditional Apache woman.

> F.   **THINKING CRITICALLY**

Select the best answer.

_____ 1. The author's tone can best be described as
   a. concerned.
   b. informative.
   c. humorous.
   d. disapproving.

_____ 2. The primary purpose of Figure A is to
   a. show that nonverbal gestures have the same or similar meanings in every culture.
   b. present gestures that are considered offensive in other cultures.
   c. illustrate cultural variations in the meanings of certain gestures.
   d. show how to communicate successfully in other cultures.

_____ 3. If this selection had been published in a popular magazine rather than a textbook, an appropriate title might have been
   a. Watch What Your Face May Reveal.
   b. Communicating Nonverbally with People from Other Cultures.
   c. Communicating with and Without Words.
   d. Gestures Tell All.

_____ 4. The author includes the list of gestures in paragraph 2 in order to show that
   a. gestures that are common and harmless in America have different meanings in other cultures.
   b. minor differences in nonverbal communication between cultures are not significant.
   c. using gestures is the best way to communicate in a foreign country.
   d. Americans are too informal in the way they communicate with others.

_____ 5. Of the following statements, the only one that is an opinion is
   a. Many studies have focused on the importance of culture in nonverbal communication.
   b. Gestures often have different meanings in different cultures.
   c. Some cultures avoid task-related touching because it is considered too intimate.
   d. People should always try to be sensitive to cultural differences in communication.

_____ 6. The author supports his thesis by using all of the following *except*

    a. examples and illustrations.

    b. research evidence.

    c. comparisons and contrasts.

    d. personal experience.

G. BUILDING VOCABULARY

▶ Context

Using context and a dictionary, if necessary, determine the meaning of each word as it is used in the selection.

_____ 1. sustained (paragraph 1)

    a. expensive

    b. continuing

    c. approved

    d. temporary

_____ 2. permissible (paragraph 3)

    a. allowed

    b. important

    c. overlooked

    d. obvious

_____ 3. neutral (paragraph 4)

    a. curious

    b. mistaken

    c. without expression

    d. unpleasant

_____ 4. aloof (paragraph 6)

    a. intelligent

    b. unfriendly

    c. pushy

    d. joyful

▶ Word Parts

> **A REVIEW OF PREFIXES**
> **NON-** means *not*
> **IN-** means *not*

Use your knowledge of word parts and the review above to fill in the blanks in the following sentences.

1. Gesture, facial expression, eye communication, touch, and silence are forms of *nonverbal* communication (paragraph 1) because they _____ words.

2. An *impolite* gesture (paragraph 2) is one that is _____ to others.

➤ **H.   SELECTING A LEARNING/STUDY STRATEGY**

Assume you will be tested on this reading on an upcoming exam. Evaluate the usefulness of comparison-contrast mapping (similar to the one you completed on page 276) as a study tool. How would you use a map to study? What additional maps would you draw?

➤ **I.   EXPLORING IDEAS THROUGH DISCUSSION AND WRITING**

1. Think about a time when you traveled to another country or interacted with someone from another country. What differences did you notice about the way people communicated both verbally and nonverbally?

2. How do you interpret silence? Write a paragraph describing whether you agree with the American perceptions of silence as discussed in paragraph 8, or if you view silence more positively.

3. Discuss how your cultural background affects the way you communicate. Is your style more typical of a contact or noncontact culture?

➤ **J.   BEYOND THE CLASSROOM TO THE WEB**

People who travel internationally for business need to be especially conscious of cultural differences in communication. Read this article on business etiquette from USA Today online (don't forget the sidebar): **http://www.usatoday.com/money/industries/travel/2007-08-23-faux-pas_N.htm.** *Pay attention to your communication behavior—verbal and nonverbal—for three days. Take notes on how you act. Use this article and the reading to analyze what habits you would have to be careful of while traveling in other countries.*

✔ Tracking Your Progress

Selection 8

Section	Number Correct	Score
A. Thesis and Main Ideas (5 items)	_____ x 4	_____
B. Details (6 items)	_____ x 4	_____
C. Organization and Transitions (4 items)	_____ x 2	_____
E. Inferred Meanings (6 items)	_____ x 3	_____
F. Thinking Critically (6 items)	_____ x 4	_____
G. Vocabulary		
1. Context (4 items)	_____ x 1	_____
2. Word Parts (2 items)	_____ x 1	_____
TOTAL SCORE		_____%

SELECTION 9

Play, Leisure, and Culture

Barbara D. Miller and Bernard Wood

From a textbook titled *Anthropology*, this reading selection explores the relationship between play, leisure, and culture.

PREVIEWING THE READING

Using the steps listed on page 29, preview the reading selection. When you have finished, complete the following items.

1. The topic of this selection is what people do for _____.

2. List at least two questions you would expect to have answered by the reading.

a. _____

b. _____

 ## MAKING CONNECTIONS

What is your favorite leisure activity? Think about what you do for fun and how you choose to spend your free time.

READING TIP

As you read, underline examples that explain cultural differences in play and leisure activities.

Play, Leisure, and Culture

1   It is impossible to draw a clear line between the concepts of play or leisure and art or performance, because they often overlap. For example, a person could paint watercolors in her leisure time yet simultaneously be creating a work of art. In most cases, though, play and leisure can be distinguished from other activities by the fact that they have no direct, utilitarian purpose for the participant. Dutch historian Johan Huizinga, in the 1930s, proposed some features of play. It is unnecessary and thus free action; it is outside of ordinary life; it is closed and limited in terms of time; it has rules for its execution; and it contains an element of tension and chance.

utilitarian
useful or practical

Leisure time and play are not limited to humans

2   Leisure activities often overlap with play, but many leisure activities, such as reading or lying on a beach, would not be considered play because they lack rules, tension, and chance. Often, depending on the context, the same activity could be considered work instead of play. For example, gardening as a hobby would be classified as a leisure activity, even though weeding, pruning, and watering are activities that could be considered work for someone else. Playing a game with a child might be considered recreational, but if one has been hired as the child's babysitter, then it is work. Professional sports are an area where the line between play and work breaks down completely because the "players" are paid to "play." Further, although play and leisure may be pursued from a nonutilitarian perspective, they are often surrounded by a wider context of commercial and political interests. For example, nonprofessional athletes competing in the Olympic games are part of a wider set of powerful interests, from advertisers to host cities to athletic equipment companies.

3   Within the broad category of play and leisure activities, several subcategories exist, including varieties of games, hobbies, and recreational travel. Cultural anthropologists study play and leisure within their cultural contexts. They ask, for example, why some leisure activities involve teams rather than individuals; what the social roles and status of people involved in particular activities are; what the "goals" of the games are and how they are achieved; how much danger or violence is involved; how certain activities are related to group identity; and how such activities link or separate different groups within or between societies or nations.

Games and Sports as Cultural Microcosm

4   Games and sports, like religious rituals and festivals, can be interpreted as reflections of social relationships and cultural ideals. In the terms of cultural anthropologist Clifford Geertz, they are both "models of" a culture, depicting basic ideals, and "models for" a culture, socializing people into adopting certain values and ideals. American football can be seen as a model for corporate culture. Leadership is vested in one person (the quarterback), and its major goal is taking territory away from the competition.

5   A comparison of baseball as played in the United States and baseball as played in Japan reveals core values about social relationships. These differences emerge dramatically when American players are hired by Japanese teams. The American players bring with them an intense sense of individualism, which promotes the value of

"doing your own thing." This conflicts with a primary value that influences the playing style in Japan: *wa,* meaning discipline and self-sacrifice for the good of the whole. In Japanese baseball, players must seek to achieve and maintain team harmony, so extremely individualistic, egotistical plays and strategies are frowned on.

Sports and Spirituality: Men's Wrestling in India

6   In many non-Western settings, sports are closely tied to aspects of religion and spirituality. Asian martial arts, for example, require forms of concentration much like meditation, leading to spiritual self-control. Men's wrestling in India, a popular form of entertainment at rural fairs and other public events, involves a strong link with spiritual development and asceticism. In some ways these wrestlers are just like other members of Indian society. They go to work, and they marry and have families, but their dedication to wrestling involves important differences.

7   Several aspects of the wrestler's life are similar to those of a Hindu sannyasi, or holy man who renounces life in the normal world. The aspiring sannyasi studies under a guru, learns to follow a strict routine of discipline and meditation called yoga, and adheres to a restricted diet to achieve control of the body and its life force. Both wrestler and sannyasi roles focus on discipline to achieve a controlled self. In India, wrestling does not involve the "dumb jock" stereotype that it sometimes does in North America; rather, the image is of perfected physical and moral health.

asceticism
the practice of strict self-denial as a measure of personal and spiritual discipline

Play, Pleasure, and Pain

8   Many leisure activities combine pleasure and pain because they may involve physical discomfort. Serious injuries may result from mountain climbing, horseback riding, or playing touch football in the backyard. A more intentionally dangerous category of sports is blood sports, competition that explicitly seeks to bring about a flow of blood or even death. Blood sports may involve human contestants, humans contesting against animal competitors, or humans hunting animal targets. In the United States and Europe, professional boxing is an example of a highly popular blood sport that has not yet been analyzed by anthropologists. Cultural anthropologists have looked more at the use of animals in blood sports such as cockfights and bullfights. These sports have been variously interpreted as providing sadistic pleasure, as offering vicarious self-validation (usually of males) through the triumph of their representative pit bulls or fighting cocks, and as the triumph of culture over nature in the symbolism of bullfighting.

vicarious
experienced or
felt through the
participation of
someone else

9   Even the seemingly pleasurable leisure experience of a Turkish bath can involve discomfort and pain. One phase involves scrubbing the skin roughly several times with a rough natural sponge, a pumice stone, or a piece of cork wood wrapped in cloth. The scrubbing removes layers of dead skin and "opens the pores" so that the skin will be beautiful. In Turkey, an option for men is a massage that can be quite violent, involving deep probes of leg muscles, cracking of the back, and being walked on by the (often hefty) masseur. In Ukraine, being struck repeatedly on bare skin with birch branches is the final stage of the bath. However, violent scrubbing, scraping, and even beating of the skin, along with radical temperature change in the water, are combined with valued social interaction at the bathhouse.

A.   UNDERSTANDING THE THESIS AND OTHER MAIN IDEAS

Select the best answer.

_____ 1. The authors' primary purpose in this article is to
   a. compare and contrast sports in different cultures.
   b. promote games and sports as leisure activities.
   c. discuss play and leisure within the context of culture.
   d. describe the effects of spirituality on sports.

_____ 2. The question that is answered in paragraph 3 is
   a. What do cultural anthropologists want to know about play and leisure?
   b. Why do some leisure activities involve teams rather than individuals?
   c. What are the goals of games and how are they achieved?
   d. How are certain activities related to group identity?

_____ 3. The main idea of paragraph 6 is expressed in the
　　　　a. first sentence.
　　　　b. second sentence.
　　　　c. third sentence.
　　　　d. last sentence.

_____ 4. The topic of paragraph 8 is
　　　　a. leisure activities.
　　　　b. sports-related injuries.
　　　　c. blood sports.
　　　　d. professional boxing.

B. IDENTIFYING DETAILS

Indicate whether each statement is true (T) or false (F).

_____ 1. According to Dutch historian Johan Huizinga, play contains an element of tension and chance.

_____ 2. Games, hobbies, and recreational travel are considered play and leisure activities.

_____ 3. According to cultural anthropologist Clifford Geertz, games and sports depict the basic ideals of a culture.

_____ 4. American baseball is the sport considered to be a model for corporate culture.

_____ 5. In Japanese baseball, individualism is valued more highly than team harmony.

_____ 6. Wrestlers in India are not allowed to marry.

_____ 7. A Hindu sannyasi is a holy man who renounces life in the normal world.

_____ 8. Blood sports are intended to bring about injury or death.

_____ 9. Anthropologists have thoroughly analyzed professional boxing.

_____ 10. The final stage of a Turkish bath in Ukraine involves being struck on the bare skin with birch branches.

C. RECOGNIZING METHODS OF ORGANIZATION AND TRANSITIONS

Select the best answer.

_____ 1. The organizational pattern used in paragraph 2 is
　　　　a. generalization and example.
　　　　b. cause and effect.
　　　　c. chronological order.
　　　　d. process.

_____ 2. The authors use the comparison-contrast organizational pattern in paragraph 5 to contrast

    a. America and Japan.

    b. amateur athletes and professional athletes.

    c. American sports and Japanese sports.

    d. American baseball and Japanese baseball.

D. REVIEWING AND ORGANIZING IDEAS: SUMMARIZING

Complete the following summary of paragraphs 6 and 7 by filling in the blanks using words and phrases from the list. Use each only once.

moral	concentration	Hindu	non-Western
martial arts	spirituality	self-control	dedication
wrestling	diet	physical	controlled self
religion	India	families	yoga

Some _____ cultures link sports to _____ and _____. In Asian _____, spiritual _____ is attained through deep _____. In _____, men's _____ involves spiritual development and self-denial; although wrestlers work and have _____, their _____ to wrestling sets them apart. The _____ holy man practices _____ and follows a strict _____; similarly, the wrestler uses discipline to gain a _____. Indian wrestlers represent the ideal of _____ and _____ health.

E. FIGURING OUT INFERRED MEANINGS

Indicate whether each statement is true (T) or false (F).

_____ 1. An important characteristic of play is that it has no useful or practical purpose.

_____ 2. Whether an activity is considered work or play often depends on the situation.

_____ 3. It can be inferred that the authors believe Olympic athletes are paid to compete.

_____ 4. The authors believe that the concepts of leisure time and play are not limited to humans.

_____ 5. It can be inferred that all American baseball players are individualistic and egotistical.

_____ 6. Indian wrestlers probably follow a strict diet.

_____ 7. The authors consider most wrestlers in North America to be dumb jocks.

> **F. THINKING CRITICALLY**

Select the best answer.

_____ 1. All of the following types of evidence are used to support the thesis *except*

   a. examples.

   b. expert opinions.

   c. personal experience.

   d. research citations.

_____ 2. The overall tone of the selection can best be described as

   a. critical.

   b. disapproving.

   c. objective.

   d. sympathetic.

_____ 3. Of the following statements from paragraph 9, the only one that is a *fact* is

   a. "Even the seemingly pleasurable leisure experience of a Turkish bath can involve discomfort and pain."

   b. "One phase involves scrubbing the skin roughly several times with a rough natural sponge, a pumice stone, or a piece of cork wood wrapped in cloth."

   c. "The scrubbing removes layers of dead skin and 'opens the pores' so that the skin will be beautiful."

   d. "In Turkey, an option for men is a massage that can be quite violent."

_____ 4. The authors include the description of blood sports in paragraph 8 in order to

   a. express their disapproval of these sports.

   b. argue that such sports should be against the law.

   c. explain the symbolism associated with blood sports.

   d. illustrate a category of sports that involves physical pain.

G. BUILDING VOCABULARY

Context

Using context and a dictionary, if necessary, determine the meaning of each word as it is used in the selection.

_____ 1. renounces (paragraph 7)

    a. proclaims   c. accuses

    b. gives up   d. promotes

_____ 2. adheres (paragraph 7)

    a. follows closely   c. brings about

    b. asks for   d. pretends

_____ 3. explicitly (paragraph 8)

    a. possibly   c. openly

    b. strongly   d. emotionally

_____ 4. radical (paragraph 9)

    a. dramatic   c. political

    b. dangerous   d. minor

Word Parts

```
A REVIEW OF PREFIXES, ROOTS, AND SUFFIXES
SUB- means under, below
ANTHROPO means human being
-LOG / -LOGY means study, thought
-IST means one who
```

Use your knowledge of word parts and the review above to fill in the blanks in the following sentences.

1. If a broad category contains several *subcategories* (paragraph 3), it has groups or classifications that fall _____ that category.

2. The term *anthropologists* (paragraph 3) refers to people who study

    _____.

Unusual Words/Understanding Idioms

*Use the meanings given below to write a sentence using the **boldface** word or phrase.*

1. The phrase **doing your own thing** (paragraph 5) means a person doing what is unique, interesting, or important to him or her.

   Your sentence: _____

   _____.

2. The term **jock** (paragraph 7) is an informal, disparaging word used to refer to an athlete, often a male athlete.

   Your sentence: _____

   _____.

➤ **H. SELECTING A LEARNING/STUDY STRATEGY**

Predict an essay question based on this selection and draft your answer to it.

➤ **I. EXPLORING IDEAS THROUGH DISCUSSION AND WRITING**

1. How do you like to spend your free time? Describe what you do for fun and/or leisure.

2. The authors assert that the line between work and play breaks down completely in professional sports because athletes are paid to "play" (paragraph 2). How do you view the work of professional athletes—as work or play?

3. In addition to activities such as yoga and tai chi, some people consider gardening or hiking to be spiritual. Write a paragraph describing one of your own leisure activities that has a spiritual aspect. Explain what makes it spiritual for you.

4. Discuss whether blood sports involving animals (bullfighting, dog-fighting) are moral.

➤ **J. BEYOND THE CLASSROOM TO THE WEB**

Read an article from Forbes *on how Americans spend their free time at* **http://www. forbes.com/2004/05/17/0517findsvpconsumers_print.html.** *Keep track of how you spend your free time over the next week. Summarize your findings and describe any surprises you encountered. Explain what changes you might make to the use of your free time.*

✔ Tracking Your Progress

Selection 9

Section	Number Correct	Score
A. Thesis and Main Ideas (4 items)	_____ x 5	_____
B. Details (10 items)	_____ x 2	_____
C. Organization and Transitions (2 items)	_____ x 2	_____
E. Inferred Meanings (7 items)	_____ x 4	_____
F. Thinking Critically (4 items)	_____ x 4	_____
G. Vocabulary		
1. Context (4 items)	_____ x 2	_____
2. Word Parts (2 items)	_____ x 2	_____
	TOTAL SCORE	_____%

13 Arts/Humanities/Literature

The **humanities and arts** are areas of knowledge concerned with human thoughts and ideas and their creative expression in written, visual, or auditory form. They deal with large, global issues such as "What is worthwhile in life?," "What is beautiful?," and "What is the meaning of human existence?" Works of art and literature are creative records of the thoughts, feelings, emotions, or experiences of other people. By studying art and reading literature you can learn about yourself and understand both joyful and painful experiences without going through them yourself. "Issue-Oriented and Street Art" focuses on two forms of modern art. In the short story "Gregory," you can experience the moral dilemma of whether a soldier should follow orders to execute a prisoner who has become a friend. In the poem "Combing" you share the experience of a woman recalling previous generations.

Use the following tips when reading and studying in the arts, humanities, and literature.

TIPS FOR READING IN THE ARTS/ HUMANITIES/ LITERATURE

- **Focus on values.** Ask yourself why the work or piece is valuable and important. In "Issue-Oriented and Street Art" you will explore new art forms and their contributions to the world of art.

- **Pay attention to the medium.** Words, sound, music, canvas, and clay are all means through which artistic expression occurs. Readings in this chapter are concerned with words and art. Three different vehicles are used in this chapter to express meaning through words: a textbook excerpt, a short story, and a poem.

- **Look for a message or an interpretation.** Works of art and literature express meaning or create a feeling or impression. "Gregory" examines important moral dilemmas that surround wartime. As you read "Combing," try to discover Cardiff's feelings about events that connect generations.

- **Read literature slowly and carefully.** Rereading may be necessary. Pay attention to the writer's choice of words, descriptions, comparisons, and arrangement of ideas. You should definitely read poetry several times.

<table>
<tr><td>SELECTION
10</td><td>Issue-Oriented and Street Art
Patrick Frank</td></tr>
</table>

Taken from a textbook titled *Prebles' Artforms: An Introduction to the Visual Arts*, this reading selection describes two movements of the present generation of modern artists.

▶ PREVIEWING THE READING

Using the steps listed on page 29, preview the reading selection. When you have finished, complete the following items.

1. The topic of this selection is _____.

2. The two categories of modern art that are discussed in this selection are:

    a. _____

    b. _____

MAKING CONNECTIONS

Think about how you define art, then consider street art and graffiti that you have seen. Would you consider them art?

▶ READING TIP

Take time to examine the different works of modern art included in this selection as you read about the artists who created them.

CHECKING YOUR READING RATE

If you plan to compute your reading rate, be sure to record your starting time in the box at the end of the exercises before you begin reading.

Issue-Oriented and Street Art

1   Today the public accepts most modern art. Exhibitions of work by such former rule-breaking radicals as Henri Matisse, Paul Gauguin, Paul Cézanne, and Claude Monet fill museums with visitors. Nine of the ten most expensive paintings ever sold at auction are modern works (three each by Picasso and van Gogh; one each by

Cézanne, Renoir, and Jackson Pollock). The modern-style Vietnam Veterans Memorial is a national shrine. Modern art is no longer controversial.

2 The impact of this situation is not yet clear. Art of our own time is always the most difficult to evaluate. In general, most artists of the present generation do not appear intent on perfecting form, creating beauty, or fine-tuning their sense of sight. They mostly want to comment on life in all of its aspects. They want to create work that illuminates the relationships between what we see and how we think. Rather than being objects of timeless beauty, most art since the 1980s consists of objects laden with information about the period in which we live. This article will present two movements of the present generation.

Issue-Oriented Art

3 Many artists in the past twenty years have sought to link their art to current social questions. Issue-oriented artists believe that if they limit their art to **aesthetic** matters, then their work will be only a distraction from pressing problems. Furthermore, they recognize that what we see influences how we think, and they do not want to miss an opportunity to influence both.

aesthetic
concerned with
what is beautiful or
pleasing in
appearance

4 Photographer Richard Misrach presents new kinds of landscape in new ways. His photograph SUBMERGED LAMPPOST, SALTON SEA captures the silent yet ironic beauty of a small town in California that was flooded by a misguided irrigation system. In other works he has documented in chilling detail the bloated carcasses of animals killed on military proving grounds in Nevada. His brand of nature photography is the opposite of the common calendars that include soothing views of pristine landscapes. He wants us to know that such scenes are fast disappearing.

5 Barbara Kruger was trained as a magazine designer, and this profession shows in her piece UNTITLED (I SHOP THEREFORE I AM). She invented the slogan, which sounds as though it came from advertising. The position of the hand, too, looks like it came from an ad for aspirin or sleeping medication. Do our

Barbara Kruger. *Untitled (I Shop Therefore I Am)*. 1987. Photographic silkscreen/vinyl. 111" × 113". Courtesy Mary Boone Gallery, New York.

products define us? Are we what we shop for? Often we buy a product because of what it will say about us and not for the thing itself. These are some of the messages present in this simple yet fascinating work. Perhaps it ultimate irony is that the artist had it silkscreened onto a shopping bag.

silkscreened
printed using a   6
special stencil
process

6   Artists who create works about racism and class bias show how common practices of museum display contribute to such problems. In 1992, the Maryland Historical Society invited African-American artist Fred Wilson to rearrange the exhibits on one floor to create an installation called MINING THE MUSEUM. He spent a year preparing for the show, rummaging through the Society's holdings and documentary records; the results were surprising. He found no portraits, for example, of noted African-American Marylanders Benjamin Banneker (who laid out the boundaries of the District of Columbia), Frederick Douglass (noted abolitionist and journalist), or Harriet Tubman (founder of the Underground Railroad). He found instead busts of Henry Clay, Andrew Jackson, and Napoleon Bonaparte, none of whom ever lived in Maryland. He exhibited those three busts next to three empty pedestals to symbolize the missing African Americans. He set out a display of Colonial Maryland silverware and tea utensils, and included a pair of slave shackles. This lesser-known form of metalwork was perhaps equally vital to the functioning of nineteenth-century Maryland. He dusted off the Society's collection of wooden cigar-store Indians and stood them, backs to viewers, facing photographs of real Native Americans who lived in Maryland. In an accompanying exhibition brochure he wrote that a museum should be a place that can make you think. When MINING THE MUSEUM went on display, attendance records soared.

installation
a work of art made
up of multiple
components, often
in different media,
and exhibited in an
arrangement
specified by the
artist

Fred Wilson. *Mining the Museum.* 1992. Installation. Cigar-store Indians facing photographs of Native American Marylanders. Museum and Library of History. Photograph: Jeff D. Goldblum.

7   The Swiss-born Thomas Hirschhorn took up the issue of the Iraq war, but only indirectly, in the context of today's media-saturated society. His 2006 installation SUPERFICIAL ENGAGEMENT filled the entire gallery space with a *dizzying* array of objects that resembled a parade float on drugs, or a cross between an insane asylum and a grocery store. Photos of mangled war dead competed for space with coffins, nail-studded mannequins, blaring headlines, and reproductions of abstract artworks. The nailed bodies refer to traditional African magic sculptures, and the abstract art was mostly copied from the Austrian mystic Emma Kunz in what the artist called "friendly piracy." The headlines shout the aimless alarmism of cable news channels: "Decision Time Approaches," "Broken Borders," "An Assault on Hypocrisy," "The Real Crisis." The artist used only cheap materials (cardboard, plastic, plywood, package tape) in an effort to avoid art-world pretense and make it more accessible. He said of his brash style, "Art is a tool, a tool to encounter the world, to confront the reality and the time I am living in." The shrill volume of this exhibition only paralleled the strident intensity of today's news, where a disaster might follow a fashion show. At the opening reception, the artist provided hammers and screwdrivers, and the crowd joined in attaching nails and screws, thus finishing the piece.

Street Art

8   In the late 1990s, many galleries in various cities began to exhibit work by artists who had previously made illegal graffiti. Many of these "street artists" were based in the culture of skateboards and Punk music, and they used materials

Shepard Fairey. *Revolution Girl*. 2006. Screenprinted temporary mural. 16' × 19'. Outdoor location, Los Angeles, Obey Grant Art, CA.

bought at the hardware store rather than the art supply house. Their creations were only rarely related to gang-oriented graffiti, which usually marks out territories of influence. Nor were they autobiographical or personal. Rather, the street artists made much broader statements about themselves and the world in a language that was widely understandable. The ancestors of the movement in the 1980s were Keith Haring and Jean-Michel Basquiat, both of whom worked illegally for years before exhibiting in galleries. By the turn of the twenty-first century, Street Art was a recognized movement, and most of its main practitioners work both indoors and out.

9   The career of Shepard Fairey is exemplary. He studied at the Rhode Island School of Design, but was never satisfied in the art world, which seemed to him closed-off and elitist. He began working outdoors, and quickly acquired notoriety for posting dozens of signs and stickers with the single word "Obey" below the ominous-looking face of wrestler Andre the Giant. His vocabulary soon expanded to include advertising symbols, propaganda posters, and currency, even as the scale of his work increased to billboard size.

10   His 2006 work REVOLUTION GIRL is an anti-war mural created on a legal wall for a three-month show in West Hollywood. The dominant motif is a huge female Communist soldier from the Vietnam War that the artist borrowed from Chinese propaganda, but her rifle has a flower protruding; her weapon has become an elaborate vase. Other motifs from Chinese propaganda decorate the center right, re-purposed for a peace campaign. In the lower corner, posters of a female face with flowery hair symbolize nurturing. The message of the mural is anti-war, but the artist made the statement positive rather than negative, expressing the hope that we can convert our weapons into flower holders. His friend and fellow street artist Blake Marquis provided the vivid leafy patterns at the left. We see the artist himself in the foreground.

11   Some of today's most skillful street art is created by Swoon, a woman who uses the pseudonym to avoid prosecution. She carves large linoleum blocks and makes life-sized relief prints from them, usually portraits of everyday people. She prints them on large sheets of cheap (usually recycled) newsprint and pastes them on urban walls, beginning on the Lower East Side of Manhattan but now in cities on every continent. Her UNTITLED installation at Deitch Projects was a recent indoor work. Against objections that her work is mostly illegal, she replies that her creations are far easier to look at than advertising, that they lack any persuasive agenda, and that they glorify common people. Moreover, the newsprint that she uses decays over time so that her work is impermanent. Although she works mostly outdoors, she sometimes shows in galleries because, she admits, "I have to make a living," but she charges far less for her work than most other artists of wide repute.

12   Probably the most famous street artist is Banksy (who also uses a pseudonym). He placed his own art in the collections of several major museums in 2005 by merely entering the galleries and sticking his pieces to the wall. His street graffiti is generally witty, as we see in his GRAFFITI REMOVAL HOTLINE, PENTONVILLE ROAD. There is no such thing as a graffiti removal hotline; the artist stenciled the words and then created the youth who seems to paint out the phone number. Banksy is currently one of the

Swoon *Untitled*. 2005. Linoleum cut, newsprint, ink, and wheat paste. Variable dimensions. Deitch Projects, New York.

most popular artists in England, and many of his outdoor works have been pre-served. When a prominent work of his was recently defaced by another graffiti artist, protests ensued and the defacer was arrested for vandalism! Thus street artists often blur the line between legal and illegal.

Banksey, *Graffiti Removal Hotline, Pentonville Road*. 2006. Steve Cotton/artofthestate.co.uk.

Source: Frank, Patrick L., *Prebles' Artforms (Book Alone)*, 9th Edition, © N/A. Reprinted by permission of Pearson Education, Inc., Upper Saddle River, NJ.

> **A. UNDERSTANDING THE THESIS AND OTHER MAIN IDEAS**

Select the best answer.

_____ 1. The author's primary purpose in this selection is to

    a. compare and contrast modern and traditional art.

    b. discuss historical events that made an impact on modern art.

    c. explore the effects of culture on art in different parts of the world.

    d. describe two types of modern art and the artists who represent each.

_____ 2. The main idea of paragraph 1 is that

    a. modern art will always be controversial.

    b. modern artists are as popular as traditional masters.

    c. most modern art has become acceptable to the public.

    d. the most expensive paintings sold at auction are modern works.

_____ 3. The main idea of paragraph 6 is expressed in the

    a. first sentence only.

    b. first and last sentence.

    c. second sentence.

    d. third sentence.

_____ 4. The topic of paragraph 7 is

    a. the Iraq war.

    b. modern media.

    c. Thomas Hirschhorn's art.

    d. the Austrian mystic Emma Kunz.

_____ 5. The main idea of paragraph 8 is that street art became an acceptable form because

    a. the artists used high-quality materials from renowned art supply stores.

    b. gangs stopped using street art to mark out their territories of influence.

    c. most street artists began working primarily indoors rather than outdoors.

    d. the art consisted of broad statements about the artists and about the world.

> **B.   IDENTIFYING DETAILS**

Select the best answer.

_____ 1. According to the selection, most artists of the present generation are intent on

   a. perfecting form.

   b. creating objects of beauty.

   c. fine-tuning their sense of sight.

   d. commenting on life in all of its aspects.

_____ 2. Issue-oriented artists link their art to

   a. current social questions.

   b. soothing views of nature.

   c. autobiographical statements.

   d. the culture of skateboards and punk music.

_____ 3. To illustrate racism, artist Fred Wilson did all of the following in his installation *Mining the Museum except*

   a. exhibit busts of white non-Marylanders next to empty pedestals symbolizing famous African-American Marylanders.

   b. include a pair of slave shackles along with silverware and tea utensils in a display of Colonial Maryland metalwork.

   c. provide hammers and screwdrivers to museum visitors so they could join in completing the installation.

   d. place a collection of wooden cigar-store Indians facing photographs of Native American Marylanders.

_____ 4. The two pieces of antiwar art in the selection were created by the artists

   a. Misrach and Kruger.

   b. Wilson and Hirschhorn.

   c. Hirschhorn and Fairey.

   d. Haring and Basquiat.

_____ 5. The street artist who placed his own work in major museums by walking in and sticking his pieces to the gallery walls is

   a. Banksy.

   b. Swoon.

   c. Shepard Fairey.

   d. Jackson Pollack.

C.   RECOGNIZING METHODS OF ORGANIZATION AND TRANSITIONS

Select the best answer.

_____ 1. In paragraph 6, the organizational pattern that is used to show the different elements of Fred Wilson's installation at the Maryland Historical Society is

a. comparison and contrast.

b. definition.

c. chronological order.

d. cause and effect.

_____ 2. A word or phrase in paragraph 6 that signals the organizational pattern is

a. In 1992.

b. the results.

c. instead.

d. next.

D.   REVIEWING AND ORGANIZING IDEAS: MAPPING

Complete the following map of paragraphs 3–7 by filling in the blanks.

Issue-Oriented Art		
Artist	**Work**	**Purpose/Focus**
_____	Nature photography: *Submerged Lamppost, Salton Sea*	How humans affect _____, in the form of disappearing landscapes
Barbara Kruger	Photographic silkscreen: _____ _____	How we define ourselves and what our purchases say about us
Fred Wilson	Installation: _____ _____	How museum displays contribute to _____
_____	Installation: _____ _____	Antiwar in the context of a modern society dominated by news and media

E.   FIGURING OUT INFERRED MEANINGS

*Each of the following **boldface** words has a strong positive or negative connotation (shade of meaning). Make inferences by indicating whether the word creates a positive (P) or negative (N) image for the reader.*

_____ 1. "Rather than being objects of timeless **beauty** . . ." (paragraph 2)

_____ 2. ". . . he has documented in **chilling** detail" (paragraph 4)

_____ 3. ". . . calendars that include **soothing** views" (paragraph 4)

_____ 4. ". . . a **dizzying** array of objects" (paragraph 7)

_____ 5. "The **shrill** volume of this exhibition . . ." (paragraph 7)

➤ F. THINKING CRITICALLY

Select the best answer.

_____ 1. The tone of the reading can best be described as

    a. critical.

    b. informative.

    c. amused.

    d. distressed.

_____ 2. The central thesis is supported primarily by

    a. research evidence.

    b. cause and effect relationships.

    c. descriptions and examples.

    d. personal experience.

_____ 3. Of the following statements from paragraph 5, the only one that does not contain an opinion is

    a. "Barbara Kruger was trained as a magazine designer. . ."

    b. "The position of the hand, too, looks like it came from an ad for aspirin or sleeping medication."

    c. "Often we buy a product because of what it will say about us and not for the thing itself."

    d. "These are some of the messages present in this simple yet fascinating work."

_____ 4. Of the following statements from paragraph 7, the only one that does not contain an opinion is

    a. "His 2006 installation . . . filled the entire gallery space with a dizzying array of objects that resembled a parade float on drugs, or a cross between an insane asylum and a grocery store."

    b. "The headlines shout the aimless alarmism of cable news channels. . ."

    c. "The shrill volume of this exhibition only paralleled the strident intensity of today's news, where a disaster might follow a fashion show."

d. "At the opening reception, the artist provided hammers and screwdrivers, and the crowd joined in attaching nails and screws. . ."

_____ 5. In paragraph 7, the artist Thomas Hirschhorn uses the term "friendly piracy" to refer to the

a. common theme of theft in his art.

b. use of another person's ideas in his art.

c. high prices charged in some art galleries.

d. practice of using stolen materials to create art.

_____ 6. In Shepard Fairey's mural "Revolution Girl," the artist's message is communicated most clearly by the

a. leafy patterns on the left of the mural.

b. use of the word "obey" at the top of the mural.

c. flower extending from the soldier's rifle in the center.

d. images of a female face in the lower corner.

_____ 7. The artists known as Swoon and Banksy use pseudonyms because

a. they are hoping to gain the attention of gallery owners.

b. their work is part of an advertising campaign.

c. much of their work is installed illegally.

d. they are already popular in other countries and wish to remain anonymous in the United States.

G. BUILDING VOCABULARY

Context

Using context and a dictionary, if necessary, determine the meaning of each word as it is used in the selection.

_____ 1. pristine (paragraph 4)

a. private

b. untouched

c. valuable

d. useful

_____ 2. pretense (paragraph 7)

a. falseness

b. concern

c. excuse

d. function

_____ 3. brash (paragraph 7)

    a. sharp

    b. easy

    c. daring

    d. cheap

_____ 4. strident (paragraph 7)

    a. pleasant

    b. harsh

    c. obvious

    d. mild

_____ 5. motif (paragraph 10)

    a. memorable tune

    b. dominant theme

    c. strong argument

    d. logical evidence

_____ 6. repute (paragraph 11)

    a. fame

    b. similarity

    c. arrangement

    d. declaration

_____ 7. defaced (paragraph 12)

    a. added

    b. lost

    c. damaged

    d. created

➤ Word Parts

A REVIEW OF PREFIXES AND SUFFIXES

MIS- means *wrongly*

IM- means *not*

PSEUDO- means *false*

-IST means *one who*

-ER means *one who*

-ARY means *pertaining to* or *referring to*

Match each word in Column A with its meaning in Column B. Write your answers in the spaces provided.

Column A

_____ 1. misguided

_____ 2. practitioner

_____ 3. exemplary

_____ 4. elitist

_____ 5. pseudonym

_____ 6. impermanent

Column B

a. referring to a typical example

b. false name

c. wrongly or mistakenly undertaken

d. temporary; not permanent

e. one who practices an art or profession

f. one who believes he or she is part of a superior or elite group

> **Unusual Words/Understanding Idioms**

*Use the meaning given below to write a sentence using the **boldface** phrase.*

1. To **blur the line** (paragraph 12) between two separate things is to make it difficult to see the difference between the two.

   Your sentence: _____

   _____

H.   SELECTING A LEARNING/STUDY STRATEGY

Using the map you completed for issue-oriented artists as a model, create a map based on the street artists described in paragraphs 8–12.

I.   EXPLORING IDEAS THROUGH DISCUSSION AND WRITING

1. Evaluate the introduction to this selection. Did it capture your attention?

2. Write your own definition of art. Does it include modern art forms such as issue-oriented art and street art? Why or why not?

3. Choose one of the pieces of art included with the selection and write a paragraph about it. Begin with a description of the piece, followed by your own interpretation of what the artist was trying to say through that particular work. End the paragraph with your response to the piece of art, explaining whether it was positive or negative and why.

4. Did this selection make you curious about other types of modern art? Discuss the types of art that you find most (and least) appealing.

➤ **J. BEYOND THE CLASSROOM TO THE WEB**

Explore the site for the Street Art exhibition at the Tate Modern in London:
http://www.tate.org.uk/modern/exhibitions/streetart/default.shtm. *Write down the words that come into your head when you view the art. What is your opinion of street art? What is your opinion of a museum-sponsored street art exhibition? Write an editorial expressing these opinions.*

✔ **Tracking Your Progress**

Selection 10

Section	Number Correct		Score
A. Thesis and Main Ideas (5 items)	_____	x 4	_____
B. Details (5 items)	_____	x 3	_____
C. Organization and Transitions (2 items)	_____	x 1	_____
E Inferred Meanings (5 items)	_____	x 3	_____
F. Thinking Critically (7 items)	_____	x 3	_____
G. Vocabulary			
1. Context (7 items)	_____	x 3	_____
2. Word Parts (6 items)	_____	x 1	_____
	TOTAL SCORE		_____%

SELECTION 11

Gregory

Panos Ioannides

This short story by Panos Ioannides, a writer born in Cyprus, gives an account of an executioner's final thoughts before killing his prisoner. The story is based on a true incident that occurred in the 1950s during a liberation struggle between Cyprus and Great Britain. The story describes the conflict a soldier experiences when he is ordered to shoot a prisoner who has saved his life and become his friend.

PREVIEWING THE READING

Short stories are not previewed in the same way as textbooks. For that reason, the headnote above gives you an overview of the plot. Based on the information in the headnote, write at least three questions you expect to be answered in the story. Answer will vary. But may include:

a. _____

b. _____

c. _____

MAKING CONNECTIONS

Think about some difficult decisions you have had to make. Have you ever had to choose between duty and friendship? What did you do?

READING TIP

As you read, create a time line of the major events in the story.

Gregory

1   My hand was sweating as I held the pistol. The curve of the trigger was biting against my finger.

2   Facing me, Gregory trembled.

3   His whole being was beseeching me, "Don't!"

4   Only his mouth did not make a sound. His lips were squeezed tight. If it had been me, I would have screamed, shouted, cursed.

5   The soldiers were watching . . . .

6   The day before, during a brief meeting, they had each given their opinions: "It's tough luck, but it has to be done. We've got no choice."

7   The order from Headquarters was clear: "As soon as Lieutenant Rafel's execution is announced, the hostage Gregory is to be shot and his body must be hanged from a telegraph pole in the main street as an exemplary punishment."

8   It was not the first time that I had to execute a hostage in this war. I had acquired experience, thanks to Headquarters which had kept entrusting me with these delicate assignments. Gregory's case was precisely the sixth.

9   The first time, I remember, I vomited. The second time I got sick and had a headache for days. The third time I drank a bottle of rum. The fourth, just two glasses of beer. The fifth time I joked about it, "This little guy, with the big pop-eyes, won't be much of a ghost!"

10   But why, dammit, when the day came did I have to start thinking that I'm not so tough, after all? The thought had come at exactly the wrong time and spoiled all my disposition to do my duty.

11   You see, this Gregory was such a miserable little creature, such a puny thing, such a nobody, damn him.

12   That very morning, although he had heard over the loudspeakers that Rafel had been executed, he believed that we would spare his life because we had been eating together so long.

mess tins
sets of eating utensils and dishes that fit together into compact units used by soldiers

13   "Those who eat from the same **mess tins** and drink from the same **water canteen**," he said, "remain good friends no matter what."

14   And a lot more of the same sort of nonsense.

15   He was a silly fool—we had smelled that out the very first day Headquarters gave him to us. The sentry guarding him had got dead drunk and had dozed off. The rest of us with **exit permits** had gone from the barracks. When we came back, there was Gregory sitting by the sleeping sentry and thumbing through a magazine.

water canteen
a flask for carrying water

16   "Why didn't you run away, Gregory?" we asked, laughing at him, several days later.

17   And he answered, "Where would I go in this freezing weather? I'm O.K. here."

18   So we started teasing him.

19   "You're dead right. The accommodations here are splendid. . . ."

20   "It's not so bad here," he replied. "The barracks where I used to be are like a sieve. The wind blows in from every side. . . ."

exit permits
passes that allow soldiers to leave their camps or bases

21   We asked him about his girl. He smiled.

22   "Maria is a wonderful person," he told us. "Before I met her she was engaged to a no-good fellow, a pig. He gave her up for another girl. Then nobody in the village wanted to marry Maria. I didn't miss my chance. So what if she is second-hand. Nonsense. Peasant ideas, my friend. She's beautiful and good-hearted. What more could I want? And didn't she load me with watermelons and cucumbers every time I passed by her vegetable garden? Well, one day I stole some cucumbers and melons and watermelons and I took them to her. 'Maria,' I said, 'from now on I'm going to take care of you.' She started crying and then me, too. But ever since that day she has given me lots of trouble—jealousy. She wouldn't let me go even to my mother's. Until the day I was recruited, she wouldn't let me go far from her apron strings. But that was just what I wanted . . . ."

23   He used to tell this story over and over, always with the same words, the same commonplace gestures. At the end he would have a good laugh and start gulping from his water jug.

24   His tongue was always wagging! When he started talking, nothing could stop him. We used to listen and nod our heads, not saying a word. But sometimes, as he was telling us about his mother and family problems, we couldn't help wondering, "Eh, well, these people have the same headaches in their country as we've got."

25   Strange, isn't it!

26   Except for his talking too much, Gregory wasn't a bad fellow. He was a marvelous cook. Once he made us some apple tarts, so delicious we licked the platter clean. And he could sew, too. He used to sew on all our buttons, patch our clothes, darn our socks, iron our ties, wash our clothes. . . .

27   How the devil could you kill such a friend?

28   Even though his name was Gregory and some people on his side had killed one of ours, even though we had left wives and children to go to war against him and his kind—but how can I explain? He was our friend. He actually liked us! A few days before, hadn't he killed with his own bare hands a scorpion that was climbing up my leg? He could have let it send me to hell!

29   "Thanks, Gregory!" I said then, "Thank God who made you. . . ."

30   When the order came, it was like a thunderbolt. Gregory was to be shot, it said, and hanged from a telegraph pole as an exemplary punishment.

31   We got together inside the barracks. We sent Gregory to wash some underwear for us.

32   "It ain't right."

33   "What is right?"

34   "Our duty!"

35   "Shit!"

Court-martial a special court for trying members of the armed forces

36   "If you dare, don't do it! They'll drag you to court-martial and then bang-bang. . . ."

37   Well, of course. The right thing is to save your skin. That's only logical. It's either your skin or his. His, of course, even if it was Gregory, the fellow you've been sharing the same plate with, eating with your fingers, and who was washing your clothes that very minute.

38   What could I do? That's war. We had seen worse things.

39   So we set the hour.

40   We didn't tell him anything when he came back from the washing. He slept peacefully. He snored for the last time. In the morning, he heard the news over the loudspeaker and he saw that we looked gloomy and he began to suspect that something was up. He tried talking to us, but he got no answers and then he stopped talking.

41   He just stood there and looked at us, stunned and lost. . . .

Now, I'll squeeze the trigger. A tiny bullet will rip through his chest. Maybe I'll lose my sleep tonight but in the morning I'll wake up alive.

Gregory seems to guess my thoughts. He puts out his hand and asks, "You're kidding, friend! Aren't you kidding?"

What a jackass! Doesn't he deserve to be cut to pieces? What a thing to ask at such a time. Your heart is about to burst and he's asking if you're kidding. How can a body be kidding about such a thing? Idiot! This is no time for jokes. And you, if you're such a fine friend, why don't you make things easier for us? Help us kill you with fewer qualms? If you would get angry—curse our **Virgin**, our God—if you'd try to escape it would be much easier for us and for you.

Virgin
the Virgin Mary,
mother of Jesus

So it is *now*.

Now, Mr. Gregory, you are going to pay for your stupidities wholesale. Because you didn't escape the day the sentry fell asleep; because you didn't escape yesterday when we sent you all alone to the laundry—we did it on purpose, you idiot! Why didn't you let me die from the sting of the scorpion?

So now don't complain. It's all your fault, nitwit.

Eh? What's happening to him now?

Gregory is crying. Tears flood his eyes and trickle down over his cleanshaven cheeks. He is turning his face and pressing his forehead against the wall. His back is shaking as he sobs. His hands cling, rigid and helpless, to the wall.

Now is my best chance, now that he knows there is no other solution and turns his face from us.

I squeeze the trigger.

Gregory jerks. His back stops shaking up and down.

I think I've finished him! How easy it is. . . . But suddenly he starts crying out loud, his hands claw at the wall and try to pull it down. He screams, "No, no. . . ."

I turn to the others. I expect them to nod, "That's enough."

They nod, "What are you waiting for?"

I squeeze the trigger again.

The bullet smashed into his neck. A thick spray of blood spurts out.

Gregory turns. His eyes are all red. He lunges at me and starts punching me with his fists.

"I hate you, hate you. . . ," he screams.

I emptied the barrel. He fell and grabbed my leg as if he wanted to hold on.

42 He died with a terrible spasm. His mouth was full of blood and so were my boots and socks.

43 We stood quietly, looking at him.

44 When we came to, we stooped and picked him up. His hands were frozen and wouldn't let my legs go.

45 I still have their imprints, red and deep, as if made by a hot knife.

46 "We will hang him tonight," the men said.

47 "Tonight or now?" they said.

48 I turned and looked at them one by one.

49 "Is that what you all want?" I asked.

50 They gave me no answer.

51 "Dig a grave," I said.

52 Headquarters did not ask for a report the next day or the day after. The top brass were sure that we had obeyed them and had left him swinging from a pole.

53 They didn't care to know what happened to that Gregory, alive or dead.

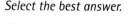 **A.   UNDERSTANDING THE THESIS AND OTHER MAIN IDEAS**

Select the best answer.

_____ 1. The central theme of "Gregory" is that

    a. friendship is more important than following orders.

    b. humans have a natural tendency to be violent.

    c. killing during wartime is justified.

    d. duty can cause people to perform acts they feel are wrong.

_____ 2. The author's primary purpose is to

    a. express support for soldiers who do their duty.

    b. criticize soldiers who do not follow orders.

    c. comment on the personal and moral conflicts that arise during war.

    d. recount a war story to show that war is wrong.

B.   IDENTIFYING DETAILS

Select the best answer.

_____ 1. Officially, Gregory was killed

    a. because he was a prisoner of war.

    b. in retaliation for Lieutenant Rafel's execution.

    c. for being "puny" and a "nobody."

    d. when he tried to escape.

_____ 2. The narrator was chosen to perform the execution because he

    a. was experienced in killing hostages.

    b. hated Gregory.

    c. never disobeyed an order.

    d. was a close friend of Lieutenant Rafel.

_____ 3. Gregory believed the soldiers would not kill him since he

    a. was their friend.

    b. had told them stories about his life.

    c. washed their underwear.

    d. begged them not to kill him.

_____ 4. When did Gregory have the chance to escape?

    a. the first day he was there.

    b. while he was off washing underwear.

    c. when the guard fell asleep while the other soldiers were away.

    d. all of the above.

_____ 5. All of the following are mentioned as tasks done by Gregory for the soldiers *except*

    a. cooking tarts.

    b. ironing.

    c. emptying garbage cans.

    d. sewing on buttons.

_____ 6. On the day he died, Gregory

    a. was stunned that his friends would kill him.

    b. wrote a letter to his family.

    c. told the soldiers to do their duty.

    d. asked the soldiers to contact Maria.

▶ C. RECOGNIZING METHODS OF ORGANIZATION AND TRANSITIONS

Select the best answer.

_____ 1. What organizational pattern is used throughout this story?

    a. comparison and contrast

    b. chronological order

    c. classification

    d. cause and effect

List one transitional word or phrase that is used in each of the following paragraphs.

    2. Paragraph 6: _____.

    3. Paragraph 9: _____.

    4. Paragraph 12: _____.

    5. Paragraph 15: _____.

▶ D. REVIEWING AND ORGANIZING IDEAS: SUMMARIZING

Use the following list of words and phrases to complete the paraphrase of paragraph 22.

left	Gregory	happy	beautiful	together
jealous	Maria	second-hand	garden	

_____ told the soldiers about his girlfriend, _____. She had been engaged, but her fiancé _____ her for another girl. Maria was then considered _____ goods by the villagers, but Gregory saw her as _____ and good-natured. She always gave him food from her _____. Finally Gregory stole some food, gave it to her, and proclaimed that they would be _____ from then on. She turned out to be a _____woman, wanting Gregory to always be with her, but Gregory was actually _____ with that.

➤ E. FIGURING OUT INFERRED MEANINGS

Indicate whether each statement is true (T) or false (F).

_____ 1. The soldiers liked Gregory.

_____ 2. Gregory liked the soldiers.

_____ 3. The war is almost over.

_____ 4. The sentry was punished for falling asleep.

_____ 5. The soldiers liked Gregory's cooking.

_____ 6. The narrator could have died from the scorpion's bite.

_____ 7. Gregory was not hung from the telephone pole.

_____ 8. The soldiers' superiors expected the soldiers to follow orders without question.

➤ F. THINKING CRITICALLY

Select the best answer.

_____ 1. The narrator's dilemma is mostly presented through
   a. personal experience.   c. analogies.
   b. historical documentation. d. expert opinion.

_____ 2. The tone of the selection can best be described as
   a. bitter.   c. light.
   b. conflicted. d. worried.

_____ 3. The author tells the story through the use of flashbacks in order to
   a. mislead the reader.
   b. describe how time stood still for Gregory during the last few minutes of his life.
   c. comment on the importance of memory in our decision-making process.
   d. show what went through the mind of the narrator when he was forced to make an important decision.

_____ 4. The story about Maria is included for all the following reasons *except*

     a. as an example of how Gregory talked so much.

     b. to show yet another side of Gregory's personality.

     c. as an example of something stupid that Gregory had done.

     d. to reveal how well the soldiers had come to know Gregory.

G. BUILDING VOCABULARY

Context

Using context and a dictionary, if necessary, determine the meaning of each word as it is used in the selection.

_____ 1. beseeching (paragraph 3)

     a. begging   c. nagging

     b. suggesting   d. opposing

_____ 2. delicate (paragraph 8)

     a. pleasant   c. classified, secret

     b. easily messed up   d. requiring special skill or tact

_____ 3. disposition (paragraph 10)

     a. fear   c. nervousness

     b. distress   d. tendency

_____ 4. imprints (paragraph 45)

     a. pressed-in shapes   c. wounds

     b. colorful drawings   d. displays

Word Parts

> **A REVIEW OF ROOTS, PREFIXES, AND SUFFIXES**
> **GRAPH** means *write*
> **TELE-** means *far, at a distance*
> **-ARY** means *pertaining to*

Use your knowledge of word parts and the review above to fill in the blanks in the following sentences.

1. An **exemplary** punishment (paragraph 7) is intended to set an _____.

2. A message sent by **telegraph** (paragraph 30) is a message that travels _____ through wires.

> **Unusual Words/Understanding Idioms**
> *Use the meanings given below to write a sentence using the* **boldface** *word or phrase.*

1. Being **dead right** (paragraph 19) means that you are absolutely certain or correct.

   Your sentence: _____.

   _____.

2. A man is said to be tied to his mother's **apron strings** (paragraph 22) when she has total control over him even during his adult life.

   Your sentence: _____.

   _____.

3. When someone **saves their skin** (paragraph 37), they do whatever it takes to prevent themselves from getting into trouble or danger.

   Your sentence: _____.

   _____.

> **H.   SELECTING A LEARNING/STUDY STRATEGY**

> *In preparation for a class discussion in a literature class, make a list of the issues or moral questions raised by this story.*

> **I.   EXPLORING IDEAS THROUGH DISCUSSION AND WRITING**

1. Discuss Gregory's motivation for helping the soldiers. Was he just trying to get on their good side or was he just a good guy?

2. Write an alternate ending to the story in which Gregory is not killed.

3. How do the last two paragraphs affect your feelings about Gregory and the narrator? What if the story had ended with paragraph 51?

4. Write an accompanying story from Gregory's point of view. Discuss how point of view affects a story's message.

➤ J. BEYOND THE CLASSROOM TO THE WEB

Explore the Web site for an online exhibit about Japanese-American internment during World War II at **http://www.lib.washington.edu/exhibits/harmony/ Exhibit/default.htm.**

You will find many points of view expressed in letters and official documents. How do these resources help you understand what life was really like in the camp?

✔ Tracking Your Progress

Selection 11

Section	Number Correct		Score
A. Thesis and Main Ideas (2 items)	_____	x 4	_____
B. Details (6 items)	_____	x 4	_____
C. Organization and Transitions (5 items)	_____	x 2	_____
E. Inferred Meanings (8 items)	_____	x 4	_____
F. Thinking Critically (4 items)	_____	x 4	_____
G. Vocabulary			
1. Context (4 items)	_____	x 2	_____
2. Word Parts (2 items)	_____	x 1	_____
	TOTAL SCORE	_____%	

SELECTION 12

Combing

Gladys Cardiff

Gladys Cardiff is an award-winning poet and author whose work often reflects her heritage: her mother was Irish and Welsh, and her father was a member of the Eastern Band of Cherokee Indians. She is a professor at Oakland University.

▶ PREVIEWING THE READING

Previewing, as described on page 29, does not work well for poetry. Instead of previewing the poem, read it through once to determine the literal content—who is doing what, when, and where. When you have finished, answer the following question.

1. Who are the four people who are featured in this poem?

    a. _____

    b. _____

    c. _____

    d. _____

MAKING CONNECTIONS

Think about a simple act you do each day, such as combing your hair or making a meal. Who taught you how to do it? How does it reflect your connection to your family?

▶ READING TIP

Read the poem out loud and notice words that sound alike (for example, bending and bow; head, hand, and hair; curls and comb). By repeating these sounds, the poet emphasizes certain words and connects them to each other.

Combing

1   Bending, I bow my head
2   And lay my hand upon
3   Her hair, combing, and think

4	How women do this for
5	Each other. My daughter's hair
6	Curls against the comb,
7	Wet and fragrant—orange

parings
the part of a
fruit or vegetable
that is pared or
cut off, especially
the skin or peel

8 **Parings**. Her face, downcast
9 Is quiet for one so young.

10 I take her place. Beneath
11 My mother's hands I feel
12 The braids drawn up tight
13 As a piano wire and singing,
14 Vinegar-rinsed. Sitting
15 Before the oven I hear
16 The orange coils tick
17 The early hour before school.

18 She combed her grandmother
19 Mathilda's hair using
20 A comb made out of bone.
21 Mathilda rocked her oak-wood
22 Chair, her face downcast,
23 Intent on tearing rags
24 In strips to braid a cotton
25 Rug from bits of orange
26 And brown. A simple act,

27 Preparing hair. Something
28 Women do for each other,
29 Plaiting the generations.

A.   UNDERSTANDING THE THESIS AND OTHER MAIN IDEAS

Select the best answer.

_____ 1. The central theme of "Combing" focuses on the
   a. differences between generations.
   b. differences between men and women.
   c. connections between generations.
   d. similarities between parents and children.

_____ 2. The person who is the subject of the first stanza is the
   a. poet herself.
   b. poet's daughter.
   c. poet's mother.
   d. poet's great-grandmother.

_____ 3. In the second stanza, the speaker is
    a. taking care of her mother.
    b. singing and playing the piano.
    c. waiting for school to start.
    d. remembering her mother braiding her hair.

_____ 4. In the third stanza, Mathilda's face was downcast because she was
    a. asleep in her chair.
    b. reading a book.
    c. concentrating on tearing rags to make a rug.
    d. unhappy about having her hair combed.

_____ 5. The color that is a recurring image throughout the poem is
    a. yellow.
    b. orange.
    c. red.
    d. brown.

B. IDENTIFYING DETAILS

Indicate whether each statement is true (T) or false (F).

_____ 1. The poet's daughter is a young child.

_____ 2. The poet's daughter is named Mathilda.

_____ 3. The poet's mother used a comb made out of bone.

_____ 4. The poet's daughter was peeling oranges.

C. RECOGNIZING METHODS OF ORGANIZATION AND TRANSITIONS

Complete the sentence by filling in the blank.

The sequence of events is arranged in _____, starting
with the most recent and moving backward.

D. REVIEWING AND ORGANIZING IDEAS: MAPPING

*Complete the following map by adding images that describe each person in the
poem.*

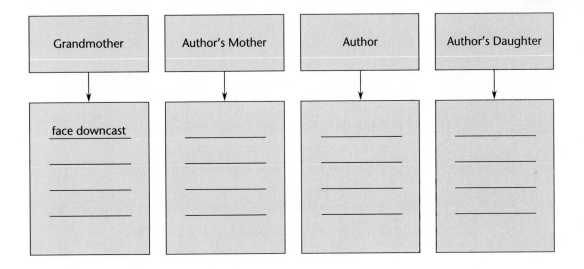

Grandmother	Author's Mother	Author	Author's Daughter
face downcast	_____	_____	_____
_____	_____	_____	_____
_____	_____	_____	_____
_____	_____	_____	_____

> ### E. FIGURING OUT INFERRED MEANINGS

Indicate whether each statement is true (T) or false (F).

It can be inferred that the poet

_____ 1. enjoys combing her daughter's hair.

_____ 2. had to braid her own hair as a child.

_____ 3. comes from a very wealthy family.

_____ 4. lives with her mother and Mathilda.

_____ 5. feels connected to the women in her family.

> ### F. THINKING CRITICALLY

Select the best answer.

_____ 1. The tone of the poem can best be described as

    a. sad.

    b. nostalgic.

    c. humorous.

    d. worried.

_____ 2. The poet uses the image of orange parings to describe

    a. what her daughter is doing.

    b. who is combing her daughter's hair.

    c. how her daughter's hair smells.

    d. how she feels about combing her daughter's hair.

_____ 3. An example of a simile (comparison) in this poem can be found in
    a. line 1.
    b. lines 12–13.
    c. line 20.
    d. lines 24–26.

_____ 4. When the speaker says, "I take her place" (line 10), she means that
    a. she is now sitting in her daughter's chair.
    b. her hair is now being combed by her daughter.
    c. her daughter must now care for her.
    d. she remembers her mother doing the same for her as a child.

_____ 5. The poet connects her daughter and Mathilda by
    a. describing them both with the word "downcast."
    b. having them both in the kitchen in the early morning.
    c. placing them both in rocking chairs.
    d. having them both working on a task.

_____ 6. Of the following words from the poem, the one with a positive connotation is
    a. bending.
    b. hair.
    c. singing.
    d. wire.

_____ 7. The poet creates the feeling of another era by describing
    a. the comb made of bone.
    b. the vinegar-rinsed hair.
    c. the rug made from strips of cotton rags.
    d. all of the above.

_____ 8. The meaning of the word "plaiting" (line 29) as it is used in this poem is
    a. twisting.
    b. interweaving.
    c. stitching.
    d. covering.

_____ 9. The lines that best capture the theme of the poem are
    a. lines 1–3.
    b. lines 14–17.
    c. lines 18–20.
    c. lines 27–29.

G. SELECTING A LEARNING/STUDY STRATEGY

How would you prepare for a class discussion of this poem?

H. EXPLORING IDEAS THROUGH DISCUSSION AND WRITING

1. Can you think of an everyday ritual that has traveled through the generations of your family from parent to child? It may be combing hair, cooking a meal, or something unique to your family. Write a paragraph or a poem describing the ritual.

2. What kind of mood does the poet create in "Combing"? How does she accomplish this?

3. In what other ways do women (and/or men) "plait" the generations? Describe some of the ways the members of your own family have created and maintained connections between the generations.

4. Discuss the colors, smells, and textures that the poet describes in this poem. How do these sensory images add to the poem?

I. EXPLORING IDEAS THROUGH DISCUSSION AND WRITING

1. Discuss who you think the "we" are in lines 17–19.

2. Write a paragraph about lines 28–30. What is the poet trying to say?

3. Discuss how you feel about the writing and study of poetry. How relevant is it to your life?

J. BEYOND THE CLASSROOM TO THE WEB

Experience the history and technique of cornrow braiding: **http://www.ccd.rpi.edu/ Eglash/csdt/african/CORNROW_CURVES/culture/african.origins.htm**

Write a paragraph that summmarizes the cultural significance of this hairstyle.

✔ Tracking Your Progress

Selection 12

Section	Number Correct	Score
A. Thesis and Main Ideas (5 items)	_____ x 5	_____
B. Details (4 items)	_____ x 5	_____
C. Organization and Transitions (1 item)	_____ x 2	_____
E. Inferred Meanings (5 items)	_____ x 7	_____
F. Thinking Critically (9 items)	_____ x 2	_____
	TOTAL SCORE	_____ %

14 Public Policy/Contemporary Issues

The field of **public policy** is concerned with the study of topics that affect the good of society. It includes laws, traditions, conventions, and procedures that affect society as a whole. **Contemporary issues** is a field that focuses on current topics of importance and interest. These fields give you an opportunity to discuss issues that affect and involve all of us in our daily lives. You might consider such questions as: "Does society have the right to take someone's life (the death penalty)?" or "Is human cloning moral?" One issue that our society faces is that of low-paid workers. The reading "The Effects of the Minimum Wage" argues that raising the minimum wage would, in the long run, be harmful. In this chapter you will also read about the right-to-die issue: "When Living Is a Fate Worse Than Death" deals with the question of when to end the life of a critically ill person. "Seoul Searching" concerns another contemporary issue—adoption.

Use the following suggestions when reading in the fields of public policy and contemporary issues.

TIPS FOR READING IN PUBLIC POLICY/ CONTEMPO-RARY ISSUES

■ **Read critically.** Some material in these fields, especially that that deals with controversial issues, is opinion, not fact. You have the right to ask questions and disagree. For example, after reading "Seoul Searching," you may agree or disagree that a child has the right to search for his or her birth mother.

■ **Look for reasons that support a position.** When an author takes a stance on an issue, examine the reasons the author offers that indicate the position is reasonable or justifiable. When reading "When Living Is a Fate Worse Than Death," look for the reasons the author offers for allowing a child to die peacefully.

■ **Consider opposing viewpoints.** When an author takes a stand on an issue, always look at the other side of the issue. Although the author of "When Living Is a Fate Worse Than Death" argues for allowing a child to die without taking extreme measures to keep her alive, consider the opposing viewpoint as well. Why shouldn't doctors do everything they can to prevent death?

SELECTION
13

The Effects of the Minimum Wage

Roger Leroy Miller, Daniel K. Benjamin,
and Douglass C. North

This selection is from the book *The Economics of Public Issues* and examines
whether the minimum wage is helpful or harmful to workers and the economy.

PREVIEWING THE READING

*Using the steps listed on page 29, preview the reading selection. When you have
finished, complete the following items.*

1. The minimum wage is _____.

2. List two questions you should be able to answer after reading this article.

   a. _____

   b. _____

 ## MAKING CONNECTIONS

*Have you ever earned minimum wage? Was it difficult to make ends meet? If mini-
mum wage were eliminated how would it have affected you?*

READING TIP

*As you read, highlight the pros and cons of the minimum wage using two different
colors of ink.*

The Effects of the Minimum Wage

1   Ask workers if they would like a raise and the answer is likely to be a resounding
yes. But ask them if they would like to be fired or have their hours or work reduced
and they would probably tell you no. The effects of the minimum wage are centered
on exactly these points.

2   Proponents of the minimum wage—the lowest hourly wage firms legally may
pay their workers—argue that low-income workers are underpaid and therefore unable to support themselves or their families. The minimum wage, they say, raises
earnings at the bottom of the wage distribution, with little disruption to workers
or business. Opponents claim that most low-wage workers are low skilled youths

without families to support. The minimum wage, they say, merely enriches a few teenagers at the far greater expense of many others, who can't get jobs. Most important, opponents argue many individuals at the bottom of the economic ladder lack the skills needed for employers to hire them at the federal minimum. Willing to work but unable to find jobs, these people never learn the basic job skills needed to move up the economic ladder to higher-paying jobs. The issues are clear—but what are the facts?

Fair Labor Standards Act (FLSA)
federal law that establishes minimum wage rates and regulates other employment issues

3   The federal minimum wage was instituted in 1938 as a provision of the Fair Labor Standards Act (FLSA). It was originally set at $0.25 per hour, about 40 percent of the average manufacturing wage at the time. Over the next 40 years, the legal minimum was raised periodically, roughly in accord with the movement of market wages throughout the economy. Typically, its level has averaged between 40 percent and 50 percent of average manufacturing wages. In response to the high inflation of the late 1970s, the minimum wage was hiked seven times between 1974 and 1981, reaching $3.35 per hour—about 42 percent of manufacturing wages. Ronald Reagan vowed to keep a lid on the minimum wage, and by the time he stepped down as president, the minimum's unchanged level left it at 31 percent of average wages. Legislation passed in 1989 raised the minimum to $3.80 in 1990 and $4.25 in 1991. Five years later, at the urging of President Clinton, Congress raised it in two steps to $5.15 per hour. By the time you read this, it is likely that the minimum wage will have been increased again.

inflation
an economic change that causes prices to rise while wages remain the same

4   Nearly 600,000 workers earn the minimum wage; another 1.6 million or so take home even less because the law doesn't cover them. Supporters of the minimum wage claim that it prevents exploitation of employees and helps people earn enough to support their families and themselves. Even so, at $5.15 per hour, a full-time worker earns less than 60 percent of what the government considers enough to keep a family of four out of poverty. In fact, to get a family of four with one wage earner up to the poverty line, the minimum wage would have to be over $9.00 per hour.

5   Yet those who oppose the minimum wage argue that such calculations are irrelevant. For example, two-thirds of the workers earning the minimum wage are single and they earn enough to put them above the poverty cutoff. Moreover, about half of these single workers are teenagers, most of whom have no financial obligations, except possibly for their clothing and car insurance expenditures. Thus opponents argue that the minimum wage chiefly benefits upper-middle class teens who are least in need of assistance at the same time that it costs the jobs of thousands of disadvantaged minority youths.

6   The debate over the minimum wage intensified a few years ago when research by David Card and Alan Krueger suggested that a change in the New Jersey minimum wage had no adverse short-run impact on employment. Further research by other scholars focusing on Canada reveals more clearly what happens when the minimum wage is hiked. In Canada there are important differences in minimum wages both over time and across different provinces. These differences enabled researchers to distinguish between the short-run and long-run effects of changes in minimum wages. The short-run effects are indeed negligible, as implied by Card and Krueger. But the Canadian research shows that in the *long run* the adverse effects of a higher minimum wage are quite substantial. In the short run, it is true that firms do not cut

their workforce by much, if at all, in response to a higher minimum. But over time, the higher costs due to a higher minimum wage force smaller firms out of business, and it is here that the drop in employment shows up clearly.

7   The Canadian results are consistent with the overwhelming bulk of the U.S. evidence on this issue, which points to a negative impact of the minimum wage on employment. After all, the number of workers demanded, like the quantity demanded for all goods, responds to price; the higher the price, the lower the number desired. There remains, however, debate over *how many* jobs are lost due to the minimum wage. For example, when the minimum wage was raised from $3.35 to $4.25, credible estimates of the number of potential job losses ranged from 50,000 all the way up to 400,000. When the minimum was hiked to $5.15, researchers suggested that at least 200,000 jobs were at stake. With a workforce of 150 million persons, numbers like these may not sound very large. But most of the people who don't have jobs as a result of the minimum wage are teenagers; they comprise only about 5 percent of the workforce but bear almost all of the burden of forgone employment alternatives.

8   Significantly, the youths most likely to lose work due to the minimum wage are disadvantaged teenagers, chiefly minorities. On average, these teens enter the workforce with the fewest job skills and the greatest need for on-the-job training. Until and unless these disadvantaged teenagers can acquire these skills, they are the most likely to be unemployed as a result of the minimum wage—and thus least likely to have the opportunity to move up the **economic ladder**. With a teen unemployment rate better than triple the overall rate, and unemployment among black youngsters hovering around 30 percent, critics argue that the minimum wage is a major impediment to long-term labor market success for minority youth.

economic ladder opportunity for employment and salary advancement

9   Indeed, the minimum wage has an aspect that its supporters are not inclined to discuss: It can make employers more likely to discriminate on the basis of sex or race. When wages are set by market forces, employers who would discriminate face a reduced, and thus more expensive, pool of workers. But when the government mandates an above-market wage, a surplus of low-skilled workers results, and it becomes easier and cheaper to discriminate. As former U.S. Treasury Secretary Lawrence Summers noted, the minimum wage "removes the economic penalty to the employer. He can choose the one who's white with blond hair."

fringe benefits employee compensation that is not salary, such as health insurance or retirement pensions

10   Critics of the minimum wage also argue that it makes firms less willing to train workers lacking basic skills. Instead, companies may choose to hire only experienced workers whose abilities justify the higher wage. Firms are also likely to become less generous with fringe benefits in an effort to hold down labor costs. The prospect of more discrimination, less job training for low-skilled workers, and fewer **fringe benefits** for entry-level workers leaves many observers uncomfortable. As economist Jacob Mincer of Columbia University notes, the minimum wage means "a loss of opportunity" for the hard-core unemployed.

standard of living the level and amount of material things a person has

11   The last time Congress and the president agreed to raise the minimum wage, it was only after a heated battle lasting months. Given the stakes involved—an improved **standard of living** for some, a loss of job opportunities for others—it is not surprising that discussions of the minimum wage soon turn to controversy. As one

former high-level U.S. Department of Labor official said, "When it comes to the minimum wage, there are no easy positions to take. Either you are in favor of more jobs, less discrimination, and more on-the-job training, or you support better wages for workers. Whatever stance you choose, you are bound to get clobbered by the opposition." When the Congress and the president face this issue, one or both parties usually feel the same way.

A. UNDERSTANDING THE THESIS AND OTHER MAIN IDEAS

Select the best answer.

_____ 1. An implied main idea in "The Effects of the Minimum Wage" is that the minimum wage is
   a. necessary.
   b. harmful.
   c. being studied.
   d. unlikely to continue.

_____ 2. The main idea of paragraph 3 is that
   a. the minimum wage has consistently been raised since it was instituted.
   b. presidents have consistently opposed raising the minimum wage.
   c. minimum wage increases have not kept up with inflation.
   d. a minimum wage decrease is likely in the future.

_____ 3. The main idea of paragraph 7 is expressed in the
   a. first sentence.
   b. second sentence.
   c. third sentence.
   d. last sentence.

_____ 4. The topic of paragraph 8 is
   a. poverty levels.
   b. minority teenagers.
   c. clothing expenses.
   d. job skills.

_____ 5. The main idea of paragraph 11 is expressed in the
   a. first sentence.
   b. second sentence.
   c. third sentence.
   d. last sentence.

B.   IDENTIFYING DETAILS

Indicate whether each statement is true (T) or false (F).

_____ 1. Those who oppose raising the minimum wage assert that most minimum wage employees have children to support.

_____ 2. Minimum wage was originally set at $0.25 per day.

_____ 3. Ronald Reagan opposed minimum wage increases.

_____ 4. In Canada, increases in the minimum wage led, in the long run, to drops in employment.

_____ 5. Increasing minimum wage makes it more difficult for employers to discriminate.

C.   RECOGNIZING METHODS OF ORGANIZATION AND TRANSITIONS

1. Paragraph 3 uses a time-sequence organizational pattern. Put these events in chronological order by placing the appropriate number (1 through 5) before each event.

   _____ a. President Clinton asked for an increase in minimum wage.

   _____ b. The Fair Labor Standards Act established a minimum wage.

   _____ c. Minimum wage remained unchanged during Reagan's presidency.

   _____ d. The minimum wage was raised during the high inflation of the 1970s.

   _____ e. The minimum wage was raised to $4.25 in 1991.

2. Identify the pattern that each of the following transitional words or phrases suggests.

   a. most important (paragraph 2) _____

   b. in fact (paragraph 4) _____

   c. yet (paragraph 5) _____

   d. for example (paragraph 5) _____

   e. moreover (paragraph 5) _____

D.   REVIEWING AND ORGANIZING IDEAS: PARAPHRASING

1. Complete the following paraphrase of the two differing positions on minimum wage described in paragraph 2.

   Those in favor of the minimum wage argue that it is necessary and important because lower-paid employees are unable to _____ themselves and their _____ because they do not earn enough.

Raising the minimum wage increases the _____ of these workers with _____ effect on business. In contrast, those opposed to the _____ argue that a minimum wage is not necessary because most of the workers affected are unskilled _____ with no _____. They say the minimum wage benefits a few teenagers and harms more by _____ and keeping them from learning the _____ they need to get better jobs.

2. Complete this paraphrase of paragraph 8 by filling in the blanks.

Minority teens are the most likely to _____ because of the minimum wage rate. Because they have the fewest _____ and the greatest need for _____, a minimum wage keeps them unemployed and economically disadvantaged. The _____ rate is three times higher than the overall rate. _____ of black teens are unemployed. Therefore, a minimum wage is a great barrier to job success for _____.

E. FIGURING OUT INFERRED MEANINGS

Indicate whether each statement is true (T) or false (F).

_____ 1. Supporters of the minimum wage believe that if no minimum wage existed, employers would pay employees less than they do now.

_____ 2. Opponents of the minimum wage believe that minimum wage allows financially secure teens to take jobs away from poorer teens.

_____ 3. Minimum wage ends up costing employers less than if they could set their own wage rates.

_____ 4. Most employers prefer to hire minorities when possible.

_____ 5. Doing away with the minimum wage is an option that should be considered.

F. THINKING CRITICALLY

Select the best answer.

_____ 1. The authors support the central thesis of "The Effects of the Minimum Wage" with

a. analogies.

b. personal anecdotes.

c. predictions.

d. statistics and studies.

_____ 2. By stating in paragraph 1 that workers want the minimum wage raised, and then going on to emphasize why the minimum wage is a bad idea, the authors may be unintentionally implying that

    a. minimum wage workers cannot understand all of the implications of the minimum wage.

    b. the minimum wage actually helps workers more than they realize.

    c. employers do not understand the increased costs minimum wage creates.

    d. the minimum wage should be optional.

_____ 3. The first sentence in paragraph 4 suggests that the minimum wage is ineffective because

    a. employees opt out of it.

    b. the population is not large enough.

    c. it does not guarantee minimum wages for all employees.

    d. it creates a second class of citizens.

_____ 4. The authors refer to the impact on minority teens in paragraph 8 in order to

    a. expose job discrimination.

    b. demonstrate who the minimum wage is hurting.

    c. urge an increase in pay for minorities.

    d. demand more job-training programs.

_____ 5. In paragraph 8, the authors suggest that the minimum wage is an important cause of

    a. employment discrimination.

    b. manufacturing costs.

    c. lifelong poverty for minorities.

    d. friction among different racial groups of teenagers.

➤ G. BUILDING VOCABULARY

➤ Context

Using context and a dictionary, if necessary, determine the meaning of each word as it is used in the selection.

_____ 1. resounding (paragraph 1)

    a. understood

    b. loud and clear

    c. barely heard

    d. uncertain

_____ 2. exploitation (paragraph 4)

    a. previous use of

    b. discovery of

    c. desegregation

    d. taking advantage of

_____ 3. expenditures (paragraph 5)

    a. income

    b. examples

    c. outcomes

    d. costs

_____ 4. distinguish (paragraph 6)

    a. recognize differences

    b. establish definitions

    c. create changes

    d. hide facts

_____ 5. negligible (paragraph 6)

    a. excessive

    b. uncertain

    c. unimportant

    d. confusing

_____ 6. impediment (paragraph 8)

    a. assistant

    b. barrier

    c. impulse

    d. reason

_____ 7. mandates (paragraph 9)

    a. avoids

    b. schedules

    c. orders

    d. discovers

➤ Word Parts

> **A REVIEW OF PREFIXES**
> **PRO-** means *in favor of*
> **DIS-** means *not*
> **IR-** means *not*

Use your knowledge of word parts and the review above to fill in the blanks in the following sentences.

1. A *proponent* (paragraph 2) of minimum wage is someone who is _____ the minimum wage.

2. If information is *irrelevant* (paragraph 5), it is _____.

3. If an advantaged person is one who has money, opportunities, and resources, then a *disadvantaged* person (paragraph 5) is one who _____.

➤ **Unusual Words/Understanding Idioms**
Use the meanings given below to write sentences using the boldface words.

1. One of the many meanings of the word **run** is an uninterrupted period of time, so the meaning of short-run and long-run effects (paragraph 6) are effects that occurred over short and long periods of time, respectively.

   Your sentence: _____

   _____

2. A **pool** (paragraph 9) is a group or supply of items or people, so a pool of workers is a shared group of people available for employment.

   Your sentence: _____

   _____

➤ **H.   SELECTING A LEARNING/STUDY STRATEGY**

_____   To prepare for a class discussion on this selection for an economics class, it would be most helpful to

   a. mark key vocabulary.

   b. summarize the evidence for both arguments.

   c. create a time line.

   d. paraphrase the quotes from government officials.

➤ **I.   EXPLORING IDEAS THROUGH DISCUSSION AND WRITING**

1. Do you think the authors present a fair and balanced perspective on both arguments? Compare the first paragraph with paragraphs 8 and 9. Do the authors use the same kind of balance throughout the selection?

2. If minimum wage were eliminated, what kind of effect do you think this would have on college students? Why?

3. Using relevant facts presented in this selection, write an argument for why a minimum wage is necessary or unnecessary.

J. BEYOND THE CLASSROOM TO THE WEB

One popular movement in the United States is for a "living wage." Visit this site from an organization at the University of Vermont that lists campus living-wage campaigns all across the country: **http://www.vtlivablewage.org/links.html# Student%20Labor%20Groups.**

After exploring the links, make a chart that compares and contrasts some of the current campaigns.

✔ **Tracking Your Progress**

Selection 13

Section	Number Correct		Score
A. Thesis and Main Ideas (5 items)	_____	x 5	_____
B. Details (5 items)	_____	x 3	_____
C. Organization and Transitions (10 items)	_____	x 1	_____
E. Inferred Meanings (5 items)	_____	x 3	_____
F. Thinking Critically (5 items)	_____	x 3	_____
G. Vocabulary			
1. Context (7 items)	_____	x 2	_____
2. Word Parts (3 items)	_____	x 2	_____
	TOTAL SCORE		_____ %

SELECTION 14

When Living Is a Fate Worse Than Death

Christine Mitchell

This reading first appeared in *Newsweek*, a weekly news magazine, in 2000. The author, a medical ethicist, describes a dilemma faced by hospital staff in treating a young child.

 PREVIEWING THE READING

Using the steps listed on page 29, preview the reading selection. When you have finished, complete the following statements.

1. The title indicates that the selection is about a situation in which living is worse than _____.

2. Most of the action in the selection takes place in a _____.

 MAKING CONNECTIONS

Imagine that you are responsible for deciding whether to withhold further treatment from someone who is terminally ill. What factors would you consider in your decision?

READING TIP

As you read, highlight reasons that support the child's right to die.

trachea
the windpipe that carries air from the larynx to the lungs

coded
the action taken by medical professionals to restart a person's heart after it has stopped beating

ICU
the intensive care unit of a hospital

When Living Is a Fate Worse Than Death

1   The baby died last winter. It was pretty terrible. Little Charlotte (not her real name) lay on a high white bed, surrounded by nurses and doctors pushing drugs into her veins, tubes into her **trachea** and needles into her heart, trying as hard as they could to take over for her failing body and brain. She was being **coded**, as they say in the **ICU**. It had happened several times before, but this time it would fail. Her parents, who were working, weren't there.

2   Charlotte was born with too few brain cells to do much more than breathe and pull away from pain. Most of her malformed brain was wrapped in a sac that grew outside her skull and had to be surgically removed to prevent immediate death.

3   Her parents were a young, unmarried couple from Haiti. They loved Charlotte and wanted her to live. The nurses and doctors thought she should be allowed to die

peacefully. They recommended that a Do Not Resuscitate order be placed in Charlotte's chart. The new parents disagreed. Surely, they thought, medical care in the United States could save their baby. They bought their daughter a doll.

4   For 16 months Charlotte bounced back and forth—between hospital, home, the ER and pediatric nursing homes. Wherever she was, every time her body tried to die, nurses and doctors staved off death. Each time, Charlotte got weaker.

ER
the emergency
room of a hospital

ethicist
a specialist in
ethics, the rules or
standards guiding
the conduct and
decisions of
members of a
profession

5   Charlotte's medical team at the hospital asked to talk with the Ethics Advisory Committee and, as the hospital's ethicist, I got involved. Is it right to keep doing painful things just to keep Charlotte alive a little longer, her doctors and nurses asked us. To whom are we most obligated: the patient or the family? The committee advised that in this case the parents' rights superseded the caregivers' beliefs about what was right. Painful procedures should be avoided, the panel believed, but the care that Charlotte's parents wanted for her should be provided unless there was a medical consensus that it would not prolong her life. Such a consensus was elusive. There's almost always another procedure that can be tried to eke out a little more time until the patient dies despite everything—as Charlotte did.

6   A week after Charlotte's death, I met with the doctors, nurses and therapists who had done everything they could for her and yet felt terrible about having done too much. We talked for almost two hours about how Charlotte had died.

7   "It was horrible," said a doctor. "We tried to resuscitate her for over an hour. It's the worst thing I've ever done. I actually felt sick." A nurse talked about the holes that were drilled in Charlotte's bones to insert lines they couldn't get in anywhere else.

8   Why didn't Charlotte's parents spare Charlotte—and us—the awfulness of her death? Because they were too young? Too hopeful? Because they were distrustful of white nurses and doctors who they thought might really be saying that their black baby wasn't worth saving? Or because they believed that a "good" death is one in which everything possible has been tried?

9   Why didn't the hospital staff, including the ethics committee, save Charlotte from that kind of death? Maybe we feared that her parents would take us to court, like the mother in Virginia who got a judge to order the hospital to provide lifesaving treatment for her anencephalic baby, who was born without most of her brain. Maybe we were afraid of seeing ourselves in the news—as the staff of a Pennsylvania hospital did when they withdrew life support, against the parents' wishes, from a comatose 3-year-old with fatal brain cancer. Maybe we were thinking about what was best for the parents, not just the child. Maybe we were wrong.

10   The nurse sitting next to me at the meeting had driven two hours from the nursing home where she used to care for Charlotte. She had attended the wake. She said the parents had sobbed; that Dad said he felt terrible because he wasn't there when his little girl died, that Mom still couldn't believe that she was dead.

11   It could have been different. They could have been there holding her. That's the way it happens most of the time in ICUs today. Family and staff make the decision together, machines are removed and death comes gently.

12   As a hospital ethicist, a large part of my job is helping staff and families distinguish between sustaining life and prolonging death. Sometimes I join the staff, as I did that night, in second-guessing decisions and drawing distinctions between the dignified death of a child held by parents who accept their child's dying, and the death that occurs amid technologically desperate measures and professional strangers.

13   Sooner or later, every person will die. I wish, and the hospital staff I work with wishes, almost beyond telling, that people could know what they are asking when they ask that "everything" be done.

Source: From *The New York Times*, August 28, 2000 © 2000 The New York Times All rights reserved. Used by permission and protected by the Copyright Laws of the United States. The printing, copying redistribution, or retransmission of the Material without express written permission is prohibited.

▶ A.   UNDERSTANDING THE THESIS AND OTHER MAIN IDEAS

Select the best answer.

_____   1. The author's primary purpose is to

  a. describe the current technology used in hospitals to prolong life.

  b. explain that hospital personnel grieve along with a patient's family when the patient dies.

  c. contrast the rights of a patient's family with the beliefs of caregivers.

  d. argue that prolonging life is sometimes worse than letting the patient die peacefully.

_____   2. The main idea of paragraph 3 is that

  a. Charlotte's parents were young and from another country.

  b. Charlotte's parents disagreed with the hospital staff about what was best for her.

  c. a Do Not Resuscitate order should have been placed in Charlotte's chart.

  d. Charlotte's parents believed that U.S. medical care should have been able to save her.

_____   3. The Ethics Advisory Board ruled that

  a. the Ethics Advisory Committee made the wrong recommendation.

  b. there are many possible procedures that can be done to prolong life.

  c. the hospital staff would have to provide the care that Charlotte's parents wanted for her.

  d. it was difficult to reach a medical consensus about Charlotte's care.

_____   4. The question that the author is asking in paragraph 9 is

  a. Would Charlotte's parents have taken the hospital staff to court?

  b. Would the hospital staff have been on the news because of their treatment of Charlotte?

  c. Was the staff thinking about what was best for the parents or for Charlotte?

  d. Why didn't the hospital staff do something to change the way that Charlotte died?

    5. The main idea of paragraph 11 is expressed in the

       a. first sentence.

       b. second sentence.

       c. third sentence.

       d. fourth sentence.

[handwritten: Pick any 3 can add 2 add'l parts for extra credit]

B. IDENTIFYING DETAILS

Indicate whether each statement is true (T) or false (F).

    1. Charlotte's parents were from Haiti.

    2. Charlotte was in the hospital because she had developed brain cancer.

    3. Charlotte lived her entire life in the hospital.

    4. The hospital's Ethics Advisory Committee believed the staff should avoid painful procedures for Charlotte.

    5. After Charlotte died, the hospital staff wished that they had tried more techniques to save her.

    6. The nurse who attended the wake said the parents were angry at the hospital.

    7. Charlotte's parents were not at the hospital with Charlotte when she died.

C. RECOGNIZING METHODS OF ORGANIZATION AND TRANSITIONS

Select the best answer.

    1. The organizational pattern that the author uses to describe events in the order in which they occurred during Charlotte's brief life is

       a. time sequence.

       b. definition.

       c. enumeration.

       d. comparison and contrast.

    2. Throughout the reading, the author uses the comparison and contrast organizational pattern to contrast the opinions of

       a. Charlotte's medical team and the Ethics Advisory Committee.

       b. Charlotte's parents and the hospital staff.

       c. Charlotte's parents and the Ethics Advisory Committee.

       d. the hospital ethicist and Charlotte's medical team.

➤ D.   REVIEWING AND ORGANIZING IDEAS: PARAPHRASING

Complete the following paraphrases of paragraphs 4 and 11 by filling in the miss-ing words or phrases.

Paragraph 4: Charlotte was moved between the _____, her _____, the hospital's _____, and pediatric _____ for _____ months. Whenever she came close to _____, nurses and _____ were able to hold it off, but she grew _____ each time it happened.

Paragraph 11: Charlotte's _____ could have been different if her _____ had been there holding her. It usually happens like that now in _____. Together, the patient's _____ and the hospital _____ decide to remove the _____ and let _____ come peacefully.

➤ E.   FIGURING OUT INFERRED MEANINGS

Indicate whether each statement is true (T) or false (F).

_____ 1. Charlotte's parents believed that the medical care in the United States was better than the medical care in Haiti.

_____ 2. Because of her condition at birth, Charlotte always would have been dependent on medical care even if she had survived longer.

_____ 3. It can be inferred that the white hospital staff was prejudiced against the black couple and their baby.

_____ 4. A hospital ethicist helps make decisions about removing life support for terminally ill patients.

_____ 5. The hospital Ethics Advisory Committee thought that Charlotte would eventually get better.

➤ F.   THINKING CRITICALLY

Select the best answer.

_____ 1. The author supports her central thesis with
  a. examples.
  b. descriptions.
  c. personal experience.
  d. all of the above.

_____ 2. The tone of the selection can best be described as
  a. angry.
  b. concerned.

_____

    c. objective.

    d. optimistic.

_____ 3. The author wrote the first paragraph in order to

    a. gain sympathy for the baby's parents.

    b. explain why the lifesaving efforts failed.

    c. describe the awfulness of the baby's death.

    d. suggest that every effort had not been made to save the baby's life.

_____ 4. Of the following statements from paragraph 1, the only one that is an *opinion* is

    a. "The baby died last winter."

    b. "It was pretty terrible."

    c. "Charlotte lay on a high white bed, surrounded by nurses and doctors."

    d. "She was being coded."

_____ 5. The author included the statement "They bought their daughter a doll" (paragraph 3) in order to indicate that

    a. the parents were not poor.

    b. Charlotte was able to play.

    c. the parents were hopeful that Charlotte would be all right.

    d. the hospital did not provide toys.

_____ 6. The author speculates that the parents let their child's death happen the way it did because they may have

    a. been too young and hopeful.

    b. distrusted the commitment of white doctors and nurses toward their black baby.

    c. believed that death should come only after every possible procedure had been tried.

    d. all of the above.

_____ 7. In paragraph 12, the author considers the decisions that were made in this case by comparing

    a. her responsibilities as an ethicist with those of the medical caregivers.

    b. her beliefs with those of the parents.

    c. the ICUs of today with the traditional ICUs of the past.

    d. a peaceful, dignified death with the kind that occurs only after desperate medical efforts have failed.

G.   BUILDING VOCABULARY

Context

Using context and a dictionary, if necessary, determine the meaning of each word as it is used in the selection.

_____ 1. resuscitate (paragraph 3)

    a. disturb   c. allow

    b. revive   d. review

_____ 2. elusive (paragraph 5)

    a. difficult to reach   c. permanent

    b. temporary   d. unlucky

_____ 3. eke (paragraph 5)

    a. harm   c. draw out

    b. leave out   d. hide

_____ 4. comatose (paragraph 9)

    a. diagnosed   c. terminally ill

    b. unconscious   d. recovering

Word Parts

> **A REVIEW OF PREFIXES AND SUFFIXES**
>
> **MAL-** means *poorly* or *wrongly*
> **SUPER-** means *above*
> **-IST** means *one who*

Use your knowledge of word parts and the review above to fill in the blanks in the following sentences.

1. The word *malformed* (paragraph 2) means _____.

2. The word *superseded* (paragraph 5) means to have been put _____ in importance.

3. A person who provides therapy is called a _____ (paragraph 6).

H.   SELECTING A LEARNING/STUDY STRATEGY

Select the best answer.

_____ 1. If you were using this article as a source for a paper on the right-to-die issue, which of the following techniques would be most helpful?

    a. highlighting useful information and quotations

    b. drawing a time line

   c. rereading the article

   d. summarizing the parents' opinions

I. EXPLORING IDEAS THROUGH DISCUSSION AND WRITING

1. What do you consider a "good" death?

2. Do you agree more with the author or with those who would do everything possible to prevent, or delay, death?

3. What did the author mean by the phrase "almost beyond telling" (paragraph 13)?

J. BEYOND THE CLASSROOM TO THE WEB

Read the policy statement of the American Academy of Pediatrics about "Infants with Anencephaly as Organ Sources: Ethical Considerations" at **http://aapolicy.aapublications.org/cgi/reprint/pediatrics;89/6/1116.pdf.**
    Anencephaly is the condition of being born with most or all of the brain missing. This article discusses the ethical considerations of using babies born in this condition as organ donors. Which of the ethical considerations mentioned in this article and in "When Living Is a Fate Worse Than Death" do you find most compelling? Why?

✔ Tracking Your Progress

Selection 14

Section	Number Correct		Score
A. Thesis and Main Ideas (5 items)	_____	x 5	_____
B. Details (7 items)	_____	x 3	_____
C. Organization and Transitions (2 items)	_____	x 2	_____
E. Inferred Meanings (5 items)	_____	x 3	_____
F. Thinking Critically (7 items)	_____	x 3	_____
G. Vocabulary			
1. Context (4 items)	_____	x 2	_____
2. Word Parts (3 items)	_____	x 2	_____
		TOTAL SCORE	_____ %

INTEGRATING THE READINGS (SELECTIONS 13 AND 14)

1. Which argument did you find more convincing? Why?

2. Evaluate the types of evidence each author provided. What additional evidence might have strengthened each article?

3. Discuss how the tone differs in the two articles.

4. Which article did you find easier to read? Why?

Seoul Searching

Rick Reilly

This article appeared in *Time* magazine in August 2000. The author, a professional writer, describes a search for his adopted daughter's birth mother in
Korea.

PREVIEWING THE READING

*Using the steps listed on page 29, preview the reading selection. When you have
finished, answer the following questions.*

1. What is the article about? _____

_____

2. Where does most of the action take place? _____

MAKING CONNECTIONS

*Do you know anyone who was adopted? If so, has that person searched for his or
her birth mother? Why?*

READING TIP

*As you read, highlight words, phrases, and dialogue that reveal the feelings of the
birth mother, of Rae, and of her adoptive parents.*

Seoul Searching

1   After 11 years and 6,000 miles, we still hadn't met our daughter's mother. We had
come only this close: staked out in a van across from a tiny Seoul coffee shop, the
mother inside with a Korean interpreter, afraid to come out, afraid of being discovered, afraid to meet her own flesh.

2   Inside the van, Rae, our 11-year-old Korean adopted daughter, was trying to
make sense of it. How could we have flown the entire family 6,000 miles from
Denver to meet a woman who was afraid to walk 20 yards across the street to meet
us? Why had we come this far if she was only going to reject Rae again?

3   We were told we had an hour. There were 40 minutes left. The cell phone rang.
"Drive the van to the alley behind the coffee shop," said the interpreter. "And wait."

birth mother
the biological
mother of a child

4 When a four-month-old Rae was hand-delivered to us at Gate B-7 at Denver's Stapleton Airport, we knew someday we would be in Korea trying to find her **birth mother**. We just never dreamed it would be this soon. Then again, since Rae was a toddler, we've told her she was adopted, and she has constantly asked about her birth mother. "Do you think my birth mother plays the piano like I do?" "Do you think my birth mother is pretty?" And then, at 10, after a day of too many stares: a teary "I just want to meet someone I'm related to."

5 "When they start asking that," the adoption therapist said, "you can start looking."

caseworker
the social worker
from the adoption
agency who is
handling the details
of the search

6 We started looking. We asked the agency that had arranged the adoption, Friends of Children of Various Nations, to begin a search. Within six months our **caseworker**, Kim Matsunaga, told us they had found the birth mother but she was highly reluctant to meet us. She had never told anyone about Rae. In Korea, the shame of unwed pregnancy is huge. The mother is disowned, the baby rootless. Kim guessed she had told her parents she was moving to the city to work and had gone to a home for unwed mothers.

7 Kim told us the agency was taking a group of Colorado and New Mexico families to Korea in the summer to meet birth relatives. She said if we went, Rae's would probably show up. "The birth mothers almost always show up," she said. Almost.

foster mother
a woman providing
care for a child who
is unrelated to her
by blood or legal
ties

8 We were unsure. And then we talked to a family who had gone the year before. They said it would be wonderful. At the very least, Rae would meet her **foster mother**, who had cared for her those four months. She would meet the doctor who delivered her. Hell, I had never met the doctor who delivered me. But meeting the birth mother was said to be the sweetest. A 16-year-old Korean-American girl told Rae, "I don't know, it just kinda fills a hole in your heart."

9 We risked it. Five plane tickets to Seoul for our two redheaded birth boys—Kellen, 15, and Jake, 13—Rae, me and my wife Linda. We steeled Rae for the chance that her birth mother wouldn't show up. Come to think of it, we steeled ourselves.

10 At first it was wonderful. We met Rae's foster mother, who swooped in and rushed for Rae as if she were her long-lost daughter, which she almost was. She bear-hugged her. She stroked her hair. She touched every little nick and scar on her tan arms and legs. "What's this from?" she asked in Korean. She had fostered 31 babies, but it was as if she'd known only Rae. Rae was half grossed out, half purring. Somebody had just rushed in with the missing four months of her life. The foster mother wept. We wept.

11 All of us, all six American families, sat in one room at a home for unwed mothers outside Seoul across from 25 unwed mothers, some who had just given up their babies, some soon to. They looked into their unmet children's futures. We looked into our unmet birth mothers' pasts. A 17-year-old Korean-American girl—roughly the same age as the distraught girls in front of her—rose and choked out, "I know it's hard for you now, but I want you to know I love my American family."

12 Another 17-year-old adoptee met not only her birth father but also her four older birth sisters. They were still a family—had always been one—but they had given her up as one mouth too many to feed. Then they told her that her birth mother had died of an aneurysm two weeks earlier. So how was she supposed to feel now? Joy at finding her father and her sisters? Grief at 17 years without them? Anger at being given up? Gratitude for her American parents? Horror at coming so close to and

then missing her birth mother? We heard her story that night on the tour bus, went to our hotel room and wept some more.

13   All these kids—even the three who never found their birth relatives—were piecing together the puzzle of their life at whiplash speed. This is where you were born. This is the woman who held you. This was the city, the food, the smells. For them, it was two parts home ("It's so nice," Rae said amid a throng of Koreans on a street. "For once, people are staring at Kel and Jake instead of me.") and three parts I'm-never-coming-here-again (a teenage boy ate dinner at his foster parents' home only to discover in mid-bite that they raise dogs for meat).

14   When the day came for our visit with Rae's birth mother, we were told "It has to be handled very, very carefully." She had three children by a husband she had never told about Rae, and she was terribly afraid someone would see her. And that's how we found ourselves hiding in that van like **Joe Friday**, waiting for the woman of a lifetime to show up. It is a very odd feeling to be staring holes in every Korean woman walking down a Korean street, thinking that your daughter may have sprung from her womb. All we knew about her was that she 1) might have her newborn girl with her, 2) was tiny—the birth certificate said she was 4 ft. 10 in.—and 3) would look slightly more nervous than a cat burglar.

Joe Friday
a deterctive on the 1950s television show *Dragnet*

15   First came a youngish, chic woman pushing a stroller. "That might be her!" yelled Rae—until she strolled by. Then a short, fat woman with a baby tied at her stomach. "There she is!" yelled Rae—until she got on a bus. Then a pretty, petite woman in yellow with an infant in a baby carrier. "I know that's her!" yelled Rae—and lo and behold the woman quick-stepped into the coffee shop across the street.

16   The only problem was, she didn't come out. She stayed in that coffee shop, talking to the interpreter for what seemed like six hours but was probably only 20 minutes. We stared at the dark windows of the shop. We stared at the cell phone. We stared at one another. What was this, **Panmunjom**? Finally, the interpreter called Kim: Drive down the alley and wait. We drove down the alley and waited. Nothing.

Panmunjom
the village in South Korea where truce negotiations for the Korean War were held

17   By this time, I could have been the centerfold for *Psychology Today*. Rae was still calm. I told her, "If she's not out here in five minutes, I want you to walk right in and introduce yourself." Rae swallowed. Suddenly, at the van window . . . and now opening the van door the woman in yellow with the baby. And just as suddenly, inside . . . sitting next to her daughter. Our daughter—all of ours. She was nervous. She wouldn't look at us, only at her baby and the interpreter. "We'll go somewhere," said the interpreter.

18   Where do you go with your deepest, darkest secret? We went to a park. Old Korean men looked up from their chess games in astonishment to see a gaggle of whites and redheads and Koreans sit down at the table next to them with cameras, gifts and notebooks. Rae presented her birth mother with a book she had made about her life—full of childhood pictures and purple-penned poems—but the woman showed no emotion as she looked at it. Rae presented her with a silver locket—a picture of herself inside but again, no eye contact, no hugs, no touches. The woman was either guarding her heart now the way she'd done 11 years ago, or she simply didn't care anymore, maybe had never cared.

19   Months before, Rae had drawn up a list of 20 questions she wanted to ask at the big moment. Now, unruffled, she pulled it out of her little purse. Some of us forgot

monsoon
the heavy rainfall that accompanies a seasonal wind system in southern Asia

all-out Noah
a reference to the biblical story of Noah's ark, built during a flood

Pusan
a city in southeast South Korea on Korea Strait southeast of Seoul

to breathe. "Why did you give me up?" Rae asked simply. All heads turned to the woman. The interpreted answer: Too young, only 19 then, no money, great shame. "Where is my birth dad?" The answer: No idea. Only knew him for two dates. Long gone. Still no emotion. I ached for Rae. How would she handle such iciness from the woman she had dreamed of, fantasized about, held on to? Finally, this one: "When I was born, did you get to hold me?" The woman's lips parted in a small gasp. She swallowed and stared at the grass. "No," she said slowly, "they took you from me." And that's when our caseworker, Kim, said, "Well, now you can."

20   That did it. That broke her. She lurched, tears running down her cheeks, reached for Rae and pulled her close, holding her as if they might take her again. "I told myself I wouldn't cry," she said. The interpreter wept. Linda wept. I wept. Right then, right at that minute, the heavens opened up, and it poured a **monsoon** starter kit on us, just an **all-out Noah**. Yeah, even the sky wept.

21   Any sane group of people would have run for the van, but none of us wanted the moment to end. We had finally got her, and we would float to **Pusan** before we would give her up. We were all crying and laughing and trying to fit all of us under the birth mother's tiny pink umbrella. But the rain was so loud you couldn't talk. We ran for the van and sat in there, Rae holding her half sister and her birth mother holding the daughter she must have thought she would never see.

22   Time was so short. Little sentences contained whole lifetimes. She thanked us for raising her baby. "You are a very good family," she said, eyeing the giants around her. "Very strong and good." And how do you thank someone for giving you her daughter? Linda said, "Thank you for the gift you gave us." The birth mother smiled bittersweetly. She held Rae with one arm and the book and the locket tight with the other.

23   Then it was over. She said she had to get back. She asked the driver to pull over so she could get out. We started pleading for more time. Meet us for dinner? No. Breakfast tomorrow? No. Send you pictures? Please, no. The van stopped at a red light. Somebody opened the door. She kissed Rae on the head, stroked her hair one last time, stepped out, finally let go of her hand and closed the door. The light turned green. We drove off and watched her shrink away from us, dropped off on the corner of Nowhere and Forever.

24   I think I was still crying when I looked at Rae. She was beaming, of course, which must be how you feel when a hole in your heart finally gets filled.

—Rick Reilly, "Seoul Searching," *Time*, August 28, 2000. © 2000 *Time* Inc.
Reprinted by permission.

▶ A.   UNDERSTANDING THE THESIS AND OTHER MAIN IDEAS

Select the best answer.

_____ 1. The author's primary purpose in "Seoul Searching" is to

    a. describe his family's search for his adopted daughter's birth mother in Korea.

    b. encourage people to consider international adoption.

    c. criticize his daughter's birth mother for giving up her baby.

    d. compare the cultures of Korea and America.

_____ 2. The birth mother gave her child up for adoption for all of the following reasons *except*

    a. she was ashamed of being unmarried and pregnant.

    b. she had kept her pregnancy a secret from her parents.

    c. she felt she was too young and had no money.

    d. she and her husband had too many children already.

_____ 3. The main idea of paragraph 8 is that

    a. the author and his wife were unsure about going to Korea.

    b. another family had made the same trip a year earlier.

    c. the author never met the doctor who had delivered him.

    d. the author's daughter would at least get to meet her foster mother.

_____ 4. The topic of paragraph 10 is

    a. the wonderful trip.

    b. Rae's foster mother.

    c. the language barrier between Rae's family and her Korean foster mother.

    d. the missing four months of Rae's life.

_____ 5. The main point of paragraph 13 is expressed in the

    a. first sentence.

    b. second sentence.

    c. third sentence.

    d. last sentence.

_____ 6. When the author and his family were waiting to meet Rae's birth mother, they were expecting all of the following about her *except* that

    a. she was petite.

    b. her newborn baby might be with her.

    c. her husband would be with her.

    d. she would be quite nervous.

_____ 7. The main idea of paragraph 19 is that

    a. Rae's birth mother refused to answer any questions.

    b. Rae forgot her list of questions.

    c. the author was angry at the birth mother's responses.

    d. Rae's birth mother at first appeared unemotional.

B.   IDENTIFYING DETAILS

Indicate whether each statement is true (T) or false (F).

_____ 1. Denver is 6,000 miles from Seoul.

_____ 2. The adoption agency refused to assist in the search for Rae's birth mother.

_____ 3. Only the author and his daughter traveled to Korea to find her birth mother.

_____ 4. Rae's birth mother had died of an aneurysm two weeks before they arrived.

_____ 5. After their meeting, Rae's birth mother promised to keep in touch.

C.   RECOGNIZING METHODS OF ORGANIZATION AND TRANSITIONS

Select the best answer.

_____ 1. Throughout the reading, the author describes the events that took place in the search for his daughter's birth mother. When he describes these events in the order in which they occurred, he is using the organizational pattern called

a. enumeration.

b. time sequence.

c. cause and effect.

d. comparison and contrast.

_____ 2. Which of the following transitional words or phrases does not suggest a direction or sequence in time?

a. after

b. and then

c. at first

d. however

D. REVIEWING AND ORGANIZING IDEAS: MAPPING

Complete the following time line of the events described in "Seoul Searching." Put the events in the correct order on the time line by writing in the number from the time line that corresponds to the event.

4-month-
old Rae is
adopted.
    1   2   3   4   5

_____ Rae's birth mother is located.

_____ Family begins search.

_____ Rae meets her foster mother.

_____ Rae meets her birth mother.

_____ Family travels to Korea.

E. FIGURING OUT INFERRED MEANINGS

Indicate whether each statement is true (T) or false (F).

_____ 1. The author never planned to try to find his daughter's birth mother.

_____ 2. The author and his wife did not want Rae to know she was adopted.

_____ 3. Rae's foster mother was thrilled to meet her.

_____ 4. Rae's birth mother had to be persuaded to meet her.

_____ 5. Rae planned to search for her birth father while she was in Korea.

F. THINKING CRITICALLY

Select the best answer.

_____ 1. The title "Seoul Searching" refers to

    a. the author's difficult decision to begin the search for his daughter's birth mother.

    b. an American family's struggle to adopt a Korean baby.

    c. the physically stressful search for Rae's birth mother.

    d. both the physical search in Seoul for Rae's birth mother and Rae's emotional search for a missing part of her heart.

_____ 2. The author supports his thesis primarily with
   a. facts and statistics.
   b. cause and effect relationships.
   c. personal experience.
   d. research evidence.

_____ 3. Of the following statements, the only one that expresses an
   opinion is
   a. "After 11 years and 6,000 miles, we still hadn't met our
       daughter's mother." (paragraph 1)
   b. "We were told we had an hour." (paragraph 3)
   c. "But meeting the birth mother was said to be the sweetest."
       (paragraph 8)
   d. "The foster mother wept." (paragraph 10)

_____ 4. Of the following statements, the only one that is a *fact* is
   a. "All of us, all six American families, sat in one room at a home
       for unwed mothers outside Seoul across from 25 unwed
       mothers, some who had just given up their babies, some soon
       to." (paragraph 11)
   b. "She had three children by a husband she had never told about
       Rae, . . . (paragraph 14)
   c. "First came a youngish, chic woman pushing a stroller."
       (paragraph 15)
   d. "By this time I could have been the centerfold for *Psychology
       Today*." (paragraph 17)

_____ 5. The most important aspect of paragraph 20 is that
   a. a monsoon had just begun.
   b. the interpreter was upset.
   c. the author and his wife were afraid they would lose their
       daughter.
   d. the birth mother finally allowed her emotions to show.

_____ 6. The statement "Little sentences contained whole lifetimes"
   (paragraph 22) means that
   a. the birth mother only knew a little English.
   b. Rae's parents and her birth mother expressed a wealth of mean-
       ing in very few words.
   c. the interpreter had trouble translating their conversation.
   d. Rae's birth mother described her life after Rae's birth in short
       sentences.

_____ 7. The best description of the author's tone throughout the reading would be

    a. lighthearted and humorous.

    b. sad and unforgiving.

    c. sympathetic and anxious.

    d. bitter and angry.

G. BUILDING VOCABULARY

➤ Context

Using context and a dictionary, if necessary, determine the meaning of each word as it is used in the selection.

_____ 1. reject (paragraph 2)

    a. take back

    b. turn away

    c. agree

    d. dislike

_____ 2. steeled (paragraph 9)

    a. deceived

    b. talked into

    c. prepared

    d. looked forward to

_____ 3. distraught (paragraph 11)

    a. childish

    b. immature

    c. distracted

    d. emotionally upset

_____ 4. throng (paragraph 13)

    a. few

    b. crowd

    c. confusion

    d. family

_____ 5. gaggle (paragraph 18)

    a. disorderly group

    b. serious mistake

    c. class

    d. annoying tourists

►Word Parts

A REVIEW OF PREFIXES AND SUFFIXES

DIS- means *not*

UN- means *not*

-EE means *one who*

-ER means *one who*

-ISH refers to a *quality*

-IST means *one who*

-LESS means *without*

Match each word in Column A with its meaning in Column B. Write your answers in the spaces provided.

Column A	Column B
_____ 1. interpreter (paragraph 1)	a. one who handles casework
_____ 2. therapist (paragraph 5)	b. without a home or "roots"
_____ 3. caseworker (paragraph 6)	c. not acknowledged or "owned"
_____ 4. unwed (paragraph 6)	d. one who provides therapy
_____ 5. disowned (paragraph 6)	e. one who interprets
_____ 6. rootless (paragraph 6)	f. not married
_____ 7. unmet (paragraph 11)	g. not flustered
_____ 8. adoptee (paragraph 12)	h. youthful
_____ 9. youngish (paragraph 15)	i. not acquainted
_____ 10. unruffled (paragraph 19)	j. one who is adopted

►Unusual Words/Understanding Idioms

Select the best answer.

_____ 1. When the author states that "Rae was half grossed out, half purring" upon meeting her foster mother (paragraph 10), he means that Rae

  a. was sick from the long flight to Korea.

  b. felt like a cat being stroked by her foster mother.

  c. wanted to get away from her foster mother.

  d. felt both pleased and repulsed by the way her foster mother treated her.

_____ 2. The phrase "staring holes" in someone (paragraph 14) means

  a. giving someone angry looks.

  b. looking hard at someone.

c. judging someone by his or her clothing.

d. frightening someone away.

_____ 3. The author describes the "iciness" that Rae's birth mother showed toward her (paragraph 19) as a way of saying that she was

a. emotionally cold to Rae.

b. chilled by the weather.

c. uncomfortable on the icy road.

d. as sweet as icing on a cake.

H. SELECTING A LEARNING/STUDY STRATEGY

Suppose you read this article in preparation for a class discussion on the pros and cons of international adoption. What techniques would you use to study the article?

I. EXPLORING IDEAS THROUGH DISCUSSION AND WRITING

1. What does the girl mean when she says finding your birth mother "fills a hole in your heart" (paragraph 8)? Why did the author repeat the phrase at the end of the story?

2. An especially poignant part of the story is described in paragraph 11: "They looked into their unmet children's futures. We looked into our unmet birth mothers' pasts." Explain the meaning of this statement.

3. How does the author illustrate the cultural differences between the visiting Americans and the Koreans?

4. Evaluate the questions Rae asked her birth mother. Would you have asked similar questions? What additional questions would you ask?

J. BEYOND THE CLASSROOM TO THE WEB

Visit the Rainbow Kids Personal Adoption Stories Web site at **http://voicesofadoption.rainbowkids.com/Articles.aspx?CatID=27.**
Read the stories posted there. How do the experiences seem similar to those of women in "Seoul Searching"?

✔ Tracking Your Progress

Selection 15

Section	Number Correct		Score
A. Thesis and Main Ideas (7 items)	_____	x 4	_____
B. Details (5 items)	_____	x 3	_____
C. Organization and Transitions (2 items)	_____	x 3	_____
E. Inferred Meanings (5 items)	_____	x 3	_____
F. Thinking Critically (7 items)	_____	x 3	_____
G. Vocabulary			
1. Context (5 items)	_____	x 1	_____
2. Word Parts (10 items)	_____	x 1	_____
	TOTAL SCORE	_____ %	

15 Political Science/Government/ History

We live in a political world shaped by history and current events. The economy, the job market, and even television sitcoms are influenced by national and international events. To study political science, government, and history is to understand factors that influence your daily life. Readings in this chapter demonstrate the relevance of these disciplines. In "The Beautiful Laughing Sisters—An Arrival Story" you will read the plight of twenty-first-century refugees arriving in America from countries with oppressive regimes. "Profile of a Terrorist" addresses an important question that has arisen since the September 11 terrorist attacks: How can we identify and cope with terrorists? "Whether to Vote: A Citizen's First Choice" examines reasons for voting and explores possible innovations in registering and voting.

Use the following suggestions when reading in the fields of political science, government, and history.

TIPS FOR READING IN POLITICAL SCIENCE/ GOVERNMENT/ HISTORY

- **Focus on the significance of events, both current and historical.** What immediate and long-range effects will or did a particular event, situation, or action have? As you read "Profile of a Terrorist," consider the impact of terrorism on American life.

- **Analyze motivations.** What causes people and groups to take political action? As you read "The Beautiful Laughing Sisters—An Arrival Story," consider why the Kurdish sisters decided to leave their homeland. What political beliefs do they hold?

- **Consider political organizations.** How and why do people organize themselves into political groups and parties? Observe how political power is distributed and who makes important political decisions. As you read "The Beautiful Laughing Sisters," you will see how political oppression affected and controlled a family's life.

- **Be alert for bias and partisanship** (support of a viewpoint or position because it is held by one's political party). "Profile of a Terrorist" presents only the viewpoint of the victims of terrorism; it does not present the viewpoint of those who commit terrorism.

- **Sort facts from opinions.** Opinions and historical interpretation are worthwhile but need to be evaluated. As you read "Whether to Vote: A Citizen's First Choice," observe how the authors provide evidence to support statements of opinion.

SELECTION 16

The Beautiful Laughing Sisters— An Arrival Story

Mary Pipher

This reading is taken from Mary Pipher's book *The Middle of Everywhere,* which examines the plight of refugees who have fled to America from countries where they have been mistreated and abused. This selection tells the story of a courageous Kurdish family.

> ## PREVIEWING THE READING

Using the steps listed on page 29, preview the reading selection. When you have finished, complete the following items.

1. This selection is about _____

2. List at least four questions you should be able to answer after reading the selection:

   a. _____

   b. _____

   c. _____

   d. _____

 ## MAKING CONNECTIONS

The sisters in the story arrive in a new place that is foreign to them. Think about a time when you visited a new place for the first time (perhaps your college campus). How did you feel? What problems or difficulties did you face?

> ## READING TIP

As you read, look at a map of the Middle East, and locate the places that are mentioned.

The Beautiful Laughing Sisters–An Arrival Story

1   One of the best ways to understand the refugee experience is to befriend a family of new arrivals and observe their experiences in our country for the first year. That first year is the hardest. Everything is new and strange, and obstacles appear like the stars appear at dusk, in an uncountable array. This story is about a family I met during their first month in our country. I became their friend and cultural broker and in the process learned a great deal about the refugee experience, and about us Americans.

cultural broker
someone who
helps people
from other
countries learn
the customs of
the new country

2   On a fall day I met Shireen and Meena, who had come to this country from Pakistan. The Kurdish sisters were slender young women with alert expressions. They wore blue jeans and clunky high-heeled shoes. Shireen was taller and bolder, Meena was smaller and more soft-spoken. Their English was limited and heavily accented. (I later learned it was their sixth language after Kurdish, Arabic, Farsi, Urdu, and Hindi.*) They communicated with each other via small quick gestures and eye movements. Although they laughed easily, they watched to see that the other was okay at all times.

3   Shireen was the youngest and the only one of the six sisters who was eligible for high school. Meena, who was twenty-one, had walked the ten blocks from their apartment to meet Shireen at school on a bitterly cold day. Shireen told the family story. Meena occasionally interrupted her answers with a reminder, an amendment, or laughter.

4   Shireen was born in Baghdad in 1979, the last of ten children. Their mother, Zeenat, had been a village girl who entered an arranged marriage at fourteen. Although their father had been well educated, Zeenat couldn't read or write in any language. The family was prosperous and "Europeanized," as Shireen put it. She said, "Before our father was in trouble, we lived just like you. Baghdad was a big city. In our group of friends, men and women were treated as equals. Our older sisters went to movies and read foreign newspapers. Our father went to cocktail parties at the embassies."

5   However, their father had opposed Saddam Hussein, and from the time of Shireen's birth, his life was in danger. After Hussein came to power, terrible things happened to families like theirs. One family of eleven was taken to jail by his security forces and tortured to death. Prisoners were often fed rice mixed with glass so that they would quietly bleed to death in their cells. Girls were raped and impregnated by the security police. Afterward, they were murdered or killed themselves.

6   It was a hideous time. Schoolteachers tried to get children to betray their parents. One night the police broke into the family's house. They tore up the beds, bookcases, and the kitchen, and they took their Western clothes and tapes. After that night, all of the family except for one married sister made a daring escape into Iran.

7   Meena said, "It was a long time ago but I can see everything today." There was no legal way to go north, so they walked through Kurdistan at night and slept under

*These languages, in addition to many others, are spoken in the Middle Eastern countries of Iran, Iraq, India, and Palestine.

Kurds
a people of the
Middle East whose
homeland is in
the mountainous
regions of Iraq,
Iran, and Turkey

bushes in the day. They found a guide who made his living escorting Kurds over the mountains. Twice they crossed rivers near flood stage. Entire families had been swept away by the waters and one of the sisters almost drowned when she fell off her horse. The trails were steep and narrow and another sister fell and broke her leg. Meena was in a bag slung over the guide's horse for three days. She remembered how stiff she felt in the bag, and Shireen remembered screaming, "I want my mama."

8   This was in the 1980s. While this was happening I was a psychologist building my private practice and a young mother taking my kids to *Sesame Street Live* and Vacation Village on Lake Okoboji. I was dancing to the music of my husband's band, Sour Mash, listening to Van Morrison and Jackson Browne and reading P. D. James and Anne Tyler. Could my life have been happening on the same planet?

Vacation Village on
Lake Okoboji
a family resort
in northwestern
Iowa

9   The family made it to a refugee camp in Iran. It was a miserable place with smelly tents and almost no supplies. Shireen said this was rough on her older siblings who had led lives of luxury. She and Meena adjusted more quickly. The sisters studied in an Iranian school for refugees.

10   They endured this makeshift camp for one very bad year. The Iranians insisted that all the women in the camp wear heavy scarves and robes and conform to strict rules. The soldiers in the camp shouted at them if they wore even a little lipstick. Shireen once saw a young girl wearing makeup stopped by a guard who rubbed it off her face. He had put ground glass in the tissue so that her cheeks bled afterward.

11   They decided to get out of Iran and traveled the only direction they could, east into Pakistan. They walked all the way with nothing to drink except salty water that made them even thirstier. I asked how long the trip took and Shireen said three days. Meena quickly corrected her: "Ten years."

12   Once in Pakistan they were settled by a relief agency in a border town called Quetta, where strangers were not welcome. The family lived in a small house with electricity that worked only sporadically. The stress of all the moves broke the family apart. The men left the women and the family has never reunited.

13   Single women in Quetta couldn't leave home unescorted and the sisters had no men to escort them. Only their mother, Zeenat, dared go out to look for food. As Meena put it, "She took good care of us and now we will take care of her."

14   The sisters almost never left the hut, but when they did, they wore robes as thick and heavy as black carpets. Meena demonstrated how hard it was to walk in these clothes and how she often fell down. Even properly dressed, they were chased by local men. When they rode the bus to buy vegetables, they were harassed.

15   Without their heroic mother, they couldn't have survived. For weeks at a time, the family was trapped inside the hut. At night the locals would break their windows with stones and taunt the sisters with threats of rape. Meena interrupted to say that every house in the village but theirs had weapons. Shireen said incredulously, "There were no laws in that place. Guns were laws."

16   One night some men broke into their hut and took what little money and jewelry they had left. They had been sleeping and woke to see guns flashing around them. The next day they reported the break-in to the police. Shireen said, "The police told us to get our own guns." Meena said, "We were nothing to them. The police slapped and pushed us. We were afraid to provoke them."

17   During the time they were there, the Pakistanis tested a nuclear bomb nearby and they all got sick. An older sister had seizures from the stress of their lives. Shireen said defiantly, "It was hard, but we got used to hard."

18   Still, the young women laughed as they told me about the black robes and the men with guns. Their laughter was a complicated mixture of anxiety, embarrassment, and relief that it was over. It was perhaps also an attempt to distance themselves from that time and place.

19   They'd studied English in the hut and made plans for their future in America or Europe. Shireen said, "I always knew that we would escape that place."

20   In Quetta the family waited ten years for papers that would allow them to immigrate. Shireen looked at me and said, "I lost my teenage years there—all my teenage years."

21   Finally, in frustration, the family went on a hunger strike. They told the relief workers they would not eat until they were allowed to leave Quetta. After a few days, the agency paperwork was delivered and the family was permitted to board a train for Islamabad.

22   In Islamabad they lived in a small apartment with no air conditioning. Every morning they would soak their curtains in water to try to cool their rooms. It was dusty and polluted and they got typhoid fever and heat sickness. They had a year of interviews and waiting before papers arrived that allowed them to leave for America. Still, it was a year of hope. Zeenat picked up cans along the roads to make money. One sister ran a beauty parlor from their home. They all watched American television, studied English, and dreamed of a good future.

23   Finally they flew to America—Islamabad to Karachi to Amsterdam to New York to St. Louis to Lincoln. Shireen said, "We came in at night. There were lights spread out over the dark land. Lincoln looked beautiful."

24   We talked about their adjustment to Lincoln. Five of the sisters had found work. They didn't have enough money though, and they didn't like the cold. Meena needed three root canals and Zeenat had many missing teeth and needed bridgework, false teeth, everything really. Still, they were enjoying the sense of possibilities unfolding. Shireen put it this way, "In America, we have rights." She pronounced "rights" as if it were a sacred word.

25   Meena mentioned that traffic here was more orderly and less dangerous than in Pakistan. The girls loved American clothes and makeup. Two of their sisters wanted to design clothes. Another was already learning to do American hairstyles so that she could work in a beauty shop. Meena wanted to be a nurse and Shireen a model or flight attendant. She said, "I have traveled so much against my will. Now I would like to see the world in a good way."

26   Shireen said that it was scary to go to the high school. Fortunately, her study of English in Pakistan made it easy for her to learn Nebraska English. She liked her teachers but said the American students mostly ignored her, especially when they heard her thick accent.

27   I was struck by the resilience of these sisters. In all the awful places they had been, they'd found ways to survive and even joke about their troubles. These young women used their intelligence to survive. Had they lived different lives, they would probably have been doctors and astrophysicists. Since they'd been in Lincoln, they'd been happy. Shireen said, "Of course we have problems, but they are easy problems."

28   I gave the sisters a ride home in my old Honda. They invited me in for tea, but I didn't have time. Instead I wrote out my phone number and told them to call if I could help them in any way.

29   When I said good-bye, I had no idea how soon and how intensely I would become involved in the lives of this family. Two weeks later Shireen called to ask about an art course advertised on a book of matches. It promised a college degree for thirty-five dollars. I said, "Don't do it." A couple of weeks later she called again. This time she had seen an ad for models. She wondered if she should pay and enter the modeling contest. Again I advised, "Don't do it." I was embarrassed to tell her that we Americans lie to people to make money. Before I hung up, we chatted for a while.

30   I wanted to make sure they learned about the good things in our city. Advertisers would direct them to the bars, the malls, and anything that cost money. I told them about what I loved: the parks and prairies, the lakes and sunsets, the sculpture garden, and the free concerts. I lent them books with Georgia O'Keeffe paintings and pictures of our national parks.

31   For a while I was so involved with the lives of the sisters that Zeenat told me that her daughters were now my daughters. I was touched that she was willing to give her daughters away so that they could advance. I tactfully suggested we could share her daughters, but that she would always be the real mother.

A. UNDERSTANDING THE THESIS AND OTHER MAIN IDEAS

Select the best answer.

_____   1. The author's primary purpose in "The Beautiful Laughing Sisters" is to

   a. examine the official channels people must go through to immigrate.

   b. comment on the racism that exists worldwide.

   c. encourage people to make friends with refugees.

   d. describe the experience of a refugee family.

_____   2. In paragraphs 2–4, the author

   a. introduces all six sisters.

   b. provides background information on the family and their early life in Iraq.

   c. describes the mother's childhood.

   d. sets out a plan for the rest of the article.

_____   3. The topic of paragraphs 5 and 6 is the

   a. conditions in Iraq under Saddam Hussein.

   b. treatment of prisoners in Iraq.

   c. tactics of the security police.

   d. night the sisters' house was broken into.

_____ 4. Paragraphs 9 and 10 focus on

a. the clothing the women were forced to wear.

b. education at the camp.

c. the journey to Iran.

d. the conditions in the Iranian refugee camp.

_____ 5. Which of the following questions is *not* answered in the paragraphs about the family's time in Quetta (paragraphs 12–16)?

a. How did the local people treat refugees?

b. What happened to the men of the family after they left?

c. Which member of the family kept them going during this time?

d. Why were these women so vulnerable?

_____ 6. Paragraph 24 is primarily concerned with

a. monetary problems.

b. social life.

c. sacred beliefs.

d. adjustment to American life.

_____ 7. The final three paragraphs (29–31) are included in order to

a. describe the author's involvement in the family's life.

b. criticize certain American businesses.

c. draw conclusions about the girls' relationship with their mother.

d. encourage the reader to learn more about the plight of refugees.

B. IDENTIFYING DETAILS

Select the best answer.

_____ 1. How many languages do Shireen and Meena know?

a. 2

b. 5

c. 6

d. 7

_____ 2. The girls' parents

a. had an arranged marriage.

b. were both from villages.

c. had been well educated.

d. were very young when they got married.

_____ 3. What finally made the family decide to escape from Iraq?

    a. the father's opposition to Hussein

    b. families being taken off to jail

    c. their own home being broken into

    d. the tactics of schoolteachers

_____ 4. On the way through Kurdistan, people

    a. had to cross mountains.

    b. could get badly injured.

    c. might be swept away by flooding rivers.

    d. all of the above

_____ 5. According to the reading, the author

    a. plays in a band.

    b. is a psychologist.

    c. does not like to read.

    d. none of the above

_____ 6. In the town of Quetta,

    a. the women had to wear heavy robes.

    b. the family finally had regular access to electricity.

    c. the sisters spent the day searching for food.

    d. the family bought guns to protect themselves.

_____ 7. After Quetta, the family went to

    a. America.

    b. Lincoln.

    c. Iran.

    d. Islamabad.

_____ 8. In Lincoln, all the sisters except Shireen

    a. had no problems.

    b. went to school.

    c. found jobs.

    d. became clothes designers.

_____ 9. In the end, the author

    a. helped the family adjust to America.

    b. hardly ever saw the sisters.

    c. adopted the sisters.

    d. bid farewell as the family moved to another state.

C.   RECOGNIZING METHODS OF ORGANIZATION AND TRANSITIONS

Select the best answer.

_____ 1. The overall organizational pattern that the author uses to describe the events in the reading is
   a. classification.
   b. time sequence.
   c. cause and effect.
   d. enumeration.

2. For the pattern you chose in #1 above, list transitions that suggest this pattern.
   a. Paragraph 4: _____
   b. Paragraph 5: _____
   c. Paragraph 6: _____
   d. Paragraph 16: _____
   e. Paragraph 21: _____

D.   REVIEWING AND ORGANIZING IDEAS: SUMMARIZING

Use the following list of words and phrases to complete the summary of paragraphs 24–26.

futures	students	Lincoln	high school	clothes
teachers	opportunities	makeup	rights	jobs

After the sisters arrived in _____, five of them found _____ while the youngest, Shireen, attended _____ where she had good experiences with the _____, but not much interaction with the _____. Despite this and money problems, they realized that _____ had once again opened up to them and they planned for bright _____. American _____ and _____ appealed to the sisters, but mostly they were happy to have _____.

E.   FIGURING OUT INFERRED MEANINGS

Indicate whether each statement is true (T) or false (F).

_____ 1. The author is an American.
_____ 2. The sisters have relatives in Lincoln.

_____ 3. The hunger strike worked for the family.

_____ 4. Shireen made lots of new friends at her Nebraska school.

_____ 5. The author regretted offering to help the family.

F.　THINKING CRITICALLY

Select the best answer.

_____ 1. The author presents information about the refugee experience primarily through

    a. figurative language.

    b. historical facts.

    c. the family's personal experience.

    d. expert opinion.

_____ 2. The author's tone can best be described as

    a. persuasive.

    b. worried.

    c. grim.

    d. sympathetic.

_____ 3. In the first paragraph the phrase, "obstacles appear like the stars appear at dusk" is an example of a(n)

    a. comparison.

    b. unimportant detail.

    c. cause and effect relationship.

    d. contrast.

_____ 4. Which of the following statements from the selection expresses an opinion?

    a. "The Kurdish sisters were slender young women with alert expressions." (paragraph 2)

    b. "Prisoners were often fed rice mixed with glass." (paragraph 5)

    c. "Even properly dressed, they were chased by local men." (paragraph 14)

    d. "They had a year of interviews and waiting." (paragraph 22)

_____ 5. When the author asks in paragraph 8, "Could my life have been happening on the same planet?" she means that

    a. it's hard to believe that there is such a big difference in lifestyles throughout the world.

    b. Americans do not understand the motives of refugees.

c. everyone on Earth is unique.

d. she was not paying attention to the current events of the time.

_____ 6. According to the reading, who was responsible for the sisters' survival?

a. their father

b. the sisters themselves

c. their mother

d. their brothers

_____ 7. What underlying feeling helped the family make it through their journey?

a. love

b. anger

c. hope

d. religious faith

_____ 8. In paragraph 24 the author states that Shireen said the word "'rights' as if it were a sacred word." Shireen felt this way because she

a. had been without rights for so long.

b. had been so focused on and worked so hard to come to America to attain her rights.

c. believes that rights are very important.

d. all of the above

_____ 9. The author was concerned that the sisters

a. were too interested in clothes and makeup.

b. spent too much money at the mall.

c. were ignoring their mother.

d. would be taken advantage of by other Americans.

> **G. BUILDING VOCABULARY**

> **Context**

Using context and a dictionary, if necessary, determine the meaning of each word as it is used in the selection.

_____ 1. amendment (paragraph 3)

a. correction

b. question

c. additional comment

d. formal statement

_____ 2. makeshift (paragraph 10)

    a. dirty and dangerous

    b. well-built and permanent

    c. temporary and rough

    d. a place for refugees

_____ 3. sporadically (paragraph 12)

    a. seldom

    b. unfailingly, reliably

    c. regularly over time

    d. at infrequent and irregular intervals

_____ 4. defiantly (paragraph 17)

    a. casually

    b. quickly

    c. boldly

    d. superficially

_____ 5. resilience (paragraph 27)

    a. the way a person copes with stress

    b. the ability to recover or adjust quickly and easily from a bad experience

    c. someone's attitude toward hard times

    d. courage, bravery

➤ Word Parts

> **A REVIEW OF ROOTS, PREFIXES, AND SUFFIXES**
> **CRED** means *believe*
> **IN-** means *not*
> **UN-** means *not*
> **-ABLE** refers to a *state, condition,* or *quality*

Use your knowledge of word parts and the review above to fill in the blanks in the following sentences.

1. If the display of stars is *uncountable* (paragraph 1) it is not able to be

    _____ or measured.

2. If someone is *incredulous* (paragraph 15) it means that he or she does not or is unwilling to _____.

➤ **Unusual Words/Understanding Idioms**

Use the meanings given below to write a sentence using the boldface word or phrase.

1. If a salesperson is **building** (paragraph 8) a clientele, she is increasing her base of customers and professional reputation.

   Your sentence: _____

   _____.

2. Groups that provide **relief** (paragraph 12) to victims of a natural disaster make sure those people receive the food, clothing, shelter, and other help that are necessary for them to get their lives back in order.

   Your sentence: _____

   _____.

➤ **H.   SELECTING A LEARNING/STUDY STRATEGY**

Suppose you were preparing to participate in a class discussion on the refugee experience in America. How could you use this reading to prepare for the discussion?

➤ **I.   EXPLORING IDEAS THROUGH DISCUSSION AND WRITING**

1. Discuss the issue of immigration. Who should be allowed to enter our country? Should our laws be stricter or more lenient?

2. What are the main immigrant groups in your community? What services are available to help them adjust? What sort of contact, if any, do you have with new people in our country?

3. Brainstorm a list of aspects of American life or culture that may have been unfamiliar to the sisters. (Pipher provides such a list later in the book, p. 90, and includes such things as what vitamins are, how to write a check, what elections are, and how to play cards.)

4. Discuss whether it would be beneficial for international students on your campus to have other students serve as culture brokers.

➤ J.   BEYOND THE CLASSROOM TO THE WEB

Read, listen to, and watch stories of refugees at the Web site of the organization Doctors Without Borders at **http://www.doctorswithoutborders.org/education/refugeecamp/home/**.
   How do these conditions compare with those described in the selection?

✔ Tracking Your Progress

Selection 16

Section	Number Correct		Score
A. Thesis and Main Ideas (7 items)	_____	x 4	_____
B. Details (9 items)	_____	x 2	_____
C. Organization and Transitions (2 items)	_____	x 2	_____
E. Inferred Meanings (5 items)	_____	x 4	_____
F. Thinking Critically (9 items)	_____	x 2	_____
G. Vocabulary			
1. Context (5 items)	_____	x 2	_____
2. Word Parts (2 items)	_____	x 1	_____
	TOTAL SCORE		_____ %

SELECTION
17

Profile of a Terrorist

Cindy C. Combs

This reading was taken from the book *Terrorism in the Twenty-First Century* by Cindy C. Combs, and offers information about the individuals behind terrorist attacks. Read it to find out what motivates different types of terrorists.

▶ PREVIEWING THE READING

Using the steps listed on page 29, preview the reading selection. When you have finished, complete the following items.

1. What is the topic of this selection? _____

2. List at least three questions you should be able to answer after reading this selection:

   a. _____

   b. _____

   c. _____

MAKING CONNECTIONS

How has the threat of terrorism affected your life?

▶ READING TIP

As you read, highlight the types of terrorists and their characteristics.

Profile of a Terrorist

Nothing is easier than to denounce the evil doer; nothing is more difficult than to understand him.

Fyodor Dostoyevsky

ideologues
people who blindly follow a certain set of theories

1 Why do people become terrorists? Are they crazy? Are they thrill seekers? Are they religious fanatics? Are they **ideologues**? Is there any way to tell who is likely to become a terrorist?

2 This final question provides a clue as to why political scientists and government officials are particularly interested in the psychological factors relating to terrorism. If

one could identify the traits most closely related to a willingness to use terrorist tactics, then one would be in a better position to predict, and prevent, the emergence of terrorist groups.

Three Types of Terrorists

3   Unfortunately, identifying such traits is not easy. Just as not all violence is terrorism, and not all revolutionaries are terrorists, not all persons who commit acts of terrorism are alike. Frederick Hacker suggested three categories of persons who commit terrorism: *crazies, criminals,* and *crusaders.* He notes that an individual carrying out a terrorist act is seldom "purely" one type or the other but that each type offers some insights into why an individual will resort to terrorism.

4   Understanding the individual who commits terrorism is vital, not only for humanitarian reasons, but also to decide how best to deal with those individuals *while they are engaged in terrorist acts.* From a law enforcement perspective, for example, it is important to appreciate the difference between a criminal and a crusading terrorist involved in a hostage-taking situation. Successful resolution of such a situation often hinges on understanding the mind of the individual perpetrating the crime.

5   Let us consider the three categories of terrorists suggested by Hacker: crazies, criminals, and crusaders. For the purposes of this study, we need to establish loose descriptions of these three types. Hacker offers some useful ideas on what is subsumed under each label. **Crazies,** he suggests, are *emotionally disturbed individuals who are driven to commit terrorism "by reasons of their own that often do not make sense to anybody else."*

6   **Criminals,** on the other hand, *perform terrorist acts for more easily understood reasons: personal gain.* Such individuals transgress the laws of society knowingly and, one assumes, in full possession of their faculties. Both their motives and their goals are usually clear, if still deplorable, to most of humanity.

7   This is not the case with the crusaders. These individuals commit terrorism for reasons that are often unclear both to themselves and to those witnessing the acts. Their ultimate goals are frequently even less understandable. Although such individuals are usually idealistically inspired, their idealism tends to be a rather mixed bag of half-understood philosophies. **Crusaders,** according to Hacker, *seek not personal gain, but prestige and power for a collective cause.* They commit terrorist acts in the belief "that they are serving a higher cause," in Hacker's assessment.

8   The distinction between criminals and crusaders with respect to terrorism needs some clarification. Clearly, when anyone breaks the law, as in the commission of a terrorist act, he or she becomes a criminal, regardless of the reason for the transgression. The distinction between criminal and crusader, though, is useful in understanding the differences in the motives and goals moving the person to commit the act.

A Trend Toward Crusaders

9   The majority of the individuals and groups carrying out terrorist acts in the world in the last decade of the twentieth and the beginning of the twenty-first century

have been crusaders. This does not mean that there are not occasional instances in which individuals who, reacting to some real or perceived injury, decide to take a machine gun to the target of their anger or kidnap or destroy anyone in sight. Nor does it mean that there are not individual criminals and criminal organizations that engage in terrorist activities.

10 Nonetheless, the majority of individuals who commit modern terrorism are, or perceive themselves to be, crusaders. According to Hacker, the typical crusading terrorist appears to be normal, no matter how crazy his or her cause or how criminal the means he or she uses for this cause may seem. He or she is neither an idiot nor a fool, neither a coward nor a weakling. Instead, the crusading terrorist is frequently a professional, well trained, well prepared, and well disciplined in the habit of blind obedience to a cause.

Negotiating with Terrorists

11 Table A indicates a few dramatic differences between the types of terrorists Hacker profiles. One is that crusaders are the least likely to negotiate a resolution to a crisis, both because such action can be viewed as a betrayal of a **sublime** cause and because there is little that the negotiator can offer, because neither personal gain nor safe passage out of the situation are particularly desired by true crusaders. Belief in the cause makes death not a penalty, but a path to reward and glory; therefore, the threat of death and destruction can have little punitive value. What can a police or military negotiator offer to a crusader to induce the release of hostages or the defusing of a bomb?

12 In terms of security devices and training, the profiles become even more vital. The events of September 11, 2001, illustrate dramatically the consequences of training and equipping for the wrong type of perpetrators. The pilots of airlines in

sublime
lofty, highly regarded

TABLE A HACKER'S TYPOLOGY OF TERRORISTS

TYPE OF TERRORIST	MOTIVE/GOAL	WILLING TO NEGOTIATE?	EXPECTATION OF SURVIVAL
Crazy	Clear only to perpetrator	Possible, but only if negotiator can understand motive and offer hope/alternatives	Strong, but not based on reality
Criminal	Personal gain/ profit	Usually, in return for profit and/or safe passage	Strong
Crusader	"Higher cause" (usually a blend of religious and political)	Seldom, because to do so could be seen as a betrayal of the cause	Minimal, because death offers reward in an afterlife

the United States had been trained to respond to attempts to take over flights as hostage situations and thus were engaged in trying to keep the situation calm and to "talk down" the plane, to initiate a hostage release without violence. But the individuals engaged in the takeover were crusaders, not criminals or crazies, who did not plan to live through the incidents. Only the passengers on the flight that crashed in Pennsylvania were able to offer substantial resistance—perhaps in part because they had not been trained to assume that a peaceful resolution could be negotiated with hostage takers.

13   This does not suggest that the pilots and crew were not vigilant and did not make every effort to save the lives of the passengers. But because the profile they had been trained to respond to did not match that with which they were confronted, they were unable to respond successfully to the demands of the situation. Thus, inaccurate profiling in pilot training was a serious contributing factor to the sequence of events on that day.

14   To political scientists, as well as to military, police, and other security and intelligence units assigned the task of coping with terrorism, an understanding of the type of person likely to commit acts of terrorism is invaluable. As our understanding of a phenomenon increases, our ability to predict its behavior with some accuracy also increases. Thus, as we try to understand who terrorists are and what they are like, we should increase our ability to anticipate their behavior patterns, thereby increasing our ability to respond effectively and to prevent more often the launching of successful terrorist attacks.

A. UNDERSTANDING THE THESIS AND OTHER MAIN IDEAS

Select the best answer.

_____ 1. The central thesis of the selection is that

    a. governments need to provide better training for terrorist situations.

    b. understanding terrorists can help prevent terrorism.

    c. all terrorists fit into one of three categories.

    d. nothing can prevent terrorism.

_____ 2. The author's primary purpose is to

    a. provide insight into what motivates terrorists and how terrorists act.

    b. criticize the government for not knowing enough about terrorism.

    c. compare our current understanding of terrorists with what we knew prior to September 11, 2001.

    d. evaluate current terrorist profile training.

_____ 3. The focus of paragraph 3 is to

    a. describe in detail the three types of terrorists.

    b. explain why it is important to understand terrorists.

    c. comment on Hacker's typology.

    d. introduce Frederick Hacker's three categories.

_____ 4. In paragraphs 5, 6, and 7, the author

    a. compares and contrasts the types of terrorists.

    b. gives Hacker's definitions of crazies, criminals, and crusaders.

    c. describes how to handle each type of terrorist.

    d. explains what law enforcement personnel know about each type of terrorist.

_____ 5. The main idea of paragraph 11 is to

    a. summarize the contents of table A.

    b. use table A to support an idea.

    c. discuss in detail one of the elements of table A.

    d. explain all the information in table A.

_____ 6. Which question is *not* answered in paragraph 12?

    a. What kind of terrorist training are pilots currently receiving?

    b. What type of terrorists were the pilots trained to respond to?

    c. What is the relationship between terrorist profiling and the September 11, 2001, attacks?

    d. What type of terrorists were involved in the September 11, 2001, attacks?

➤ B.   IDENTIFYING DETAILS

Select the best answer.

_____ 1. Which of the following is *not* a type of terrorist as described by Hacker?

    a. crusader

    b. crazy

    c. professional

    d. criminal

_____ 2. According to the reading, it is important to understand the types of terrorists in order to

    a. deal with them effectively.

    b. write articles about them.

    c. identify children who might grow up to be terrorists.

    d. keep government files on them.

_____ 3. All of the following are characteristics of Hacker's crusader type of terrorists *except*

    a. They are acting on behalf of a "higher cause."

    b. Death as a penalty is not feared.

    c. They are always religiously motivated.

    d. Negotiation is seen as a betrayal to the cause.

_____ 4. The motive of the crazy type of terrorist

    a. may be understood only by the terrorist himself/herself.

    b. is clearly defined.

    c. is not important to the negotiation process.

    d. almost always has a political basis.

_____ 5. According to the reading, the passengers on the flight that crashed in Pennsylvania

    a. understood that they had crusader terrorists aboard their flight.

    b. did not try to reach a peaceful resolution with the terrorists.

    c. understood the terrorists' motives.

    d. knew more about handling terrorists than the pilots.

► C.   RECOGNIZING METHODS OF ORGANIZATION AND TRANSITIONS

Fill in the blanks.

1. The author uses one primary organizational pattern. _____ is used to divide terrorists into categories. Transitional words or phrases used for this pattern are

   Paragraph 3: _____

   Paragraph 5: _____

2. The author also uses _____ to show the similarities and differences among the types of terrorists. Transitional words or phrases used for this type of pattern are

   Paragraph 6: _____

   Paragraph 8: _____

➤ **D.   REVIEWING AND ORGANIZING IDEAS: MAPPING**

Complete the following map by filling in the missing words.

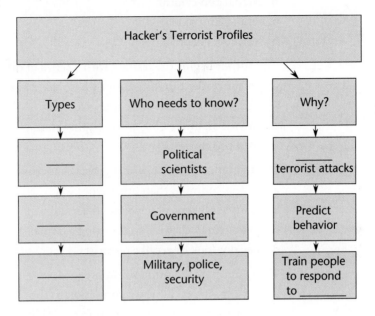

➤ **E.   FIGURING OUT INFERRED MEANINGS**

Indicate whether each statement is true (T) or false (F).

_____ 1. Terrorists are born, not made.

_____ 2. Frederick Hacker is an expert on terrorist types.

_____ 3. The "crazies" type of terrorists are mentally ill.

_____ 4. It can be inferred that terrorism is the primary problem the U.S.
government faces this century.

_____ 5. Some terrorists are not afraid to die.

➤ **F.   THINKING CRITICALLY**

Select the best answer.

_____ 1. The author supports the central thesis of "Profile of a Terrorist"
primarily by

a. citing statistics.

b. describing a personal experience.

c. providing expert opinion.

d. offering reasons.

_____ 2. The tone of the selection can best be described as

    a. informative and hopeful.

    b. factual and cynical.

    c. serious and outraged.

    d. tragic and depressing.

_____ 3. The author begins the reading with a series of questions in order to

    a. get the reader thinking about what makes a terrorist.

    b. briefly mention the basic terrorist types.

    c. provide an interesting and engaging start.

    d. all of the above

_____ 4. In paragraph 10, the author suggests that crusader terrorists

    a. are less common than other types.

    b. are the only type of terrorist we should worry about.

    c. do not think they are committing a crime.

    d. may not look or act like terrorists.

_____ 5. Table A is included primarily in order to

    a. add a great deal of new information to the reading.

    b. compare and contrast the terrorist types in a simple, clear way.

    c. have the reader refer to it several times throughout the reading.

    d. stimulate further discussion.

_____ 6. The events of September 11, 2001, are mentioned in order to

    a. offer praise for the passengers who showed resistance.

    b. evaluate the training of the pilots.

    c. remind the readers of a tragic event involving terrorists.

    d. give an example of a time when proper terrorist profile training would have been useful.

➤ G. BUILDING VOCABULARY

➤ Context

Using context and a dictionary, if necessary, determine the meaning of each word as it is used in the selection.

_____ 1. vital (paragraph 4)

    a. prerequisite

    b. logical

    c. inherent

    d. essential

_____ 2. perpetrating (paragraph 4)

    a. committing

    b. entrusting

    c. perpetuating

    d. delivering

_____ 3. faculties (paragraph 6)

    a. teachers

    b. mental abilities

    c. physical skills

    d. qualifications

_____ 4. deplorable (paragraph 6)

    a. to be weird

    b. to be overwhelming

    c. to be condemned

    d. to be beneficial

_____ 5. resolution (paragraph 11)

    a. cause

    b. distinction

    c. solution

    d. motive

_____ 6. punitive (paragraph 11)

    a. correcting

    b. causing fame

    c. punishing

    d. frightening

_____ 7. vigilant (paragraph 13)

    a. alert to danger

    b. awake and lively

    c. brave, courageous

    d. intelligent and fast-thinking

➤ Word Parts

> **A REVIEW OF PREFIXES**
> **DE-** means *away, from*
> **TRANS-** means *across, over*

Use your knowledge of word parts and the review on the preceding page to fill in the blanks in the following sentences.

1. If you *transgress* (paragraph 6) a law, you go _____ established legal boundaries and commit a crime.

2. To *defuse* (paragraph 11) a bomb, you take _____ its harmfulness by removing its detonating device.

➤ Unusual Words/Understanding Idioms

Use the context of each sentence to discover the meaning of the boldface word or phrase and to write your own sentence.

1. When a job applicant possesses a **mixed bag** (paragraph 7) of qualifications, she can do an assortment of tasks that may not be related to each other.

   Your sentence: _____

   _____.

2. People who follow a leader with **blind obedience** (paragraph 10) will unquestioningly do and believe what the leader tells them.

   Your sentence: _____

   _____.

➤ H. SELECTING A LEARNING/STUDY STRATEGY

Select the best answer.

_____ What part of the reading could best be expanded and used as a study aid?

a. paragraph 1

b. paragraph 4

c. paragraph 12

d. Table A

➤ I. EXPLORING IDEAS THROUGH DISCUSSION AND WRITING

1. Evaluate the government's role in protecting us against terrorism. What should our leaders be doing? Are they doing enough? How far should they go in areas such as airport security and immigration?

2. Write a few paragraphs discussing the current war on terrorism. Be sure to include factual information as well as your emotional responses to the events.

3. Discuss Hacker's categories of terrorists. How useful do you think they are?

> **J.   BEYOND THE CLASSROOM TO THE WEB**

Visit the Patterns of Global Terrorism 2003 report on the Web site of the U.S. Department of State at **http://www.state.gov/s/ct/rls/crt/2003/.** *Explore sections of the report. Does the number of terrorist groups surprise you? How do you think Hacker's typology fits in with the information contained in this report?*

✔ **Tracking Your Progress**

Selection 17

Section	Number Correct		Score
A. Thesis and Main Ideas (6 items)	_____	x 4	_____
B. Details (5 items)	_____	x 3	_____
C. Organization and Transitions (6 items)	_____	x 1	_____
E. Inferred Meanings (5 items)	_____	x 3	_____
F. Thinking Critically (6 items)	_____	x 4	_____
G. Vocabulary			
1. Context (7 items)	_____	x 2	_____
2. Word Parts (2 items)	_____	x 1	_____
	TOTAL SCORE		_____%

SELECTION 18

Whether to Vote:
A Citizen's First Choice

George C. Edwards III, Martin P. Wattenberg, and Robert L. Lineberry

This reading is taken from the "Elections and Voting Behavior" chapter of the textbook *Government in America*. Read it to discover why voting is important, how voting turnout in the U.S. compares to other countries, and how technology may change the voting process.

> ## PREVIEWING THE READING

Using the steps listed on page 29, preview the reading selection. When you have finished, complete the following items.

1. What is the topic of this selection? _____

2. Why should citizens vote? List two reasons.

    a. _____

    b. _____

MAKING CONNECTIONS

Do you vote? Why or why not? Explain your reasons.

> ## READING TIP

As you read keep track of the dates and statistics that are provided.

---

suffrage
the legal right to vote, extended to African-Americans by the Fifteenth Amendment, to women by the Nineteenth Amendment, and to people over the age of 18 by the Twenty-sixth Amendment

Whether to Vote: A Citizen's First Choice

1   Two centuries of American electoral history include greatly expanded suffrage—the right to vote. In the election of 1800, only property-owning White males over the age of 21 were typically allowed to vote. Now virtually everyone over the age of 18—male or female, White or non-White, rich or poor—has the right to vote. The two major exceptions concern noncitizens and convicted criminals. No state currently permits residents who are not citizens to vote. Some immigrant groups feel that this ought to at least be changed at the local level. State law varies widely when it comes to crime and voting: 46 states deny prisoners the right to vote,

32 states extend the ban to people on parole, and 10 states impose a lifetime ban on convicted felons.

2   Interestingly, as the right to vote has been extended, proportionately fewer of those eligible have chosen to exercise that right. In the past 100 years, the 80 percent turnout in the 1896 election was the high point of electoral participation. In 2004, only 55 percent of the adult population voted in the presidential election (see Figure A).

Deciding Whether to Vote

3   Realistically, when over 100 million people vote in a presidential election, as they did in 2004, the chance of one vote affecting the outcome is very, very slight. Once in a while, of course, an election is decided by a small number of votes, as occurred in Florida in 2000. It is more likely, however, that you will be struck by lightning during your lifetime than participate in an election decided by a single vote.

4   Not only does your vote probably not make much difference to the outcome, but voting is somewhat costly. You have to spend some of your valuable time becoming informed, making up your mind, and getting to the polls. If you carefully calculate

FIGURE A   THE DECLINE OF TURNOUT 1892–2004

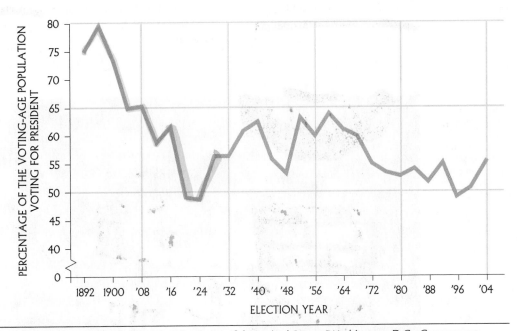

Sources: For data up to 1968, Historical Statistics of the United States (Washington, D.C.: Government Printing Office, 1975), part 2, 1071. For 1972–1988, *Statistical Abstract of the United States, 1990* (Washington, D.C.: Government Printing Office, 1990), 264. Subsequent years from census reports and authors' calculations.

your time and energy, you might rationally decide that the costs of voting outweigh the benefits. Indeed, the most frequent response given by nonvoters in the 2000 Census Bureau survey on turnout was that they could not take time off from work or school that day. Some scholars have therefore proposed that one of the easiest ways to increase American turnout levels would be to move election day to Saturday or make it a holiday.

5   Economist Anthony Downs, in his model of democracy, tries to explain why a rational person would ever bother to vote. He argues that rational people vote if they believe that the policies of one party will bring more benefits than the policies of the other party. Thus people who see policy differences between the parties are more likely to join the ranks of voters. If you are an environmentalist and you expect the Democrats to pass more environmental legislation than the Republicans, then you have an additional incentive to go to the polls. On the other hand, if you are truly indifferent—that is, if you see no difference whatsoever between the two parties— you may rationally decide to abstain.

political efficacy
the belief that one's political participation really matters—that one's vote can actually make a difference

civic duty
the belief that in order to support democratic government, a citizen should always vote

6   Another reason why many people vote is that they have a high sense of **political efficacy**—the belief that ordinary people can influence the government. Efficacy is measured by asking people to agree or disagree with statements such as "I don't think public officials care much what people like me think." Those who lack strong feelings of efficacy are being quite rational in staying home on Election Day because they don't think they can make a difference. Yet even some of these people will vote anyway, simply to support democratic government. In this case, people are impelled to vote by a sense of **civic duty.** The benefit from doing one's duty is the long term contribution made toward preserving democracy.

Young people have one of the lowest rates of election turnout. Music stars like P. Diddy have tried to change this by actively participating in events that encourage young people to vote.

Why Turnout in the United States Is So Low Compared to Other Countries

7   Despite living in a culture that encourages participation, Americans have a woefully low turnout rate compared to other democracies. There are several reasons given for Americans' abysmally low turnout rate. Probably the reason most often cited is the American requirement of voter registration. The governments of many, but not all, other democracies take the responsibility of seeing to it that all their eligible citizens are on the voting lists. In America, the responsibility for registration lies solely with the individual. If we were to be like the Scandinavian countries and have the government take care of registering every eligible citizen, no doubt our turnout rate would be higher.

8   A second difference between the United States and other countries is that the American government asks citizens to vote far more often. Whereas the typical European voter may be called upon to cast two or three ballots in a four-year period, many Americans are faced with a dozen or more separate elections in the space of four years. Furthermore, Americans are expected to vote for a much wider range of political offices. With 1 elected official for every 442 citizens and elections held somewhere virtually every week, it is no wonder that it is so difficult to get Americans to the polls. It is probably no coincidence that the one European country that has a lower turnout rate—Switzerland—has also overwhelmed its citizens with voting opportunities, typically asking people to vote three times every year.

9   Finally, the stimulus to vote is low in the United States because the choices offered Americans are not as stark as in other countries. This is because the United States is quite unusual in that it has always lacked a major left-wing socialist party. When European voters go to the polls, they are deciding on whether their country will be run by parties with socialist goals or by conservative (and in some cases religious) parties. The consequences of their vote for redistribution of income and the scope of government are far greater than the ordinary American voter can imagine.

Registering and Voting by E-mail?

10   Future reform designed to increase turnout may well focus on conducting elections through e-mail. Although modern technology is widely available, Americans have not harnessed much of it to improve democracy. Though many precincts now use computer touch screens to record votes, the high-tech age has not yet made much of an impact on the voting process. There is good reason to expect that this will change in the twenty-first century.

11   The development of the personal computer and the World Wide Web are likely to facilitate the process of voter registration. Already, one can go to the website of the Federal Election Commission (http://www.fec.gov/votregis/vr.htm) and download the "National Mail Voter Registration Form." Twenty-two states currently accept copies of this application printed from the computer image, signed by the applicant, and mailed in the old-fashioned way. As e-mail becomes ever more popular and "snail mail" fades into a method reserved for packages, the entire voter registration process may someday be conducted mostly through electronic means. In an age where personal computers in the home are nearly as common as television sets are today, this technology would clearly make registering to vote more user-friendly.

12   If people can register by computer, the next step is voting by e-mail. A growing trend in the Pacific Coast states has been voting by mail. In 1998, Oregon voters approved a **referendum** to eliminate traditional polling places and conduct all future elections by mail. In California, approximately 25 percent of the votes cast currently come in via the post office. Again, as e-mail takes the place of regular mail, why not have people cast their votes through cyberspace?

referendum
a vote on a specific
question or issue

13   Voting through the Internet would be less costly for the state, as well as easier for the average citizen—assuming that computer literacy reaches near-universal proportions sometime in the future. The major concerns, of course, would be ensuring that no one votes more than once and preserving the confidentiality of the vote. These security concerns are currently being addressed by some of the world's top computer programmers, as commercial enterprises look toward using the Internet to conduct business. If the technology can be perfected to allow trillions of dollars of business to be conducted via the Internet, then it seems reasonable that similar problems can be overcome with regard to the voting process.

14   Whether these possible developments will improve democracy in America is debatable. Making voting more user-friendly should encourage turnout, but people will still have to be interested enough in the elections of the future to send in their e-mail ballots. If old-style polling places are relegated to the history books and everyone votes electronically in the convenience of their own homes, the sense of community on Election Day may be lost. This loss could lead to even lower turnout. You be the policymaker: Do the benefits of voting by e-mail outweigh the potential costs?

A. UNDERSTANDING THE THESIS AND OTHER MAIN IDEAS

Select the best answer.

_____ 1. The central thesis of this selection is that

   a. computer voting will increase turnout.

   b. voter turnout in the United States is low.

   c. people in other countries are more inclined to vote.

   d. voting is a right that not everyone chooses to exercise.

_____ 2. The authors' primary purpose is to

   a. present information on voting history, statistics, and innovations.

   b. convince readers they should exercise their right to vote.

   c. explain why voter turnout is lower in the United States than in Europe.

   d. argue that today's citizens do not deserve the right to vote.

_____ 3. The first paragraph

   a. grabs the reader's attention with interesting trivia.

   b. provides important background information on voting rights.

    c. explains how women and African-Americans struggled for the right to vote.

    d. introduces the issues surrounding low voter turnout.

_____ 4. The main idea of paragraph 4 is that

    a. election day should be a national holiday.

    b. not everyone can take time off from work to vote.

    c. elections decided by one vote are very rare.

    d. reasons people offer for not voting include lack of time and energy.

_____ 5. In paragraph 7, the authors focus on

    a. the way in which Scandinavian countries register their citizens to vote.

    b. the main reasons for poor voter turnout.

    c. the voter registration process.

    d. voter turnout statistics.

_____ 6. In the last paragraph, the authors

    a. doubt that we will ever raise voter turnout.

    b. conclude that people will be more interested in voting if we use e-mail ballots.

    c. lament the possible loss of community if we go to computer-based voting.

    d. offer a solution to the lack of voter motivation and interest.

➤ B. IDENTIFYING DETAILS

Select the best answer.

_____ 1. Which group cannot vote in any state?

    a. convicted felons

    b. prisoners

    c. noncitizens

    d. people on parole

_____ 2. As more types of people have been given the right to vote, the voter turnout has

    a. increased.

    b. decreased.

    c. stayed the same.

    d. varied considerably.

_____ 3. The Florida 2000 election (paragraph 3) was a

    a. presidential election.

    b. gubernatorial election.

    c. senatorial election.

    d. judicial election.

_____ 4. According to economist Anthony Downs,

    a. the voter registration process is too complicated for the average citizen.

    b. environmentalists vote more than other groups.

    c. voters only consider issues that are important to them.

    d. people vote if they perceive a difference between parties.

_____ 5. One reason people vote that is not included in the reading is

    a. civic duty.

    b. political efficacy.

    c. peer pressure.

    d. support of democratic process.

_____ 6. A difference between United States and European elections _not_ mentioned in the selection is

    a. American voters are more apathetic than Europeans.

    b. the voter registration process is more difficult in the United States.

    c. voters in the United States are overwhelmed by the number of elections in which they are expected to participate.

    d. Europeans have more distinct choices with more significant consequences.

_____ 7. What technologies do the authors mention are used or could be used in the election process?

    a. touch-screen recording, Internet registration, and e-mail voting

    b. touch-screen voting and voting by instant message

    c. Internet registration, e-mail voting, and voting by text message

    d. Internet registration, touch-screen voting, and RFID tracking of absentee ballots

_____ 8. Electronic voting is

    a. a sure way to increase voter turnout.

    b. unconstitutional.

    c. a potential security concern.

    d. impossible to implement.

C.   RECOGNIZING METHODS OF ORGANIZATION AND TRANSITIONS

Select the best answer.

_____ 1. What is the organizational pattern used to discuss the reasons why Americans choose to vote?

    a. listing

    b. time sequence

    c. cause and effect

    d. comparison and contrast

_____ 2. What pattern is used to organize the information in paragraphs 7 through 10?

    a. listing

    b. time sequence

    c. definition

    d. comparison and contrast

D.   REVIEWING AND ORGANIZING IDEAS: SUMMARIZING

Complete the time line of significant voting events described in the selection.

DATE	EVENT
1800	Only _____ over the age of _____ were allowed to vote.
1896	The voter turnout was _____, representing the _____ of electoral participation ever.
1998	In the state of _____, voters decided to conduct future elections by _____.
2000	Census information indicates that people who cannot take off from _____ are _____ to vote.
2000	The presidential election in the state of _____ is decided by a _____ of votes.
2004	Over _____ people voted in the presidential election.

E. FIGURING OUT INFERRED MEANINGS

Indicate whether each statement is true (T) or false (F).

_____ 1. American women could not vote before 1800.

_____ 2. The election results in Florida in 2000 were unusual.

_____ 3. Republicans do not pass environmental legislation.

_____ 4. European countries do not elect as many officials as the United States.

_____ 5. In the future Americans might vote via the Internet.

F. THINKING CRITICALLY

Select the best answer.

_____ 1. The authors support the central thesis of "Whether to Vote" primarily by

   a. citing authorities.

   b. citing personal experience.

   c. making comparisons.

   d. reporting facts and statistics.

_____ 2. The tone of the selection can best be described as

   a. bitter.

   b. excited.

   c. informative.

   d. sympathetic.

_____ 3. Of the following statements from the reading, which is an opinion?

   a. "State law varies widely when it comes to crime and voting." (paragraph 1)

   b. "Interestingly, as the right to vote has been extended, proportionally fewer of those eligible have chosen to exercise that right." (paragraph 2)

   c. "Some scholars have therefore proposed that one of the easiest ways to increase American turnout levels would be to move election day to Saturday or make it a holiday." (paragraph 4)

   d. "If we were to be like the Scandinavian countries and have the government take care of registering every eligible citizen, no doubt our turnout rate would be higher." (paragraph 7)

_____ 4. The authors include statistics in the reading in order to

   a. provide supporting evidence.

   b. impress the reader with startling facts.

     c. show how misleading statistics can be.

     d. relate the most important information that someone should know about voting behavior.

_____ 5. The authors compare the United States with other countries

     a. to embarrass American voters.

     b. to explain why American voter turnout might be so low.

     c. to describe places to which civic-minded Americans might want to move.

     d. to prove that no country is perfect when it comes to voter turnout.

_____ 6. Overall, the authors' attitude toward voter turnout in the United States seems to be

     a. indifferent.   c. concerned.

     b. hopeful.   d. amused.

G. BUILDING VOCABULARY

Context

Using context and a dictionary, if necessary, determine the meaning of each word as it is used in the selection.

_____ 1. rationally (paragraph 4)

     a. simply   c. mindlessly

     b. practically   d. reasonably

_____ 2. woefully (paragraph 7)

     a. distressingly   c. dangerously

     b. carelessly   d. recklessly

_____ 3. abysmally (paragraph 7)

     a. secretly   c. incomprehensibly

     b. profoundly   d. superficially

_____ 4. harnessed (paragraph 10)

     a. powered   c. benefited from

     b. tried   d. made use of

_____ 5. facilitate (paragraph 11)

     a. increase   c. make easier

     b. speed up   d. resolve

_____ 6. relegated (paragraph 14)

     a. banished   c. elected

     b. chosen for   d. dedicated

▶ **Word Parts**

A REVIEW OF PREFIXES AND ROOTS
IN-, IM- means *into*
CYBER- refers to *computers*
PELL means *drive, move*

Use your knowledge of word parts and the review above to fill in the blanks in the following sentences.

1. *Immigrants* (paragraph 1) are people who have moved _____ a new country.

2. Some citizens are *impelled* (paragraph 6) by civic duty to __Move into__ action and vote.

3. *Cyberspace* (paragraph 12) is the medium in which electronic data from _____ exists or is exchanged.

▶ **Unusual Words/Understanding Idioms**
Use the meanings given below to write a sentence using the boldface word or phrase.

1. If you have recently **joined the ranks** (paragraph 5) of new college students you are in a new group of people all doing the same thing.

   Your sentence: _____

   _____

2. **Snail mail** (paragraph 11) is a term used to refer to regular paper mail sent through the U.S. Postal Service.

   Your sentence: _____

   _____

▶ **H. SELECTING A LEARNING/STUDY STRATEGY**

Select the best answer.

_____ This reading contains many facts about voting behavior. What would be the best way to learn these facts?

a. visualize the scene at a polling place on election day

b. record the facts on a study sheet

c. read the facts over and over

d. summarize the reading

➤ I. EXPLORING IDEAS THROUGH DISCUSSION AND WRITING

1. Discuss the situation of low voter turnout. Why do you think more eligible Americans do not vote? What do you think would boost voter turnout?

2. Pick a target group. Discuss factors/strategies that would encourage that group to vote.

3. Interview someone from another country about voting behavior. Summarize your findings.

➤ J. BEYOND THE CLASSROOM TO THE WEB

Visit the site for Voter Call, an organization that seeks to register young, low-income, minority voters at **http://www.votercall.org/.** *Review the FAQs and then write a brief description of the organization and its activities.*

Also, if you need voter registration information for yourself or someone you know, visit Just Vote, a site with links to registration materials for all states that make them available at **http://www.justvote.org/.**

✔ Tracking Your Progress

Selection 18

Section	Number Correct		Score
A. Thesis and Main Ideas (6 items)	_____	x 4	_____
B. Details (8 items)	_____	x 3	_____
C. Organization and Transitions (2 items)	_____	x 2	_____
E. Inferred Meanings (5 items)	_____	x 3	_____
F. Thinking Critically (6 items)	_____	x 3	_____
G. Vocabulary			
1. Context (6 items)	_____	x 2	_____
2. Word Parts (3 items)	_____	x 1	_____
	TOTAL SCORE		_____ %

16 Business/Advertising/Economics

Business is a diverse field that includes business management, marketing, finance, statistics, retailing, information systems, and organizational behavior. In general, **business** is concerned with the production and sale of goods and services. All of us are in contact with businesses on a daily basis. When you stop for gas, buy a sandwich, or pick up the telephone, you are involved in a business transaction. In "Four Simple Words That Guarantee the Job of Your Dreams," you will learn how to pursue a career that will bring satisfaction as well as a paycheck. Studying business can also make you a savvy, better-informed consumer. When you read "McDonald's Makes a Lot of People Angry for a Lot of Different Reasons," you will learn how McDonald's, a popular fast food chain, has not acted as a responsible business leader in the opinion of the authors. Business courses can help you make career decisions and discover a wide range of employment opportunities. Business courses also examine the issue of ethnic and cultural diversity since today's workforce consists of individuals from a variety of cultural and ethnic groups. As you read "Product Placement," you will see how product advertisement through placement seeps into popular culture.

Use the following techniques for reading in business.

TIPS FOR READING IN BUSINESS/ ADVERTISING/ ECONOMICS

- **Focus on process.** Many courses in business examine how things work and how things get done. In "Product Placement" you will learn how specific products and brand names are used in movies, television, and other media. In "Four Simple Words That Guarantee the Job of Your Dreams," you will discover how to find a rewarding job.

- **Focus on the theme of globalization.** Growing numbers of U.S. businesses are doing business with firms in other countries and are competing in foreign markets. In "McDonald's Makes a Lot of People Angry for a Lot of Different Reasons," you will see that McDonald's has become a global corporation.

- **Consider ethical decision making and social responsibility.** The application of moral standards to business activities and operations is of increasing importance in the field of business. Issues of honesty, fairness, environmental safety, and public health are often discussed in business courses. In "McDonald's Makes a Lot of People Angry for a Lot of Different Reasons," the authors suggest that McDonald's has acted irresponsibly in a number of different areas.

SELECTION 19

Four Simple Words That Guarantee the Job of Your Dreams

Martha I. Finney

This article first appeared in *Career Magazine*. Read it to discover how to find the ideal job.

▶ PREVIEWING THE READING

Using the steps listed on page 29, preview the reading selection. When you have finished, answer the following questions.

1. What are the "four simple words" from the title? _____

2. The topic of the reading is _____.

MAKING CONNECTIONS

With a classmate, discuss what you know about how to find a good job.

▶ READING TIP

As you read, highlight tips that will help you find the ideal job.

Four Simple Words That Guarantee the Job of Your Dreams

1   Actually, these are also the most exasperating words. Say you meet up with a friend who just landed the all-time best job: the responsibilities suit your friend perfectly; the hours are right; the company is congenial; and there's a future in the position, complete with raises and promotions. So, you ask, how did you get that job? The answer, always delivered in an infuriatingly cagey, off-hand sort of way:

2   I dunno, right time/right place, I guess.

3   Right time/right place. That magic formula is about as elusive as true love.

4   I had a right time/right place experience once. Although I wouldn't recommend that anyone else duplicate this particular incident. Especially these days. I interviewed for my first real adult job in my underwear. And I landed a job as a writer for the **Cousteau Society**.

Cousteau Society
an organization devoted to continuing the work begun by underwater pioneer Jacques Cousteau

5   Let me explain: I was working as a lowly, underpaid, over-abused receptionist for a nasty public relations firm in Manhattan. About the only perk that came with the job is that sometimes the owners would receive boxes of designer clothes . . . samples, they were. And we could buy them cheap. So now and then I would take a bundle into the ladies room and try them on. But to get to the ladies room, I'd always pass the closed door of our neighboring office, the Cousteau Society. And I would sigh. Saving whales seemed much more up my alley than promoting fiction about fashion. And I bet the people inside were nice, too.

6   One day I was in the ladies' room, in my scivvies, about to try on some ridiculous new fashion idea. And in walked the woman who would become my future boss. Just like in **Ally McBeal.** By the sinks, in between the flushes, we got an interview done. And I got the job as member correspondent. It was a cool job, complete with a desk on the 32nd floor right by a gigantic window overlooking the East River, with a view of the 59th Street Bridge.

Ally McBeal
a popular contemporary television program about the life of a young female lawyer named Ally McBeal

7   That was about the coolest way I ever got a job, except for the time I made my interviewer cry by telling him the storyline of the **Twilight Zone** episode that aired the night before. But that's a different story.

8   So how do you get to right time/right place (besides standing around in your underwear)? There must be a secret. Yes, there is. And here it is, another four words: Do what you love.

Twilight Zone
a popular television program from the 1960s featuring a new mystery/science fiction plot each week

9   That's it, it's that simple. So, if it's that simple, why doesn't everyone do it? I have my theories. But it boils down to our tendencies to put our marketable skills ahead of what poet William Blake called our divine spark—that passion, that interest, that cause that ignites our eyes.

10   Somewhere along the line we were trained that marketable skills and divine spark were mutually exclusive. Don't mix work with pleasure, and all that rot. Well, we find ourselves at the right place at the right time when we combine our skills with our love of life. It's in the fun where we discover the part of ourselves that has wings. And wouldn't it be nice to be able to take our wings to work?

11   Unrealistic, you say? Just about every activity that brings us joy has an industry that supports it. Snowboarding, eating chocolate, going to the movies, even sex. Whatever you love to do, there's a job description with your name on it.

12   Take sailing, for instance. (Indulge me here. I live in one of the most beautiful sailing grounds on the planet. But I'm 1,000 miles away and I'm homesick at the moment.) Say you loved to sail while you were a kid. But you gave it up in favor of investing time to learn a profession. And now you're as far away from that old life as you could possibly be. And there's a hollow in your heart that used to be filled by days under the mainsail.

cartographer
mapmaker

13   Okay, what professions support sailing? Racing, yes. Sailboat delivery, yes. Sailing instructor, yes. Okay, let's stretch our imaginations just a little bit. How about: chef, physician, economist, computer programmer, chemist, **cartographer, meteorologist,** club manager, construction worker, secretary, writer, advertising executive, physical therapist, statistician.

meteorologist
one who studies and reports on the weather

14   See what I mean? All these professionals can find a lucrative career in the sailing world if they don't lose sight of the fact they love the sailing world. So they hang out. And they make friends. And one day they're in the right place at the right time.

15   Here's how indulging your passions makes you happy and gets you at the right place at the right time:

- You spend time and work in an environment that fascinates you.
- You spend time with kindred spirits who share your values and mission. They're your playmates and they like you. How mentally healthy is that?
- You become a learning sponge. And you never obsolete yourself. You would never pass up the chance to learn something new if it had something to do with your passion.
- Your network of contacts will be gigantic and it will cross all the hierarchical barriers that you typically find in a strictly corporate relationship.
- Your reputation will precede you everywhere you go.
- You'll know who the up-and-comers are . . . the ones behind you, the ones you will help bring up through the ranks.

16   Even if your next job is found through the classifieds or computer listings, the depth of experience you get by indulging your loves will make you stand out from among the other, more generic, candidates. Say you're a chemist with a passion for sailboat racing. And Gore-Tex announces an opening for a chemist to develop formulas for high-performance sailcloth. Who do you think they're going to pick?

17   Four words to guarantee you the job of your dreams: Right place/right time.

18   Four more words to unlock that marvelous coincidence: Do what you love.

A.   UNDERSTANDING THE THESIS AND OTHER MAIN IDEAS

Select the best answer.

_____ 1. The central thesis of "Four Simple Words" is that
   a. most jobs are not meant to be fun.
   b. the "perfect" job is impossible to find.
   c. the demands of most jobs leave no time for the pursuit of hobbies.
   d. it is important and possible to find a job that you love.

_____ 2. The author's primary purpose in "Four Simple Words" is to
   a. describe her job search.
   b. report employment trends.
   c. urge readers to find work that they love.
   d. persuade employers to make jobs more interesting.

_____ 3. The main idea of paragraph 5 is that the
   a. author was unhappy in her job as a receptionist.
   b. author enjoyed all the perks that came with her job.
   c. author wanted to save whales.
   d. owners of the public relations firm received clothing samples.

_____ 4. The topic of paragraph 12 is
    a. the best sailing locations.
    b. a passion for sailing.
    c. sailing as a child.
    d. learning a profession.

_____ 5. According to the author, indulging your passions allows you to
    a. spend time in an interesting environment with people you like.
    b. be happy while improving your chances of getting a job you love.
    c. widen your network of contacts outside a corporate setting.
    d. do all of the above.

B. IDENTIFYING DETAILS

Indicate whether each statement is true (T) or false (F).

_____ 1. The author currently works as a receptionist in a public relations firm.

_____ 2. The author was interviewed in a restroom for her job at the Cousteau Society.

_____ 3. The author believes that you shouldn't mix work with pleasure.

_____ 4. When she wrote this article, the author was 1,000 miles away from home.

_____ 5. The author's office at the Cousteau Society had a view of the East River.

C. RECOGNIZING METHODS OF ORGANIZATION AND TRANSITIONS

Methods of Organization
Select the best answer.

_____ 1. In paragraph 13, the author describes many professions that support a love of sailing. The type of organizational pattern used in this paragraph is
    a. cause and effect.
    b. definition.
    c. time sequence.
    d. enumeration.

_____ 2. In paragraphs 5 and 6, the author describes her interview for the Cousteau Society. The type of organizational pattern used in these paragraphs is

    a. time sequence.

    b. comparison and contrast.

    c. definition.

    d. cause and effect.

> **Transitional Words and Phrases**
> *Complete the following statements by filling in the blanks.*

1. In paragraph 5, the phrase _____ indicates that an explanation is to follow.

2. In paragraph 12, the phrase _____ indicates that the paragraph contains an example.

D.   REVIEWING AND ORGANIZING IDEAS: PARAPHRASING

Complete the following paraphrase of paragraphs 1 and 2 by filling in the missing words and phrases.

These _____ words are simple but _____. Assume you run into a _____ who has just gotten the _____, with _____ that perfectly _____ him. The job features excellent _____ at a _____ company, and the job has a _____ that includes raises and _____. When you ask _____ your friend got the _____, the _____, which is given in an irritatingly casual way, is that your friend doesn't know but _____ he was in the _____ at the _____.

E.   FIGURING OUT INFERRED MEANINGS

Each of the following boldface words has a strong positive or negative connotation (shade of meaning). Make inferences by indicating whether the word creates a positive (P) or negative (N) image for the reader.

_____ 1. ". . . the Job of Your **Dreams**" (title)

_____ 2. "I was working as a **lowly** . . . receptionist" (paragraph 5)

_____ 3. ". . . about to try on some **ridiculous** new fashion idea"
(paragraph 6)

_____ 4. "That was about the **coolest** way I ever got a job . . ."
(paragraph 7)

_____ 5. ". . . it's that **simple.**" (paragraph 9)

_____ 6. ". . . and all that **rot.**" (paragraph 10)

_____ 7. ". . . the part of ourselves that has **wings.**" (paragraph 10)

_____ 8. "And there's a **hollow** in your heart . . ." (paragraph 12)

_____ 9. "They're your **playmates** . . ." (paragraph 15)

➤ F.   THINKING CRITICALLY

Select the best answer.

_____ 1. One way the author supports her ideas is by

　　a. describing her personal experience.

　　b. reporting statistics.

　　c. quoting authorities.

　　d. defining terms.

_____ 2. The author's tone throughout the article can best be described as

　　a. sharp and sarcastic.

　　b. informal and friendly.

　　c. cold and impersonal.

　　d. dull and serious.

_____ 3. Of the following statements from paragraph 6, the only one that is
an *opinion* is

　　a. "One day I was in the ladies' room."

　　b. "And in walked the woman who would become my future
boss."

　　c. "And I got the job as member correspondent."

　　d. "It was a cool job."

_____ 4. When the author asks, "How mentally healthy is that?" (paragraph 15),
she means that

　　a. it is not actually healthy.

　　b. she doesn't know if it is healthy.

　　c. it is actually very healthy.

　　d. she doubts whether it is mentally or physically healthy.

> ➤ **G. BUILDING VOCABULARY**

> ➤ **Context**
> *Using context and a dictionary, if necessary, determine the meaning of each word as it is used in the selection.*

_____ 1. congenial (paragraph 1)

    a. sharp   c. unlike

    b. pleasant   d. complex

_____ 2. elusive (paragraph 3)

    a. difficult to grasp   c. within reach

    b. easy to see   d. under control

_____ 3. tendencies (paragraph 9)

    a. inclinations   c. reluctance

    b. attitudes   d. abilities

_____ 4. lucrative (paragraph 14)

    a. lucky   c. profitable

    b. fancy   d. challenging

_____ 5. hierarchical (paragraph 15)

    a. educational   c. having levels of authority

    b. displaying social skills   d. physical

_____ 6. generic (paragraph 16)

    a. distinctive   c. minor

    b. common   d. untrained

> ➤ **Word Parts**

A REVIEW OF PREFIXES AND SUFFIXES

UN- means *not*

-IAN means *one who*

Use your knowledge of word parts and the review above to fill in the blanks in the following sentences.

1. Statistics refers to numerical data. A _____ is a person who collects and interprets numerical data.

2. Realistic ideas are practical; _____ ideas are _____.

➤ Unusual Words/Understanding Idioms

Use context to match each word or phrase in Column A with its meaning in Column B. Write your answers in the spaces provided. Note that there is one extra meaning.

Column A	Column B
_____ 1. cagey (paragraph 1)	a. underwear
_____ 2. up my alley (paragraph 5)	b. people who are moving up professionally
_____ 3. scivvies (paragraph 6)	c. someone who feels trapped in his or her job
_____ 4. kindred spirits (paragraph 15)	d. suits me perfectly
_____ 5. up-and-comers (paragraph 15)	e. people who have the same interests
	f. sly or secretive

➤ H.   SELECTING A LEARNING/STUDY STRATEGY

Discuss the best way to record useful information from this reading.

➤ I.   EXPLORING IDEAS THROUGH DISCUSSION AND WRITING

1. Have you ever been in the right place at the right time? If so, describe the experience and explain its outcomes.

2. Do you agree or disagree with Finney's method of finding an ideal job?

3. Write a list of ten things you love that might help you find an ideal job.

➤ J.   BEYOND THE CLASSROOM TO THE WEB

Visit the University Career Services office at the University of Virginia at **http://www.career.virginia.edu/students/resources/handouts/.**
    Read one of the handouts posted at the career services center. Does the general view of how a person gets a good job seem similar to or different from the idea that one just has to be in the "right place at the right time"? Why?

✔ Tracking Your Progress

Selection 19

Section	Number Correct		Score
A. Thesis and Main Ideas (5 items)	_____	x 5	_____
B. Details (5 items)	_____	x 4	_____
C. Organization and Transitions (4 items)	_____	x 2	_____
E. Inferred Meanings (9 items)	_____	x 3	_____
F. Thinking Critically (4 items)	_____	x 3	_____
G. Vocabulary			
1. Context (6 items)	_____	x 1	_____
2. Word Parts (2 items)	_____	x 1	_____
TOTAL SCORE			_____ %

<table>
<tr><td>SELECTION
20</td><td>McDonald's Makes
a Lot of People Angry for
a Lot of Different Reasons</td></tr>
</table>

This article appears on the McSpotlight Web site, a site sponsored by McInformation Network, a volunteer organization dedicated to collecting information and encouraging debate about the workings, policies, and practices of the McDonald's Corporation.

▶ PREVIEWING THE READING

Using the steps listed on page 29, preview the reading selection. When you have finished, complete the following items.

1. What question do you expect the reading to answer?

   _____

2. List at least four issues addressed in the reading.

   a. _____

   b. _____

   c. _____

   d. _____

MAKING CONNECTIONS

Do the customers look satisfied?

> ## READING TIP

This reading uses emotional language to present information. Be sure to note whether the authors' statements are based on facts or opinions.

McDonald's Makes a Lot of People Angry for a Lot of Different Reasons

1   McDonald's makes a lot of people angry for a lot of different reasons.

Nutrition

nutritionists
experts in the field
of nutrition

2   **Nutritionists,** for example, argue that the type of high fat, low fiber diet promoted by McDonald's is linked to serious diseases such as cancer, heart disease, obesity, and diabetes—the sort of diseases that are now responsible for nearly three-quarters of premature deaths in the western world. McDonald's responds that the scientific evidence is not conclusive and that its food can be a valuable part of a balanced diet.

3   Some people say McDonald's is entitled to sell junk food in exactly the same way that chocolate or cream cake manufacturers do: if people want to buy it that's their decision. But should McDonald's be allowed to advertise its products as nutritious? Why does it sponsor sports events when it sells unhealthy products? And what on earth is McDonald's doing opening restaurants in hospitals?

Environment

conservationists
people who
advocate the
conservation of
natural resources

4   **Conservationists** have often focused on McDonald's as an industry leader promoting business practices detrimental to the environment. And yet the company spends a fortune promoting itself as environmentally friendly. What's the story?

5   One of the most well-known and sensitive questions about McDonald's is: is McDonald's responsible for the destruction of tropical forests to make way for cattle ranching? McDonald's says no. Many people say yes. So McDonald's sues them. Not so many people say yes anymore, but does this mean McDonald's isn't responsible?

6   McDonald's annually produces over a million tons of packaging, used for just a few minutes before being discarded. What environmental effect does the production and disposal of all this have? Is its record on recycling and recycled products as green as it makes out? Is McDonald's responsible for litter on the streets, or is that the fault of the customer who drops it? Can any multinational company operating on McDonald's scale *not* contribute to global warming, ozone destruction, depletion of mineral resources and the destruction of natural habitats?

Advertising

7   McDonald's spends over two billion dollars each year on advertising: the Golden Arches are now more recognized than the Christian cross. Using collectible toys, television ads, promotional schemes in schools, and figures such as Ronald McDonald,

the company bombards its main target group: children. Many parents object strongly to the influence this has over their own children.

8   McDonald's argues that its advertising is no worse than anyone else's and that it adheres to all the advertising codes in each country. But others argue it still amounts to cynical exploitation of children—some consumer organizations are calling for a ban on advertising to children. Why does McDonald's sponsor so many school events and learning programs? Is its Children's Charities genuine **philanthropy** or is there a more explicit publicity and profit motive?

philanthropy
an activity or institution intended for the good of humankind

Employment

9   The Corporation has pioneered a global, highly standardized and fast production-line system, geared to maximum turnover of products and profits. McDonald's now employs more than a million mostly young people around the world. Some say a million people might otherwise be out of work; others, however, consider that McDonald's is in fact a net destroyer of jobs by using low wages and the huge size of its business to undercut local food outlets and thereby force them out of business. Is McDonald's a great job opportunity or is it taking advantage of high unemployment to exploit the most vulnerable people in society, working them very hard for very little money? Complaints from employees range from discrimination and lack of rights, to understaffing, few breaks and illegal hours, to poor safety conditions and kitchens flooded with sewage, to the sale of food that has been dropped on the floor. This type of low-paid work has even been termed "McJobs."

trade unionists
members of a labor union, especially those in the same trade

10   **Trade unionists** don't like McDonald's either. The company is notorious for the vehemence with which it tries to crush any unionization attempt. McDonald's argues that all its workers are happy and that any problems can be worked out directly without the need for interference from a third party, but is McDonald's in fact just desperate to prevent any efforts by the workers to improve wages and conditions?

Animals

vegetarians
people who maintain a meat-free diet

11   **Vegetarians** and animal welfare campaigners aren't too keen on McDonald's—for obvious reasons. As the world's largest user of beef McDonald's is responsible for the slaughter of hundreds of thousands of cows per year. In Europe alone McDonald's uses half a million chickens every week, all from windowless factory farms. All such animals suffer great cruelty during their unnatural, painful and short lives, many being kept inside with no access to fresh air and sunshine, and no freedom of movement—how can such cruelty be measured? Is it acceptable for the food industry to exploit animals at all? Again, McDonald's argues that it sticks to the letter of the law and if there are any problems it is a matter for government. McDonald's also claims to be concerned with animal welfare.

Expansion

12   In 1996 McDonald's opened in India for the first time: a country where the majority of the population is vegetarian and the cow is sacred. This is just one example of the inexorable spread of western multinationals into every corner of the globe, a

capitalism
an economic
system in which
the means of
production
and distribution
are privately or
corporately
owned

13

socialism
a social system in
which the means
of producing and
distributing goods
are owned
collectively and
political power is
exercised by the
whole community

14

anarchism
the theory or
doctrine that
all forms of
government are
oppressive and
undesirable and
should be abolished

spread which is creating a globalized system in which wealth is drained out of local economies into the hands of a very few, very rich elite. Can people challenge the undermining of long-lived and stable cultures and regional diversity? Self-sufficient and sustainable farming is replaced by cash crops and agribusiness under control of multinationals—but how are people fighting back?

Free Speech

So, it seems as though lots of people are opposed to the way McDonald's goes about its business. So there is a big global debate going on about them, right? Wrong. McDonald's knows full well how important its public image is and how damaging it would be if any of the allegations started becoming well-known among its customers. So McDonald's uses its financial clout to influence the media and legal powers to intimidate people into not speaking out, directly threatening free speech. The list of media organizations who have been sued in the past is daunting, and the number of publications suppressed or pulped is frightening. But what are the lessons of the successful and ever-growing anti-McDonald's campaign for those also determined to challenge those institutions which currently dominate society?

Capitalism

Nobody is arguing that the huge and growing global environmental and social crisis is entirely the fault of one high-profile burger chain, or even just the whole food industry. McDonald's is, of course, simply a particularly arrogant, shiny and self-important example of a system that values profits at the expense of anything else. Even if McDonald's were to close down tomorrow, someone else would simply slip straight into its position. There is a much more fundamental problem than Big Macs and French fries: capitalism. But what about anti-capitalist beliefs like socialism and anarchism? Is it possible to create a world run by ordinary people themselves, without multinationals and governments—a world based on sharing, freedom and respect for all life?

A. UNDERSTANDING THE THESIS AND OTHER MAIN IDEAS

Select the best answer.

_____ 1. The central thesis of "McDonald's Makes a Lot of People Angry for a Lot of Different Reasons" is that

    a. many customers are unhappy with the service they get at McDonald's.

    b. competitors, such as Burger King and Hardee's, resent the success of McDonald's.

    c. McDonald's restaurants have been a target for robbery, vandalism, and other serious crimes.

    d. many different groups of people are disturbed by the global effects of McDonald's and other multinational corporations.

_____ 2. The authors' primary purpose in the article is to

    a. describe their efforts to bring about reform.

    b. compare McDonald's with more environmentally sensitive corporations.

    c. describe the harmful effects of McDonald's.

    d. persuade consumers to boycott McDonald's and other fast-food restaurants.

_____ 3. The topic of paragraph 6 is

    a. McDonald's environmental effects.

    b. consumers who litter.

    c. recycling.

    d. global warming.

_____ 4. The topic of paragraph 8 is

    a. children's charities.

    b. consumer organizations.

    c. philanthropy.

    d. advertising.

_____ 5. The main idea of paragraph 11 is expressed in the

    a. first sentence.   c. third sentence.

    b. second sentence.   d. last sentence.

_____ 6. The main idea of paragraph 13 is that

    a. there is currently a global debate about McDonald's practices.

    b. McDonald's uses its power to silence critics, thus threatening free speech.

    c. a lot of people are opposed to the way McDonald's conducts business.

    d. the anti-McDonald's campaign is successful and ever-growing.

_____ 7. The statement that best expresses the main idea of paragraph 14 is

    a. "Nobody is arguing that the huge and growing global environmental and social crisis is entirely the fault of one high-profile burger chain . . ."

    b. "McDonald's is, of course, simply a particularly arrogant . . . example . . ."

    c. "Even if McDonald's were to close down tomorrow, someone else would simply slip straight into its position."

    d. "There is a much more fundamental problem than Big Macs and French fries: capitalism."

B.   IDENTIFYING DETAILS

Indicate whether each statement is true (T) or false (F).

_____ 1. The term "McJobs" has been used to describe a type of low-paid work.

_____ 2. McDonald's is not permitted to open restaurants in hospitals.

_____ 3. According to the authors, McDonald's annually spends more than two billion dollars on advertising.

_____ 4. McDonald's opened in India for the first time in 1996.

_____ 5. McDonald's employs more than a million people in America.

C.   RECOGNIZING METHODS OF ORGANIZATION AND TRANSITIONS

Fill in the blanks to complete the following statements.

1. In paragraph 2, the authors report that nutritionists believe McDonald's food can be linked to serious diseases and that McDonald's disagrees. This organizational pattern is _____, because the authors present both points of view.

2. In paragraph 9, the authors use _____ to present opposing points of view about McDonald's employment.

3. The transitional phrase in paragraph 9 that indicates a contrast between two ideas is _____.

D.   REVIEWING AND ORGANIZING IDEAS: OUTLINING

Complete the following outline of the "Employment" section (paragraphs 9 and 10) by filling in the missing words.

I. McDonald's system

   A. Global _____

   B. Highly _____

   C. Fast _____

   D. Geared to _____ of products and _____

II. Employees

   A. More than _____ employees worldwide

      1. Great job opportunity for people who would otherwise be

      _____

2. Net _____ of jobs

    a. Uses _____ wages

    b. Huge size forces _____ out of business

    c. Exploiting most _____ people in society

3. _____

    a. Discrimination

    b. Lack of _____

    c. _____

    d. Few _____

    e. _____ hours

    f. Poor _____ conditions

    g. Kitchens flooded with _____

    h. Sale of food that has been _____

4. Low-paid work called _____

III. _____

  A. Don't like McDonald's

  B. McDonald's prevents _____

    1. Argues that employees are _____

    2. _____ can be worked out without the need for _____ interference

    3. Desperate to prevent _____ from improving _____

E.   FIGURING OUT INFERRED MEANINGS

Make inferences by indicating whether each of the following boldface words creates a positive (P) or negative (N) image for the reader.

_____ 1. ". . . part of a **balanced** diet." (paragraph 2)

_____ 2. ". . . environmentally **friendly**." (paragraph 4)

_____ 3. ". . . the company **bombards** its main target group . . ." (paragraph 7)

_____ 4. ". . . is McDonald's in fact just **desperate** . . ." (paragraph 10)

_____ 5. ". . . wealth is **drained** out of local economies . . ." (paragraph 12)

➤ F. THINKING CRITICALLY

Select the best answer.

_____ 1. The authors' tone throughout the article can best be described as
   a. critical and concerned.
   b. sympathetic.
   c. realistic and honest.
   d. objective and unbiased.

_____ 2. When the authors ask questions throughout the reading, they are primarily trying to
   a. add humor to the article.
   b. emphasize how curious they are.
   c. provoke thought about the issues.
   d. show that they don't know the answers.

_____ 3. The authors refer to all of the following groups to support their thesis *except*
   a. nutritionists.
   b. politicians.
   c. conservationists.
   d. animal welfare campaigners.

_____ 4. According to the authors, McDonald's has responded to critics in environmental groups and the media by
   a. ignoring them.
   b. bribing them.
   c. suing them.
   d. amending its operations.

➤ G. BUILDING VOCABULARY

➤ Context
Using context and a dictionary, if necessary, determine the meaning of each word as it is used in the selection.

_____ 1. detrimental (paragraph 4)
   a. advantageous   c. harmful
   b. minor   d. intense

_____ 2. depletion (paragraph 6)
   a. discussion   c. replacement
   b. reduction   d. contribution

_____ 3. adhere (paragraph 8)

    a. abide by   c. separate

    b. explain   d. market

_____ 4. notorious (paragraph 10)

    a. having a common trait

    b. famous for something undesirable

    c. well respected

    d. strong and forceful

_____ 5. vehemence (paragraph 10)

    a. forcefulness   c. sympathy

    b. professionalism   d. calmness

_____ 6. diversity (paragraph 12)

    a. agreement   c. variety

    b. similarity   d. divisions

_____ 7. daunting (paragraph 13)

    a. lengthening   c. harmful

    b. diminishing   d. intimidating

Word Parts

> **A REVIEW OF PREFIXES**
> **ANTI-** means *against*
> **IN-** means *not*
> **MULTI-** means *many*
> **PRE-** means *before*
> **UN-** means *not*

Match each word in Column A with its meaning in Column B. Write your answers in the spaces provided.

Column A

_____ 1. anticapitalist

_____ 2. multinational

_____ 3. inexorable

_____ 4. premature

_____ 5. unemployment

Column B

a. lack of work

b. before the normal time

c. against capitalism

d. having operations or investments in more than two countries

e. not preventable, relentless

Unusual Words/Understanding Idioms

Select the best answer.

_____ 1. When the authors ask if McDonald's has a record on recycling that is as "**green**" as it claims (paragraph 6), the word "green" refers to

    a. the color green.

    b. the environment.

    c. money.

    d. a lack of experience.

_____ 2. The word "**pulped**" (paragraph 13) means

    a. inflated.

    b. reduced.

    c. crushed.

    d. turned to paper.

H. SELECTING A LEARNING/STUDY STRATEGY

Suppose you have been asked to evaluate the evidence the authors provide to support their accusations against McDonald's. For each accusation, highlight the specific evidence the authors provide. For each statement you highlight, decide whether there is sufficient or insufficient evidence to support the claim.

I. EXPLORING IDEAS THROUGH DISCUSSION AND WRITING

1. The authors are biased against McDonald's. In what ways is this bias revealed?

2. What ethical or moral issues does this selection raise?

3. What is the opposing viewpoint not presented in this article? That is, in what ways does McDonald's benefit society?

J. BEYOND THE CLASSROOM TO THE WEB

Visit the McSpotlight Web site at **http://www.mcspotlight.org/campaigns/current/mckids.html.**

    The selection you have just read was posted on the McSpotlight Web site. Another selection from that site is "What's Wrong with Ronald McDonald?" This selection includes much of the same basic information as the article you just read, but presents the information in a very different way. How do the two readings differ and why?

✔ Tracking Your Progress

Selection 20

Section	Number Correct		Score
A. Thesis and Main Ideas (7 items)	_____	x 4	_____
B. Details (5 items)	_____	x 3	_____
C. Organization and Transitions (3 items)	_____	x 2	_____
E. Inferred Meanings (5 items)	_____	x 3	_____
F. Thinking Critically (4 items)	_____	x 3	_____
G. Vocabulary			
1. Context (7 items)	_____	x 2	_____
2. Word Parts (5 items)	_____	x 2	_____
	TOTAL SCORE		_____%

SELECTION
21

Product Placement

Michael R. Solomon

Taken from a textbook titled *Consumer Behavior*, this reading selection describes how specific products and brand names are used in movies, television, and other media.

▶ PREVIEWING THE READING

Using the steps listed on page 29, preview the reading selection. When you have finished, complete the following items.

1. The topic of this selection is _____.

2. List two questions you should be able to answer after reading this selection.

   a. _____

   b. _____

MAKING CONNECTIONS

Think about a movie or television show that you have seen recently and try to recall whether you noticed the particular products or brands being shown.

▶ READING TIP

This selection contains many examples of the "what"—in other words, the particular products and brands that appear in different types of media. As you read, be sure to notice the "why"—the reasons given for the use of product placement in each type of media.

Product Placement

1   Traditionally, TV networks demanded that producers "geek" (alter) brand names before they could appear in a show, as when *Melrose Place* changed a Nokia cell phone to a "Nokiao." Nowadays, though, real products pop up everywhere. In many cases, these "plugs" are no accident. **Product placement** is the insertion of real products in fictional movies, TV shows, books, and plays. Many types of products play starring (or at least supporting) roles in our culture; in 2007 for example the most visible brands ranged from Coca-Cola and Nike apparel to the Chicago

Art imitates life. life imitates art: ABC distributed laundry bags to promote the TV show *Desperate Housewives*. The idea became part of the plot in a later episode of the show.

Bears football team and the Pussycat Dolls band. This practice is so commonplace (and profitable) now that it's evolving into a new form of promotion we call **branded entertainment,** where advertisers showcase their products in longer-form narrative films instead of brief commercials. For example, *SportsCenter* on ESPN showed installments of "The Scout presented by Craftsman at Sears," a 6-minute story about a washed-up baseball scout who discovers a stunningly talented stadium groundskeeper.

2   Today most major releases brim with real products, even though a majority of consumers believe the line between advertising and programming is becoming too fuzzy and distracting (though as we might expect, concerns about this blurring of boundaries are more pronounced among older people than younger). A 2006 study reported that consumers respond well to placements when the show's plot makes the product's benefit clear. It found that the year's most effective brand integration occurred on ABC's now-cancelled *Miracle Workers* reality show, where physicians performed novel, life-changing surgeries. Audiences reacted strongly to CVS Pharmacy's role in covering the costs of medications that patients needed after the procedures. Similarly, audiences had favorable impressions when retailers provided furniture, clothes, appliances, and other staples for struggling families who got help on ABC's *Extreme Makeover: Home Edition.*

3   Although we hear a lot of buzz today about product placement, in reality it's a long-standing cinematic tradition. The difference is that today the placements are

more blatant and financially lucrative. In the heyday of the major Hollywood studios, brands such as Bell telephone, Buick, Chesterfield cigarettes, Coca-Cola, De Beers diamonds, and White Owl cigars regularly appeared in films. For example, in a scene in the classic *Double Indemnity* (1944) that takes place in a grocery store, the director Billy Wilder made some products such as Green Giant vegetables face the camera whereas others "mysteriously" were turned around to hide their labels. Indeed, the practice dates at least as far back as 1896, when an early movie shows a cart bearing the brand name Sunlight (a Lever Brothers brand) parked on a street. Perhaps the greatest product placement success story was Reese's Pieces; sales jumped by 65 percent after the candy appeared in the film *E.T.*

Props 4
items used by actors on the set of plays, movies, or television shows

Directors like to incorporate branded **props** because they contribute to the film's realism. When Stephen Spielberg directed the movie *Minority Report* (2002) he used brands such as Nokia, Lexus, Pepsi, Guinness, Reebok, and American Express to lend familiarity to the plot's futuristic settings. Lexus even created a new sports car model just for the film. And new technologies even let Hollywood studios dub product placements into films so they can substitute one product plug for another in the domestic and overseas versions of the same movie. This first occurred in the futuristic police drama *Demolition Man* (1993). In the U.S. release, PepsiCo Inc. bought a major role for its Taco Bell brand, which a character in the movie described as "the only restaurant to survive the franchise wars." The overseas version of the movie featured Pizza Hut instead.

5   Some researchers claim that product placement aids consumer decision making because the familiarity of these props creates a sense of cultural belonging while generating feelings of emotional security. Another study found that placements consistent with a show's plot do enhance brand attitudes, but incongruent placements that aren't consistent with the plot affect brand attitudes *negatively* because they seem out of place.

6   For better or worse, products are popping up everywhere. Worldwide product placement in all media was worth $3.5 billion in 2004, a 200 percent increase from 1994. In 2005, there were 108,000 instances of product placement in television programming, up 30 percent from the year before. Here are a few recent placements:

- During the first 4 months of 2006, TV shows mentioned or showed Apple products at least 250 times.
- Entire episodes of NBC's *The Apprentice* revolve around one brand: Instead of selling lemonade or giving rickshaw rides, the aspiring business tycoons now sell Mars's newest candy bar, hawk Crest toothpaste, and construct a new toy for Mattel. Pontiac sold 1,000 Solstices in less than an hour following an episode that featured the car.
- In *Shrek 2*, the ogre and his bride-to-be drive through a town that has a Baskin-Robbins storefront. Out in the real world, the ice cream retailer created three flavors—Fiona's Fairytale, Puss in Boots Chocolate Mousse, and Shrek's Swirl—named for characters in the film.
- A script for ABC's soap opera *All My Children* was reworked so that one of the characters would plug a new Wal-Mart perfume called Enchantment. Daytime TV stars eat Butterball turkeys, wear NASCAR shirts, and use Kleenex tissue. And the characters on *All My Children* have been drinking a lot of Florida orange juice—not only because they're thirsty.

- Colleges are selling advertising space on everything from basketball nets (State Farm) to student apartments. One company throws parties for prospective tenants at two buildings adjacent to Marquette and DePaul Universities. The apartments feature Herman Miller furniture and the company stocks them with Vitamin Water and Bliss and Kiehl's cosmetics.
- DC Comics' "Rush City" miniseries includes visible promotional support from Pontiac. "The Rush," a new hero, drives a Pontiac Solstice in the comic book. Meanwhile, Marvel Entertainment Inc. puts Nike's "swoosh" logo in the scenes of some titles, such as "New X-Men."

7   New advances in technology are taking product placement to the next level, as producers can insert brands into shows after filming them. Virtual product placement put a box of Club Crackers into an episode of *Yes, Dear* producers also inserted Cheez-Its, a can of Star-Kist tuna, and Nutri-Grain bars into the show. This new procedure means that a brand doesn't have to be written into the script and it can't be deleted by late editing changes.

Solomon, Michael, *Consumer Behavior*, 7th Edition, © 2007. Reprinted by permission of Pearson education, Inc., Upper Saddle River, NJ.

A.   UNDERSTANDING THE THESIS AND OTHER MAIN IDEAS

Select the best answer.

_____ 1. The author's primary purpose in this selection is to

     a. discuss the use of real products and brands in fictional movies, television shows, and other media.

     b. compare and contrast product placement in movies with conventional advertising methods.

     c. explore the controversy surrounding the use of advertising in children's television programming.

     d. describe the latest advances in technology used for film and television production.

_____ 2. The main idea of paragraph 1 is that

     a. brand names must be altered before they can be used on television shows.

     b. branded entertainment is taking the place of typical commercials.

     c. Coca-Cola and Nike are the most visible brands in advertising.

     d. product placement has become common in our culture.

_____ 3. Paragraph 2 is primarily concerned with

     a. consumers' response to placement.

     b. impressions of consumers.

     c. competition among advertisers.

     d. the distinction between programming and advertising.

_____ 4. The topic of paragraph 3 is
   a. Hollywood.
   b. product placement.
   c. popular brands.
   d. popular films.

_____ 5. The main idea of paragraph 4 is expressed in the
   a. first sentence.
   b. second sentence.
   c. fourth sentence.
   d. last sentence.

_____ 6. The question that is answered in paragraph 7 is
   a. What types of products are used most commonly in television shows?
   b. How do producers insert brands into television shows after filming them?
   c. How have advances in technology affected the use of product placement?
   d. Who chooses the products that are used in television shows and movies?

B. IDENTIFYING DETAILS

Match each brand with the television show or movie in which it appeared, according to the selection. Write your answers in the spaces provided. Note that four of the brand names will not be used.

TV Show or Movie

_____ 1. _Double Indemnity_
_____ 2. _The Apprentice_
_____ 3. _All My Children_
_____ 4. _Miracle Workers_
_____ 5. _Melrose Place_
_____ 6. _Demolition Man_
_____ 7. _Shrek 2_
_____ 8. _Minority Report_

Brand

a. Nokia
b. CVS Pharmacy
c. Sears
d. Green Giant
e. Taco Bell
f. Wal-Mart
g. Lexus
h. Apple
i. Coca-Cola
j. Baskin-Robbins
k. Pontiac
l. Nike

C.   RECOGNIZING METHODS OF ORGANIZATION AND TRANSITIONS

Select the best answer.

_____ 1. In paragraph 1, the author explains the meanings of *product placement* and *branded entertainment* using the organizational pattern called

a. cause and effect.

b. comparison and contrast.

c. definition.

d. process.

_____ 2. In paragraph 1, a word or phrase that signals that the author will illustrate the terms he has defined is

a. nowadays.

b. though.

c. in 2007.

d. for example.

_____ 3. In paragraph 3, the difference between traditional and modern product placement is described using the organizational pattern called

a. cause and effect.

b. comparison and contrast.

c. classification.

d. enumeration.

_____ 4. In paragraph 4, the word or phrase that indicates the author is about to provide examples is

a. because.

b. such as.

c. first.

d. instead.

➤ D. REVIEWING AND ORGANIZING IDEAS: MAPPING

Complete the following map by filling in the blanks.

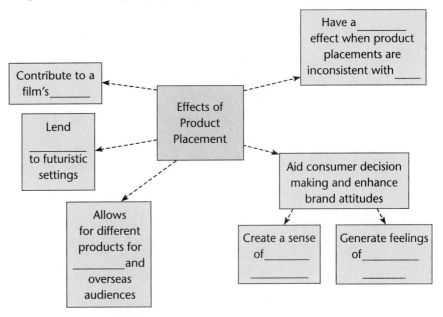

➤ E. FIGURING OUT INFERRED MEANINGS

Complete each inference by underlining the correct answer in the parentheses.

1. Product placement will probably become (more / less) common in movies and on television.

2. Older people are generally (more / less) responsive to product placement than are younger people.

3. Audiences had a (positive / negative) reaction to CVS Pharmacy's role in the reality show *Miracle Workers*.

4. Sales of products that appear in movies are typically (helped / hurt) by the product placement.

5. Based on product placement in the movie *Demolition Man*, it can be inferred that Pizza Hut is (more / less) popular overseas than Taco Bell.

6. Technology will make product placement (more / less) likely to be used in popular television shows.

➤ **F. THINKING CRITICALLY**

Select the best answer.

_____ 1. The tone of the reading can best be described as

    a. arrogant.

    b. informal.

    c. pessimistic.

    d. sympathetic.

_____ 2. The central thesis is supported by all of the following *except*

    a. examples.

    b. statistical data.

    c. descriptions.

    d. personal experience.

_____ 3. In paragraph 3, when the author says that the labels of some products were "mysteriously" hidden from the camera in *Double Indemnity,* he means that

    a. no one is sure why they were turned around.

    b. the hidden product labels were intended to be a mystery to reflect the plot of the movie.

    c. the director intentionally obscured some product labels to draw attention to others, such as Green Giant.

    d. the director was experimenting with special effects during the filming of the movie.

_____ 4. In paragraph 6, the author uses the phrase "For better or worse" to indicate that he

    a. disapproves of the widespread use of product placement.

    b. believes that most people are unhappy about product placement in the media.

    c. believes that product placement is the best form of advertising.

    d. is not making a value judgment about the increase in product placement.

_____ 5. This selection describes product placement in all of the following settings *except*

    a. television soap operas.

    b. video games.

    c. comic books.

    d. basketball nets.

G. BUILDING VOCABULARY

▶ Context

Using context and a dictionary, if necessary, determine the meaning of each word as it is used in the selection.

_____ 1. evolving (paragraph 1)
- a. preventing
- b. growing
- c. allowing
- d. performing

_____ 2. brim (paragraph 2)
- a. remove
- b. substitute
- c. are full of
- d. cover up

_____ 3. novel (paragraph 2)
- a. charming
- b. unusual
- c. complicated
- d. pleasant

_____ 4. staples (paragraph 2)
- a. necessities
- b. problems
- c. obstructions
- d. devices

_____ 5. blatant (paragraph 3)
- a. timely
- b. obvious
- c. offensive
- d. private

_____ 6. lucrative (paragraph 3)
- a. profitable
- b. similar
- c. destructive
- d. unnecessary

_____ 7. dub (paragraph 4)

    a. speak

    b. damage

    c. substitute

    d. delete

_____ 8. aspiring (paragraph 6)

    a. striving

    b. proving

    c. arriving

    d. deceiving

_____ 9. hawk (paragraph 6)

    a. watch

    b. guard

    c. sell

    d. cancel

➤ Word Parts

> ### A REVIEW OF PREFIXES, ROOTS, AND SUFFIXES
> **IN-** means *not*
> **SPECT** means *look, see*
> **-IVE** means *a state, condition, or quality*
> **-IC** means *a state, condition, or quality*

Use your knowledge of word parts and the review above to fill in the blanks in the following sentences.

1. If *narrate* means "tell a story," then a **narrative** film (paragraph 1) is one that tells a _____.

2. If the term *cinema* refers to films or movies, then a **cinematic** tradition (paragraph 3) is one having to do with _____.

3. If something is *congruent*, it is fitting or compatible with something else; therefore, **incongruent** placements (paragraph 5) are ones that are _____ with others.

4. The term *prospect* has to do with looking forward or having a belief about the future, so a **prospective** tenant (paragraph 6) is a person who may become a _____.

> **Unusual Words/Understanding Idioms**

Write a sentence using the underlined word or phrase.

1. The word **plugs** (paragraph 1) is an informal term that refers to favorable publicity for something in order to sell or promote it.

   Your sentence: _____

   _____.

2. The word **buzz** (paragraph 3) refers to excited talk or attention surrounding a new product or event.

   Your sentence: _____

   _____.

3. The word **heyday** (paragraph 3) means the period of greatest popularity or prosperity for someone or something.

   Your sentence: _____

   _____.

> ## H.   SELECTING A LEARNING/STUDY STRATEGY

Predict an essay question that might be asked on an exam about this selection.

> ## I.   EXPLORING IDEAS THROUGH DISCUSSION AND WRITING

1. Choose one or two television shows to watch for product placement in the next week. Make a list of the products or brands used during the show and indicate whether they were part of the storyline or simply used as props for the characters. If they were props, what do you think they were intended to reveal about the character or story? If they were part of the storyline, what did they add to the plot?

2. Discuss the pros and cons of product placement. For example, do you think using a product that is currently popular will make a movie or TV show seem outdated in a year or two?

3. Why do you think networks no longer require producers to alter brand names?

4. Do you think that product placement has had an effect on your own decisions as a consumer? Why or why not?

➤ J.   BEYOND THE CLASSROOM TO THE WEB

*Read over some facts about product placement at h*ttp://www.motherjones.com/
news/exhibit/2007/01/exhibit.html. *Choose one that particularly interests you and
find out more about it. Try clicking on the "Sources" link at the very beginning of
the article or doing an Internet search using the keywords from the statistic. Write
a short news story about product placement and your chosen fact.*

✔ Tracking Your Progress

Selection 21

Section	Number Correct		Score
A. Thesis and Main Ideas (6 items)	_____	x 4	_____
B. Details (8 items)	_____	x 3	_____
C. Organization and Transitions (4 items)	_____	x 2	_____
E. Inferred Meanings (6 items)	_____	x 2	_____
F. Thinking Critically (5 items)	_____	x 3	_____
G. Vocabulary			
1. Context (9 items)	_____	x 1	_____
2. Word Parts (4 items)	_____	x 2	_____
	TOTAL SCORE	_____	%

17 Technology/Computers

Technology has become an important part of our daily lives. In some cases, technology directly controls our lives. For example, if your car does not start or the bus breaks down, you may miss class. People's lives have been saved by medical technology: for example, when a person's heart has stopped and been restarted by a machine. In other situations, technology influences the quality of our lives. Without technology we would lack many conveniences that we take for granted. For example, we would not have computers, elevators, automated teller machines, or microwave ovens. Technology affects our communication through radio, television, and the Internet; our comfort through furnaces, air conditioners, and plumbing systems; our health through vaccines, drugs, and medical research; and our jobs through computers, copiers, and fax machines. In fact, it is difficult to think of any aspect of our daily lives untouched by technology.

In this chapter you will explore the effects of technology and read about upcoming innovations. In "Blogger Beware" you will discover some of the risks and dangers faced by people who write Web-logs, also called blogs. "Hold It Right There, and Drop That Camera" describes attempts to curb the misuses of camera phones that violate the privacy of others. As you read "DNA Fingerprinting: Cracking Our Genetic 'Barcode,'" you will learn how DNA fingerprinting works.

Use the following suggestions when reading technical material.

TIPS FOR READING IN TECHNOLOGY/ COMPUTERS	■ **Read slowly.** Technical material tends to be factually dense and requires careful, slow reading.
	■ **Pay attention to technical vocabulary.** "Blogger Beware," for example, includes some specialized computer terms as well as legal terminology.
	■ **Focus on process.** Much technical writing focuses on how things work. "DNA Fingerprinting: Cracking Our Genetic 'Barcode,'" explains how DNA fingerprinting works.
	■ **Use visualization.** Visualization is a process of creating mental pictures or images. As you read, try to picture in your mind the process or procedure that is being described. Visualization makes reading these descriptions easier and will improve your ability to recall details. As you read "Hold It Right There, and Drop That Camera," try visualizing possible misuses of camera phones.

SELECTION 22

Blogger Beware

George H. Pike

This article, which first appeared in *Information Today* (December 2005), describes the legal risks associated with Web-logs, or blogs. The author is director of the Barco Law Library and assistant professor of law at the University of Pittsburgh School of Law.

▶ PREVIEWING THE READING

Using the steps listed on page 29, preview the reading selection. When you have finished, complete the following items.

1. The topic of this selection is _____.

2. The headings indicate that the three specific issues that will be discussed in this selection are _____,
_____, and _____.

 ### MAKING CONNECTIONS

Have you ever read another person's blog or created your own blog? Consider what legal issues may have been raised by what you read in someone else's blog or by what you created yourself.

▶ READING TIP

As you read, highlight examples of legal risks associated with blogging.

Blogger Beware

1   A person standing on a soapbox in the middle of the town square is the historic and romantic embodiment of the First Amendment's right to free speech. The freedom to comment on political and social issues of the day, even in opposition to government or majority views, is essential to the foundation of American principles. Many people might consider the blog to be the modern embodiment of the soapbox. Web-logs use a simple Web-based format to let individuals post comments, images, and links on any subject. They also allow other users to post comments and generate continuing threads of discussion.

soapbox
platform for
speaking publically

2   The growth of blogs has been phenomenal. Some estimates calculate that there are as many as 60 million blogs. Blog readership was recently described by the Associated Press as "relatively small, but influential." Stanford law professor Lawrence Lessig's Lessig Blog, however, is widely read by many information industry experts, and Matt Drudge's Drudge Report played an active role in the 2004 elections. The growth of blogging, however, has been accompanied by a growth of legal threats to bloggers. Free speech is not as broad as it is often perceived, as many bloggers have found out in a number of ways. These cautionary tales warn bloggers to be aware of what their free speech rights actually permit—and prohibit—them to blog.

Workplace Blogging

3   Blogging in and about the workplace has emerged as the most likely venue for legal difficulties. Blogging about "life at work" is a fairly common practice, because a person's workday is a major element of their daily experience. Under law, the use of company computers, software, and e-mail is under the employer's control. Employees who blog on company time and/or with company computers run a strong risk of being sanctioned. Employers with legitimate concerns about productivity, network security, and potential liability have every legal right to regulate blogging and other computer activity.

proprietary information confidential information related to a company's products, business, or activities and considered the property of the company

4   But how about blogging from home on work life and activities? In late August, a "hip, Web-savvy company" terminated an employee for blogging about company activities. The blogger mentioned her work on redesigning her company's Web architecture and indicated that the redesign would improve site performance. The blog did not release any **proprietary information**, but it could still be considered critical of the company's product.

5   While this case has not resulted in a legal claim (yet), employment law gives the employer some latitude for sanctioning employees for off-work blogging. Any release of proprietary or confidential information could readily be grounds for sanction. Damage to the company's reputation is more nebulous. Specific, negative comments about the company, its personnel, or products are more dangerous than general comments like "I had a lousy day."

whistle-blogging a reference to "whistle-blowing," in which a person reveals wrongdoing within an organization, in this case through a blog

6   However, comments on political or social issues may be entitled to free speech protection even if they disagree with a company position. Promoting union activities or "**whistle-blogging**" may also be protected under certain state and federal laws. Still, caution is advised when blogging specifically about work life and activities.

Defamation

dot-com company a company that operates its business primarily on the Internet

7   Defamation and revealing trade secrets is another area that has captured the attention of the blogging community. A State College, PA, blogger was recently sued for allegedly posting defamatory remarks about—and trade secrets from—a **dot-com company**. The blogger did not work for the company but posted critical comments about the company's service and received other comments that were similarly critical and allegedly contained proprietary information. The suit alleges (without distinguishing between blogger and follow-up commentator) that the

libelous
involving
statements that
are harmful and
untrue in order
to damage a
person's
reputation

trade secrets
secret formulas,
methods, devices,
or information
belonging to a
company that
give it an
advantage
over its
competition

defamation
making false
statements
about a person
that damage
the person's
reputation or
deter others
from associating
with that person

8   information published on the blog was false, libelous, and included illegally obtained trade secrets.

By definition, defamation must contain false statements. The First Amendment is far less sympathetic to false statements than it is to opinions or statements of fact. A number of cases have arisen from postings on Internet bulletins and message boards that upheld the right of defamation victims to sue message board posters, even when the posting is done anonymously. Similar principles would apply to bloggers and to the comments made on blogs by third parties.

9   The First Amendment does provide some protection for blogging about public figures. The Supreme Court held that public figures must show that the alleged defamation is not only false, but also malicious. The blogger must know or recklessly avoid knowing that the statements are false. If the blog regularly reports on public issues or figures, the blogger might also be able to seek legal protection under the same shield laws that protect journals under the First Amendment's free press clause.

International Blogging

10   Global access to the Internet has raised concerns about worldwide reaction to blogs. In October 2005, two Singapore men were jailed for comments posted on their blogs that were found to have racial overtones. The First Amendment limits sanctions for such postings, although it may not protect threats, discrimination, and intimidation. However, seemingly innocent posts (such as a disparaging put-down) that target individuals or groups in countries with narrower free speech provisions could conceivably lead to criminal or civil liability. It may be difficult for a country or individual to get jurisdiction over a U.S. resident, but an Australian court recently allowed an American company to be sued in Australia for online defamation.

11   These are not the only legal risks that bloggers may face. Publication of private information, some forms of election-related activities, use of copyrighted or trademark content, or publication of adult content all raise liability concerns. For most day-to-day bloggers, these concerns may be minimal, but they still exist.

12   Blogging is now a pervasive activity on the Internet. When I was researching this column, many of the hits on my various searches were to blogs—which often contained helpful information or links. But bloggers who might wish to tread in legally dangerous waters should heed the lesson that their blog comments of questionable legality can readily be found by anyone who is looking—and that the soapbox can only help you so much.

➤ A.   UNDERSTANDING THE THESIS AND OTHER MAIN IDEAS

Select the best answer.

_____ 1. The statement that best expresses the central thesis of the selection is

   a. The freedom to comment on current political and social issues is essential to the foundation of American principles.

   b. The growth of blogging has been accompanied by an increase in legal threats to bloggers.

c. Blogging about the workplace is a common practice despite the risk of employer sanctions.

d. Bloggers who publish private or copyrighted information should be concerned about liability.

_____ 2. The author's primary purpose is to

a. convince bloggers that legal risks associated with blogging are minor.

b. criticize people who use blogs to make false or defamatory statements.

c. describe the legal risks and difficulties that bloggers may face.

d. persuade lawmakers to provide better protection for bloggers.

_____ 3. The topic of paragraph 2 is

a. the Associated Press.

b. the information industry.

c. the 2004 elections.

d. the growth of blogs.

_____ 4. The main idea of paragraph 7 is that

a. defamation and trade secrets represent another area of concern for bloggers.

b. a blogger was recently sued for posting defamatory remarks about a company.

c. only bloggers who are not employed by a company may post critical comments about the company.

d. bloggers are held liable for comments made by others in response to a blog.

_____ 5. According to the selection, the situation most likely to be associated with legal difficulties is blogging

a. from home about personal matters.

b. in and about the workplace.

c. on political or social issues.

d. about public issues or figures.

_____ 6. The main idea of paragraph 10 is expressed in the

a. first sentence.

b. second sentence.

c. fourth sentence.

d. last sentence.

> **B.   IDENTIFYING DETAILS**

Complete each of the following statements by filling in the blanks.

1. Paragraph 1: On a Web-log (blog), users can post comments,

   _____ or _____ on any

   subject. In addition, other users are allowed to post comments or continue

   a _____.

2. Paragraph 11: Other legal risks that bloggers may face include the

   _____, some forms of

   _____, use of _____,

   or publication of adult content.

> **C.   RECOGNIZING METHODS OF ORGANIZATION AND TRANSITIONS**

Select the best answer.

_____ 1. In paragraph 1, the author explains what a blog is by using the or-
         ganizational pattern called

   a. definition.

   b. cause and effect.

   c. classification.

   d. comparison and contrast.

_____ 2. In paragraph 10, the transition indicating that the author is provid-
         ing a contrasting idea is

   a. in October 2005.

   b. however.

   c. such as.

   d. lead to.

> **D.   REVIEWING AND ORGANIZING IDEAS: MAPPING**

*Complete the map of paragraphs 3–6 on the next page by filling in the missing
words or phrases using the words in the box.*

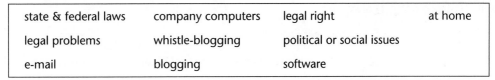

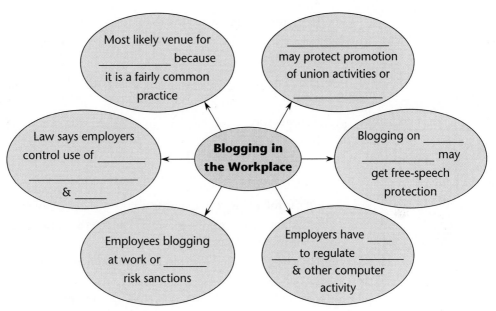

> E.   FIGURING OUT INFERRED MEANINGS

Indicate whether each statement is true (T) or false (F).

_____ 1. It can be inferred that the author is qualified to write about different aspects of the law.

_____ 2. Web architecture refers to the way a company has designed or "built" its site.

_____ 3. It can be inferred that the author admires the role that the Drudge Report played in the 2004 elections.

_____ 4. The employee terminated for blogging about company activities may file a legal claim.

_____ 5. The person who published trade secrets about a dot-com company worked for a competitor.

_____ 6. The First Amendment is more likely to protect opinions than false statements.

F. THINKING CRITICALLY

Select the best answer.

_____ 1. The central thesis of the selection is supported primarily by

   a. personal experience.

   b. examples and illustrative situations.

   c. statistical data.

   d. expert opinions.

_____ 2. Of the following words in paragraph 1, the only one that has a negative connotation is

   a. romantic.

   b. right.

   c. freedom.

   d. opposition.

_____ 3. Of the following statements from the selection, which one is a fact?

   a. "Many people might consider the blog to be the modern embodiment of the soapbox." (paragraph 1)

   b. "The growth of blogs has been phenomenal." (paragraph 2)

   c. "Under law, the use of company computers, software, and e-mail is under the employer's control." (paragraph 3)

   d. "The soapbox can only help you so much." (paragraph 12)

_____ 4. The author's tone can best be described as

   a. formal.

   b. condescending.

   c. cautionary.

   d. sensational.

G. BUILDING VOCABULARY

Context

Using context and a dictionary, if necessary, determine the meaning of each word as it is used in the selection.

_____ 1. embodiment (paragraph 1)

   a. imitation

   b. representation

   c. opposite

   d. container

_____   2. phenomenal (paragraph 2)

      a. extraordinary   c. threatening

      b. mysterious   d. illegal

_____   3. prohibit (paragraph 2)

      a. promote   c. prevent

      b. reveal   d. revise

_____   4. venue (paragraph 3)

      a. street   c. publication

      b. problem   d. place

_____   5. sanctioned (paragraph 3)

      a. rewarded   c. punished

      b. questioned   d. protected

_____   6. nebulous (paragraph 5)

      a. unclear   c. critical

      b. suspicious   d. fortunate

_____   7. malicious (paragraph 9)

      a. intending to harm   c. anonymous

      b. without knowledge   d. dissatisfied

_____   8. disparaging (paragraph 10)

      a. generous   c. insulting

      b. exciting   d. unequal

_____   9. pervasive (paragraph 12)

      a. unusual   c. confusing

      b. widespread   d. difficult

➤ Word Parts

Read the following statements from the selection again, and then use the hints to fill in the meaning of the boldface words.

1. "The suit alleges (without distinguishing between **blogger** and follow-up **commentator**) that the information published on the blog was false . . . ." (paragraph 7)

    Hints: The suffixes _-er_ and _-or_ mean _one who._

             A blogger is a _____.

             A commentator is a _____.

2. "It may be difficult for a country or individual to get **jurisdiction** over a U.S. resident, but an Australian court recently allowed an American company to be sued in Australia for online defamation." (paragraph 10)

Hints: The root *juris* means law.

The root *dict* means *tell* or *say*.

Therefore, a person or country trying to get jurisdiction wants to be able to _____ what the _____ should be regarding a particular issue or individual.

➤ Unusual Words/Understanding Idioms
Use the meanings given below to write a sentence using the boldface word or phrase.

1. When someone is given **latitude** (paragraph 5) regarding an issue, he or she is allowed some freedom in how the issue is addressed.

Your sentence: _____

_____.

2. A person who wishes to **tread in legally dangerous waters** (paragraph 12) is taking a risk that may have serious effects; in this case, the effects would involve legal consequences.

Your sentence: _____

_____.

➤ H.   SELECTING A LEARNING/STUDY STRATEGY

How would you prepare if you knew you had to answer the following essay question?
Discuss the First Amendment as it applies to online activities, especially blogging.

➤ I.   EXPLORING IDEAS THROUGH DISCUSSION AND WRITING

1. Evaluate the title of this piece: "Blogger Beware." What other title(s) might be appropriate for this selection?

2. Do you agree with those who "consider the blog to be the modern embodiment of the soapbox" (paragraph 1)? Why or why not?

3. Discuss each of the following situations described in the selection: a person was fired for blogging about her work (paragraph 4), a person was sued for

posting critical and possibly defamatory comments (paragraph 7), and two men were put in jail for posting comments with racial overtones (paragraph 10). What is your opinion of each case? How do you think each one should be resolved?

4. How do you think blogging should be regulated? Do you favor more or less protection for the rights of bloggers?

J.   BEYOND THE CLASSROOM TO THE WEB

Do a search for your school using the Google Blog Search at **http://blogsearch. google.com/**. *Categorize the results (for example, sports results, prospective students, alumni, etc.). Who is writing about your school and why? Should your school officials be concerned? Why or why not?*

✔ Tracking Your Progress

Selection 22

Section	Number Correct		Score
A. Thesis and Main Ideas (6 items)	_____	x 4	_____
B. Details (6 items)	_____	x 2	_____
C. Organization and Transitions (2 items)	_____	x 2	_____
E. Inferred Meanings (6 items)	_____	x 3	_____
F. Thinking Critically (4 items)	_____	x 4	_____
G. Vocabulary			
1. Context (9 items)	_____	x 2	_____
2. Word Parts (2 items)	_____	x 4	_____
	TOTAL SCORE	_____%	

<table>
<tr><td>SELECTION
23</td><td>Hold It Right There,
and Drop That Camera

Jo Napolitano</td></tr>
</table>

This article first appeared in the *New York Times*. Read the article to find out about the issues surrounding the use of cell phone cameras in public spaces.

▷ PREVIEWING THE READING

Using the steps listed on page 29, preview the reading selection. When you have finished, complete the following items.

1. The subject of this article is _____.

2. List several places you think might be discussed in the article as being off limits to cell phone camera users.

    a. _____

    b. _____

    c. _____

 MAKING CONNECTIONS

If you have ever used a cell phone camera, describe the circumstances in which you used it. Did your use violate the privacy of others?

▷ READING TIP

As you read, highlight the reasons why camera phones should and should not be banned.

Hold It Right There, and Drop That Camera

alderman
a member of
Chicago's city
council

1   "What grabbed my attention," said **Alderman** Edward M. Burke, "was that TV commercial when the guy is eating the pasta like a slob, and the girl sends a photo of him acting like a slob to the fiancee." The commercial, for Sprint PCS, was meant to convey the spontaneity and reach afforded by the wireless world's latest craze, the camera phone. But what Mr. Burke saw was the peril. "If I'm in a locker room changing clothes," he said, "there shouldn't be some pervert taking photos of me that

could wind up on the Internet." Accordingly, as early as Dec. 17, the Chicago City Council is to vote on a proposal by Mr. Burke to ban the use of camera phones in public bathrooms, locker rooms, and showers. There will be no provision to protect messy restaurant patrons. But Mr. Burke wanted to ban the use of camera phones in places where "the average Chicagoan would expect a reasonable right to privacy."

2   Not that tiny cameras couldn't be spirited into intimate settings before. But now it is a matter of numbers: only a year after camera phones began to appear in the United States, there were six million of them, according to the market-research firm IDC. And when you marry a camera to a phone that can transmit the pictures instantly, legislation increasingly results. The Chicago proposal, setting a fine of $5 to $500 for offenders, echoes restrictions adopted in several smaller jurisdictions. What remains to be seen is how and when such laws will be enforced.

American Civil Liberties Union a nonprofit organization that works to preserve the constitutional guaranteed rights of Americans, especially those of free speech and privacy

3   While privacy experts, municipalities and the American Civil Liberties Union agree that photos should not be taken without consent in public bathrooms and showers, there is no consensus on the best method of balancing the camera owner's rights with those of the unsuspecting citizen. The town of Seven Hills, Ohio, backed down less than two weeks after proposing a ban to avoid possibly costly court challenges. The mayor, David A. Bentkowski, said he would leave the matter to state and federal legislation.

4   Trying to distinguish between a camera phone and any other cell phone has also complicated matters. The Elk Grove Park District in suburban Chicago enacted a ban in November that covered the possession of any cell phone—not just camera phones—in park-owned restrooms, locker rooms, and showers. "There is no reason to have a cell phone while you're changing and showering," said Ron Nunes, one of the park district's commissioners. "I'd rather protect the children and the public more than someone who wants to call home and see what's for dinner." Fresh in the town's memory was a 2001 incident in which a man used a fiber-optic camera to secretly take pictures of children in a park shower.

5   So far, there have been no complaints in Elk Grove about cell phone transgressions. But Mr. Nunes concedes, "It's darn near impossible to enforce." There will be no searches of bags, he said, and park officials will not summon the police if a cell phone is found in a restricted area. "We're not going to arrest someone for making a phone call in a locker room," he said. "We're counting on people to just say, 'Shut it off.'" Though they are permitted in gym areas, patrons say they often leave their phones in the car when they work out there because they usually have to use the changing room first, where the phones are not permitted. Nancy Funteas, a business owner, said she was worried about missing calls while at the park district gym. "You feel protected in the locker room, but out here if you need it for business it's not a good idea," she said after finishing an upper-body workout. Desi Leyba, a 30-year-old gym member, admitted, "Sometimes I forget and I bring it in. I wonder if they're going to make a case of it."

6   L. Richard Fischer, a Washington lawyer who deals with privacy issues, said the park district's ban goes too far. "People have to pass laws very carefully and recognize there is a broad but flexible standard of reasonable expectation of privacy," he said. "You have to do it very selectively or you really are treading on people's rights." Banning cell phones from some locations could invite lawsuits from people who might have to use

a phone in an emergency and be unable to summon help, he said. "What they've done is go to the extreme," he said. "They've threatened the rights of the majority of people to try to control the conduct of a few, and that's just beyond the balance." He added that the only way to deter people from taking photos of others was to punish them for taking surreptitious pictures rather than banning the phones.

7   Des Peres, Mo., a St. Louis suburb, passed a more limited and specific law in September that bans taking photos of a person who is partly unclothed without consent in an area where they should expect privacy. "The ordinance would provide the city with some teeth for the ability to prosecute someone," said Jason McConachie, the assistant city administrator, adding, "I don't believe there is any way to proactively enforce it, like putting police officers in locker rooms." He said the city would help an aggrieved citizen pursue legal action against someone for taking pictures in a restricted area without consent—an occurrence as yet unreported.

8   Some courthouses have extended existing bans on picture taking to include camera phones. Representative Michael G. Oxley of Ohio felt that the federal government should draft its own provision, so he and a fellow Ohio Republican, Senator Mike DeWine, broadened the language in a law proposed by Mr. Oxley, the Video Voyeurism Prevention Act of 2003, to include camera phones. "I think if we can nip it in the bud, we can avoid a lot of embarrassing situations or gross invasions of privacy," Mr. Oxley said. "Our bill would only apply to federal property, but it would spur the states to pass similar legislation." The law would prohibit the use of camera phones in restrooms in federal park districts and federal buildings. Breaking the law would result in a fine, up to a year in prison, or both.

9   Chris J. Hoofnagle, legislative counsel for the Electronic Privacy Information Center, a nonprofit group in Washington, acknowledged that the proliferation of camera phones had helped give new life to "up skirt" or "down blouse" photography. "Clearly, this is going to get worse," Mr. Hoofnagle said. "There is a remarkable lack of sensitivity to the subjects of the photographs." But he said changing the norms of society, rather than its laws, was likely to be a more effective response.

10   Barry Steinhardt, director of the year-old technology and liberty program for

the A.C.L.U., suggested that the camera-phone quandary reflected a larger problem: that technology has developed at the speed of light and American law is "stuck in the Stone Ages." "The rest of the developed world have fairly advanced laws that incorporate privacy and fair information that we invented in the 1960's but didn't implement," he said. While he would not comment on specific measures in Chicago and elsewhere, he said that privacy laws were justifiable but had to be very specific. What the United States needs, he added, is to establish a privacy commissioner to enforce existing rules and investigate the need for new ones. Technology for surveillance and data gathering is "becoming more powerful every day," he said. "In the U.S., our response to this has been to bury our heads in the sand and say, 'It'll all work out.'"

11   Meanwhile, cameras are becoming not only more numerous among the nation's 160 million cell phones, but also more capable. Alex Slawsby, an analyst with IDC, said that by next year the typical camera phone sold in the United States would have a resolution of at least one megapixel, about three times the current average—doing wonders, no doubt, for the rendering of sloppy restaurant patrons.

12   Whatever indiscretions arise in a camera phone's use, the makers plead, don't blame the equipment. "There are people who would use things they shouldn't," said Keith Nowak, a spokesman for **Nokia**. "There is not a product made that somebody somewhere with a good enough imagination couldn't figure out how to misuse."

> **Nokia**
> major wireless company; manufactures cell phones, multimedia systems, and business networks

From The New York Times, December 11, 2003. © 2003. The New York Times. All rights reserved. Used by permission and protected by the Copyright Laws of the United States. The printing, copying, redistribution, or retransmission of the Material without express written permission is prohibited.

➤ A.   UNDERSTANDING THE THESIS AND OTHER MAIN IDEAS

Select the best answer.

_____   1. The central thesis of this selection is that

    a. legislation against cell phone camera use should be enforced.

    b. not enough has been done to protect Americans from cell phone camera users.

    c. cell phone cameras should be banned from public spaces.

    d. there is growing concern about the use of cell phone cameras in public spaces and violation of privacy.

_____   2. The author's primary purpose is to

    a. offer personal opinion on a current topic of interest.

    b. argue in favor of a particular position.

    c. make a comparison.

    d. explore a problem.

_____   3. The main idea of paragraph 3 is that

    a. the American Civil Liberties Union is trying to protect the rights of people who use cell phone cameras inappropriately.

    b. towns are afraid of getting sued over this issue.

    c. there is disagreement over how to protect the privacy of citizens.

    d. the federal government should enact legislation for the entire nation.

_____ 4. The main idea of paragraph 6 is that

    a. people will not be able to call 911 for help if they cannot use a cell phone in a park.

    b. one lawyer thinks that the district's ban goes too far in its restrictions.

    c. the majority are being punished.

    d. cell phones should not be banned; taking pictures with cell phones should be banned.

_____ 5. The main idea of paragraph 10 is expressed in the

    a. first sentence.   c. fourth sentence.

    b. second sentence.   d. last sentence.

B. IDENTIFYING DETAILS

Select the best answer.

_____ 1. Alderman Burke was moved to action against cell phone camera use because of a

    a. magazine article.

    b. television commercial.

    c. news story.

    d. radio call-in show.

_____ 2. Which of the following is *not* true about the Elk Grove situation?

    a. People cannot have any kind of cell phone in a park-owned locker room.

    b. Children were the victims of a man using a camera in park-owned showers.

    c. The new law is being enforced frequently and strictly.

    d. Locker room users are leaving their cell phones in their cars.

_____ 3. According to the article, the Video Voyeurism Prevention Act of 2003 would

    a. prohibit the use of video cameras in federal courtrooms.

    b. penalize violators with fines from $5 to $500.

    c. require states to enact similar legislation.

    d. ban camera phones from restrooms in federal buildings.

_____ 4. One concern not mentioned in the article is

    a. whether private establishments should make rules about camera phone use.

    b. the lack of sensitivity towards those who have been the subjects of photographs.

c. a person's right to expect a reasonable amount of privacy in a public setting.

d. the rights of camera phone owners.

_____ 5. The Nokia spokesperson feels that

a. people will come up with ways to misuse a product no matter what laws are in place.

b. cameras will have such high resolution in the future that offensive pictures will be even more common.

c. cell phone manufacturers should take more responsibility for how their products are used.

d. federal legislators are not doing enough to protect the privacy of Americans.

C. RECOGNIZING METHODS OF ORGANIZATION AND TRANSITIONS

Complete the following statements by filling in the blanks.

1. The author uses the _____ pattern of organization to present the relevant situations, problems, and opinions on the camera phone issue.

2. An example of a transition for this pattern in paragraph 4 is _____.

D. REVIEWING AND ORGANIZING IDEAS: PARAPHRASING

Complete the following paraphrase of paragraphs 4 and 5 by filling in the missing words or phrases.

In a suburb of _____, the Elk Grove Park District has banned any _____ in park-owned _____, locker rooms, and showers. There had been an incident involving a man taking pictures of _____ in a park _____ that prompted park district commissioners like _____ to create the policy. Because it is hard to _____ between types of cell phones, the park district does not allow any. Nunes feels that the policy protects children and the _____; he is less concerned about inconveniencing the casual cell phone user. No one has _____ about cell phone use in _____ parks, and Nunes admits that the rule is difficult to _____. He expects residents to police themselves and each _____. Many exercisers leave their phones in their _____ , but sometimes they forget and bring them into the changing _____ , hoping not to get in _____ . This seems unlikely, because bags are not _____ and the police are not _____ .

E.   FIGURING OUT INFERRED MEANINGS

Indicate whether each statement is true (T) or false (F).

_____ 1. The Sprint commercial made Alderman Burke think about negative uses for a camera phone.

_____ 2. In the past people have been able to get small cameras into private places.

_____ 3. People in Chicago will feel safer if camera phones are restricted in public spaces.

_____ 4. It can be inferred that Ron Nunes is responsible for the enforcement of cell phone use in Elk Grove Park District.

_____ 5. No one has brought charges against anyone in Des Peres for inappropriate camera phone use.

_____ 6. It is clear that Mr. Fischer has worked on numerous cases involving camera phones.

_____ 7. The better a camera phone's resolution, the more likely it will be used to take inappropriate photographs.

F.   THINKING CRITICALLY

Select the best answer.

_____ 1. The author began the article with Alderman Burke's experience in order to

a. grab the reader's attention with an interesting example.

b. present an opposing viewpoint.

c. establish a time frame for the article.

d. make a comparison.

_____ 2. Ron Nunes's remarks are included to

a. present evidence against cell phone bans.

b. show an alternate point of view.

c. explain the reasoning behind Elk Grove's ban on all cell phones.

d. add humor to the article.

_____ 3. Fisher and Hoofnagle would agree that

    a. nothing can be done to stop people from taking inappropriate photos.

    b. camera phones don't take inappropriate photos; people take inappropriate photos.

    c. only federal legislation will solve the camera phone problem.

    d. not enough has been done to stop privacy violations.

_____ 4. The overall tone of this article is

    a. informative.

    b. alarmist.

    c. indifferent.

    d. angry.

➤ G. BUILDING VOCABULARY

➤ Context

Using context and a dictionary, if necessary, determine the meaning of each word as it is used in the selection.

_____ 1. provision (paragraph 1)

    a. change   c. notice

    b. idea   d. legal clause

_____ 2. spirited (paragraph 2)

    a. banned   c. secretly carried

    b. openly brought   d. animated

_____ 3. echoes (paragraph 2)

    a. sounds   c. authorizes

    b. imitates   d. distinguishes

_____ 4. consensus (paragraph 3)

    a. dispute   c. announcement

    b. agreement   d. direction

_____ 5. surreptitious (paragraph 6)

    a. secret   c. inappropriate

    b. silly   d. obvious

_____ 6. aggrieved (paragraph 7)

    a. wronged   c. angry

    b. sad   d. frustrated

_____ 7. indiscretions (paragraph 12)

    a. confusions or mistakes   c. mean behaviors

    b. moral errors   d. actions showing poor judgment

Word Parts

> **A REVIEW OF PREFIXES**
> **TRANS-** means *across* or *beyond*
> **PRO-** means *to come before*

Use your knowledge of word parts and the review above to fill in the blanks in the following sentences.

1. When someone commits a *transgression* (paragraph 5), he _____ what is allowable by law.

2. To work *proactively* (paragraph 7) on a potential problem means to take action _____ to prevent or avert the problem.

Unusual Words/Understanding Idioms
Use the meanings given below to write a sentence using the boldface word or phrase.

1. When teachers have the backing of their principal for enforcing rules, then they have some **teeth** (paragraph 7) to support their actions.

Your sentence: _____

_____

2. A business person who exhibits **gross** (paragraph 8) misconduct has absolutely no regard for ethics or the law.

Your sentence: _____

_____

H. SELECTING A LEARNING/STUDY STRATEGY

Select the best answer.

_____ If you were writing a research paper on camera phones and privacy using this article as one of your sources, the most useful strategy would be to

  a. record details of the various bans.

  b. outline the selection.

  c. draw a concept map of the main ideas.

  d. paraphrase useful information.

I. EXPLORING IDEAS THROUGH DISCUSSION AND WRITING

1. Discuss the use of cell phones in public places. Where on campus should they be used or not used? What about camera phones?

2. Write a policy for camera phone use in various places on your campus.

3. Discuss with your classmates how you could find out more information about some of the bans and legislation mentioned in the article. Do some follow-up work to find out what has happened in these communities since the article was written. Ask your librarian for help, if necessary.

J. BEYOND THE CLASSROOM TO THE WEB

Visit Reiter's Camera Phone Report Archives at **http://www.cameraphonereport.com/archives.html.**

Read a few months worth of posts. Make a list of the main categories that the posts fit into. What was the most interesting post you read? What surprised you about this site?

✔ Tracking Your Progress

Selection 23

Section	Number Correct		Score
A. Thesis and Main Ideas (5 items)	_____	x 5	_____
B. Details (5 items)	_____	x 4	_____
C. Organization and Transitions (2 items)	_____	x 2	_____
E. Inferred Meanings (7 items)	_____	x 3	_____
F. Thinking Critically (4 items)	_____	x 3	_____
G. Vocabulary			
1. Context (7 items)	_____	x 2	_____
2. Word Parts (2 items)	_____	x 2	_____
TOTAL SCORE		_____%	

SELECTION 24

DNA Fingerprinting: Cracking Our Genetic "Barcode"

Elaine N. Marieb

This selection is taken from a textbook titled *Essentials of Human Anatomy and Physiology*, by Elaine N. Marieb, published in 2009. Read the selection to find out about the process known as DNA fingerprinting.

PREVIEWING THE READING

Using the steps listed on page 29, preview the reading selection. When you have finished, complete the following items.

1. The topic of this selection is _____.

2. List at least three questions you expect to be able to answer after reading the selection.

   a. _____

   b. _____

   c. _____

 ## MAKING CONNECTIONS

What do you already know about DNA fingerprinting? How is it like traditional fingerprinting? With a classmate, make a list of the ways that you think DNA fingerprinting is used in the world today.

READING TIP

As you read, highlight unfamiliar terms and their definitions. If a definition is not given, be sure to look up the term in a dictionary so that you can understand the passage.

DNA Fingerprinting: Cracking Our Genetic "Barcode"

1   The terrorist attacks on New York City's World Trade Center killed more than 3,000 people, their bodies buried in millions of tons of rubble. As weeks passed, it became clear that even if victims could be recovered from the wreckage, their bodies would

probably be mangled, burned, or decomposed to a point where even family members would not recognize them.

2   In a situation like this, how can we identify individuals with any certainty? The New York Medical Examiner's Office turned to DNA fingerprinting, a technique for analyzing tiny samples of DNA taken from semen, skin, blood, or other body tissues. DNA fingerprinting is based on the fact that no two human beings, except for identical twins, possess identical sets of genetic material. In effect, DNA fingerprinting creates a unique genetic "barcode" that distinguishes each of us from all other humans. Let's see how it works.

DNA
deoxyribonucleic acid, the long string of genetic material found in the nucleus of a cell

barcode
a series of vertical bars printed on consumer products to identify the item for pricing and inventory purposes

nucleotides
the basic structural units of nucleic acids such as DNA

Creating a DNA Profile

3   Recall that DNA contains four nucleotides—A, G, C, and T—that form complementary base pairs. In members of the same species, 99.9 percent of DNA is identical. This means that only 0.1 percent of your DNA differs from that of other humans—even close relatives, but this is enough to make you genetically unique. In a DNA string 3 billion units long, that 0.1 percent translates into 3 million variations that differ slightly from everyone else's. Unless you're an identical sibling, your set of DNA is yours alone. DNA fingerprinting involves analyzing an individual's DNA, mapping its unique pattern, and comparing it to other DNA profiles to determine whether there's a match.

4   A standard technique for creating a DNA profile focuses on 13 specific sites on our chromosomes where short segments of nuclear DNA are arranged in a repeating sequence. Although it is theoretically possible that unrelated people could show identical repeats at all 13 sites, the odds are less than 1 in 1 trillion.

5   Sometimes it can be difficult to obtain sufficient nuclear DNA for analysis. DNA samples recovered from crime scenes or disaster sites, for example, are frequently contaminated with dirt, fibers, and debris, or badly decomposed, limiting the amount of testable tissue. DNA retrievel can become a race against time as microbes, enzymes, insects, and environmental factors such as heat and humidity accelerate the process of decomposition.

Sorting and Identifying DNA

6   For DNA to be profiled, it must first be cut into manageable fragments by *restriction enzymes*, enzymes that recognize a specific base sequence and cleave the DNA at this location. This breaks down chromosomes into millions of pieces of different sizes that are then subjected to *gel electrophoresis*, which sorts the pieces by length. The DNA is placed on a gel and positioned in an electric field. The negatively charged fragments of DNA are attracted to the positively charged electrode and migrate toward it. Because the smaller pieces move more quickly than the larger pieces, the fragments end up sorted by size.

7   To locate a specific repeating sequence, researchers make a *DNA probe* with a complementary sequence and tag it with a radioactive compound. Because their sequences are complementary, the probe binds to the site; and when exposed to X-ray film, the image shows dark bands where the probe bound to the DNA.

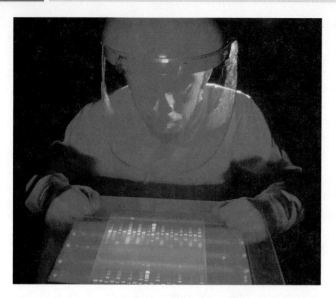

DNA electrophoresis. A scientist looking at DNA fragments in an electrophoresis gel.

8   A victim's DNA profile is then compared to known references to find one that matches. In the case of the World Trade Center attack, DNA references were obtained from victims' personal effects (such as toothbrushes and combs), entered into a computer, and sorted to find a match.

DNA Fingerprinting and Forensics

9   DNA fingerprinting has become a vital tool in forensic medicine (the application of medical knowledge to questions of law). For example, DNA fingerprinting is used to identify "John and Jane Does," unknown human remains. The U.S. military takes blood and saliva samples from every recruit so it can identify soldiers killed in the line of duty. DNA fingerprinting can also identify victims of mass disasters such as airplane crashes. The World Trade Center tragedy called for genetic analysis on an unprecedented scale.

10   DNA fingerprinting can prove that a suspect was actually at the scene of a crime. In the United States, some communities now require certain criminal offenders to provide DNA samples, which are classified and stored. DNA profiles can also establish innocence. At least 10 people in the United States have been released from death row after genetic evidence exonerated them.

11   DNA fingerprinting can also verify relationships in cases of disputed property, identify long-lost relatives, and establish paternity, even in paternity cases that are centuries old. For example, historians have fiercely debated whether Thomas Jefferson, our third president, fathered any children by his slave Sally Hemings. Modern DNA researchers entered the fray by profiling Jefferson's Y chromosome. A comparison of 19 genetic markers on the Jefferson Y chromosomes and those of Hemings's descendants found identical matches between the Jefferson line and Hemings's youngest son. Could it be chance? Hardly!

A. UNDERSTANDING THE THESIS AND OTHER MAIN IDEAS

Select the best answer.

_____ 1. The central thesis of this selection is that DNA fingerprinting is
   a. a legal tool primarily for use in the criminal justice system.
   b. a process that makes it possible to identify individuals through their genetic material.
   c. one of several methods used to analyze an individual's DNA.
   d. a new technology that may become useful in the future.

_____ 2. The author's primary purpose is to
   a. compare traditional and DNA fingerprinting.
   b. argue that DNA profiling should be against the law.
   c. describe the process and uses of DNA fingerprinting.
   d. discuss a variety of techniques used in forensic medicine.

_____ 3. The topic of paragraph 2 is
   a. the New York Medical Examiner's Office.
   b. DNA fingerprinting.
   c. identical twins.
   d. genetic barcodes.

_____ 4. According to the selection, DNA fingerprinting involves
   a. analyzing an individual's DNA.
   b. mapping the unique pattern of an individual's DNA.
   c. comparing an individual's DNA profile to others to find a match.
   d. all of the above.

_____ 5. The topic of paragraph 9 is expressed in the
   a. first sentence.
   b. second sentence.
   c. third sentence.
   d. last sentence.

_____ 6. The question that is answered in paragraph 9 is
   a. What is DNA fingerprinting?
   b. How is DNA fingerprinting used in forensic medicine?
   c. How is DNA obtained for matching purposes?
   d. Why is DNA fingerprinting important in criminal cases?

_____ 7. The main idea of paragraph 11 is expressed in the
   a. first sentence.
   b. second sentence.
   c. third sentence.
   d. fourth sentence.

_____ 8. According to the selection, DNA fingerprinting was used to find out whether Thomas Jefferson
   a. had an identical brother.
   b. died of natural causes.
   c. was the son of a slaveowner.
   d. fathered a child by Sally Hemings.

B. IDENTIFYING DETAILS

Complete each of the following statements by underlining the correct answer in parentheses.

1. DNA contains (4 / 100) nucleotides that form complementary base pairs.

2. In members of the same species, (0.1 / 99.9) percent of DNA is identical.

3. A DNA string is three (thousand / billion) units long.

4. A standard technique for creating a DNA profile focuses on (4 / 13) specific sites where DNA repeats.

5. The odds of unrelated people showing identical repeats are less than 1 in (3 million / 1 trillion).

C. RECOGNIZING METHODS OF ORGANIZATION AND TRANSITIONS

Select the best answer.

_____ 1. In paragraph 2, the author explains what DNA fingerprinting is by using the organizational pattern called
   a. cause and effect.
   b. definition.
   c. comparison and contrast.
   d. chronological order.

_____ 2. In paragraphs 6–8, the author describes how DNA is sorted and identified using the organizational pattern called
   a. process.
   b. listing.

    c. classification.

    d. comparison and contrast.

_____ 3. In paragraph 9, the transition indicating the author's organizational pattern is

    a. has become.

    b. for example.

    c. also.

    d. called for.

➤ D. REVIEWING AND ORGANIZING IDEAS: SUMMARIZING

Use the following list of words and phrases to complete the summary of paragraphs 6–8.

size	restriction enzymes	probe
gel electrophoresis	X-rays	radioactive compound

The first step in profiling DNA is to break it down using _____.
The pieces of chromosomes are then subjected to _____,
which uses an electric field to sort the pieces by _____. To find a
specific repeating sequence, a DNA _____ with a complementary
sequence is made and tagged with a _____. The probe
then binds to the complementary DNA site and _____ reveal
dark bands where the probe and DNA are bound. Finally, this DNA profile is
compared to known references to find a match.

➤ E. FIGURING OUT INFERRED MEANINGS

Indicate whether each statement is true (T) or false (F).

_____ 1. Identifying some victims of the World Trade Center attacks would have been impossible without DNA fingerprinting.

_____ 2. The DNA profiles of siblings and other closely related family members are more similar than those of unrelated people.

_____ 3. The technique is called DNA fingerprinting because it relies primarily on fingerprints for identification.

_____ 4. It is extremely unlikely that unrelated people would have matching DNA profiles.

_____ 5. A person does not need any special training to conduct DNA profiling.

_____ 6. It is impossible to analyze DNA that is more than 100 years old.

_____ 7. In a criminal trial, DNA evidence can establish guilt, but cannot establish innocence.

F. THINKING CRITICALLY

Select the best answer.

_____ 1. The tone of the selection can best be described as
   a. grim.
   b. sympathetic.
   c. informative.
   d. cheerful.

_____ 2. The primary purpose of the photograph on page 448 is to
   a. present evidence of the importance of DNA fingerprinting.
   b. illustrate how simple the DNA fingerprinting process is.
   c. show what DNA electrophoresis looks like.
   d. compare DNA fingerprinting to other identification techniques.

_____ 3. The central thesis of "DNA Fingerprinting: Cracking Our Genetic 'Barcode' " is supported by
   a. facts.
   b. examples.
   c. descriptions.
   d. all of the above.

_____ 4. Of the following statements, the only one that is an *opinion* is
   a. DNA samples recovered from crime scenes or disaster sites are frequently contaminated with dirt, fibers, and debris.
   b. A victim's DNA profile is compared with known references to find one that matches.
   c. DNA profiles can also establish innocence.
   d. Historians have fiercely debated whether Thomas Jefferson fathered children by Sally Hemings.

_____ 5. The author began the selection with a reference to the World Trade Center attacks in order to
   a. compare different types of historical events.
   b. illustrate the importance of DNA fingerprinting.
   c. introduce her own point of view.
   d. establish a setting for the selection.

➤ G. BUILDING VOCABULARY

➤Context

Using context and a dictionary, if necessary, determine the meaning of each word as it is used in the selection.

_____ 1. accelerate (paragraph 5)

     a. affect

     b. speed up

     c. improve

     d. recover

_____ 2. cleave (paragraph 6)

     a. split

     b. appear

     c. cover

     d. harm

_____ 3. migrate (paragraph 6)

     a. match

     b. show

     c. move

     d. limit

_____ 4. exonerated (paragraph 10)

     a. attacked

     b. cleared

     c. removed

     d. identified

_____ 5. fray (paragraph 11)

     a. tool

     b. location

     c. proof

     d. fight

➤Word Parts

> ### A REVIEW OF PREFIXES AND SUFFIXES
> **DE-** means *away, from*
> **UN-** means *not*
> **PRE-** means *before*
> **-ANT** means *one who*

Use your knowledge of word parts and the review on the previous page to fill in the blanks in the following sentences.

1. Something that is *decomposed* (paragraph 1) or in the process of *decomposition* (paragraph 5) is breaking down; it is changing its composition _____ one form to another.

2. If an event happens on an *unprecedented* scale (paragraph 9), it is something that has _____ happened before to such an extent.

3. A person's *descendants* (paragraph 11) may include children, grandchildren, and so on down through a family line. A *descendant* is _____ comes from an ancestor or a race.

►Unusual Words/Understanding Idioms

Use the meanings given below to write a sentence using the boldface word or phrase.

1. A **barcode** (paragraph 2) is usually an identification given to a product so that it can be priced or identified for inventory. In this selection it refers to our unique set of genetic material.

   Your sentence: _____

   _____.

2. When there is a **race against time** (paragraph 5), an urgency exists that makes it important to complete a task before it is too late.

   Your sentence: _____

   _____.

► H.   SELECTING A LEARNING/STUDY STRATEGY

Predict an essay question that might be asked on this selection.

► I.   EXPLORING IDEAS THROUGH DISCUSSION AND WRITING

1. Evaluate the introduction to the selection. Did it capture your interest? Why or why not?

2. Discuss the title of the selection, "DNA Fingerprinting: Cracking Our Genetic 'Barcode.'" Can you think of another title that would be as effective?

3. Do you think it would be interesting to work in DNA profiling or forensic medicine? Describe why it would or would not appeal to you.

4. Discuss the importance of DNA fingerprinting to the justice system. Do you think that all criminal offenders should be required to provide DNA samples?

➤ J. BEYOND THE CLASSROOM TO THE WEB

Explore the applications of DNA research in online modules at **http://www.dnai. org/d/index.html.**

Using this site and the reading, write a paragraph that summarizes one way in which DNA is used.

✔ Tracking Your Progress

Selection 24

Section	Number Correct		Score
A. Thesis and Main Ideas (8 items)	_____	x 3	_____
B. Details (5 items)	_____	x 3	_____
C. Organization and Transitions (3 items)	_____	x 2	_____
E. Inferred Meanings (7 items)	_____	x 3	_____
F. Thinking Critically (5 items)	_____	x 3	_____
G. Vocabulary			
1. Context (5 items)	_____	x 2	_____
2. Word Parts (3 items)	_____	x 3	_____
	TOTAL SCORE	_____%	

18 Health-Related Fields

"Nothing can be more important than your health." This is an overused saying, but it remains meaningful. As the medical field and health-care systems become more complex and as medical knowledge expands, it is becoming necessary for you to assume greater responsibility in your health-care management. Doctors expect you to be able to report your symptoms and many assume you have some basic knowledge of the functioning of the human body. Certainly keeping yourself healthy on a day-to-day basis by eating properly and getting adequate exercise is your responsibility. In "Use It and Lose It" you will read about a woman who decided to take charge of her body through an exercise program. Making sure you get the right prescription and that your medications do not interact is also important. As you will learn in "Make No Mistake: Medical Errors Can Be Deadly Serious," medical errors do occur, and patient awareness is a primary means of prevention. Use and misuse of drugs is also an individual responsibility. "Athletes Looking Good and Doing Better with Anabolic Steroids?" describes the use of anabolic steroids by athletes to improve their strength and endurance.

Use the following tips when reading in health-related fields.

TIPS FOR READING IN HEALTH-RELATED FIELDS

- **Learn necessary terminology.** Each of the articles in this chapter uses some technical and specialized terms. Reading in the field and speaking with health care professionals will be much easier if you have a mastery of basic terminology.

- **Learn about basic human body systems.** You have to know how your body works in order to take care of it and to understand readings in the field. For example, in reading "Athletes Looking Good and Doing Better with Anabolic Steroids?" you need to know about hormonal and muscular systems of the body.

- **Read critically.** There are many different viewpoints, different proposed cures, numerous lose-20-pounds-in-a-week diets, and many "miracle" exercise programs. Read critically, ask questions, and look for supporting evidence. As you read "Use It and Lose It," for example, you will read about one woman's fitness program. Can you be sure that what worked for her will work for you? Ask yourself, "On what principles of diet and exercise was her fitness program based?"

SELECTION
25

Use It and Lose It

Bonnie Schiedel

This reading was taken from the women's magazine, *Chatelaine*. Read it to learn how one woman became healthier and more physically fit.

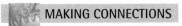

PREVIEWING THE READING

Using the steps listed on page 29, preview the reading selection. When you have finished, complete the following items.

1. The woman featured in the article is named _____.

2. List at least three questions you expect to be able to answer after reading "Use It and Lose It."

   a. _____

   b. _____

   c. _____

MAKING CONNECTIONS

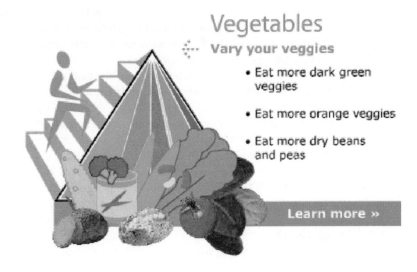

Vegetables

Vary your veggies

- Eat more dark green veggies
- Eat more orange veggies
- Eat more dry beans and peas

Learn more »

One component of maintaining a fit body is eating the right amounts of different kinds of food. MyPyramid, published by the U.S. Department of Agriculture in 2008, recommends personalized eating plans. Think about your own eating habits. Do they fit into a plan? What other behaviors lead to good health?

> **READING TIP**

As you read, highlight advice the author offers that would help someone become more physically fit.

Use It and Lose It

1   Five dress sizes and 100 pounds later, fitness instructor Marilee Arthur is trimmer and more vibrant than ever, thanks to smart and sensible new habits that turn fat to muscle. Read on to learn her secrets.

2   Marilee Arthur knows about breaking the rules. She's been doing it all her life, as a plus-size fitness instructor who won aerobics competitions, taught exercise classes and ran 25 kilometers a week. Baffled doctors and trainers told her that she had the **cardiovascular** system of a high-level athlete and the body fat of a high-level couch potato. She was fat—and fit.

cardiovascular
involving the
heart and the
blood vessels

3   When Marilee, now 37, was profiled in the June 1997 issue of *Chatelaine,* she told us she wanted to lose weight. "But," she added, "I think this is the body I have to live with." Then a little over two years ago, going through a split with her husband and frustrated with her inability to lose weight no matter how active she was, the Plattsville, Ont., resident decided she was fed up with being the exception to the rule. "I wanted to attain some semblance of normalcy."

4   She consulted an exercise physiologist, and together they worked out a customized plan to reduce her overall body fat and gain muscle. "I decided the numbers on the scale were no longer significant. I wanted a healthy body that was strong and well defined with a good distribution of lean body mass to body fat."

5   There was no magic formula that melted the excess body fat. "I tried new things, constantly tweaked my routine, consulted so many different people and books. I refused to give up." And her determination has paid off. Now in the third year of her program, she's gone from a high of 267 pounds down to about 175 pounds (she doesn't know her exact weight because she doesn't look at a scale), trimmed 70 inches from all over her five-foot-seven frame (including nearly 12 from her abdomen and six and a half from each thigh) and dropped five dress sizes, from 24 to 16. Most important, she's reduced her body fat percentage from an obese 38 to a healthy 24 and is well on her way to her goal of 20 percent.

6   "I have a fairly large bone structure and I put on muscle easily, so I realized early on I'd never be one of those 120-pound women," says the mother of two children. "But I love being strong and active and not having to carry all that extra weight around anymore."

7   Here are the secrets to her success—with tips on how to make them work for you.

The Menu: Squelching Starch

8   Like many athletes looking to fuel their activities, Marilee used to load up on starchy carbohydrates such as pasta, rice, potatoes and bagels. "I didn't dump anything fattening on these carbs, but they were the mainstay of my diet. I didn't give much thought to getting enough protein."

9   Carbohydrates are not the enemy—our bodies need them for energy. "If your body doesn't get enough carbohydrates, it will start using fat and protein to provide energy instead. Then that protein isn't being used to build muscle. It's an inefficient system," explains Pam Lynch, a professional dietitian and sports nutritionist in Halifax. The problem is the quantity of carbs you reach for the most—pasta, rice and bread. You can easily eat too much of them at one meal, sometimes taking seconds. Your body uses carbohydrates (or any food) first for immediate energy, then stores the excess as glycogen in your muscles and liver. Whatever the liver and muscles don't use is converted to fat.

glycogen
a compound stored in the liver and muscles that is converted to glucose when the body needs energy

10   Now Marilee enjoys rye bread, baked potatoes and brown rice in moderation—two servings a day—and gets the majority of her carbs from other sources such as fruit and vegetables. They are packed with vitamins and minerals as well as fiber, which fills you up faster, cleanses your system and keeps you regular. She also eats several daily servings of good-quality lean protein such as turkey, fish and beans. Fish, olive oil, a daily flaxseed-oil capsule and almonds supply the monounsaturated "good" fat her body needs. "I'm actually eating a greater volume of food now. And I really enjoy what I eat. I don't feel like I'm depriving myself." She's disciplined but not fanatical. "I don't work out on Sunday and if I feel like having a small amount of ice cream or a couple cookies, that's the day I do it."

The Meals: Timing Is Everything

11   Marilee eats regular healthful meals to keep her blood sugar level on an even keel. Our bodies strive to keep blood sugar within a certain range. If you reach for a sugary treat when you're starving, your blood sugar will go up, then crash down, leaving you cranky, headachy and hungry again.

12   Dinner is her smallest meal of the day, and she tries to eat by 6 p.m.—advice many personal trainers swear by. "If you're loading up on calories at the end of the day when you're relaxing, you're not burning them off," says Susan Cantwell, a Fredericton personal trainer.

13   If you simply must have a starchy carb such as bread, Marilee advises eating it shortly following exercise, when your body is looking to replenish energy. "There's a 15-minute window immediately after exercise," says Lynch. "Your body is more receptive to replacing the glycogen in the muscles and liver, rather than converting it to fat."

The Workout: Busting a Rut

14   Marilee was a fitness nut, but she hadn't changed her aerobics-and-running routine much for years. "I see a lot of fitness instructors who get stuck in a rut and get frustrated because they aren't seeing results anymore," says Cantwell. "You should

change your routine every six to eight weeks. Otherwise your body adapts and the exercise isn't as effective." Marilee added interval training to her thrice-weekly runs (see "Kick It Up a Notch,"). Cantwell approves. "This is an excellent way to burn more calories because you're increasing your intensity without having to increase the duration. It shakes up your routine and can be applied to most forms of exercise."

Tae Bo 15
a type of aerobic exercise that combines a modified form of martial arts with boxing

Marilee also began to develop a Tae-Bo-like routine with her business partner, Terry Yanke. They drew on her aerobics background and his martial arts knowledge and created Ty-Jitsu, a kicking-punching-hee-yaw aerobic-martial arts workout that's easier on the joints than Tae-Bo. "My body changed—my hips, thighs and abdomen got more toned and defined. I was using new muscles in new ways," she says. Her experience doesn't surprise Heather Long, owner of Adventure Fitness, a Winnipeg fitness-consultation business. "Your body likes change and responds to it. You tap into a pool of underused muscles and see a more visible improvement."

The Routine: Early Birds Catch the Burn

16
Conventional wisdom says you should exercise whenever you can fit it into your day. The new thinking is that exercising first thing in the morning burns stored fat, whereas exercising later tends to burn calories that you consumed over the course of the day. Long tells her clients to set their alarms earlier than usual. "If you can't manage a full-length workout in the morning, divide it and have a short workout in the morning and a short one in the evening," she says. "Morning workouts increase your heart rate and keep it at a higher level during the day, which keeps your metabolism revved up."

17
Marilee's running routine consists of a 30-minute high-intensity or interval run at 5:30 a.m. three days a week. She exercises on an empty stomach. For those people who would otherwise end up light-headed or with an acidic stomach after exercising on an empty stomach, Long suggests eating an apple or banana or drinking a glass of juice 15 to 20 minutes before the workout.

bicep
the muscle at the front of the upper arm that flexes the forearm, and also the muscle at the back of the thigh that flexes the knee joint

Weights: The Secret Weapon

18
Marilee also added more weight training (using both free weights and weight machines) to her exercise mix three times a week. Smart move: a muscular body burns more calories than a fat body, even at rest. Why? Muscle tissue requires more oxygen than fatty tissue does, and you use more calories to get this oxygen. The result: a pound of muscle burns between 20 and 50 calories a day, while a pound of fat burns less than 10. "Weight training has been called the 'missing link' for weight loss," explains Cantwell. "Not only does muscle burn calories at rest, but after you lift weights, your muscles use energy to repair themselves for up to three hours. That burns calories too."

curls 19
a weightlifting exercise using a barbell

The key to building muscle is to progressively overload it. As she works out, Marilee increases the amount of weight she lifts and decreases the number of repetitions. She was already a strong woman, so she's able to heft some heavy weights: bicep easy curls, for instance, consist of 12 reps of 27 pounds, 10 reps of 35 pounds, eight reps of 44 pounds and six reps of 50 pounds. Between each set there is a one-minute rest. Beginners, of course, would start at about two-pound weights and work up from there.

reps
short for repetitions

20   It's important to do each lift up and back down smoothly and slowly, resisting both ways. Those bicep curls should take about eight seconds—four to lift and four to lower.

21   "It's important to work your muscles to fatigue, otherwise you're just increasing endurance, not strength," says Cantwell. "The last two or three reps should be really challenging. This tears the muscle fibers microscopically, and then your body expends energy to repair them."

Kick It Up a Notch

22   Whether you're running, biking or swimming you can maximize your workout benefit by varying the intensity of your routine in specific time segments. By doing so, you increase the amount of calories burned without increasing the duration of your workout. Here's what Marilee does over a 30-minute interval run with her running partners and a stopwatch:

- **Warm-up:** Walk or jog for five minutes
- **Intensify pace minute by minute:** Total of five minutes
- **Decrease pace minute by minute:** Total of five minutes until she reaches her original pace. Repeat increasing/decreasing cycle.
- **All-out sprint:** One minute
- **Walking cool-down:** Three to five minutes

Fat and Fit Revisited

23   *Chatelaine*'s first article on Marilee Arthur ("Fat and Fit" by Kim Pittaway, June 1997) discussed new research, most notably a 1995 study by the Cooper Institute for Aerobics Research in Dallas, that indicated overweight but fit men lived longer than unfit men. A subsequent study by the Cooper Institute, published in the International Journal of Obesity in 1998, followed more than 20,000 men aged 30 to 83 over eight years. They found, not surprisingly, that fit men of normal weight had the lowest rate of cardiovascular disease mortality, while unfit and overweight men experienced the highest cardiovascular disease mortality. Bottom line: being obese (BMI 30-plus) is never a good idea because you put yourself at high risk for disease.

mortality
the rate of death associated with a certain cause, such as cardiovascular disease

A.   UNDERSTANDING THE THESIS AND OTHER MAIN IDEAS

Select the best answer.

_____   1. The author's primary purpose in "Use It and Lose It" is to

a. promote weight loss programs offered by local health clubs.

b. describe ways to successfully build muscle while reducing body fat.

c. compare traditional methods of losing weight with new theories of weight loss.

d. inform readers about the health risks associated with obesity.

_____ 2. Marilee Arthur is

    a. the author of "Use It and Lose It."

    b. an exercise physiologist.

    c. a fitness instructor who wanted to lose weight.

    d. a professional dietician.

_____ 3. The main idea of paragraph 3 is that Marilee

    a. was resigned to being overweight.

    b. had not lost weight since her original interview several years earlier.

    c. was frustrated by her inability to lose weight.

    d. made the decision to lose weight.

_____ 4. The topic of paragraph 9 is

    a. carbohydrates.

    b. energy.

    c. protein.

    d. fat.

_____ 5. The statement that best expresses the main idea of paragraph 14 is

    a. "Marilee was a fitness nut but she hadn't changed her aerobics-and-running routine much for years."

    b. "You should change your routine every six to eight weeks."

    c. "Marilee added interval training to her thrice-weekly runs."

    d. "It shakes up your routine and can be applied to most forms of exercise."

_____ 6. The main idea of paragraph 22 is that

    a. you can maximize your workout by running, biking, and swimming.

    b. Marilee's workout is about 30 minutes long, including warming up, sprinting, and cooling down.

    c. you can get the most out of your workout by varying the intensity of your routine in specific intervals.

    d. it is impossible to increase the number of calories burned without increasing the duration of your workout.

_____ 7. The main idea of paragraph 23 is expressed in the

    a. first sentence.

    b. second sentence.

    c. third sentence.

    d. last sentence.

> **B. IDENTIFYING DETAILS**

Select the best answer.

_____ 1. According to the author, the most important result of Marilee's weight loss is that she has
   a. lost almost 100 pounds.
   b. taken a total of 70 inches off her frame.
   c. gone down five dress sizes.
   d. reduced her body fat to a healthy percentage.

_____ 2. Marilee adjusted her diet in all of the following ways *except*
   a. eliminating monounsaturated fats from her diet.
   b. reducing the amount of starch she consumes.
   c. eating regular meals.
   d. making dinner her smallest meal of the day.

_____ 3. Fruits and vegetables provide Marilee with all of the following *except*
   a. vitamins and minerals.   c. carbohydrates.
   b. fiber.   d. protein.

_____ 4. The key to building muscle is to
   a. progressively overload it.
   b. avoid working your muscles to fatigue.
   c. focus on increasing endurance rather than strength.
   d. use light weights that can be lifted quickly.

_____ 5. According to the selection, it is best to exercise
   a. early in the day, because you will be burning stored fat.
   b. late in the day, because you will be burning calories that you consumed during the day.
   c. whenever you can fit it in during the day.
   d. late in the day, and only on a full stomach.

> **C. RECOGNIZING METHODS OF ORGANIZATION AND TRANSITIONS**

Select the best answer.

_____ 1. In paragraph 9, the author uses the cause and effect organizational pattern. In this paragraph, the cause is
   a. too many carbohydrates and the effect is fat.
   b. protein and the effect is energy.
   c. energy and the effect is glycogen.
   d. too much fiber and the effect is low blood sugar.

_____ 2. In paragraph 16, the author makes a comparison between exercising early in the day and exercising later. The transitional word she uses to indicate the comparison is

a. whenever.

b. whereas.

c. earlier.

d. If.

D.   REVIEWING AND ORGANIZING IDEAS: MAPPING

Fill in the blanks to complete the following process diagram based on paragraph 9.

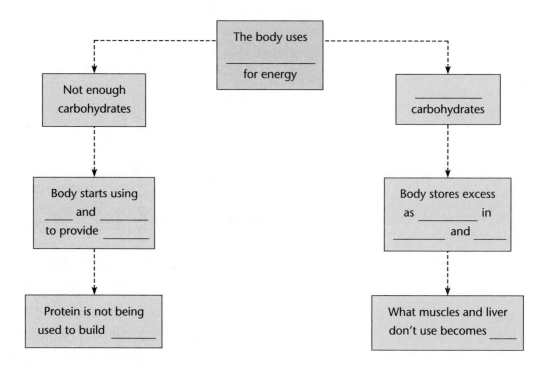

E.   FIGURING OUT INFERRED MEANINGS

Indicate whether each statement is true (T) or false (F).

_____ 1. It can be inferred that a "plus-size" person is one who wears large sizes in clothing.

_____ 2. Doctors and trainers were baffled by Marilee Arthur because she was very strong even though she never exercised.

_____ 3. Marilee considered herself to be abnormally overweight.

_____ 4. Marilee doesn't look at a scale because she's afraid to know how much she weighs now.

_____ 5. Personal trainers encourage their clients to eat dinner by 6 p.m.

➤ F. THINKING CRITICALLY

Select the best answer.

_____ 1. The author supports her thesis with all of the following types of evidence *except*

a. giving examples.

b. quoting authorities.

c. citing facts.

d. describing her own personal experience.

_____ 2. Of the following excerpts from the selection, the only one that is a *fact* is

a. "Fitness instructor Marilee Arthur is trimmer and more vibrant than ever." (paragraph 1)

b. "She consulted an exercise physiologist and together they worked out a customized plan." (paragraph 4)

c. "She's disciplined but not fanatical." (paragraph 10)

d. "Marilee was a fitness nut . . ." (paragraph 14)

_____ 3. Of the following excerpts from the selection, the only one that is an *opinion* is

a. "Our bodies strive to keep blood sugar within a certain range." (paragraph 11)

b. "There's a 15-minute window immediately after exercise." (paragraph 13)

c. "Marilee was a fitness nut . . ." (paragraph 14)

d. "Morning workouts increase your heart rate and keep it at a higher level during the day." (paragraph 16)

_____ 4. The author includes references to weight training as the "missing link" and the "secret weapon" in order to

a. explain that weight training incorporates elements of the martial arts.

b. inject a note of humor into the discussion about workout programs.

c. emphasize that weight lifting is more important than diet in any weight loss program.

d. imply that many people are unaware of the benefits of weight training as part of a weight loss program.

G.   BUILDING VOCABULARY

Context

Using context and a dictionary, if necessary, determine the meaning of each word as it is used in the selection.

_____ 1. vibrant (paragraph 1)

    a. calm

    b. lively

    c. nervous

    d. colorful

_____ 2. attain (paragraph 3)

    a. eliminate

    b. achieve

    c. let go

    d. replace

_____ 3. obese (paragraph 5)

    a. average

    b. unhealthy

    c. overweight

    d. underweight

_____ 4. mainstay (paragraph 8)

    a. chief support

    b. downfall

    c. minor aspect

    d. reward

_____ 5. replenish (paragraph 13)

    a. overlook

    b. eliminate

    c. use up

    d. restore

_____ 6. receptive (paragraph 13)

    a. dishonest

    b. obvious

    c. open to

    d. unavailable

_____ 7. heft (paragraph 19)

    a. weight

    b. push

    c. build

    d. lift

_____ 8. fatigue (paragraph 21)

    a. strength

    b. exhaustion

    c. illness

    d. exercise

➤ Word Parts

> ### A REVIEW OF PREFIXES AND SUFFIXES
> **EX-** means *out*
> **IN-** means *out*
> **-AL** means *characteristic of*
> **-ANCE** means *the quality of*
> **-IST** means *a person who*

Use your knowledge of word parts and the review above to fill in the blanks in the following sentences.

1. A **physiologist** (paragraph 4) is _____ studies physiology, or the functions of living organisms and their parts.

2. A system that is **inefficient** (paragraph 9) is _____ efficient; it does not work well.

3. Someone who is **fanatical** (paragraph 10) behaves in a way that is _____ a fanatic, or a person who is extreme in his or her enthusiasm for a subject.

4. When you are trying to increase your **endurance** (paragraph 21), you are trying to improve _____ your ability to endure something.

5. When your body **expends** (paragraph 21) energy to repair torn muscle fibers, it puts _____, or spends, energy.

➤ **Unusual Words/Understanding Idioms**
Use the meanings given below to write a sentence using the boldface word or phrase.

1. The term **couch potato** (paragraph 2) refers to a person who spends a lot of time sitting or lying down, usually watching television, rather than engaging in physical activity.

   Your sentence: _____

   _____.

2. The word **tweak** (paragraph 5) means to adjust or fine-tune something.

   Your sentence: _____

   _____.

3. The author uses the word **fuel** (paragraph 8) as a verb, meaning to stimulate or sustain an activity.

   Your sentence: _____

   _____.

4. The word **nut** (paragraph 14) is used in the selection to mean a person who is very enthusiastic about something; in this case, fitness.

   Your sentence: _____

   _____.

5. To be **stuck in a rut** (paragraph 14) is to remain in the same, boring routine.

   Your sentence: _____

   _____.

➤ **H. SELECTING A LEARNING/STUDY STRATEGY**

Suppose you were taking a health and fitness class to meet your physical education requirements. Discuss what method(s) you would use to learn this material in preparation for a multiple-choice test.

➤ **I. EXPLORING IDEAS THROUGH DISCUSSION AND WRITING**

1. Why is the information about mortality and cardiovascular disease included at the end of the selection? How do you think Marilee Arthur has lessened her chances of developing cardiovascular disease?

2. Did you find any parts of this information useful? If so, which ones?

3. Discuss whether Americans are overly concerned with body image.

> **J.   BEYOND THE CLASSROOM TO THE WEB**

Visit Karate Tournament Central at **http://www.karatetournaments.com/ artic001.htm**.
   Read this interview with Master Billy Blanks, the person who invented Tae-Bo. What three areas of physical conditioning did he draw on to create Tae-Bo?

✔ **Tracking Your Progress**

Selection 25

Section	Number Correct		Score
A. Thesis and Main Ideas (7 items)	_____	x 4	_____
B. Details (5 items)	_____	x 3	_____
C. Organization and Transitions (2 items)	_____	x 2	_____
E. Inferred Meanings (5 items)	_____	x 3	_____
F. Thinking Critically (4 items)	_____	x 3	_____
G. Vocabulary			
1. Context (8 items)	_____	x 2	_____
2. Word Parts (5 items)	_____	x 2	_____
	TOTAL SCORE	_____ %	

SELECTION 26

Make No Mistake: Medical Errors Can Be Deadly Serious

Tamar Nordenberg

This article appeared on the Federal Drug Administration (FDA) consumer magazine Web site. Read it to learn why you must be a wary consumer, even in a hospital.

▶ PREVIEWING THE READING

Using the steps listed on page 29, preview the reading selection. When you have finished, complete the following items.

1. The topic of this selection is _____.

2. Based on the subheadings, list three questions you expect to be able to answer after reading the selection:

   a. _____

   _____

   b. _____

   _____

   c. _____

   _____

MAKING CONNECTIONS

What is one type of medical mistake that can cause problems for patients, as suggested by the image on the next page? What others can you think of?

▶ READING TIP

As you read, highlight the types of medical errors that can occur.

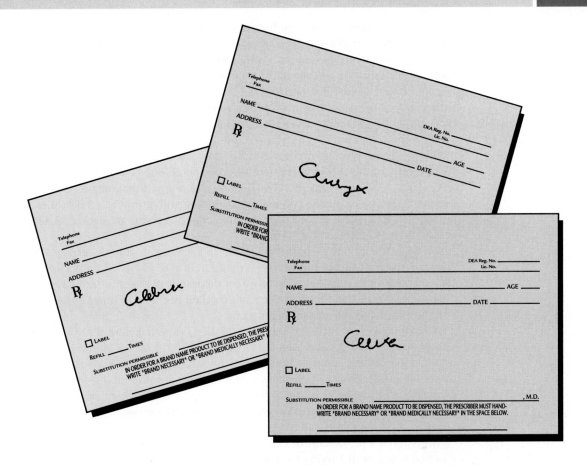

double bypass heart operation
a surgical procedure to create alternative passages for diverting blood around obstructions in coronary arteries

artery
a vessel that carries oxygenated blood from the heart to the rest of the body

Make No Mistake: Medical Errors Can Be Deadly Serious

1   Two months after a double bypass heart operation that was supposed to save his life, comedian and former *Saturday Night Live* cast member Dana Carvey got some disheartening news: the cardiac surgeon had bypassed the wrong artery. It took another emergency operation to clear the blockage that was threatening to kill the 45-year-old funnyman and father of two young kids. Responding to a $7.5 million lawsuit Carvey brought against him, the surgeon said he'd made an honest mistake because Carvey's artery was unusually situated in his heart. But Carvey didn't see it that way. "It's like removing the wrong kidney. It's that big a mistake," the entertainer told *People* magazine.

2   Based on a recent report on medical mistakes from the National Academy of Sciences' Institute of Medicine, Carvey might fairly be characterized as one of the lucky survivors. In its report, "To Err Is Human: Building a Safer Health System," the IOM estimates that 44,000 to 98,000 Americans die each year not from the medical

conditions they checked in with, but from preventable medical errors. A medical error, under the report's definition, could mean a health-care provider chose an inappropriate method of care, such as giving a patient a certain asthma drug without knowing that he or she was allergic to it. Or it could mean the health provider chose the right course of care but carried it out incorrectly, such as intending to infuse a patient with diluted potassium chloride—a potassium supplement—but inadvertently giving the patient a concentrated, lethal overdose.

3   The Institute of Medicine (IOM) estimates that fully half of adverse reactions to medicines are the result of medical errors. Other adverse reactions—those that are unexpected and not preventable—are not considered errors. The statistics in the IOM report, which were based on two large studies, suggest that medical errors are the eighth leading cause of death among Americans, with error-caused deaths each year in hospitals alone exceeding those from motor vehicle accidents (43,458), breast cancer (42,297), or AIDS (16,516).

4   But the numbers in the report don't tell the whole story, its authors acknowledge. People in the hospital are just a small proportion of those at risk. Doctors' offices, clinics, and outpatient surgical centers treat thousands of patients each day; retail pharmacies fill countless prescriptions; and nursing homes and other institutional settings serve vulnerable patient populations.

5   Despite the recent focus on the IOM statistics, experts assure that the health system in the United States is safe. But its safety record is a far cry from the enviable record of the similarly complex aviation industry, which is being held up as an example for the medical world. A person would have to fly nonstop for 438 years before expecting to be involved in a deadly airplane crash, based on recent airline accident statistics. That, IOM says, places health-care at least a decade behind aviation in safeguarding consumers' lives and health.

6   The report is a self-described "call to action" for the health-care system. "Whether a person is sick or just trying to stay healthy, he or she should not have to worry about being harmed by the health system itself," its authors say.

Medication Mistakes

7   Even the seemingly simple process of giving a patient medicine—the right drug, in the right dose, to the right patient, at the right time—is, in reality, teeming with opportunities for error. The IOM estimates that preventable medication errors result in more than 7,000 deaths each year in hospitals alone, and tens of thousands more in outpatient facilities.

8   Name confusion is among the most common causes of drug-related errors, says Peter Honig, M.D., an FDA expert on drug risk-assessment. A recent example: the sound-alike names for the antiepileptic drug Lamictal and the antifungal drug Lamisil. The volume of dispensing errors involving these two drugs prompted the manufacturer of Lamictal, Glaxo Wellcome Inc., of Research Triangle Park, N.C., to launch a campaign warning pharmacists of the potential confusion. The possible consequences of prescribing the wrong drug are grave: Epileptic patients receiving the anti-fungal drug Lamisil by mistake could experience continuous seizures. Patients erroneously receiving the antiepileptic drug

Lamictal might experience a serious rash, blood pressure changes, or other side effects.

9   Under FDA's authority to regulate drug labeling, the agency's new Office of Postmarketing Drug Risk Assessment evaluates medicines' brand names in an attempt to avoid sound-alike and look-alike names. If FDA considers the name of a new medical product to be potentially confusing to health professionals, the agency works with the drug company to change the product's name. FDA is developing new standards to prevent such name mix-ups, as well as to prevent confusion between similar-looking drug packaging. Also, the agency is developing new label standards to highlight common interactions between drugs so that doctors are less likely to mistakenly prescribe dangerous combinations. And even after a drug is approved, FDA monitors its use to see if unexpected adverse events occur and whether any labeling changes are required to help avoid medication mishaps.

10   So where does FDA's responsibility end and the health professionals' judgment take over? "FDA must do everything within its authority to maximize the likelihood that approved products will be used correctly in the real world," says Honig. But, he notes, "We don't regulate the practice of medicine, such as the sloppy handwriting when prescribing a drug." The real-world practice of medicine occurs within an intricate system, says Janet Woodcock. "It's that complexity," she says, "coupled with the limitations of humans, that makes avoiding mistakes a consuming task."

Human Limitations

11   As its title—To Err Is Human—suggests, the IOM report supports moving away from the traditional culture of "naming, shaming, and blaming" individual health providers who make mistakes. Instead, the institute believes that preventing future errors is best achieved by designing a safer overall system.

12   Some medical centers have begun using computer programs and other system supports to curtail medical mishaps by double-checking the care decisions doctors and nurses make. Even simple computer systems that use electronic prescriptions in place of handwritten ones have in some cases already paid off with substantial error reductions.

13   But systems, too, can fail, cautions Raymond L. Woosley, M.D., a professor and chairman of pharmacology at Georgetown University Medical Center. Woosley's example: "It's true that if you have a prescription drug with an electronic bar code on it—the right code—it can help prevent errors. But if the wrong code is on there, you may have even more errors. There will always be mistakes, though they will be different mistakes as the systems change. You've got to be ready to handle them."

pharmacology the study of drugs, including their compositions, uses, and effects

14   Despite technological advances, preventing mistakes will always depend on the vigilance of health professionals, Woosley says. Otherwise, human carelessness can render useless the very systems designed to avert mistakes. Even among pharmacies with a computer program to highlight dangerous drug interactions, according to a study published in the *Journal of the American Medical Association,* one-third of pharmacists nevertheless continued to fill prescriptions for a known killer combination: the prescription antihistamine Seldane (terfenadine) with the antibiotic

erythromycin. (Seldane has since been removed from the market.) "The pharmacists would get the computer warnings and zip right on by them," Woosley says. "Or they would turn off the program entirely." Why turn off the computer program? Because, Woosley explains, it was slowing down the pharmacists when they wanted to print labels.

15   Health professionals "are trained to memorize everything and are rewarded for it," says the pharmacology professor. "The medical student who says, 'I don't know; I've got to look it up,' is likely to fail an exam, yet that's the one who is less likely to make an error." Woosley hopes medical students will be taught to accept their limitations and admit their mistakes. Under the current system, however, some people call that goal pie-in-the-sky.

To Improve Is Human

16   Woodcock (head of the FDA's Center for Drug Evaluation and Research) encourages consumers to help prevent errors by being vigilant about their health care—understanding their treatment, keeping organized records of what doctors they see and what medications they take, and asking questions when things don't seem right. For example, "If your pills look different than they have in the past, they might be the right medication, and they might not. But raise the issue."

17   Honig calls consumer education the "secret weapon" in the war against medical errors. "It's unfortunate that people research buying a car better than they research health-care decisions. They're willing to tolerate more uncertainty with their health care than their mode of transportation." He encourages patients to feel comfortable asking more questions about their medical care.

18   With everyone from pharmaceutical manufacturers to consumers playing a role in improving the safety of the health system, Woodcock believes that the already "very safe" medical system in the United States will become even safer. "There are fixes," she says. "We know that from other industries." The spotlight on the health system's problems might be just what the system needs to transform itself, says Woodcock. After all, as the IOM report notes, "It may be part of human nature to err, but it is also part of human nature to create solutions, find better alternatives, and meet the challenges ahead."

A.   UNDERSTANDING THE THESIS AND OTHER MAIN IDEAS

Select the best answer.

_____ 1. The central thesis of "Make No Mistake" is that

a. thousands of dollars are lost every year because of billing errors in America's health system.

b. physicians and pharmacists should be held accountable for the medical errors they make.

c. preventable medical errors cause thousands of deaths in America each year.

     d. the Food and Drug Administration (FDA) must set standards for evaluating new medical products.

_____ 2. The author's primary purpose is to

     a. compare America's health-care system with that of other countries.

     b. report on the types and causes of medical mistakes as well as efforts to address those mistakes.

     c. assign blame to the medical professionals who are most at fault.

     d. urge people to sue medical professionals who have misdiagnosed or mistreated patients.

_____ 3. The topic of paragraph 4 is

     a. the Institute of Medicine (IOM) report.

     b. hospital patients.

     c. outpatients.

     d. at-risk patients.

_____ 4. The main idea of paragraph 8 is expressed in the

     a. first sentence.

     b. second sentence.

     c. third sentence.

     d. last sentence.

_____ 5. The statement that best expresses the main idea of paragraph 14 is

     a. "Despite technological advances, preventing mistakes will always depend on the vigilance of health professionals."

     b. "Otherwise, human carelessness can render useless the very systems designed to avert mistakes."

     c. "Even among pharmacies with a computer program to highlight dangerous drug interactions, one-third of pharmacists nevertheless continued to fill prescriptions for a known killer combination."

     d. "It was slowing down the pharmacists when they wanted to print labels."

_____ 6. The main idea of paragraph 15 is that health professionals

     a. are trained to memorize everything.

     b. should learn to accept their limitations.

     c. are rewarded for their memorization skills.

     d. will never admit their mistakes.

_____ 7. The topic of paragraph 18 is

    a. pharmaceutical manufacturers.

    b. consumers.

    c. improving safety of the health system.

    d. the IOM report.

➤ B. IDENTIFYING DETAILS

Select the best answer.

_____ 1. Under the definition given in the IOM's report, all of the following would be considered medical errors *except*

    a. an inappropriate method of care chosen by a health-care provider.

    b. a method of care incorrectly carried out by a health-care provider.

    c. unexpected and unpreventable adverse reactions to medicines.

    d. dispensing the wrong medication because of name confusion.

_____ 2. Of the following causes of death, the greatest number of deaths resulted from

    a. car accidents.

    b. medical errors.

    c. breast cancer.

    d. AIDS.

_____ 3. In the example describing prescription errors for the sound-alike drugs Lamictal and Lamisil, the drug manufacturer decided to

    a. take both drugs off the market.

    b. launch a campaign warning pharmacists of the potential confusion.

    c. rename one of the drugs.

    d. disclaim all responsibility for any mistakes.

_____ 4. The Food and Drug Administration (FDA) and its Office of Postmarketing Drug Risk Assessment address the problem of medical mistakes in all of the following ways *except*

    a. monitoring the use of approved drugs to see whether labeling changes are necessary.

    b. working with drug companies to change potentially confusing product names and packaging.

    c. reprimanding individual health-care providers who make prescription mistakes or write difficult-to-read prescriptions.

    d. developing new label standards that highlight common interactions between drugs.

_____ 5. According to FDA expert Peter Honig, the secret weapon in the war against medical errors is

    a. medical lawsuits.

    b. electronic prescription-writing.

    c. the FDA's new label standards.

    d. consumer education.

C. RECOGNIZING METHODS OF ORGANIZATION AND TRANSITIONS

Fill in the blanks in the following statements.

1. In paragraph 2, the author describes what constitutes a medical error according to the IOM report. The organizational pattern in this paragraph is _____.

2. In paragraph 5, the author uses the _____ organizational pattern to contrast the safety record of America's health system with the safety record of the aviation industry.

3. In paragraph 8, the author uses cause and effect to describe one type of medical mistake. In this paragraph, the cause is _____ and the effects are the serious physical reactions of patients who receive the wrong drug.

4. In paragraph 16, the phrase that indicates that Janet Woodcock's point about consumer vigilance will be illustrated is _____.

D. REVIEWING AND ORGANIZING IDEAS: PARAPHRASING

Complete the paraphrase of paragraph 1 by filling in the missing words and phrases.

Comedian and former _____ cast member Dana Carvey had to have a _____ to save his life. Two _____ later, the 45-year-old _____ of two young _____ found out that the _____ had bypassed the wrong _____; Carvey would have to have an emergency _____ to clear the life-threatening blockage. When Carvey _____ the surgeon for $7.5 million, the _____ said that the unusual placement of Carvey's _____ in his _____ caused the mistake. Carvey disagreed, telling _____ that it was as major a _____ as removing the wrong _____ would be.

E. FIGURING OUT INFERRED MEANINGS

Indicate whether each statement is true (T) or false (F).

_____ 1. It can be inferred that many more deaths from medical mistakes probably occur outside hospital settings.

_____ 2. A person has a much greater chance of being in an airplane crash than being the victim of a serious medical mistake.

_____ 3. The health-care industry requested that the IOM conduct research into medical mistakes.

_____ 4. The volume of dispensing errors for the two similarly named drugs (Lamictal and Lamisil) was significant.

_____ 5. The IOM believes that the traditional culture of punishing health-care providers who made mistakes was not effective in preventing future mistakes.

F. THINKING CRITICALLY

Select the best answer.

_____ 1. Most of the evidence supporting the central thesis is based on

a. interviews with health-care providers.

b. interviews with victims of medical mistakes.

c. a report by the National Academy of Sciences' Institute of Medicine.

d. the personal experiences of the author.

_____ 2. The tone of the reading can best be described as

a. cautionary.

b. bitter.

c. angry.

d. humorous.

_____ 3. When this selection first appeared, its intended audience most likely was

a. health-care providers.

b. health-care consumers.

c. lawyers.

d. medical students.

_____ 4. The author captures the reader's attention by beginning the article with

a. a funny story about medical mistakes.

b. several quotations from health-care providers.

       c. shocking statistics about medical mistakes.

       d. the serious account of a medical mishap affecting a popular entertainer.

_____ 5. By calling their IOM report a "call to action," the report's authors mean that the report is intended to

       a. put pressure on the health-care system to improve its safety.

       b. challenge health-care providers to dispute the IOM findings.

       c. encourage consumers to pursue legal action against their health-care providers.

       d. prompt the government to become less involved in regulating the safety of the health-care system.

G.   BUILDING VOCABULARY

Context

Using context and a dictionary, if necessary, determine the meaning of each word as it is used in the selection.

_____ 1. infuse (paragraph 2)

       a. connect

       b. recover

       c. inject

       d. diagnose

_____ 2. lethal (paragraph 2)

       a. effective

       b. deadly

       c. illegal

       d. unfortunate

_____ 3. adverse (paragraph 3)

       a. likely

       b. common

       c. expected

       d. harmful

_____ 4. teeming (paragraph 7)

       a. filled with

       b. searching

       c. leaving

       d. forming

_____ 5. erroneously (paragraph 8)

    a. occasionally

    b. purposely

    c. repeatedly

    d. mistakenly

_____ 6. intricate (paragraph 10)

    a. expensive

    b. old-fashioned

    c. dangerous

    d. complicated

_____ 7. curtail (paragraph 12)

    a. encourage

    b. limit

    c. hide

    d. find

➤ Word Parts

> **A REVIEW OF PREFIXES**
> **ANTI-** mean *against*
> **DIS-** means *not*
> **IN-** means *not*

Match each word in Column A with its meaning in Column B. Write your answers in the spaces provided.

Column A	Column B
_____ 1. inappropriate	a. not encouraging
_____ 2. antifungal	b. unsuitable
_____ 3. disheartening	c. not on purpose
_____ 4. antibiotic	d. destroys fungi
_____ 5. inadvertently	e. destroys harmful bacteria

➤ Unusual Words/Understanding Idioms
Use the meanings given below to write a sentence using the boldface phrase.

1. The phrase **tell the whole story** (paragraph 4) means to give a complete account of the facts of the situation.

    Your sentence: _____

    _____.

2. The phrase **pie-in-the-sky** (paragraph 15) describes an unrealistic wish or an empty promise.

Your sentence: _____

_____.

> **H. SELECTING A LEARNING/STUDY STRATEGY**

Select the best answer.

_____   If you were preparing for an essay exam in a health class and the material in this selection was to be covered on the exam, which of the following strategies would be most useful?

a. making a list of specific medical errors described in the article

b. preparing a chart listing types of medical errors and means of prevention

c. making a list of IOM report findings

d. writing a list of quotations by medical experts cited in the article.

> **I. EXPLORING IDEAS THROUGH DISCUSSION AND WRITING**

1. How will this reading change the way you view your health care? Do you think the author presented an unbiased account of medical mistakes?

2. Do you agree with the health-care experts who say the American health-care system is safe?

3. Explain what is meant by a "culture of 'naming, shaming, and blaming.'" What do you think happened to the health-care providers who made mistakes in that environment?

4. Explain why the medical student who has to look up the answers is more likely to fail the exam but less likely to make a mistake. Why do you think some people believe it is unrealistic to expect medical students to learn to accept their limitations?

> **J. BEYOND THE CLASSROOM TO THE WEB**

Visit FDA Consumer magazine, published by the U.S. Food and Drug Administration at **http://www.fda.gov/fdac/features/1999/599_med.html**.

Read the article on this page, "When Is a Medical Product Too Risky?" (This article was referred to in paragraph 3 of "Make No Mistake.") What are two reasons FDA Commissioner Jane Henney gives for the risks associated with a drug not being completely known before the medication becomes available for sale?

✔ Tracking Your Progress

Selection 26

Section	Number Correct		Score
A. Thesis and Main Ideas (7 items)	_____	x 4	_____
B. Details (5 items)	_____	x 3	_____
C. Organization and Transitions (4 items)	_____	x 2	_____
E. Inferred Meanings (5 items)	_____	x 3	_____
F. Thinking Critically (5 items)	_____	x 3	_____
G. Vocabulary			
1. Context (7 items)	_____	x 2	_____
2. Word Parts (5 items)	_____	x 1	_____
TOTAL SCORE			_____ %

SELECTION 27

Athletes Looking Good and Doing Better with Anabolic Steroids?

Elaine Marieb

This reading was taken from a biology book titled *Human Anatomy and Physiology*. It appears as a boxed insert in the chapter titled "Muscles and Muscle Tissue."

▶ PREVIEWING THE READING

Using the steps listed on page 29, preview the reading selection. When you have finished, complete the following items.

1. The topic of this selection is _____.

2. List three questions you expect to be able to answer after reading the article.

   a. _____

   b. _____

   c. _____

MAKING CONNECTIONS

What would you be willing to do in order to win an athletic competition—a weight-lifting contest, a race, a football game? Would you be willing to take drugs? Why or why not?

anobolic steroids
synthetic hormones
that promote
protein storage and
tissue growth

testosterone
the male hormone
that causes
increased muscle
and bone mass
and other
physical changes
during male puberty
and maintains
masculine traits
throughout life

anemia
condition
in which an
abnormally
low amount of
hemoglobin or a
low number of red
blood cells results
in the body's cells
not receiving
enough oxygen

muscle atrophy
the deterioration
of a muscle due
to disease, injury,
or lack of use

shot put
athletic event
involving
throwing a heavy
metal ball

isometric
a form of exercise
in which muscles
are pushed
against something
or against other
muscles to
strengthen them

> **READING TIP**

This selection contains many examples of the effects of steroid use, both positive and negative. Create two columns in your notes, one labeled "Benefits" and the other labeled "Risks," so you can keep track of both types of effects as you read.

Athletes Looking Good and Doing Better with Anabolic Steroids?

1   Society loves a winner and top athletes reap large social and monetary rewards. Thus, it is not surprising that some will grasp at anything that will increase their performance—including **anabolic steroids.** Anabolic steroids, variants of the male sex hormone **testosterone** engineered by pharmaceutical companies, were introduced in the 1950s to treat victims of **anemia** and certain muscle-wasting diseases and to prevent **muscle atrophy** in patients immobilized after surgery. Testosterone is responsible for the increase in muscle and bone mass and other physical changes that occur during puberty and convert boys into men. Convinced that megadoses of the steroids could produce enhanced masculinizing effects in grown men, many athletes and bodybuilders were using the steroids by the early 1960s, and the practice is still going strong today. Indeed, it has been estimated that nearly one in every ten young men has tried steroids, so use is no longer confined to athletes looking for the edge.

2   It has been difficult to determine the incidence of anabolic steroid use among athletes because the use of drugs has been banned by most international competitions, and users (and prescribing physicians or drug dealers) are naturally reluctant to talk about it. Nonetheless, there is little question that many professional bodybuilders and athletes competing in events that require muscle strength (e.g., **shot put**, discus throwing, and weight lifting) are heavy users. Sports figures such as football players have also admitted to using steroids as an adjunct to training, diet, and psychological preparation for games. Advantages of anabolic steroids cited by athletes include enhanced muscle mass and strength, increased oxygen-carrying capability owing to greater red blood cell volume, and an increase in aggressive behavior.

3   Typically, bodybuilders who use steroids combine high doses (up to 200 mg/day) with heavy resistance training. Intermittent use begins several months before an event, and commonly entails the use of many anabolic steroid supplements (a method called stacking). Injected or transdermal (taken via a skin patch) steroid doses are increased gradually as the competition nears.

4   But do the drugs do all that is claimed for them? Research studies have reported increases in **isometric** strength and a rise in body weight in steroid users. While these are results weight lifters dream about, there is a hot dispute over whether this also translates into athletic performance requiring the fine muscle coordination and endurance needed by runners, etc. The "jury is still out" on this question, but if you ask users, the answer will most likely be a resounding yes.

5   Do the proclaimed advantages conferred by steroid use outweigh the risks? Absolutely not. Physicians say they cause bloated faces (Cushingoid sign of steroid excess); shriveled testes and infertility; damage to the liver that promotes liver cancer; and changes in blood cholesterol levels (which may predispose long-term users to coronary heart disease). The psychiatric hazards of anabolic steroid use may be equally threatening: Recent studies have indicated that one-third of users have serious mental problems. Manic behavior in which the users undergo Jekyll-Hyde personality swings and become extremely violent (termed the 'roid rage) is common, as are depression and delusions.

6   A recent arrival on the scene, sold over the counter and touted as a "nutritional performance-enhancer," is **androstenedione,** which is converted to testosterone in the body. Though it is taken orally (and much of it is destroyed by the liver soon after ingestion), the few milligrams that survive temporarily boost testosterone levels. Reports of its use by baseball great Mark McGwire in the summer of '98, and of athletic wannabes from the fifth grade up recently sweeping the supplement off the drugstore shelves are troubling, particularly since it is not regulated by the FDA and its long-term effects are unpredictable and untested.

androstenedione an oral supplement that temporarily raises testosterone levels by converting to testosterone in the body

7   The question of why some athletes use these drugs is easy to answer. Some admit to a willingness to do almost anything to win, short of killing themselves. Are they unwittingly doing this as well?

➤ A. UNDERSTANDING THE THESIS AND OTHER MAIN IDEAS

Select the best answer.

_____ 1. The central thesis of the selection is that

    a. steroid use is common among professional athletes.

    b. the risks of anabolic steroid use are much greater than the benefits.

    c. synthetic steroids such as androstenedione should be regulated by the FDA.

    d. most international athletic competitions ban the use of steroids.

_____ 2. The author's primary purpose is to

    a. describe the history of anabolic steroids.

    b. reassure readers that the effects of anabolic steroids are not as serious as some people think.

    c. inform readers about the benefits and risks of anabolic steroid use.

    d. criticize the professional athletes who have popularized the use of anabolic steroids.

Match each question in Column A with the paragraph in the selection that primarily answers that question in Column B.

Column A	Column B
_____ 3. What are the risks/hazards of anabolic steroid use?	a. paragraph 1
_____ 4. What are anabolic steroids?	b. paragraph 2
_____ 5. Who uses anabolic steroids?	c. paragraph 3
_____ 6. How and when do athletes use anabolic steroids?	d. paragraphs 2 and 4
_____ 7. Why do athletes use anabolic steroids?	e. paragraph 5

➤ B. IDENTIFYING DETAILS

Complete the following statement by filling in the blanks.

1. Anabolic steroids were first introduced in the _____.

2. Anabolic steroids were originally intended to treat victims of _____ and certain muscle-wasting diseases and to prevent _____ in patients immobilized after surgery.

3. It has been estimated that nearly one out of every _____ young men has tried steroids.

4. The use of many anabolic steroid supplements is called _____.

5. A high dose of steroids is up to _____.

6. The steroid androstenedione is converted to _____ in the body.

7. The long-term effects of androstenedione are _____ and untested.

➤ C. RECOGNIZING METHODS OF ORGANIZATION AND TRANSITIONS

Select the best answer.

_____ 1. In paragraph 2, the organizational pattern the author uses to present the advantages of anabolic steroids cited by athletes is
     a. time sequence.
     b. enumeration.
     c. cause and effect.
     d. problem–solution.

_____ 2. The author uses the cause and effect organizational pattern in paragraph 5. The cause in this paragraph is

a. steroid use and the effects are increased strength and weight.

b. athletic competition and the effects are steroid use.

c. steroid use and the effects are physical and psychiatric hazards.

d. athletes and the effects are improved performance.

D.   REVIEWING AND ORGANIZING IDEAS: OUTLINING

Complete the following outline of paragraphs 4 and 5 by filling in the missing words and phrases.

Results of Anabolic Steroid Use

I.   Benefits

   A. For weight lifters

     1. Increase in _____ strength

     2. Rise in _____

   B. For _____ and other athletes

     1. Uncertain effects

II.   Hazards/Risks

   A. Physical

     1. Bloated _____

       a. Cushingoid sign of _____

     2. Shriveled testes and _____

     3. Damage to _____

       a. Promotes liver _____

     4. Changes in _____ levels

       a. May predispose _____ to

       _____

   B. _____

     1. One-third of users have serious _____

2. _____ behavior

   a. Jekyll-Hyde _____ swings

   b. Extreme _____ or 'roid rage

3. Depression

4. _____

E. FIGURING OUT INFERRED MEANINGS

Indicate whether each statement is true (T) or false (F).

_____ 1. Most athletes are proud of their steroid use.

_____ 2. Increased isometric strength and body weight are goals of weight lifters.

_____ 3. Steroid users believe runners and other athletes whose performance depends on fine muscle coordination and endurance do not benefit from steroids.

_____ 4. Many young athletes do not know about the risks of steroid use.

F. THINKING CRITICALLY

Select the best answer.

_____ 1. The thesis is supported primarily by
   a. personal experience.
   b. statistics.
   c. analogies.
   d. facts and examples.

_____ 2. The tone of the selection can best be described as
   a. pessimistic.
   b. serious.
   c. admiring.
   d. disgusted.

_____ 3. The author opens with the words "Society loves a winner" in order to
   a. add humor to the subject of steroid use.
   b. defend steroid use by athletes.
   c. offer a possible motivation for steroid use.
   d. ridicule steroid users.

_____ 4. In paragraph 2, the statement that "users are naturally reluctant to talk about it" means that

    a. these athletes don't want to give away the secrets of their success.

    b. athletes who use steroids are breaking the rules of most international competitions.

    c. these athletes would be arrested if they talked about their steroid use.

    d. athletes who do not use steroids would criticize the ones who do.

_____ 5. Of the following statements based on paragraph 6, the only one that is an _opinion_ is

    a. Androstenedione is sold over the counter as a nutritional supplement.

    b. Although androstenedione is taken orally, the liver destroys much of it soon after ingestion.

    c. Androstenedione is not regulated by the FDA.

    d. Reports of its use by baseball great Mark McGwire are troubling.

_____ 6. The author ends the selection with a question primarily to

    a. prompt readers and possibly athletes to think about the effects of steroid use.

    b. reveal why some athletes use steroids.

    c. demonstrate sympathy for athletes who use steroids.

    d. present another side of the issue.

G. BUILDING VOCABULARY

Context

Using context and a dictionary, if necessary, determine the meaning of each word as it is used in the selection.

_____ 1. monetary (paragraph 1)

    a. emotional

    b. financial

    c. status

    d. social

_____ 2. masculinizing (paragraph 1)

    a. strengthening

    b. hormone-altering

    c. giving a masculine appearance

    d. taking away masculinity

_____ 3. adjunct (paragraph 2)

    a. replacement

    b. supplement

    c. alternative

    d. advantage

_____ 4. intermittent (paragraph 3)

    a. periodic

    b. constant

    c. intensive

    d. careful

_____ 5. entails (paragraph 3)

    a. realizes

    b. eliminates

    c. involves

    d. relaxes

_____ 6. resounding (paragraph 4)

    a. strong and forceful

    b. slow and hesitant

    c. suspicious or doubtful

    d. restricted and limited

_____ 7. touted (paragraph 6)

    a. counted

    b. promoted

    c. respected

    d. performed

➤ Word Parts

> **A REVIEW OF PREFIXES**
>
> **IM-** means *not*
> **IN-** means *in, into*
> **MEGA-** means *large*
> **PRE-** means *before, in advance*
> **TRANS-** means *across, over, through*
> **UN-** means *not*

Match each word in Column A with its meaning in Column B. Write your answers in the spaces provided.

Column A

_____ 1. transdermal

_____ 2. unwittingly

_____ 3. predispose

_____ 4. ingestion

_____ 5. immobilized

_____ 6. megadoses

Column B

a. taking into the body by the mouth

b. exceptionally large quantities

c. not able to move

d. through the skin

e. not knowingly or not intentionally

f. make someone susceptible in advance

Unusual Words/Understanding Idioms

Read each of the statements from the selection again, and then use the hints to fill in the meaning of the boldface word or phrase.

1. "[Anabolic steroid] use is no longer confined to athletes looking for the **edge**." (paragraph 1)

   Hint: An *edge* means an advantage or a margin of superiority over someone or something.

   Therefore, athletes who are looking for the edge are hoping to find

   _____.

2. "The '**jury is still out**' on this question." (paragraph 4)

   Hint: The expression refers to a situation in which the jury for a case presented in court has not yet agreed upon its decision.

   Therefore, there has not yet been _____ about this particular question.

3. "Reports of . . . athletic **wannabes** from the fifth grade up recently sweeping the supplement off the drugstore shelves are troubling." (paragraph 6)

   Hint: The term *wannabe* is a shortened version of the phrase "want to be."

   Therefore, athletic *wannabes* are young people who _____.

H. SELECTING A LEARNING/STUDY STRATEGY

Evaluate the two-column list you created as a study aid. For what types of exams would it be most and least useful?

➤ I.   EXPLORING IDEAS THROUGH DISCUSSION AND WRITING

1. Why do you think so many young men have tried steroids? Does society do more to promote steroid use or discourage it?

2. How can you tell that the author disapproves of steroid use? Give an example.

3. Do you think the advantages of steroid use outweigh the disadvantages? Defend your opinion.

➤ J.   BEYOND THE CLASSROOM TO THE WEB

Visit Anabolic Steroid Abuse, published by the National Institute on Drug Abuse at **http://steroidabuse.org/**.
    According to the home page of this organization's Web site, what are at least five risks for women who take anabolic steroids?

✔ Tracking Your Progress

Selection 27

Section	Number Correct		Score
A. Thesis and Main Ideas (7 items)	_____	x 4	_____
B. Details (7 items)	_____	x 3	_____
C. Organization and Transitions (2 items)	_____	x 1	_____
E. Inferred Meanings (4 items)	_____	x 3	_____
F. Thinking Critically (6 items)	_____	x 3	_____
G. Vocabulary			
1. Context (7 items)	_____	x 1	_____
2. Word Parts (6 items)	_____	x 2	_____
	TOTAL SCORE	_____ %	

Life Sciences

The sciences investigate the physical world around us. The **life sciences** are concerned with living organisms—how they grow, develop, and function. The life sciences explore many important questions that affect our daily lives and are essential to our well-being. The study of science is fun and rewarding because you come to understand more about yourself and how you interact with other living things around you. "Honor Among Beasts" explores whether animals exhibit moral traits of fairness, cooperation, and altruism. "Bugs in Your Pillow," in addition to encouraging you to go pillow shopping, examines the unseen world of micro-organisms. "Resolving the Debate: Adult vs. Embryonic Stem Cells" discusses the current issue of the use of stem cells.

Use the following suggestions for reading in the life sciences.

TIPS FOR READING IN LIFE SCIENCES

- **Adopt a scientific mind-set.** To read successfully in the sciences, get in the habit of asking questions and seeking answers, analyzing problems, and looking for solutions or explanations. For example, when reading "Resolving the Debate: Adult vs. Embryonic Stem Cells," focus on the issues and evidence presented.

- **Learn new terminology.** To read in the sciences, you have to learn the language of science. Science is exact and precise, and scientists use specific terminology to make communication as error free as possible. In "Bugs in Your Pillow," for example, you will encounter biological terms used to name particular species of bugs.

- **Focus on cause and effect and process.** Since science is concerned with how and why things happen, cause and effect and process are most always important. In "Bugs in Your Pillow," for example, you will learn how tiny bugs inhabit your pillows.

SELECTION 28

Honor Among Beasts

Michael D. Lemonick, Dan Cray, and Wendy Grossman

This article first appeared in the July 11, 2005, issue of *Time* magazine. Read it to learn about how certain rules of behavior operate in the animal world.

> ## PREVIEWING THE READING

Using the steps listed on page 29, preview the reading selection. When you have finished, complete the following items.

1. What is the topic of this reading? _____

2. Name at least three types of animals discussed in the reading.

   _____

 ## MAKING CONNECTIONS

Songbirds. If they sing with the wrong local accent, the flock will chase them away. Is it territorial behavior or a sense of what's fair?

➤ READING TIP

As you read, look for and highlight each behavior that is mentioned. Also highlight the information or message that the animal seems to be communicating through its behavior.

Honor Among Beasts

Think Altruism, Empathy and a Sense of Fair Play Are Traits Only Humans Possess? Think Again.

1   Anyone who has owned dogs or spent much time watching them is familiar with the posture: hind end up, chest down on the ground, forelegs stretched forward, an eager expression on the face. It's obviously a friendly, playful gesture, and for most dog lovers, that's all you need to know. Ethologists—animal-behavior experts—go a step further. They call this move the "play bow" and know it's used not just by dogs but also by wolves and coyotes to signal an interest in the romping, pretend-fighting sort of games that canines of all kinds seem to love.

2   But Marc Bekoff, an ethologist at the University of Colorado, always suspected there was something more going on. True, the posture happens most often at the beginning of a bout of canine play. But it also happens in the middle, and not randomly. And the more closely Bekoff observed dog behavior, the more he began to recognize other ritualized motions and postures—some of them so fleeting that he couldn't really keep track. So he began making videotapes, then playing them back one frame at a time. "The more details I saw, the more interesting it got," he recalls.

When dogs grab each other with forepaws, it's a clear sign that nobody is mad. If they meant to inflict pain, they would use their powerful jaws.

"It wasn't just dogs playing; it was also dogs exchanging an incredible amount of information as they played."

3   In short, Bekoff was able to show—after at least a decade of painstaking observation and analysis—that canine play is actually a complex social interaction in which the participants constantly signal their intentions and check to make sure their behavior is correctly interpreted. Dogs that cheat—promising a playful bite but delivering a harsh one, for example—tend to be ostracized.

4   That understanding is nothing short of revolutionary. Only a decade or so ago, scientists were arguing vigorously over whether animals had emotions: just because a dog looks sad or a chimp appears to be embarrassed doesn't mean it really is, the skeptics said. That argument is pretty much over. The idea of animal emotion is now accepted as part of mainstream biology. And thanks to Bekoff and other researchers, ethologists are also starting to accept the once radical idea that some animals—primarily the social ones such as dogs, chimps, hyenas, monkeys, dolphins, birds, and even rats—possess not just raw emotions but also subtler and more sophisticated mental states, including envy, empathy, altruism, and a sense of fairness. "They have the ingredients we use for morality," says Frans De Waal, a professor of primate behavior at Emory University in Atlanta, referring to the monkeys and chimps he studies.

5   That doesn't mean animals necessarily have a fully developed moral or ethical sense. "I don't say dogs are fair the way you and I are fair, or have the same moral systems," says Bekoff. But it does mean that—just as with so many other attributes once considered unique to humans, including toolmaking and language—animals have at least rudimentary versions of what we call morality. That would conform to **Darwin's** ideas of evolution, and indeed, Darwin himself was convinced this must be true. "It would be bad evolutionary biology," says Bekoff, "to assume that moral behavior just pops on the scene only with us."

Darwin
a biologist who developed the theory that species evolve and change in response to the environment

6   Study after study bears him out. In one of De Waal's experiments at Atlanta's Yerkes Regional Primate Research Center, for example, pairs of **capuchin** monkeys (the species favored by organ grinders) have to cooperate in dragging a heavy tray so they can get the food on it. They quickly figure out how to do so, sharing the effort and the food. But when the food is placed on one side of the tray, giving only one monkey access to it, they still share. "There is no need for the one who gets all the food to do it," says De Waal. "He could sit in the corner and eat all by himself."

capuchin
intelligent, longtailed monkey from Central and South America

7   In another experiment, De Waal and his students reward two monkeys for a task by giving them cucumber. It's not a favorite food, but they happily go on doing the task anyway. Then the scientists begin giving one of the monkeys grapes—like caviar for a capuchin. At that point, the monkey that is still getting cucumber refuses to play. Says De Waal, "It's like me discovering my colleague, who works just as hard as I do, gets a salary that is twice the size of mine. I was perfectly happy before."

8   Both those results can be explained in part by self-interest. But De Waal has also observed behavior that can be seen only as empathetic. When a male loses a fight and sits on the floor screaming, the other chimps will comfort it. "They come over to these distressed individuals and embrace them and kiss them and groom them, and try to calm them down," De Waal says. True, there's an implied benefit for the comforters—the hope that others will do the same for them if they end up in that

situation—but that's a level of emotional abstraction that would once have been presumed impossible.

9   At TerraMar Research on Bainbridge Island, Washington, animal behaviorist Toni Frohoff has also observed dolphins behaving with what appears to be altruism—although not predictably. In one case, she recalls, she and her colleagues watched a group of dolphins assemble around a female swimmer the researchers later learned was exhausted to the point at which she was afraid for her life. "Conversely," Frohoff says, "I have been 'abandoned' [by dolphins], where all of a sudden they'd disappear and I'd see a shark."

10   Does that mean the supposed altruism of dolphins—not just in Frohoff's studies but also in anecdotal reports of the animals' rescuing sailors—is a myth? No, she says: "The mythology in some cases is true." But dolphins have adapted so long in such a different environment to humans that there's reason to suppose that their ethics might be equally different to ours.

11   Dolphins, dogs, and primates are the usual suspects when scientists talk about higher mental functions, but fairness, at least, extends even deeper into the lower animal kingdom. If you watch rats wrestle, says Steven Sivy, a biologist at Gettysburg College, you'll see that the bigger rat lets the smaller rat win every now and then so that the smaller rat will keep playing. That, he says, could be interpreted as a sense of fair play, although he emphasizes that a rat's behavior is probably Darwinian—based not on thoughtful consideration but on what has worked in the past to keep species alive. "I can't see a rat sitting around and contemplating the ethical consequences of what it's doing," he says.

12   At Bowling Green State University in Kentucky, psychologist Jaak Panskepp is similarly leery of using words like morality and ethics to describe animal behavior. He is sure that rats and other animals do experience joy, sadness, anger, and fear—

Dolphins. They have been known to both save and abandon swimmers who are drowning, baffling scientists about what ethical rules they live by.

because the wiring of the brain is set up to generate those feelings. (Actually, Panskepp discovered a few years ago that rats chirp in laughter, albeit in response to tickling, and in a register too high for the human ear to detect.)

13   Nobody has yet found the neurocircuits for ethics or morality, however, so Panskepp is reluctant to comment about those qualities. But he does accept that some animals have strict rules of behavior. "Cockroaches probably don't have a sense of justice," says Panskepp. But dogs and rats, which are social animals, clearly do.

14   So do birds, says Dan Blumstein, a former student of Bekoff's, now studying animal behavior at UCLA. While he hasn't addressed the question through formal research, Blumstein has seen hints of behavioral rules in songbirds. A given species tends to have similar songs but with local "dialects" that vary from one territory to another. If a bird sings with a nonlocal accent, he says, "everybody knows: 'Oh, my God, there's an invader.' Then they get upset and kick it out." The question, Blumstein says, is whether that's a sign of ethics or just instinct.

15   While some behaviors are obviously instinctive, Bekoff is convinced that others are not. "If you study animals in the complex social environments in which they live," he says, "it's impossible for everything they do to be hardwired, with no conscious thought. It really is." And once again, he cites play as perhaps the most obvious example. Play between dogs involves extremely complex, precise behavior, he says. "They're really close, they're mouthing, but they don't bite their own lips; they almost never bite the lip of the other animal hard, nor the eyes, nor the ears." And that requires communication and constant feedback. "Just think of basketball players faking left and going right," says Bekoff. "There's no way you could be doing that by pure instinct."

16   As for the play bow, his guess that it meant more than just "Let's play" turned out to be correct. "It says, 'I want to play with you' but also 'I'm sorry I bit you so hard' or 'I'm going to bite you hard, but don't take it seriously.'" It even works between species: Bekoff has seen wild coyotes bow to dogs—and vice versa—before they engage in something like play. "At least they don't fight," says Bekoff. "The play bow changes the whole mood."

Lucy 17
the name given to
skeletal remains of
a female hominid
found in Tanzania
in 1974 and dated
at about 3 million
years

17   Meanwhile, dishonesty is punished across all canid species. "I know coyotes best," says Bekoff. "Coyotes will signal play and then try to fight or mate with others, but if they do that enough, they can't get other animals to play." Does that behavior rise to the level of ethics or morality? If morality is simply living by the rules of a society, says hyena expert Christine Drea of Duke University, then yes, animals do that. But just because animals have rules and bad things can happen when those aren't followed, she says, "doesn't mean they're ethical creatures."

18

Einstein
Nobel
Prize–winning
scientist who
developed the
foundation for
atomic energy

18   But while animals may not possess true ethics or morality, Bekoff, De Waal, and a growing number of their colleagues think fairness and cooperation may be the forerunners of those qualities, just as the apelike brain of our distant ancestor Lucy was the forerunner of our own, much more sophisticated minds. After all, Lucy was no Einstein—but without her, the leap from the tiny brains of primitive mammals to the subtle intelligence of an Einstein could never have occurred.

—Michael Lemonick, "Honor Among Beasts," *Time,* July 11, 2005. © 2005 Time Inc.
Reprinted by permission.

> ## A.   UNDERSTANDING THE THESIS AND OTHER MAIN IDEAS

Select the best answer.

_____ 1. The central thesis of this selection is that animals
   a. have fully developed moral and ethical systems.
   b. act according to certain rules of behavior.
   c. can be taught to communicate their emotions.
   d. learn moral behavior through interactions with humans.

_____ 2. The authors' primary purpose is to
   a. argue that only humans have a sense of morality.
   b. debate the idea that animals possess emotions.
   c. compare the behavior of social animals and antisocial animals.
   d. describe animal behavior in terms of moral and ethical traits.

_____ 3. An ethologist is a person who studies
   a. ethics.
   b. social systems.
   c. animal behavior.
   d. language and communication.

_____ 4. Research by Marc Bekoff indicates that canine play is actually
   a. a complex social interaction.
   b. a form of fighting.
   c. a series of random motions and postures.
   d. an expression of emotion.

_____ 5. The main idea of paragraph 4 is that scientists
   a. disagree about whether animals have emotions.
   b. consider dogs, hyenas, and monkeys social animals.
   c. agree that some animals possess mental traits associated with morality.
   d. think studies of primate behavior are inconclusive.

_____ 6. The main idea of paragraph 5 is expressed in the
   a. first sentence.
   b. second sentence.
   c. fourth sentence.
   d. fifth sentence.

_____ 7. The topic of paragraph 11 is
   a. dolphins.
   b. dogs.
   c. primates.
   d. rats.

_____ 8. The main idea of paragraph 15 is that
   a. animal behaviors are based purely on instinct.
   b. animals live in complex social environments.
   c. certain animal behaviors are not simply instinctive.
   d. play between dogs involves communication and feedback.

B.   IDENTIFYING DETAILS

Indicate whether each statement is true (T) or false (F).

_____ 1. The play bow posture in canines occurs only at the beginning of a play session.

_____ 2. The idea that animals have emotions is now considered acceptable in mainstream biology.

_____ 3. Researchers use food to motivate monkeys to perform specific tasks.

_____ 4. Stories of dolphins rescuing sailors are myths.

_____ 5. Rats probably behave a certain way based on what has worked in the past to keep the species alive.

C.   RECOGNIZING METHODS OF ORGANIZATION AND TRANSITIONS

Complete the following statements by filling in the blanks.

1. This selection is concerned with how animals demonstrate certain rules of behavior. For each type of animal, the authors provide _____ to illustrate the concept that animals behave according to established rules.

2. One transitional phrase suggesting that the authors will illustrate their ideas with an example is _____.

3. In paragraph 7, the authors describe what happens when monkeys are rewarded unfairly. The organizational pattern in this paragraph is _____.

4. One transitional word in paragraph 13 that indicates a contrasting idea is _____.

D.   REVIEWING AND ORGANIZING IDEAS: MAPPING

The following conceptual map is a useful way to organize the ideas presented in the article. Complete the following map of the reading by filling in the blanks.

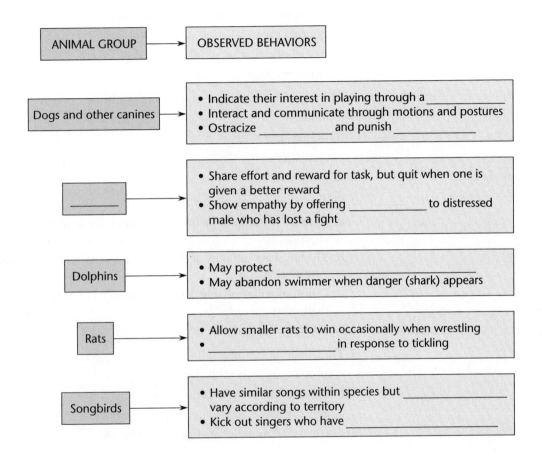

ANIMAL GROUP → OBSERVED BEHAVIORS

Dogs and other canines
- Indicate their interest in playing through a _____
- Interact and communicate through motions and postures
- Ostracize _____ and punish _____

_____
- Share effort and reward for task, but quit when one is given a better reward
- Show empathy by offering _____ to distressed male who has lost a fight

Dolphins
- May protect _____
- May abandon swimmer when danger (shark) appears

Rats
- Allow smaller rats to win occasionally when wrestling
- _____ in response to tickling

Songbirds
- Have similar songs within species but _____ vary according to territory
- Kick out singers who have _____

E.   FIGURING OUT INFERRED MEANINGS

Indicate whether each statement is true (T) or false (F).

_____ 1. Based on the article, it can be inferred that not all animal experts are convinced that animals possess higher mental functions.

_____ 2. Because dogs seem to behave according to certain rules, it is reasonable to infer that cats and other pets behave according to the same rules.

_____ 3. Some of the behaviors described in the article could be attributed to instinct rather than a sense of morals or ethics.

F.   THINKING CRITICALLY

Select the best answer.

_____ 1. The authors support their thesis by doing all of the following *except*
  a. giving examples and illustrations.
  b. quoting experts.
  c. describing their personal experiences.
  d. citing research.

_____ 2. The overall tone of the selection can best be described as
  a. amused.
  b. informative.
  c. sarcastic.
  d. pessimistic.

_____ 3. Of the following statements, the only one that is a *fact* is
  a. Animals should not be forced to participate in research experiments.
  b. The monkeys in Frans de Waal's experiment cooperated in dragging a heavy tray.
  c. Dolphins will probably develop a sense of ethics more quickly than other animals.
  d. Cockroaches may never develop a sense of justice.

_____ 4. The concluding paragraph of the article suggests that
  a. animals are truly ethical creatures.
  b. fairness and cooperation are instinctive behaviors.
  c. animals may evolve to develop true ethics and morality.
  d. ethics and morality are unique to humans.

G.   BUILDING VOCABULARY

Context
Using context and a dictionary, if necessary, determine the meaning of each word as it is used in the selection.

_____ 1. ostracized (paragraph 3)
  a. helped   c. imitated
  b. excluded   d. rewarded

_____ 2. rudimentary (paragraph 5)
  a. intelligent   c. colorful
  b. distant   d. basic

_____ 3. empathetic (paragraph 8)

    a. causing distress

    b. avoiding aggression

    c. understanding another's feelings

    d. being a mind reader

_____ 4. anecdotal (paragraph 10)

    a. based on casual observations

    b. based on scientific analysis

    c. based on false information

    d. based on medical research

_____ 5. leery (paragraph 12)

    a. angry   c. truthful

    b. mistrustful   d. successful

_____ 6. dialects (paragraph 14)

    a. changes in pitch   c. rhyming sounds

    b. formal language   d. regional variations in language

➤ Word Parts

> **A REVIEW OF PREFIXES, SUFFIXES, AND ROOTS**
> **IN-** mean *not*
> **FORE-** means *front*
> **-LOGY** means *study, thought*
> **CRED** means *believe*
> **NEURO** means *nerve*

Use your knowledge of word parts and the review above to fill in the blanks in the following sentences.

1. Something that is described as *incredible* (paragraph 2) _____

   _____; it is amazing.

2. *Mythology* (paragraph 10) is the _____ myths; it also refers to the collection of stories associated with a culture or group.

3. The *neurocircuits* (paragraph 13) of the brain refer to a system of _____.

4. Anything that precedes or comes _____ something similar is considered a *forerunner* (paragraph 18).

➤ **Unusual Words/Understanding Idioms**
Use the meanings given below to write a sentence using the boldface phrase.

1. The authors use the expression **the usual suspects** (paragraph 11) to mean the people (or animals, in this case) one would expect to be present in a certain place or doing a particular thing.

   Your sentence: _____

   _____.

2. When the authors state that "Lucy was **no Einstein**" (paragraph 18), they are comparing a distant ancestor of modern humans to a highly intelligent individual called Albert Einstein.

   Your sentence: _____

   _____.

➤ **H.   SELECTING A LEARNING/STUDY STRATEGY**

Assume you will be tested on this reading on an upcoming exam. Evaluate the usefulness of the conceptual map you completed on page 501 as a study tool. How would you use it to study?

➤ **I.   EXPLORING IDEAS THROUGH DISCUSSION AND WRITING**

1. Do you believe that animals are capable of moral or ethical behavior? Why or why not? How did this selection affect your point of view?

2. Discuss the authors' tone. Point to examples in the selection in which the authors' language reveals their attitude toward the subject.

3. Explain Marc Bekoff's statement, "It would be bad evolutionary biology to assume that moral behavior just pops on the scene only with us" (paragraph 5).

4. Discuss the title, "Honor Among Beasts." What other titles would be appropriate for this article?

➤ **J.   BEYOND THE CLASSROOM TO THE WEB**

Visit and explore the Public Broadcasting Service Web site at
http://www.pbs.org/wnet/nature/excats/cats.html. *The site describes a program on cats. Identify five facts about cats you did not know before. Click on the "Critter" button to learn more about other animals.*

✔ Tracking Your Progress

Selection 28

Section	Number Correct		Score
A. Thesis and Main Ideas (8 items)	_____	x 4	_____
B. Details (5 items)	_____	x 3	_____
C. Organization and Transitions (4 items)	_____	x 3	_____
E. Inferred Meanings (3 items)	_____	x 3	_____
F. Thinking Critically (4 items)	_____	x 3	_____
G. Vocabulary			
1. Context (6 items)	_____	x 2	_____
2. Word Parts (4 items)	_____	x 2	_____
TOTAL SCORE			_____ %

SELECTION 29

Bugs in Your Pillow
David Bodanis

This reading is taken from a book titled *The Secret Family*. The book follows a typical family for a 24 hour period, exposing real-life science behind our everyday routines and surroundings.

▶ PREVIEWING THE READING

Using the steps listed on page 29, preview the reading selection. When you have finished, complete the following items.

1. The topic of this selection is _____.

2. List three questions you expect to be able to answer after reading the article.

   a. _____

   b. _____

   c. _____

MAKING CONNECTIONS

Have you ever encountered a "bug" infestation in your home or in a place you have stayed overnight? What was your response?

▶ READING TIP

As you read, highlight startling or unusual facts about the contents of pillows.

Bugs in Your Pillow

1   There's an entire neo-dinosaur landscape of lumbering creatures deep inside the pillows, even in the cleanest of homes. We nourish our pillows with hours of moisture-rich exhaled air each night—a drenching half pint per night is typical—and that, combined with the skin oils and surface skin flakes we can't help but scrape loose, is enough to keep their population at levels immensely greater than the hair-follicle dwelling demodex we saw at breakfast. The demodex existed by the mere hundreds; here, on the pillow, the human family is cozily surrounded by a world—mercifully invisible to the naked eye—with hundreds of thousands of busy inhabitants.

2   These are *Dermatophagoides pteronyssinus*—the flesh-eating pillow mites. Unlike the cuddly rounded demodex, a microscope reveals the *Dermatophagoides* as hulking armored beasts, with eight legs and massive rhinolike necks. They're also superbly equipped for life inside the pillow—their feet even have flaring pads, like a *Star Wars* desert planet beast, to keep them from suddenly sinking in the soft filling—and despite the forbidding name and appearance, they are actually quite mild.

3   As it's difficult to see well in the dim light reaching their depths, they signal romantic availability not by crude bellowing calls, but by the polite release of a floating vapor. The targeted one swivels its huge neck to get a directional fix, and then, as gracefully and balletically as an armored monster is able, trundles shyly forward for the hopeful tryst that awaits.

4   It seems to be a near perfect life, with several generations of these bulky creatures—from gnarled grandparents to thin-walled frisky juveniles—resting, strolling, romancing, or, greatest of pleasures and definitely greatest use of time, tilting their heads up to grab the gently swirling skin flakes tumbling down. But paradise is not for our planet, and there's also one other sort of creature in the pillow: the dreaded, jaw-slobbering *Cheyletus*—a relative giant in this subvisible domain, that lives by tracking down the ordinary peaceable mites in our pillows, and eating them. Let a *Dermatophagoides* adult release a mate-luring **pheromone** cloud, and this *Cheyletus* will hurry along faster than the intended, to wait, jaws ready, there in the dark, till one of the hopeful suitors lumbers into reach. If the *Cheyletus* can't find suitably nutritious adults it'll simply pick off bite-size morsels of baby *Dermatophagoides*.

5   If this were all that happened, it wouldn't matter much that this odd world is so busily active beneath us. But the mother plumps up the pillow for her and her baby son. Any such plumping, or even any twists and turns we take on the clutched pillow at night, forces windstorm velocity air gusts into that hidden world. The air then whooshes back up, forming great arcing **parabolas** that rise a full three inches or even more above the pillowcase, loaded with thousands of the discreetly named "anal pellets" each *Cheyletus* has produced. They explode apart in our open air and then float. Since they were recently inside the digestive system of an enzyme-secreting arthropod, they're not especially healthy to have floating around, especially as they're exactly the right size to get breathed in.

6   Adults are fairly well protected by their developed immune systems, but kids, and especially babies, can suffer, as the gut enzymes slip loose from the floating pellets or land on insufficiently blinking eyes. The baby's cells that will later be powerful **histamine** producers can become oversensitized when enough pellets touch and will stay that way for years. The effect is greater than that of anything else the baby encountered in the hallway: a large **epidemiological** study in Britain, tracing several hundred Southampton families over the years, found that one of the best predictors of getting asthma as an adolescent was living in a home with large numbers of pillow mites as a baby. It's not just a problem in the bedroom, for the haze of broken pellets floats to all the rooms, settling on baby-exposed carpets everywhere in the house. Regularly allowing the dog or cat to sleep on the bed during the day provides further supplies of warmth and nutrient breath vapor when the animals rest their heads on the pillows, thus incubating even greater numbers of pillow mites. A teenager who spends hours leaning on her pillow during her life-sustaining phone

pheromone
a chemical secreted by an animal, especially an insect, that influences the behavior of other members of its species

parabolas
curves

histamine
a chemical released from cells in the immune system as part of an allergic reaction

epidemiological
related to the branch of medicine that studies the causes, distribution, and control of disease in populations

Pillow mite. Too small to see, colonies of 40,000 or more pillow mites inhabit the warmth of even the cleanest household pillows. Most are harmless scavengers, living on our scraped-loose skin, though a small number of microcarnivores—hunting these skin-eaters—rampage through their midst under our resting heads each night.

calls—her body thereby acting as a radiant heating coil for the life underneath her—will be guaranteed supremely high numbers in her room.

7   The results of these studies make people inquire about the price of **flamethrowers**. The populations are impressive, for the pillow mites have been found in virtually 100 percent of the homes studied, be it in Germany, America, or Britain. There are usually at least 10,000 mites per pillow in the most hygienic of traditional homes. If it is a house where busy professional parents only change the pillow*cases,* but somehow have forgotten to ever rinse, soak, boil, or in the faintest way wash the pillow *itself*—thereby letting the sheltered inhabitants be discreetly fruitful and multiply for weeks, months, or years on end—then the pillows they're using, and considerably providing for the rest of the family, will be home to 400,000 or more creatures. In the distressing estimate of Britain's leading pillow-mite specialist, an unwashed pillow can end up being stuffed with up to 10 percent living or deceased *Dermatophagoides* by weight over the years. Along with cleaning one's pillows, at least occasionally, it's also good to keep the windows open sometimes. Double-glazed windows and central heating encourage the warm, moist conditions the mites like, and wherever that's kept down, their numbers fall too. Arizona and the Alps work as resorts, partly because their dry air helps kill off the **asthma**-production machines of such pillows.

8   The wife hears a call from downstairs, glances at her bedside clock to confirm the late time, and quickly gets up, one soothed baby son happy in her arms. A number of the mites come along too, clinging tightly to wife and baby alike. Habitat destruction is a continual threat. In a pillow not used for five or six months, the entire population of mites will starve. A proportion of the population valiantly travels with us all the time as a safeguard against such disasters. Most die before they're ever brought to another pillow for recolonization. But a number will survive, for the species is photophobic (averse to light) and so without quite knowing why, they do try to hunker down, tiny feet working their way down from any sun or artificial light, to clamp around our clothing fibers—wool and brushed cotton do best—till they're at least partially protected.

flamethrowers
weapons that project a stream of burning liquid

asthma
a chronic respiratory disease often resulting from allergies

9   We accordingly are the vehicles that transport these city-state populations around from room to room in our homes, as well as carrying them to offices, schools, and one of the most fruitful switching stations: hotel rooms, with their nice, constantly reinvigorated, traveler-awaiting pillows. Here in this house representatives of the several different pillow colonies are being carried on the human family as they begin to assemble downstairs; adults and babies and juveniles and even some of the awful *Cheyletus* predators, though humbled now, and cowering away from the light as much as the others. All the movement is just a vague blur to the diverse *Dermatophagoides* holding on, as the humans collect money and jackets and candy bars and shopping lists; as the baby's bag is rechecked for extra diapers, and the dad tries not to be too impatient, holding the car keys, as the daughter comes down. Even she's been willing to hurry up, for the sake of what's coming next. The traveling mites are going to get a treat today.

10   This family is going to the mall.

A.   UNDERSTANDING THE THESIS AND OTHER MAIN IDEAS

Select the best answer.

_____ 1. The author's primary purpose is to
   a. entertain readers with a story about tiny mites.
   b. describe pillow mites and their effect on human health.
   c. urge readers to have their homes inspected for pests.
   d. compare two types of microscopic insects that live in most homes.

_____ 2. The topic of paragraph 2 is
   a. the *Dermatophagoides pteronyssinus* (pillow mites).
   b. the demodex.
   c. a *Star Wars* character.
   d. flesh-eaters.

_____ 3. The main idea of paragraph 4 is that *Dermatophagoides*
   a. lives harmlessly in pillows.
   b. lures mates by releasing pheromones.
   c. has a natural predator in *Cheyletus*.
   d. typically lives with several generations of other *Dermatophagoides*.

_____ 4. The main idea of paragraph 6 is expressed in the
   a. first sentence.
   b. second sentence.
   c. third sentence.
   d. last sentence.

_____ 5. The question that is answered in paragraph 7 is

    a. What do pillow mites look like?

    b. Who is most at risk from the effects of pillow mites?

    c. How do pillow mites form new colonies?

    d. What can be done about pillow mites?

_____ 6. The topic of paragraph 9 is the

    a. pillows in hotel rooms.

    b. transportation of pillow mites.

    c. photophobia of pillow mites.

    d. human family.

B.   IDENTIFYING DETAILS

Indicate whether each statement is true (T) or false (F).

_____ 1. Pillow mites exist even in households that are kept very clean.

_____ 2. Pillow mites are microscopic creatures.

_____ 3. Pillow mites attract other mites by bellowing crudely.

_____ 4. Pillow mites are called flesh-eaters because they bite humans while we are sleeping.

_____ 5. The *Cheyletus* only eats adult *Dermatophagoides*.

_____ 6. According to a British study, one of the best predictors of getting asthma as an adolescent was living in a home with large populations of pillow mites as a baby.

_____ 7. The anal pellets produced by *Cheyletus* are typically only a problem in the bedroom.

_____ 8. Pillow mites have been found in practically 100 percent of the homes studied.

_____ 9. The number of mites per pillow ranges from at least 10,000 to 400,000 or more.

C.   RECOGNIZING METHODS OF ORGANIZATION AND TRANSITIONS

Select the best answer.

_____ 1. In paragraph 2, the author describes the *Dermatophagoides pteronyssinus* using the organizational pattern known as

    a. time sequence.

    b. enumeration.

    c. cause and effect.

    d. definition.

_____ 2. In paragraphs 5–6, the author describes what happens when a pillow is plumped. The author is using the organization pattern known as

    a. cause and effect.

    b. problem and solution.

    c. definition.

    d. enumeration.

➤ D. REVIEWING AND ORGANIZING IDEAS: PARAPHRASING

Complete the following paraphrases of paragraphs 2 and 3 and paragraph 6 by filling in the missing words.

Paragraphs 2 and 3: The _____ *pteronyssinus*, or flesh-eating _____, appears under a _____ to have a protective covering, eight _____, and a thick _____. It also has _____ on its _____ that flare to prevent it from going down into the pillow's _____. Although it may seem to be dangerous, it is really harmless.

Paragraph 6: When a _____ is fluffed up, air rushes into it and forces out thousands of _____ produced by _____. The pellets break apart in the air and drift around, where they can be _____ in by humans and cause health problems.

➤ E. FIGURING OUT INFERRED MEANINGS

Indicate whether each phrase from the selection is meant to be taken literally (L) or figuratively (F). Literal statements are facts. Figurative expressions are imaginative comparisons (see Section 6g).

_____ 1. "We nourish our pillows . . ." (paragraph 1)

_____ 2. "They signal romantic availability . . ." (paragraph 3)

_____ 3. ". . . as gracefully and balletically as an armored monster is able, [it] trundles shyly forward . . ." (paragraph 3)

_____ 4. "They're exactly the right size to get breathed in." (paragraph 5)

_____ 5. "The baby's cells that will later be powerful histamine producers can become oversensitized when enough pellets touch." (paragraph 6)

_____ 6. "The traveling mites are going to get a treat today." (paragraph 9)

➤ **F.   THINKING CRITICALLY**

Select the best answer.

_____   1. The author supports the thesis of "Bugs in Your Pillow" by
   a. making comparisons.
   b. quoting authorities.
   c. including descriptions.
   d. all of the above.

_____   2. The author writes the selection in a way that appeals to the reader's sense of
   a. humor.   c. horror.
   b. imagination.   d. all of the above.

_____   3. The author uses the phrase "mercifully invisible" (paragraph 1) in order to imply that
   a. people would kill the mites without mercy if they could see them.
   b. it is fortunate that microscopes can show us what the mites look like.
   c. people would rather not be able to see these mites.
   d. the mites would be even more unhealthy if they were large enough to see.

_____   4. The phrase "But paradise is not for our planet" (paragraph 4) is the author's way of saying with
   a. sincere regret that people are not meant to be completely happy on Earth.
   b. humor that the pillow mite's life would be almost perfect if not for its predator *Cheyletus*.
   c. disgust that our planet would be perfect without insects like pillow mites.
   d. sympathy that there is no way we can completely eliminate pillow mites in our homes.

_____   5. The statement "The results of these studies make people inquire about the price of flamethrowers" (paragraph 7) means that people
   a. are referring to pest control companies as flamethrowers.
   b. believe the money spent on the pillow mite studies was wasted.
   c. are so disgusted with the results that they want to take immediate and drastic action to destroy the mites.
   d. are asking seriously for information on how to set fire to their pillows.

_____ 6. In paragraphs 7–8, one word that indicates the author's true feelings about pillow mites is

    a. impressive.

    b. distressing.

    c. fruitful.

    d. valiantly.

_____ 7. The author ends the selection (paragraphs 8–9) with an image of pillow mites as

    a. allergy-producing agents.

    b. microscopic household pests.

    c. filthy and dangerous parasites.

    d. brave and civilized members of a colony of creatures.

G. BUILDING VOCABULARY

Context

Using context and a dictionary, if necessary, determine the meaning of each word as it is used in the selection.

_____ 1. lumbering (paragraph 1)

    a. sleeping   c. snoring

    b. moving clumsily   d. reproducing

_____ 2. vapor (paragraph 3)

    a. signal   c. mist

    b. flash   d. color

_____ 3. balletically (paragraph 3)

    a. noisily   c. hopefully

    b. gracefully   d. anxiously

_____ 4. trundles (paragraph 3)

    a. moves slowly and heavily   c. avoids carefully

    b. crunches loudly and forcefully   d. changes quickly

_____ 5. tryst (paragraph 3)

    a. victory   c. meeting

    b. effort   d. reward

_____ 6. velocity (paragraph 5)

    a. speed   c. shadow

    b. dustiness   d. damage

_____ 7. incubating (paragraph 6)

    a. counting   c. destroying

    b. heating   d. introducing

_____ 8. predators (paragraph 9)

    a. victims   c. hunters

    b. pests   d. insects

➤ Word Parts

> **A REVIEW OF PREFIXES AND ROOTS**
> **ARTHRO** means *jointed*
> **MICRO-** means *tiny*
> **NEO-** means *new, recent*
> **PHOTO** means *light*
> **RE-** means *again*
> **SUB-** means *under, beneath*

Match each word in Column A with its meaning in Column B. Write your answers in the spaces provided.

Column A	Column B
_____ 1. recolonization	a. beneath our normal vision
_____ 2. arthropod	b. new kind of dinosaur
_____ 3. neodinosaur	c. creature with jointed legs
_____ 4. subvisible	d. establishment of a new colony
_____ 5. photophobic	e. given new life
_____ 6. microcarnivores	f. fearing light
_____ 7. reinvigorated	g. tiny flesh-eaters

➤ H. SELECTING A LEARNING/STUDY STRATEGY

1. You probably had little or no difficulty concentrating while reading this selection. Why?

2. The author provides a photo and a description of a pillow mite. Which was more memorable and meaningful? What does this suggest about your learning style (how you learn)?

➤ I. EXPLORING IDEAS THROUGH DISCUSSION AND WRITING

1. How does the author's tone affect how you feel about the information in the selection? Does the descriptive language affect the author's credibility, or simply make the selection more entertaining?

2. Did this information make you wonder about other "creatures" that may be living in your house? Describe your reaction to some of the statistics quoted in the selection.

➤ J. BEYOND THE CLASSROOM TO THE WEB

Visit the Excite search engine at **http://www.excite.com.**

Dust mite feces is only one of many proposed causes of asthma. Search on Excite for Web sites related to "asthma+cause" (include the quotation marks and the plus sign in your search phrase). How many proposed causes for asthma can you list from the first ten search results shown?

✔ Tracking Your Progress

Selection 29

Section	Number Correct		Score
A. Thesis and Main Ideas (6 items)	_____	x 4	_____
B. Details (9 items)	_____	x 2	_____
C. Organization and Transitions (2 items)	_____	x 2	_____
E. Inferred Meanings (6 items)	_____	x 3	_____
F. Thinking Critically (7 items)	_____	x 3	_____
G. Vocabulary			
1. Context (8 items)	_____	x 1	_____
2. Word Parts (7 items)	_____	x 1	_____
	TOTAL SCORE	_____	%

SELECTION 30

Resolving the Debate: Adult vs. Embryonic Stem Cells

Michael Bellomo

This selection is taken from a book titled *The Stem Cell Divide: The Facts, the Fiction, and the Fear Driving the Greatest Scientific, Political, and Religious Debate of Our Time,* by Michael Bellomo. Read the selection to find out more about the stem cell debate.

PREVIEWING THE READING

Using the steps listed on page 29, preview the reading selection. When you have finished, complete the following items.

1. The topic of this selection is _____ .

2. List at least three questions you expect to be able to answer after reading the selection.

   a. _____

   b. _____

   c. _____

MAKING CONNECTIONS

What do you already know about stem cells? How do you feel about stem cell research in general?

READING TIP

As you read, highlight sections that describe the benefits and limitations of each of the two types of stem cells.

Resolving the Debate: Adult vs. Embryonic Stem Cells

1   At the most basic level, the promise that stem cells hold is also the source of the controversy over them. The idea that replacement parts for our bodies might one day be as easy to create as ordering prescription medication from the local drugstore is breathtaking. But if these same cells can only work their magic through the

regenerative medicine
the process of creating living, functional tissues to repair or replace damaged tissues and organs in the body

blastocyst
a stage of early embryonic development before cells have formed into specific types

stem cell line
a family of cells formed from a single parent group of stem cells and grown in laboratory cultures

venture capital
money invested or available for investment in new enterprises

pluripotent
capable of changing from a single cell into one of the many cell types that make up the body

immune reaction
a bodily defense reaction that recognizes an invading substance, such as a virus or transplanted tissue, and produces antibodies against it

2   destruction of human embryos, then cure and curse will be one and the same to many people. To those who see a human being's life as starting from the moment of fertilization, regenerative medicine via stem cells is nothing more than *high-tech cannibalism.*

There is an alternative, imperfect though it may be. In recent years, scientists have discovered that similar kinds of cells can be found outside the holy sphere of the human embryo's blastocyst. These "adult" stem cells can be found in the blood, the pockets of our bone marrow, the umbilical cord, under the dermis of the skin, and, just perhaps, buried deep in the brain.

ASC Pros and Cons

3   Adult stem cells (ASCs) are the technology of choice among those who morally object to the use of embryonic stem cells. At a May 2005 White House press conference, President Bush reaffirmed his opposition to funding embryonic stem cell research outside of the existing stem cell lines, but praised the use of "alternative sources" of stem cells. The ones mentioned in the above paragraph, such as stem cells from bone marrow and umbilical cord blood, are classic examples of ASCs.

4   "With the right policies and the right techniques," Bush asserted, "we can pursue scientific progress while still fulfilling our moral duties." But is this indeed the case, or is it wishful thinking? As with many complex subjects, there is no clear-out answer.

5   The degree to which adult stem cells can be put to use often depends on who is being interviewed. However, if one sticks as closely as possible to what has been reliably reproduced in multiple laboratories over time, some hard facts do become available. That is, at least as "hard" as the facts can be, before the technology advances yet further and changes reality yet again.

6   A fair number of therapies involving adult stem cells are in human clinical trials at present, and the number continues to grow. It is likely that these therapies will make their appearance at the local hospital or health clinic long before embryonic stem cells can even begin to make it to human trials. At the third annual meeting of the International Society for Stem Cell Research, held in 2005, the clear majority of the presentations dealt with therapies related to adult stem cells. Clearly, the interest— and, not coincidentally, the private sector venture capital—lies in ASCs for now.

7   Adult stem cells have something of a trade-off in their makeup. They simply do not have the pluripotent ability to morph into any kinds of cell. However, this one-track orientation allows them to be admirably well-suited building blocks for a limited number of therapies. For example, blood-specific illnesses such as leukemia stand to benefit from the use of adult stem cells collected from bone marrow.[1]

8   A major limitation of adult stem cells that their boosters fail to mention is that being a full-grown cell, the biological markers of an individual have matured. This means that an adult stem cell is more likely to cause a dangerous immune reaction if transplanted into another person. To avoid this, adult stem cell transplants could only be carried out using a patient's own cells.

---

[1] These particular kinds of adult stem cells are also known as *hematopoietic* stem cells.

FIGURE A   THE PROCESS FOR CULTURING ADULT STEM CELLS

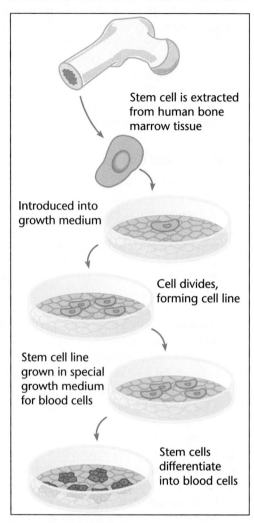

Stem cell is extracted from human bone marrow tissue

Introduced into growth medium

Cell divides, forming cell line

Stem cell line grown in special growth medium for blood cells

Stem cells differentiate into blood cells

9   Some researchers claim that adult stem cells do, in fact, have the ability to produce different kinds of cells. The trick, so the argument goes, is to get them to regress to the point that they become pluripotent, or developmentally plastic once again.

10   A few researchers, such as Dr. Catherine Verfaillie, the director of the University of Minnesota's Stem Cell Institute, have been able to persuade bone marrow stem cells to produce other types of organ tissue. However, until these results are replicated in many other labs, it is difficult to evaluate whether this can be done in a systematic way.

11   David Traver, a stem cell researcher at the University of California at San Diego, admits that there are no hard answers yet. "The more conservative thing to say is that each human organ probably has a specific stem cell system behind it, and there probably isn't a lot of 'cross-talk' between them," says Traver.

12   Traver reiterates that more research has to be done, and that the field is not as advanced as many outside the scientific community would think. "The bottom line," he says, "is that we haven't learned much from studying human stem cells. Most of what we know comes from studying mice, fish, and flies."

13   Adult stem cells are also harder to study in some ways. Because they do not renew themselves indefinitely in the lab, as embryonic stem cells [ESCs] do, they must constantly be replenished if they are to be studied.

14   On the other hand, embryonic stem cells come with their own price tag in sweat and hard work. In order to keep them renewing themselves indefinitely, constant feeding and attention must be performed, or the relatively fragile embryonic stem cells will either die off or twist themselves into a grotesque **teratomatic** growth in the **petri dish.**

teratomatic
a tumor consisting of different types of tissue

15   While scientists, admittedly, are still groping for ways to reliably "reprogram" the blank slate of the embryonic stem cell, the possibilities just seem too great to ignore. And embryonic stem cells, since they come from a point where the organism has yet to mature, simply provide much more insight into the complexities of stem cell function and development.

petri dish
a shallow dish used in laboratories to grow cultures of bacteria or other microorganisms

16   Ironically, years of research spent on embryonic stem cells are very likely to teach scientists how to best reprogram an *adult* stem cell to make tissues as easily as an embryonic stem cell can. Put another way, embryonic stem cells may very well be needed . . . so that they will never be needed again.

17   In the meantime, it's worth moving beyond the sound bites of the researchers to review what both ASCs and ESCs are being used for at this time. Given how fast the field moves, the list is less a definitive catalog of therapies than a snapshot in time. In five years or less, the balance of treatments and knowledge between the two may have shifted, and the total number of treatments available will have expanded beyond belief.

➤ A.   UNDERSTANDING THE THESIS AND OTHER MAIN IDEAS

Select the best answer.

_____   1. The central thesis of this selection is that
   a. stem cell research is controversial for many reasons.
   b. adult stem cells (ASCs) have too many limitations to be useful.
   c. embryonic stem cells (ESCs) are becoming more widely accepted.
   d. ASCs offer an imperfect alternative to ESCs.

_____   2. The author's primary purpose is to
   a. argue that stem cell research should receive federal funding.
   b. compare traditional medical treatments with stem cell therapies.
   c. describe the pros and cons of ASCs and ESCs.
   d. present the most current medical applications for stem cells.

_____ 3. The topic of paragraph 3 is
   a. President Bush.
   b. ASCs.
   c. ESCs.
   d. funding for stem cell research.

_____ 4. The topic of paragraph 7 is expressed in the
   a. first sentence.
   b. second sentence.
   c. third sentence.
   d. last sentence.

_____ 5. According to the selection, a major limitation of ASCs is that they
   a. can be obtained only by destroying human embryos.
   b. produce too many different kinds of cells.
   c. are buried deep in the human brain.
   d. may cause a dangerous reaction if transplanted into another person.

B.   IDENTIFYING DETAILS

Next to each of the following phrases, indicate whether it describes adult stem cells (ASCs) or embryonic stem cells (ESCs).

_____ 1. The type of stem cells found in the bone marrow and the umbilical cord

_____ 2. The type of stem cells used in therapies that are currently in human clinical trials

_____ 3. The only type of stem cells that are capable of changing into different kinds of cells

_____ 4. The type of stem cells that renew themselves indefinitely in the lab

_____ 5. The type of stem cells that have a "one-track" orientation useful for specific therapies

C.   RECOGNIZING METHODS OF ORGANIZATION AND TRANSITIONS

Select the best answer.

_____ 1. In paragraph 7, the transitional word or phrase that indicates that the author will introduce a contrasting idea is
   a. any kinds.   c. for example.
   b. however.   d. such as.

_____ 2. In paragraph 8, the author describes a major limitation of ASCs using the organizational pattern called

    a. statement and clarification.

    b. comparison and contrast.

    c. classification.

    d. order of importance.

_____ 3. In paragraph 13, the author describes the difficulty of working with ASCs using the organizational pattern called

    a. classification.

    b. cause and effect.

    c. definition.

    d. spatial order.

_____ 4. In paragraph 14, the transitional word or phrase that indicates that a contrast is to follow is

    a. on the other hand.

    b. in order to.

    c. indefinitely.

    d. must be performed.

▶ D. REVIEWING AND ORGANIZING IDEAS: OUTLINING

Complete the following outline based on paragraphs 3–8 and 13.

Advantages and Disadvantages of ASCs

I.   Advantages of ASCs

    A. Morally acceptable alternative to _____

       1. Do not require destruction of _____

    B. Therapies already being tested in _____

    C. Focus of current research and private funding

    D. _____ orientation well suited for specific therapies

II.   Disadvantages of ASCs

    A. Unable to _____

    B. Biological markers have matured

1. Transplants may cause _____

    in others

2. Transplants limited to patient's own cells

C. Hard to study in the lab

1. Do not _____ indefinitely

2. Must constantly be replenished

E. FIGURING OUT INFERRED MEANINGS

Indicate whether each statement is true (T) or false (F).

_____ 1. Many people reject the idea of using stem cells from embryos because of moral or religious beliefs.

_____ 2. President Bush is opposed to all forms of stem cell research.

_____ 3. Researchers disagree about how successfully ASCs can be put to use.

_____ 4. Therapies based on ASCs will probably be available much sooner than those based on ESCs.

_____ 5. Most private funding for stem cell research is directed toward ASCs because of their unlimited potential.

_____ 6. Within the scientific community, most of the knowledge about stem cells has come primarily from studying human cells.

_____ 7. The field of stem cell research is rapidly changing.

F. THINKING CRITICALLY

Select the best answer.

_____ 1. The central thesis of this selection is supported by
    a. facts.
    b. examples.
    c. expert opinions.
    d. all of the above.

_____ 2. The primary question answered by Figure A is:
    a. How do adult stem cells differ from embryonic cells?
    b. How are stem cells extracted from bone marrow tissue?
    c. What is the process for culturing adult stem cells?
    d. At what point do stem cells differentiate into blood cells?

_____ 3. In paragraph 1, the author uses the phrase *high-tech cannibalism* in order to

    a. create a sense of fear and dread about the subject of stem cell research.

    b. indicate that his own attitude toward stem cell research is critical and disapproving.

    c. illustrate the viewpoint of many people that using embryonic cells in medicine is immoral and wrong.

    d. introduce a sense of humor and sarcasm into the discussion of stem cell research.

Indicate whether each of the following quotes from the selection is fact (F) or opinion (O).

_____ 4. "The idea that replacement parts for our bodies might one day be as easy to create as ordering prescription medication from the local drugstore is breathtaking." (paragraph 1)

_____ 5. "At the third annual meeting of the International Society for Stem Cell Research . . . the clear majority of the presentations dealt with therapies related to adult stem cells." (paragraph 6)

_____ 6. "A few researchers . . . have been able to persuade bone marrow stem cells to produce other types of organ tissue." (paragraph 10)

_____ 7. "While scientists . . . are still groping for ways to reliably 'reprogram' the blank slate of the embryonic stem cell, the possibilities just seem too great to ignore." (paragraph 15)

➤ G. BUILDING VOCABULARY

➤ Context

Using context and a dictionary, if necessary, determine the meaning of each word as it is used in the selection.

_____ 1. asserted (paragraph 4)

    a. questioned   c. disagreed

    b. claimed   d. removed

_____ 2. sector (paragraph 6)

    a. area   c. report

    b. number   d. technique

_____ 3. morph (paragraph 7)

    a. disappear   c. control

    b. harm   d. change

_____ 4. boosters (paragraph 8)

     a. critics   c. researchers

     b. supporters   d. markers

_____ 5. replicated (paragraph 10)

     a. prohibited   c. repeated

     b. abandoned   d. stolen

_____ 6. grotesque (paragraph 14)

     a. useful   c. limited

     b. simple   d. bizarre

_____ 7. groping (paragraph 15)

     a. feeling   c. starting

     b. searching   d. confusing

➤ Word Parts

A REVIEW OF PREFIXES AND SUFFIXES

IM- means *not*

RE- means *back, again*

-IVE means *a state, condition, or quality*

Use your knowledge of word parts and the review above to fill in the blanks in the following sentences.

1. An alternative that is *imperfect* (paragraph 2) is one that has flaws or is somehow _____ perfect.

2. If a person has affirmed something, he or she has expressed commitment to it; when it is *reaffirmed* (paragraph 3), that commitment is expressed _____.

3. To make progress is to move forward, so to *regress* (paragraph 9) is to move _____.

4. When a person *reiterates* a statement (paragraph 12), he or she repeats it or says it _____.

5. Stem cells that do not renew themselves must be *replenished* (paragraph 13); in other words, the supply of cells must be filled up _____ or added to.

6. Something that is definite is known for certain, so a *definitive* list (paragraph 17) is one that has the _____ of being complete or certain. ·

▶ **Unusual Words/Understanding Idioms**
Use the meanings given below to write a sentence using the boldface word or phrase.

1. The term **bottom line** (paragraph 12) refers to the last line of a financial statement, which shows net profit or loss. It is often used to indicate the main point or most important aspect of a topic of debate.

   Your sentence: _____

   _____

2. To describe stem cells as coming **with their own price tag** (paragraph 14) is to say that they have a cost associated with them. In the case of embryonic stem cells, the cost is the effort—"sweat and hard work"—required to study them.

   Your sentence: _____

   _____

3. The term **sound bites** (paragraph 17) refers to brief comments or statements taken from longer speeches or interviews; sound bites may be interesting excerpts, but they may also leave out important information.

   Your sentence: _____

   _____

▶ **H.   SELECTING A LEARNING/STUDY STRATEGY**

Suppose you were preparing for a class discussion on the pros and cons of different types of stem cell research. How would you use this selection to prepare for the discussion?

▶ **I.   EXPLORING IDEAS THROUGH DISCUSSION AND WRITING**

1. Discuss the title of the book from which this selection was taken *(The Stem Cell Divide: The Facts, the Fiction, and the Fear Driving the Greatest Scientific, Political, and Religious Debate of Our Time)*. Do you agree that stem cell research is the greatest debate of our time? Discuss each aspect of the debate cited in the title: scientific, political, and religious.

2. Evaluate the introduction. What captured your interest in the opening paragraphs?

3. What do you think the author meant by the phrase "holy sphere" in paragraph 2? Discuss his meaning and purpose in using that term.

4. The author is careful to present information about the advantages and disadvantages of both types of stem cells, but which type do you think he believes is preferable? Explain your answer with support from the selection.

5. Discuss some of the predictions the author makes in this selection. Together with a classmate, come up with your own list of predictions, either about medical treatments or another aspect of life such as transportation, housing, work, and so on.

J. BEYOND THE CLASSROOM TO THE WEB

Read "Key Moments in the Stem Cell Debate" at http://www.npr.org/templates/ story/story.php?storyId=5252449.

Using this site and the reading for inspiration, write a list of words that reflects your feelings about the stem cell debate. Use these words to create a short persuasive speech for your side of the argument.

✔ Tracking Your Progress

Selection 30

Section	Number Correct	Score
A. Thesis and Main Ideas (5 items)	———— x 4	————
B. Details (5 items)	———— x 3	————
C. Organization and Transitions (4 items)	———— x 1	————
E. Inferred Meanings (7 items)	———— x 3	————
F. Thinking Critically (7 items)	———— x 3	————
G. Vocabulary		
1. Context (7 items)	———— x 1	————
2. Word Parts (6 items)	———— x 2	————
TOTAL SCORE		————%

20 Physical Sciences/Mathematics

The **physical sciences** are concerned with the properties, functions, structure, and composition of matter, substances, and energy. They include physics, chemistry, astronomy, physical geography, and geology. **Mathematics** is the study of relationships among numbers, quantities, and shapes using signs, symbols, and proofs (logical solutions of problems). Often mathematics and physical science work together to address interesting questions important to our life and well-being. "Are Lotteries Fair?" uses mathematics to examine a popular American pastime—playing the lottery. The reading "Is There Life Elsewhere?" addresses the issue of the possibility of extraterrestrial life. "Air Pollution May Result in Global Warming" explains how the greenhouse effect is contributing to a rise in global temperatures.

Use the following suggestions for reading in the physical sciences.

TIPS FOR READING IN PHYSICAL SCIENCES/ MATHEMATICS

- **Read slowly and reread if necessary.** Both mathematics and the physical sciences are technical and detailed. Do not expect to understand everything on your first reading. When reading "Are Lotteries Fair?" you might read it once to grasp the overall issue—fairness of lotteries—and then reread, concentrating on the role mathematics plays in examining the issue.

- **Focus on new terminology.** To read mathematics and the physical sciences, you have to learn the language of science. Mathematics and physical science are exact and precise, using terminology to make communication as error free as possible. In "Air Pollution May Result in Global Warming," you will encounter technical terms describing the greenhouse effect, carbon dioxide emission, and weather patterns, for example.

- **Use writing to learn.** Reading alone is often not sufficient for learning mathematics and physical sciences. While highlighting and annotating a text work well for many subjects, they do not for math and science textbooks where everything seems important. Try writing; express ideas in your own words. This method will test your understanding, too. If you cannot explain an idea in your own words, you probably do not understand it. After reading "Is There Life Elsewhere?" try to explain in your own words why life on other planets seems likely.

One of the most challenging things to read in mathematics textbooks is word problems. This task requires both reading skills and knowledge of mathematics, as well as reasoning skills. To read and solve word problems more effectively, use the following steps.

TIPS FOR READING WORD PROBLEMS

- **Identify what is being asked for.** You may need to read the problem several times in order to do so. Often the information asked for occurs at the end of the problem.

- **Locate the useful information contained in the problem.** Underline useful information. Many problems also contain irrelevant information that will not help you solve the problem; cross out this information. Also note what information you do not have.

- **Visualize the problem.** Draw a picture or diagram that will make the problem real and practical. Label its parts, and include measurements and any other relevant information.

- **Estimate your answer.** Decide what would and would not be a reasonable answer.

- **Decide how to solve the problem.** Recall formulas you have learned that are related to the problem. You may have to translate ordinary words into mathematical language. For example, the phrase "percent of" usually suggests multiplication; the word "decreased by" means subtraction. Look for clue words that suggest a particular process. For example, the phrase "how fast" means *rate;* you may be able to use the formula $r = d/t$ to solve the problem.

- **Solve the problem.** Set up an equation and choose variables to represent unknown quantities.

- **Verify your answer.** Compare your answer with your estimate. If there is a large discrepancy, it is a signal that you have made an error. Be sure to check your arithmetic.

SELECTION

31

Are Lotteries Fair?

Jeffrey O. Bennett, William L. Briggs,
and Mario F. Triola

Taken from the college mathematics textbook, *Statistical Reasoning for Everyday Life,* this reading looks at lotteries from a statistical perspective.

PREVIEWING THE READING

Using the steps listed on page 29, preview the reading selection. When you have finished, complete the following items.

1. The title of this selection suggests that the author will be discussing

   _____.

2. List at least three questions that you should be able to answer after reading the selection:

   a. _____

   b. _____

   c. _____

MAKING CONNECTIONS

Have you ever played the lottery or some type of game of chance? If so, did you feel you had a good chance of winning? If not, why not? If you did not win, how did you react?

READING TIP

Be sure to refer to the charts mentioned in the reading; they will help you grasp the concepts presented in the reading.

Are Lotteries Fair?

1   Lotteries have become part of the American way of life. Most states now have legal lotteries, including multi-state lotteries such as Powerball and the Big Game. National statistics show that per capita (average per person) lottery spending is

approaching $200 per year. Since many people do not play lotteries at all, this means that active players tend to spend much more than $200 per year.

2   The mathematics of lottery odds involves counting the various combinations of numbers that are winners. While these calculations can become complex, the essential conclusion is always the same: The probability of winning a big prize is infinitesimally small. Advertisements may make lotteries sound like a good deal, but the expected value associated with a lottery is always negative. On average, those who play regularly can expect to lose about half of what they spend.

3   Lottery proponents point to several positive aspects. For example, lotteries produce billions of dollars of revenue that states use for education, recreation, and environmental initiatives. This revenue allows states to keep tax rates lower than they would be otherwise. Proponents also point out that lottery participation is voluntary and enjoyed by a **representative cross-section** of society. Indeed, a recent Gallup poll shows that three-fourths of Americans approve of state lotteries (two-thirds approve of legal gambling in general).

4   This favorable picture is part of the marketing and public relations of state lotteries. For example, Colorado state lottery officials offer statistics on the age, income, and education of lottery players compared to the general population (Figure A). Within a few percentage points, the age of lottery players parallels that of the population as a whole. Similarly, the **histogram** of the income of lottery players gives the impression that lottery players as a whole are typical citizens—with the exception of the bars for incomes of $15,000-$25,000 and $25,000-$35,000, which show that the poor tend to play more than we would expect for their proportion of the population.

5   Despite the apparent benefits of lotteries, critics have long argued that lotteries are merely an unfair form of taxation. Some support for this view comes from a recent report by the National Gambling Impact Study Commission and a *New York*

representative cross-section
a particular part that displays the characteristics of and typifies the whole

histogram
a bar graph used for large sets of data to show relationships and frequencies

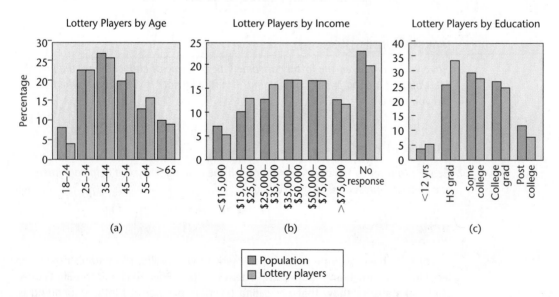

Figure A   Three figures showing (a) age, (b) income, and (c) education of Colorado lottery players compared to population.

Times study of lotteries in New Jersey. Both of these studies focus on the *amount* of money spent on lotteries by individuals.

6   The *New York Times* study was based on data from 48,875 people who had won at least $600 in New Jersey lottery games. (In an ingenious bit of sampling, these winners were to be a random sample of all lottery players; after all, lottery winners are determined randomly. However, the sample is not really representative of all lottery players because winners tend to buy more than an average number of tickets.) By identifying the home zip codes of the lottery players, researchers were able to determine whether players came from areas with high or low income, high or low average education, and various demographic characteristics. The overwhelming conclusion of the *New York Times* study is that lottery spending has a much greater impact in *relative terms* on those players with lower incomes and lower educational background. For example, the following were among the specific findings:

* People in the state's lowest income areas spend five times as much of their income on lotteries as those in the state's highest income areas. Spending in the lowest income areas on one particular lottery game was $29 per $10,000 of annual income, compared to less than $5 per $10,000 of annual income in the highest income areas.
* The number of lottery sales outlets (where lottery tickets can be purchased) is nearly twice as high per 10,000 people in low-income areas as in high-income areas.
* People in areas with the lowest percentage of college education spent over five times as much per $10,000 of annual income as those in areas with the highest percentage of college education.
* Advertising and promotion of lotteries is focused in low-income areas.

7   Some of the results of the *New York Times* study summarized in Figure B suggests that while New Jersey has a progressive tax system (higher-income people pay a

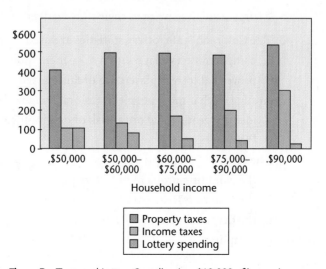

Figure B   Taxes and Lottery Spending (per $10,000 of income)

regressive
describing a tax
in which the tax
rate goes down
as the amount
of income being
taxed increases

8

greater percentage of their income in taxes), the "lottery tax" is **regressive**. Moreover, the study also found that the areas that generate the largest percentage of lottery revenues do not receive a proportional share of state funding.

Similar studies reveal the same patterns in other states. The overall conclusions are inescapable: While lotteries provide many benefits to state governments, the revenue they produce comes disproportionately from poorer and less educated individuals. Indeed, a report by the National Gambling Impact Study Commission concluded that lotteries are "the most widespread form of gambling in the United States" and that state governments have "irresponsibly intruded gambling into society on a massive scale . . . through such measures as incessant advertising and the ubiquitous placement of lottery machines in neighborhood stores."

▶ A. UNDERSTANDING THE THESIS AND OTHER MAIN IDEAS

Select the best answer.

_____ 1. The central thesis of "Are Lotteries Fair"? is that

  a. the chances of winning the lottery are very slim.

  b. it is poor, undereducated people who play the lottery but do not receive its benefits.

  c. lotteries are an acceptable form of gambling.

  d. advertising for lotteries is too aggressive.

_____ 2. The authors' primary purpose is to

  a. stop people from playing the lottery.

  b. criticize the government's promotion of the lottery.

  c. report on research that finds lotteries to be unfair.

  d. urge readers to write to their state leaders about this issue.

_____ 3. The Colorado state lottery statistics are used in the reading to

  a. compare lottery players with the general public.

  b. prove that lottery players are unfairly taxed.

  c. suggest that most people in Colorado are well educated.

  d. identify groups that are at risk of developing gambling problems.

_____ 4. The topic of paragraph 6 is

  a. the gambling problem of lottery players.

  b. the *New York Times* study.

  c. the tax structure in New Jersey.

  d. sampling.

_____ 5. In the final paragraph, the authors

   a. refer to other studies and reports.

   b. restate the first paragraph.

   c. recommend ways to make the lottery more fair.

   d. suggest a plan for abolishing the lottery.

B.   IDENTIFYING DETAILS

Match each statement with the study to which it refers.

a. Colorado state lottery statistics

b. The *New York Times* study

c. The National Gambling Impact Study Commission Report

_____ 1. stated that lotteries are "the most widespread form of gambling in the United States."

_____ 2. indicates that "the age of lottery players parallels that of the population as a whole."

_____ 3. suggests that lottery advertising is never-ending.

_____ 4. determined that lottery revenues do not go to the areas that need them most.

_____ 5. compared lottery players with the general population.

_____ 6. looked at demographic factors of lottery winners.

_____ 7. found that lottery advertising is aimed at poor people.

C.   RECOGNIZING METHODS OF ORGANIZATION AND TRANSITIONS

1. The authors make use of the generalization and example organizational pattern to make statements and then give specific instances of the idea expressed in the statement. Place an "X" next to the number of each paragraph that illustrates this pattern.

   _____ 1   _____ 5

   _____ 2   _____ 6

   _____ 3   _____ 7

   _____ 4   _____ 8

2. The authors also use _____to describe factors that lead to lottery playing and show what happens as a result of playing the lottery.

D. REVIEWING AND ORGANIZING IDEAS: PARAPHRASING

Complete the following paraphrase of paragraphs 1 and 2 from the selection by filling in the blanks.

_____ are very _____ in our _____. There are legal state lotteries and multistate lotteries such as _____ and _____. Regular _____ spend well over $200 per _____. The odds of winning are computed by _____ how many combinations of numbers are possible to produce a winner. The odds of _____ a large payout are extremely slim. People still play, though, partially due to _____ that _____ the lottery as a good _____. These regular players end up losing _____ of what they _____.

E. FIGURING OUT INFERRED MEANINGS

Indicate whether each statement is true (T) or false (F).

_____ 1. Rich people do not play the lottery.

_____ 2. In Colorado, no one under 18 plays the lottery.

_____ 3. It can be inferred that the property tax rate in New Jersey is high.

_____ 4. The reading suggests that state governments are not forthcoming in their ads about the real chances of winning the lottery.

_____ 5. Going to college will teach you not to buy lottery tickets.

F. THINKING CRITICALLY

Select the best answer.

_____ 1. The authors of "Are Lotteries Fair?" support the thesis primarily with

    a. research evidence.

    b. personal experience.

    c. historical information.

    d. expert opinion.

_____ 2. The tone of the selection can best be described as

    a. apathetic.

    b. frustrated.

    c. serious.

    d. indirect.

_____ 3. Of the following statements from the reading, which is an opinion?

    a. "The mathematics of lottery odds involves counting the various combinations of numbers that are winners." (paragraph 2)

    b. "Advertising and promotion of lotteries is focused in low-income areas." (paragraph 6)

    c. "Similar studies reveal the same patterns in other states." (paragraph 8)

    d. "State governments have 'irresponsibly intruded gambling into our society on a massive scale.'" (paragraph 8)

_____ 4. The authors

    a. present strong data as evidence that lotteries are unfair.

    b. do not offer any information from the proponents of lotteries.

    c. are biased against state government.

    d. twist the findings of the studies to fit their opinion.

_____ 5. The final quotations from the National Gambling Impact Study Commission are intended to

    a. shock the reader.

    b. reinforce the central thesis with a powerful conclusion.

    c. provide more statistical data.

    d. contradict the main argument of the reading.

➤ G. BUILDING VOCABULARY

➤ Context

Using context and a dictionary, if necessary, determine the meaning of each word as it is used in the selection.

_____ 1. infinitesimally (paragraph 2)

    a. definitely

    b. a tiny amount

    c. very unlikely

    d. amazingly

_____ 2. ingenious (paragraph 6)

    a. clever

    b. mean-spirited

    c. dishonest

    d. suitable

_____   3. disproportionately (paragraph 8)

    a. unresponsively

    b. conveniently

    c. logically

    d. unequally

_____   4. ubiquitous (paragraph 8)

    a. careful

    b. underhanded

    c. skillful

    d. widespread

➤ Word Parts

> ### A REVIEW OF ROOTS AND PREFIXES
> **POS, PON** means *place, put*
> **PRO-** means *forth, in front of*
> **IN-** means *not*

Use your knowledge of word parts and the review above to fill in the blanks in the following sentences.

1. If you are a *proponent* (paragraph 3) of a new subway system in your city, you _____ yourself _____ in favor of the cause.

2. The *incessant* (paragraph 8) barking of your neighbor's dog does _____ ever stop!

➤ Unusual Words/Understanding Idioms
Use the meanings given below to write a sentence using the boldface word or phrase.

1. An **essential** (paragraph 2) text in a field of study is one that is fundamental to the basic understanding of that field.

   Your sentence: _____

   _____.

2. When something is **intruded** (paragraph 8) it is put where it does not belong or where it would be wrong or rude for it to be.

   Your sentence: _____

   _____.

H.   SELECTING A LEARNING/STUDY STRATEGY

Select the best answer.

_____   This reading appears in a college mathematics textbook in a chapter on probability. As a class activity you can most likely expect your mathematics professor to ask you to

a. read the National Impact Study Commission report.

b. buy a lottery ticket and report on your process of choosing numbers.

c. solve a word problem that asks you to calculate the odds of wining a certain lottery.

d. research systems lottery players use to attempt to enhance their winnings.

I.   EXPLORING IDEAS THROUGH DISCUSSION AND WRITING

1. Some billboards that advertise the lottery show outrageous items that a person could buy with his or her winnings. Design a billboard that shows alternative uses for the money.

2. Write a list of other types of "gambling" that we engage in (for example, church bingo).

3. Discuss what factors motivate people to gamble, despite the poor odds of winning.

J.   BEYOND THE CLASSROOM TO THE WEB

Visit the home page of the New York State Lottery at **http://www.nylottery.org/index.php.**

How easy is it to find information on where the money raised by the lottery goes? Is there any information about the dangers of gambling? What information is missing from this site?

✔ Tracking Your Progress

Selection 31

Section	Number Correct		Score
A. Thesis and Main Ideas (5 items)	_____	x 5	_____
B. Details (7 items)	_____	x 3	_____
C. Organization and Transitions (2 items)	_____	x 2	_____
E. Inferred Meanings (5 items)	_____	x 4	_____
F. Thinking Critically (5 items)	_____	x 4	_____
G. Vocabulary			
1. Context (4 items)	_____	x 2	_____
2. Word Parts (2 items)	_____	x 1	_____
	TOTAL SCORE	_____%	

SELECTION 32

Is There Life Elsewhere?

Jeffrey Bennett, Seth Shostak, and Bruce Jakosky

Originally appearing in the textbook *Life in the Universe,* this reading addresses the idea of finding life beyond Earth.

PREVIEWING THE READING

Using the steps listed on page 29, preview the reading selection. When you have finished, complete the following items.

1. This selection is about _____.

2. List at least three questions you should be able to answer after reading this selection:

   a. _____

   b. _____

   c. _____

MAKING CONNECTIONS

Do you think that we should search for life on other planets? Why or why not?

READING TIP

As you read, keep track of the names of planets, moons, and spacecraft that are mentioned.

Is There Life Elsewhere?

1   We know of only one example of life existing in the universe—life here on Earth. No matter how reasonable and plausible the idea that life exists elsewhere might seem, we still don't know for sure that it does. Because of this uncertainty, all we can do today is discuss the issues that could determine whether extraterrestrial life is likely or unlikely to exist and how we might search for evidence of it.

2   Despite these limitations, we are at a unique point in the long history of the debate over the possibility of extraterrestrial life. We have the technological capability to explore Mars and much of the rest of our solar system, and we are rapidly developing technology that might allow us to find evidence about whether life exists on

planets around other stars. After millennia of speculation about life beyond Earth, we have the potential to discover life on another planet within perhaps the next one or two decades. This remarkable prospect calls us to discuss the philosophical and cultural consequences of finding life elsewhere. But first let's summarize the key issues in our discussion about the prospects of finding life and the search for life in the universe.

Why Life Seems Likely

3   Why do we think life might exist elsewhere? Although we don't know for sure whether it does, current science offers reasons for optimism. We can examine the nature of life on Earth—its building blocks and how it originated—and understand the environmental conditions in which life can exist. We can look at the other planets and satellites in our solar system and determine whether the conditions **conducive** to life exist there. And we can look for planets around other stars, learn how abundant they are and how they form, and determine whether some of them might be Earth-like planets (that is, rocky planets in the inner regions of their solar systems that might have liquid water at the surface) that could be capable of supporting life.

4   When we do these things, we find three key pieces of evidence that point to the idea that life should be common in the universe. We'll list them and then discuss each briefly in turn:

1. The chemical elements that comprise life are common throughout the universe, and complex, carbon-bearing molecules important to life on Earth appear to form easily and naturally under conditions that should be common on many planets.
2. Life on Earth thrives under a wide range of environmental conditions that we once considered too extreme to be capable of supporting life, and many of these types of environments are likely to be found on other planets in our own solar system and beyond.
3. It seems that life appeared on Earth quite quickly once the conditions became conducive to supporting life (that is, after the end of the heavy bombardment), implying that the origin of life took place rapidly and making it seem **plausible** that life would arise quickly elsewhere when the right conditions exist.

Prospects for Finding Life in Our Solar System

5   At least two worlds in our solar system—Mars and **Europa**—seem to be good candidates for having life today or for having had it at some time in the past, and several other worlds seem to be possible candidates for life. As a result, NASA and other space agencies have embarked on a program to try to determine whether life might actually exist elsewhere in our solar system. Spacecraft are being developed for missions to Mars, with launches planned approximately every two years (at the times when Earth and Mars line up to make the trip relatively easy). Numerous other spacecraft are exploring or are being developed to explore other worlds, including the Cassini spacecraft currently en route to Saturn and **Titan**. Such missions will help

---

Marginal glossary notes:

conducive
favorable; tending to bring about

plausible
believable or credible

Europa
one of Jupiter's moons

Titan
one of Saturn's moons

us learn not only whether life can exist on various worlds, but also how interior, surface, and atmospheric processes play out on different planets and moons. This knowledge will help us understand why some worlds end up habitable and others don't. It will also provide guidance to us as we seek to answer the question of what planets in other solar systems might be like.

The Impact of Finding Life on Human Perspective

6   People have long speculated about life beyond Earth, and many people—including many scientists—have at times been convinced that life exists on the Moon, on Mars, or on other worlds. Why, then, would the discovery of extraterrestrial life have a major impact on human perspective? The answer lies in the difference between guessing and knowing. As long as there is uncertainty about the existence of life on other worlds, people are free to hold a wide range of opinions. People living before the time of **Copernicus** could continue to believe in an Earth-centered world, but it was very hard to continue to do so after **Galileo**, **Kepler**, and **Newton** offered convincing proof to the contrary. An actual discovery of life beyond Earth would force us, both as individuals and as a society, to reconsider the place of our planet and our species in the cosmos.

7   In contemplating the significance of finding life elsewhere, let's begin by considering what would happen if we found **microbial** life on Mars. The first question we would probably ask is whether the life was genetically related to terrestrial life (suggesting that it had migrated between planets on meteorites) or instead represented an independent origin of life on Mars. We could answer this question by determining the structure of the molecules that make up the martian life. Does it use DNA and RNA molecules similar to those used by terrestrial life? Does it use the same amino acids or the same proteins to carry out enzymatic reactions? Do the molecules that participate in life have the same "handedness" to them? It seems unlikely that there would be only one solution to the problems of containing and passing on the genetic information required for life to reproduce, of **catalyzing** the chemical reactions that comprise life, and of storing and using energy in metabolism. We would expect life that had an origin independent from life on Earth to have a different chemical structure.

8   While a discovery of life on Mars that was genetically related to terrestrial life would be exciting, it would not have as great an impact as a discovery of life that showed evidence of an independent origin. If and when such a discovery occurs, it likely will seem to be the final step in recognizing that we on Earth are not so special. Life would be seen as just another example of the types of chemistry that can occur in a planetary environment, albeit an especially interesting one. A discovery of non-terrestrial-based life on Mars would be consistent with the views that have been put forward about the ease of formation of life and would suggest that at least microbial life was common throughout the galaxy.

9   Would a discovery of alien microbial life have the same philosophical impact as a discovery of extraterrestrial intelligence? In informal polls, many people indicate that only the discovery of alien intelligence would have truly profound significance

Copernicus
first scientist to believe that Earth revolves around the sun

Galileo
proved Copernicus's theory by using a telescope to observe the solar system

Kepler
used math to prove that the planets move around the sun

Newton
developed the law of gravitation, which explains how planets move

microbial
relating to microscopic organisms

catalyzing
increasing or bringing about, initiating

nascent
emerging

for them. Many scientists working in the nascent field of astrobiology disagree, however, feeling that the discovery of even the simplest single-celled organism on another planet would have profound significance for us. If this life had an origin independent from terrestrial life, it would tell us that the origin of life was not a unique event. With proof that life has originated twice, we would have every reason to think it has originated many times and thus that life is widespread in the universe. A discovery of alien microbial life would also help us better understand life in general. We would learn more about the conditions under which life can arise and persist, as well as the conditions under which it can evolve into more complex forms. That knowledge, in turn, would have implications for whether intelligent life might be common.

Significance of the Search Itself

10   A discovery of extraterrestrial life would undoubtedly bring important practical benefits. For example, studying it will help us understand what characteristics of terrestrial life are unique to Earth and what characteristics apply generally to life anywhere. If we find intelligent life elsewhere, we would learn much more about the nature of intelligence and might be exposed to cultures and societies very different from those of humans. If we could communicate with more advanced beings, we could possibly learn the secrets of the nature of the universe, the nature of consciousness and the mind, and technological marvels that could dramatically change our life here on Earth.

11   However, for many people excited by the scientific search for life in the universe, the search itself is much more than a means to an end. For them the search is just one more critical component in our exploration of the world around us. Other components in astronomy and space science include exploring the planets and moons in our solar system as a way to understand how planets work and exploring stars and galaxies as a way to determine the nature of our universe. Other components in biology include exploring the origin and evolution of life on Earth so that we can understand how we ourselves came to exist.

12   In all these cases, our exploration does not seem to be driven solely by the desire to find specific answers to the scientific questions we are asking, because in each case we end up asking more questions. Instead, we seem to be driven by our inherent curiosity, our desire to understand the world around us (Figure A). Sometimes our curiosity leads to discoveries with practical applications, while at other times it simply helps us understand how or why the world is as it is. Understanding the world around us means learning about the broader-scale environment in which humans exist. Understanding the occurrence of planets orbiting other stars helps us understand the significance of the occurrence of planets orbiting the Sun, including Earth. Understanding the occurrence of life elsewhere allows us to understand the significance of the occurrence of life on Earth. And understanding the potential for intelligent life beyond Earth brings with it an understanding of the meaning of the occurrence of intelligent life here on Earth. In essence, by learning about the world around us we are learning about ourselves and about what it means to be human.

inherent
innate, native, inbred

Figure A The Earth as viewed in space from the Apollo 17 spacecraft. Seen from this perspective, we recognize the strong connections between the terrestrial ecosystem and the planet itself, and we recognize that life, indeed, is a planetary phenomenon. As we explore the universe, we will learn whether the formations of planets around stars and the occurrence of life on planets are rare or commonplace. We may then finally answer the question of whether we are alone.

A. UNDERSTANDING THE THESIS AND OTHER MAIN IDEAS

Select the best answer.

_____ 1. The central thesis of this selection is that

   a. no one knows if life exists on other planets.

   b. NASA runs many programs intended to find life elsewhere in the solar system.

   c. if extraterrestrial life is discovered, what is learned will have important implications for life on Earth.

   d. finding microbial life that originated on another planet is more significant than finding life that migrated to a planet.

_____ 2. The authors' primary purpose is to

   a. describe what types of life might exist in the universe.

   b. explain why searching for life on other planets is important and worthwhile.

    c. persuade students to choose a career in astrobiology.

    d. present evidence for the existence of life on other planets.

_____ 3. The topic of paragraph 6 is

    a. famous scientists and their theories.

    b. beliefs concerning life beyond Earth.

    c. the impact of the discovery of extraterrestrial life.

    d. a response to aliens.

_____ 4. The topic sentence of paragraph 7 is expressed in the

    a. first sentence.   c. third sentence.

    b. second sentence.   d. last sentence.

_____ 5. What is the main idea of paragraph 9?

    a. Discovery of any kind of life on another planet would be very important.

    b. Only the discovery of intelligent life is significant to scientists.

    c. The general public does not understand the importance of alien microbial life.

    d. The existence of microbial life on another planet implies the existence of intelligent life elsewhere.

_____ 6. The final paragraph

    a. states that all our questions about human life can be answered by learning more about the universe.

    b. gives a negative view of space exploration.

    c. provides the reader with places to look for more information on the topic of the reading.

    d. summarizes the importance of understanding the world around us.

B. IDENTIFYING DETAILS

Fill in each of the blanks using the words and phrases listed below. Each word may be used only once. Not all words and phrases will be used.

Cassini	astrobiology	Mars and Europa
NASA	carbon–bearing molecules	life on Earth
universe	cultures and societies	slowly
conditions	Earth	Venus
quickly		

1. The _____ was once thought to be the center of our planetary system.

2. One practical benefit of the discovery of intelligent life elsewhere could be to expose us to different _____.

3. _____ is the study of life in space.

4. _____ are good candidates for having life today or in the past.

5. _____ is a spacecraft on its way to explore Saturn.

6. Discovery of extraterrestrial life would force us to reconsider our place in the _____.

7. _____ is a space agency interested in exploring for life beyond Earth.

8. _____ should be common on other planets.

9. Life on Earth seems to have appeared quite _____.

10. Life on Earth exists under a large number of different _____.

C. RECOGNIZING METHODS OF ORGANIZATION AND TRANSITIONS

Select the best answer.

_____ 1. The organizational pattern used in paragraph 3 is
   a. classification.
   b. time sequence.
   c. cause and effect.
   d. enumeration.

_____ 2. The organizational pattern used in paragraph 4 is
   a. comparison and contrast.
   b. classification.
   c. time sequence.
   d. enumeration.

➤ D. REVIEWING AND ORGANIZING IDEAS: MAPPING

Complete the following map of the main issues and details in the reading.

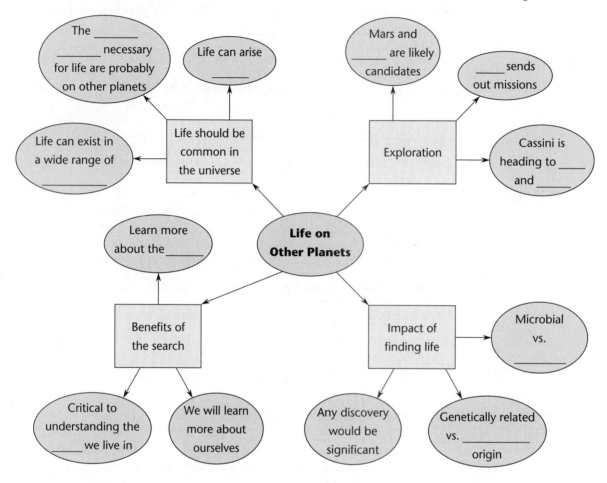

➤ E. FIGURING OUT INFERRED MEANINGS

Indicate whether each statement is true (T) or false (F).

_____ 1. Life might exist on other planets.

_____ 2. NASA scientists know that life exists beyond Earth.

_____ 3. It can be inferred that the spacecraft exploring other planets will send back data relevant to the search for life.

_____ 4. Not everyone believed Copernicus's theories.

_____ 5. From paragraph 7, it can be inferred that life on other planets could be completely different from life on Earth.

_____ 6. Scientists only want to find intelligent life.

➤ **F.   THINKING CRITICALLY**

Indicate whether each statement is fact (F) or opinion (O).

_____ 1. "We have the potential to discover life on another planet within perhaps the next one or two decades." (paragraph 2)

_____ 2. "Spacecraft are being developed for missions to Mars." (paragraph 5)

_____ 3. "It seems unlikely that there would be only one solution to the problems of containing and passing on the genetic information." (paragraph 7)

_____ 4. "If and when such a discovery occurs, it likely will seem to be the final step in recognizing that we on Earth are not so special." (paragraph 8)

_____ 5. "Many scientists working in the nascent field of astrobiology disagree." (paragraph 9)

_____ 6. "A discovery of extraterrestrial life would undoubtedly bring important practical benefits." (paragraph 10)

➤ **G.   BUILDING VOCABULARY**

➤ **Context**
Using context and a dictionary, if necessary, determine the meaning of each word as it is used in the selection.

_____ 1. plausible (paragraph 1)

   a. believable

   b. unlikely

   c. exciting

   d. necessary

_____ 2. millennia (paragraph 2)

   a. one hundred years

   b. thousands of years

   c. every million years

   d. one century

_____ 3. abundant (paragraph 3)

   a. large

   b. plentiful

   c. full of life

   d. wealthy

_____ 4. speculated (paragraph 6)

    a. showed concern

    b. imagined

    c. talked about

    d. theorized

➤ Word Parts

> **A REVIEW OF PREFIXES, ROOTS, AND SUFFIXES**
> **EXTRA-** means *out of*
> **TERRE** means *earth*
> **-ABLE** means *fit for*

Use your knowledge of word parts and the review above to fill in the blanks in the following sentences.

1. *Extraterrestrial* life (paragraph 2) refers to life that exists outside the boundaries of _____.

2. A planet that is *habitable* (paragraph 5) is one that is _____ life.

➤ H.   SELECTING A LEARNING/STUDY STRATEGY

Select the best answer.

_____ The best way to study for an essay exam on this selection would be to

    a. list all the facts.

    b. visualize creatures from outer space and their habitats.

    c. write a summary of the main issues discussed in the reading.

    d. reread the selection several times.

➤ I.   EXPLORING IDEAS THROUGH DISCUSSION AND WRITING

1. Discuss the ethical issues surrounding the exploration for life on other planets. For example, would it be acceptable to colonize other planets that could support life?

2. Write a paragraph describing your beliefs about life beyond Earth. Do you think it exists? Why or why not? Compare your response with that of classmates.

3. Discuss the depiction of alien life in TV, movies, and books. How does science fiction help us deal with the unknown? How does it prepare us for possible discoveries?

J. BEYOND THE CLASSROOM TO THE WEB

Visit the NASA home page at **http://www.nasa.gov/home/**. *Look for information on space exploration, especially as it relates to the hunt for life on other planets. Identify at least three pieces of new information you find.*

✔ **Tracking Your Progress**

Selection 32

Section	Number Correct	Score
A. Thesis and Main Ideas (6 items)	_____ x 5	_____
B. Details (10 items)	_____ x 2	_____
C. Organization and Transitions (2 items)	_____ x 2	_____
E. Inferred Meanings (6 items)	_____ x 3	_____
F. Thinking Critically (6 items)	_____ x 3	_____
G. Vocabulary		
1. Context (4 items)	_____ x 2	_____
2. Word Parts (2 items)	_____ x 1	_____
	TOTAL SCORE	_____ %

SELECTION 33

Air Pollution May Result in Global Warming

John Suchocki

This selection was taken from a college chemistry textbook titled *Conceptual Chemistry* by John Suchoki. Read it to discover how global warming affects us all.

PREVIEWING THE READING

Using the steps listed on page 29, preview the reading selection. When you have finished, complete the following items.

1. This selection is about _____
_____.

2. List at least three questions you should be able to answer after reading the selection:

   a. _____

   b. _____

   c. _____

MAKING CONNECTIONS

Crystals of ice photographed in polarized light reveal tiny air bubbles containing ancient air. What can we learn about global warming from these crystals?

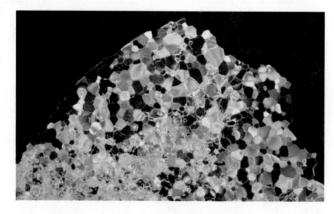

➤ READING TIP

As you read, highlight the topic sentence of each paragraph.

Air Pollution May Result in Global Warming

1   Park your car with its windows closed in the bright sun, and its interior soon becomes quite toasty. The inside of a greenhouse is similarly toasty. This happens because glass is transparent to visible light but not to **infrared**, as illustrated in Figure A. As you may recall, wavelengths of visible light are shorter than **wavelengths** of infrared. Visible light wavelengths range from 400 **nanometers** to 740 nanometers, while infrared wavelengths range from 740 nanometers to a million nanometers. Short-wavelength visible light from the sun enters your car or a greenhouse and is absorbed by various objects—car seats, plants, soil, whatever. The warmed objects then emit infrared energy, which cannot escape through the glass, and so the infrared energy builds up inside, increasing the temperature.

infrared
invisible radiation wavelengths

wavelengths
the lengths of light waves, which affect whether they are visible

nanometers
billionths of a meter

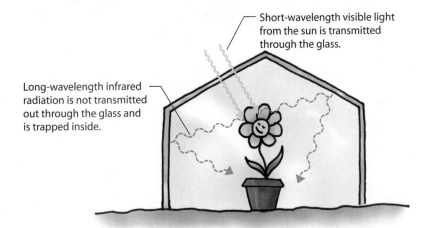

Short-wavelength visible light from the sun is transmitted through the glass.

Long-wavelength infrared radiation is not transmitted out through the glass and is trapped inside.

Figure A   Glass acts as a one-way valve, letting visible light in and preventing infrared energy from existing.

2   A similar effect occurs in the Earth's atmosphere, which, like glass, is transparent to visible light emitted by the sun. The ground absorbs this energy but radiates infrared waves. Atmospheric carbon dioxide, water vapor, and other select gases absorb and re-emit much of this infrared energy back to the ground, as Figure B illustrates. This process, called the greenhouse effect, helps keep the Earth warm. The greenhouse effect is quite desirable because the Earth's average temperature would be a frigid $-18°C$ otherwise. Greenhouse warming also occurs on Venus but to a far greater extent. The atmosphere surrounding Venus is much thicker than the Earth's atmosphere, and its composition is 95 percent carbon dioxide, which brings surface temperatures to a scorching $450°C$.

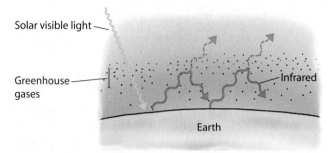

Figure B   The greenhouse effect in the Earth's atmosphere. Visible light from the sun is absorbed by the ground, which then emits infrared radiation. Carbon dioxide, water vapor, and other greenhouse gases in the atmosphere absorb and re-emit heat that would otherwise be radiated from the Earth into space.

Atmospheric Carbon Dioxide Is a Greenhouse Gas

3   The role of carbon dioxide as a greenhouse gas is well documented. Core samples from polar ice sheets, for example, show a close relationship between atmospheric levels of carbon dioxide and global temperatures over the past 160,000 years. This relationship is graphed in Figure C.

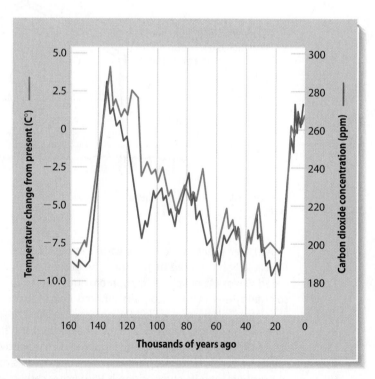

Figure C   Levels of atmospheric carbon dioxide and global temperatures appear to be closely related to each other.

fossil fuels
hydrocarbon
deposits from
formerly living
objects used to
create heat or
power

**Industrial
Revolution**
the period in
the late 1700s
when a shift
from home-
based
manufacturing
to large-scale
factories took
place

4   There is strong evidence that recent human activities, such as the burning of fossil fuels and deforestation, are responsible for some dramatic increases in atmospheric carbon dioxide levels. Prior to the Industrial Revolution, carbon dioxide levels were fairly constant at about 280 parts per million. During the 1800s, however, levels began to climb, as Figure D shows, reaching a level of 300 parts per million in about 1910. Today's level is a worrisome 360 parts per million! Interestingly, as can be seen in Figure C, ice samples dating as far back as 160,000 years ago do not show atmospheric carbon dioxide levels ever exceeding 300 parts per million. In step with these increases, average global temperatures since 1860 have increased by about 0.8°C. Current estimates are that a doubling of today's atmospheric carbon dioxide levels will increase the average global temperature by an additional 1.5 to 4.5°C.

5   Carbon dioxide ranks as the number-one gas emitted by human activities. When speaking of atmospheric pollutants such as sulfur dioxide, we talk in terms of millions of tons. The amount of carbon dioxide we pump into the atmosphere, however, is measured in *billions* of tons, as Figure D shows. A single tank of gasoline in an automobile produces up to 90 kilograms of carbon dioxide. A jet flying from New York to Los Angeles releases more than 200,000 kilograms (about 300 tons). Above all, our population increases by about 236,000 individuals every day, which is about 86 million individuals every year. In 1999, we passed the milestone of 6 billion humans, each of us responsible for activities that result in the output of carbon dioxide.

6   When direct monitoring of atmospheric carbon dioxide began in 1958, the global atmospheric reservoir of carbon dioxide was about 671 billion tons, a figure

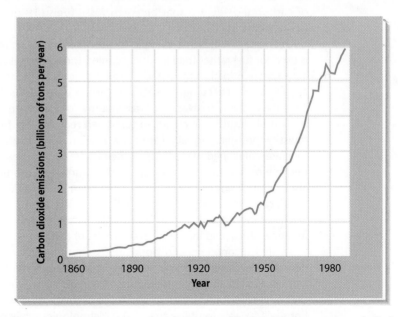

Figure D   Carbon dioxide emissions from the burning of fossil fuels have grown dramatically since 1860.

calculated from the observed concentration of 315 parts per million. By 1995, this amount had grown to 767 billion tons, which simple subtraction tells us is an increase of 96 billion tons:

1995 Global atmospheric reservoir of CO_2:	767 billion tons
1958 Global atmospheric reservoir of CO_2:	−671 billion tons
Net increase:	+ 96 billion tons

Over the same period, humans released about 175 billion tons of atmospheric carbon dioxide from fossil-fuel emissions alone. From these data, we can get a feel for nature's ability to absorb carbon dioxide. Even though we pumped out 175 billion tons of carbon dioxide, the total quantity in the atmosphere went up by only 96 billion tons. Models suggest that most of the difference was absorbed by the oceans. The ocean, because its water is **alkaline**, can absorb carbon dioxide. Carbon dioxide can also be absorbed by vegetation during photosynthesis. It has been shown, for example, that trees grow more rapidly when exposed to higher concentrations of carbon dioxide.

alkaline
able to neutralize and absorb acid

7   That levels of atmospheric carbon dioxide have gone up by 96 billion tons tells us that we are exceeding nature's absorbing power. Bear in mind, 96 out of 767 is about 12 percent. Take a deep breath—at least 12 percent of the carbon dioxide you just inhaled came from the combustion of fossil fuels and deforestation.

8   With less than 5 percent of the world's population, the United States ranks first in carbon dioxide emissions and is responsible for about 25 percent of global carbon dioxide emissions. Industrial nations worldwide are responsible for about 58 percent of carbon dioxide emissions, primarily from the combustion of fossil fuels. Developing nations account for the remaining 42 percent, but their sources of carbon dioxide are split between fossil fuels (19 percent) and deforestation (23 percent).

9   Deforestation presents multiple threats to atmospheric resources. If the cut wood is used for fuel rather than lumber, burning the fuel releases carbon dioxide into the atmosphere. Whether the wood is used for fuel or for lumber, though, cutting down any forest destroys a net absorber of carbon dioxide. Furthermore, tropical forests have the capacity to evaporate vast volumes of water vapor, which assist in the formation of clouds. The clouds in turn keep regions cool by reflecting sunlight and moist by precipitating rain. Farmers who burn down rainforests for farmland, therefore, are simultaneously cutting off their future supply of rainwater. When their farms become desert, they are then spurred to burn even more of the rainforest. So far, about 65 percent of all rainforests have been destroyed. At present rates, within a few decades remaining rainforests will not be able to sustain regional climates, which will leave more than a billion citizens of the rapidly growing communities of South America, Africa, and Indonesia in the midst of arid land.

10   As their economies and populations continue to grow over the next several decades, developing nations will likely surpass industrial nations in the amounts of carbon dioxide and other pollutants they emit. New energy-efficient technologies that minimize emissions are now available. In a best-case scenario, developing nations will be able to utilize these new technologies while maintaining needed economic growth.

The Potential Effects of Global Warming Are Uncertain

11   There is general consensus that increased levels of atmospheric carbon dioxide and other greenhouse gases will result in global warming. How much temperatures may rise, however, is uncertain, as are the potential effects of the temperature increases. This uncertainty is due to the large number of variables that determine global weather. The sun's intensity, for example, changes over time, as does the ocean's ability to absorb and distribute greenhouse heat. Another variable is the cooling effect of cloud cover, atmospheric dust, **aerosols,** and ice sheets, which all serve to reflect incoming solar radiation.

aerosols
fine solid or liquid particles suspended in air

12   An average global temperature increase of only a few degrees would not be felt uniformly around the world. Instead, some places would experience wider fluctuations than others. For example, the number of days temperatures reach above 32°C (90°F) might double in New York City but remain unchanged in Los Angeles. The number of days in polar regions when temperatures rise above 0°C might double or even triple, causing glaciers and polar ice sheets to melt. Melting ice combined with the thermal expansion of ocean waters would lead to an increase in sea level. Many climatologists project that a global temperature increase of a few degrees over the next 50 to 100 years may raise sea level by about 1 meter, enough to inundate many coastal regions and displace millions of people.

13   Small changes in average global temperatures would also change weather patterns. The warming of the equatorial eastern Pacific Ocean during an El Niño, for example, is already known to change local weather patterns throughout the world. If the whole planet were to warm by a few degrees, the impact would be far greater. What is now fertile agricultural land may turn barren while land now barren may turn fertile. Over the past several decades, for example, average global temperatures have edged up by about 0.2°C. In step with this warming trend, the growing seasons of the Great Plains of Canada are now more than one week longer than they were just several decades ago. As weather patterns change, one nation's gain may well be another nation's loss. Developing nations lacking the resources to make adjustments, however, would be the hardest hit.

Figure E   Which weather extreme might become more prevalent as greenhouse gases continue to increase? Either one is possible.

➤ **A.   UNDERSTANDING THE THESIS AND OTHER MAIN IDEAS**

Select the best answer.

_____ 1. The central thesis of the selection is that
   a. Earth is naturally becoming a warmer place.
   b. human activities are increasing global warming.
   c. global warming poses no great danger.
   d. human activities improve Earth's ability to regulate temperature.

_____ 2. The author's primary purpose is to
   a. recommend lifestyle steps that will reduce global warming.
   b. examine research about the effect of aerosols on global warming.
   c. reassure readers about global warming.
   d. explain the causes and effects of global warming.

_____ 3. The topic of paragraph 2 is
   a. the greenhouse effect in Earth's atmosphere.
   b. the greenhouse effect in outer space.
   c. changes in light wavelengths.
   d. the dangers of infrared energy.

_____ 4. Which of the following questions is *not* answered in paragraph 4?
   a. What human activities have caused carbon dioxide levels to rise?
   b. How does the use of fossil fuel increase carbon dioxide levels?
   c. How have carbon dioxide levels changed since the Industrial Revolution?
   d. How will an increase in carbon dioxide affect temperatures in the future?

_____ 5. What is the main idea of paragraph 6?
   a. Nature can absorb some but not all of the carbon dioxide humans produce.
   b. Fossil fuel emissions are a primary cause of air pollution.
   c. Direct monitoring of carbon dioxide has improved.
   d. Deforestation is the largest factor in carbon dioxide increases.

_____ 6. The purpose of paragraph 8 is to
   a. explain how deforestation is more dangerous than fossil fuels.
   b. examine the impact of industrial nations on carbon dioxide emissions.
   c. examine who and what is contributing to increased carbon dioxide.
   d. blame the United States for global warming.

_____ 7. The topic of paragraph 12 is

    a. increases in sea level.

    b. danger to coastal regions.

    c. impacts of global temperature increase.

    d. polar temperature changes.

B. IDENTIFYING DETAILS

Select the best answer.

_____ 1. Most visible light waves are

    a. absorbed by the ground.

    b. emitted by reflection.

    c. caused by fossil fuel.

    d. invisible to the naked eye.

_____ 2. The relationship between carbon dioxide and global temperatures was examined using

    a. fossil fuel residue.

    b. core samples from polar ice sheets.

    c. thermometers in several global positions.

    d. measurement of sulfur dioxide.

_____ 3. If today's carbon dioxide levels double, it will increase global temperatures by

    a. no noticeable amount.

    b. 5.1 to 7.2°C.

    c. 1.5 to 4.5°C.

    d. 20 to 30°C.

_____ 4. The United States has less than 5% of the world's population yet produces

    a. 35% of global carbon dioxide emissions.

    b. 25% of global carbon dioxide emissions.

    c. 35% of global deforestation.

    d. 25% of global deforestation.

_____ 5. Deforestation is an important factor in global warming because

    a. trees are a net absorber of carbon dioxide.

    b. it destroys animal habitats.

    c. it increases the price of lumber.

    d. trees effectively reflect infrared rays.

_____ 6. Global temperature increases could cause the oceans to
   a. evaporate more quickly.
   b. create more hurricanes.
   c. grow more algae.
   d. rise by one meter.

C.   RECOGNIZING METHODS OF ORGANIZATION AND TRANSITIONS

Select the best answer.

_____ 1. The main organizational pattern used throughout this selection is
   a. listing/enumeration.
   b. classification.
   c. definition.
   d. cause and effect.

_____ 2. The organizational pattern used to describe the greenhouse effect in paragraphs 1 and 2 is
   a. comparison and contrast.
   b. process.
   c. classification.
   d. spatial order.

D.   REVIEWING AND ORGANIZING IDEAS: OUTLINING

Fill in this outline about the effects of global warming (paragraph 11).

I. Increased levels of _____ gases result in global warming.

   A. Amount of _____ and potential effects are uncertain due to several variables

      1. _____ changes over time

      2. _____ changes

      3. Cooling effect and reflection of incoming solar radiation by

         a. _____

         b. _____

         c. _____

         d. _____

➤ **E.   FIGURING OUT INFERRED MEANINGS**

Indicate whether each statement is true (T) or false (F).

_____ 1. Carbon dioxide is a natural part of the atmosphere.

_____ 2. Although today's carbon dioxide levels are higher than those 160,000 years ago, scientists are not concerned.

_____ 3. Increased carbon dioxide levels mean plants will grow faster.

_____ 4. The United States produces a proportionate share of carbon dioxide compared to other countries.

_____ 5. Humans have the capability to take actions that would reduce global warming.

➤ **F.   THINKING CRITICALLY**

Select the best answer.

_____ 1. The author supports the central thesis with

    a. facts and statistics.   c. opinions.

    b. analogies.   d. research citations.

_____ 2. The tone of the selection is

    a. worried.   c. uncomfortable.

    b. persuasive.   d. informative.

_____ 3. In paragraph 5, the author explains carbon dioxide amounts by

    a. making inferences.   c. giving examples.

    b. repeating information.   d. offering opinions.

_____ 4. Which of the following statements from the reading is an opinion?

    a. "Prior to the Industrial Revolution, carbon dioxide levels were fairly constant at about 280 parts per million." (paragraph 4)

    b. "A single tank of gasoline in an automobile produces up to 90 kilograms of carbon dioxide." (paragraph 5)

    c. "In 1999, we passed the milestone of 6 billion humans, each of us responsible for activities that result in the output of carbon dioxide." (paragraph 5)

    d. "Carbon dioxide can also be absorbed by vegetation during photosynthesis." (paragraph 6)

_____ 5. In the last paragraph, the author

    a. discusses the impact of global warming on weather patterns.

    b. summarizes the entire reading.

    c. rephrases the first paragraph.

    d. identifies the impact to polar ice caps of global warming.

G.   BUILDING VOCABULARY

Context

Using context and a dictionary, if necessary, determine the meaning of each word as it is used in the selection.

_____   1. estimates (paragraph 4)

    a. measurements   c. answers

    b. opinions   d. approximate calculations

_____   2. reservoir (paragraph 6)

    a. body of water   c. emergency amount

    b. amount set aside   d. extra supply

_____   3. arid (paragraph 9)

    a. heavily populated   c. lacking rainfall

    b. breezy   d. neglected

_____   4. fluctuations (paragraph 12)

    a. variations   c. scientific measurements

    b. durations   d. water levels

Word Parts

A REVIEW OF ROOTS AND SUFFIXES

PHOTO means *light*

-OLOGY means *the study of*

Use your knowledge of word parts and the review above to fill in the blanks in the following sentences.

1. If synthesis is a process that combines things, then *photosynthesis* (paragraph 6) is a process involving plants and _____.

2. *Climatologists* (paragraph 12) are people who _____ the weather.

H.   SELECTING A LEARNING/STUDY STRATEGY

Select the best answer.

_____   What is the best way to learn the meanings of all the technical terms in the reading, such as *thermal expansion*?

    a. Write a paragraph using as many of the words as possible.

    b. Highlight each as you read.

c. Write the terms and their definitions on index cards and test yourself.

d. Recopy each several times.

I. EXPLORING IDEAS THROUGH DISCUSSION AND WRITING

1. Discuss how global warming would affect your area of the world.

2. Write a list of ways you could reduce carbon dioxide emissions.

3. What can be done to educate people about the dangers of global warming?

J. BEYOND THE CLASSROOM TO THE WEB

Explore the Environmental Protection Agency's site on climate change at **http://www.epa.gov/climatechange/.**

How does the information presented here compare with the information from the reading and popular media? Write a list of the main issues in the global warming debate and how different groups view these issues.

✔ Tracking Your Progress

Selection 33

Section	Number Correct		Score
A. Thesis and Main Ideas (7 items)	_____	x 4	_____
B. Details (6 items)	_____	x 3	_____
C. Organization and Transitions (2 items)	_____	x 2	_____
E. Inferred Meanings (5 items)	_____	x 4	_____
F. Thinking Critically (5 items)	_____	x 4	_____
G. Vocabulary			
1. Context (4 items)	_____	x 2	_____
2. Word Parts (2 items)	_____	x 1	_____
	TOTAL SCORE	_____	%

21 Workplace/Career Fields

Work is a complex, important part of our lives and serves a number of different functions. It provides essential income to purchase life's necessities. It also offers an outlet for creative expression, helps us learn new skills, and allows us to explore new interests and talents. Jobs can be a source of personal satisfaction, a means of demonstrating that we are competent, self-sufficient individuals. Work can also make leisure time valuable and meaningful. Finally, work can lead to new friends, new relationships, new experiences, and new realizations.

The readings in this chapter provide several different perspectives on work and the workplace. The article "Building Toward a Career" offers partial suggestions to help you prepare for the career of your choice while you are attending college. In "Rx for Anger at Work" you will learn causes of anger on the job and discover ways to cope with anger. "The Sandman Is Dead—Long Live the Sleep Deprived Walking Zombie" addresses a serious problem many of us with hectic lives face—sleep deprivation.

Use the following tips when reading about the workplace.

TIPS FOR READING IN WORKPLACE/ CAREER FIELDS

- **Focus on practical information.** As you read the selections in this chapter, try to find techniques and strategies that you can use on the job or to find a better job. You may find some practical suggestions for coping with anger and frustrations on the job in "Rx for Anger at Work."

- **Pay attention to trends and projections.** The workplace is constantly changing and evolving. The job you have today may not exist in 20 years. Read to find out how to make yourself marketable and competitive.

- **Apply what you learn.** The information in the readings on sleep deprivation and anger management can be put to immediate use, both in the workplace and in the college environment.

SELECTION 34	**Building Toward a Career**
	Courtland L. Bovee, John V. Thill, and Barbara E. Shatzman

This article originally appeared in a business textbook titled *Business Communication Today*. Read it to discover what you can do now to discover the right career choice and prepare for that career upon graduation.

▶ PREVIEWING THE READING

Using the steps listed on page 29, preview the reading selection. When you have finished, answer the following questions.

1. This selection is primarily about _____.

2. List at least three questions you should be able to answer after reading the selection:

   a. _____

   b. _____

   c. _____

MAKING CONNECTIONS

Fill in the following chart with what you have done and what you plan to do toward obtaining several jobs that interest you.

Potential careers Categories of experience			
COURSES			
INTERNSHIPS			
EMPLOYMENT PORTFOLIO			
JOBS			

> READING TIP

As you read, highlight specific actions you can take to choose a career that is best suited to your interests and prepare for a job in that career field.

Building Toward a Career

1   Getting the job that is right for you takes more than sending out a few resumes and application letters. Before entering the workplace, you need to learn as much as you can about your capabilities and the job marketplace.

Adapting to the Changing Workplace

2   Do you have what employers are looking for? Before you limit your employment search to a particular industry or job, it's a good idea to analyze what you have to offer and what you hope to get from your work. This advance preparation allows you to identify employers who are likely to want you and vice versa.

What Do You Have to Offer?

3   Get started by jotting down 10 achievements you're proud of, such as learning to ski, taking a prize-winning photo, tutoring a child, or editing your school paper. Think carefully about what specific skills these achievements demanded. For example, leadership skills, speaking ability, and artistic talent may have helped you coordinate a winning presentation to your school's administration. As you analyze your achievements, you'll begin to recognize a pattern of skills. Which of them might be valuable to potential employers?

4   Next, look at your educational preparation, work experience, and extracurricular activities. What do your knowledge and experience qualify you to do? What have you learned from volunteer work or class projects that could benefit you on the job? Have you held any offices, won any awards or scholarships, mastered a second language?

5   Take stock of your personal characteristics. Are you aggressive, a born leader? Or would you rather follow? Are you outgoing, articulate, great with people? Or do you prefer working alone? Make a list of what you believe are your four or five most important qualities. Ask a relative or friend to rate your traits as well.

6   If you're having difficulty figuring out your interests, characteristics, or capabilities, consult your college placement office. Many campuses administer a variety of tests to help you identify interests, aptitudes, and personality traits. These tests won't reveal your "perfect" job, but they'll help you focus on the types of work best suited to your personality.

What Do You Want to Do?

7   Knowing what you can do is one thing. Knowing what you want to do is another. Don't lose sight of your own values. Discover the things that will bring you satisfaction and happiness on the job.

- What would you like to do every day? Talk to people in various occupations about their typical workday. You might consult relatives, local businesses, or former graduates (through your school's alumni relations office). Read about various occupations. Start with your college library or placement office.
- How would you like to work? Consider how much independence you want on the job, how much variety you like, and whether you prefer to work with products, machines, people, ideas, figures, or some combination thereof. Do you like physical work, mental work, or a mix? Constant change or a predictable role?
- What specific compensation do you expect? What do you hope to earn in your first year? What kind of pay increase do you expect each year? What's your ultimate earnings goal? Would you be comfortable getting paid on commission, or do you prefer a steady paycheck? Are you willing to settle for less money in order to do something you really love?
- Can you establish some general career goals? Consider where you'd like to start, where you'd like to go from there, and the ultimate position you'd like to attain. How soon after joining the company would you like to receive your first promotion? Your next one? What additional training or preparation will you need to achieve them?
- What size company would you prefer? Do you like the idea of working for a small, entrepreneurial operation? Or would you prefer a large corporation?
- What type of operation is appealing to you? Would you prefer to work for a profit-making company or a nonprofit organization? Are you attracted to service businesses or manufacturing operations? Do you want regular, predictable hours, or do you thrive on flexible, varied hours? Would you enjoy a seasonally varied job such as education (which may give you summers off) or retailing (with its selling cycles)?
- What location would you like? Would you like to work in a city, a suburb, a small town, an industrial area, or an uptown setting? Do you favor a particular part of the country? A country abroad? Do you like working indoors or outdoors?
- What facilities do you envision? Is it important to you to work in an attractive place, or will simple, functional quarters suffice? Do you need a quiet office to work effectively, or can you concentrate in a noisy, open setting? Is access to public transportation or freeways important?
- What sort of corporate culture are you most comfortable with? Would you be happy in a formal hierarchy with clear reporting relationships? Or do you prefer less structure? Are you looking for a paternalistic firm or one that fosters individualism? Do you like a competitive environment? One that rewards teamwork? What qualities do you want in a boss?

How Can You Make Yourself More Valuable to Employers?

8   While you're figuring out what you can offer an employer and what you want from a job, you can take positive steps toward building your career. There is a lot you can

do before you graduate from college and while you are seeking employment. The following suggestions will help potential employers recognize the value of hiring you:

9   Keep an employment portfolio. Get a three-ring notebook and a package of plastic sleeves that open at the top. Collect anything that shows your ability to perform (classroom or work evaluations, certificates, awards, papers you've written). Your portfolio is a great resource for writing your resume, and it gives employers tangible evidence of your professionalism.

10   Take interim assignments. As you search for a permanent job, consider temporary or freelance work. Also gain a competitive edge by participating in an internship program. These temporary assignments not only help you gain valuable experience and relevant contacts but also provide you with important references and with items for your portfolio.

11   Work on polishing and updating your skills. Whenever possible, join networks of professional colleagues and friends who can help you keep up with your occupation and industry. While waiting for responses to your resume, take a computer course or seek out other educational or life experiences that would be hard to get while working full-time.

12   Even after an employer hires you, continue improving your skills to distinguish yourself from your peers and to make yourself more valuable to current and potential employers. Becoming a lifelong learner will help you reach your personal goals in the workplace.

A.   UNDERSTANDING THE THESIS AND OTHER MAIN IDEAS

Select the best answer.

_____   1. The central thesis of the selection is that

a. recruiters are looking for well-rounded candidates, not those with specific skills.

b. students should analyze their skills and values and take steps toward preparing for a career while in college.

c. you should plan to update your skills regularly.

d. an employment portfolio is an employee's strongest asset.

_____   2. The authors' primary purpose is to

a. discourage students from focusing only on salary.

b. explain how to polish your skills.

c. encourage students to plan ahead when pursing a career.

d. advise job seekers on the fundamentals of networking and business etiquette.

_____   3. What topic do the authors address in paragraph 5?

a. aggression.

b. leadership.

       c. personal traits.

       d. work preferences.

_____ 4. The main idea of paragraph 7 is

       a. start your job search at your college's placement office.

       b. you should set a salary goal before you go job hunting.

       c. you should consider whether you prefer mental or physical tasks.

       d. you should identify things that bring you happiness and job satisfaction.

_____ 5. The main idea of paragraph 8 is

       a. temporary jobs often lead to permanent ones.

       b. if students find careers they love, the money will follow.

       c. an employment portfolio demonstrates your professionalism.

       d. students should take steps while in college that will enable them to demonstrate their value to employers.

➤ B.   IDENTIFYING DETAILS

Indicate whether each statement is true (T) or false (F).

_____ 1. Listing achievements you are proud of will help you discover skills you have to offer employers.

_____ 2. Tests offered by the college placement office may identify the perfect job for you.

_____ 3. It is helpful to develop a career plan that includes long-term goals.

_____ 4. An employment portfolio should contain testimonials from friends and family who are familiar with your personal traits.

_____ 5. Part-time or temporary jobs provide important contacts and useful references.

➤ C.   RECOGNIZING METHODS OF ORGANIZATION AND TRANSITIONS

Select the best answer.

_____ 1. The overall general organizational pattern that the authors use to explain what students need to do to build toward a career is

       a. classification.

       b. order of importance.

       c. process.

       d. comparison and contrast.

_____ 2. An example of a transition for this overall pattern in paragraphs 3–6 is
   a. As you analyze.
   b. for example.
   c. If you're having difficulty.
   d. next.

D.   REVIEWING AND ORGANIZING IDEAS: SUMMARIZING

Complete the following summary of paragraphs 8–11 by filling in the missing words or phrases.

Before you graduate from _____ and while you are looking for a

_____, there are _____ steps you can take to help

_____ recognize your value. First, prepare an employment

_____. It is a collection of documents that demonstrate your

ability to _____. Second, when looking for a permanent job, ac-

cept _____ jobs or internships. Third, polish and update your

_____.

E.   FIGURING OUT INFERRED MEANINGS

Indicate whether each statement is probably true (T) or probably false (F) based on information contained in the reading.

_____ 1. Friends or relatives are capable of assessing your personal characteristics.

_____ 2. Tests offered by the college placement office are unfair and often misused.

_____ 3. A student who prefers physical tasks probably would not be happy as a stock market analyst.

_____ 4. Volunteer work can help you learn what is involved in a particular job.

_____ 5. Speaking a second language is probably not a career asset.

_____ 6. If you are proud that you learned to drive a race car, then you should include awards that you have won in your employment portfolio in preparation for a job in accounting.

_____ 7. While searching for a full-time job, you should consider taking a part time-job.

_____ 8. If a student likes regular, predictable hours, he or she might be happy with a career in nursing.

➤ **F.   THINKING CRITICALLY**

Select the best answer.

_____ 1. The tone of the reading can best be described as

     a. encouraging.   c. biased.

     b. anxious.   d. eager.

_____ 2. Of the following statements based on the reading, the only one that is a *fact* is

     a. your values are your most important asset.

     b. making a list of achievements is one way to discover your values and skills.

     c. advance job preparation is always a good idea for everyone.

     d. job location is more important than the job itself.

_____ 3. Another accurate and descriptive title for the entire reading would be

     a. The Workplace: A Changing Scene.

     b. Getting Back to Basics.

     c. Analyzing Your Talents.

     d. Advance Preparation for the Job Market.

_____ 4. The authors end the selection with a(n)

     a. summary statement.

     b. example of a student who followed his advice.

     c. look ahead to after you get your first career position.

     d. warning to be cautious in the workplace.

_____ 5. The authors ask numerous questions throughout the reading primarily to

     a. encourage readers to analyze their skills and values.

     b. give themselves an opportunity to provide answers.

     c. help readers stay focused on the subject.

     d. avoid sounding too authoritative.

➤ **G.   BUILDING VOCABULARY**

➤ **Context**

Using context and a dictionary, if necessary, determine the meaning of each word as it is used in the selection.

_____ 1. alumni (paragraph 7)

     a. organization of professors

     b. graduates or former students

     c. students' rights group

     d. group of high achieving students

_____ 2. suffice (paragraph 7)

     a. be enough

     b. be expensive

     c. be beneficial

     d. be productive

_____ 3. hierarchy (paragraph 7)

     a. group ranked by authority

     b. group with equal power

     c. group without a mission

     d. group to replace another group

_____ 4. tangible (paragraph 9)

     a. replaceable

     b. reachable

     c. portable

     d. touchable

_____ 5. interim (paragraph 10)

     a. convenient

     b. important

     c. temporary

     d. instructive

➤ Word Parts

> ### A REVIEW OF PREFIXES AND ROOTS
> **EXTRA-** means *out of*
> **VIS** means *see*

Use your knowledge of word parts and the review above to fill in the blanks in the following sentences.

1. *Extracurricular* activities (paragraph 4) occur _____ the regular school curriculum.

2. If you can *envision* (paragraph 7) the office you would like to work in, you can see or form a mental _____ of it.

➤ Unusual Words/Understanding Idioms

Use the meanings given below to write a sentence using the boldface word or phrase.

1. **Vice versa** (paragraph 2) means the other way around.

   Your sentence: _____

   _____.

2. A **born leader** (paragraph 5) is someone who naturally possesses many of the qualities of an effective leader.

   Your sentence: _____

   _____.

➤ H. SELECTING A LEARNING/STUDY STRATEGY

Select the best answer.

_____ What would be the best way to remember all the tips described in this selection?

   a. Visualize each piece of advice.

   b. Remember the individual pieces by grouping them into more general, broader categories.

   c. Make a chart listing ideas you agree and disagree with.

   d. Write an essay summarizing what you have already decided about your career.

➤ I. EXPLORING IDEAS THROUGH DISCUSSION AND WRITING

1. Discuss whether any of the ideas in this article were new or surprised you.

2. Explain the ways in which you have already worked toward attaining your career goals.

3. Evaluate how useful this advice is as you work toward your career.

➤ J. BEYOND THE CLASSROOM TO THE WEB

Explore a career of interest to you on the Web. You can start by selecting the "Careers" section of a browser or search engine or by typing in a keyword search. Visit several sites that explain how to prepare for or what to expect in a particular career. Then write a paragraph that describes what you learned.

✔ Tracking Your Progress

Selection 34

Section	Number Correct	Score
A. Thesis and Main Ideas (5 items)	_____ x 4	_____
B. Details (5 items)	_____ x 4	_____
C. Organization and Transitions (2 items)	_____ x 2	_____
E. Inferred Meanings (8 items)	_____ x 3	_____
F. Thinking Critically (5 items)	_____ x 3	_____
G. Vocabulary		
1. Context (5 items)	_____ x 3	_____
2. Word Parts (2 items)	_____ x 1	_____
TOTAL SCORE	_____%	

SELECTION 35

Rx for Anger at Work

Kathy Simmons

This reading appears on *Career Magazine*'s Web site. Read it to discover how anger works and how to control it.

> ### PREVIEWING THE READING

Using the steps listed on page 29, preview the reading selection. When you have finished, complete the following items.

1. The selection is about _____.

2. List three questions you should be able to answer after reading the article:

   a. _____

   b. _____

   c. _____

 ### MAKING CONNECTIONS

Have you ever gotten angry at work? Who or what provoked your anger? How did you express your anger?

> ### READING TIP

This selection includes the work of several experts on the subject of anger. Keep track of who said what, and in what context (for example, three books are mentioned, and all three have a slightly different focus).

Rx for Anger at Work

Rx
the abbreviation
for prescription

1   A fable is told about a young lion and a cougar. The animals arrived at their usual water hole at the same time. They were both very thirsty, and immediately began to argue about who should take the first drink. The argument escalated rapidly. As they stubbornly clung to their anger, it quickly turned to rage. Their vicious attacks on each other were suddenly interrupted when they both looked up. Circling overhead was a flock of vultures waiting for the loser to fall. Quietly, the two beasts turned and walked away. The thought of being devoured was all they needed to end their quarrel.

2   Have you ever lost your cool at work? Warning: Seeing red too often might lead to seeing pink: the **pink slip**, that is. The workplace can be a regular breeding ground for anger, considering the amount of time we are around people of different value systems, deadlines, competitive co-workers, gossip and misunderstandings. The ugly consequences of mishandled anger include such "vultures" as lost credibility, damaged relationships, and stress.

pink slip
a notice of termination of employment

3   A solid understanding of anger is a giant leap toward mastering this "most misunderstood emotion." You can strengthen your anger IQ with the following information.

What Makes Us Angry at Work?

4   According to Dr. Hendrie Weisinger, author of *The Anger Work-Out Book,* there are five work situations that provoke anger.

5   **Being left out.** Not being accepted by your peers provokes anger for two reasons: 1) It severely limits how effective you can be on the job, and 2) It shakes your fundamental need for acceptance and a sense of belonging.

6   **The critical boss.** Nit-picking bosses are infuriating. To add insult to injury, you are severely restricted in how much anger you can express toward him or her. Weisinger comments, "We tend to get back at our boss by taking a passive-aggressive stance. We do everything the job dictates, but not one iota more." This often makes the boss even more critical, and the vicious cycle continues.

7   **Not getting the promotion you deserve.** You bust your butt and it's not acknowledged. Who wouldn't feel cheated? Most people handle this perceived injustice poorly by becoming negative—and angry—**martyrs**.

martyr
one who endures great suffering for the sake of a belief or principle, or one who makes a show of suffering in order to gain sympathy

8   **Being maligned by co-workers.** Dr. Weisinger points out that "being victimized by false rumors is a consistent anger arouser. It is abusive and unjust. And the rumors frequently cause irrevocable damage."

9   **Dealing with an incompetent boss.** Everyone has an innate need to admire their leader and follow their direction confidently and cheerfully. An incompetent boss can stifle your enthusiasm, and bring down the effectiveness of your organization.

Is There Such a Thing as Bad Anger?

10   Dr. Paul Meier, M.D., author of *Don't Let Jerks Get the Best of You,* offers three main causes of illegitimate anger: selfishness, perfectionism, and paranoia.

11   Selfishness carries the unrealistic expectation that people should never disagree with you, get to go first, or receive more recognition than you. You expect too much, and inevitably end up angry.

12   Perfectionists also have a difficult time with anger. According to Meier, "Some of the angriest people I know are perfectionists." When perfectionism rules your life, the person you are hardest on is yourself. Expecting flawless results causes continual anger, which accelerates as the same unrealistic demands are imposed on those with whom you work.

13   Paranoid people misinterpret situations—a glance from the boss or a co-worker passing by without saying hello, for instance. Too much energy is spent on insignificant and meaningless trivia, which can lead to a high anger level.

How Can You Avoid Feeling Out of Control When Angry?

Accept the Anger

14   Susanna McMahon, Ph.D., author of *The Portable Therapist,* points to the importance of acknowledging angry feelings. "Give yourself permission to feel angry. You do not always know when and why and how you will feel angry. Sometimes you may feel angry without knowing why. And sometimes, when you would expect to feel angry, you do not."

15   McMahon explains that anger lives inside of you along with your other feelings. Accepting anger does not mean you express it. You can control what you choose to do when you are angry. The reality is that most of us are afraid of what we might do when we are angry. As a result, we deny rage until it finally explodes into destructive behavior. You can be sure this will affect your career success.

16   A study by the Center of Creative Leadership indicates the primary reason executives were fired or forced to retire was their inability to handle anger—especially under pressure. Accepting the angry feeling as it occurs means that we do not accumulate the feelings until they become rage.

Acknowledge Your Choices

17   Don't repeat helpless statements like "I can't do anything about it." *The Anger Work-Out Book* encourages readers to keep one fact in mind: When angry, you must acknowledge that you want to keep your job. However **cathartic** it might be to "tell someone off," the more rational choice is to avoid doing permanent damage to your career.

cathartic producing emotional release

18   Weisinger explains, "This allows you to get angry and yet keep things in perspective as coming with the territory. 'I don't like it, but I will learn to deal with it' is much more productive than 'Nothing I can do about it, it's not that bad.' The latter statement denies the anger where the former is task oriented. You can then move on to workable solutions, in other words considering the fact I am angry, but I also want to keep my job, what is the best way to handle the situation?"

19   Your focus should be on keeping your job, *and* refusing to let unconstructive anger derail your career success. In the words of Roman philosopher Seneca, "The greatest cure of anger is delay."

Cool Your Anger with Humor

20   Steven Sultanoff, Ph.D., licensed psychologist and president of The American Association for Therapeutic Humor explains, "Anger and the experience of humor cannot occupy the same psychological space." Can you recall a situation when you were really angry with someone, and they spontaneously did something to make you laugh? In that moment you probably had a split second of disappointment—you wanted to be angry!

21   Sultanoff explains, "When we experience humor, distressing emotions like anger disappear. When we are angry, if we can look to our funny bone we will experience some relief." The root cause of anger at work is a belief that everything should be fair. Laughing at the "unfairness" will help you gain perspective and dissipate your anger.

Practice Forgiveness

22   When you are mistreated at work, the last thing you want to do is practice forgiveness. While it may be absolutely true that the offender does not deserve your kindness, remember this: *You do!*

23   By forgiving abusive jerks, you are actually giving yourself a break.

24   It has been said that recovering from wounds makes us extremely powerful. With this in mind, can you look at others' assaults against you that way? Rather than wallowing in despair and focusing on the inequity of the situation, can you view those painful wounds as growth opportunities?

25   Anger is a natural part of being human, but success-minded people have a healthy respect for—and control of—this emotion. By raising your awareness of what provokes your anger, and determining ways to handle it well, you can see clearly—even when you see red!

Ways to Deal with Your Anger

26   1. *Physically*. Get a tennis racquet and hit a pillow. Work out. Break something. I once broke all the dishes in my cabinet. It was a mess, but I felt good.

27   2. *Mentally*. Talk out your anger, with a confidante or with yourself. Ask yourself, "How is holding on to this anger serving me? Do I want to stay in this state?"

28   3. *Emotionally*. Underneath anger is pain, and underneath pain are tears. Have a good cry.

29   4. *Spiritually*. Seek guidance from a higher power. If you believe in God, pray for help. Ask that your anger be lifted, or imagine that your anger is like a lump of dough that you heave out into space. See your anger as something outside of you. Ask God to take it from you. (From: *Since Strangling Isn't an Option* by Sandra A. Crowe, M.A.)

A.   UNDERSTANDING THE THESIS AND OTHER MAIN IDEAS

Select the best answer.

_____   1. The central thesis of the selection is that

    a. employees who lose their temper at work often end up being fired.

    b. certain work situations can provoke anger that is justified.

    c. most anger in the workplace is based on misunderstandings that are easily resolved with proper communication.

    d. mishandled anger in the workplace can have serious consequences and workers can learn to manage their anger.

_____   2. The author's primary purpose is to

    a. describe anger in the workplace and how to cope with it.

    b. compare various strategies for coping with disappointment at work.

    c. report on the best types of therapy for anger management.

    d. urge people who feel mistreated at work to express their emotions.

_____ 3. The topic of paragraph 12 is

    a. Paul Meier.

    b. illegitimate anger.

    c. perfectionism.

    d. paranoia.

_____ 4. The main idea of paragraph 15 is that

    a. angry feelings do not have to be expressed.

    b. most people are afraid of their anger.

    c. destructive behavior can ruin your career.

    d. denying rage is better than expressing it.

_____ 5. The method promoted by Steven Sultanoff in paragraphs 20 and 21 to deal with anger is

    a. delay.

    b. denial.

    c. humor.

    d. acceptance.

B. IDENTIFYING DETAILS

Indicate whether each statement is true (T) or false (F).

_____ 1. Kathy Simmons wrote _The Anger Work-Out Book._

_____ 2. According to Dr. Hendrie Weisinger, not being accepted by peers at work severely limits a person's effectiveness.

_____ 3. The two main causes of illegitimate anger identified by Dr. Paul Meier are false rumors and an incompetent boss.

_____ 4. The author of _The Portable Therapist_ emphasizes the importance of acknowledging angry feelings.

_____ 5. A study by the Center of Creative Leadership indicated that the primary reason executives were fired was their inability to adapt to the stress of new technology.

C. RECOGNIZING METHODS OF ORGANIZATION AND TRANSITIONS

Select the best answer.

_____ 1. In paragraph 2, the organizational pattern the author uses to describe the consequences of mishandled anger at work is

    a. time sequence.   c. problem and solution.

    b. cause and effect.   d. definition.

——— 2. In paragraphs 4–9, the organizational pattern the author uses to describe the five anger-provoking work situations identified by Dr. Weisinger is

    a. time sequence.

    b. definition.

    c. enumeration.

    d. comparison and contrast.

D. REVIEWING AND ORGANIZING IDEAS: OUTLINING

Complete the following outline of the selection by filling in the missing words and phrases.

I. What Makes Us Angry at Work?

    A. Hendrie Weisinger—*The Anger Work-Out Book*

    B. _____

        1. Being left out by your peers

        2. _____

        3. Not getting the _____ you deserve

        4. _____

        5. Dealing with the _____

II. Is There Such a Thing as Bad Anger?

    A. _____—*Don't Let Jerks Get the Best of You*

    B. Main causes of _____

        1. Selfishness

        2. _____

        3. Paranoia

III. How Can You Avoid Feeling Out of Control When Angry?

    A. Accept the anger

        1. Susanna McMahon—_____

B. Acknowledge your choices

    1. *The Anger Work-Out Book*

C. _____

    1. Steven Sultanoff—The American Association for Therapeutic Humor

D. Practice forgiveness

➤ E. FIGURING OUT INFERRED MEANINGS

Indicate whether each statement is true (T) or false (F).

_____ 1. When the author refers to "your anger IQ," she means your understanding of what anger is.

_____ 2. It can be inferred that *The Anger Work-Out Book* is primarily a book about exercising and working out.

_____ 3. Taking a passive-aggressive stance is an effective way to express anger toward one's co-workers.

_____ 4. A lack of respect for one's boss can affect the success of the entire organization.

_____ 5. Perfectionists set impossible standards for themselves and others.

_____ 6. Humor can help people deal with other distressing emotions in addition to anger.

➤ F. THINKING CRITICALLY

Select the best answer.

_____ 1. The central thesis of "Rx for Anger at Work" is supported primarily by
    a. the personal experience of the author.
    b. statistics from the Center of Creative Leadership.
    c. interviews with employees.
    d. evidence from authorities on anger.

_____ 2. The author begins with a fable in order to
    a. show that many work situations can be described in fable form.
    b. illustrate her point about the consequences of anger at work.
    c. introduce the idea that co-workers can be like vultures.
    d. appeal to very young readers.

_____ 3. The tone of the selection can best be described as

    a. humorous.

    b. encouraging.

    c. anxious.

    d. angry.

_____ 4. The author chose the title in order to

    a. advocate the use of prescription medication to cope with anger at work.

    b. imply that the "ingredients" for anger are in the workplace.

    c. indicate that the selection offers remedies or treatments for anger at work.

    d. suggest that society's reliance on prescription medication is one of the causes of anger in the workplace.

_____ 5. The quote by Seneca (paragraph 19) means that

    a. anger becomes even more intense with the passage of time.

    b. letting time pass is the best way to get over anger.

    c. the best way to make people angry is to make them wait.

    d. it is impossible to hold people back from expressing their anger.

G. BUILDING VOCABULARY

Context

Using context and a dictionary, if necessary, determine the meaning of each word as it is used in the selection.

_____ 1. escalated (paragraph 1)

    a. provoked   c. avoided

    b. intensified   d. improved

_____ 2. fundamental (paragraph 5)

    a. basic   c. creative

    b. hidden   d. purposeful

_____ 3. infuriating (paragraph 6)

    a. harmful   c. maddening

    b. uncertain   d. humorous

_____ 4. accelerates (paragraph 12)

    a. improves   c. threatens

    b. increases   d. deflates

_____ 5. derail (paragraph 19)

    a. promote

    b. speed up

    c. cause questions

    d. go off course

_____ 6. dissipate (paragraph 21)

    a. dissolve

    b. spread

    c. encourage

    d. replace

_____ 7. wallowing (paragraph 24)

    a. wondering

    b. indulging

    c. recovering

    d. planning

➤ **Word Parts**

A REVIEW OF PREFIXES THAT MEAN _NOT_
IL-
IN-
IR-
UN-

For each word in Column A, write the correct prefix (il-, in-, ir-, or un-) in the blank before the word. Then select the new word's meaning from Column B and write the letter in the space to the left of the number.

Column A	Column B
_____ 1. _____ justice	a. not according to rules or laws
_____ 2. _____ revocable	b. not qualified or effective
_____ 3. _____ competent	c. impossible to undo or take back
_____ 4. _____ legitimate	d. lack of fair treatment
_____ 5. _____ realistic	e. not important or meaningful
_____ 6. _____ evitable	f. lack of fairness
_____ 7. _____ significant	g. not reasonable or practical
_____ 8. _____ equity	h. impossible to avoid or prevent

➤ **Unusual Words/Understanding Idioms**
Use the meanings below to write a sentence using the boldface word or phrase.

1. To **lose your cool** (paragraph 2) is to lose your composure or self-control, in other words, to become angry.

   Your sentence: _____

   _____.

2. Red is a color associated with rage, so when someone is **seeing red** (paragraph 2), that person has become angry.

   Your sentence: _____

   _____.

3. A **nit-picking** person (paragraph 6) doesn't literally pick nits, which are the tiny eggs of lice; the person figuratively "picks nits" by focusing on minor or trivial details, usually in order to criticize.

   Your sentence: _____

   _____.

4. When you **bust your butt** (paragraph 7) for someone or something, you put forth a lot of effort, or work very hard.

   Your sentence: _____

   _____.

5. The **funny bone** (paragraph 21) in this case is not an actual bone, but an expression that means a sense of humor.

   Your sentence: _____

   _____.

➤ **H.   SELECTING A LEARNING/STUDY STRATEGY**

Discuss methods of studying the outline shown on page 578 in preparation for an exam that covers this reading.

➤ **I.   EXPLORING IDEAS THROUGH DISCUSSION AND WRITING**

1. Anger management is a timely topic in today's world, especially in light of the number of crimes committed in recent years by enraged employees at the workplace. Describe a situation in which you have observed anger expressed at work.

2. Discuss the author's tone. Does the author's language reveal her attitude toward the subject?

3. What does the author mean when she says, "By forgiving abusive jerks, you are actually giving yourself a break" (paragraph 23)?

➤ J.   BEYOND THE CLASSROOM TO THE WEB

Visit ITworld.com at **http://www.itworld.com/ITW0305joch/.**
    Read the article "Defuse Workplace Anger." What factors does this article list as being the most likely causes of workplace anger?

✔ Tracking Your Progress

Selection 35

Section	Number Correct		Score
A. Thesis and Main Ideas (5 items)	————	x 4	————
B. Details (5 items)	————	x 3	————
C. Organization and Transitions (2 items)	————	x 1	————
E. Inferred Meanings (6 items)	————	x 3	————
F. Thinking Critically (5 items)	————	x 3	————
G. Vocabulary			
1. Context (7 items)	————	x 2	————
2. Word Parts (8 items)	————	x 2	————
	TOTAL SCORE		———— %

SELECTION 36

The Sandman Is Dead—Long Live the Sleep Deprived Walking Zombie

Dorrit T. Walsh

This reading appears on HR Plaza, a Web site for professionals in the human resources (recruiting and managing employees) field. Read it to find out if you are getting enough sleep and the effects of sleep deprivation.

PREVIEWING THE READING

Using the steps listed on page 29, preview the reading selection. When you have finished, complete the following items.

1. The topic of this selection is _____.

2. List four questions you should be able to answer after reading the selection:

   a. _____

   b. _____

   c. _____

   d. _____

MAKING CONNECTIONS

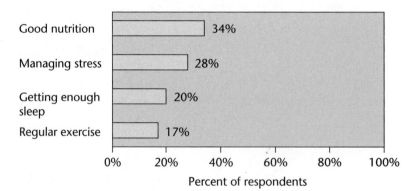

MOST IMPORTANT FACTORS IN MAINTAINING HEALTH

Good nutrition	34%
Managing stress	28%
Getting enough sleep	20%
Regular exercise	17%

Percent of respondents

This graph is part of the results of the National Sleep Foundation's 2000 survey of Americans and sleep. It shows what factors U.S. adults consider most important in maintaining good health. How would you rank these four factors?

> **READING TIP**

This selection contains a lot of information about the effects of sleeplessness on individuals and on businesses. Highlight or write a list of these effects as you read.

Sleep Deprived Walking Zombie

1   Back in 1954, the Chordettes had a number one hit singing the praises of "Mr. Sandman," but today he's dead. It was a slow death; gradually, over a few decades, Americans killed him. Farewell sweet dreams and golden slumbers—we've entered into the age of waking up tired. Don't assume it's not you, either. Here's a quick quiz: do you get less than eight hours of sleep a night? Fall asleep almost as soon as your head hits the pillow? Need an alarm clock to wake up? And sometimes that doesn't even work? A "yes" to any of those questions means you're probably one of the chronically sleep deprived.

2   Before I continue, let me clarify why an article on lack of sleep is on a business Website. After all, not getting enough sleep is a personal problem, right? Wrong. While it is up to the individual to control his or her sleeping habits, unfortunately, for various reasons that I'll discuss in this article, today more than 100 million Americans are sleep deprived. And this lack of sleep has a direct and substantial effect on American businesses. In 1990 the National Commission on Sleep Disorders put the direct costs of sleep loss at $15.9 billion, and the indirect costs, such as higher stress and diminished productivity, clocked in at $150 billion. One hundred and fifty billion dollars is way more than a "personal problem."

The Basics: Why Sleep Is Important

3   Before going into the facts about why Americans aren't getting enough sleep, or the problems sleep deprivation causes, the first logical step is a brief explanation of exactly why sleep is so important to humans.

4   Contrary to popular belief, sleep isn't just a wasteful state of inertness. In fact, your brain when it's "sleeping" is often more active than when you're awake—**neural** activity drops by about only 10 percent when we're asleep. Sleeping consists of five cycles, one through four and REM sleep, so depending on how long you sleep at night you may experience anywhere from three to five cycles. The most significant stages are Stage 4, the deepest phase of sleep, and REM or Rapid Eye Movement Sleep. Stage 4 plays a major part in maintenance of our general health, including our natural **immune system**. REM sleep is when we dream, but more importantly, it's the key player in maintaining the various aspects of memory. It also has a lot to do with how we're able to learn new things and general mental performance.

neural
related to the body's nervous system

immune system
the system of organs, tissues, cells, and cell products that works as the body's defense against infections and disease

5   Sleep restores and rejuvenates us, and affects everything from our creativity and communication skills to reaction times and energy levels.

How Much Sleep Do We Need? How Much Are We Getting?

6   The simple answer to this question is: more than we're getting. According to Dr. James B. Maas, Cornell University professor and author of the book *Power Sleep*,

the optimal amount of sleep we should be getting nightly is ten hours. Although ten hours of sleep per night may seem high by today's standards, it actually used to be the standard in this country. Before the invention of the electric light in 1879, most people slept ten hours per night. In fact, Einstein said that he could only function well if he had a full ten hours of sleep every night.

7   Since the late 1800s we've gradually cut back the time we sleep each night by a full 20 percent, to eight hours. However, even with a "standard" at two hours less than optimal, according to the National Sleep Foundation's "1998 Omnibus Sleep in America" poll, most Americans now average seven hours (actually only six hours and fifty-seven minutes) of sleep per night during the work week, or 30 percent less than the ideal. Nearly 32 percent only get six hours of sleep during the work week.

8   As far as why we're getting less sleep, there's no one single answer. Part of it's due to increased workloads (since 1977 Americans have added 158 hours annually to our working/commuting time), and then there's the stress that comes from the increased workloads. Or the fact that many people today, especially a number of "motivational speakers," downplay the need for sleep, so we don't want to be perceived as lazy. Or it could be what's on TV, or the book we just "have" to read, or the kids, or whatever.

Effects of Sleeplessness

9   Because many adults have never gotten sufficient sleep, or have gotten so used to getting by on less sleep than they need, many of the effects often go unnoticed. They don't realize that if they got more sleep, they could be in a better mood, be more productive, more creative, and think more clearly.

10   However, there are far reaching, quantifiable consequences that result from not getting enough sleep. Some of the most significant are:

- Thirty-one percent of all drivers say they've fallen asleep at the wheel at least once.
- Accidents resulting from falling asleep at the wheel cost Americans more than $30 billion each year.
- The National Transportation Safety Board cited fatigue as the number one factor detrimentally affecting airline pilots.
- Shiftworkers are particularly affected by lack of sleep. Fifty-six percent of them say they fall asleep on the job at least once a week.
- According to the *Wall Street Journal,* $70 billion is lost annually in productivity, health costs and accidents, a direct result of shiftworkers' not being able to adjust to late-night schedules.
- Forty percent of adults say that they're so sleepy during the day that it interferes with their daily activities, including work (remember, these are only the people who acknowledge or realize that their productivity is lessened).
- Research done at Leicestershire, England's Sleep Research Center found that not getting enough sleep has noticeable negative effects on our ability to understand situations that change rapidly. They found sleep deprivation also made us more likely to be distracted, makes us think less flexibly, and hampers our ability to solve problems innovatively.

- Studies at Loughborough University have shown a direct connection between our abilities to remember and concentrate, and sleep deprivation.
- The U.S. National Highway Traffic Safety Administration has proven that there's a direct connection between hand-eye coordination (a necessity when you're driving) and lack of sleep.

11   And according to the National Sleep Foundation survey, an incredible one-third of American adults tested reached levels of sleepiness that are known to be dangerous.

What To Do?

12   Again, there's no one simple answer to this question. Obviously people need more sleep. And one of the problems is that many people simply don't realize how important sleep is to us, or how serious the effects of sleep deprivation are. The National Sleep Foundation's "1998 Omnibus Sleep in America Poll" rated the sleep knowledge of 1,027 Americans, and it showed that Americans are generally ignorant when it comes to sleep and many sleep myths (e.g., that you need more sleep as you get older—you don't; sleep needs remain the same throughout adulthood).

13   Along with self education, employers could help both by providing the facts about sleep to employees and stressing how important an adequate amount of sleep is to everyday performance. Don't equate sleepiness with laziness; they're two totally different issues. Sleepy workers are more likely to cause accidents, make mistakes, and are more susceptible to heart attacks. Lazy workers, for whatever reason, just don't do their jobs.

14   One thing employers can do is give the okay to napping at work. This doesn't have to be the old kindergarten version with blankets on the floor; just closing the door and sitting in your chair with your eyes closed and trying to sleep for fifteen minutes will help to restore your energy. That's all you need, 15–30 minutes. Besides relieving stress, naps increase your ability to make important decisions and pay sufficient attention to details.

15   If you employ shift workers, realize that shift work simply isn't natural and humans cannot simply adapt to just any work cycle. Also, get more information on recommendations (the National Sleep Foundation Web site and/or the book *Power Sleep* are good places to start) on how to help arrange shift working schedules to help your employees stay alert and healthy.

16   It's time that Americans, both as individuals and businesses, start to acknowledge the vital importance sleep plays in our everyday lives and in our society. Although he wrote in the 1600s, Miguel de Cervantes may have described the importance of sleep best in *Don Quixote de la Mancha:*

17   "Now blessings light on him that first invented this same

sleep! It covers a man all over, thoughts and all, like a cloak;

'tis meat for the hungry, drink for the thirsty, heat for the cold,

and cold for the hot . . . and the balance that sets the kind and

the shepherd, the fool and the wise man even."*

*From *Bartlett's Familiar Quotations.* Little, Brown and Company.

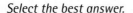

A.   UNDERSTANDING THE THESIS AND OTHER MAIN IDEAS

Select the best answer.

_____ 1. The central thesis of "The Sandman Is Dead" is that

a. sleep loss costs American businesses millions of dollars a year.

b. most people don't realize the importance of sleep.

c. Americans are not getting enough sleep.

d. sleep is essential to human health.

_____ 2. The author's primary purpose is to

a. compare sleep statistics in America with statistics in other countries.

b. educate people about the importance of sleep and the effects of sleeplessness.

c. entertain readers with humorous anecdotes about sleeplessness.

d. encourage employers to stress the importance of sleep to their employees.

Match each question in Column A with the paragraph listed in Column B that answers that question.

Column A	Column B
_____ 3. How much sleep do Americans average per night?	a. paragraph 4
_____ 4. What is the optimal amount of sleep per night?	b. paragraphs 4–5
_____ 5. What are the consequences of insufficient sleep?	c. paragraph 6
_____ 6. Why is sleep important to humans?	d. paragraph 7
_____ 7. What are the stages of sleep?	e. paragraph 10

B.   IDENTIFYING DETAILS

Select the best answer.

_____ 1. According to the National Commission on Sleep Disorders, the *indirect* costs of sleep loss to American businesses in 1990 equaled

a. $15.9 billion.

b. $30 billion.

c. $70 billion.

d. $150 billion.

_____ 2. The most significant stages of sleep are
   a. Stages 1 and 2.   c. Stages 3 and 4.
   b. Stages 2 and 3.   d. Stage 4 and REM sleep.

_____ 3. The selection links all of the following aspects of health to REM
         sleep *except*
   a. memory.   c. learning.
   b. immune system.   d. general mental performance.

_____ 4. According to the selection, the U.S. National Highway Traffic
         Safety Administration has proven that there is a direct connection
         between a lack of sleep and our
   a. ability to understand situations that change rapidly.
   b. hand-eye coordination.
   c. ability to solve problems innovatively.
   d. productivity at work.

_____ 5. According to the selection, employers could help reduce the effects
         of sleeplessness in all of the following ways *except*
   a. allowing 15–30 minute naps at work.
   b. emphasizing how important an adequate night's sleep is to
      everyday performance.
   c. informing employees that they need more sleep as they get older.
   d. arranging shift working schedules to help employees stay alert
      and healthy.

C.   RECOGNIZING METHODS OF ORGANIZATION AND TRANSITIONS

Select the best answer.

_____ 1. The overall organizational pattern used throughout this selection is
   a. comparison and contrast.
   b. cause and effect.
   c. definition.
   d. time sequence.

_____ 2. In paragraphs 12–16, the organizational pattern the author uses to
         offer suggestions of what to do about sleep deprivation is
   a. time sequence.
   b. definition.
   c. comparison and contrast.
   d. enumeration.

D.   REVIEWING AND ORGANIZING IDEAS: MAPPING

Fill in the blanks to complete the map of the quantifiable effects of sleeplessness described in paragraph 10 of the reading.

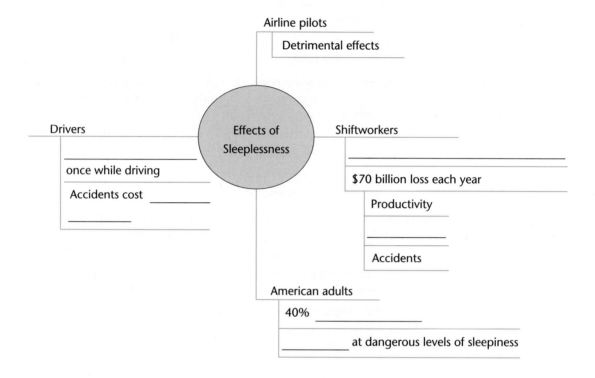

E.   FIGURING OUT INFERRED MEANINGS

Indicate whether each statement is true (T) or false (F).

_____ 1. It can be inferred that people who are sleep deprived have a more difficult time fighting infection.

_____ 2. The percentage of adults whose sleepiness interferes with their daily activities is probably much smaller than the number reported.

_____ 3. It can be inferred that sleep-deprived students have difficulty studying and learning.

_____ 4. It can be inferred that sleep needs for children are the same as those for adults.

> **F. THINKING CRITICALLY**

Select the best answer.

_____ 1. The title of the selection is intended to
   a. project a sense of horror about chronic sleeplessness in America.
   b. establish a tone of dread about the serious consequences of sleep deprivation.
   c. capture the reader's attention with a humorous reference to an old song and a horror movie.
   d. introduce the subject of myths.

_____ 2. The thesis of the selection is supported by
   a. statistics.
   b. appeals to authority.
   c. research evidence.
   d. all of the above.

_____ 3. The tone of the selection can best be described as
   a. informal but concerned.
   b. critical but objective.
   c. optimistic and humorous.
   d. alarmed and distressed.

_____ 4. Of the following statements from paragraphs 1 and 2, the only one that is an *opinion* is
   a. "In 1954, the Chordettes had a number one hit [called] 'Mr. Sandman.'"
   b. "It is up to the individual to control his or her sleeping habits."
   c. "Today more than 100 million Americans are sleep deprived."
   d. "One hundred and fifty billion dollars is way more than a 'personal problem.'"

_____ 5. The author puts quotation marks around the phrase "motivational speakers" (paragraph 8) in order to
   a. show respect for the title.
   b. indicate that motivational speakers are popular in today's culture.
   c. signify that this is one of many names for public speakers.
   d. point out that any speaker who discourages the need for sleep is not truly being motivational.

_____ 6. The statement that an "incredible one-third of American adults" have reached dangerous levels of sleepiness (paragraph 11) means that

    a. these adults are amazing because they are still able to work.

    b. this number represents a startlingly large fraction of the population.

    c. this number represents a reassuringly small fraction of the population.

    d. the survey did not include the other two-thirds of the population.

_____ 7. The author includes the quote by Miguel de Cervantes in order to

    a. end the selection with a thoughtful and historical perspective on the importance of sleep.

    b. point out that sleep is really a more light-hearted topic than the statistics seem to indicate.

    c. prove that sleep was much more important to people in the 1600s.

    d. appeal to Cervantes' authority as a writer.

G.   BUILDING VOCABULARY

Context

Using context and a dictionary, if necessary, determine the meaning of each word as it is used in the selection.

_____ 1. chronically (paragraph 1)

    a. temporarily

    b. undiagnosed

    c. continually

    d. suddenly

_____ 2. diminished (paragraph 2)

    a. insulted

    b. improved

    c. expected

    d. lessened

_____ 3. inertness (paragraph 4)

    a. animation

    b. similarity

    c. inactivity

    d. productivity

_____ 4. rejuvenates (paragraph 5)

    a. refreshes

    b. calms

    c. pleases

    d. entertains

_____ 5. optimal (paragraph 6)

    a. occasional

    b. likely

    c. standard

    d. ideal

_____ 6. detrimentally (paragraph 10)

    a. purposefully

    b. actively

    c. harmfully

    d. helpfully

_____ 7. susceptible (paragraph 13)

    a. vulnerable

    b. ignorant

    c. careless

    d. unhealthy

➤ Word Parts

> ### A REVIEW OF SUFFIXES
> **-ABLE** means *capable of*
> **-ANCE** means *state* or *condition*
> **-ITY** means *state* or *quality*

Use your knowledge of word parts and the review above to fill in the blanks in the following sentences.

1. Creativity is the state of being _____.

2. An automobile maintenance agreement specifies the
_____ in which the car is maintained.

3. If a heap of junk from the attic is quantifiable, then you are
_____ count the items and assign a value.

➤ **Unusual Words/Understanding Idioms**
Use the meanings given below to write a sentence using the boldface phrase.

1. The phrase **clocked in at** (paragraph 2) usually refers to the finish time of a race. (For example, "In the 50-yard dash, Jamal clocked in at 5:30 seconds.") In this case, it is used to show what the costs of sleep loss *amounted* to.

    Your sentence: _____

    _____.

2. The phrase **key player** (paragraph 4) can mean a person in a game who played an important role ("Gus was the key player in our baseball game last night"), or one who had an important role in a certain situation ("Maria was the key player in the real estate deal"). In this case, it is used to describe REM sleep as the most important *element* in the maintenance of memory.

    Your sentence: _____

    _____.

➤ **H.   SELECTING A LEARNING/STUDY STRATEGY**

Select the best answer.

_____   This reading contains numerous statistics about sleeplessness. The best way to learn these statistics for an upcoming multiple-choice exam would be to

a. map the entire reading.

b. reread the selection.

c. summarize the reading.

d. prepare a study sheet.

➤ **I.   EXPLORING IDEAS THROUGH DISCUSSION AND WRITING**

1. How did you do on the quiz in the first paragraph of the selection? Was the quiz successful in capturing your attention?

2. Have you ever experienced the effects of sleep deprivation? How do you think it affected your judgment? Your ability to learn? Your memory?

> **J. BEYOND THE CLASSROOM TO THE WEB**

Visit the 2008 Omnibus Sleep in America Poll Summary Findings at
http://www.sleepfoundation.org/site/c.hulXKjM0IxF/b.3933533/.
Study the tables in the Work and Sleep section of this survey report. What problems do workers report that stem from not getting enough sleep? Which of these problems are most widespread?

✔ Tracking Your Progress

Selection 36

Section	Number Correct		Score
A. Thesis and Main Ideas (7 items)	————	x 4	————
B. Details (5 items)	————	x 3	————
C. Organization and Transitions (2 items)	————	x 2	————
E. Inferred Meanings (4 items)	————	x 3	————
F. Thinking Critically (7 items)	————	x 3	————
G. Vocabulary			
1. Context (7 items)	————	x 2	————
2. Word Parts (3 items)	————	x 2	————
	TOTAL SCORE		————%

PART THREE

Textbook Chapter Reading

This part of the book contains a complete psychology textbook chapter. Questions are included for each major section of the chapter, but these sets of questions appear at the end of the entire chapter, not after each section.

To work through the chapter, first turn to Psychology Selection 1 and note which pages in the chapter it covers. Then read Previewing the Section, Making Connections, and the Reading Tip. After you complete these exercises, turn to the appropriate section of the psychology chapter and read the material. After you have finished reading, go to the After Reading exercises, begin with Understanding Main Ideas, and work through the remainder of the questions. Work through the other selections the same way.

Please note that the page numbers mentioned in the exercises refer to the page numbering of the textbook chapter itself, not to the pages of this book.

22   Psychology Textbook Chapter

22 Psychology Textbook Chapter

Chapter 9

Memory

From
PSYCHOLOGY

Lester A. Lefton
Linda Brannon

CHAPTER 9

Memory

Chapter 8 pointed out that learning is a relatively permanent change in an organism that occurs as a result of experience and is often, but not always, expressed in overt behavior. *Memory* is the ability to recall past events, images, ideas, or previously learned information or skills. Memory is also the storage system that allows a person to retain and retrieve previously learned information. Learning and memory are two facets of the process of acquiring information, storing it, and using it. The acquisition part is learning, and the storage and accessing of learned information comprise memory.

Memory ■ The ability to recall past events, images, ideas, or previously learned information or skills; the storage system that allows for retention and retrieval of previously learned information.

321

How Does the Memory Process Begin?

Traditionally, psychologists have considered memory as a type of storage and have sought to understand its structure and limits. Studies of memory at the beginning of the 20th century focused on factors related to how quickly people learned and forgot lists of nonsense words (Robinson-Riegler & Robinson-Riegler, 2004). Physiological psychologists sought to discover locations in the brain corresponding to the functions of memory. During the 1950s, research became more practical, focusing on variables such as how the organization of material affects retention. Today, research still focuses on understanding the complex processes of memory but also considers practical issues, including how people can code information and use memory aids, imagery, and other learning cues to retrieve information from memory more effectively. Researchers are also using brain-imaging techniques to pinpoint the specific areas in the brain that become more active when people are in the process of remembering.

The Brain as Information Processor

In this age of computers and information technology, it is not surprising that psychologists have likened the brain to a computer—an information processor. This analogy has influenced the study of memory since the 1960s and 1970s, when researchers began to recognize the brain's complex interconnections and information-processing abilities. Psychologists use the term *information processing* to refer to organizing, interpreting, and responding to information coming from the environment (Lachman, Lachman, & Butterfield, 1979). Of course, human brains are not computers—no computer has yet come close to the sophistication of the human brain. In addition, brains do not work exactly as computers do. Brains make mistakes, and they are influenced by biological, environmental, and interpersonal events. Computers complete some operations much faster than brains can, and they always get the same answer when they are given a problem repeatedly. Nevertheless, there are enough similarities between human brains and computers for psychologists to discuss perception, learning, and memory in terms of information processing.

The information-processing approach typically focuses on the flow of information, beginning with the sensory systems, where information from the outside world first impinges on the body. This approach describes and analyzes a sequence of stages for key memory processes and assumes that the stages and processes are related but separate. Although psychologists once considered memory a step-by-step, linear process, they now recognize that many of the steps take place simultaneously, in parallel (Rumelhart & McClelland, 1986).

Virtually every approach to understanding memory offered by researchers has proposed that memory involves three key processes. The names of these processes derive from information technology and will sound familiar to you if you know how computers work. The first process is *encoding*, the second is placement of information in some type of *storage* (either temporary or permanent), and the third is making the information available through *retrieval*. We'll use this three-process model to guide our exploration of memory.

Encoding

I (L.B.) tell my students to think of their memory as a filing cabinet, and I point out that how well a filing cabinet works depends on several factors. A filing cabinet can be very useful if you have a good system of organization so that when you put papers away, you will know how to retrieve them. You need folders and a system of labels that will allow you to find each folder in the cabinet. If you put papers in a folder and file it away in the cabinet without labeling it, your filing cabinet will be useful as a place to move folders off your desk, but little more. Labeling, or coding, the folders is critical.

The conversion of sensory stimuli into neural impulses is a type of coding, the first step of establishing a memory. *Encoding* is the organizing of sensory information so that the nervous system can process it, much as a computer programmer devises code that a computer can understand. The sensory information can be of any type: visual, auditory, olfactory, and so on. The type and extent of encoding affect what we remember. Encoding is not a discrete step that happens all at once. Rather, some levels of encoding happen quickly and easily, whereas others take longer and are more complex. Your brain may continue to encode information while storing previously encoded information.

Attention is important for encoding (Brown & Craik, 2000; Craik, 2002). In general, *attention* refers to the process of directing mental focus to some features of the environment and not to others. People can focus their attention on one idea, one event, one person, or one memory task, or they can shift their attention among several tasks or events. Dividing one's attention during encoding interferes with the process, and people who are forced to divide their attention during encoding tend to perform more poorly during retrieval—they experience a type of memory problem known as *encoding failure*. Such failures are very common, because many stimuli compete for a person's attention.

Encoding ■ The organizing of sensory information so that the nervous system can process it.

Levels of Processing

Does the human brain encode and process different kinds of information in different ways? Do thinking processes depend on different types of analysis? Researchers Fergus Craik and Robert Lockhart (1972) argued that the brain encodes and processes stimuli (information) in different ways, to different extents, and at different levels. They called their theory the *levels-of-processing approach*. According to this view of encoding, how information is processed determines how it will be stored for later retrieval.

Cognitive psychologists equate the level of processing with the depth of analysis involved. When the level of processing becomes more complex, they theorize, the code goes deeper into memory.

The levels-of-processing approach has generated an enormous amount of research (Craik, 2002). It explains why you retain some information, such as your family history, for long periods, whereas you quickly forget other information, such as the dry cleaner's phone number. It shows that when people are asked to encode information in only one way, they do not encode it in other ways. However, the levels-of-processing approach focuses on encoding and largely

Levels-of-processing approach ■ Theory of memory that suggests that the brain encodes and processes stimuli (information) in different ways, to different extents, and at different levels.

Transfer-appropriate processing ■ Processing of information that is similar for both encoding and retrieval of the information.

ignores retrieval, which led to the development of alternative views of how information is processed.

One variation is the idea of *transfer-appropriate processing*, which occurs when the processing for encoding of information is similar to the process for retrieval of the information. When there is a close relationship between the form of the information encoded (whether it is visual, auditory, or in some other form) and the processing required to retrieve it, retrieval improves. For example, when researchers give participants instructions to encode words for sound and then ask participants to recall the meaning of the words, performance is worse than when participants are asked to code for sound and to recall sound (Franks et al., 2000; Morris, Bransford, & Franks, 1977; Rajaram, Srinivas, & Roediger, 1998).

Other researchers also questioned the levels-of-processing approach, suggesting that differences in recall originate from how memories are elaborated on, or made distinctive. The *encoding specificity principle* explains the link between encoding and retrieval by stating that the effectiveness of a specific cue for retrieving information depends on how well it matches up with the originally encoded information (Tulving & Thompson 1973). The more sharply such cues are defined and the more closely they are paired with memory stores, the better your recall will be and the less likely you will be to experience retrieval failures. For example, my (L.B.'s) students sometimes fail to recognize me when they meet me in the grocery store or at the movies, but they always recognize me on campus. On campus, the circumstances in which we meet match those in which they first knew me, but off campus, the circumstances are different. Thus, some of them experience retrieval difficulties because of the type of encoding they have done.

Encoding specificity principle ■ The principle that the effectiveness of a specific retrieval cue depends on how well it matches up with the originally encoded information.

The research on the levels-of-processing approach and its subsequent refinements and extensions have influenced the study of memory by emphasizing the importance of encoding. Researchers are aware that the encoding process is flexible. This process is affected by both the cues provided and the demands of the retrieval tasks, as well as by people's preconceived biases. Humans tend to notice and encode information that confirms beliefs they already hold—a tendency called *confirmation bias* (Jonas et al., 2001). This tendency to "see what you expect to see" is a powerful force in allowing people to retain inaccurate beliefs.

Neuroscience and Encoding

Memories are retained because they take some form in the brain. Many researchers are using brain-imaging techniques to explore the neurobiological bases of memory. Positron emission tomography (PET) and functional magnetic resonance imaging (fMRI) (described in Chapter 3) have allowed researchers to examine the brain during the process of encoding.

A general rule about brain functioning is that structures toward the top of the brain tend to control functions that are more complex and abstract. This principle has led researchers to concentrate on the cerebral cortex in their efforts to understand memory. Specifically, researchers have directed their attention to the prefrontal lobes with their overlying cortex—the large areas on the left and right at the top front of the brain, behind the forehead.

In the view of Endel Tulving and his colleagues, the left prefrontal cortex is used more in the encoding of new information into memory, whereas the right prefrontal cortex is involved more in memory retrieval (Habib, Nyberg, & Tulving, 2003; Nyberg, Cabeza, & Tulving, 1996). Research using PET and fMRI imaging shows that when participants engage in various tasks, brain scans of the left and right hemispheres are quite different—that is, patterns of blood flow differ in different portions of the prefrontal cortex. These differences are generally consistent with Tulving's view—the left prefrontal cortex is more active when people encode information, especially meaningful verbal information (Otten, Henson, & Rugg, 2002). The left prefrontal cortex is also more active during encoding of information that is later recalled correctly than during encoding of information that is not recalled correctly (Casino et al., 2002; Reynolds et al., 2004).

Researchers have long known that the temporal lobes of the cerebral cortex are related to memory (Squire & Kandel, 1999), and brain-imaging studies have furnished more specific knowledge of how the temporal lobes interact with other brain structures. (**Figure 9.1** shows several of the brain structures that are important to memory.) An fMRI study demonstrated that the anterior (front) part of the medial (middle) temporal lobes is activated during the process of successfully encoding information in memory (Jackson & Schacter, 2004). This type of association is critical for learning associations, for example, between a name and a face or a car and a parking space. Indeed, the medial temporal lobes may be important for encoding information about setting and context (Davachi, Mitchell, & Wagner, 2003).

One study that used PET scanning of the brain during encoding showed that more of the brain was activated when people encode fact-based information than when they merely listened to sentences (Maguire & Frith, 2004). The areas of greater activation included several regions of the prefrontal cortex, part of the thalamus, and the temporal cortex. Reasonably enough, your brain works harder when

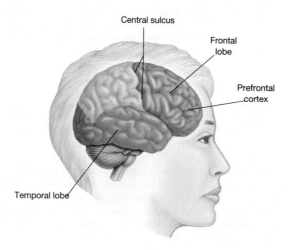

Central sulcus

Frontal lobe

Prefrontal cortex

Temporal lobe

Figure 9.1
Areas of the Brain Involved in Encoding
The prefrontal cortex and the temporal lobes are involved in the process of encoding.

you are encoding information than when you are listening passively. Just as the levels-of-processing approach predicts, people's brains are activated in different ways when they process information on a superficial level than when they process it on a deeper level (Weiser & Weiser, 2003).

Learners encode information to store it. If they do a good job of encoding, then they will be able to retrieve the information from storage. Thus, encoding is the first step in the flow of information through the memory system. Storage is the next step.

What Are the Types of Memory Storage?

If you think of memory as a filing cabinet, its storage capacity consists of the drawers of the cabinet. Once a folder is created and labeled, it is filed away in a drawer. *Storage* is the process of maintaining or keeping information readily available. It also refers to the locations where information is held, which researchers call memory stores. The duration of storage may be a few seconds or many years, but whenever people have access to information they no longer sense, memory is involved. For example, if you look up a telephone number, go to the telephone, and dial the number while no longer looking at it, then memory is involved, even if only for seconds.

Researchers have conceptualized a three-stage model for memory storage: (1) sensory memory, (2) short-term storage, and (3) long-term memory. Each type of storage has different characteristics and limits.

Storage ■ The process of maintaining or keeping information readily available, as well as the locations where information is held, also known as *memory stores.*

Sensory Memory

Sensory memory ■ The mechanism that performs initial encoding of sensory stimuli and provides brief storage of them; also known as the *sensory register.*

Sensory memory, sometimes called the *sensory register*, is the mechanism that performs initial encoding of sensory stimuli and provides brief storage of them. When you hear a song, see a photograph, or touch a piece of silk, sensory memory starts. This very brief storage allows the attention and coding processes to begin. The brief image of a stimulus appears the way lightning does on a dark evening: The lightning flashes, and you retain a brief visual image of it.

Research on sensory memory can be traced back to the early 1960s, when George Sperling (1960) briefly presented research participants with a visual display consisting of three rows of letters, which they saw for only a fraction of a second. He asked the participants to recite the letters, and they typically responded by reciting three or four letters from the first row. This limit on their performance suggests that they recorded only three or four items in their sensory register. But when Sperling cued them (with a tone that varied for each row), he found that participants were able to recall three out of four letters from *any* of the rows. This result suggests that the sensory register records a complete picture but that the image fades too rapidly for people to "read" the information before it fades. When Sperling delayed the cue that signaled which row to report, recall decreased, which again suggests a picture that fades rapidly (see **Figure 9.2**). From Sperling's studies and others that followed, researchers concluded that humans have a brief (250 milliseconds, or 0.25 second), rapidly fading sensory memory for visual stimuli. Current research on sensory memory concentrates on finding the underlying neural basis for the immediate processing of this type of stimuli (Schall et al., 2003; Ulanovsky, Lars, & Nelken, 2003).

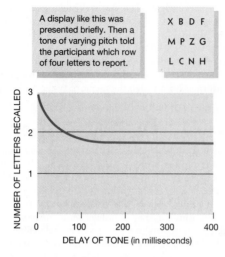

Figure 9.2
Sperling's Discovery of a Visual Sensory Memory
The graph plots participants' accuracy in reporting a specified row of letters. At best, participants recalled about three out of the four letters in a row. As the tone was delayed, the accuracy of recall decreased. But note that there were no further decreases in accuracy when the tone was delayed more than 200 milliseconds. (Based on data from Sperling, 1960, p. 11.)

Sensory memory captures a visual, auditory, tactile, or chemical stimulus (such as an odor) in a form the brain can interpret. In the visual system, the initial coding usually contains information in the form of a picture stored for 0.25 second in a form almost like a photograph. This visual sensory representation is sometimes called an *icon*, and the storage mechanism is called *iconic storage*. For the auditory system, the storage mechanism is called *echoic storage*, which holds an auditory representation for about 3 seconds.

Sensory memory lasts very briefly. Once information is established there, it must be transferred elsewhere for additional encoding and storage, or it will be lost. For example, when you locate a phone number on a computer screen or phone book page, the number is established in your visual sensory memory (in iconic storage), but unless you quickly transfer it to short-term storage by repeating it over and over to yourself, writing it down, or associating it with something else in your memory, you will forget it. **Building Table 9.1** summarizes key processes in sensory memory.

Building Table 9.1

KEY PROCESSES IN SENSORY MEMORY

Stage	Encoding	Storage	Retrieval	Duration	Forgetting
Sensory Memory	Visual or auditory (iconic or echoic storage)	Brief, fragile, and temporary	Information is extracted from stimulus and transferred to short-term storage.	Visual stimuli: 250 milliseconds; auditory stimuli: about 3 seconds	Rapid decay of information; interference is possible if a new stimulus is presented.

Short-Term Storage

Once captured in sensory memory, stimuli either fade or are transferred to a second stage—short-term storage. This storage is similar to a computer's random access memory (RAM)—it is where information is held for processing. Another similarity between your memory and your computer's RAM is their fragility—information in short-term storage is easily lost, just as information in RAM is when the electricity goes off unexpectedly. Similarly, if you look up a telephone number but do not dial it immediately, you quickly lose that information. In terms of our filing cabinet analogy, short-term storage is equivalent to the process of creating folders for the papers on your desk, and deciding what to use as labels on the folders.

Initially, researchers spoke of *short-term memory*, to emphasize its brief duration. After extensive research demonstrated its active nature, however, some began to call it *working memory*. Both terms apply to the brief, fragile storage that occurs between sensory memory and long-term memory, but the two terms have slightly different meanings to some researchers in the field (Baddeley, 2002; Kail & Hall, 2001). This text uses *short-term storage* as a general term to refer to this type of brief memory; the terms *short-term memory* and *working memory* are used when discussing research on those specific topics.

Early Research on Short-Term Memory

Thousands of researchers have studied the components and characteristics of storage in short-term memory. Early research focused on its duration, its capacity, and its relationship to rehearsal. In 1959, Lloyd and Margaret Peterson presented experimental evidence for the existence of a separate memory store they called short-term memory. In a laboratory study, the Petersons asked participants to recall a three-consonant sequence, such as *xbd*, either immediately following its presentation or after a time interval ranging from 1 to 18 seconds. During the interval, the participants had to count backward by threes to prevent them from repeating (rehearsing) the consonant sequence. The Petersons wanted to examine recall when rehearsal was not possible. **Figure 9.3** shows that, as the interval between presentation and recall increased, accuracy of recall decreased until it fell to levels that could have been due to chance. The Petersons' experiment, like many others that followed, showed that information contained in short-term memory is available for 20–30 seconds at most. After that, the information must be transferred to long-term memory, or it will be lost.

In 1956, George Miller argued that human beings can retain about seven (plus or minus two) items in short-term memory. The number of items that a person can reproduce from short-term memory is the **memory span**. But what constitutes an "item" is not consistent. For example, a person can recall about five letters, about five words, and about five sentences. Therefore, people can group information in ways that expand short-term memory capacity. The groupings are called **chunks**—manageable and meaningful units of information organized in a familiar way for easy encoding, storage, and retrieval. Short-term memory will hold one or two chunks. Many people remember their Social Security number in three chunks (a really difficult task for short-term memory) and telephone numbers in two chunks (a much easier task). When ten-digit

Memory span ■ The number of items that a person can reproduce from short-term memory, usually consisting of one or two chunks.

Chunks ■ Manageable and meaningful units of information organized in a familiar way for easy encoding, storage, and retrieval.

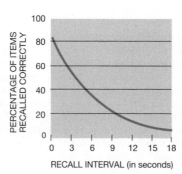

Figure 9.3
Results of Peterson and Peterson's Classic Experiment
Peterson and Peterson (1959) found that when they delayed the report of three-letter syllables by having participants count backward, accuracy of recall decreased over the first 18 seconds.

telephone numbers came into existence, people had trouble remembering them because of their short-term memory limit. But because they could think of the area code as a chunk, people got around that limit and dealt with ten-digit dialing. Chunks can be organized on the basis of meaning, past associations, rhythm, or some arbitrary strategy a person devises to help encode large amounts of data (Brown & Craik, 2000). Determining what constitutes a chunk is sometimes difficult, though, because it varies according to each individual's perceptual and cognitive groupings.

Psychologists agree that a key operation—rehearsal—is especially important in memory (Robinson-Riegler & Robinson-Riegler, 2004). *Rehearsal* is the process of repeatedly verbalizing, thinking about, or otherwise acting on or transforming information in order to keep that information active in memory. Rehearsal usually involves more than simply repeating information. Psychologists distinguish two important types of rehearsal: maintenance rehearsal and elaborative rehearsal. *Maintenance rehearsal* is the repetitive review of information with little or no interpretation. This shallow form of rehearsal focuses only on the physical stimuli, not their underlying meaning. It generally occurs just after initial encoding has taken place—for example, when you repeat a phone number just long enough to dial it. *Elaborative rehearsal* involves repetition plus analysis, in which the stimulus may be associated with (linked to) other information and further processed. When a grocery shopper attempts to remember the things he needs in order to make dinner, he may organize them in a meaningful mental pattern, such as the ingredients required for each recipe. Elaborative rehearsal, during which information is made personally meaningful, is especially important in the encoding processes. Maintenance rehearsal alone is usually not sufficient to allow information to be permanently stored, but elaborative rehearsal allows information to be transferred into long-term memory. In general, information held in short-term memory is either transferred to long-term memory or lost.

For example, you can repeat the term *suprachiasmatic nucleus* until you can recognize it and connect it with the regulation of circadian rhythms, but to remember this term and its meaning beyond the date of the test on Chapter 7, you need to do more. One strategy would be to analyze the term, breaking it down into parts and developing an understanding of each one. *Chiasm* means "intersection," and it refers to the place in the brain where the optic nerves from the two eyes come

Rehearsal ■ The process of repeatedly verbalizing, thinking about, or otherwise acting on or transforming information in order to keep that information active in memory.

Maintenance rehearsal ■ Repetitive review of information with little or no interpretation.

Elaborative rehearsal ■ Rehearsal involving repetition and analysis, in which a stimulus may be associated with (linked to) other information and further processed.

together. *Supra* means "above," and *nucleus* is a formation of neurons within the brain. So the term *suprachiasmatic nucleus* describes a brain structure that lies above the optic chiasm. Though it requires some work, this level of elaboration will boost memory for this information.

The Emergence of Working Memory

Until the 1970s, psychologists used the term *short-term memory* to refer to memory that lasts for less than a minute. In the 1970s researchers Alan Baddeley and Graham Hitch (1974; Baddeley, 2002) began to reconceptualize short-term memory as a more complex type of brief storage they called **working memory**, the storage mechanism that temporarily holds current or recent information for immediate or short-term use. Their model conceives of working memory as several substructures that operate simultaneously to maintain information while it is being processed. The concept of working memory goes beyond individual stages of encoding, storage, and retrieval to describe the active integration of both conscious processes (such as repetition) and unconscious processes. This model of memory emphasizes how human memory meets the demands of real-life activities such as listening to the radio, reading, and mentally calculating the sum of 74 plus 782.

Working memory ▪ The storage mechanism that temporarily holds current or recent information for immediate or short-term use.

In working memory, information is not simply stored; it is further encoded and then maintained for about 20–30 seconds while active processing takes place. A person may decide that a specific piece of information is important; if it is complicated or lengthy, the person will need to actively rehearse it to keep it in working memory. The addition of new information may interfere with the recall of other information in working memory. Baddeley and Hitch (1974) demonstrated the limited capabilities of several components, or subsystems, of working memory by having participants recall digits while doing some other type of reasoning task. If one subsystem is given a demanding task, the performance of the others will suffer.

One subsystem in working memory is the phonological loop, which encodes, rehearses, and holds auditory information such as a person's name or phone number. Another subsystem is a visual-spatial "scratchpad," which stores visual and spatial information, such as the appearance and location of objects, for a brief time and then is erased to allow new information to be stored. A third subsystem is an episodic buffer that holds integrated episodes or scenes and provides a limited-capacity storage system. Each of these subsystems also receives information from long-term memory. A fourth subsystem is a central executive mechanism; it balances the information flow, controlling attention. Research confirms the existence of these four separable components of working memory and also shows that they are functioning by the time a child is 6 years old (Gathercole et al., 2004).

Figure 9.4 illustrates the current form of the model of short-term storage as working memory (Baddeley, 2002). **Building Table 9.2** summarizes key processes in the first two stages of memory. Recent research on working memory has concentrated on the brain activity that underlies this type of processing (Bor et al., 2003) and on the episodic buffer, which allows a better explanation of how working memory relates to long-term memory (Baddeley, 2002).

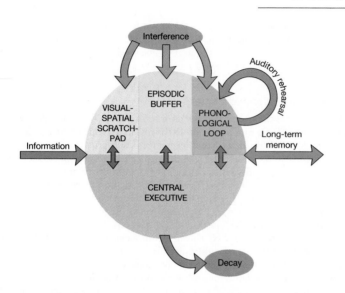

**Figure 9.4
Working
Memory**
Active processing
occurs in working
memory.
Information is held
in the visual-spatial
scratchpad, the
episodic buffer, or
the phonological
loop, depending on
the type of input.
This information is
monitored by the
central executive.

Building Table 9.2

KEY PROCESSES IN THE FIRST TWO STAGES OF MEMORY

Stage	Encoding	Storage	Retrieval	Duration	Forgetting
Sensory Memory	Visual or auditory (iconic or echoic storage)	Brief, fragile, and temporary	Information is extracted from stimulus and transferred to short-term storage.	Visual stimuli: 250 milliseconds; auditory stimuli: about 3 seconds	Rapid decay of information; interference is possible if a new stimulus is presented.
Short-Term Storage	Visual and auditory	Repetitive rehearsal maintains information in storage, in either visual or verbal form, so that further encoding can take place.	Maintenance and elaborative rehearsal can keep information available for retrieval; retrieval is enhanced through elaboration and further encoding.	No more than 30 seconds, probably less than 20 seconds; depends on specific task and stimulus	Interference and decay affect memory; new stimulation causes rapid loss of information unless it is especially important.

Long-Term Memory

Long-term memory The storage mechanism that keeps a relatively permanent record of information.

In a computer, information is stored for long periods of time on the hard drive. In the brain, information is stored in *long-term memory*, the storage mechanism that keeps a relatively permanent record of information from which a person can recall, retrieve, and reconstruct previous experiences. Names, faces, dates, places, smells, and events are stored in long-term memory. In contrast to the limitations of sensory memory and short-term storage, long-term memory may last a lifetime, and its capacity seems unlimited. Using our filing cabinet analogy, we can say that long-term memory includes all the folders in the cabinet. Like folders in a filing cabinet, information in long-term memory can be lost (misfiled) or unavailable for some other reason (the drawers can get stuck). However, unlike a filing cabinet, human long-term memory is an active rather than a passive storage system that is subject to distortion—as if the information on the papers in the folders developed errors while in the filing cabinet.

A wide variety of information is stored in long-term memory—the words to "The Star-Spangled Banner," the meaning of the word *sanguine*, how to operate a CD player, where your psychology class meets, what you did to celebrate your high school graduation—the list is endless and, of course, unique for each individual. Different types of information seem to be stored and called on in different ways. Based on how information is stored and retrieved, psychologists have made a number of distinctions among types of long-term memories.

Procedural and Declarative Memory

Procedural memory Memory for skills, including the perceptual, motor, and cognitive skills required to complete complex tasks.

Declarative memory Memory for specific information.

Procedural memory is memory for skills, including the perceptual, motor, and cognitive skills required to complete complex tasks (see **Figure 9.5** on p. 333). Driving a car, riding a bike, or cooking a meal involves a series of steps that include perceptual, motor, and cognitive skills—and thus procedural memories. Acquiring such skills is usually time-consuming and difficult at first; but once the skills are learned, they are relatively permanent and automatic. *Declarative memory* is memory for specific information, such as what Abu Gharaib is (an American prison camp in Iraq), who tore off Janet Jackson's costume during halftime at the 2004 Superbowl (Justin Timberlake), and the meaning of the word *sanguine* (hopeful and confident). Declarative memories may be established quickly, but the information is more likely to be forgotten over time than is the information in procedural memory. Some researchers subdivide declarative memory into episodic memory and semantic memory.

Episodic and Semantic Memory

Episodic [ep-ih-SAW-dick] memory Memory for specific personal events and situations (episodes), tagged with information about time.

Episodic memory is memory for specific personal events and situations (episodes), tagged with information about time (Tulving, 1972, 2002). An episodic memory includes where and when the episode occurred; the chronological dating, or tagging, lets you know the sequence of events within your episodic memory. Examples of episodic memories include memories of having breakfast this morning, seeing a movie last night, and being on vacation two summers ago. Episodic memory is often highly detailed: You may recall not only the plot of the movie you saw last night and who starred in it, but also the temperature of

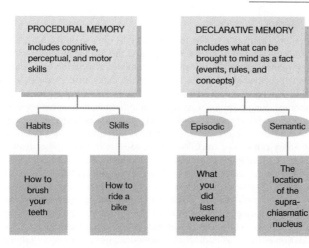

Figure 9.5
Procedural and
Declarative
Long-Term
Memory

the theater, the smell of the popcorn, what you were wearing, who accompanied you, and many other details of the experience.

Episodic memories about ourselves—our own personal stories—are called *autobiographical memories*. In some sense, we *are* our autobiographical memories; we need these memories to construct our sense of self (Nelson & Fivush, 2004). Cognitive abilities such as understanding time are required for the development of autobiographical memory, and this capacity develops during early childhood. People's autobiographical memories can last for many years (Neisser & Libby, 2000), and when people lose autobiographical memory, they lose some of their sense of self. This type of long-term memory storage is durable and fairly easy to access if a helpful retrieval cue, such as a smell associated with an event, is available. These memories are also subject to a variety of distortions (which we'll consider in a later section).

Semantic memory is memory for ideas, rules, words, and general concepts about the world. It is your set of generalized knowledge, based on concepts about the world, about previous events, experiences, and learned information (Tulving, 1972, 2002). It is not time-specific. Semantic memory contains knowledge that may have been gathered over days or weeks, and it continues to be modified and expanded over a lifetime. Your knowledge of what a horse typically looks like comes from semantic memory, whereas your knowledge of your last encounter with a horse is episodic memory. Semantic memory develops earlier in childhood than does episodic memory (Wheeler, 2000).

Semantic memory ■
Memory for ideas, rules, words, and general concepts about the world.

Explicit and Implicit Memory

Explicit memory is conscious memory that a person is aware of, such as a memory of a word in a list or an event that occurred in the past. Both semantic and episodic memories are explicit, resulting from voluntary, active memory storage. When you tap semantic memory to recall, for example, the year the Declaration of Independence was signed, you are accessing explicit memory. In contrast, *implicit memory* is memory a

Explicit memory ■
Conscious memory that a person is aware of.

Implicit memory ■
Memory a person is not aware of possessing.

person is not aware that he or she possesses. Implicit memory is accessed automatically and sometimes unintentionally.

For example, you may remember things you are supposed to remember (explicit memories), but you are also likely to recall things you did not deliberately attempt to learn—the color of a book you are studying or the name of the book's publisher, the size of a piece of cake you were served, or perhaps the make of a computer in the office of a professor you have visited. Such implicit memories are formed without conscious awareness, which demonstrates that people can learn without intentional effort (Boronat & Logan, 1997). What they learn explicitly and how they are asked to recall it may affect their implicit memories (Nelson, McKinney, & Gee, 1998). The hippocampus and structures in the medial temporal lobe are necessary for the formation of most explicit memories but are not necessary for all implicit memories (Adeyemo, 2002). For example, people with damage to the hippocampus can still learn skills and motor associations. That different brain structures are required for forming explicit versus implicit memories confirms that these types of memory are separable.

The distinction between explicit and implicit memory adds another dimension to researchers' understanding of long-term memory, suggesting that this storage is varied and complex. The distinction also suggests that these different types of memory may have differing representations in the brain and that the functioning of each system is independent of others.

Practice

Obviously, practice is a factor in storage, but research indicates that the timing of practice is also an important factor. One early study (Baddeley & Longman, 1978) investigated which of two types of practice resulted in more optimal learning and retention: intensive practice at one time (massed practice) or the same amount of practice divided into several intervals (distributed practice). To answer this question, the researchers taught postal workers to type.

The participants were divided into four groups, each member of which practiced the same number of hours but spread over different numbers of days, to create either distributed practice or massed practice. One group practiced typing for 1 hour a day; the second practiced for 2 hours a day; the third practiced for 1 hour twice a day; the fourth practiced for 2 hours twice a day. Given the same total number hours of practice, did the distribution of those practice hours over days make a difference? The dependent variable was how well participants learned to type—that is, the number of accurate keystrokes per minute. A typing test showed that distributed practice (typing 1 hour a day for several days) was most effective. From this experiment and others, researchers have learned that the effectiveness of distributed practice depends on many variables, but it is typically more effective than massed practice. Distributed practice is especially effective for perceptual motor skills, where eye–hand coordination is important.

Neuroscience and Storage

Using both PET and fMRI, researchers can now monitor the neural machinery that underlies brain functions, and this technology has been applied to the study of both working memory and long-term memory. Brain-imaging studies of working memory reveal a complex pattern of activity in several different brain regions, which is compatible with the phonological loop and visual-spatial scratchpad of Baddeley's model (Wagner & Smith, 2003). Other research suggests that various parts of the frontal cortex as well as parts of the parietal cortex (see **Figure 3.9**) are activated when working memory is being used (Collette & Van der Linden, 2002). This diffusion of function is consistent with the concept of a central executive function that draws on several parts of the brain.

One patient with brain damage has been very important in understanding the brain mechanisms underlying the transition of information from short-term storage to long-term memory. Brenda Milner (1966) reported the case of H.M., a man whose brain was damaged as a result of surgery to control his epilepsy. His short-term storage was intact, but he was unable to form new long-term declarative memories. As long as H.M. was able to rehearse information and keep it in short-term storage, his recall performance was normal. For example, he could recall a telephone number as long as he kept repeating it. However, as soon as he could no longer rehearse, his recall became poor. His ability to shift information from short-term to long-term storage was impaired. He would have no memory that he had even heard the phone number 5 minutes after hearing it. (His procedural memory was not so severely affected, and he was able to learn new motor skills such as tracing and coordination tasks, but much more slowly than people with no brain damage.) Milner's account of this case provides support for a neurological distinction between short-term and long-term memory and focused researchers' attention on the role of the *hippocampus*, a brain structure in the medial (middle part of the) temporal lobes. Subsequent research has shown that this brain structure is an important component in memory formation, especially the transfer of information from short-term to long-term storage (Zeineh et al., 2003).

The process of changing a temporary memory to a permanent one is called *consolidation*. This concept plays an important role in one of the leading theories of storage, formulated by psychologist Donald Hebb. Hebb (1949) suggested that when groups of neurons are stimulated, they form patterns of neural activity. When specific groups of neurons fire frequently, this activity establishes regular neural circuits through the process of consolidation. According to Hebb, this process must occur for short-term memory to become long-term memory. When key neurons and neurotransmitters are repeatedly stimulated by various events, those events tend to be remembered and more easily accessed—this may be part of the reason that practiced behaviors are so easily recalled (Kandel, 2001).

Consolidation [kon-SOL-ih-DAY-shun] ■ The process of changing a temporary (short-term) memory to a permanent (long-term) one.

If a neuron is stimulated, the biochemical processes involved make it more likely to respond again later. This increase in responsiveness is referred to as *long-term potentiation*, and it is especially evident in areas of the brain such as the hippocampus. In addition, clear evidence exists that specific proteins are synthesized in the brain just after learning and that long-term memory depends on this synthesis (Kandel, 2001). Psychologists now generally accept the idea that synapses undergo structural changes after learning, and especially after repeated learning experiences. As Hebb (1949) said, "Some memories are both instantaneously established and permanent. To account for the permanence, some structural change seems necessary" (p. 62).

Long-term potentiation ■ An increase in responsiveness of a neuron after it has been stimulated.

If the physical changes in the brain that form the basis for memory occur at the level of the synapse, then no particular brain structure should be specifically associated with long-term memory. This conclusion seems true. Researchers worked for years trying to find a structure in the cerebral cortex associated with the formation of memory. They failed (Lashley, 1950). Although complete agreement has not been reached, many researchers accept that memory is distributed throughout the brain rather than localized in one spot. As we have seen, structures in the medial temporal lobe, including the hippocampus, are critically important to long-term storage, but the temporal lobes are not the site of long-term memory (Markowitsch, 2000). Memories are distributed over the cerebral cortex and other brain structures, and their encoding and retrieval activate pathways that include the prefrontal cortex and the medial temporal lobes.

Building Table 9.3 summarizes key processes in the three stages of memory.

Building Table 9.3

KEY PROCESSES IN THE THREE STAGES OF MEMORY

Stage	Encoding	Storage	Retrieval	Duration	Forgetting
Sensory Memory	Visual or auditory (iconic or echoic storage)	Brief, fragile, and temporary	Information is extracted from stimulus and transferred to short-term storage.	Visual stimuli: 250 milliseconds; auditory stimuli: about 3 seconds	Rapid decay of information; interference is possible if a new stimulus is presented.
Short-Term Storage	Visual and auditory	Repetitive rehearsal maintains information in storage, in either visual or verbal form, so that further encoding can take place.	Maintenance and elaborative rehearsal can keep information available for retrieval; retrieval is enhanced through elaboration and further encoding.	No more than 30 seconds, probably less than 20 seconds; depends on specific task and stimulus	Interference and decay affect memory; new stimulation causes rapid loss of information unless it is especially important.
Long-Term Memory	Important information processed by short-term storage is transferred into long-term memory through elaborative rehearsal.	Storage is organized on logical and semantic lines for rapid recall; organization of information by categories, events, and other structures aids retrieval.	Retrieval is aided by cues and careful organization; errors in retrieval can be introduced: long-term memory is fallible.	Indefinite: many events will be recalled in great detail for a lifetime.	Both decay and interference contribute to retrieval failure.

What Influences Memory Retrieval?

If memory is like a filing cabinet, then retrieval is like the process of opening the drawer and finding a folder. The retrieval operation usually goes smoothly: You know which drawer to open and you can find the folder, pull it out, and look at the information, which matches the coded label. Likewise, most memory retrieval is fairly easy: We consciously and deliberately try to remember something, and it becomes available with little effort. But things *can* get in the way of remembering—you realize this when you take a test and cannot remember a fact or a concept, even though you know you have it "filed away." Like everyone, you experience many retrieval failures, situations in which you know that you know the information—it's "on the tip of your tongue," yet you cannot access it (Brown, 1991).

Retrieval is the process by which stored information is recovered from memory. Recalling your Social Security number, remembering the details of an assignment, and listing the names of all Seven Dwarfs are retrieval tasks. Information may be encoded quickly, dealt with in working memory, and entered into long-term memory, but then the person must be able to retrieve the information and use it in a meaningful way. It turns out that the ability to retrieve information depends on how retention is measured and how the information is encoded and stored.

Retrieval ■ The process by which stored information is recovered from memory.

Retention: Measures of Retrieval

Are you a fan of *Jeopardy*, or did you tune in regularly to *Who Wants to Be a Millionaire?* Does your preference relate to the difference in difficulty of the two? These two television shows are similar—both require participants to retrieve information that they have stored in memory. They differ in rules and format, but a major difference is the way that each asks participants to access information. *Jeopardy* asks participants to recall information by reproducing it, whereas *Who Wants to Be a Millionaire?* required participants to recognize information. Psychologists use these two measures of *retention*, as well as another called *relearning*, in studies of memory retrieval.

Recall

In memory tasks using *recall*, participants have to retrieve previously presented information by reproducing it. In addition to *Jeopardy*, fill-in-the-blank and essay exams require the recall of information. In experiments, the information to be recalled usually consists of strings (lists) of digits or letters. A typical study might ask participants to remember 10 items, one of which appears on a screen every half-second. The participants would then try to repeat the list of 10 items at the end of the 5-second presentation period.

Three widely used recall tasks involve free recall, serial recall, and paired associates. In *free recall tasks*, participants may recall items in any order, much as you might recall the items on a grocery list. *Serial recall tasks* are more difficult, because the items must be recalled in the order in which they were presented, as when

Recall ■ A method of measuring memory in which participants have to retrieve previously presented information by reproducing it.

recalling the digits in a telephone number. In *paired associate tasks*, participants must learn the association of items in pairs and be able to produce the second item in each pair when cued with the first item. For example, in the learning phase of a paired associate study, the experimenter might pair the words *tree* and *shoe*. In the testing phase, participants would be presented with the word *tree* and would have to respond with the correct answer, *shoe*.

Recognition

Recognition ▪ A method of measuring memory in which participants select previously presented information from other unfamiliar information.

On *Who Wants to Be a Millionaire?* people must recognize the correct information from a set of four possibilities. Psychologists study ***recognition*** by using memory tasks that also require participants to select previously presented information from other unfamiliar information, as in a multiple-choice test. Recognition tasks are better than recall tasks for showing subtle differences in memory ability. Although a person may be unable to recall the details of previously learned material, he or she may recognize them (Robinson-Riegler & Robinson-Riegler, 2004). If a question involved the identity of the capital of Maine, more people would succeed on *Millionaire* than on *Jeopardy*. The chance of answering correctly is better when presented with four names to choose from: Columbus, Annapolis, Helena, or Augusta. (Final answer: Augusta.)

Relearning

Relearning ▪ A method of assessing memory by measuring how long it takes participants to relearn material they have learned previously.

No game show uses ***relearning*** as a memory task—it wouldn't make a very exciting program. A relearning task assesses memory by measuring how long it takes a participant to relearn material that was learned previously. The rationale for this assessment is that rapid relearning indicates some residual memory. For example, let's say you receive a list of 12 words to memorize, and you study them until you can recite them perfectly. You report back two days later and are asked to recall the list. Unless you have rehearsed the list during the two-day interval, your performance will be far from perfect. However, you will probably relearn the material more quickly than you originally learned it, indicating that you have some memory of the items, even though you cannot recall them.

Retrieval Success and Failure: Encoding Specificity

Some contemporary researchers assert that every memory is retained but that some memories are less accessible than others. Think of the filing cabinet analogy: You may be unable to find some of the folders in the cabinet (perhaps because they are misfiled, or perhaps the drawer is stuck temporarily), making retrieval difficult or impossible. When retrieval of information is blocked, the information is effectively forgotten. It is not gone, however—just inaccessible.

Research on retrieval focuses on how people encode information and on the cues that help them recall it—on the interaction between encoding and retrieval. If you are given a cue for retrieval that relates to some aspect of the originally stored information, retrieval will be easier, faster, and more accurate. For example, if asked what stage of sleep is usually associated with dreams, you might find it fairly easy to recall because you may have known about the association between REM sleep and dreaming even before you studied Chapter 7. But recalling which brain structure is associated with the regulation of the sleep–wakefulness cycle would likely be harder for you, because the term *suprachiasmatic nucleus* is much less familiar than the concept of REM sleep.

Retrieval cues make recall easier. This evidence supports the *encoding specificity principle*, which asserts that the effectiveness of a specific retrieval cue depends on how well it matches up with information in the original encoded memory. This principle predicts that people who encode information under one set of circumstances will find it easier to retrieve that information under the same circumstances. This prediction is supported by studies of state-dependent learning and retrieval.

State-Dependent Learning and Retrieval

Psychologist Gordon Bower (1981) used the following story to describe a phenomenon known as *state-dependent learning*:

> When I was a kid I saw the movie *City Lights* in which Charlie Chaplin plays the little tramp. In one very funny sequence, Charlie saves a drunk from leaping to his death. The drunk turns out to be a millionaire who befriends Charlie, and the two spend the evening together drinking and carousing. The next day, when sober, the millionaire does not recognize Charlie and even snubs him. Later the millionaire gets drunk again, and when he spots Charlie, treats him as his long-lost companion. So the two of them spend another evening together carousing and drinking and then stagger back to the millionaire's mansion to sleep. In the morning, of course, the sober millionaire again does not recognize Charlie, treats him as an intruder, and has the butler kick him out by the seat of his pants. The scene ends with the little tramp telling the camera his opinion of high society and the evils of drunkenness. (p. 129)

The millionaire remembers Charlie only when he is intoxicated, the same state he was in when he originally met him. Psychologists find that information learned while a person is in a particular physiological or emotional state is recalled most accurately when the person is again in that state. This phenomenon is known as *state-dependent learning*. This dependence of retrieval on learning state is associated not only with alcohol but also with caffeine (Kelemen & Creeley, 2003), with emotional states (Lang et al., 2001), and with language spoken (Schrauf, 2000). Mood is an example of an emotional state that affects learning and recall.

In a typical study of state-dependent learning, Weingartner and colleagues (1976) had four groups of participants learn and recall lists of words. Participants in the control group learned and recalled the words while they were sober; those in a second group learned and recalled while they were intoxicated; a third group learned while sober and recalled while intoxicated; a fourth group learned while intoxicated and recalled while sober. The results showed that participants recalled the words best when they were in the state in which they had learned them. (This does not mean your memory works better when you're drunk! All else being equal, recall is better in sober individuals.) The finding that certain states affect retrieval brings up questions about what makes retrieval easier.

State-dependent learning ■ The tendency to recall information learned while in a particular physiological or emotional state most accurately when one is again in that state.

What Facilitates Retrieval?

Long-term memory studies have brought forth some interesting findings about retrieval and have generated hundreds of other studies focusing on factors that can facilitate or inhibit accurate recall. Two of these factors are (1) primacy and recency effects and (2) imagery.

Primacy and Recency Effects

In a typical memory experiment, a participant is asked to do some type of memory task, such as study a list of words and recall as many of the items as possible so that the researcher can determine whether the information was transferred from short-term storage to long-term memory. If the list is 30 or 40 items long, such experiments typically show an overall recall rate of 20%, but the recall rate is not even throughout the list. Recall is higher for words at the beginning of a series than for those in the middle, a phenomenon termed the ***primacy effect*** (Robinson-Riegler & Robinson-Riegler, 2004). This occurs because when a person begins a new memory task, no information related to the task is already in short-term storage, and so attention to new stimuli is at its peak. In addition, words at the beginning of a series get to be rehearsed more thoroughly, allowing them to be transferred to long-term memory.

However, recall is *even higher* for words at the end of a series—a phenomenon termed the ***recency effect*** (Robinson-Riegler & Robinson-Riegler, 2004). These more recently presented items are still being held in short-term storage, where they can be actively rehearsed without interference. These items are easy to retrieve from short-term storage. **Figure 9.6** is a graph showing the recall rate for words in various positions in a list. It is called a ***serial position curve*** and presents the probability of recall as a function of an item's position in a list (series) of presented items.

There is an exception to the serial position curve: When one item in a list differs from the others—for example, an adjective in a series of common nouns or a longer

Primacy effect ■ The more accurate recall of items presented at the beginning of a series.

Recency effect ■ The more accurate recall of items presented at the end of a series.

Serial position curve ■ A bow-shaped curve that represents the probability of recall as a function of an item's position in a list (series) of presented items.

Figure 9.6
A Serial Position Curve
The probability of recalling an item is plotted as a function of its position in a series (list) of items. Generally, the first several items are fairly likely to be recalled (the primacy effect), and the last several are recalled very well (the recency effect).

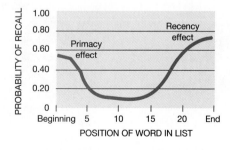

word in a series of short ones—the different item is learned more easily (Hunt & Lamb, 2001). This phenomenon is called the *von Restorff effect*.

Imagery

People use perceptual imagery every day as an aid to long-term memory retrieval. *Imagery* is the creation or re-creation of a mental picture of a sensory or perceptual experience. People constantly invoke images to recall things they did, said, read, or saw. People's imagery systems can be activated not only by visual stimuli but also by auditory stimuli (Tranel et al., 2003) or olfactory stimuli (Kosslyn, 2003). Imagery helps you answer questions such as these: Which is darker green, a pea or a Christmas tree? Which is bigger, a tennis ball or a baseball? Does the person you met last night have brown eyes or blue?

One technique researchers use to study imagery is to ask participants to imagine objects of various sizes—for example, an animal such as a rabbit next to either an elephant or a fly. In a 1975 study by Stephen Kosslyn of Harvard University, participants reported that when they imagined a fly, plenty of room remained in their mental image for a rabbit. However, when they imagined an elephant, it took up most of the space. One particularly interesting result was that the participants required more time and found it harder to see a rabbit's nose when the rabbit was next to an elephant than when it was next to a fly, because the nose appeared to be extremely small in the first instance (see **Figure 9.7**).

Imagery ■ The creation or re-creation of a mental picture of a sensory or perceptual experience.

Kosslyn had subjects imagine elephants, flies, and rabbits. An imagined rabbit appeared small in size next to an elephant.

Next to a fly, however, an imagined rabbit appeared large in size.

Figure 9.7
Kosslyn's Imagery Studies (Kosslyn, 1975)

Imagery is an important aid for retrieval of perceptual memories. In fact, a large body of evidence suggests that it is a means of preserving perceptual information that might otherwise decay. According to Allan Paivio (1971), a person told to remember two words may form an image combining those words. Someone told to remember the words *house* and *hamburger*, for example, may form an image of a house made of hamburgers or of a hamburger on top of a house. When the person is later presented with the word *house*, the word *hamburger* will be easy to retrieve because the imagery will aid retrieval. Paivio suggests that words paired in this way become conceptually linked, with the image as the crucial factor. How images facilitate recall and recognition is not yet fully understood, but one possibility is that an image may provide an easy way to elaborate information, which relates to effective encoding (Willoughby et al., 1997).

Figure 9.8 presents an overall view of the memory processes of encoding, storage, and retrieval. However, some extreme situations seem to create memories that are exceptions to the typical processes of memory.

Flashbulb Memories

Where were you when you heard about the attacks on the World Trade Center and the Pentagon on September 11, 2001? How did you hear about these events? What were you doing? What were your first thoughts? Do you remember those details more vividly than you remember what you had for lunch two days ago? These terrorist attacks made a life-long impression on most Americans as well as on many people around the world. Are these public, dramatic events the basis of a special kind of memory?

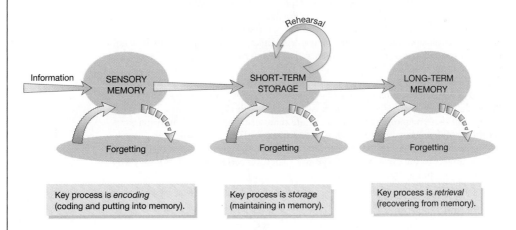

Figure 9.8
Encoding, Storage, and Retrieval in Memory
Information proceeds from sensory memory to short-term storage and then to long-term memory.

Your memory of first hearing about the terrorist attacks may be the type referred to as a *flashbulb memory*, a detailed memory of circumstances at the time of some dramatic major event. Such memories are vivid, and people have great confidence that they are accurate (Talarico & Rubin, 2003).

Brown and Kulik (1977) were the first to research this type of memory. They argued that there is a special type of memory for events that have a critical level of emotional impact. Most people immediately understand the concept of flashbulb memories and can identify personal examples. In addition to the attacks on the World Trade Center, the Columbine shootings and the death of Princess Diana were also dramatic, public events about which many people have flashbulb memories. The types of events that are likely to create flashbulb memories vary among individuals and even among countries. For example, people living in the United Kingdom are more likely to have such a memory for the death of Princess Diana than are people living in Italy (Kvavilashvili et al., 2003). Not only has there been a great deal of research on the concept of flashbulb memories, there has also been debate over its validity.

The concept of flashbulb memory holds that people will have complete, detailed, accurate memories about dramatic events. Brown and Kulik claimed that a special memory mechanism creates flashbulb memories, which explains their special characteristics. Other psychologists argue that the processes of encoding and retrieval can account for flashbulb memories, just as for other memories (Schooler & Eich, 2000). The emotional component of these memories makes them more distinctive (affecting encoding), and research has confirmed distinctiveness as a characteristic of flashbulb memories (Edery-Halpern, & Nachson, 2004).

Another point of debate involves the accuracy of flashbulb memories. Brown and Kulik argued that the special mechanism for creating these memories should make them very accurate—just as a photograph made with a flashbulb accurately captures details of a scene. Researchers have focused on collecting people's memories of various public events that generated emotion (assassinations, the space shuttle *Challenger* explosion, the September 11 terrorist attacks) and comparing their detail and accuracy to those of other memories and assessing these factors over time. Results indicate that flashbulb memories are far from perfectly accurate, and they change over time. For example, an examination of President George W. Bush's reports of the terrorist attacks showed evidence of changes over time (Greenberg, 2004). People retain a feeling of vividness associated with these memories, and they believe that these memories are more accurate than memories of other information, but this confidence is misplaced (Talarico & Rubin, 2003). Thus, flashbulb memories are probably created by the same mechanisms that form other memories and are subject to the same type of forgetting. They are certainly vivid, but they are probably not a unique type of memory.

Flashbulb memory ■
A detailed memory for circumstances at the time of some dramatic event.

Gender and Memory

The emotional vividness of flashbulb memories may be the component that relates to gender differences in this type of memory. When asked to report their most vivid memories, women and men show some differences (Niedzwienska, 2003). Gender differences also appeared in a study of autobiographical memory among older people; women's reports were more vivid, contained more details, and were longer than men's (Pillemer et al., 2003). Perhaps these gender differences do not indicate that women have better memories than men but rather that women attend better to emotional factors or are more willing to report them than men are, making their memory reports more detailed and longer.

Several studies confirm how memory can be influenced by gender stereotypes. For example, one study asked women and men to memorize a shopping list and the directions to a particular place (Herrmann, Crawford, & Holdsworth, 1992). The results showed the expected stereotypical differences: Women performed slightly better on the shopping list and men on the directions. But the study also showed that memory performance could be manipulated along stereotypical lines. Among the participants who were told that the shopping list related to groceries, women did better at remembering its items, but among participants who were told that the list pertained to hardware, men remembered the items better. A similar study (Colley et al., 2002) showed that both men and women were affected by being told that either men or women were better at the memory task being studied. Therefore, memory is influenced by gender-stereotypical information and by gender-related expectations.

When memory tests do not evoke gender stereotypes, gender differences in memory are very small or nonexistent. For example, some studies have found small gender differences in favor of women for memory related to verbal information (Larsson, Lövdén, & Nilsson, 2003) and in favor of men for memory related to the position of objects in space (Postma et al., 2004). Other studies have failed to find gender differences. For example, no gender difference appeared in one study of short-term memory in children and adolescents (Lowe, Mayfield, & Reynolds, 2003). Another study found no gender differences when women and men recalled pictures and words (Ionescu, 2000). Thus, gender differences in memory are likely to be based on differences in attention and motivation related to the specific tasks.

Culture and Memory

The effects of culture on memory may be stronger than those of gender. Many of the studies on culture and memory explore the differences between people in individualist Western cultures and those in collectivist Asian cultures. These studies examine the possibility that these differing cultural views become personalized in ways that affect memory. For example, Asian Canadians were slower to recognize individual traits but quicker to recognize collective traits than European Canadians, suggesting that culture influences what information becomes encoded into long-term memory or how it is encoded (Wagar & Cohen, 2003).

This cultural difference also appears in examinations of the types of information that individuals from the United States and China recall in their personal memories (Lang, 2001). People from China tend to give brief accounts that focus on collective activities, whereas people from the United States tend to give longer reports in which the individual is the center of the story. In addition, an individualistic or collectivist orientation may also influence the development of memory. One study showed that adults from an individualist Western culture reported childhood memories from earlier ages than did adults from a collectivist Asian culture, suggesting that an emphasis on the individual made a difference in the early organization of memory during childhood (MacDonald, Uesiliana, & Hayne, 2000). On an even more profound level, research using brain-imaging technology showed that Chinese and American participants exhibited different patterns of brain activity during a memory recall task, even when their behavioral performance was alike (Grön et al., 2003). Therefore, individuals from different cultures may have the same memory ability, but what they remember and how they recall this information is influenced by their culture.

What Causes People to Forget?

Quick! Name your first-grade teacher. Recite your Social Security number. Tell where you went on your last vacation. Did you have any problems remembering what you needed to answer these questions? In general, our memories function well, but we tend to take good memory for granted and to complain about memory lapses. Everyone experiences memory failures, and forgetting has been a focus of research in psychology since its early years.

Early Studies

Starting with pioneering work over 100 years ago, in the late 19th century, many psychologists have studied forgetting—and their work has not been forgotten! Such research has revealed a great deal, not only about forgetting in particular, but about memory processes in general. Some of the memory tasks used in the early studies required paper and pencil, but most merely involved the experimenter, a participant, and some information to be learned.

Ebbinghaus and Forgetting

Hermann Ebbinghaus (1850–1909) studied how well people retain stored information. Ebbinghaus earnestly believed that the contents of consciousness could be studied by scientific methods. He tried to quantify how quickly participants could learn, relearn, and forget information. Ebbinghaus (1885) was the first person to investigate memory scientifically and systematically, which made his technique as important as his findings.

In his early studies, in which he was both researcher and participant, Ebbinghaus assigned himself the task of learning lists of letters in order of their presentation. First, he strung together groups of three letters to make nonsense syllables such as *nak*, *dib*, *mip*, and *daf*, because he believed that these would carry no previous associations to contaminate the measurement of learning. Next, he recorded how many times he had to present lists of these nonsense syllables to himself before he could remember them perfectly. Ebbinghaus found that when the lists were short, his learning was nearly perfect after one or two trials. When the lists contained more than seven items, however, he had to present them over and over to achieve accurate recall.

Later, Ebbinghaus did learning experiments with other participants, using the technique of *relearning*. He had the participants learn a list of syllables and then,

Figure 9.9
Ebbinghaus's Forgetting Curve
Ebbinghaus found that most forgetting occurs during the first 9 hours after learning.

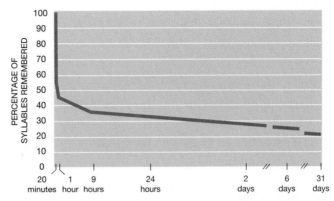

ELAPSED TIME BETWEEN LEARNING OF SYLLABLES AND MEMORY TEST

after varying amounts of time, measured how quickly they relearned the original list. He called this method the *savings method*, because it revealed what was saved in memory from the initial learning. Ebbinghaus's research showed that forgetting occurs very rapidly. Recall falls from 100% to less than 50% correct within 20 minutes. After the first several hours, forgetting levels off and shows a very slow decrease after that, indicating that most forgetting occurs quickly. (See **Figure 9.9**, which shows Ebbinghaus's "forgetting curve.")

Bartlett and Forgetting

In 1932, English psychologist Sir Frederick Bartlett reported that when college students tried to recall stories they had just read, they changed the stories in several interesting ways. First, they shortened and simplified details, a process Bartlett called *leveling*. Second, they focused on or emphasized certain details, a process he called *sharpening*. Third, they altered facts to make the stories fit their own views of the world, a process he called *assimilation*. In other words, the students constructed memories of the stories that distorted their details.

Contemporary explanations of this distortion have centered on the reconstructive nature of the memory process—the idea that memory retrieval is more like a reconstruction than a replay. Reconstruction may have to be the means for retrieval because memory formation often relies on a *schema*—a conceptual framework that organizes information and allows a person to make sense of the world. Because people cannot remember *all* the details of an event or situation, they retain key facts and lose minor details. Schemas group together key pieces of information. In general, people try to fit an entire memory into some framework to make it more readily available for later recall. Distortion is important in forgetting, but so is the type of decay that Ebbinghaus researched.

Schema [SKEEM-uh]
A conceptual framework that organizes information and allows a person to make sense of the world.

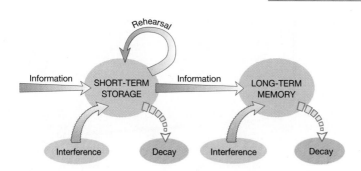

Figure 9.10
Decay and Interference in Short-Term Storage and Long-Term Memory
The transfer of information from short-term storage to long-term memory is crucial for accurate recall. Note that decay and interference affect both stages of memory.

Key Causes of Forgetting

Daniel Schacter (2001) wrote about the types of problems that can plague memory, referring to them as "sins of memory." Schacter's memory sins include the reasons that people fail to retrieve information when they need it and the processes that make memory inaccurate. Two such processes—decay and interference—can affect both short-term storage and long-term memory. (See **Figure 9.10**.)

Decay of Information

Decay is the loss of information from memory as a result of disuse and the passage of time. Decay theory asserts that unimportant events fade from memory, and details become lost, confused, or fuzzy if not called up from time to time. Another way to look at decay theory is to think of a memory as existing in the brain in a physiological form known as a *memory trace*. With the passage of time and a lack of active use, the trace disintegrates or fades and is lost. Despite the logic of disuse leading to decay, research indicates that decay is not the main way that information in memory is lost. Decay does affect information in short-term storage more than that in long-term memory (Robinson-Riegler & Robinson-Riegler, 2004). However, decay is less important to forgetting than other processes, such as interference.

Decay ■ Loss of information from memory as a result of disuse and the passage of time.

Interference in Memory

Interference is the suppression of one bit of information by another that is received either earlier or later or the confusion caused by the input of more than one piece of information. Interference theory suggests that the limited capacity of short-term storage makes it susceptible to interference when stimuli are coming in at a high rate. That is, when competing information is stored in short-term storage, the crowding that results affects a person's memory for particular items. The person experiences *encoding failure*—a memory failure attributable to encoding problems. For example, if you look up a friend's home telephone number and then her cell phone number as well, the second number will probably interfere with your ability to remember the first one. Moreover, interference in memory is more likely to occur

Interference ■ The suppression of one bit of information by another that is received either earlier or later or the confusion caused by the input of more than one piece of information.

when a person is presented with a great deal of new information, such as meeting a group of new people and trying to remember all of their names. Situations that present an overload of information tend to produce encoding failures.

A person's memory for information learned at a specific time will be influenced by information encountered both before and after that learning. For example, if you studied French on Tuesday morning and Spanish on Tuesday night and took a test on Wednesday morning, you would likely experience some interference on your exam, depending on which language you were tested on. Psychologists call these interference effects proactive and retroactive interference (or inhibition). *Proactive interference*, or *proactive inhibition*, is a decrease in accurate recall of information as a result of the effects of previously learned or presented information (the interference you experience from studying French before you studied Spanish). *Retroactive interference*, or *retroactive inhibition*, is a decrease in accurate recall of information as a result of the subsequent presentation of different information (the interference you experience from studying Spanish after you studied French). The similarities of these two languages make the interference worse. **Figure 9.11** illustrates both types of interference. Proactive and retroactive interference help explain most failures to recall information from long-term memory.

The effects of proactive and retroactive interference apply to many situations. For example, suppose you hear a series of speeches, each 5 minutes long. According to research on interference, you will be most likely to remember the first and last speeches. There will be no proactive interference with the first speech and no retroactive interference with the last speech. Your memory of the middle speeches, however, will suffer from both proactive and retroactive interference. Political campaign managers attempt to capitalize on these effects in scheduling their candidates' speeches. For example, they urge the candidates to speak both very early in the

Proactive [pro-AK-tiv] interference ■ A decrease in accurate recall of information as a result of the effects of previously learned or presented information; also known as *proactive inhibition*.

Retroactive [RET-ro-AK-tiv] interference ■ A decrease in accurate recall of information as a result of the subsequent presentation of different information; also known as *retroactive inhibition*.

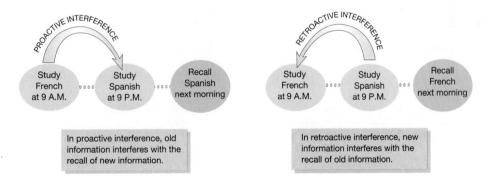

In proactive interference, old information interferes with the recall of new information.

In retroactive interference, new information interferes with the recall of old information.

Figure 9.11
Proactive and Retroactive Interference
Proactive and retroactive interference occur when information interferes with (inhibits recall of) other information in memory.

campaign and very late, just before people vote. If several candidates are to speak in succession at one event, knowledgeable campaign managers try to schedule their candidate either first or last.

Interference with Attention

According to Schacter (2001), interference with attention is responsible for one of the most annoying types of memory failure—absentmindedness. This problem plagues almost everyone, even people who have excellent memories, because this type of interference prevents information from getting into long-term memory. That is, absentmindedness is encoding failure. You really can't remember where you put your keys because that information is not there to retrieve. This problem is common, because the competition for our attention leads us to ignore some stimuli at critical points in the flow of information through the memory system. Thus, we do not remember where we put our keys, whether we locked the car, what time we agreed to meet a friend for coffee, and so on.

When people try to attend to more than one thing at a time, their attention is divided, which is another way that interference affects attention. Divided attention presents a problem for both encoding and retrieval processes, but these effects are not equal: Distraction during encoding is a much bigger problem than distraction during retrieval (Brown & Craik, 2000; Fernandes & Moscovitch, 2002).

For many years, interference with attention was used to explain what is called the *Stroop effect* (Stroop, 1935). In the Stroop test, people are presented with the names of colors, printed in different colors of ink. When reading the color names in column A aloud, most people find it difficult to attend to the word and ignore the color of ink (the Stroop effect). Their performance for column A is slower and has more errors than when they read column B, where all the words are printed in black ink, or when they read column C, where all the words are printed in the color of ink that matches the name of the color. The color of the ink produces interference. This explanation seems reasonable, but a more recent explanation of the Stroop effect has focused on a more complex interaction of selective attention and cognitive processing (Melara & Algom, 2003).

Special Types of Forgetting

Psychologists have learned that some kinds of forgetting are not easily explained by decay or interference. Sometimes the problem is not an inability to retrieve information from memory, but rather, remembering incorrectly.

Eyewitness Testimony

The police and the courts have generally accepted *eyewitness testimony* as some of the best evidence. Eyewitnesses are people who saw a particular crime occurring, often have no bias or grudge, and are sworn to tell (and to recall) the truth. Eyewitness testimony is considered very credible, and both jurors and judges place confidence in eyewitnesses (Wise & Safer, 2004). But research indicates that eyewitnesses are far from accurate, both in experimental studies (Yarmey, 2004) and in the recalling of actual crimes (Wagstaff et al., 2003). Approximately 75% of all wrongful convictions are based on eyewitness testimony (Wells & Olson, 2003).

Beginning in the 1970s, psychologists such as Elizabeth Loftus (1975, 1979) investigated the accuracy of eyewitness testimony and the circumstances that lead witnesses to make mistakes. She discovered that people who witness an event may have inaccurate memories of it. One of her early studies presented a video of a traffic accident and asked people to answer questions about what they saw. Loftus found that the wording of questions influenced witnesses' reports. For example, witnesses who answered the question "How fast were the cars going when they *contacted* each other?" gave significantly lower speed estimates than the witnesses who answered the question "How fast were the cars going when they *crashed into* each other?" All participants saw the same videotape, but their responses were influenced by the wording of the questions. This distortion of memory is sometimes referred to as the *misinformation effect*, and it is not the only type of memory distortion that eyewitnesses experience.

Someone who witnesses (or is the victim) of a crime may not get a good look at the culprit but may be strongly motivated (and even urged by authorities) to identify a suspect. Research indicates that repeated and prolonged attempts to remember details of an event can actually blur the details rather than sharpen them (Henkel, 2004). Thus, being presented with leading questions and making repeated attempts to remember can create false memories and lead eyewitnesses to mistakenly identify suspects. In addition, witnesses who make mistakes tend to believe their self-generated misinformation, and after time has passed, they no longer know what they have constructed and what they have actually observed (Pickel, 2004).

Mistakes in witness identification occur with similar frequency in women and men and in all age groups, although young children and older individuals are somewhat less accurate than those of other ages (Wells & Olson, 2003). Unfortunately, accuracy and confidence in one's accuracy are not strongly associated: People can have a great deal of confidence that they saw something when, in fact, they did not (Wells, Olson, & Charman, 2002). However, confidence tends to sway juries and judges, creating additional potential for wrongful convictions. Research indicates that speed of identification is a better indicator of accuracy than confidence is (Dunning & Perretta, 2002). Witnesses who identify culprits (from photos or police lineups) within 10 seconds are 90% accurate, whereas those who take longer than 12 seconds are only 50% accurate.

Research on eyewitness testimony suggests that memory is routinely inaccurate. People reconstruct events, and those reconstructions may vary sharply from what actually occurred. This type of error is definitely one of the "sins of memory," highlighting the need for applying research findings from psychology to the procedures of the criminal justice system. A related memory issue has generated a great deal of controversy: Can traumatic events lead people to experience a special type of forgetting in which the memory is buried in the unconscious but then later recovered?

Motivated Forgetting

Freud (1964/1933) was the first to propose the occurrence of *motivated forgetting*—that frightening, traumatic events might be forgotten simply because people want (or need) to forget them. He stated that such memory loss occurs through ***repression***—the burying of traumatic events in the unconscious, where they remain but are inaccessible to conscious memory. The concept of repressed memories caught the public's attention when the topic of sexual abuse of children began to get widespread media publicity.

Repression ▪ The burying of traumatic events in the unconscious, where they remain but are inaccessible to conscious memory.

Confirming the existence of motivated forgetting has been a challenge. Research on this topic presents ethical and practical problems—it would be unethical to attempt to traumatize participants, and it would require follow-ups over time to determine if an experience had resulted in repression. Therefore, researchers have been restricted to creating false memories of incidents that are not traumatic. Studies have succeeded in demonstrating false memories for a variety of situations in college-aged students, including false memories of the occurrence of a specific childhood event (Lindsay et al., 2004) and for the existence of a nonexistent friend during adolescence (Nourkova, Bernstein, & Loftus, 2004).

Other evidence of motivated forgetting of traumatic events comes from clinical psychologists who study people who have lived through such events, in childhood and later in life. However, some researchers are reluctant to accept this type of clinical evidence (Pope, 2000). Thus, that motivated forgetting occurs as a result of repression is controversial within psychology, and many psychologists are critical of claims of recovered memories of childhood abuse.

To further complicate this complex issue, repression is not necessary for the creation of false memories, nor are repressed memories limited to traumatic experiences.

Why are memories so vulnerable to interference, distortion, and error? The adaptive benefits of memory are obvious (Klein et al., 2002). In addition, the existence of multiple memory systems and their relative independence are consistent with the view that each system evolved to solve some specific adaptive problem during evolution. Evolutionary psychologists approach the study of memory by trying to understand the function of memory rather than by concentrating on its many capabilities. However, some of the evolutionary benefit of a complex memory system is negated by memory problems.

Examined another way, perhaps the problems of memory are not so serious (Anderson & Schooler, 2000). The processes that produce memory problems may have advantages; or, alternatively, these problems are not damaging enough to hamper reproductive success. For example, most of the information that we cannot recall is not critically important, at least not life-threatening, and we seem to be able to retrieve the information that is important at any given time. We might forget information that we need to remember during a test, but we do not forget that walking into traffic is dangerous. Indeed, even people with profound types of memory loss rarely lose memory to the extent that they endanger themselves.

def.
causes
2 types
define each

Neuroscience and Forgetting: Studies of Amnesia

Much of the early work on the neuroscience of memory began with the study of patients who for one reason or another had developed *amnesia*, the inability to remember information, usually because of physiological trauma. Popular beliefs about amnesia contain a number of inaccuracies, many created by media portrayals. There are two basic kinds of amnesia: retrograde and anterograde.

Retrograde amnesia is the inability to remember events and experiences that preceded a damaging event, such as a blow to the head. The loss of memory can cover a period ranging from a few minutes to several years. Recovery tends to begin quickly, and memory returns over a period of days to weeks, with earlier events being remembered before more recent ones.

Anterograde amnesia is the inability to remember events and experiences that occur *after* an injury or brain damage; that is, anterograde amnesia is the inability to form new memories. People suffering from anterograde amnesia are stuck in the lives they lived before being injured because they cannot form new memories. H.M., discussed earlier in the chapter, had anterograde amnesia. People with anterograde amnesia are able to learn some new information, but they tend to be much better at forming new procedural memories than declarative memories (Squire & Kandel, 1999). H.M. could meet someone for the hundredth time and still believe the individual to be a perfect stranger, but he was able to learn new motor skills. Interestingly, he would have no recall of the experience of practicing a new skill, so he would believe that he could not perform it even though he could.

The existence of different types of amnesia produced by different types of brain damage supports the view that memory includes many types of coding and creates many types of memories. The range of events that affect memory suggests that memory is a complex process rather than a single thing.

Amnesia [am-NEE-zhuh] ▪ Inability to remember information (typically all events within a specific period), usually because of physiological trauma.

Retrograde [RET-ro-grade] amnesia ▪ Inability to remember events and experiences that preceded a blow to the head or other event causing brain damage.

Anterograde amnesia ▪ Inability to remember events and experiences that occur after brain damage.

Summary and Review

HOW DOES THE MEMORY PROCESS BEGIN?

What is memory, and what is the information-processing view of memory?

Memory is defined as the ability to remember past events, images, ideas, or previously learned information or skills; it is also the storage system that allows retention and retrieval of information. p. 321

The information-processing approach assumes that each stage of learning and memory is separate, though related, and that information flows through this series of stages. p. 322

What is the encoding process in memory?

Encoding is the organizing of sensory information so that the nervous system can process it. The extent and type of encoding affect what we remember. p. 323

What are the underlying assumptions of the levels-of-processing approach?

The *levels-of-processing approach* holds that the brain encodes and processes stimuli (information) in different ways, to different extents, and at different levels. The deeper the level of processing, the better the retrieval of the memory. The *encoding specificity principle* asserts that the effectiveness of a specific retrieval cue depends on how well it matches up with the originally encoded information. The more clearly and sharply retrieval cues are defined, the better recall will be. *Transfer-appropriate processing* is an alternative explanation of this effect. pp. 323–324

What is the neurological basis of encoding?

PET and fMRI brain-imaging techniques indicate that the left prefrontal cortex and areas in the medial temporal lobes are involved in encoding, but different areas are activated during retrieval. pp. 324–326

WHAT ARE THE TYPES OF MEMORY STORAGE?

Describe the role of sensory memory.

Storage refers to the process of maintaining information as well as the locations where information is held. *Sensory memory* is the mechanism that performs initial encoding and brief storage of sensory information. Once information is established in sensory memory, it must be transferred elsewhere for additional encoding or it will be lost. pp. 326–327

Describe short-term storage.

Short-term storage, initially conceptualized as short-term memory, maintains a limited amount of information (seven plus or minus two items) for about 20–30 seconds. The limited number of items that can be reproduced easily after presentation is called the *memory span*. *Chunks* are manageable and meaningful units of information. *Rehearsal* is the process of repeatedly verbalizing, thinking about, or otherwise acting on or transforming information in order to remember it. *Maintenance rehearsal* is the repetitive review of information with little or no interpretation; this shallow form of rehearsal involves the physical stimulus, not its underlying meaning. *Elaborative rehearsal* involves repetition and analysis in which the stimulus may be associated with other information and further processed. This type of rehearsal is usually necessary to transfer information to long-term memory. pp. 328–330

Working memory is a more recent conceptualization that is seen as consisting of four subsystems: a phonological loop to encode and rehearse auditory information, a visual-spatial scratchpad, an episodic buffer, and a central executive to balance the information flow. p. 330

What is long-term memory, and what are the different types of long-term storage?

Long-term memory is the storage mechanism that keeps a relatively permanent record of information. It is divided into procedural memory and declarative memory. *Procedural memory* is memory for the perceptual, motor, and cognitive skills necessary to complete complex tasks; *declarative memory* is memory for specific facts, which can be subdivided into episodic and semantic memory. p. 332

Episodic memory is memory for specific personal events and situations, including their time sequence. *Semantic memory* is memory for ideas, rules, words and general concepts about the world, based on experiences and learned information. pp. 332–333

Explicit memory is conscious memory that a person is aware of, such as memory of a word in a list or an event that occurred in the past; generally speaking, most recall tasks require participants to recall explicit information. Explicit memory is a voluntary, active memory store. In contrast, *implicit memory* is memory a person is not aware of possessing; implicit memory occurs unintentionally and almost automatically. pp. 333–334

What is the neurological basis of memory storage?

Structures in the frontal cortex and the parietal cortex are important for working memory, and the hippocampus, a structure in the medial temporal lobes, is critical in transferring memories from short-term to long-term storage. *Consolidation* is the transformation of temporary memory into permanent memory. The repeated stimulation of neurons may produce changes in the synapses of neurons and *long-term potentiation*, which may be the underlying neurological basis for memory. pp. 334–336

WHAT INFLUENCES MEMORY RETRIEVAL?

How do psychologists measure retrieval?

Retrieval is the process by which stored information is recovered from memory. Recall, recognition, and relearning can be used to assess retrieval success. *Recall* is a type of memory task that requires reproducing previously presented information (usually without any cues or aids). *Recognition* requires distinguishing information that one has previously encountered from other, unfamiliar information. After information has been learned, *relearning* can determine how long it takes to reacquire the information. pp. 337–339

What is state-dependent learning?

Physiological and emotional states affect retrieval. *State-dependent learning* is the tendency to recall information learned in a particular physiological or emotional state most accurately when one is again in that state. p. 339

What factors facilitate retrieval?

Timing influences retrieval. The *primacy effect* is the more accurate recall of items presented first in a series; the *recency effect* is the more accurate recall of items presented last. A combination of these two effects produces the *serial position curve*, a graph illustrating the probability of recall of different items in a list. *Imagery*, the cognitive process of creating a mental picture of a sensory event (visual, auditory, or olfactory), can facilitate memory. pp. 340–342

What are flashbulb memories?

Flashbulb memories are vivid memories associated with some dramatic major event. Their formation and recall are subject to the same factors as other memories. pp. 342–343

Are gender and culture factors in memory?

Gender is not a very important factor in memory, but gender stereotypes have an impact on attention, which can affect memory. pp. 343–344

Culture has an influence on memory, and reports of personal memories of people from collectivist cultures are less self-centered than those of people from individualistic cultures. pp. 344–345

WHAT CAUSES PEOPLE TO FORGET?

What factors influence memory failures?

Distortions of memory are common and occur in part because people develop a *schema*, a way to organize information, that fails to include all details of a situation. pp. 346–347

Decay may result in forgetting, but *interference* is a more common source of memory failure. *Proactive interference* is a decrease in accurate recall as a result of the effects of previously learned or presented information. *Retroactive interference* is a decrease in accurate recall as a result of the subsequent presentation of different information. Interference may also affect attention, which influences memory. pp. 347–349

What do eyewitness testimony and false memories reveal about the memory process?

Both eyewitness testimony and false memories show that memory is subject to errors, including distortion and suggestibility. These errors indicate that memory is more of a reconstruction than a replay. An extreme type of memory distortion is motivated forgetting through *repression*. Everyone is subject to these memory problems, but memory is an evolutionary adaptation that has many more advantages than disadvantages. pp. 349–351

Distinguish retrograde from anterograde amnesia.

Amnesia is the inability to remember information, usually because of some physiological trauma (such as a blow to the head). *Retrograde amnesia* is the inability to remember events that preceded a traumatizing event. *Anterograde amnesia* is the inability to form new memories after the trauma has occurred. p. 352

PSYCHOLOGY SELECTION 1

How Does the Memory Process Begin?

(pages 322–326)

This set of questions refers to material from the beginning of the chapter up to the heading "What Are the Types of Memory Storage?" To locate a paragraph by number as referred to in an exercise, start counting with the first paragraph on the page, regardless of whether it is an incomplete paragraph continuing from a preceding page or a new, full paragraph. Please note that page numbers refer to the pages of the textbook chapter, not to the pages of this book.

BEFORE READING

➤ PREVIEWING THE SECTION

Using the steps listed on page 29, preview pages 322–326 of Psychology. *When you have finished, complete the following items.*

1. What is the topic of this section of the chapter? _____

2. List at least four questions you should be able to answer after reading this section of the chapter.

   a. _____

   b. _____

   c. _____

   d. _____

MAKING CONNECTIONS

In what ways is your brain like a computer? What do you do to keep your brain working at its best?

➤ READING TIP

As you read, highlight the findings of each of the studies described in this section.

> ## VOCABULARY

neural (page 323, paragraph 2) related to a nerve or the nervous system

olfactory (page 323, paragraph 2) related to the sense of smell

cognitive psychologists (page 323, paragraph 5) psychologists whose approach emphasizes internal mental processes

positron emission topography (PET) (page 324, paragraph 5) a computerized radiographic technique used to examine metabolic and physiological functions in tissues

functional magnetic resonance imaging (fMRI) (page 324, paragraph 5) a form of magnetic resonance imaging that registers blood flow to functioning areas of the brain

AFTER READING

> ## A. UNDERSTANDING MAIN IDEAS

Select the best answer.

_____ 1. The primary purpose of this section of the chapter is to
   a. identify sensory factors that affect memory.
   b. describe how the memory process begins.
   c. explain how short- and long-term memory work.
   d. discuss why we forget some things and remember others.

_____ 2. Most researchers propose that the three key processes involved in memory are
   a. encoding, interpreting, and responding.
   b. perception, learning, and memorizing.
   c. encoding, storage, and retrieval.
   d. organizing, analyzing, and processing.

_____ 3. The main idea of the levels-of-processing approach is that the brain
   a. has one level specifically for processing information and another level for retrieving it.
   b. encodes and processes information in different ways, to different extents, and at different levels.
   c. is constantly moving information from one level to another depending on its importance to the learner.
   d. uses only the large lobes in the top right and left areas behind the forehead for processing information.

B. IDENTIFYING DETAILS

Use the list of terms below to complete the following statements. One term will not be used.

confirmation bias	encoding	information processing
attention	retrieval	encoding failure

1. The organizing of sensory information so that the nervous system can respond to it is known as _____.

2. The process of directing mental focus to some features of the environment and not to others is called _____.

3. The human tendency to "see what you expect to see" is known as _____.

4. A type of memory problem that results when people divide their attention during encoding is known as _____.

5. The term that refers to organizing, interpreting, and responding to information coming from the environment is _____.

C. RECOGNIZING METHODS OF ORGANIZATION AND TRANSITIONS

Select the best answer.

_____ 1. In paragraph 2 of the section titled "The Brain as Information Processor" (page 322), the authors primarily use the organizational pattern called

a. cause and effect.

b. order of importance.

c. comparison and contrast.

d. classification.

_____ 2. The authors organize paragraphs 2 and 3 on page 324 in the same way, by using

a. definition and example.

b. comparison and contrast.

c. chronological and spatial order.

d. cause and effect.

➤ D.   REVIEWING AND ORGANIZING IDEAS: MAPPING

Complete the following map based on the section titled "Levels of Processing"
(pages 323 and 324) by filling in the blanks.

How Information Is Processed

Levels-of-Processing Approach	Transfer-Appropriate Processing	Encoding Specificity Principle
How information is processed determines how _____ . _____ .	Occurs when the process for information encoding is similar to _____ .	The effectiveness of a retrieval cue depends on how well it matches up with _____ .
The code goes deeper into memory when the level of processing becomes _____ .	Retrieval improves when there is a close relationship between _____ and the processing required to retrieve it.	Retrieval improves when cues are defined more sharply and paired more closely with _____ .

➤ E.   FIGURING OUT INFERRED MEANINGS

Indicate whether each statement is true (T) or false (F) by making inferences based
on the section "Neuroscience and Encoding" (pages 324–326).

_____ 1. It can be inferred that brain-imaging techniques such as PET and
fMRI are harmful to the brain.

_____ 2. The functions of the cerebral cortex are probably limited to
memory-related tasks only.

_____ 3. The left and right prefrontal cortexes are probably engaged in different ways during learning.

_____ 4. It can be inferred that people learn better when they actively encode
information rather than passively listen to it.

_____ 5. It can be inferred from the selection that most headaches take place
in a person's cerebral cortex.

F. THINKING CRITICALLY

Select the best answer.

_____ 1. The authors support the main ideas in this section of the chapter primarily with

a. statistics.   c. analogies.

b. research evidence.   d. personal experience.

_____ 2. In the introduction to the section, the authors describe how memory was studied in the past in order to

a. illustrate how little early researchers understood about memory.

b. provide evidence that past studies were based on faulty information.

c. show how memory research has changed over the years.

d. establish the parallels between computers and brains.

_____ 3. The authors include the analogy of a filing cabinet (paragraph 1, page 323) in order to illustrate the concept of

a. brain-imaging techniques.   c. the brain.

b. encoding.   d. the nervous system.

_____ 4. According to one of the authors, students sometimes fail to recognize her in off-campus settings because of

a. the encoding specificity principle.

b. confirmation bias.

c. encoding failure.

d. sensory stimuli.

_____ 5. The purpose of Figure 9.1 on page 325 is to illustrate the

a. different stages of memory.

b. development of the brain.

c. effects of PET and fMRI imaging on the brain.

d. areas of the brain that are important to memory.

G. BUILDING VOCABULARY

➤ Context

Using context and a dictionary, if necessary, determine the meaning of each word as it is used in the selection.

_____ 1. impinges (page 322, paragraph 3)

a. avoids   c. makes a sound

b. has an effect   d. breaks apart

_____ 2. derive (page 322, paragraph 4)

    a. come from   c. improve

    b. contradict   d. complain

_____ 3. discrete (page 323, paragraph 2)

    a. unnoticeable   c. separate

    b. natural   d. sudden

_____ 4. stimuli (page 323, paragraph 4)

    a. problem   c. distraction

    b. information   d. barrier

_____ 5. anterior (page 325, paragraph 2)

    a. front   c. middle

    b. inside   d. behind

▶ Word Parts

> ### A REVIEW OF PREFIXES AND ROOTS
> **INTER-** means *between*
> **PRE-** means *before*
> **RE-** means *back, again*
> **EX-** means *from, out of*
> **IN-** means *not*
> **SUPER-** means *above*
> **AUD** means *hear*
> **LOG** means *study, thought*
> **TENT/TENS** means *stretch* or *strain*

Match each word in Column A with its meaning in Column B. Write your answers in the spaces provided.

Column A	Column B
_____ 1. physiological	a. not correct
_____ 2. retention	b. additions to or expansions of a subject
_____ 3. interconnections	c. related to the study of living organisms
_____ 4. auditory	d. formed beforehand
_____ 5. extensions	e. on the surface only; not deep
_____ 6. preconceived	f. the ability to recall past experience (memory)
_____ 7. inaccurate	g. related to hearing
_____ 8. superficial	h. links between different parts

➤ **H.   SELECTING A LEARNING/STUDY STRATEGY**

Predict an essay question that might be asked on this section of the chapter.

➤ **I.   EXPLORING IDEAS THROUGH DISCUSSION AND WRITING**

1. Discuss the similarities and differences between the human brain and a computer or information processor.

2. Have you ever tried to improve your memory? Describe your technique and whether or not it was successful.

3. Evaluate Figure 9.1 in this section of the chapter. Was it helpful to you? Did it make you curious about the parts of the brain that were not labeled or depicted in this figure?

✔ Tracking Your Progress

Psychology Selection 1

Section	Number Correct	Score
A. Main Ideas (3 items)	_____ x 4	_____
B. Details (5 items)	_____ x 4	_____
C. Organization and Transitions (2 items)	_____ x 2	_____
E. Inferred Meanings (5 items)	_____ x 3	_____
F. Thinking Critically (5 items)	_____ x 3	_____
G. Vocabulary		
1. Context (5 items)	_____ x 2	_____
2. Word Parts (8 items)	_____ x 3	_____
	TOTAL SCORE	_____%

PSYCHOLOGY SELECTION 2

What Are the Types of Memory Storage?

(pages 326–336)

To locate a paragraph by number as referred to in an exercise, start counting with the first paragraph on the page, regardless of whether it is an incomplete paragraph continuing from a preceding page or a new, full paragraph. Please note that page numbers refer to the pages of the textbook chapter, not to the pages of this book.

BEFORE READING

➤ PREVIEWING THE SECTION

Using the steps listed on page 29, preview pages 326–336 of Psychology. *When you have finished, complete the following items.*

1. What is the topic of this section of the chapter? _____

2. List the three types of memory that are discussed in this section of the chapter.

    a. _____

    b. _____

    c. _____

MAKING CONNECTIONS

How do you memorize information that you need to remember? Do you use different techniques for different types of information?

➤ READING TIP

This section of the chapter has several graphic aids to help you understand the material you are reading. Be sure to take time to study the figures and tables as you read.

AFTER READING

> **A.   UNDERSTANDING MAIN IDEAS**

Select the best answer.

_____ 1. The primary purpose of this section of the chapter is to

    a. compare early studies on memory to more recent research using modern methods.

    b. discuss the relationship between learning and forgetting.

    c. describe the characteristics and limits of the different types of memory storage.

    d. explore the effects of brain damage on short-term and long-term memory.

_____ 2. The three-stage model for memory storage consists of

    a. storage, rehearsal, and memory span.

    b. sensory memory, sensory register, and working memory.

    c. sensory memory, short-term storage, and long-term memory.

    d. procedural memory, declarative memory, and long-term memory.

_____ 3. The difference between maintenance rehearsal and elaborative rehearsal is that *elaborative rehearsal*

    a. focuses only on the physical stimuli, not their underlying meaning.

    b. makes information meaningful so it can be transferred into long-term memory.

    c. repetitively reviews information with little or no interpretation.

    d. generally occurs just after initial encoding has taken place.

_____ 4. The type of memory that demonstrates that people can learn without intentional effort is called

    a. implicit memory.   c. episodic memory.

    b. semantic memory.   d. explicit memory.

_____ 5. According to the selection, the case of the patient with brain damage was important to understanding the

    a. effects of interference and decay during the encoding process.

    b. role of brain structures in the transfer of information from short-term to long-term storage.

    c. similarities between short-term storage and a computer's random access memory (RAM).

    d. use of retrieval cues, such as a smell associated with an event, in accessing long-term memory.

_____ 6. The process of changing a temporary memory to a permanent one is called

    a. iconic storage.

    b. long-term potentiation.

    c. echoic storage.

    d. consolidation.

B. IDENTIFYING DETAILS

Match the last names of the researchers in Column A with their corresponding research findings in Column B.

Column A	Column B
_____ 1. Sperling (1960)	a. Humans can retain about seven items in short-term memory.
_____ 2. Petersons (1959)	
_____ 3. Miller (1956)	b. Working memory consists of substructures that operate simultaneously to maintain information while it is being processed.
_____ 4. Baddeley/Hitch (1970s)	
	c. Humans have a brief, rapidly fading sensory memory for visual stimuli.
	d. Information contained in short-term memory is available for no more than 20–30 seconds before it must be transferred to long-term memory or lost.

C. RECOGNIZING METHODS OF ORGANIZATION AND TRANSITIONS

Select the best answer.

_____ 1. The primary organizational pattern in paragraph 1 on page 328 is

    a. comparison and contrast.

    b. process.

    c. order of importance.

    d. summary.

_____ 2. In paragraph 4 on page 330, the authors describe the subsystems in working memory using the organizational pattern called

    a. cause and effect.

    b. listing/enumeration.

    c. comparison and contrast.

    d. chronological order.

_____ 3. In paragraph 1 on page 332, the transitional words and phrases that indicate the authors' organizational pattern include

    a. In contrast.

    b. Like.

    c. However.

    d. all of the above.

_____ 4. The primary organizational pattern used in paragraphs 3 and 4 on page 335 is

    a. classification.

    b. chronological order.

    c. spatial order.

    d. cause and effect.

➤ D. REVIEWING AND ORGANIZING IDEAS: OUTLINING

Fill in the blanks to complete the following outline based on the section "Long-Term Memory" (pages 332–334).

Long-Term Memory

I. Procedural Memory

    A. For skills required to complete complex tasks

        1. Perceptual

        2. _____

        3. _____

    B. Memory acquisition

        1. Time-consuming, difficult

        2. Once acquired, permanent and automatic

II. Declarative Memory

    A. For specific information

        1. Episodic—events and situations

        2. _____—generalized knowledge

B. Memory acquisition

    1. Established _____

    2. May be forgotten over time

III. Explicit vs. Implicit Memory

    A. _____—conscious memory

    B. _____—formed without conscious awareness

    C. Different brain structures used for explicit and implicit

E.   FIGURING OUT INFERRED MEANINGS

Complete each statement by underlining the correct answer in parentheses.

1. The type of rehearsal you would need to remember a zip code just long enough to write it on an envelope is (elaborative / maintenance) rehearsal.

2. To learn a skill such as typing or playing guitar, it would probably be more effective to engage in (massed / distributed) practice.

3. Remembering the color of the hat your professor wore into class before a recent lecture is an example of an (implicit / explicit) memory.

4. Knowing what an ice cream cone looks like is an example of (semantic / episodic) memory, and remembering the last time you ate an ice cream cone is (semantic / episodic) memory.

F.   THINKING CRITICALLY

Select the best answer.

_____ 1. The primary purpose of Figure 9.2 on page 327 is to

    a. illustrate the effects of chemical stimuli on recall and memory.

    b. show that people can remember words better than random letters.

    c. depict the results of a study on visual sensory memory.

    d. explain the importance of practice on short-term memory.

_____ 2. According to Figure 9.3 on page 329, participants correctly recalled about 40 percent of test items after an interval of

    a. 18 seconds.

    b. 12 seconds.

    c. 6 seconds.

    d. 1 second.

_____ 3. The working memory subsystem that controls attention by balancing the flow of information is known as the

    a. phonological loop.

    b. visual-spatial scratchpad.

    c. episodic buffer.

    d. central executive mechanism.

_____ 4. An example of the type of information that would be stored in your semantic memory is

    a. how to ice-skate.

    b. the definition of the word _deluge_.

    c. what you did on your last birthday.

    d. what velvet feels like.

_____ 5. The units of information called "chunks" are helpful to learning because they allow a person to

    a. associate a retrieval cue with a memory.

    b. group information into more manageable segments.

    c. repeatedly review information without interpreting it.

    d. hold auditory information indefinitely in short-term memory.

_____ 6. According to Tables 9.1–9.3 (pp. 327, 331, 336), a sound stays in your sensory memory for

    a. about 250 milliseconds.

    b. about 3 seconds.

    c. 20 seconds.

    d. 30 seconds.

G. BUILDING VOCABULARY

Context

Using context and a dictionary, if necessary, determine the meaning of each word as it is used in the selection.

_____ 1. duration (page 326, paragraph 3)

    a. property   c. difficulty

    b. length   d. storage

_____ 2. tactile (page 327, paragraph 1)

    a. related to sound   c. related to smell

    b. related to vision   d. related to touch

_____ 3. icon (page 327, paragraph 1)

    a. image   c. letter

    b. tone   d. character

_____ 4. fragility (page 328, paragraph 1)

    a. transparency   c. delicateness

    b. urgency   d. damage

_____ 5. arbitrary (page 329, paragraph 1)

    a. missing a part   c. based on individual preference

    b. established by a judge   d. limited by law

_____ 6. integrated (page 330, paragraph 4)

    a. combined   c. limited

    b. awkward   d. divided

_____ 7. distortion (page 332, paragraph 1)

    a. distraction   c. illustration

    b. interruption   d. change for the worse

_____ 8. monitor (page 334, paragraph 6)

    a. move   c. agree

    b. observe   d. alter

➤ Word Parts

> **A REVIEW OF PREFIXES AND ROOTS**
> **RE-** means *again*
> **SUB-** means *under, below*
> **CAP** means *take*
> **PHONO** means *sound*
> **LOG** means *study, thought*
> **BIO** means *life*
> **GRAPH** means *write*

Match each word in Column A with its meaning in Column B. Write your answers in the spaces provided.

Column A	Column B
_____ 1. phonological	a. the amount of information that can be taken in
_____ 2. reproduce	b. related to stories about one's own life
_____ 3. capacity	c. related to sound
_____ 4. autobiographical	d. underlying or supporting parts
_____ 5. substructures	e. to create again

H. SELECTING A LEARNING/STUDY STRATEGY

Evaluate the usefulness of Table 9.3. How would you use this table to help you learn the material?

I. EXPLORING IDEAS THROUGH DISCUSSION AND WRITING

1. Discuss each of the graphic aids in this section of the chapter. Which ones were most helpful and which were least helpful? Explain your answers.

2. What is your earliest memory? Why do you think it has stayed in your long-term memory? Make a list of some of your autobiographical memories and any retrieval cues that accompany those memories.

3. Discuss the statements, "We need these memories to construct our sense of self" and "When people lose autobiographical memory, they lose some of their sense of self" (paragraph 2, page 333). How important are your memories to your own sense of self?

✔ **Tracking Your Progress**

Psychology Selection 1

Section	Number Correct	Score
A. Main Ideas (6 items)	_____ x 4	_____
B. Details (4 items)	_____ x 3	_____
C. Organization and Transitions (4 items)	_____ x 3	_____
E. Inferred Meanings (4 items)	_____ x 2	_____
F. Thinking Critically (6 items)	_____ x 3	_____
G. Vocabulary		
1. Context (8 items)	_____ x 2	_____
2. Word Parts (5 items)	_____ x 2	_____
	TOTAL SCORE	_____ %

PSYCHOLOGY SELECTION 3

What Influences Memory Retrieval?

(pages 337–345)

To locate a paragraph by number as referred to in an exercise, start counting with the first paragraph on the page, regardless of whether it is an incomplete paragraph continuing from a preceding page or a new, full paragraph. Please note that page numbers refer to the pages of the textbook chapter, not to the pages of this book.

BEFORE READING

➤ PREVIEWING THE SECTION

Using the steps listed on page 29, preview pages 337–345 of Psychology. *When you have finished, complete the following items.*

1. What is the topic of this section of the chapter? _____
   List five questions you expect to be able to answer after reading this section of the chapter.

   a. _____

   b. _____

   c. _____

   d. _____

   e. _____

 ### MAKING CONNECTIONS

Practice perceptual imagery by answering the questions posed in this section: Which is darker green, a pea or a Christmas tree? Which is bigger, a tennis ball or a baseball? Does the person you met last night have brown eyes or blue?

➤ READING TIP

As you read, highlight new terms and their definitions. Note that not all of these definitions are given in the margin; you may want to create your own marginal notes as well.

> **VOCABULARY**

stereotypes (page 344, paragraph 2) standardized mental pictures that represent an oversimplified opinion, prejudiced attitude, or uncritical judgment about a group

individualist cultures (page 344, paragraph 4) cultures that emphasize the rights and responsibilities of the individual over those of the group

collectivist cultures (page 344, paragraph 4) cultures that emphasize the rights and responsibilities of the group over those of the individual

AFTER READING

> **A.　UNDERSTANDING MAIN IDEAS**

Select the best answer.

_____ 1. In this section of the chapter, the authors focus on all of the following topics *except*
   a. measures of retrieval.
   b. gender differences in memory.
   c. specific brain structures involved in memory.
   d. cultural effects on memory.

_____ 2. A free recall task is one in which participants are asked to
   a. recall items in any order.
   b. recognize the correct information from a set of possibilities.
   c. remember items in the order in which they were presented.
   d. learn the association of items in pairs and recall one of the items when cued.

_____ 3. All of the following statements about flashbulb memories are true *except*
   a. The types of events that create flashbulb memories can vary among individuals and among countries.
   b. Research has confirmed distinctiveness as a characteristic of flashbulb memories.
   c. Flashbulb memories are detailed, accurate, and unchanging over time.
   d. Flashbulb memories are probably created by the same mechanisms that form other memories.

_____ 4. The topic of paragraph 1 on page 342 is

    a. encoding.   c. memory decay.

    b. imagery.   d. recognition.

_____ 5. The main idea of paragraph 2 on page 344 is expressed in the

    a. first sentence only.

    b. second sentence only.

    c. first and last sentences.

    d. last sentence only.

▶ B. IDENTIFYING DETAILS

Using the key below, indicate which memory task is associated with each of the following examples.

A = Recall   B = Recognition   C = Relearning

_____ 1. Answering a question on the television show *Who Wants to Be a Millionaire?*

_____ 2. Writing the answer to an essay question on an exam

_____ 3. Reviewing a list of terms for a final exam after learning them earlier in the year for a quiz

_____ 4. Choosing the correct answer to a multiple-choice question

_____ 5. Remembering the nine digits in your Social Security number

_____ 6. Matching a list of terms to the correct definitions on a test

_____ 7. Giving the right answer on the television show *Jeopardy*

▶ C. RECOGNIZING METHODS OF ORGANIZATION AND TRANSITIONS

Select the best answer.

_____ 1. The organizational pattern used in paragraph 5 on page 337 is

    a. spatial order.   c. chronological order.

    b. listing.   d. cause and effect.

_____ 2. In the section titled "Culture and Memory" (page 344, paragraph 4, through page 345, paragraph 1) the authors use comparison and contrast to describe differences between

    a. men and women.

    b. Americans and Europeans.

    c. individualist and collectivist cultures.

    d. children and adults.

_____ 3. In the same section ("Culture and Memory"), the transitional word or phrase that signals the comparison and contrast organization pattern is

    a. The effects.   c. In addition.

    b. whereas.   d. Therefore.

➤ D.   REVIEWING AND ORGANIZING IDEAS: SUMMARIZING

Fill in the blanks to complete the following summary based on paragraph 2 on page 340, in the section titled "Primacy and Recency Effects."

Participants in memory experiments typically do a memory task to demonstrate whether information has been transferred from _____ to long-term memory. The overall _____ is typically 20%, but the rate is _____ for items at the beginning of a list than for those in the _____. This is the _____ effect, which occurs because attention to _____ is at its peak and because items at the beginning of a list are _____ more thoroughly, allowing them to be transferred to _____.

➤ E.   FIGURING OUT INFERRED MEANINGS

Indicate whether each statement is true (T) or false (F).

_____ 1. Women may appear to have better memories because they may be more willing to report their memories than men are.

_____ 2. Once gender stereotypes are removed from a memory test, there seems to be very little difference between how well men and women can remember.

_____ 3. Culture seems to have little or no effect on how people recall their personal memories.

_____ 4. It can be inferred that people from collectivist cultures are more willing to talk about their personal memories than are people from individualist cultures.

➤ F.   THINKING CRITICALLY

Select the best answer.

_____ 1. The authors use the television shows _Jeopardy_ and _Who Wants to Be a Millionaire?_ to explain

    a. the importance of relearning.

    b. the duration of sensory memory.

c. types of long-term memory.

d. measures of retention.

_____ 2. According to Figure 9.6 on page 340, the probability of recall for a word at the beginning of a list is

a. higher than for one at the end of the list.

b. lower than for one at the end of the list.

c. the same as for one at the end of the list.

d. lower than for one in the middle of the list.

_____ 3. The story about Charlie Chaplin in the movie *City Lights* is included primarily to

a. add humor to the material.

b. demonstrate the effects of culture on memory.

c. illustrate the concept of state-dependent learning.

d. show how alcohol affects the brain.

_____ 4. The purpose of Figure 9.7 on page 341 is to illustrate

a. the von Restorff effect.

b. imagery.

c. gender differences.

d. the primacy effect.

_____ 5. According to Figure 9.8 on page 342, the key process that takes place in long-term memory is

a. encoding.

b. retrieval.

c. storage.

d. rehearsal.

G. BUILDING VOCABULARY

Context

Using context and a dictionary, if necessary, determine the meaning of each word as it is used in the selection.

_____ 1. rationale (page 338, paragraph 3)

a. property

b. departure

c. production

d. explanation

_____ 2. residual (page 338, paragraph 3)

    a. expense

    b. rapid

    c. leftover

    d. digital

_____ 3. facilitate (page 340, paragraph 1)

    a. change for the worse

    b. make easier

    c. lose importance

    d. complete

_____ 4. primacy (page 340, paragraph 2)

    a. being first in order

    b. being most recent

    c. being last in order

    d. being most probable

_____ 5. invoke (page 341, paragraph 2)

    a. refuse

    b. mistake

    c. think of

    d. prevent

_____ 6. manipulated (page 344, paragraph 2)

    a. changed

    b. forced

    c. feared

    d. criticized

_____ 7. evoke (page 344, paragraph 3)

    a. withhold

    b. limit

    c. understate

    d. call forth

_____ 8. profound (page 345, paragraph 1)

    a. fundamental

    b. missing

    c. plentiful

    d. average

▶ Word Parts

> ### A REVIEW OF PREFIXES
> **IN-** means *not*
> **NON-** means *not*

Use your knowledge of word parts and the review above to fill in the blanks in the following sentences.

1. If *accessible* means "capable of being reached," then something that is <u>inaccessible</u> (page 338, paragraph 4) is _____.

2. If *existent* means "actually occurring," then to describe something as <u>nonexistent</u> (page 344, paragraph 3) is to say it _____.

▶ Unusual Words/Understanding Idioms
Use the meanings given below to write a sentence using the boldface phrase.

1. To say that something is **on the tip of your tongue** (page 337, paragraph 1) means that you believe you know the information but you are unable to recall it or say it at that moment.

   Your sentence: _____

   _____.

2. The term **flashbulb memory** (343, paragraph 1) refers to the use of a flashbulb on a camera; the flash of light is used to make the scene more vivid and the details more clear.

   Your sentence: _____

   _____.

3. To say that one's **confidence is misplaced** (page 343, paragraph 4) means that as convincing as something may seem or as firmly as one believes it, it is not actually true or valid.

   Your sentence: _____

   _____.

▶ H.   SELECTING A LEARNING/STUDY STRATEGY

Predict an essay question that might be asked on this section of the chapter and outline your answer to it.

I. EXPLORING IDEAS THROUGH DISCUSSION AND WRITING

1. Reread the section about flashbulb memories (paragraph 3 on page 342 through paragraph 4 on page 343). Choose one or two of the events described in those paragraphs, or come up with other instances of dramatic events, and recall your own flashbulb memories related to those events.

2. Discuss the gender differences in memory. Do you believe the differences are valid or based on other factors, such as stereotypes about women and men?

3. Consider whether your own culture is individualist or collectivist. Do the findings about memory and culture make sense with what you know about your culture?

4. Choose one of the memory tasks to recreate with several classmates. How do your results compare with the ones described in this section of the reading?

✔ Tracking Your Progress

Psychology Selection 3

Section	Number Correct		Score
A. Main Ideas (5 items)	_____	x 4	_____
B. Details (7 items)	_____	x 3	_____
C. Organization and Transitions (3 items)	_____	x 2	_____
E. Inferred Meanings (4 items)	_____	x 5	_____
F. Thinking Critically (5 items)	_____	x 3	_____
G. Vocabulary			
1. Context (8 items)	_____	x 2	_____
2. Word Parts (2 items)	_____	x 1	_____
	TOTAL SCORE	_____ %	

PSYCHOLOGY SELECTION 4

What Causes People to Forget?

(page 345–352)

To locate a paragraph by number as referred to in an exercise, start counting with the first paragraph on the page, regardless of whether it is an incomplete paragraph continuing from a preceding page or a new, full paragraph. Please note that page numbers refer to the pages of the textbook chapter, not to the pages of this book.

BEFORE READING

➤ PREVIEWING THE SECTION

Using the steps listed on page 29, preview pages 345–352 of Psychology. *When you have finished, complete the following items.*

1. What is the topic of this section of the chapter? _____

2. List at least three questions you expect to be able to answer after reading this section of the chapter .

    a. _____

    b. _____

    c. _____

MAKING CONNECTIONS

Try to recall the names of each of your teachers from kindergarten to high school. Which names do you have the most difficulty remembering?

➤ READING TIP

Be sure to refer to the tables and figures as you read; they will help you grasp the concepts presented in the selection.

AFTER READING

A. UNDERSTANDING MAIN IDEAS

Select the best answer.

_____ 1. In this section of the chapter, the authors focus on
   a. what causes amnesia.
   b. why we forget.
   c. how information is stored.
   d. all of the above.

_____ 2. In a study by Bartlett, the process by which college students shortened and simplified the details of stories is called
   a. leveling.
   b. sharpening.
   c. assimilation.
   d. suppression.

_____ 3. The main idea of paragraph 3 on page 348 (continued on page 349) is expressed in the
   a. first sentence.
   b. second sentence.
   c. third sentence.
   d. last sentence.

_____ 4. The study by Elizabeth Loftus (page 350, paragraph 2) investigated how eyewitness testimony of an event is affected by the
   a. gender of the witnesses.
   b. age of the witnesses.
   c. way questions are worded.
   d. level of trauma associated with the event.

_____ 5. The main idea of paragraphs 5 and 6 on page 351 is that
   a. our memory system will improve as it continues to evolve.
   b. the benefits of our complex memory system are greater than its problems.
   c. understanding the function of memory is more important than studying its capabilities.
   d. memory problems typically are not life-threatening.

B. IDENTIFYING DETAILS

Complete each statement by underlining the correct answer in the parentheses.

1. Retrograde amnesia is the inability to remember events and experiences that occurred (before / after) a damaging event.

2. Recovery from retrograde amnesia usually begins (slowly / quickly).

3. People recovering from retrograde amnesia tend to recall events that happened (earlier / more recently).

4. Anterograde amnesia is the inability to remember events and experiences that occurred (before / after) an injury or brain damage.

5. People suffering from anterograde amnesia (can / cannot) form new memories.

6. People with anterograde amnesia are better at forming (procedural / declarative) memories.

C. RECOGNIZING METHODS OF ORGANIZATION AND TRANSITIONS

Complete the following statements based on the section titled "Early Studies" (pages 345 and 346) by filling in the blanks.

In paragraph 5 on page 345, the authors describe the early studies of Ebbinghaus using the _____ pattern of organization. The transition words that indicate this pattern are _____ and _____. In paragraph 2 on page 346, the authors explain Bartlett's study of forgetting using the _____ pattern of organization, as shown by the transition words *first, second,* and *third.*

D. REVIEWING AND ORGANIZING IDEAS: OUTLINING

Fill in the blanks to complete the following outline based on the section titled "Key Causes of Forgetting" (pages 347–349).

Key Causes of Forgetting

I. Decay of Information

A. Disuse

B. _____

II. Interference in Memory

    A. _____ interference

      1. Old information interferes with recall of new information

    B. _____ interference

      2. New information interferes with recall of old information

III. Interference with Attention

    A. Absentmindedness

      1. Encoding failure

      2. Information prevented from _____

    B. Distraction / divided attention

      1. Encoding and _____ failure

      2. Distraction during encoding is bigger problem

    C. _____

      1. Color of ink produces interference

      2. May be more complex interaction

➤ E. FIGURING OUT INFERRED MEANINGS

Indicate whether each statement based on the section "Special Types of Forgetting" (pages 349–351) is true (T) or false (F).

_____ 1. Eyewitness testimony may be one of the least reliable forms of evidence.

_____ 2. The longer it takes a witness to identify a suspect, the better the chances that the witness's memory is accurate.

_____ 3. Most eyewitnesses give inaccurate information because they have a grudge against the suspect.

_____ 4. Psychologists disagree about the validity of repression and motivated forgetting.

➤ F. THINKING CRITICALLY

Select the best answer.

_____ 1. The authors' overall tone throughout the chapter can best be described as

a. pessimistic.   c. formal.

b. objective.   d. excited.

_____ 2. According to Figure 9.9 on page 346, the percentage of syllables remembered after nine hours is about

a. 90 percent.   c. 35 percent.

b. 45 percent.   d. 25 percent.

_____ 3. One purpose of Figure 9.10 on page 347 is to show that

a. most information in short-term memory is not transferred to long-term memory.

b. decay and interference affect both short-term and long-term memory.

c. rehearsal takes place in both short-term and long-term memory.

d. only short-term memory is affected by decay.

_____ 4. The purpose of Figure 9.11 on page 348 is to illustrate the

a. best way to study for a test.

b. best times of day to study for a test.

c. difference between interference and decay.

d. difference between proactive and retroactive interference.

_____ 5. The authors included the section about motivated forgetting in order to

a. provide evidence that the concept of repressed memories is real.

b. argue that the creation of false memories is unethical.

c. challenge psychologists to study the subject further.

d. present information about a timely and controversial subject.

➤ G. BUILDING VOCABULARY

➤ Context
Using context and a dictionary, if necessary, determine the meaning of each word as it is used in the selection.

_____ 1. lapses (page 345, paragraph 2)

a. actions   c. results

b. patterns   d. failures

_____ 2. earnestly (page 345, paragraph 4)

    a. falsely

    b. usually

    c. seriously

    d. initially

_____ 3. contaminate (page 345, paragraph 5)

    a. record

    b. taint or spoil

    c. explore

    d. improve

_____ 4. plague (page 347, paragraph 1)

    a. bother

    b. reward

    c. engage

    d. finish

_____ 5. suppression (page 347, paragraph 3)

    a. treatment

    b. exclusion

    c. transfer

    d. interference

_____ 6. susceptible (page 347, paragraph 3)

    a. against

    b. open to

    c. fearful

    d. critical

_____ 7. negated (page 351, paragraph 5)

    a. canceled

    b. supported

    c. balanced

    d. hoped

_____ 8. hamper (page 351, paragraph 6)

    a. create

    b. cover

    c. identify

    d. restrict

➤ **Word Parts**

> **A REVIEW OF PREFIXES AND ROOTS**
> **MIS-** means *wrongly*
> **DIS-** means *apart, away, not*
> **RE-** means *again*
> **CRED** means *believe*

Match each word in Column A with its meaning in Column B. Write your answers in the spaces provided.

Column A	**Column B**
_____ 1. reconstructive	a. comes apart
_____ 2. disuse	b. building or putting together again
_____ 3. disintegrates	c. information that is incorrect
_____ 4. misinformation	d. believable
_____ 5. credible	e. neglect; not being in use

➤ **H.   SELECTING A LEARNING/STUDY STRATEGY**

Discuss methods of learning the new terminology introduced in this section.

➤ **I.   EXPLORING IDEAS THROUGH DISCUSSION AND WRITING**

1. Discuss Daniel Schacter's term for memory problems: "the sins of memory" (page 347, paragraph 1). Can you think of other terms that are used to describe memory problems, or can you come up with your own?

2. Have you ever had to provide eyewitness testimony? If you have siblings, have you ever compared their "eyewitness account" of events from childhood with your own version? Discuss how and why your accounts may differ.

3. Popular culture has addressed the topic of amnesia in films such as *50 First Dates* and *Regarding Henry*. If you have seen a film or read a book about amnesia, how accurate does it seem in light of what you have learned in this section of the chapter? Discuss what makes amnesia an interesting subject for many people.

4. Throughout this chapter the authors have used the analogy of a filing cabinet to explain various aspects of memory. How effective has this analogy been in helping you understand the different concepts related to memory and apply them to your own experience?

✔ Tracking Your Progress

Psychology Selection 4

Section	Number Correct		Score
A. Main Ideas (5 items)	_____	x 4	_____
B. Details (6 items)	_____	x 3	_____
C. Organization and Transitions (4 items)	_____	x 2	_____
E. Inferred Meanings (4 items)	_____	x 4	_____
F. Thinking Critically (5 items)	_____	x 4	_____
G. Vocabulary			
1. Context (8 items)	_____	x 1	_____
2. Word Parts (5 items)	_____	x 2	_____
	TOTAL SCORE	_____ %	

Appendix

Assessing Your Reading Progress

This appendix contains a Reading Progress Graph.

Use the Reading Progress Graph to chart your progress as you work through the reading selections in the book, including Chapter 22. For each reading selection you complete, record the date and the selection number. Then write your Total Score from the Tracking Your Progress boxes in the appropriate columns.

Reading Progress Graph

Reading Progress Chart

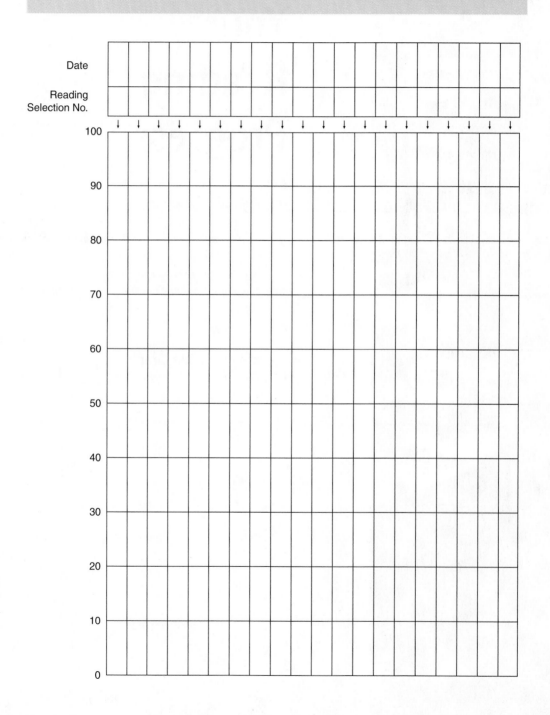

Reading Progress Chart *(continued)*

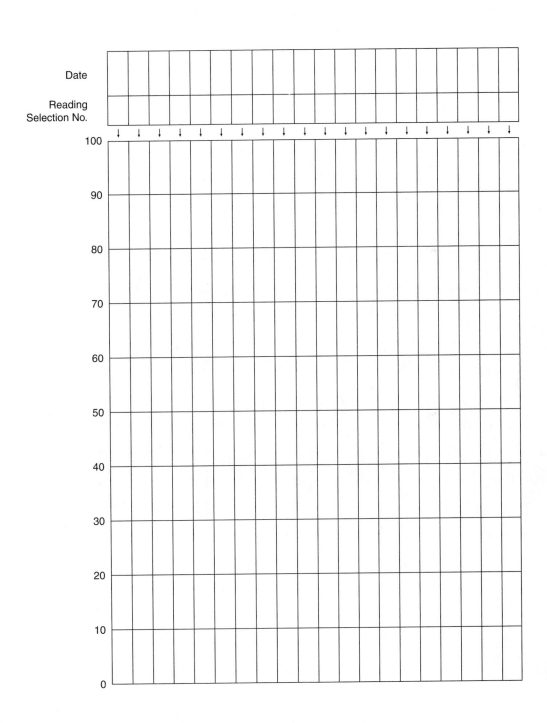

Credits

Text Credits

Chapter 1

30: Joseph A. DeVito, from *The Interpersonal Communication Book,* 9/e. Published by Allyn and Bacon, Boston, MA. Copyright © 2001 by Pearson Education. Copyright © 2001 by Pearson Education. Reprinted by permission of the publisher.
33: Ayah Young, "Deadly Silence: Stop Snitching's Fatal Legacy. Reprinted from WiretapMag.org.

Chapter 2

43: F. Philip Rice and Kim Gale Dolgin, from *The Adolescent: Development, Relationships, and Culture,* 10/e, pp. 250–251. Boston: Allyn and Bacon, 2002.
45: Teresa Audesirk, Gerald Audesirk, and Bruce E. Byers, from *Life on Earth,* 3/e, pp. 622–624, 632. Copyright © 2003. Adapted by permission of Pearson Education, Inc., Upper Saddle River, NJ.
47: Mark C. Carnes and John A. Garraty, from *The American Nation: A History of the United States,* 11/e, p. 267. New York: Longman, 2003.
49: Edward F. Bergman and William H. Renwick, from *Introduction to Geography: People, Places, and Environment,* 2/e, p. 263. Copyright © 2002. Adapted by permission of Pearson Education, Inc., Upper Saddle River, NJ.
54: William J. Germann and Cindy L. Stanfield, *Principles of Human Physiology,* 1/e, p. 173. San Francisco: Benjamin Cummings, 2002.
57: Jeffrey Bennett, Megan Donahue, Nicholas Schneider, and Mark Voit, *The Cosmic Perspective,* 2/e, p. 218. San Francisco: Addison-Wesley, 2002.
61: Teresa Audesirk, Gerald Audesirk, and Bruce E. Byers, from *Life on Earth,* 3/e, p. 237. Copyright © 2003. Adapted by permission of Pearson Education, Inc., Upper Saddle River, NJ.

Chapter 3

64: Leon Baradat, from *Understanding American Democracy,* p. 163. Copyright © 1992. Reprinted by permission of Pearson Education, Inc., Upper Saddle River, NJ.
65: Josh R. Gerow, from *Psychology: An Introduction,* 5/e, p. 553. Copyright © 1997. Reprinted by permission of Pearson Education, Inc., Upper Saddle River, NJ.
66: Joseph A. DeVito, from *The Interpersonal Communication Book,* 9/e, p. 182. Published by Allyn and Bacon, Boston, MA. Copyright © 2001 by Pearson Education. Reprinted by permission of the publisher.
66: Josh R. Gerow, from *Psychology: An Introduction,* 5/e, p. 700. Copyright © 1997. Reprinted by permission of Pearson Education, Inc., Upper Saddle River, NJ.
67: Robert A. Wallace, from *Biology: The World of Life,* 6/e, p. 283. Copyright © 1992 HarperCollins College Publishers. Reprinted by permission of Pearson Education, Inc.
67: James Coleman and Donald Cressey, *Social Problems,* 6/e, p. 277. New York: HarperCollins College Publishers, 1996.
68: William Keefe, et al., *American Democracy,* 3/e, p. 178. New York: Harper & Row, 1990.
68: Josh R. Gerow, from *Psychology: An Introduction,* 5/e, p. 250. Copyright © 1997. Reprinted by permission of Pearson Education, Inc., Upper Saddle River, NJ.
68: Karen Timberlake, *Chemistry: An Introduction to General, Organic, and Biological Chemistry,* 6/e, p. 30. New York: HarperCollins College Publishers, 1996.
68: Mix, et al, from *Biology: The Network of Life,* 2/e, p. 532. Copyright © 1992 Michael Mix, Paul Farber, and Keith I. King. Reprinted by permission of Pearson Education, Inc.

69: William Keefe, et al., *American Democracy*, 3/e, p. 186. New York: Harper & Row, 1990.

69: William E. Thompson and Joseph V. Hickey, from *Society in Focus*, 4/e, p. 198. Published by Allyn and Bacon, Boston, MA. Copyright © 2002 by Pearson Education, Inc. Reprinted by permission of the publisher.

69: Joseph A. DeVito, *Human Communication: The Basic Course*, 9/e, p. 217. Boston: Allyn and Bacon, 2003.

69: Ebert and Griffin, from *Business Essentials*, 4/e, p. 64. Copyright © 2003. Reprinted by permission of Pearson Education, Inc., Upper Saddle River, NJ.

69: Barbara Miller, from *Cultural Anthropology*, 2/e, pp. 145–146. Boston: Allyn and Bacon, 2004.

70: Paul G. Hewitt, from *Conceptual Physics*, 9/e, p. 39. San Francisco: Addison Wesley, 2002.

70: Michael R. Solomon and Elnora W. Stuart, from *Marketing: Real People, Real Choices*, 3/e, p. 108. Copyright © 2003. Reprinted by permission of Pearson Education, Inc., Upper Saddle River, NJ.

71: Rebecca Donatelle, from *Health: The Basics*, 5/e, p. 105. Copyright © 2003 by Pearson Education, publishing as Benjamin Cummings. Reprinted by permission.

73: Nora Newcombe, from *Child Development: Change Over Time*, p. 354. New York: HarperCollins College Publishers, 1996.

73: Michael R. Solomon, 1 par. "The average American . . ." from *Consumer Behavior: Buying, Having, and Being*, 5/e, p. 184. Upper Saddle River, NJ: Prentice Hall, 2002.

74: Jeffrey Bennett, Megan Donahue, Nicholas Schneider, and Mark Voit, *The Cosmic Perspective*, Brief Edition, p. 28. New York: Longman, 2000.

75: Nandy Bandyo-Padhyay, from *Computing for Non-Specialists*, 1/e, p. 4. New York: Addison-Wesley, 2000.

76: William E. Thompson and Joseph V. Hickey, from *Society in Focus*, 3/e, p. 162. New York: Longman, 1999.

77: Roger LeRoy Miller, *Economics Today*, 8/e, p. 184. New York: HarperCollins College Publishers, 1994.

77: Roger LeRoy Miller, *Economics Today*, 8/e, p. 513. New York: HarperCollins College Publishers, 1994.

77: Josh R. Gerow, from *Psychology: An Introduction*, 5/e, p. 319. Copyright © 1997. Reprinted by permission of Pearson Education, Inc., Upper Saddle River, NJ.

78: George C. Edwards III, Martin P. Wattenberg, and Robert L. Lineberry, *Government in America: People, Politics, and Policy*, 10/e, p. 422; New York: Longman, 2002.

78: Roy A. Cook, Laura J. Yale, and Joseph J. Marqua, *Tourism: The Business of Travel*, 2/e, p. 370. Upper Saddle River, NJ: Prentice Hall, 2002.

79: Elaine Marieb, from *Human Anatomy and Physiology*, 5/e, p. 9. Copyright © 2001 The Benjamin Cummings Publishing Company. Reprinted by permission of Pearson Education, Inc.

80: Joseph A. DeVito, *Messages: Building Interpersonal Communication Skills*, 5/e, p. 161. Boston, MA: Allyn and Bacon, 2002.

84: James Geiwitz, from *Psychology: Looking at Ourselves*, 2/e, p. 512. Boston: Little, Brown, 1980.

84: James Geiwitz, from *Psychology: Looking at Ourselves*, 2/e, p. 513. Boston: Little, Brown, 1980.

84: James Geiwitz, from *Psychology: Looking at Ourselves*, 2/e, p. 229. Boston: Little, Brown, 1980.

85: Richard George, *The New Consumer Survival Kit*, p. 14. Boston: Little, Brown, 1978.

85: "ABC's of How a President is Chosen," *U.S. News & World Report*, February 18, 1980.

85: Edward H. Reiley and Carroll Shry, from *Introductory Horticulture*, p. 114. Albany, NY: Delmar Publishers, 1979.

Chapter 4

91: Michael Mix, Paul Farber, and Keith I. King, from *Biology: The Network of Life*, 2/e, p. 262. Copyright © 1992 Michael Mix, Paul Farber, and Keith I. King. Reprinted by permission of Pearson Education, Inc.

92: Barbara Miller, from *Cultural Anthropology*, 2/e, pp. 308–309. Boston: Allyn and Bacon, 2004.

92: Elaine Marieb, from *Essentials of Human Anatomy and Physiology*, 6/e, p. 3. San Francisco: Benjamin Cummings, 2000.

93: Gerard Tortora, *Introduction to the Human Body: The Essentials of Anatomy and Physiology*, 2/e, p. 56. New York: HarperCollins College Publishers, 1991.

94: Edward Tarbuck and Frederick Lutgens, from *Earth Science*, 9/e, p. 309. Copyright © 2000. Reprinted by permission of Pearson Education, Inc., Upper Saddle River, NJ.

95: Edward Tarbuck and Frederick Lutgens, from *Earth Science*, 9/e, pp. 620–621. Copyright © 2000. Reprinted by permission of Pearson Education, Inc., Upper Saddle River, NJ.

96: Gary B. Nash et al., from *The American People: Creating a Nation and Society*, p. 1099. Copyright © 2004 by Pearson Education, Inc. Reprinted by permission.

97: Gary B. Nash et al., from *The American People: Creating a Nation and Society*, pp. 611–612. Copyright © 2004 by Pearson Education, Inc. Reprinted by permission.

97: Jackson R. Wilson et al., *The Pursuit of Liberty: A History of the American People*, 3/e, p. 493. New York: HarperCollins College Publishers, 1996.

99: Philip Zimbardo and Richard Gerrig, from *Psychology and Life*, 14/e, p. 115. New York: HarperCollins College Publishers, 1996.

99: Bishop, from *Introduction to Chemistry*, 1/e, p. 749. San Francisco: Benjamin Cummings, 2002.

100: Rebecca Donatelle, from *Access to Health*, 7/e, p. 264. Copyright © 2002, Pearson Education, Inc., publishing as Benjamin Cummings. Reprinted by permission.

100: Alex Thio, from *Sociology*, 4/e, p. 255. New York: HarperCollins College Publishers, 1996.

101: Wilson Dizard, from *Old Media, New Media*, 3/e, p. 179. New York: Longman, 2000.

102: Michael Mix, Paul Farber, and Keith I. King, from *Biology: The Network of Life*, 2/e, pp. 663–664. Copyright © 1992 Michael Mix, Paul Farber, and Keith I. King. Reprinted by permission of Pearson Education, Inc.

103: Gerard Tortora, from *Introduction to the Human Body: The Essentials of Anatomy and Physiology*, 2/e, p. 77. New York: HarperCollins College Publishers, 1991.

104: Alex Thio, from *Sociology*, 4/e, p. 534. New York: HarperCollins College Publishers, 1996.

105: Paul G. Hewitt, from *Conceptual Physics*, 9/e, p. 272. San Francisco: Addison Wesley, 2002.

105: Rebecca Donatelle, from *Access to Health*, 7/e, p. 516. Copyright © 2002, Pearson Education, Inc., publishing as Benjamin Cummings. Reprinted by permission.

107: Thomas C. Kinnear, Thomas C. Bernhardt, and Kathleen Krentler, from *Principles of Marketing*, 4/e, p. 218. Copyright © 1995. Reprinted by permission of Pearson Education, Inc., Upper Saddle River, NJ.

108: Leon Baradat, from *Understanding American Democracy*, p. 300. Copyright © 1992. Reprinted by permission of Pearson Education, Inc., Upper Saddle River, NJ.

109: James M. Henslin, from *Social Problems*, 5/e, p. 154. Copyright © 2000. Reprinted by permission of Pearson Education, Inc., Upper Saddle River, NJ.

110: William Pride, Robert Hughes, and Jack Kapoor, from *Business*, 5/e, p. 189. Boston: Houghton Mifflin, 1996.

110: James M. Henslin, from *Social Problems*, 5/e, p. 252. Copyright © 2000. Reprinted by permission of Pearson Education, Inc., Upper Saddle River, NJ.

111: George C. Edwards III, Martin P. Wattenberg, and Robert L. Lineberry, *Government in America: People, Politics, and Policy*, 9/e, p. 330. New York: Longman, 2000.

113: Edward S. Greenberg, and Benjamin I. Page, from *The Struggle for Democracy*, Brief 2/e, p. 71. New York: Longman, 1999.

113: Gerard Tortora, from *Introduction to the Human Body: The Essentials of Anatomy and Physiology*, 2/e, p. 77. New York: HarperCollins College Publishers, 1991.

113: William J. Germann and Cindy L. Stanfield, from *Principles of Human Physiology*, 1/e, pp. 606–607. San Francisco: Benjamin Cummings, 2002.

114: Leon Baradat, from *Understanding American Democracy*, p. 202. Copyright © 1992. Reprinted by permission of Pearson Education, Inc., Upper Saddle River, NJ.

114: Rebecca Donatelle, adapted excerpt from *Health: The Basics*, 5/e. Copyright © 2003 Pearson Education Inc. Reproduced by permission of Pearson Education, Inc.

115: Edward F. Bergman and William H. Renwick, from *Introduction to Geography: People, Places, and Environment*, 2/e, p. 185. Copyright © 2002. Adapted by permission of Pearson Education, Inc., Upper Saddle River, NJ.

115: Wilson Dizard, from *Old Media, New Media*, 3/e, p. 169. New York: Longman, 2000.

116: Stephen F. Davis and Joseph J. Palladino, from *Psychology*, 3/e, p. 210. Upper Saddle River, NJ: Prentice Hall 2000.

117: Edward F. Bergman and William H. Renwick, from *Introduction to Geography: People, Places, and Environment*, 2/e, p. 182. Copyright © 2002. Adapted by permission of Pearson Education, Inc., Upper Saddle River, NJ.

118: Rebecca Donatelle, from *Access to Health*, 7/e, p. 81. Copyright © 2002, Pearson Education, Inc., publishing as Benjamin Cummings. Reprinted by permission.

118: Henslin, James M., from *Social Problems*, 5/e, p. 93. Copyright © 2000. Reprinted by permission of Pearson Education, Inc., Upper Saddle River, NJ.

119: James M. Henslin, from *Social Problems*, 5/e, p. 91. Copyright © 2000. Reprinted by permission of Pearson Education, Inc., Upper Saddle River, NJ.

119: Edward F. Bergman and William H. Renwick, from *Introduction to Geography: People, Places, and Environment*, 2/e, p. 197. Copyright © 2002. Adapted by permission of Pearson Education, Inc., Upper Saddle River, NJ.

119: Joseph A. DeVito, from *Human Communication: The Basic Course*, 7/e, p. 103. New York: Longman, 1997.

Chapter 5

126: Thomas C. Kinnear, Thomas C. Bernhardt, and Kathleen Krentler, from *Principles of Marketing*, 4/e, p. 301. Copyright © 1995. Reprinted by permission of Pearson Education, Inc., Upper Saddle River, NJ.
129: William E. Thompson and Joseph V. Hickey, from *Society in Focus*, 4/e, p. 544. Published by Allyn and Bacon, Boston, MA. Copyright © 2002 by Pearson Education, Inc. Reprinted by permission of the publisher.
129: William J. Germann, and Cindy L. Stanfield, from *Principles of Human Physiology*, 1/e, p. 185. San Francisco: Benjamin Cummings, 2002.
129: Joseph A. DeVito, from *Essentials of Human Communication*, 4/e, pp. 36–37. Boston: Allyn and Bacon, 2002.
130: Gini Stephens Frings, from *Fashion: From Concepts to Consumer*, 6/e, p. 11. Upper Saddle River, NJ: Prentice Hall, 1999.
130: Duane Preble and Sarah Preble, from *Artforms: An Introduction to the Visual Arts*, 7/e, p. 34. Upper Saddle River, NJ: Prentice Hall, 2002.
131: James A. Fagin, from *Criminal Justice*, 1/e, p. 195. Published by Allyn and Bacon, Boston, MA. Copyright © 2003 by Pearson Education. Reprinted by permission of the publisher.

Chapter 6

134: Arlene Skolnick, from *The Intimate Environment: Exploring Marriage and the Family*, 6/e, p. 96. New York: HarperCollins College Publishers, 1996.
134: Robert L. Lineberry and George C. Edwards III, from *Government in America: People, Politics, and Policy*, 4/e, p. 540. Glenview, IL: Scott, Foresman, 1989.
135: Rebecca Donatelle, from *Health: The Basics*, 5/e, p. 215. Copyright © 2003 by Pearson Education, publishing as Benjamin Cummings. Reprinted by permission.
136: Rebecca Donatelle, from *Access to Health*, 8/e, pp. 372–373. Copyright © 2004 by Pearson Education, publishing as Benjamin Cummings. Reprinted by permission.
136: B.E. Pruitt, and Jane J. Stein, from *Health Styles: Decisions for Living Well*, 2/e, pp. 572–573. Boston: Allyn and Bacon, 1999.
137: William E. Thompson and Joseph V.Hickey, Joseph V., from *Society in Focus*, 4/e, p. 364. Published by Allyn and Bacon, Boston, MA. Copyright © 2002 by Pearson Education, Inc. Reprinted by permission of the publisher.
143: Bess Armstrong, from essay in *The Choices We Made*, edited by Angela Bonavoglia, p. 165. New York: Random House, 1991.
144: Robert A. Wallace, from *Biology: The World of Life*, 6/e, p. 518. Copyright © 1992 HarperCollins College Publishers. Reprinted by permission of Pearson Education, Inc.
145: Marie Winn, from *The Plug-In-Drug*. New York: Viking Press, 1977.
149: Jane Kenyon, excerpt from "The Suitor." Copyright 2005 by the Estate of Jane Kenyon. Reprinted from *Collected Poems* with the permission of Graywolf Press, Saint Paul, Minnesota.
149: Shelley, Percy Bysshe, "Adonais," 1821.
150: Emily Dickinson, from "My Life Had Stood a Loaded Gun." Reprinted by permission of the publishers and the Trustees of Amherst College from *The Poems of Emily Dickinson*, Johnson, Thomas H., ed., J754, Cambridge, Mass.: The Belknap Press of Harvard University Press, Copyright © 1951, 1955, 1979, 1983 by the President and Fellows of Harvard College.
150: Gustave Flaubert, *The Legend of Saint Julian the Hospitaller*, 1838.

Chapter 7

154: Robert A. Wallace, from *Biology: The World of Life*, 6/e, pp. 708, 710. Copyright © 1992 HarperCollins College Publishers. Reprinted by permission of Pearson Education, Inc.
155: Robert A. Wallace, from *Biology: The World of Life*, 6/e, pp. 712–713. Copyright © 1992 HarperCollins College Publishers. Reprinted by permission of Pearson Education, Inc.
155: James A. Fagin, from *Criminal Justice*, 1/e, p. 89. Published by Allyn and Bacon, Boston, MA. Copyright © 2003 by Pearson Education. Reprinted by permission of the publisher.
155: Ronald J. Ebert and Ricky W. Griffin, *Business Essentials*, 4/e, p. 71. Upper Saddle River, NJ: Prentice Hall, 2003.

156: "How Commercial Jingles Work" by Tim Faulkner from HowStuffWorks.com. Reprinted courtesy of HowStuffWorks.com.

164: Miller, Barbara, from *Cultural Anthropology*, 2/e, p. 302. Boston: Allyn and Bacon, 2004.

164: William E. Thompson and Joseph V. Hickey, from *Society in Focus*, 4/e, p. 355. Published by Allyn and Bacon, Boston, MA. Copyright © 2002 by Pearson Education, Inc. Reprinted by permission of the publisher.

167: William E. Thompson and Joseph V. Hickey, from *Society in Focus*, 4/e, p. 285. Published by Allyn and Bacon, Boston, MA. Copyright © 2002 by Pearson Education, Inc. Reprinted by permission of the publisher.

169: Alex Thio, from *Sociology: A Brief Introduction*, 5/e, pp. 35–36. Boston: Allyn and Bacon, 2003.

170: James A. Fagin, from *Criminal Justice*, 1/e, p. 107. Published by Allyn and Bacon, Boston, MA. Copyright © 2003 by Pearson Education. Reprinted by permission of the publisher.

172: Rebecca Donatelle, from *Health: The Basics*, 5/e, p. 179. Copyright © 2003 by Pearson Education, publishing as Benjamin Cummings. Reprinted by permission.

173: Robert Divine et al., from *America Past and Present*, 4/e, pp. 890–891. Copyright © 1996 by HarperCollins College Publishers. Reprinted by permission of Pearson Education, Inc.

174: Louis Berman and J.C. Evans, from *Exploring the Cosmos*, 5/e, p. 145.Boston: Little, Brown, 1986.

Chapter 9

183: United Nations Foundation home page from http://www.unfoundation.org. © 2006 UN Foundation. All Rights Reserved. Reprinted by permission.

Chapter 10

200: Samuel E. Wood, Ellen Green Wood, and Denise Boyd, "Mastering the World of Psychology," pp. 145–146. © 2008 Pearson Education, Inc. Reproduced by permission of Pearson Education, Inc.

209: Deborah A. Lott, from "The New Flirting Game," *Psychology Today*, January 1999. Reprinted with permission from Psychology Today, Copyright © 2006. www.psychologytoday.com.

220: Dr. Benjamin Carson, "Coming Into My Own." Taken from *Gifted Hands: The Ben Carson Story* by Dr. Benjamin Carson, pp. 115–117. Copyright 1990 by Review and Herald ® Publishing Association. Used by permission of the Zondervan Corporation.

Chapter 11

229: Aubree Rankin, excerpts adapted from *Reality TV: Race to the Bottom: A Content Analysis of Prime Time Broadcast Reality Series*.www.parentstv.org. © 2004 Parents Television Council. Image and text reprinted by permission.

239: Brian Faler, "War: The Mother of All Words." Reprinted with permission from National Journal, February 2, 2002. Copyright © 2008 by National Journal Group, Inc. All rights reserved.

250: Joseph A. DeVito, *Interpersonal Messages: Communication and Relationship Skills,* 1/e Published by Allyn and Bacon, Boston, MA. Copyright © 2008 by Pearson Education. Reprinted by permission of the publisher.

Chapter 12

262: Michelle Kearns, "To Love and to Cherish," *Buffalo News*, June 7, 2003. Reprinted by permission of Buffalo News.

271: Joseph A. DeVito, "Culture and Nonverbal Communication" from *Human Communication: The Basic Course,* 11/e Published by Allyn and Bacon, Boston, MA. Copyright © 2009 by Pearson Education. Reprinted by permission of the publisher.

281: Barbara D. Miller and Bernard Wood, from "Play, Leisure and Culture" in *Anthropology*, 1/e, Pgs. 566–568. © 2006, Reprinted by permission of Pearson Education, Inc., Upper Saddle River, NJ.

Chapter 13

292: Patrick Frank, "Issue-Oriented and Street Art," from *Prebles' Artforms: An Introduction to the Visual Arts*, pp. 460, 474–479 © N/A Reprinted by permission of Pearson Education, Inc., Upper Saddle River, NJ.

306: Panos Ioannides, "Gregory," translated by Marion Byron and Catherine Raizis, from *The Charioteer: A Review of Modern Greek Literature.* Copyright © 1989 by Panos Ioannides. English translation copyright © 1989 by Marion Byron and Catherine Raizis. Reprinted by permission of Pella Publishing, New York, NY.
316: Gladys Cardiff, "Combing," first published in *To Frighten a Storm* by Copper Canyon Press. Copyright © 1976. Reprinted by permission of the author.

Chapter 14

324: Roger LeRoy Miller, Daniel K. Benjamin, and Douglass C. North, "The Effects of the Minimum Wage" from *The Economics of Public Issues* , 14/e pp. 88–91. © 2005, 2003, 2001 Pearson Education, Inc. publishing as Pearson Addison-Wesley. Reprinted by permission of Pearson Education, Inc. All rights reserved.
334: Christine Mitchell, "When Living Is a Fate Worse Than Death." From *Newsweek*, August 28, 2000. © 2000 Newsweek, Inc. All rights reserved. Reprinted by permission.
343: Rick Reilly, "Seoul Searching,"from *Time Magazine*, August 28, 2000. Copyright © 2000, Time Inc. All rights reserved. Reprinted by permission.

Chapter 15

356: Mary Pipher, Excerpts from "The Beautiful Laughing Sisters – An Arrival Story" in *The Middle of Everywhere*, copyright © 2002 by Mary Pipher. Reprinted by permission of Houghton Mifflin Harcourt Publishing Company.
369: Cindy C. Combs, "Profile of a Terrorist" from *Terrorism in the Twenty-First Century*, 3/e, pp. 50–54. Copyright © 2003. Reprinted by permission of Pearson Education, Inc., Upper Saddle River, NJ.
380: George C. Edwards III, Martin P. Wattenberg, and Robert L. Lineberry, from "Whether to Vote: A Citizen's Choice," pp. 304–309. Copyright © 2006 by Pearson Education, Inc. Reprinted by permission.
383: "Why Turnout in the United States Is So Low Compared to Other Countries" is reprinted by permission of the publisher of *Where Have All the Voters Gone?* by Martin P. Wattenberg, p. 15, Cambridge, Mass.: Harvard University Press, Copyright © 2002 by the President and Fellows of Harvard College.

Chapter 16

393: Marta Finney, "Four Simple Words That Guarantee the Job of Your Dreams," *Career Magazine*, August 24, 1999. Reprinted by permission of the author.
402: McSpotlight, "McDonald's Makes a Lot of People Angry for a Lot of Different Reasons." From www.mcspotlight.org, The Issues: Introduction. Used by permission.
413: Michael Solomon, "Product Placement, from *Consumer Behavior*, 7/e © 2007. Reprinted by permission of Pearson education, Inc., Upper Saddle River, NJ.

Chapter 17

426: George H. Pike, "Blogger Beware," *Information Today*, Vol. 22, Issue 11, December 2005, pp. 17-19. Reprinted by permission of Information Today, Inc.
436: Jo Napolitano, "Hold It Right There, and Drop That Camera" *The New York Times*, December 11, 2003. All Rights Reserved. Used by permission and protected by the Copyright Laws of the United States. The printing, copying, redistribution, or retransmission of the Material without express written permission is prohibited.
446: Elaine N. Marieb, from "DNA Fingerprinting: Cracking Our 'Genetic Barcode'," from *Essentials of Human Anatomy & Physiology*. Copyright © 2009. Reprinted by permission of Pearson Education.

Chapter 18

457: Bonnie Schiedel, "Use It and Lose It," *Chatelaine*, July 2000, Vol. 73, No. 7. © Rogers Publishing Ltd. Reprinted by permission.
470: Tamar Nordenberg "Make No Mistake: Medical Errors Can Be Deadly Serious," *FDA Consumer*, October 16, 2000. www.fda.gov.

483: Elaine Marieb, "Athletes Looking Good and Doing Better with Anabolic Steroids?" from *Human Anatomy and Physiology*, 5/e. Copyright © 2001 by The Benjamin Cummings Publishing Company. Reprinted by permission of Pearson Education, Inc.

Chapter 19

494: Michael D. Lemonick, Dan Cray, and Wendy Grossman, "Honor Among Beasts," from *Time Magazine*, July 14, 2005. Copyright © 2005, Time Inc. All rights reserved. Reprinted by permission.
506: David Bodanis, "Bugs In Your Pillow," from *The Secret Family: Twenty-Four Hours Inside the Mysterious World of Our Minds and Bodies*. Copyright © 1997 by David Bodanis. Reprinted with the permission of Simon & Schuster Adult Publishing Group.
516: Michael Bellomo, "Resolving the Debate: Adult Vs. Embryonic Stem Cells," from *The Stem Cell Divide: The Facts, the Fiction and the Fear Driving the Greatest Scientific, Political and Religious Debate of Our Time*. Copyright © 2006 AMACOM Books. Reprinted by permission.

Chapter 20

529: Jeffrey O. Bennett, William L. Briggs, and Mario F. Triola, "Are Lotteries Fair?" from *Statistical Reasoning for Everyday Life*, 2/e, pp. 266–268. © 2003, 2001 Pearson Education, Inc. Reprinted by permission of Pearson Education, Inc. All rights reserved.
539: Jeffrey Bennett, Seth Shostak, and Bruce Jakosky, "Is There Life Elsewhere?" from *Life in the Universe*, pp. 338–345. Copyright © 2003 Pearson Education, Inc., publishing as Addison Wesley. Reprinted by permission.
550: John Suchocki, "Air Pollution May Result in Global Warming," from *Conceptual Chemistry*, 2/e, pp. 575–581. Copyright © by John A. Suchocki. Reprinted by permission of Pearson Education, Inc.

Chapter 21

563: Courtland L. Bovee, John V. Thill, and Barbara Schatzman, "Building Toward a Career," from *Business Communication Today*, 7/e, pp. 543–545. Copyright © 2003. Reprinted by permission of Pearson Education, Inc.
573: Kathy Simmons, "RX for Anger at Work," as it appeared on the *Career Magazine* Web site. Reprinted by permission of the author.
584: Dorrit T. Walsh, from "The Sandman Is Dead—Long Live the Sleep Deprived Walking Zombie" as it appeared on the *HR Plaza* Web site. Copyright © 2000 Bernard Hodes Group. Reprinted by permission of Bernard Hodes Group, http://www.hodes.com.

Chapter 22

Lester A. Lefton and Linda Brannon, "Memory" form *Psychology* pp. 321–355 © 2008 Pearson Education Inc. Reproduced by permission of Pearson Education, Inc.

Photo Credits

1 top: D. Hurst/Alamy; **1 center:** Getty Images; **1 bottom:** Mario Tama/Getty Images; **2 top left:** Erich Lessing/Art Resource; **2 top right:** Alamy; **2 bottom left:** Ali Yussef/Getty Images; **2 bottom right:** David Mdzinarishvili/Corbis; **3 top left:** Justin Sullivan/Getty Images; **3 top right:** Penny Tweedie/Corbis; **3 bottom left:** Istockphoto **3 bottom right:** Arnd Weigmann/Corbis; **4:** age footstock; **11:** Dennis Kunkel/Phototake; **13:** David R. Frazier Photolibrary, Inc./Alamy; **15:** Photolibrary; **18:** Alamy; **20:** vario images GmbH & Co.KG/Alamy; **22:** Andrew Holt/Alamy; **34:** Michael S. Wirtz/Phladelphia Inquirer/Newscom; **122:** Bob Deammrich/The Image Works; **123:** Associated Press; **127:** The New Yorker Collection 2008 David Borchart from cartoonbank.com. All Rights Reserved.; **157:** Tim Boyle/Getty Images; **158:** Business Wire/Getty Images; **159:** Justin Sullivan/Getty Images; **201:** Marilynn K. Yee/The New York Times; **209:** Raffaele Celentano/laif/Redux; **220:** The Baltimore Sun; **229:** David Young-Wolff/PhotoEdit; **230:** NBC Universal Photo Bank; **239:** Khalid Mohammed/Associated Press; **253:** Jeff Greenberg/PhotoEdit; **262:** Louise Gubb/Corbis; **282:** Frans Lanting/Minden Pictures; **283:** Gordon Wiltsie/Getty Images; **294:** Barbara Kruger, Untitled (I shop therefore I am). 1987. Photographic sildscreen/vinyl, 111″ × 113″, Courtesy Mary Boone Gallery, NY; 294: Fred Wilson, Mining The Museum, 1992. Museum and Library of Maryland History. Photograph by Jeff D. Goldman.; **296:** Shepard Fairey, Revolution Girl. Outdoor location, Los Angeles. Obey Giant Art, CA. **297:** Swoon, Untitled, 2005. Linoleum cut, newsprint, ink and wheat paste. Variable dimensions. Deitch Projects, New York.; **297:** Banksy, Graffittii Removal Hotline, Pentonville Road, 2006. Steve Colton/artofthestate.co.uk; **382:** Mary Altaffer/Associated Press; **402:** Claude Paris/Associated Press; **414:** Advertising Savants, St. Louis, MO; **438:** Alex Brandon/Associated Press; **448:** Geoff Tompkinson/Photo Researchers; **483:** Mark Allen Johnson/ZUMA/Corbis; **494:** John Canacolosi/Peter Arnold; **495:** Mark Bekoff; **497:** Klein & Hubert/BIOS/Peter Arnold; **508:** Mackes/Ottawa/Photo Researchers; **543:** NASA; **550:** Perennou Nuridsany/Photo Researchers; **555 left:** Tony Buxton/Photo Researchers; **555 right:** B.&C. Alexander/Photo Researchers.

Index